Everyone's an Author

THIRD EDITION

ANDREA LUNSFORD
STANFORD UNIVERSITY

MICHAL BRODY

LISA EDE
OREGON STATE UNIVERSITY

BEVERLY J. MOSS
THE OHIO STATE UNIVERSITY

CAROLE CLARK PAPPER

KEITH WALTERS
PORTLAND STATE UNIVERSITY

W. W. NORTON & COMPANY
Independent Publishers Since 1923

W. W. Norton & Company has been independent since its founding in 1923, when William Warder Norton and Mary D. Herter Norton first published lectures delivered at the People's Institute, the adult education division of New York City's Cooper Union. The firm soon expanded its program beyond the Institute, publishing books by celebrated academics from America and abroad. By midcentury, the two major pillars of Norton's publishing program—trade books and college texts—were firmly established. In the 1950s, the Norton family transferred control of the company to its employees, and today—with a staff of five hundred and hundreds of trade, college, and professional titles published each year—W. W. Norton & Company stands as the largest and oldest publishing house owned wholly by its employees.

Editor: Erica Wnek
Project Editor: Christine D'Antonio
Assistant Editor: Edwin Jeng
Managing Editor, College: Marian Johnson
Managing Editor, College Digital Media: Kim Yi
Production Manager: Jane Searle
Media Editor: Samantha Held, Joy Cranshaw
Media Project Editor: Cooper Wilhelm
Media Editorial Assistant: Katie Bolger
Ebook Manager: Michael Hicks

Marketing Manager, Composition: Michele Dobbins
Design Director: Rubina Yeh
Designer: Lissi Sigillo
Director of College Permissions: Megan Schindel
Permissions Specialist: Elizabeth Trammell
Photo Editor: Ted Szczepanski
Photo Research: Elyse Rieder
Composition: Six Red Marbles
Manufacturing: LSC Communications—
   Crawfordsville

Permission to use copyrighted material is included in the credits section of this book, which begins on p. 821.

Library of Congress Cataloging-in-Publication Data

Names: Lunsford, Andrea A., 1942- author. | Brody, Michal, author. | Ede,
   Lisa S., 1947- author. | Moss, Beverly J., author. | Papper, Carole
   Clark, author. | Walters, Keith, author.
Title: Everyone's an author / Andrea Lunsford, Michal Brody, Lisa Ede,
   Beverly J. Moss, Carole Clark Papper, Keith Walters.
Description: Third edition. | New York : W. W. Norton & Company, [2020] |
   Includes bibliographical references and index.
Identifiers: LCCN 2019044442 | ISBN 9780393680850 (paperback)
Subjects: LCSH: English language—Rhetoric. | Report writing. | Authorship. |
   College readers.
Classification: LCC PE1408 .L874 2020 | DDC 808/.0427—dc23
LC record available at https://lccn.loc.gov/2019044442

W. W. Norton & Company, Inc., 500 Fifth Avenue, New York, NY 10110

wwnorton.com

W. W. Norton & Company Ltd., 15 Carlisle Street, London W1D 3BS

1 2 3 4 5 6 7 8 9 0

For our students, authors all.

Preface

VERYONE'S AN AUTHOR grew out of a growing concern for the mismatch we perceived between the kinds of writing students were asked to do in school and the kinds of writing they were doing everywhere else. They were doing more writing than ever as they tweeted, texted, blogged, and posted to all manner of social media—venturing well beyond "just words" to include photos, drawings, maps, sound, video, and visuals of all kinds. In addition, they were clearly aware that they could reach an audience far beyond their classrooms. In short, we were responding to a sea change we saw in students as they entered enthusiastically into what media scholar Henry Jenkins refers to as our "participatory culture."

So we set out to create a text that would introduce students to the joy and power and responsibility of authorship, that would present writing as it really is today—multimodal, multimedia, multilingual, and deeply digitized—and that would show students how the basic insights of rhetoric are applicable to writing in any media, any genre, any language. Our book's title argues that today, *everyone* with access to the internet can become an author who can reach broad audiences. And it aims to speak to every student who will use it: we want all students to see themselves in the pages of this book.

So these have been the overarching goals for our text. We aim to connect to students where they are, with the kinds of reading and writing they do *outside* the classroom; to acknowledge the communities they belong to; and to show respect for their linguistic and cultural diversity. We've included examples of language at work (and play) everywhere, from *YouTube* videos to ads, from hip-hop to classical genres, from pickup basketball to the Olympics. In the pages of our book, students meet a community college student working two jobs while attending school full-time; a man who walks 21 miles every day to work; an ex-con who became a successful college student and published author; and many more. On every page, we try to show that *every* student has important ideas and significant things to say, and that we stand ready to help them do so.

Everyone's an Author thus acknowledges the primacy of writing and verbal communication in today's world, echoing the findings of Deborah Brandt and other researchers who demonstrate that writing has surpassed reading as the most significant literate practice of our time. For teachers of writing and rhetoric everywhere, this is good news indeed. But there's also an underbelly of bad news: as writing has exploded exponentially through social media, the ability to spread untrustworthy, mean-spirited, and dangerous ideas has also exploded.

We came to work on this third edition of *Everyone's an Author*, then, with a sense of urgency. Could we find ways to help students resist the lure of clickbait and misinformation, help them rev up their critical-thinking engines and become hardheaded fact-checkers who are not taken in by misleading and false stories? Could we do this while at the same time helping students remain open to ideas that differ from theirs and to people with different backgrounds and convictions? These two issues—being open to new and different ideas yet capable of critical skepticism—are two sides of the same "ethos" coin perhaps captured best in the Russian proverb: "Trust, but verify." We hope this edition answers "yes, we can, and yes, we did" to these questions—primarily in two new chapters.

Chapter 2, **"Engaging Respectfully with Others,"** provides concrete guidance to help students listen actively and respectfully so they can really hear what others are saying and can understand, as much as possible, why they are saying it.

But even as students practice empathy and look for common ground, they also must be strong critical thinkers. So in Chapter 8, **"Distinguishing Facts from Misinformation,"** students learn first to look closely at their own beliefs and values—questioning where those beliefs came from and considering whether to uphold those ideas or let them go—and then learn practical steps for reading *defensively*.

Knowing how to find and verify what media critic Howard Rheingold calls "the good stuff" calls for strong reading abilities, and that's one reason we have included a new part on **"Reading Processes"** (now Part 2) in this edition. This part comprises three chapters that provide advice for active, engaged reading; annotating texts; writing summary/response essays; and much more.

This edition continues to see students as resourceful writers and readers who bring strengths to the work they do in college. One such strength is linguistic versatility. Students are coming to college today with multiple languages and the abilities that go along with them. In addition, all students bring with them some regional, ethnic, occupational, or other dialects. A new chapter, "**Mixing Languages and Dialects**," recognizes this fact of contemporary life and shows students how to put their linguistic versatility to work in college and beyond. Throughout, this chapter encourages students to draw on their own home languages and dialects to connect to audiences and to present their messages most effectively.

And, as always, this third edition of *Everyone's an Author* is grounded in rhetoric, which we define as "the art, theory, and practice of ethical communication." Of course rhetoric can be (and often is) used for nefarious, harmful, even evil purposes: in fact, as our book rolls off the presses, the use of rhetoric to humiliate and belittle, to confuse and distract, to distort and mislead is on the rise. But giving in to these misuses would mean giving up on rhetoric as ethical communication. And that we cannot do. Never has it been more important for teachers to embrace and practice ethical communication and to pass it on to their students. Teachers of writing everywhere have an urgent obligation to help students understand the pervasive forces appealing to people's worst instincts and build tools capable of revealing these negative and destructive forces for what they are. This means providing students with the rhetorical knowledge and strategies that can lead to true, honest, honorable, and good communication.

We believe that the third edition of *Everyone's an Author* embodies these aims and ideals and that teachers and students will respond to its message and become authors who are always—always!—ethical communicators.

Other Highlights

- *NEW advice on developing academic habits of mind* now appears in Chapter 4, "Meeting the Expectations of Academic Writing."

- *A NEW chapter on "Editing the Errors That Matter"* covers 14 errors that teachers identified as ones that undermine a writer's authority and explains why these errors matter, how to spot them in a draft, and how to edit them out. InQuizitive activities give students more practice editing the same errors online.

- *NEW readings and examples* students will relate to. From a rhetorical analysis of smart speakers with female voices and a student's narrative about growing up in his family's nail salon business to a review of *Black Panther* and an argument for deleting social media accounts, we hope that all students will find examples and images that will make them smile—and inspire them to read and write.

- *On the need for rhetoric.* From Chapter 1 on "Thinking Rhetorically" to the many prompts throughout the book that help students reflect on their own rhetorical situations and choices, this book makes students aware of the importance of rhetoric and shows them the power of understanding and using it.

- *On research.* The challenge today's students face is not gathering data but making sense of massive amounts of information and using it effectively in support of their own arguments. Chapters 20 to 29 cover all stages of research, from finding and evaluating sources to citing and documenting them. Guidelines for evaluating sources have been updated to help students judge accuracy and avoid misinformation.

- *On argument.* Chapter 12 covers "Arguing a Position," Chapter 18 covers "Analyzing and Constructing Arguments," and Chapter 19 offers "Strategies for Supporting an Argument."

- *On writing in multiple modes.* Chapter 35 provides practical advice on writing illustrated essays, blogs, wikis, audio and video essays, and posters, and Chapter 36 covers oral presentations. The companion *Tumblr* site provides a regularly updated source of multimodal readings.

- *On social justice.* Minimum wages, safe drinking water, Black Lives Matter, safety at school: many of the examples in this book demonstrate how people use writing in ways that strive to create "a more perfect union," a society that is just and equitable for all its members. We don't always agree on how to go about reaching those goals, and that's why rhetoric and civic discourse matter.

- *Menus, directories, documentation templates, and a glossary / index* make the book easy to use—and to understand.

Everyone's an Author is available in two versions, with and without an anthology of 32 readings. Readings are arranged alphabetically by author, with menus indexing the readings by genre and theme. And the book is formatted as two books in one, rhetoric in front and readings in the back. You can therefore center your course on either the rhetoric or the readings, since links in the margins will help you draw from the other part as you wish to.

What's Online

Ebooks, available for both versions of the text, provide an enhanced reading experience at a fraction of the cost of a print textbook. Norton ebooks allow students to access the entire book, highlight, bookmark, and take notes with ease, allowing students to practice active reading as it's modeled in *Everyone's an Author.* The ebooks can be viewed on—and synced between— all computers and mobile devices and include links to online multimodal examples referenced in the text. Ebook access comes free with all new copies of this textbook. See the bind-in card in the front of this book for more information.

InQuizitive for Writers delivers a game-like approach to practicing sentence editing and working with sources. After practicing with InQuizitive, students will be better prepared to find and edit errors in their own writing, and they will approach research projects with more focus and confidence. The activities are adaptive so students receive additional practice in the areas where they need more help. And explanatory feedback offers advice precisely when it's needed. The learning objectives covered in InQuizitive for Writers align with the "Editing the Errors That Matter" chapter in *Everyone's an Author.* InQuizitive for Writers access comes free with all new copies of this textbook. See the bind-in card in the front of this book for more information.

Everyonesanauthor.tumblr.com, a dynamic collection of online media curated by book author Michal Brody, provides a rich, regularly updated source of readings—including articles, speeches, advertisements, and more—for inspiration, analysis, and response. Readings are sortable by theme, genre, and medium, and each reading is accompanied by a headnote and prompts that guide students to evaluate, reflect, and develop arguments. "Conversation" clusters pair multiple readings with diverse viewpoints on contemporary topics. Find a chapter-by-chapter menu of the online examples in this book by clicking "Links from the Book." See you and your students at *everyonesanauthor.tumblr.com!*

Resources for your LMS. You can easily add high-quality Norton digital resources to your online, hybrid, or lecture course. All activities can be accessed within your existing learning management system, and many components are customizable. The *Everyone's an Author* coursepack files include reading comprehension quizzes for every chapter and reading in the book; assignable short-answer prompts and discussion questions that ask students to apply skills discussed in the text, some tied to "Think Beyond Words" and "Reflect" prompts from the book; model student papers; quizzes and exercises on grammar and research; documentation guidelines; revision worksheets, and more.

Author videos. Andrea Lunsford, Lisa Ede, Beverly Moss, Carole Clark Papper, and Keith Walters answer questions they're often asked by other instructors: about fostering collaboration, teaching multimodal writing, taking advantage of the writing center, teaching classes that include both L1 and L2 students, and more. View the videos at *everyonesanauthor.tumblr.com*.

The Guide to Teaching *Everyone's an Author*

Written by the book's authors, the *Everyone's an Author* Instructor's Guide includes specific advice for teaching every chapter and reading in the text and general advice for teaching first-year writing. It now includes new suggested classroom activities and writing assignments; more sample syllabi; and new coverage of teaching reading, maintaining a respectful classroom environment, and teaching facts versus misinformation. Available online and in print.

Find all of the resources at **wwnorton.com/instructors**.

Acknowledgments

We are profoundly grateful to the many people who have helped bring *Everyone's an Author* into existence. Indeed, this text provides a perfect example of what an eighteenth-century German encyclopedia meant when it defined *book* as "the work of many hands." Certainly this one is the work of many hands, and among those hands none have been more instrumental than those of Marilyn Moller: the breadth of her vision is matched by her meticulous attention to detail, keen sense of style and design, and ability to get more work done than anyone we have ever known. Throughout the process of conceiving and composing this text, she has set the bar high for us, and we've tried hard to reach it. For this edition, we have been graced with the editorial wisdom, wit, generosity, and organizational acumen of Erica Wnek, who has guided us in all the best ways and managed to keep us on track throughout this complex process of group revision. A big thank-you as well to Marian Johnson for making time to read and respond to many of the chapters in the first edition.

We are similarly grateful to many others who contributed their talents to this book, especially Christine D'Antonio and Jane Searle, for all they did to produce this book (no small undertaking). Thanks as well to Elizabeth Trammell for her work clearing the many text permissions and to Ted Szczepanski and Elyse Rieder for their work finding and clearing permissions for the many images. Last but certainly not least, we thank Edwin Jeng for undertaking countless tasks large and small with efficiency, conscientiousness, and smarts.

Everyone's an Author is more than just a print book, and we thank Sam Held as well as Joy Cranshaw, Katie Bolger, Cooper Wilhelm, and Michael Hicks for producing the superb resources that support the text, including the ebook, InQuizitive, LMS resources, and instructor's guide. And we again want to thank Cliff Landesman for his work in imagining and creating the fantastic *Tumblr* site.

The design of this book is something we are particularly proud of, and for that we offer very special thanks to several amazing designers. Stephen Doyle created the spectacular cover that embodies a key message of our book: that we live in a world made of words and images. Carin Berger created the illuminated alphabet, also made of text, that opens every chapter. JoAnne Metsch and Lissi Sigillo did the lovely interior design. And Debra Morton-Hoyt, Rubina Yeh, and Michael Wood oversaw the whole thing as well as adding their own elegant—and whimsical!—touches inside and out. Best thanks to all of them.

Special thanks to the fabled Norton Travelers, who have worked so hard to consult with teachers across the country about what *Everyone's an Author* can offer them. And a big thank-you to Michele Dobbins, Elizabeth Pieslor, Emily Rowan, and Lib Triplett for helping us keep our eye on our audience: teachers and students at colleges where rhetorics of this kind are assigned. Finally, we are grateful to Roby Harrington, Julia Reidhead, Steve

Dunn, and Mike Wright, who have given their unwavering support to this project for more than a decade now. We are fortunate indeed to have had the talent and hard work of this distinguished Norton team.

An astute and extremely helpful group of reviewers has helped us more than we can say: we have depended on their good pedagogical sense and advice in revising every chapter of this book. Special thanks to Forster Agama, Tallahassee Community College; Jacob Babb, Indiana University Southeast; Edward Baldwin, College of Southern Nevada; Brooke Ballard, Lone Star College–CyFair; Nancy Barendse, Charleston Southern University; Dawn Bergeron, St. Johns River State College; J. Andrew Briseño, Northwestern State University; Paul Cook, Indiana University Kokomo; Adrienne J. Daly, University of Rhode Island; Christine Davis, Northern Arizona University; James M. Decker, Illinois Central College; Sara DiCaglio, Texas A&M University; Beth Ebersbaker, Lee College; Michael Emerson, Northwestern Michigan College; Michael Faris, Texas Tech University; Wioleta Fedeczko, Utah Valley University; Bill FitzGerald, Rutgers University–Camden; Stephanie Freuler, Valencia State College; Jennifer Holly-Wells, Montclair State University; Debra Knutson, Shawnee State University; Lynn C. Lewis, Oklahoma State University; Cathy Mahaffey, University of North Carolina, Charlotte; Sadeem El Nahhas, Northwestern State University; Nicole F. Oechslin, Piedmont Virginia Community College; Kate Pantelides, Middle Tennessee State University; Jerry Petersen, Utah Valley University; Mary Jo Reiff, University of Kansas; Thomas Reynolds, Northwestern State University; Janice Rieman, University of North Carolina, Charlotte; Mary Elizabeth Rogers, Florida Gateway College; Pamela Saunders, Suffolk University; Emerson Schroeter, Northern Arizona University; Shawna Shapiro, Middlebury College; Kaia Simon, University of Wisconsin–Eau Claire; Kristen Snoddy, Indiana University Kokomo; Daniel Stanford, Pitt Community College; Shannon C. Stewart, Coastal Carolina University; Emily Suh, Texas State University; Edwin Turner, St. Johns River State College; Verne Underwood, Rogue Community College; Melanie Verner, Lee College; Courtney Wooten, George Mason University; Craig Wynne, Hampton University; and Vershawn Ashanti Young, University of Waterloo.

We'd also like to thank those reviewers who helped us to shape the previous editions: Stevens Amidon, Indiana University–Purdue Fort Wayne; Georgana Atkins, University of Mississippi; Michelle Ballif, University of Georgia; Larry Beason, University of South Alabama, Mobile; Kristen Belcher, University of Colorado, Denver; Samantha Bell, Johnson County Community College; Cassandra Bishop, Southern Illinois University; Kevin Boyle, College of Southern Nevada; Erin Breaux, South Louisiana Community College; Elizabeth Brockman, Central Michigan University; Stephen Brown, University of Nevada, Las Vegas; Ellie Bunting, Edison State College; Vicki Byard, Northeastern Illinois University; Maggie Callahan, Louisiana State University; Laura Chartier, University of Alaska, Anchorage; Tera Joy Cole, Idaho State University; Beth Daniell, Kennesaw State University; Anne-Marie Deitering, Oregon State University; Nancy DeJoy, Michigan State University; Debra Dew, Valparaiso University; Robyn DeWall, Idaho State University; Ronda Dively, Southern Illinois University, Carbondale; Patrick Dolan Jr., University of Iowa; Douglas Downs, Montana State University; Suellynn Duffey, University of Missouri, St. Louis; Anne Dvorak, Longview Community College; Maryam El-Shall, Jamestown Community College; Patricia Ericsson, Washington State University; Frank Farmer, University of Kansas; Casie Fedukovich, North Carolina State University; Lindsay Ferrara, Fairfield University; Lauren Fitzgerald, Yeshiva University; Maureen Fitzpatrick, Johnson County Community College; Kitty Flowers, University of Indianapolis; Robin Gallaher, Northwest Missouri State University; Diana Grumbles, Southern Methodist University; Ann Guess, Alvin Community College; Michael Harker, Georgia State University; Samuel Head, Idaho State University; Tara Hembrough, Southern Illinois University; Charlotte Hogg, Texas Christian University; Emma Howes, Coastal Carolina University; Melissa Ianetta, University of Delaware; Joyce Inman, University of Southern Mississippi; Jordynn Jack, University of North Carolina, Chapel Hill; Sara Jameson, Oregon State University; David A. Jolliffe, University of Arkansas; Ann Jurecic, Rutgers University; Connie Kendall, University of Cincinnati; William Lalicker, West Chester University; Michelle S. Lee, Daytona State College; Sonja Lynch, Wartburg College; Phillip Marzluf, Kansas State University; Richard Matzen, Woodbury University; Moriah McCracken, The University of Texas, Pan American; Mary Pat McQueeney, Johnson County Community College; Clyde Moneyhun, Boise State University; Chelsea Murdock, University of Kansas; Whitney Myers, Texas Wesleyan University; Carroll Ferguson Nardone, Sam Houston State University; Jessie Nixon, University of Alaska, Anchorage; Rolf Norgaard, University of Colorado, Boulder; Katherine Durham Oldmixon, Huston-Tillotson University; Matthew Oliver, Old Dominion University; Gary Olson, Idaho State University; Paula Patch, Elon University; Scott Payne, University of Central Arkansas; Albert Rouzie, Ohio University; Alison Russell, Xavier University; Kathleen J. Ryan, University of Montana; Matthew Schmeer, Johnson County Community College; Emily Robins Sharpe, Penn State University; John Sherrill, Purdue University;

Mary Lourdes Silva, Ithaca College; Marc Simoes, California State University, Long Beach; Eddie Singleton, The Ohio State University; Allison Smith, Middle Tennessee State University; Susan Smith, Georgia Southern University; Tracie Smith, University of Indianapolis; Paulette Swartzfager, Rochester Institute of Technology; Deborah Coxwell Teague, Florida State University; Jason Tham, St. Cloud State University; Tom Thompson, The Citadel; Jennifer Vala, Georgia State University; Rex Veeder, St. Cloud State University; Emily Ward, Idaho State University; Matthew Wiles, University of Louisville; Lauren Woolbright, Clemson University; and Mary Wright, Christopher Newport University.

Collectively, we have taught for over 150 years: that's a lot of classes, a lot of students—and we are grateful for every single one of them. We owe some of the best moments of our lives to them—and in our most challenging moments, they have inspired us to carry on. In *Everyone's an Author,* we are particularly grateful to the student writers whose work adds so much to this text: Ade Adegboyega, Rutgers University; Crystal Aymelek, Portland State University; Halle Edwards, Stanford University; Ryan Joy, Portland State University; Julia Landauer, Stanford University; Larry Lehna, University of Michigan, Dearborn; Melanie Luken, The Ohio State University; David Pasini, The Ohio State University; Walter Przybylowski, Rutgers University; Melissa Rubin, Hofstra University; Shuqiao Song, Stanford University; Katryn Sheppard, Portland State University; Katherine Spriggs, Stanford University; Manisha Ummadi, University of California, Berkeley; Saurabh Vaish, Hofstra University; Yuliya Vayner, Hunter College; and Kameron Wiles, Ball State University.

Each of us also has special debts of gratitude. Andrea Lunsford thanks her students and colleagues at the Bread Loaf Graduate School of English and in the Program in Writing and Rhetoric at Stanford, along with her sisters Ellen Ashdown and Liz Middleton, editor and friend Marilyn Moller, friends and life supporters Shirley Brice Heath, Betty Bailey, Cheryl Glenn, Beverly Moss, Marvin Diogenes, and Adam Banks; and especially—and forever—her grandnieces Audrey and Lila Ashdown, already compelling authors.

Michal Brody would like to thank her two wonderful families in the United States and Yucatán who so graciously support (and endure) her crazy and restless transnational life. Her conversations with each and all of those loved ones provide the constant impetus to reach for clarity and honesty of expression. She also thanks her students in both countries, who remind her every day that we are all teachers, all learners.

Lisa Ede thanks her husband, Greg Pfarr, for his support, for his commitment to his own art, and for their year-round vegetable garden. Thanks as well to her siblings, who have stuck together through thick and thin: Leni Ede Smith, Andrew Ede, Sara Ede Rowkamp, Michele Ede Smith, Laurie Ede Drake, Robert Ede, and Julie Ede Campbell. She also thanks her colleagues in the Oregon State School of Writing, Literature, and Film for their encouragement and support.

Beverly Moss thanks her parents, Harry and Sarah Moss, for their love, encouragement, and confidence in her when her own wavered. In addition, she thanks her Ohio State and Bread Loaf students, who inspire her and teach her so much about teaching. She also wants to express gratitude to her colleagues in Rhetoric, Composition, and Literacy at Ohio State for their incredible support. Finally, she thanks two of her own former English teachers, Dorothy Bratton and Jackie Royster, for the way they modeled excellence inside and outside the classroom.

Carole Clark Papper would like to thank her husband, Bob, and wonderful children—Dana, Matt, Zack, and Kate—without whose loving support little would happen and nothing would matter. In addition, she is grateful for the inspiration and support over the years of teachers, colleagues, and students at Ohio State, Ball State, and Hofstra, but especially for Beverly Moss and Andrea Lunsford for launching her on this journey.

Keith Walters thanks his partner of thirty-seven years and husband of fourteen, Jonathan Tamez, for sharing a love of life, language, travel, flowers, and beauty. He is also grateful to his students in Tunisia, South Carolina, Texas, Oregon, and Palestine who have challenged him to find ways of talking about what good writing is and how to do it.

Finally, we thank those who have taught us—who first helped us learn to hold a pencil and print our names, who inspired a love of language and of reading and writing, who encouraged us to take chances in writing our lives as best we could, who prodded and pushed when we needed it, and who most of all set brilliant examples for us to follow. One person who taught almost all of us—about rhetoric, about writing, and about life—was Edward P. J. Corbett. We remember him with love and with gratitude

—Andrea Lunsford, Michal Brody, Lisa Ede,
Beverly Moss, Carole Clark Papper, Keith Walters

CONTENTS

Preface   *v*

Introduction: Is Everyone an Author?   *xxix*

PART I   The Need for Rhetoric and Writing   *1*

1   Thinking Rhetorically   *5*

First, Listen   *8*
Hear What Others Are Saying—and Think about Why   *9*
What Do You Think—and Why?   *10*
Do Your Homework   *11*
Give Credit   *13*
Be Imaginative   *13*
Put In Your Oar   *15*

2   Engaging Respectfully with Others   *18*

Get to Know People Different from You   *19*
Practice Empathy   *21*
Demonstrate Respect   *23*
Search for Common Ground   *24*
Invite Response   *26*
Join the Conversation   *27*

3   Rhetorical Situations   *28*

Genre   *30*
Audience   *31*
Purpose   *32*

Stance *33*
Context *33*
Medium and Design *34*

4 Meeting the Expectations of Academic Writing 35
Habits of Mind for Academic Success *36*
So Just What Is Edited Academic Writing? *38*
Joining US Academic Conversations *39*
CHARACTERISTIC FEATURES *42*
Use edited academic English / Use clear patterns of organization / Mark
logical relationships between ideas / State claims explicitly and provide
appropriate support / Present your ideas as a response to others / Express
ideas clearly and directly / Be aware of how genres and conventions vary
across disciplines / Document sources using appropriate citation style

5 Writing and Rhetoric in the Workplace 50
Consider Your Rhetorical Situation *52*
Be Professional *53*
Job Letters *53*
Résumés *58*
References *60*
Writing Samples *60*
Job Interviews *61*
Writing on the Job *62*

PART II Reading Processes 65

6 Reading Rhetorically 67
Thinking about Your Rhetorical Situation *69*
Becoming an Active, Engaged Reader *69*
Fast—and Slow—Reading *70*
Unfamiliar or Difficult Texts *72*
On-Screen and Off *72*
Across Genres *76*
Across Academic Disciplines *77*

7 Annotating, Summarizing, Responding 79
Annotating *80*

Summarizing *86*
Responding *88*
Summary/Response Essays *90*
YULIYA VAYNER, *The Higher Price of Buying Local* *93*

8 Distinguishing Facts from Misinformation 98
Defining Facts and Misinformation *98*
Think about Your Own Beliefs *100*
Read Defensively and Find the Good Stuff *101*
Fact-Check Photos and Videos *105*

PART III Writing Processes 109

9 Managing the Writing Process 113
A ROADMAP *115*
Approach Your Writing Pragmatically *122*

10 The Need for Collaboration / "Here Comes Everybody!" 123
What Collaboration Means for Authors—and Audiences *125*
What Collaboration Means for You as a Student *127*
Collaboration with a Writing Tutor *127*
Collaboration at Work *128*
Some Tips for Collaborating Effectively *130*

PART IV Genres of Writing 133

11 Choosing Genres 137
What You Need to Know about Genres of Writing *138*
Deciding Which Genres to Use *140*

12 Arguing a Position / "This Is Where I Stand" 143
Across Academic Disciplines / Media / Cultures and Communities / Genres

CHARACTERISTIC FEATURES   *147*

An explicit position / A response to what others have said or done /
Appropriate background information / A clear indication of why the
topic matters / Good reasons and evidence / Attention to more than one
point of view / An authoritative tone / An appeal to readers' values

A ROADMAP   *164*

READINGS

RUSSEL HONORÉ, *Work Is a Blessing*   *162*

JARON LANIER, *Delete Your Social Media Accounts Right Now*   *172*

KATHERINE SPRIGGS, *On Buying Local*   *177*

13   Writing a Narrative / "Here's What Happened"   *186*

Across Academic Disciplines / Media / Cultures and Communities / Genres

CHARACTERISTIC FEATURES   *192*

A clearly identified event / A clearly described setting / Vivid, descriptive
details / A consistent point of view / A clear point

LITERACY NARRATIVES   *208*

A well-told story / A firsthand account /
An indication of the narrative's significance

A ROADMAP   *214*

READINGS

RAYA ELFADEL KHEIRBEK, *Healing the Doctor-Patient Relationship*   *202*

MELANIE LUKEN, *Literacy: A Lineage*   *209*

CONNOR COYNE, *Bathtime*   *219*

LARRY LEHNA, *The Look*   *224*

14   Writing Analytically / "Let's Take a Closer Look"   *229*

Across Academic Disciplines / Media / Cultures and Communities / Genres

CHARACTERISTIC FEATURES   *234*

A question that prompts a closer look / Some description of the subject /
Evidence drawn from close examination of the subject / Insight gained from
your analysis / Clear, precise language

VISUAL ANALYSIS *256*

A description of the visual / Some contextual information / Attention to any words / Close analysis of the message / Insight into what the visual "says" / Precise language

A ROADMAP *262*

READINGS

EAMONN FORDE, *Why Pharrell's "Happy" Has Grabbed the Nation* *252*
SOMINI SENGUPTA, *Why Is Everyone Focused on Zuckerberg's Hoodie?* *259*
JOHNA PAOLINO, *Google Home vs Alexa* *272*
MELISSA RUBIN, *Advertisements R Us* *276*

15 Reporting Information / "Just the Facts" 282

Across Academic Disciplines / Media / Cultures and Communities / Genres

CHARACTERISTIC FEATURES *288*

A topic carefully focused for a specific audience / Definitions of key terms / Trustworthy information / Appropriate organization and design / A confident, informative tone

PROFILES *301*

A firsthand account / Detailed information about the subject / An interesting angle

A ROADMAP *311*

READINGS

WIKIPEDIA, *Gender* *298*
BILL LAITNER, *Heart and Sole: Detroiter Walks 21 Miles to Work* *304*
BARRY ESTABROOK, *Selling the Farm* *318*
RYAN JOY, *The Right to Preach on a College Campus* *324*

16 Writing a Review / "Two Thumbs Up" 328

Across Academic Disciplines / Media / Cultures and Communities / Genres

CHARACTERISTIC FEATURES *333*

Relevant information about the subject / Criteria for the evaluation / A well-supported evaluation / Attention to the audience's needs and expectations / An authoritative tone / Awareness of the ethics of reviewing

LITERATURE REVIEWS   *348*

A survey of relevant research on a carefully focused topic / An objective summary of the literature / An evaluation of the literature / An appropriate organization / Careful, accurate documentation

A ROADMAP   *356*

READINGS

TIM ALAMENCIAK, *Monopoly: The Scandal behind the Game*   *345*

CRYSTAL AYMELEK, *The Effects of Mindfulness Meditation on Memory*   *350*

MARC BERNARDIN, Black Panther *Gets So Much Right*   *362*

MANISHA UMMADI, *Indie Gem Expertly Captures Mental Illness*   *367*

17   Making a Proposal / "Here's What I Recommend"   371

Across Academic Disciplines / Media / Cultures and Communities / Genres

CHARACTERISTIC FEATURES   *374*

A precise description of the problem / A clear and compelling solution / Evidence that your solution will address the problem / Acknowledgment of other possible solutions / A statement of what your proposal will accomplish

PROJECT PROPOSALS   *386*

An indication of your topic and focus / An explanation of why you're interested in the topic / A plan / A schedule

A ROADMAP   *391*

READINGS

INTERDISCIPLINARY GROUP ON PREVENTING SCHOOL AND COMMUNITY VIOLENCE, *Call for Action to Prevent Gun Violence*   *383*

DAVID PASINI, *The Economic Impact of Investing in Sports Franchises*   *387*

SHERYL SANDBERG / ADAM GRANT, *Speaking While Female*   *396*

SHAWNA SHAPIRO, *Snowflakes and Free Speech on Campuses*   *400*

PART V   The Centrality of Argument   405

18   Analyzing and Constructing Arguments   411

Where's the Argument Coming From?   *412*

What's the Claim?   *415*

What's at Stake? *419*
Means of Persuasion: Emotional, Ethical, and Logical Appeals *421*
What about Other Perspectives? *434*
Ways of Structuring Arguments *438*
Classical / Toulmin / Rogerian / Invitational
Matters of Style *448*

19 Strategies for Supporting an Argument 451
Analogy *451*
Cause / Effect *453*
Classification *455*
Comparison / Contrast *457*
Definition *460*
Description *462*
Examples *464*
Humor *466*
Narration *468*
Problem / Solution *469*
Reiteration *471*

PART VI Research 475

20 Starting Your Research / Joining the Conversation 477
Find a Topic That Fascinates You *478*
Consider Your Rhetorical Situation *479*
Narrow Your Topic *480*
Do Some Background Research *482*
Articulate a Question Your Research Will Answer *482*
Plot Out a Working Thesis *484*
Establish a Schedule *485*

21 Finding Sources / Online, at the Library, in the Field 486
Starting with *Wikipedia*—or Social Media *487*
What Kind of Sources Do You Need? *488*
Determining If a Source Is Scholarly *490*
Types of Sources—and Where to Find Them *493*

Research Sites: On the Internet, in the Library   *497*
Running Searches   *503*
Conducting Field Research   *506*

22 Keeping Track / Managing Information Overload   *515*
Keep Track of Your Sources   *515*
Take Notes   *516*
Maintain a Working Bibliography   *518*

23 Evaluating Sources   *520*
Is the Source Worth Your Attention?   *521*
Reading Sources with a Critical Eye   *526*

24 Annotating a Bibliography   *529*
CHARACTERISTIC FEATURES   *529*
Complete bibliographic information / A brief summary or description of each work / Evaluative comments / Some indication of how each source will inform your research / A consistent and concise presentation
SAURABH VAISH, *Renewable and Sustainable Energy in Rural India*   *531*

25 Synthesizing Ideas   *534*
Synthesizing the Ideas in Your Sources   *535*
Moving from What Your Sources Say to What You Say   *537*
Entering the Conversation You've Been Researching   *539*

26 Quoting, Paraphrasing, Summarizing   *541*
Deciding Whether to Quote, Paraphrase, or Summarize   *542*
Quoting   *543*
Paraphrasing   *547*
Summarizing   *549*
Incorporating Source Material   *551*
Incorporating Visual and Audio Sources   *553*

27 Giving Credit, Avoiding Plagiarism   *555*
Knowing What You Must Acknowledge   *556*
Fair Use and the Internet   *557*
Avoiding Plagiarism   *558*
Documenting Sources   *562*

28 MLA Style *563*

A Directory to MLA Style *563*
In-Text Documentation *565*
Notes *571*
List of Works Cited *572*
Formatting a Research Paper *598*
WALTER PRZYBYLOWSKI, *Holding Up the Hollywood Stagecoach* *601*

29 APA Style *618*

A Directory to APA Style *618*
In-Text Documentation *620*
Notes *625*
Reference List *625*
Formatting a Research Essay *644*
KATRYN SHEPPARD, *A Study of One Child's Word Productions* *647*

PART VII Style *663*

30 What's Your Style? *667*

Appropriateness and Correctness *668*
Connecting with Audiences *671*
Level of Formality *673*
Stance *674*
Tone *676*
Across Media *677*
Across Disciplines *679*
Thinking about Your Own Style *680*

31 Mixing Languages and Dialects *683*

Using Edited Academic English and Other Dialects *685*
Connecting with Audiences *686*
Providing Translation *687*
Illustrating a Point *689*
Drawing Attention *691*
Quoting People Directly and Respectfully *691*
Evoking a Particular Person, Place, or Community *692*

32 How to Craft Good Sentences 694

Four Common Sentence Patterns *695*

Ways of Emphasizing the Main Idea in a Sentence *701*

Opening Sentences *704*

Closing Sentences *707*

Varying Your Sentences *709*

33 Editing the Errors That Matter 713

Sentences *714*

Pronouns *725*

Verbs *734*

Quotations *740*

Commas *746*

Words That Are Often Confused *750*

PART VIII Design and Delivery 755

34 Designing What You Write 757

Thinking Rhetorically about Design *758*

Choosing Fonts *760*

Adding Headings *760*

Using Color *761*

Using Visuals *763*

Putting It All Together *771*

Getting Response to Your Design *773*

35 Writing in Multiple Modes 776

Defining Multimodal Writing *776*

Considering Your Rhetorical Situation *778*

Illustrated Essays *779*

Blogs *781*

Wikis *784*

Audio Essays *786*

Video Essays *788*

Posters *790*

Managing a Multimodal Project *792*

36 Making Presentations   *794*

HALLE EDWARDS, *The Rise of Female Heroes in Shoujo Manga*   *797*

A ROADMAP   *803*

37 Assembling a Portfolio   *809*

What to Include in a Writing Portfolio   *810*
Collecting Your Work   *811*
Reflecting on Your Writing   *812*
Organizing a Portfolio   *815*

38 Publishing Your Writing   *818*

Credits   *821*

About the Authors   *826*

About the Alphabet   *828*

Submitting Papers   *831*

Author / Title Index   *833*

Glossary / Index   *845*

MLA and APA Directories   *878*

Is Everyone an Author?

 E'VE CHOSEN A PROVOCATIVE TITLE for this book, so it's fair to ask if we've gotten it right, if everyone is an author. Let's take just a few examples that can help to make the point:

- A student creates an *Instagram* account, which immediately finds a large audience of other interested people.

- A visitor to the United States sends an email to a few friends and family members in Slovakia—and they begin forwarding it. The message circles the globe in a day.

- A professor assigns students in her class to work together to write a number of entries for *Wikipedia*, and they are surprised to find how quickly their entries are revised by others.

- An airline executive writes a letter of apology for unconscionable delays in service and publishes the letter in newspapers, where millions will read it.

- A small group of high school students who are keen on cooking post their recipe for Crispy Candy Cookies on their *Cook's Corner* blog and are overwhelmed by the number of responses to their invention.

- Five women nominated for the Academy Award for Best Actress prepare acceptance speeches: one of them will deliver the speech live before an international audience.

- You get your next assignment in your college writing class and set out to do the research necessary to complete it. When you're finished, you turn in your twelve-page argument to your instructor and classmates for their responses—and you also post a short excerpt from it on *Twitter*.

All of these examples represent important messages written by people who probably do not consider themselves authors. Yet they illustrate what we mean when we say that today "everyone's an author." Once upon a time, the ability to compose a message that reached wide and varied audiences was restricted to a small group; now, however, this opportunity is available to anyone with access to the internet.

The word *author* has a long history, but it is most associated with the rise of print and the ability of writers to claim what they have written as property. The first copyright act, in the early eighteenth century, ruled that authors held the primary rights to their work. And while anyone could potentially be a writer, an author was someone whose work had been published. That rough definition worked pretty well until recently, when traditional copyright laws began to show the strain of their 300-year history, most notably with the simple and easy file sharing that the internet makes possible.

In fact, the web has blurred the distinction between writers and authors, offering anyone with access to the internet the opportunity to publish what they write. If you have access to the internet (at school, at a library, at home), you can publish what you write and thus make what you say available to readers around the world.

Think for a minute about the impact of blogs, which first appeared in 1997. When this book was first published, there were more than 156 million public blogs, and as this new edition goes to press, there are more than 478 million blogs on *Tumblr* alone. Add to blogs the rise of *Twitter, YouTube, Instagram, Facebook,* and other social networking sites for even more evidence to support our claim: today, everyone's an author. Moreover, twenty-first-century authors just don't fit the image of the Romantic writer, alone in a garret, struggling to bring forth something unique. Rather, today's authors are part of a huge, often global, conversation; they build on what others have thought and written, they create mash-ups and remixes, and they practice teamwork at almost every turn. They are authoring for the digital age.

Redefining Writing

If the definition of *author* has changed in recent years, so has our understanding of the definition, nature, and scope of *writing*.

Writing, for example, now includes much more than words, as images and graphics take on an important part of the job of conveying meaning. In addition, writing now includes sound, video, and other media. Perhaps more important, writing now often contains many voices, as information from the internet is incorporated into the texts we write with ease. Finally, as we noted above, writing today is almost always part of a larger conversation. Rather than rising mysteriously from the depths of a writer's original thoughts, a stereotype made popular during the Romantic period, writing almost always responds to some other written piece or to other ideas. If "no man [or woman] is an island, entire of itself," then the same holds true for writing.

Writing now is also often highly collaborative. You work with a team to produce an illustrated report, the basis of which is used by members of the team to make a key presentation to management; you and a classmate carry out an experiment, argue over and write up the results together, and present your findings to the class; a business class project calls on you and others in your group to divide up the work along lines of expertise and then to pool your efforts in meeting the assignment. In all of these cases, writing is also performative—it performs an action or, in the words of many students we have talked with, it "makes something happen in the world."

Perhaps most notable, this expanded sense of writing challenges us to think very carefully about what our writing is for and whom it can and might reach. Email provides a good case in point. In the aftermath of the September 11 attacks, Tamim Ansary, a writer who was born in Afghanistan, found himself stunned by the number of people calling for bombing Afghanistan "back to the Stone Age." He sent an email to a few friends expressing his horror at the events, his condemnation of Osama bin Laden and the Taliban, and his hope that those in the United States would not act on the basis of gross stereotyping. The few dozen friends to whom Ansary wrote hit their forward buttons. Within days, the letter had circled the globe more than once, and Ansary's words were published by the Africa News Service, the *Philippine Daily Inquirer*, the *Evening Standard* in London, the *San Francisco Chronicle* and many other papers in the United States, as well as on many websites.

Authors whose messages can be instantly transported around the world need to consider those who will receive those messages. As the example of Tamim Ansary shows, no longer can writers assume that they write only to a specified audience or that they can easily control the dissemination of their messages. We now live not only in a city, a state, and a country but in a global community as well—and we write, intentionally or not, to speakers of many languages, to members of many cultures, to believers of many creeds.

Everyone's a Researcher

Since all writing responds to the ideas and words of others, it usually draws on some kind of research. Think for a moment of how often you carry out research. We're guessing that a little reflection will turn up lots of examples: you may find yourself digging up information on the pricing of new cars, searching *Craigslist* or the want ads for a good job, comparing two new smartphones, looking up statistics on a favorite sports figure, or searching for a recipe for tabbouleh. All of these everyday activities involve research. In addition, many of your most important life decisions involve research— what colleges to apply to, what jobs to pursue, where to live, and more. Once you begin to think about research in this broad way—as a form of inquiry related to important decisions—you'll probably find that research is something you do almost every day. Moreover, you'll see the ways in which the research you do adds to your credibility—giving you the authority that goes along with being an author.

But research today is very different from the research of only a few decades ago. Take the example of the concordance, an alphabetized listing of every instance of all topics and words in a work. Before the computer age, concordances were done by hand: the first full concordance to the works of Shakespeare took decades of eye-straining, painstaking research, counting, and sorting. Some scholars spent years, even whole careers, developing concordances that then served as major resources for other scholars. As soon as Shakespeare's plays and poems were in digital form—voilà!—a concordance could be produced automatically and accessed by writers with the click of a mouse.

To take a more recent example, first-year college students not too long ago had no access to the internet. Just think of how easy it is now to check temperatures around the world, track a news story, or keep up to the minute on stock prices. These are items that you can google, but you may also have many expensive subscription databases available to you through your school's library. It's not too much of an exaggeration to say that the world is literally at your fingertips.

What has *not* changed is the need to carry out research with great care, to read all sources with a critical eye, and to evaluate sources before depending on them for an important decision or using them in your own work. What also has not changed is the sheer thrill research can bring: while much research work can seem plodding and even repetitious, the excitement of discovering materials you didn't know existed, of analyzing information in a new way, or of tracing a question through one particular historical period brings its own reward. Moreover, your research adds to what philosopher Kenneth Burke calls "the conversation of humankind," as you build on what others have done and begin to make significant contributions of your own to the world's accumulated knowledge.

Everyone's a Student

More than 2,000 years ago, the Roman writer Quintilian set out a plan for education, beginning with birth and ending only with old age and death. Surprisingly enough, Quintilian's recommendation for a lifelong education has never been more relevant than it is in the twenty-first century, as knowledge is increasing and changing so fast that most people must continue to be active learners long after they graduate from college. This explosion of knowledge also puts great demands on communication. As a result, one of your biggest challenges will be learning how to learn and how to communicate what you have learned across wider distances, to larger and increasingly diverse sets of audiences, and using an expanding range of media and genres.

When did you first decide to attend college, and what paths did you take to achieve that goal? Chances are greater today than at any time in our past that you may have taken time off to work before beginning college, or that you returned to college for new training when your job changed, or that you are attending college while working part-time or even full-time. These characteristics of college students are not new, but they are increasingly important, indicating that the path to college is not as straightforward as it was once thought to be. In addition, college is now clearly a part of a process of lifetime learning: you are likely to hold a number of positions—and each new position will call for new learning.

Citizens today need more years of education and more advanced skills than ever before: even entry-level jobs now call for a college diploma. But what you'll need isn't just a college education. Instead, you'll need an education that puts you in a position to take responsibility for your own learning and to take a direct, hands-on approach to that learning. Most of us learn best by *doing* what we're trying to learn rather than just being told about it. What does this change mean in practice? First, it means you will be doing much more writing, speaking, and researching than ever before. You may, for instance, conduct research on an economic trend and then use that research to create a theory capable of accounting for the trend; you may join a research group in an electrical engineering class that designs, tests, and implements a new system; you may be a member of a writing class that works to build a website for the local fire department, writes brochures for a nonprofit agency, or makes presentations before municipal boards. In each case, you will be doing what you are studying, whether it is economics, engineering, or writing.

Without a doubt, the challenges and opportunities for students today are immense. The chapters that follow try to keep these challenges and opportunities in the foreground, offering you concrete ways to think about yourself as a writer—and yes, as an author; to think carefully about the rhetorical situations you face and about the many and varied audiences for your work; and to expand your writing repertoire to include new genres, new media, and new ways of producing and communicating knowledge.

PART I

The Need for Rhetoric and Writing

CLOSE YOUR EYES and imagine a world without any form of language—no spoken or written words, no drawings, no mathematical formulas, no music—no way, that is, to communicate or express yourself. It's pretty hard to imagine such a world, and with good reason. For better or worse, we seem to be hardwired to communicate, to long to express ourselves to others. That's why philosopher Kenneth Burke says that people are, at their essence, "symbol-using animals" who have a basic need to communicate.

We can look across history and find early attempts to create systems of communication. Think, for instance, of the

Horses in prehistoric art: Uffington White Horse, Oxfordshire, England (approx. 3,000 years old); Chauvet Cave, near Vallon-Pont-d'Arc, France (approx. 30,000 years old); rock paintings, Bhimbetka, India (approx. 30,000 years old).

chalk horses of England, huge figures carved into trenches that were then filled with white chalk some 3,000 years ago. What do they say? Do they act as maps or road signs? Do they celebrate, or commemorate, or tell a story? Whatever their original intent, they echo the need to communicate to us from millennia away.

Cave paintings, many of them hauntingly beautiful, have been discovered across Europe, some thought to be 30,000 years old. Such communicative art—all early forms of writing—has been discovered in many other places, from Africa to Australia to South America to Asia.

While these carvings and paintings have been interpreted in many different ways, they all attest to the human desire to leave messages. And we don't need to look far to find other very early attempts to communicate—from makeshift drums and whistles to early pictographic languages to the symbols associated with the earliest astronomers.

As languages and other symbolic forms of communication like our own alphabet evolved, so did a need for ways to interpret and organize these forms and to use them in effective and meaningful ways. And out of these needs grew rhetoric—the art, theory, and practice of communication. In discussing rhetoric, Aristotle says we need to understand this art for two main reasons: first, in order to express our own ideas and thoughts, and second, to protect ourselves from those who would try to manipulate or harm us. Language, then, can be used for good or ill, to provide information that may help someone—or to deliberately mislead.

We believe the need for understanding rhetoric may be greater today than at any time in our history. At first glance, it may look as if communication has never been easier. We can send messages in a nanosecond, reaching people in all parts of the world with ease. We can broadcast our thoughts, hopes, and dreams—and invectives—in emails, *YouTube* videos, status updates, tweets, text messages, and a plethora of other ways.

So far, perhaps, so good. But consider the story of the Tower of Babel, told in different ways in both the Qur'an and the Bible. When the people sought to build a tower that would reach to the heavens, God responded to their hubris by creating so many languages that communication became impossible and the tower had to be abandoned. Like the languages in Babel, the means of communication are proliferating today, bringing with them the potential for miscommunication. From the struggle to sift through the amount of information created in a day—more than was previously created in several lifetimes—to the difficulty of trying to communicate across vast differences in languages and cultures, we face challenges that our parents and grandparents never did.

Pieter Brueghel the Elder, *Tower of Babel*, 1563.

"The need for rhetoric" translated from English to Japanese.

In a time when new (and sometimes confusing) forms of communication are available, many of us are looking for help with making our messages known. *Google Translate* and *Bing Translator*, for example, are attempts to offer instant translation of texts from one language to another.

Such new technologies and tools can certainly help us as we navigate twenty-first-century global villages. But they are not likely to reduce the need for an art and a theory that can inform the conversations we have there—that can encourage thoughtfulness, empathy, and responsible use of such technologies. Rhetoric responds to this need. Along with writing, which we define broadly to include speaking and drawing and performing as well as the literal inscription of words, rhetoric offers you solid ground on which to build both your education and your communicative ability and style. The chapters that follow will introduce you more fully to rhetoric and writing—and engage you in acquiring and using their powers.

ONE

Thinking Rhetorically

The only real alternative to war is rhetoric.

—WAYNE BOOTH

ROFESSOR WAYNE BOOTH made this statement at a conference of scholars and teachers of writing held only months after 9/11, and it quickly drew a range of responses. Just what did Booth mean by this stark statement? How could rhetoric—the art and practice of persuasion—act as a counter to war?

A noted critic and scholar, Booth explored these questions throughout his career, identifying rhetoric as an ethical art that begins with intense listening and that searches for mutual understanding and common ground as alternatives to violence and war. Put another way, two of the most potent tools we have for persuasion are language—and violence: when words fail us, violence often wins the day. Booth sees the careful and ethical use of language as our best approach to keeping violence and war at bay.

Over the past several years, Booth's words echoed again, as the Myanmar army renewed attacks that killed and maimed legions of Rohingyas, forcing hundreds of thousands to flee. In the United States, demonstrators used signs and chants—"Black Lives Matter!" and "3 shots to the back—how do you justify that?"—to demand justice for African Americans killed at the hands of police. Following the 2018 shooting in Parkland, Florida, young activists took to social media using #NeverAgain, held "March for Our Lives" protests, and founded a movement devoted to preventing gun violence. And as this book goes to press, people across the country are protesting the treatment of immigrant children and families. All these

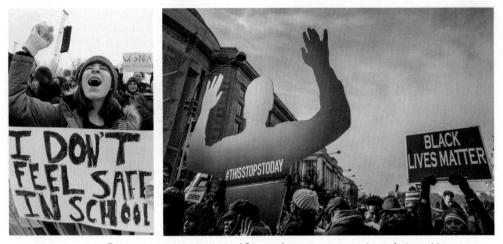

Protesters use posters, raised fists, and more to communicate their positions.

groups are using dramatic, memorable statements as rhetorical strategies to capture and hold the attention of millions of people.

Note that while Booth speaks of rhetoric as an "ethical art," rhetoric can also be used for unethical purposes, as Hitler and other dictators have done; in fact, rhetoric used in unethical ways can itself lead to violence. That's why Aristotle cautioned that people need to understand rhetoric—both to get their own ethical messages across *and* to be able to recognize and resist unethical messages that others attempt to use against them. We take Aristotle's point and focus in this book on how to think rhetorically both as readers and writers. In addition, we define rhetoric as the art, theory, and practice of ethical communication—the ethical language use that Booth speaks of.

So how can you go about developing your own careful, ethical use of language? Our short answer: by learning to think and act rhetorically, that is, by developing habits of mind that begin with listening and searching for understanding before you decide what you yourself think, and by thinking hard about your own beliefs before trying to persuade others to listen to and act on what you say.

Learning to think rhetorically can serve you well as you negotiate the complexities of life today. In many everyday situations, you'll need to communicate successfully with others in order to get things done, and done in a responsible and ethical way. On the job, for example, you may need to bring coworkers to consensus on how best to raise productivity when there

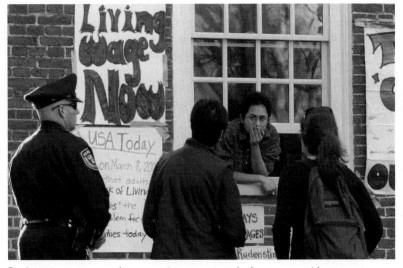

Students use posters and conversation to protest the low wages paid to campus workers.

is little, if any, money for raises. Or in your college community, you may find yourself negotiating difficult waters.

When a group of students became aware of how little the temporary workers on their campus were paid, for example, they met with the workers and listened to gather information about the issue. They then mounted a campaign using flyers, speeches, and sit-ins—in other words, using the available means of persuasion—to win attention and convince the administration to raise the workers' pay. These students were thinking and acting rhetorically, and doing so responsibly and ethically. Note that these students, like the protesters from Parkland, worked together, both with the workers and with each other. In other words, none of us can manage such actions all by ourselves; we need to engage in conversation with others and listen hard to what they say. Perhaps that's what philosopher Kenneth Burke had in mind when he created his famous "parlor" metaphor:

> Imagine that you enter a parlor. You come late. When you arrive, others have long preceded you, and they are engaged in a heated discussion, a discussion too heated for them to pause and tell you exactly what it is about. . . . You listen for a while, until you decide that you have caught the tenor of the argument; then you put in your oar.
>
> —KENNETH BURKE, *The Philosophy of Literary Form*

In this parable, each of us is the person arriving late to a room full of animated conversation; we don't understand what is going on. Yet instead of butting in or trying to take over, we listen closely until we catch on to what people are saying. Then we join in, using language and rhetorical strategies to engage with others as we add our own voices to the conversation.

This book aims to teach you to *think and act rhetorically*—to listen carefully and respectfully and then to "put in your oar," join conversations about important issues, and develop strong critical and ethical habits of mind that will help you engage with others in responsible ways. This chapter will help you develop the habit of thinking rhetorically.

First, Listen

> We have two ears and one mouth so we may listen more and talk less.
>
> —EPICTETUS

Thinking rhetorically begins with listening, with being willing to hear the words of others in an open and understanding way. It means paying attention to what others say before and even *as a way* of making your own contributions to a conversation. Think of the times you are grateful to others for listening closely to you: when you're talking through a conflict with a family member, for instance, or even when you're trying to explain to a salesperson what you're looking for. On those occasions, you want the person you're addressing to really *listen* to what you say.

This is a kind of listening that rhetorician Krista Ratcliffe dubs "rhetorical listening," opening yourself to the thoughts of others and making the effort not only to hear their words but to take those words in and fully understand what people are saying. It means paying attention to what others say as a way of establishing good will and acknowledging the importance of their views. And yes, it means taking seriously and engaging with views that differ, sometimes radically, from your own.

Rhetorical listening is what middle school teacher Julia Blount asked for in a *Facebook* post following the 2015 riots in Baltimore after the death of Freddie Gray, who suffered fatal spinal injuries while in police custody:

> Every comment or post I have read today voicing some version of disdain for the people of Baltimore—"I can't understand" or "They're destroying their own community"—tells me that many of you are not listening. I am not asking you to condone or agree with violence. I just need you

to listen. . . . If you are not listening, not exposing yourself to unfamiliar perspectives . . . not engaging in conversation, then you are perpetuating white privilege. . . . It is exactly your ability to *not* hear, to ignore the situation, that is a mark of your privilege.

—JULIA BLOUNT, "Dear White *Facebook* Friends: I Need You to Respect What Black America Is Feeling Right Now"

Hear What Others Are Saying—and Think about Why

When you enter any conversation, whether academic, professional, or personal, take the time to understand what is being said rather than rushing to a conclusion or a judgment. Listen carefully to what others are saying and consider what motivates them: where are they coming from?

Developing such habits of mind will be useful to you almost every day, whether you are participating in a class discussion, negotiating with friends over what movie is most worth watching, or studying a local ballot issue to decide how you'll vote. In each case, thinking rhetorically means being flexible and fair, able to hear and consider varying—and sometimes conflicting—points of view.

In ancient Rome, Cicero argued that considering alternative points of view and counterarguments was key to making a successful argument, and it is just as important today. Even when you disagree with a point of view—perhaps especially when you disagree with it—allow yourself to see the issue from the viewpoint of its advocates before you reject their positions. You may be skeptical that hydrogen fuel will be the solution to global warming—but don't reject the idea until you have thought hard about others' perspectives and carefully considered alternative solutions.

Thinking hard about others' views also includes considering the larger context and how it shapes what they are saying. This aspect of rhetorical thinking goes beyond the kind of reading you probably learned to do in high school literature classes, where you looked very closely at a particular text and interpreted it on its own terms, without looking at secondary sources. When you think rhetorically, you go one step further and put that close analysis into a larger context—historical, political, or cultural, for example—to recognize and consider where the analysis is "coming from."

In analyzing the issue of gun control, for instance, you would not merely consider your own thinking or do a close reading of texts that address the issue. In addition, you would look at the whole debate in context by considering its historical development over time, thinking about the broader political agendas of both those who advocate for and those who oppose stricter gun control, asking what economic ramifications adopting—or rejecting—new gun restrictions might have, examining the role of constitutional rights in the debate, and so on. In short, you would try to see the issue from as many different perspectives and in as broad a context as possible before you formulate your own stance. When you write, you draw on these sources—what others have said about the issue—to support your own position and to help you consider counterarguments to it.

REFLECT. Go to everyonesanauthor.tumblr.com *and read "The 'Other Side' Is Not Dumb" by blogger Sean Blanda, who warns that many of us gravitate on social media to those who think like we do, which often leads to the belief that we are right and that those with other worldviews are "dumb." He argues that we need to "make an honest effort to understand those who are not like us" and to remember that "we might be wrong." Look at some of your own recent posts. How many different perspectives do you see represented? What might you do to listen—and think—more rhetorically?*

What Do You Think—and Why?

Examining all points of view on any issue will engage you in some tough thinking about your own stance—literally, where you are coming from on an issue—and why you think as you do. Such self-scrutiny can eventually clarify your stance or perhaps even change your mind; in either case, you stand to gain. Just as you need to think hard about the motivations of others, it's important to examine your own motivations in detail, asking yourself what influences in your life lead you to think as you do or to take certain positions. Then you can reconsider your positions and reflect on how they relate to those of others, including your audience—those you wish to engage respectfully in conversation or debate.

In your college assignments, you probably have multiple motivations and purposes, one of which is to convince your instructor that you are a serious and hardworking student. But think about additional purposes as well: What could you learn from doing the assignment? How can doing it help you attain goals you have?

Examining your own stance and motivation is equally important outside the classroom. Suppose you are urging fellow members of a campus group to lobby for a rigorous set of procedures to deal with accusations of sexual harassment. On one level, you're alarmed by the statistics showing a steep increase in cases of rape on college campuses and you want to do something about it. But when you think a bit more, you might find that you have additional motivations. Perhaps you've long wanted to become a leader of this group. You may have just seen *The Hunting Ground*, a documentary about rape on US college campuses, and found it deeply upsetting—and persuasive. These realizations shouldn't necessarily change your mind about what action you want your group to take, but examining what you think and why will help you to challenge your own position—and to make sure that it is fair and appropriate.

Do Your Homework

Rhetorical thinking calls on you to do some homework, to find out everything you can about what's been said about your topic, to **ANALYZE** what you find, and then to **SYNTHESIZE** that information to inform your own ideas. To put it another way, you want your own thinking to be aware and deeply informed, to reflect more than just your own opinion.

To take an everyday example, you should do some pretty serious thinking when deciding on a major purchase, such as a new car. You'll want to begin by considering the purchase in the larger context of your life. What motivates you to buy a car? Do you need one for work? Do you want it in part as a status symbol? Are you concerned about the environment and want to switch to an electric vehicle? Who besides you might be affected by this decision? A thoughtful analysis of the context and your specific motivations and purposes can guide you in drawing up a preliminary list of cars to consider.

Then you'll need to do some research, checking out product reviews and reports on safety records, efficiency, cost, and so on. Sometimes it can be hard to evaluate such sources: how much should you trust the mileage statistics provided by the carmaker, for example, or one particular reviewer's evaluation? For this reason, you should consult multiple sources and check them against one another.

You will also want to consider your findings in light of your priorities. Cost, for instance, may not be as high on your priority list as fuel efficiency. Such careful thinking will help you come to a sound decision, and then to explain it to others. If your parents, for instance, are helping you buy the car,

TAKE A LOOK *at the 2011 Super Bowl Chrysler ad at* everyonesanauthor.tumblr
.com. *You'll see many scenes from Detroit and hear a voiceover say, "What does this
city know about luxury? What does a town that's been to hell and back know about the
finer things in life? I'll tell you, more than most." What kind of rhetorical thinking did
the ad writers do? Who was their target audience, and how did they go about appealing
to them? This was an award-winning ad—but how successful do you think it was as an
ad? In other words, do you think it sold a lot of cars? If you were looking to buy a car,
what would this ad tell you about Chryslers—and what would you have to find out
from other sources?*

you'll want to consider what their responses to your decision will be, antici-
pating questions they may ask and how to respond.

  Doing your homework also means taking an analytic approach, focusing on *how* various rhetorical strategies work to persuade you. You may have
been won over by a funny car commercial you saw on Super Bowl Sunday.
So what made that advertisement so memorable? To answer that question,
you'll need to study the ad closely, determining just what qualities—a clever
script? memorable music? celebrity actors? cute animals? a provocative
message?—made the ad so persuasive. Once you've determined that, you'll
want to consider whether the car will actually live up to the advertiser's
promises. This is the kind of analysis and research you will do when you
engage in rhetorical thinking.

Give Credit

As part of engaging with what others have thought and said, you'll want to give credit where credit is due. Acknowledging the work of others will help build your own ethos, or character, showing that you have not only done your homework but that you want to credit those who have influenced you. The great physicist Isaac Newton famously and graciously gave credit when he wrote to his rival Robert Hooke in 1676, saying:

> What Descartes did was a good step. You have added much in several ways, and especially in taking the colours of thin plates into philosophical consideration. If I have seen a little further it is by standing on the shoulders of giants. —ISAAC NEWTON, letter to Robert Hooke

In this letter, Newton acknowledges the work of Descartes as well as of Hooke before saying, with a fair amount of modesty, that his own advancements were made possible by their work. In doing so, he is thinking—and acting—rhetorically.

You can give credit informally, as Newton did in this letter, or you can do so formally with a full citation. Which method you choose will depend on your purpose and context. Academic writing, for instance, usually calls for formal citations, but if you are writing for a personal blog, you might embed a link that connects to another's work—or give an informal shout-out to a friend who contributed to your thinking. In each case, you'll want to be specific about what ideas or words you've drawn from others, as Newton does in referring to Hooke's consideration of the colors of thin plates. Such care in crediting your sources contributes to your credibility—and is an important part of ethical, careful rhetorical thinking.

Be Imaginative

Remember that intuition and imagination can often lead to great insights. While you want to think carefully and analytically, don't be afraid to take chances. A little imagination can lead you to new ideas about a topic you're studying and suggest how to approach it in a way that will interest others. Such insights and intuitions can often pay off big-time. One student athlete we know was interested in how the mass media covered the Olympics, and he began doing research on the coverage in *Sports Illustrated* from different periods. So far, so good: he was gathering information and would be able to write an essay showing that the magazine had been a major promoter of the Olympics.

While looking through old issues of *Sports Illustrated*, however, he kept feeling that something he was seeing in the early issues was different from what he saw in current issues of the magazine . . . something that felt important to him though he couldn't quite articulate it. This hunch led him to make an imaginative leap, to study that difference even though it was outside of the topic he had set out to examine. Excited that he was on to something, he returned to his chronological examination of the magazine. On closer inspection, he found that over the decades, *Sports Illustrated* had slowly but surely moved from focusing on teams to depicting *only* individual stars.

This discovery led him to make an argument he would never have made had he not followed his creative hunch—that the evolution of sports from a focus on the team to a focus on individual stars is perfectly captured

Two *Sports Illustrated* covers depicting hockey players. The cover on the left, from the 1980 Winter Olympics, showcases the US team's "miracle on ice" victory over the heavily favored USSR team. The one on the right, from 2018, pictures Washington Capitals captain Alexander Ovechkin, who was named MVP in the Stanley Cup play-offs for leading the team to victory against the Vegas Golden Knights.

in the pages of *Sports Illustrated*. It also helped him write a much more interesting—and more persuasive—essay, one that captured the attention not only of his instructor and classmates but of a local sports newsmagazine, which reprinted his essay. Like this student, you can benefit by using your imagination and listening to your intuition. You could stumble upon something exciting.

Put In Your Oar

So rhetorical thinking offers a way of entering any situation with a tool kit of strategies that will help you understand it and "put in your oar." When you think rhetorically, you ask yourself certain questions:

- How do you want to come across to your audience?
- What can you do to represent yourself as knowledgeable and credible?
- What can you do to show respect both for your audience and for those whose work and thinking you engage with?
- How can you show that you have your audience's best interests at heart?

This kind of rhetorical thinking will help ensure that your words will be listened to and taken seriously.

We can find examples of such a rhetorical approach in all fields of study. Take, for instance, the landmark essay by James Watson and Francis Crick on the discovery of DNA, published in *Nature* in 1953. This essay shows Watson and Crick to be thinking rhetorically throughout, acutely aware of their audience (major scientists throughout the world), including competitors who were simultaneously working on the same issue.

Here is Wayne Booth's analysis of Watson and Crick's use of rhetoric:

> In [Watson and Crick's] report, what do we find? Actually scores of *rhetorical* choices that they made to strengthen the appeal of their scientific claim. (Biographies and autobiographies have by now revealed that they did a lot of conscientious revising, not of the data but of the mode of presentation; and their lives were filled, before and after the triumph, with a great deal of rhetoric-charged conflict.) We could easily compose a dozen different versions of their report, all proclaiming the

same scientific results. But most alternatives would prove less engaging to the intended audience. They open, for example, with

> "*We wish to suggest* a structure" that has "*novel* features which are of *considerable* biological *interest*." *(My italics, of course)*

Why didn't they say, instead: "We shall here demonstrate a *startling, totally new structure* that will *shatter* everyone's conception of the biological world"? Well, obviously their rhetorical choice presents an ethos much more attractive to most cautious readers than does my exaggerated alternative. A bit later they say

> "We have made the *usual chemical assumptions,* namely . . ."

Why didn't they say, "*As we all know*"? Both expressions acknowledge reliance on warrants, commonplaces within a given rhetorical domain. But their version sounds more thoughtful and authoritative, especially with the word "chemical." Referring to Pauling and Corey, they say

> "They *kindly* have made their manuscript available."

The original sketch showing the structure of DNA that appeared in Watson and Crick's article.

Okay, guys, drop the rhetoric and just cut that word "kindly." What has that got to do with your scientific case? Well, it obviously strengthens the authors' ethos: we are nice guys dealing trustfully with other nice guys, in a rhetorical community.

And on they go, with "*In our opinion*" (rather than "We proclaim" or "We insist" or "We have miraculously discovered": again ethos—we're not dogmatic); and Fraser's "*suggested*" structure is "*rather ill-defined*" (rather than "his structure is stupid" or "obviously faulty"—we *are* nice guys, right?).

And on to scores of other such choices.

—WAYNE BOOTH, *The Rhetoric of Rhetoric*

Booth shows in each instance that Watson and Crick's exquisite understanding of their rhetorical situation—especially of their audience and of the stakes involved in making their claim—had a great deal to do with how that claim was received. (They won the Nobel Prize!)

As the example of Watson and Crick illustrates, rhetorical thinking involves certain habits of mind that can and should lead to something—often to an action, to making something happen. And when it comes to taking action, those who think rhetorically are in a very strong position. They have listened attentively, engaged with the words and ideas of others, viewed their topic from many alternate perspectives, and done their homework. This kind of rhetorical thinking will set you up to contribute to conversations—and will increase the likelihood that your ideas will be heard and will inspire real action.

Indeed, the ability to think rhetorically is of great importance in today's global world, as professors Gerald Graff and Cathy Birkenstein explain:

> The ability to enter complex, many-sided conversations has taken on a special urgency in today's diverse, post-9/11 world, where the future for all of us may depend on our ability to put ourselves in the shoes of those who think very differently from us. Listening carefully to others, including those who disagree with us, and then engaging with them thoughtfully and respectfully . . . can help us see beyond our own pet beliefs, which may not be shared by everyone. The mere act of acknowledging that some-one might disagree with us may not seem like a way to change the world; but it does have the potential to jog us out of our comfort zones, to get us thinking critically about our own beliefs, and perhaps even to change our minds.   —GERALD GRAFF AND CATHY BIRKENSTEIN, *"They Say / I Say"*

In the long run, if enough of us learn to think rhetorically, we just might achieve Booth's goal—to use words (and images) in thoughtful and con-structive ways as an alternative to violence and war.

⟋⟍ REFLECT. *Read Margaret Mead's words below, and then think of at least one historical example in which a "small group of thoughtful citizens" has changed the world for the better. Then think about your own life and the ways in which you have worked with others to bring about some kind of change. In what ways were you called upon to think and act rhetorically in order to do so?*

Never doubt that a small group of thoughtful

committed citizens can change the world;

indeed, it's the only thing that ever has.

—MARGARET MEAD

TWO

Engaging Respectfully with Others

 N THE LATE spring of 2017, Oprah Winfrey, standing before a cheering crowd of graduating students at Agnes Scott College in Atlanta, urged them to learn to engage respectfully with others. She told the assembled crowd that "two weeks after the election last year" she had invited a group of women voters—half on the right and half on the left, politically—to join her at a diner for "great croissants with jam." But none of the women wanted to come, saying they'd "never sat this close" to someone from the other side and didn't want to start now. Winfrey eventually prevailed and brought the women together, even though they came in "all tight and hardened." As she goes on to tell it in her speech,

> After two and a half hours . . . the women were sitting around the table, listening to each other's stories, hearing both sides, and by the end they were holding hands, exchanging emails and phone numbers, and singing "Reach Out and Touch." . . . Which means it's possible; it can happen. So I want you to work in your own way to change the world in respectful conversations with others. And I want you to enter every situation aware of its context, open to hear the truths of others and most important open to letting the process of changing the world change you.
>
> —OPRAH WINFREY, Agnes Scott College
> Commencement Address, 2017

The goal of this chapter is to encourage and guide you as you engage with others: respectfully listening to their stories, their truths, and contributing to a process that may, indeed, change the world. Here are some steps you can take to realize this goal.

Get to Know People Different from You

It's a commonplace today to point out that we often live and act in "silos" where we encounter only people who think like we do, who hold the same values. While the internet has made the whole world available to us, we increasingly choose to interact with like-minded people—online and in person. We are in what some call "filter bubbles" or "echo chambers," where we hear our views echoed back to us from every direction. In such an atmosphere, it can be easy—and comforting—to think this is the real world, but it's not!

Beyond your own bubble of posts and tweets and conversations lie countless other people with different views and values.

So one of the big challenges we face today is finding ways to get out of our own echo chambers and get to know people who take different positions, hold different values. But simply encountering people who think differently is just the start. Breaking out of our bubbles calls for making the effort to understand those different perspectives, to listen with openness and empathy, and to hear where others are coming from. As Winfrey notes in her commencement address, even the first step is hard: she had to work to convince the women simply to meet one another, and then she had to persuade them to listen, as she says, with respect. Once they did, things changed: they realized that it's not as easy to dislike or dismiss someone when you are sitting face-to-face.

That's certainly what one Canadian student found when she spent a semester in Washington, DC. Shauna Vert had expected the highlights of her semester to be visiting places like the museums of the Smithsonian Institution or the Library of Congress, but her greatest experience, as she describes it in a blog post, turned out to be an "unexpected gift: While in DC, I became close, close friends with people I disagree with on almost everything." As she got to know these people, she found that they were:

> funny, smart, and kind. We all really liked music. . . . We even lived together. We ate dinner together, every single night. So I couldn't look down on them. I couldn't even consider it. And when you can't look down on someone who fundamentally disagrees with you, when you're busy breaking bread, sharing your days, laughing about the weather . . . well.
>
> —SHAUNA VERT, "Making Friends Who Disagree with You (Is the Healthiest Thing in the World)"

Read Shauna Vert's blog by visiting everyonesan author.tumblr.com.

During a conversation with one of her housemates, a deeply conservative Christian from Mississippi, Vert mentioned that she was "pro-choice," realizing as she did so that this was "dangerous territory." To her surprise, she met not resistance or rebuke but curiosity:

> She wanted to know more. Her curiosity fueled my curiosity, and we talked. We didn't argue—we debated gently, very gently. . . . We

laughed at nuance, we self-deprecated, we trusted each other. And we liked each other. Before the conversation, and after the conversation. To recap: Left-wing Canadian meets Bible Belt Republican. Discusses controversial political issues for over an hour. Walks away with a new friend.

This kind of careful, responsible, respectful exchange seems hard in today's highly polarized society, where anger and hate are fueled by incendiary messages coming from social media and highly partisan news organizations. Just finding people outside our silos to talk with can be hard. But like Vert, some people have taken up the challenge of finding ways to bring people with different views together.

One group aiming to create conversation rather than conflict is the Living Room Conversations project, which offers guidelines for engaging in meaningful discussions on more than eighty specific topics—free speech on campus, the opportunity gap, privacy and security, climate change, and more. The founders want these conversations between people who disagree to "increase understanding, reveal common ground and allow us to discuss possible solutions." Visit livingroomconversations.org to find the resources to start a "living room" conversation yourself.

The point is that it's worth making the time to try to find and engage with those who hold different ideas and values than you do. And this means becoming familiar with sources other people read, too. Get out of your comfort zone and look beyond the sources you know; look carefully at what the "the other side" is reading. Sites like *AllSides* can help. It's time to shut down the echo chambers and seek out people outside of our silos.

Practice Empathy

The examples in this chapter suggest the power of empathy, the ability to share the feelings of someone else. Dylan Marron is someone who directly addresses empathy and shows how it works. As the creator and host of several popular video series on controversial social issues, Marron has gained quite a bit of attention and, he says, "a lot of hate." Early on, he tried to ignore hateful comments, but then he got interested and began visiting commenter profiles to learn about the people behind them. Doing so, he said, led him to realize "there was a human on the other side of the screen"—and prompted him to call some of these people on the phone, conversations he shares on his podcast *Conversations with People Who Hate Me.*

In one of these talks, Marron learned that Josh, who in a comment had called Marron a "moron" and said that being gay was a sin, had recently graduated from high school. When Marron asked him, "How was high school for you?" Josh replied that "it was hell" because he'd been bullied by kids who made fun of him for being "bigger." Marron shared his own experiences of being bullied too, and as the conversation progressed, empathy laid the groundwork that helped them relate to each other.

At the end of another conversation, a man who had called Marron a "talentless hack" reflected on the ubiquitous comment fields where such statements are often made, saying "the comment sections are really a way to get your anger at the world out on random strangers"—an insight "that made me rethink the way I interact with people online."

Marron's work shows that comment sections are used to release anger—and often hate, the very opposite of the kind of empathy that can bring people together. More than that, his work demonstrates the power of practicing empathy and how it can help us to see one another as human, even in the most negative and nasty places. In a 2018 TED talk, Marron again stressed the importance of empathy, noting, however, that "empathy is not endorsement" and doesn't require us to compromise our deeply held values but rather to acknowledge the views of "someone raised to think

↗ Watch Marron's TED talk and listen to his podcast by visiting everyonesanauthor .tumblr.com.

Dylan Marron, creator and host of *Conversations with People Who Hate Me*, a podcast featuring conversations between people who disagree.

very differently" than we do. That's the power and the promise of practicing empathy.

Demonstrate Respect

"R-E-S-P-E-C-T." That spells respect. If you've never heard Aretha Franklin belt out these lyrics, take time to look her up on *YouTube*. Franklin added this now-famous line to her 1967 rendition of Otis Redding's original song, inspiring millions to expect and to demand R-E-S-P-E-C-T.

Franklin's message is still a timely one today, when *dis*respect seems common, especially between those who don't agree. But respect is a two-way street: if we need to stand up and ask for the respect of others, we also need to respect them. Moreover, we need to invite (and deserve!) respect. Easy to say, but harder to do. So just how can you demonstrate respect for others? Not surprisingly, the first tip for showing respect is listening, open-mindedly and generously, without interrupting or making snap judgments. You should also strive to:

Aretha Franklin performs onstage in 1968.

- Be helpful and cooperative.
- Be sincere, and remember to say "thank you."
- Be on time: even something as simple as that is a sign of respect.
- Follow through and do what you say you'll do. Keep your promises!
- Be careful to represent other people's views fairly and generously—and acknowledge their accomplishments whenever you can.
- Ask questions rather than issuing orders or challenges.
- Apologize if you say or do something you regret. We all make mistakes.

If you respect others in these ways, you will invite their respect for you. As the French philosopher Voltaire is reported to have said, "I may disapprove of what you say, but I will defend to the death your right to say it."

Search for Common Ground

Even children learn early on that digging in to opposing positions doesn't usually get them far: "No, you can't!" "Yes, I can!" can go on forever, without going anywhere. Rhetoricians in the ancient world understood this very well and thus argued that for conversations to progress, it's necessary to establish some COMMON GROUND, no matter how small. If "No, you can't!" moves on to "Well, you can't do that in this particular situation," then maybe a conversation can begin.

This is a strategy musician Daryl Davis discovered in his high-stakes work researching the Ku Klux Klan, a white supremacist group that's terrorized African Americans. Davis decided to try to meet some Klansmen, listen to them, and engage with what they said. As he says, finding common ground is essential:

> Look for commonalities. You can find something in five minutes, even with your worst enemy. And build on those. Say I don't like you because you're white and I'm black. . . . And so our contention is based upon our races. But if you say "How do you feel about all these drugs on the street" and I say "I think the law needs to crack down on things that people can get addicted to very easily" . . . and you say "Well, yeah, I agree with that" . . . You might even tell me your son started dabbling in drugs. So now I see

Daryl Davis with former KKK member Scott Sheperd. Because Davis was willing to listen to, respect, and talk with him, Sheperd listened, respected, and talked with Davis, a process that led to his leaving the KKK.

that you want what I want, that drugs are affecting your family the same way they affect my family. So let's focus on that. And as we focus more and more and find more things in common, things we have in contrast, such as skin color, matter less and less.

—DARYL DAVIS, "How to Argue"

So Davis urges us to seek out areas of agreement and then areas of compromise, all the while listening carefully and respectfully to one another. He reminds us that argument doesn't need to be abusive, insulting, or condescending—stances that usually only make things worse. But he notes as well that looking for areas of compromise doesn't mean giving in to ideas you know are not right. As Davis says, "you're going to hear things that you know are absolutely wrong. You will also hear opinions put out as facts." In such cases, Davis suggests offering facts or other **EVIDENCE** that disprove the opinion being put forward. Then, if the other person still holds to the opinion, try saying something like "I believe you are wrong, but if you think you're right, then bring me the data." Such a response invites the person to supply information that may actually carry the conversation forward.

So when you hear things you believe to be wrong, try to respond in a civil way, showing data that refute what other people say or asking them to show you evidence that *you* are wrong—with the hope of continuing the conversation based on evidence.

REFLECT. Some would say it's pointless or even wrong to try to find common ground with people whose views they find hateful or dangerous. Daryl Davis might disagree. Based on your own experiences, what do you think—and why?

Invite Response

All the examples we've provided in this chapter feature dialogue and conversation: the road to understanding is never a one-way street. That's why long speeches often have little effect on anyone who doesn't already agree with you. But tuning out is a lot harder in "live" conversations. So if

ATTENTIVE EYES   RESPECTFUL VOICE   LISTENING

OPEN MIND   KIND HEART   PATIENCE

Graphic from a website devoted to helping children learn to communicate respectfully.

you want to engage successfully with people who think differently from you, then inviting them to respond is a good way forward.

To invite response, you have to make time for it. Rather than rushing forward or talking over others, make a space for others to chime in: pause, make eye contact, even ask for response directly: "How do you feel about what I've just said?" You can also invite response online, turning commenting features on, for example, and even explicitly asking for responses to social media posts—and then responding respectfully to those who leave comments for you. In doing so, you are showing that you are open to what others think and that you really want to understand their views.

Join the Conversation: Collaborate! Engage! Participate!

Especially in times of deep societal divisions, it may be tempting to retreat, to put our heads in the sand and hope that, somehow, things will get better. But don't give in to that temptation. Your voice is important, your thoughts are important, and you can best make them heard if you engage and join with other people. That may mean working with groups of like-minded people to speak out—for or against—on issues such as immigration bans, gun control, or environmental policies. That kind of civic engagement and participation is important in a democracy. But there are smaller ways, too, like looking beyond those who think as you do, seeking to collaborate with them, listening with empathy, understanding their reasons for thinking as they do—and then looking hard for a shared goal that you can work toward together.

As a country, as a world, we have a lot riding on our willingness to reach across barriers, work together for the common good, and keep on trying even in the most difficult circumstances. And as writers, readers, and thinkers, we all have much to offer in this endeavor. So let's get going!

REFLECT. Look back through the examples in this chapter of people working out disagreements or finding ways to empathize with one another. Then think about your own experiences interacting with people who think differently than you do or with whom you disagree. How did you handle those encounters? Were you satisfied with the results? What would you do differently if you could replay them? What will you try and do differently next time? How can you apply this advice when engaging with the ideas of others in writing?

THREE

Rhetorical Situations

S PART OF A COLLEGE APPLICATION, a high school student writes a personal statement about what she plans to study, and why. A baseball fan comments on an article that analyzes data to show why a beloved New York Yankees pitcher probably won't be elected to the Hall of Fame. Eighty-seven readers respond, some praising his analysis, others questioning his conclusions and offering their own analyses. The officers of a small company address the annual shareholders' meeting to report how the firm is doing, using *PowerPoint* slides to call attention to their most important points. They take questions afterward, and two people raise their hands. The student in our first example takes a deep breath and logs in to the website of the college she wants to attend to see if she's been accepted. Good news: she's in. Come September she's at the library, working on an essay for her first-year composition course—and texting her friends as she works.

In each of these scenarios, an author is writing (or speaking) in a different set of specific circumstances—addressing certain audiences for a particular purpose, using certain technologies, and so on. So it is whenever we write. Whether we're texting a friend, outlining an oral presentation, or writing an essay, we do so within a specific rhetorical situation.

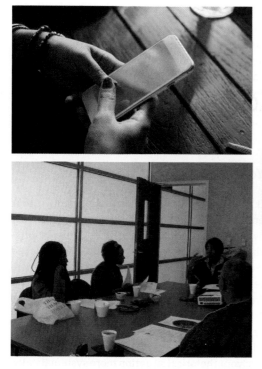

Three different rhetorical situations: a lone writer texting (*top left*); a student giving an oral presentation in class (*right*); and members of a community group collaborating on a project (*bottom left*).

We have a purpose, an audience, a stance, a genre, a medium, a design—all of which exist in some larger context. This chapter covers each of these elements and provides prompts to help you think about some of the choices you have as you negotiate your own rhetorical situations.

Every rhetorical situation presents its own unique constraints and opportunities, and as authors, we need to think strategically about our own situation. Adding to a class discussion thread presents a different challenge from writing an in-class essay exam, putting together a résumé and cover letter for a job, or working with fellow members of a campus choir to draft a grant proposal to the student government requesting funding to go on tour. A group of neighbors developing a proposal to present at a community meeting will need to attend to both the written text they will submit and the oral arguments they will make. They may also need to create slides or other visuals to support their proposal.

The workplace creates still other kinds of rhetorical situations with their own distinctive features. Reporters, for instance, must always consider their deadlines as well as their ethical obligations—to the public, to the persons or institutions they write about, and to the story they are reporting. A reporter working for six months to investigate corporate wrongdoing faces different challenges from one who covers local sports day to day. The medium—print, video, radio, podcast, social media feed, or some combination of these or other media—also influences how reporters write their stories.

Think about Your Own Rhetorical Situation

It is important to start thinking about your rhetorical situation early in your writing process. As a student, you'll often be given assignments with very specific guidelines—to follow the conventions of a particular genre, in a certain medium, by a specific date. Nevertheless, even the most fully developed assignment cannot specify every aspect of any particular rhetorical situation.

Effective writers—whether students, teachers, or journalists—know how to analyze their rhetorical situations. They may conduct this analysis unconsciously, drawing on the rhetorical common sense they have developed as writers, readers, speakers, and listeners. Particularly when you are writing in a new genre or discipline—a situation that you'll surely face in college—it can help to analyze your rhetorical situation more systematically.

THINK ABOUT YOUR GENRE

- *Have you been assigned a specific genre?* If not, do any words in the assignment imply a certain genre? *Evaluate* may signal a review, for example, and *explain why* could indicate a causal analysis.

- *If you get to choose your genre,* consider your PURPOSE. If you want to convince readers to recycle their trash, you would probably write an argument. If, however, you want to explain how to recycle food waste into compost, your purpose would call for a process analysis.

- *Does your genre require a certain organization?* A process analysis, for instance, is often organized CHRONOLOGICALLY, whereas a visual analysis may be organized SPATIALLY —and an annotated bibliography is almost always organized alphabetically.

- *How does your genre affect your* TONE *?* A lab report, for example, generally calls for a more matter-of-fact tone than a film review.

- *Are certain* DESIGN *features expected in your genre?* You would likely need to include images in a review of an art show, for instance, or be required to use a standard font for a research paper.

THINK ABOUT YOUR AUDIENCE

- *Who is your intended audience?* An instructor? A supervisor? Classmates? Members of a particular organization? Visitors to a website? Who else might see or hear what you say?

- *How are members of your audience like and unlike you?* Consider demographics such as age, gender, religion, income, education, occupation, and political attitudes.

- *What's your relationship with your audience?* An instructor or supervisor, for example, holds considerable authority over you. Other audiences may be friends, coworkers, or even strangers. What expectations about the text might they have because of your relationship?

- *If you have a choice of* MEDIUM, which one(s) would best reach your intended audience?

- *What do you want your audience to think or do* as a result of what you say? Take your ideas seriously? Reflect on their beliefs? Respond to you? Take some kind of action? How will you signal to them what you want?

- *Can you assume your audience will be interested* in what you say, or will you need to get them interested? Are they likely to resist any of your ideas?

- *How much does your audience know about your topic?* How much background information do they need? Will they expect—or be put off by—the use of technical jargon? Will you need to define any terms?

- *Will your audience expect a particular* GENRE *?* If you're writing about Mozart for a music class, you might analyze a piece he composed; if, however, you're commenting on a music video posted on *YouTube*, you'd be more likely to write some kind of review.

To quote further from People's Exhibit A, your Twitter feed, "@holdupguy82 I'm in the getaway vehicle with the money and hostages. Where R U?"

- *What about audience members you don't or can't know?* It goes without saying that you won't always know who could potentially read your writing, especially if you're writing on a site that anyone can access. The ability to reach hundreds, even thousands of readers is part of the internet's power, but you will want to take special care when your writing might reach unknown audiences. Remember as well that anything posted on the internet may easily be shared and read out of context, as the above cartoon shows!

THINK ABOUT YOUR PURPOSE

- *How would you describe your own motivation for writing?* To fulfill a course assignment? To meet a personal or professional commitment? To express your ideas to someone?

- *What is your primary goal?* To inform your audience about something? To persuade them to think a certain way? To call them to action? To entertain them? Something else?

- *How do your goals influence your choice of genre, medium, and design?* For example, if you want to persuade neighbors to recycle, you may choose to make colorful posters for display in public places. If you want to inform a corporation about what recycling programs accomplish, you may want to write a report using charts and data.

THINK ABOUT YOUR STANCE

- *What's your attitude toward your topic?* Objective? Strongly supportive? Mildly skeptical? Amused? Angry?

- *What's your relationship with your* AUDIENCE *?* Do they know you, and if so, how? Are you a student? a friend? a mentor? an interested community member? How do they see you, and how do you want to be seen?

- *How can you best convey your stance in your writing?* What TONE do you want it to have?

- *How will your stance and tone be received by your audience?* Will they be drawn in by it?

THINK ABOUT THE LARGER CONTEXT

- *What else has been said about your topic,* and how does that affect what you will say? What would be the most effective way for you to add your voice to the conversation?

- *Do you have any constraints?* When is this writing due and how much time and energy can you put into it? How many pages (or minutes) do you have to deliver your message?

- *How much independence do you have as a writer* in this situation? To what extent do you need to meet the expectations of others, such as an instructor or a supervisor? If this writing is an assignment, how can you approach it in a way that makes it matter to you?

THINK ABOUT YOUR **MEDIUM** AND **DESIGN**

- *If you get to choose your medium,* which one will work best for your audience and purpose? Print? Spoken? Digital? Some combination?

- *How will the medium determine what you can and cannot do?* For example, if you're submitting an essay online, you could include video, but if you were writing the same essay in print, you'd only be able to include a still shot from the video.

- *Does your medium favor certain conventions?* Paragraphs work well in print, but *PowerPoint* presentations usually rely on images or bulleted phrases instead. If you are writing online, you can include links to sources and background information.

- *What's the most appropriate look for your writing given your* RHETORICAL SITUATION*?* Plain and serious? Warm and inviting? What design elements will help you project that look?

- *Should you include visuals?* Would any part of your text benefit from them? Will your audience expect them? What kind would be appropriate—photographs? videos? maps? Is there any statistical data that would be easier to understand as a table, chart, or graph?

- *If you're writing a spoken or digital text,* should you include sound? still images? moving images?

REFLECT. Make a list of all the writing that you remember doing in the last week. Be sure to include everything from texts and posts to more formal academic or work-related writing. Choose three examples that strike you as quite different from one another and analyze the rhetorical situation you faced for each one, drawing upon the guidelines in this chapter.

FOUR

Meeting the Expectations of Academic Writing

"It's Like Learning a New Language"

LLEN MacNAMARA ARRIVED AT COLLEGE excited but also anxious. She had grown up in a small town far from the college, had not taken calculus, and had never written more than a five-paragraph essay. So when she got her first college writing assignment— in a political science class, to write a ten-page essay on how the relationship among the three branches of the US government has evolved—she felt a little panic. She had read all her assignments and done some research, and she had even met with her instructor during office hours. She had quite a bit of material. But her first attempts at writing just didn't sound right. She wasn't sure what college writing sounded like, but this wasn't it.

Following her instructor's advice, MacNamara studied several of the political science articles on her course reading list. Compared to her usual writing, they were much more formal, full of complicated sentences. What she eventually came up with wasn't a particularly good essay (and she knew it), but it served its purpose: it had gotten her thinking about college-level writing. Looking back at the work she had done to get this far, she thought, "Wow, this is almost like learning a new language."

MacNamara had a point. Many students have experiences similar to hers, especially multilingual students who've grown up in other cultures. One Romanian student we know put it this way:

> In my country we care very much about the beauty of what we write. Even with academic and business writing, we try to make our texts poetic in some way. When I got to the U.S.A., I discovered that writing that I thought was beautiful struck my teachers as wordy and off-task. I was surprised about this.

This student, like Ellen MacNamara, needed to set about learning a new language—in this case, the language of US academic writing.

Habits of Mind for Academic Success

Learning the language of US academic writing is key to succeeding in college. Luckily, you don't need to guess at what strategies will lead to success. In *Framework for Success in Postsecondary Writing*, researchers and scholars have identified several key habits characteristic of students who do well in college—and beyond. Practice these habits in your coursework and you'll be "approaching learning from an active stance." In other words, you'll be on the path to succeed as an active, engaged writer and thinker.

- *Be curious.* Inquire, investigate, poke and pry until you find answers to questions you have or until you discover or create something new. Without curiosity, you'll miss much of what is really going on around you—in the courses you take and the sources you read. You can practice curiosity by asking questions: Why are the dorms on your campus so far away from the academic buildings? Who makes such decisions? How does the distance affect students who don't have bikes, for instance, or those with physical disabilities?

- *Be open & flexible.* Look at all sides of an issue. Consider fairly ideas that at first seem strange, foreign, or incorrect. Don't simply gather sources that agree with your position; instead, look for opposing views. And don't accept easy answers or those that occur to you first. In a discussion about campus safety, for example, listen and try to put yourself in the position of people with different perspectives—perhaps a young woman visitor, an older faculty member, or a student who works in a lab late at night.

- *Be engaged.* Grapple with the ideas of others, responding to them and finding connections between them. And don't give in to boredom—seek out something that really interests you in each course and assignment. A student we know was taking a course on ancient religious texts, primarily to fulfill a requirement, but when he read the Samson and Delilah story in different traditions, he used his interest in comics to create a graphic narrative of his favorite version. A topic that didn't draw him in at first became one he was excited about.

- *Be creative.* Try a new method or approach. Use a different medium for representing an idea. Take a risk investigating an idea or topic outside your comfort zone. If you think for a minute or two about your most successful school endeavors, you'll probably find that creativity played an important role: that geology project you created and presented that was unlike anything anyone else had done; the decision you made to create hip-hop lyrics to illustrate a point in a history essay.

- *Be persistent.* Keep at it. Follow through. Take advantage of opportunities to redo and improve. Keep track of what's challenging or hard for you—and look for ways to overcome those specific obstacles. You've probably already seen the positive effects of persistence in your life: they will count double (or triple) in college. Successful students don't give up but keep on keeping on. A student searching for information on a distant relative who had played a role in the civil rights movement kept coming up empty-handed and was about to give up on the project. But she decided to try one last lead on an ancestry website—and came up with a crucial piece of information that led to a big breakthrough and a sense of personal satisfaction. Persistence pays off!

- *Be responsible.* You're in control of your own learning—own it. Hold yourself responsible for making the most of your education. And be a responsible participant in the academic conversation by both incorporating and acknowledging the words and ideas of others in your own work.

- *Think about your own thinking.* Reflect on how you learn and think—and develop a habit of doing so often. Several major studies identify this kind of purposeful reflection as instrumental to becoming well educated. Many students find that keeping an informal journal to write about what they are learning, how they are learning it, and how they are learning to overcome obstacles leads to better comprehension and better success.

It's no coincidence that these habits of mind overlap with what it means to think and act rhetorically. The same practices that make us careful, ethical, and effective communicators (listen, search for understanding, put in your oar) also lead to success in college. You'll have opportunities to practice and develop these habits in your college writing. And doing so means you'll be well on your way to learning the "new language" of academic writing Ellen MacNamara described.

REFLECT. Think about a writing task you've recently been assigned or you're working on now. Which of the habits of mind have you used? And which ones are missing? Which habits of mind seem to come most naturally to you and which do you need to develop? Is there a habit you could put to better use? How will you do so next time?

So Just What Is Edited Academic Writing?

Academic writing is the kind of writing you do for school (and sometimes for work). It follows a set of conventions, such as using fairly formal edited English, following patterns of organization, and providing support for the points you make. But academic writing is also rather flexible, reaching beyond the classroom: it's used in many journals, newspapers, and books as well as online, especially on sites that address serious topics like politics, research, or cultural analysis. So "academic writing" is a broad category, one flexible enough to accommodate differences across disciplines, for example, while still remaining recognizably "academic." This chapter considers some of the assumptions that lie behind academic writing in the United States and describes some of the most common characteristics of that writing.

We're giving so much attention to academic writing for a couple of important reasons. First, becoming fluent in it will be of great help to you both in college and well beyond; and second, it poses challenges to both native and nonnative speakers of English. We want to acknowledge these challenges without making them seem difficult to overcome. Instead, we want to demystify some of the assumptions and conventions of academic writing and get you started thinking about how to use them to your advantage.

Though edited academic English is used in most academic and professional situations in the United States, the multilingual nature of our society often leads writers to bring other dialects of English and other languages into their writing and to take what Professors Jerry Won Lee and Christopher Jenks refer to as "translingual dispositions." This term refers to a pretty simple concept: those who adopt such a way of thinking are open and receptive to language differences, including differences among varieties of any language. Taking such a flexible approach to language difference is now characteristic of many college writing programs as well as much of the best writing occurring today. This mindset recognizes that there's usually more than one effective way to say or write something. And while edited academic English is one way (and a very common one in academic writing), it's not objectively better or worse than other ways. Ultimately, your audience and purpose should always inform your language choices.

Joining US Academic Conversations

If you are new to college, you'll want to learn to "talk the talk" of academic writing so that you can join the conversations in progress all around you. Doing so calls for understanding some common expectations that most of your instructors likely hold.

You're expected to respond. One important assumption underlying the kind of writing expected in American colleges is that reading and writing are active processes in which students not only absorb information but also respond to and even question it. Not all educational systems view reading and writing in this way. In some cultures, students are penalized if they attempt to read established texts critically or disagree with authorities or insert their own views. If you are from such a background, you may find it difficult to engage in this kind of active reading and writing. It may feel rude, disrespectful, or risky, particularly if you would be reprimanded for such engagement in your home culture.

Remember, however, that the kind of engagement your instructors want is not hostile or combative; it's not about showing off by beating down the ideas of others. Rather, they expect you to demonstrate your active engagement with the texts you read—and an awareness that in doing so you are joining an academic conversation, one that has been going on for a long time and that will continue. It's fine to express strong opinions, but it's also important to remember—and acknowledge—that there is value in perspectives other than your own.

You're expected to ask questions. Because US culture emphasizes individual achievement, students are expected to develop authority and independence, often by asking questions. In contrast to cultures where the best students never ask questions because they have already studied the material and worked hard to learn it, students in American academic contexts are expected and encouraged to voice their questions. In other words, don't assume you have to figure everything out by yourself. Do take responsibility for your own learning whenever possible, but it's fine to ask questions about what you don't understand, especially specific assignments.

You're expected to say what *you* think. American instructors expect that students will progress from relying on the thoughts of others to formulating ideas and arguments of their own. One important way to make that move is to engage in dialogue with other students and teachers. In these dialogues, teachers are not looking for you to express the "right" position; instead, they're looking for you to say what *you* think and provide adequate and appropriate support for that point of view.

You're expected to focus from the start. In contrast to many cultures, where writers start with fairly general background information, American academic writing immediately focuses in on the topic at hand. Thus, even in the introduction of an essay, you begin at a relatively focused level, providing even greater detail in the paragraphs that follow. The point is not to show how much you know but instead to provide the information your audience needs to understand the point easily.

Because American academic writers generally open their discussions at a fairly specific level, you wouldn't want to begin with a sentence like "All over the world and in many places, there are families," a thesis statement in an essay one of us once received from a native speaker of Arabic. (Translated into Arabic, this would make a beautiful sentence and an appropriate opening statement for an essay.) Students educated in Spanish or Portuguese and, to an even greater extent, those educated in Arabic are accustomed to providing a great deal more background information than those educated in English. If you are from one of these cultural backgrounds, do not be surprised if your instructor encourages you to delete most of the first few pages of a draft, for example, and to begin instead by addressing your topic more directly and specifically.

Academic writers at work in (*clockwise from top left*) India, Chile, Burkina Faso, the United States, Thailand, and Italy.

You're expected to state your point explicitly. In US academic English, writers are usually expected to provide direct and explicit statements that lead readers, step by step, through the text—in contrast to cultures that value indirectness, circling around the topic rather than addressing it head-on. A Brazilian student we knew wasn't inclined to state the point of an essay up front and explicitly. From his cultural perspective, it made more sense to develop an argument by building suspense and stating his position only at the end of the essay. As he said, "It took a lot of practice for me to learn how to write the very direct way that professors in the USA want."

All these expectations suggest that American academic discourse puts much of the burden for successful communication on the author rather than on members of the audience. So with these expectations in mind, let's take a close look at eight common characteristics of US academic writing.

CHARACTERISTIC FEATURES

No list of characteristics can describe all the kinds of texts you'll be expected to write in college, particularly given the differences among disciplines. But there are certain things you're expected to do in college writing:

- Use edited academic English.
- Use clear and recognizable patterns of organization.
- Mark logical relationships between ideas.
- State claims explicitly and provide appropriate support.
- Present your ideas as a response to others.
- Express your ideas clearly and directly.
- Be aware of how genres and conventions vary across disciplines.
- Document sources using the appropriate citation style.

Use Edited Academic English

Academic writing usually follows the conventions of **EDITED ACADEMIC ENGLISH** in terms of spelling, grammar, and punctuation. In addition, it is often more rather than less formal. Thus, the kinds of abbreviations and other shortcuts you use while texting or posting to social media usually aren't appropriate in academic writing: you'll have to write out "in my opinion" rather than "IMHO," and you'll also want to avoid emojis. Likewise, slang isn't usually appropriate. In some contexts, you'll discover that even contractions aren't appropriate—although we use them in this book because we're aiming for a conversational tone, one that is formal to some degree but not stuffy.

Thinking about the term itself—edited academic English—will give you some insights into the goal you are trying to accomplish. In general, this **DIALECT** of language, like its counterpart in many other cultures, is the one used in formal contexts, including academic ones, by educated people.

There is a logic behind using such an academic dialect: if everyone can agree on and follow the same basic conventions, whether for spelling or subject-verb agreement, we should all be able to communicate successfully with a broad range of people. It's helpful but not perfect, since as you know if you have been to Canada or the United Kingdom or Australia, academic English varies from country to country. *Edited* reminds you that this variety of English is one that has been looked at very carefully. Most writers, especially those who grew up speaking other varieties of English and those whose first language is not English, re-read their writing several times with great care. This is also, of course, the role that good editors play: they read someone else's work and make suggestions about how to improve the quality, whether at the level of the sentence, the paragraph, or the text as a whole. Few of us pay such careful attention to our writing when we tweet or text—but we *all* need to do so with our academic writing, even if it's in the form of email.

Use Clear and Recognizable Patterns of Organization

Academic writing is often organized in a way that's clear and easy for readers to recognize. In fact, writers generally describe the pattern explicitly early in a text by including a **THESIS** sentence that states the main point and says how the text is structured.

At the paragraph level, the opening sentence generally serves as a **TOPIC SENTENCE**, which announces what the paragraph is about. Readers of academic writing expect such signals for the text as a whole and within each paragraph, even in shorter texts like essay exams. Sometimes you'll want to include headings to make it easy for readers to locate sections of text.

Readers of academic writing look for organization not only to be clear but also to follow some kind of logical progression. For example:

- Beginning with the simplest ideas and then moving step by step to the most complex ideas
- Starting with the weakest claims or evidence and progressing to the strongest ones
- Treating some topics early in the text because readers must have them as background to understand ideas introduced later
- Arranging the text chronologically, starting with the earliest events and ending with the latest ones

Some academic documents in the sciences and social sciences require a specific organization known as **IMRAD** for its specific headings: introduction, methods, results, and discussion. Although there are many possible logical patterns to use, readers will expect to be able to see that pattern with little or no difficulty. Likewise, they generally expect the **TRANSITIONS** between sections and ideas to be indicated in some way, whether with words like *first*, *next*, or *finally*, or even with full sentences like "Having considered three reasons to support this position, I will now present some alternative positions."

Finally, remember that you need to conclude your text by somehow reminding your readers of the main point(s) you want them to take away. Often, these reminders explicitly link the conclusion back to the thesis statement or introduction.

Mark Logical Relationships between Ideas

Academic writers usually strive to make clear how the ideas they present relate to one another. Thus, in addition to marking the structure of the text, you need to mark the links between ideas and to do so explicitly. If you say in casual conversation, "It was raining, and we didn't go on the picnic," listeners will interpret *and* to mean *so* or *therefore*. In academic writing, however, you have to help readers understand how your ideas are related to one another. For this reason, you'll want to use **TRANSITIONS** like *therefore*, *however*, or *in addition*. Marking the relationships among your ideas clearly and explicitly helps readers recognize and appreciate the logic of your arguments.

State Claims Explicitly and Provide Appropriate Support

One of the most important conventions of academic writing is to present **CLAIMS** explicitly and support them with **EVIDENCE**, such as examples or statistics, or by citing authorities of various kinds. Notice the two distinct parts: presenting claims clearly and supporting them appropriately. In academic writing, authors don't generally give hints; instead, they state what is on their minds, often in a **THESIS** statement. If you are from a culture that values indirection and communicates by hinting or by repeating proverbs or telling stories to make a point, you'll need to check to be sure that you have stated your claims explicitly. Don't assume that readers will be able to understand what you're saying, especially if they do not have the same cultural background knowledge that you do.

Qualify your statements. Note that being clear and explicit doesn't mean being dogmatic or closed-minded. You'll generally want to moderate your claims by using qualifying words like *frequently, often, generally, sometimes,* or *rarely* to indicate how strong a claim you are making. Note as well that it is much easier to provide adequate support for a qualified claim than it is to provide support for a broad unqualified claim.

Choose evidence your audience will trust. Whatever your claim, you'll need to use **EVIDENCE** that will be considered trustworthy and persuasive by your audience. And keep in mind that what counts as acceptable and appropriate evidence in academic writing often differs from what works in other contexts. Generally, for example, you wouldn't cite sacred religious texts as a primary source for academic arguments. In addition, writers today need more than ever to act as fact-checkers, making certain that their sources are accurate and credible rather than based on misinformation or lies.

Consider multiple perspectives. You should be aware that your readers may have a range of opinions on any topic, and you should write accordingly. Thus, citing only sources that reflect one perspective won't be sufficient in most academic contexts. Be sure to consider and acknowledge **COUNTER-ARGUMENTS** and viewpoints other than your own.

Organize information strategically. One common way of supporting a claim is by moving from a general statement to more specific information.

When you see words like *for example* or *for instance*, the author is moving from a more general statement to a more specific example.

In considering what kind of evidence to use in supporting your claims, remember that the goal is not to amass and present large quantities of evidence but instead to sift through all the available evidence, choose the evidence that will be most persuasive to your audience, and arrange and present it all strategically. Resist the temptation to include information or **ANECDOTES** that do not contribute to your argument. Your instructor may see these as digressions and encourage you to delete them.

Present Your Ideas as a Response to Others

Strong academic writers do more than just make well-supported claims. They present their ideas as a response to what else has been said (or might be said) about their topic. One common pattern, introduced by professors Gerald Graff and Cathy Birkenstein, is to start with what others are saying and then to present your ideas as a response. If, as noted earlier in this chapter, academic writing is a way of entering a conversation—of engaging with the ideas of others—you need to include their ideas with your own.

In fact, providing support for your claims will often involve **SYNTHESIS**: weaving the ideas and even the words of others into the argument you are making. And since academic arguments are part of a larger conversation, all of us are always responding to and borrowing from others, even as we are developing our own individual ideas.

Express Your Ideas Clearly and Directly

Another characteristic of academic writing is clarity. You want to be sure that readers can understand exactly what you are writing about. Have you ever begun a sentence by writing "This shows . . ." only to have your teacher ask, "What does this refer to?" Such a comment is evidence that the reader isn't sure what the author—you—is referring to: this argument? this evidence? this analysis? Be specific in your language. You'll also want to **DEFINE** terms you use, both to be sure readers will not be confused and to clarify your own positions—much as we defined "edited academic English" earlier in this chapter.

Clarity of expression in academic writing also means being direct and concise. Academic writers in the United States avoid highly elaborate sentence structures or flowery language, and they don't let the metaphors and similes they use get the best of them either, as this author did:

> Cheryl's mind turned like the vanes of a wind-powered turbine, chopping her sparrowlike thoughts into bloody pieces that fell onto a growing pile of forgotten memories.

In fact, this sentence was the winner of an annual "bad writing" contest in which writers try to write the worst sentence they can. It's easy to see why this one was a winner: it has way too much figurative language—chopping wind turbines, bleeding sparrows, thoughts in a pile, forgotten memories—and the metaphors get in the way of one another. Use metaphors carefully in academic writing, making sure they add to what you're trying to say. Here's one way the prize-winning sentence might be revised to be clearer and more direct: "Cheryl's mind worked incessantly, thought after thought piling up until she couldn't keep track of them all."

Be Aware of How Genres and Conventions Vary across Disciplines

While we can identify common characteristics of all academic writing, some genres and conventions vary across disciplines. Thus, an analytic essay in psychology is similar to one in a literature class, but it is also different in crucial ways. The same will be true for lab reports or position papers in various fields. In this regard, different disciplines are like different cultures, sharing many things but unique in specific ways. Therefore, part of becoming a biologist or an engineer—or even an electrical engineer instead of a civil engineer—is learning the discipline's particular rules and rituals as well as its preferred ways of presenting, organizing, and documenting information.

You'll also find that some rhetorical moves vary across genres. In the humanities, for example, writers often use a quotation to open an essay, as a way of launching an argument—or to close one, as a way of inspiring the audience. Such a move occurs far less often in the sciences or social sciences.

Despite these differences in genres across academic disciplines, you'll also find there are some common rhetorical moves you'll make in much of the academic writing you do. You'll find that short essays and research articles generally open with three such moves:

- First, you give the **CONTEXT** or general topic of whatever you are writing; frequently, you will do this by discussing the existing research or commentary on the topic you are writing about.

- Second, you point out some aspect of this topic that merits additional attention, often because it is poorly understood or because there is a problem that needs to be solved—that is, you'll show there is a problem or gap of some kind in our understanding.

- Finally, you'll explain how your text addresses that problem or fills that gap. This explanation often happens within the first paragraph or two of the text.

Document Sources Using the Appropriate Citation Style

Finally, academic writers credit and **DOCUMENT** all sources carefully. Understanding how Western academic culture defines intellectual property and **PLAGIARISM** is complicated. Although you never need to provide a source for common knowledge that no one disputes (for example, that the US Declaration of Independence was approved by Congress on July 4, 1776, in Philadelphia), you will need to document words, information, or ideas that you get from others, including, of course, any content (words or images) you find on the internet.

What else do you need to learn about academic writing? While we hope this chapter gives you a good idea of the major features of academic writing in the United States, you may still find yourself asking questions. What kinds of evidence are necessary to support a claim sufficiently? How much documentation is needed? Should a review of literature primarily describe and summarize existing research, or should it go one step further and critique this research? You will begin to learn the answers to these questions in time, as you advance through college, and especially when you choose your major. But don't be surprised that the immediate answer to questions like these will very often be "It depends." And "it" will always depend on your purpose for writing and on the audience you wish to reach.

In the meantime, even as you work to become fluent in US academic writing, it's worth returning to a note we have sounded frequently in this chapter: the US way of writing academically is not the only way. Nor is it a better way. Rather, it is a different way. As you learn about other cultures and languages, you may have an opportunity to learn and practice the conventions those cultures use to guide their own forms of academic writing. When you do so, you'll be learning yet another "new" language, just as you have learned the "academic writing" language of the United States.

FIVE

Writing and Rhetoric in the Workplace

LASH FORWARD FIVE OR TEN YEARS. You've graduated from college, maybe from graduate or professional school as well; you're on the job. And whatever that job is, one thing is certain: your ability to communicate— through writing, speaking, and other means—will be crucial to your success. If you're an engineer, you'll likely be writing **PRO- POSALS**, specifications, and directions and maybe giving presentations to prospective clients. If you're a teacher, you'll be writing lesson plans and student **EVALUATIONS**. If you're a health-care practitioner, you'll be writing medical **NARRATIVES** and patient charts and speaking with patients and their families. If you're an accountant, you'll be **ANALYZING** data. If you're a sales representative, you'll be writing **REPORTS** as well as pre- senting pitches to customers. So strong is the demand for good communi- cators that virtually every survey of employers reports that the ability to write and speak well is the skill they value most.

Becoming a strong writer, speaker, and presenter isn't rocket sci- ence or a gift from the gods: it's a product of careful choices, hard work, and lots of practice. This chapter offers advice on some of the writing and speaking you'll need to do for work, first to get hired and then to succeed once you're on the job.

Strong writing and speaking skills are essential in the workplace—from finding a job to performing the tasks that job will require.

Consider Your Rhetorical Situation

Whether you have a job or are searching for one, you'll be communicating with many different audiences for many different purposes—and so you should get in the habit of thinking systematically about your rhetorical situation. Here are some questions that can guide you:

- *What's your* PURPOSE*?* Are you seeking information? an interview? a specific job? Are you asking someone to do something for you? Are you discussing a possible job, plan, or project? Are you presenting a proposal? asking for a raise?

- *Who's your* AUDIENCE*?* Someone you know or have been referred to? A human resources director? A colleague? A person you would report to? Someone you know nothing about? What can you assume about someone you don't know—and what can you find out by looking on a company website? If you don't know whose desk your message will land on, or if it's likely to be read by multiple people, err on the side of caution: it's better to come across as too formal than too casual.

- *What* GENRES *should you use?* Are you writing a letter? composing a résumé? reporting information? arguing a position or proposing some kind of action? reviewing someone's work (or being reviewed)? Thinking about genre can help you know what is expected in any of these instances.

- *What's your* STANCE*?* How do you want to present yourself—as eager? curious? confident? knowledgeable? professional? friendly? earnest? If you're looking for a job, what experience do you bring—and how can you demonstrate what you could contribute?

- *What's the* CONTEXT*?* Are you responding to an ad? writing a cover letter to go with an application or a proposal? presenting to a large group? If you're applying for a job, what can you find out about the organization online?

- *What* MEDIA *will you use?* If you're sending a letter or résumé, should you use email or snail mail? Or are you required to upload your application to a website? If you're participating in a discussion or interview, will it be face-to-face? on the phone? in a webinar? If you're giving a presentation, should you include slides or handouts?

Be Professional

The words you choose, the sentences you write, the way you design a letter or résumé, even your email address create an impression for prospective employers—and you want it to be a good one. The impression you make is even more important once you're on the job, for then you'll be representing both yourself and the organization you work for. Careless errors that might result in a few points off a grade at school can have greater consequences in the working world, from not getting an interview to not winning a contract to actually losing a job or a promotion. Whether you're on the job or applying for one, every word is crucial for making your goals clear and establishing credibility with employers, colleagues, or clients.

Job Letters

Letters are an important part of a job search. You will almost certainly write letters to gather information or ask about possible positions, to apply for specific jobs, and to thank those with whom you have interviewed. For all the job-related letters you'll write, here are some tried-and-true tips:

- Be direct and brief. Say what you want, and why. Assume that your readers will be scanning for just the information they need; make it easy for them to find it.

- Focus more on how you can help the company or organization than on why working there would be good for you. Be careful not to start too many sentences with I.

- State your interest and qualifications in a way that makes your readers want to speak with you—and hire you.

- Design letters carefully, making sure they look neat and professional. Use a single typeface—Times New Roman or **Arial** are always appropriate. Remember that the look of your letters says a lot about you.

- Use capitalization and punctuation the way you would in an academic essay. Don't include emojis or too many exclamation points.

- Address readers by name and title (Dear Ms. Willett) or by first name and last if you're not sure about the correct title (Dear Mary Helen

Willett). If an advertisement lists only an office, use that in your salutation (Dear Office of Human Resources). If you can't find a person or an office to use, check the company's website—or make a call to the company headquarters to find out more about whom you should address.

- Proofread, proofread, proofread! Make sure that nothing is misspelled.

Inquiry letters. Sometimes you may want to send a letter looking for information about a position, an industry, an organization, or something else. If you admire someone's work or are interested in a particular company, do some research. You can probably find contact information online and some specific names on *LinkedIn*. Write to ask if they would speak with you.

Inquiry letters should be brief. Introduce yourself, and explain your interest in the organization or the person's work. Be enthusiastic but direct about what you're asking for—information about an organization? an opportunity to meet with someone? Remember to include your contact information.

Shuqiao Song read a book on designing presentations that she liked very much and that helped her improve her own presentation skills. When she noticed in the book that the author had a business near her college, Song sent the following email:

From: Shuqiao Song <ssong@gmail.com>

Date: Sunday, May 26, 2019 8:28 PM

To: Nancy Duarte <nduarte@presentations.com>

Subject: Interested in communications design

Dear Ms. Duarte:

I'm a sophomore at Stanford, where I recently took a rhetoric course in which we studied your book *slide:ology* for examples of successful presentations. I loved your book and was inspired to incorporate your suggestions and model my own presentation and slides on the advice you give.

The words and images in the graphic novel that I analyzed in my presentation interact in unusual and fascinating ways. My research on this topic led me to some insights about the way that speech, written text, and images could interact in my presentation. I've attached a video file of the presentation, which I hope you'll find interesting. My performance is far from perfect, but reading your book changed the way I thought about presenting and helped me analyze the elements of good (and bad) presentations.

Your book also made me aware of the field of communications design, and I'm interested to learn more about it. Would you be willing to meet with me to tell me about your work and how I can learn more about the field?

Thank you so much for considering this request. I hope to have the opportunity to speak with you.

Sincerely yours,
Shuqiao Song
650-555-5555

Application letters. When you're writing to apply for a job, a grant, or something else, you'll usually need to write an application letter. This kind of letter is ordinarily sent along with a résumé, so it should be relatively short and to the point, saying what you are applying for and why you are interested in it. Most important of all, try to show readers why they should consider your application—and here you need to focus on why hiring you would be good for them, not for you. Finally, identify anything you are including with your letter: your résumé, a writing sample, and so on.

Ade Adegboyega saw an advertisement for a summer internship at a ticket sales and service company. He was majoring in exercise science and sport management and had some experience in ticket sales and related services, so he was quick to apply. See the letter he sent on the next page.

An Application Letter

89 Laurel Ave.
Irvington, NJ 07111
April 14, 2019

Frank Miller, Sales Manager
The ASR Group
3120 Industrial Blvd.
Suite A200
Atlanta, GA 30318

Dear Mr. Miller:

I am writing in response to your Teamworkonline.com posting for a summer intern in ticket sales and services. I believe that I have skills and experience that would enable me to contribute to your organization, and I am interested in this position.

I am a sophomore at Rutgers University, majoring in exercise science and sport management, graduating in May 2021. The enclosed résumé provides details of my skills, education, and work experience. One item that may be of particular interest to you is my work in the ticket sales department at the Prudential Center. This experience taught me how to analyze sales patterns and meet sales quotas and promotional objectives. I've also worked as an office assistant and would also be able to contribute to the production of reports. All my jobs have helped me learn to communicate effectively with both colleagues and vendors.

I would welcome the opportunity to put my experience and abilities to work for the ASR Group sport management department and to discuss the position further with you. I can be reached at 862-555-5555 or ade.adegbo@gmail.com. Thank you for considering my application.

Sincerely,

Ade Adegboyega

Ade Adegboyega

Thank-you letters. Send a thank-you letter to anyone you speak with or who helps you when you're looking for a job. Whether you talk to people in person, on the phone, or in an email, you should thank them in writing. Doing so is a sign of respect and demonstrates your seriousness and your ability to follow through. When you're writing to someone who's interviewed you, try to reference something discussed in the interview, to raise a new question that might extend the conversation, and to provide additional thoughts about why the position would be an excellent match for your abilities and interests. And be sure to send a thank-you promptly, within a day or two of your interview. A handwritten note is a nice touch, but it's perfectly appropriate to send the thank-you via email, especially if the employer will be making a decision soon. When Scott Williams was looking for a job, he was careful to write thank-you emails like this one after every interview.

From: Scott Williams <sjwilliams@optonline.net>

Date: Friday, March 23, 2018 4:35 PM

To: Yuri Davison <davisony@graceco.com>

Subject: Thank You

Dear Mr. Davison,

Thank you for meeting with me yesterday and for taking so much time to explain the work your firm does. My studies as an economics major were mostly theoretical, so I was especially interested to hear about the day-to-day work at a private equity firm.

It's exciting to know that Grace & Company might be looking for a junior analyst in the near future, and I'm pleased to attach a sample of my writing, as you requested. It's an analytical paper I wrote about the music of Franz Liszt.

Thank you again for your time and consideration. I hope you'll keep me in mind if you do decide you need a junior analyst.

Sincerely,
Scott Williams
203-555-5555

Résumés

Your résumé provides an overview of your education and work experience—and thus is usually your most important chance to create a strong and favorable impression. While busy employers may not take time to read all the materials you send them, they will certainly take a close look at your résumé. For that reason, you'll need to write and design it carefully. As a piece of writing that represents you, your résumé should look good and be easy to read. Keep it to one page—just enough to showcase your experience and to present yourself thoughtfully. The sample résumé on the next page lists experience in chronological order, but you might consider using reverse-chronological order if your recent experiences relate directly to the kind of job you'd like to attain.

Format. Be prepared to submit your document in a variety of ways: Word, rich text format (RTF) or plain text, PDF, or HTML. Because browsers or company systems can translate files in different ways, having a clean, simple setup will prevent your résumé from being relegated to the "toss pile" because it has defaulted to something that's difficult to read. If you're submitting your résumé online, check how it looks once uploaded. If a company you're applying to wants résumés in a particular format, be sure you deliver yours that way.

Design. Use headings to organize your information and highlight key information with bullets. Make your design as simple as possible: fonts and indents won't always carry over, and simpler can often be more readable. Many companies rely on scanning technology to filter résumés for a specific position. A simple design means your résumé will be easy for automatic scanners to read. These systems search keywords to find candidates with the most appropriate experience, so mention skills, qualities, and qualifications listed in the job description when detailing your own experience.

If you have a specific job objective, you might list that objective at the top, just under your name and contact information. Be sure to mention any courses and experience that are relevant to that objective. If you're applying to be a teaching assistant at an elementary school, for example, you'll want to list any substitute teaching or babysitting experience and your CPR certification. And you might want to put experience that is most relevant to your goals first, as Ade Adegboyega did on the résumé he sent in for an internship at a ticket sales and service company.

A Print Résumé

Ade Adegboyega
89 Laurel Ave.
Irvington, NJ 07111
862-555-5555
ade.adegbo@gmail.com

OBJECTIVE
To obtain an internship related to the field of sport management

EDUCATION
Rutgers University, New Brunswick, NJ (2017–present)
* School of Arts and Science
* Major: Exercise Science and Sport Management
* Minor: Economics
* Bachelor of Science expected May 2021

EXPERIENCE
Prudential Center, Newark, NJ (Oct. 2015–Sept. 2017)
Ticket Sales Associate
* Responded to inbound sales calls and inquiries, and provided information and/or follow-up materials as requested
* Maintained knowledge of ticket plan programs and ticket holder preferences

Answer, Rutgers University Center for Applied Psychology, Piscataway, NJ (Sept. 2017–present)
Office Assistant at national organization for sex education
* Oversee database management for quality assurance
* Assist staff with administrative duties as requested
* Compile statistical information for program coordinators
* Distribute incoming mail and prepare outgoing mail

Rutgers Recreation, New Brunswick, NJ (Jan. 2018–present)
Intramural Referee
* Look for violations of rules during play
* Impose penalties on players as necessary
* Explain the rules governing a specific sport

COMPUTER SKILLS
Microsoft Office, Adobe InDesign, HTML coding

ACTIVITIES
Intramural soccer
Rutgers Brazilian Jiu Jitsu Club

References

Often prospective employers will ask for references—professors or supervisors who can speak about your work and your work ethic. Your first step is to develop relationships with teachers and others who might serve as references. Start early in your college career; visit your teachers during office hours, discuss your goals with them—and keep in touch. When you feel comfortable enough, ask if they would be willing to be a reference for you.

When it comes time to apply for a specific job, be sure to provide your references with helpful information: a description of the position, your résumé and cover letter, and samples of your work. Give ample notice—never less than a week or two to write a letter. If the letter will be mailed, be sure to provide stamped, addressed envelopes. Remember to thank your references at every step: when they agree to be a reference, after they recommend you, and when you get the position!

Writing Samples

You may be asked to submit a writing sample or even a **PORTFOLIO** of your work. For some positions, you may want to choose writing that relates in some way to the position you're seeking, but often you'll just need to show something that demonstrates your writing ability. Include a brief cover note with your sample explaining what it is, why you are proud of it, and why you've chosen to submit it. Label the sample with your name and contact information, and take care with its presentation: place it in a folder if you're delivering it in person or make sure it's a neatly designed document if you're sending it via email.

When Elizabeth Sanders interviewed for a position as a student events coordinator for a campus research institute that specified "experience organizing and publicizing campus events" as a qualification, she was asked to bring a portfolio of her work along. She chose work that showcased writing that would matter for that job—two brochures she wrote, designed, and produced; an interview she'd conducted with a visiting speaker; and a press release—and then wrote a cover statement listing what was in her portfolio and describing how each item addressed the job she was applying for.

Job Interviews

When it comes time to interview, you'll need to prepare. Review the job description and plan how you will talk about your experiences. Research the department and organization that you'd be working for. Make a list of questions you can imagine being asked and come up with answers to each. Prepare your own list of questions that you'd like to ask. You may even want to ask a friend to do a mock interview with you for practice.

The day of the interview, be on time, dress appropriately, and bring extra copies of your résumé, cover letter, references, and any other materials that were requested. Of course you'll be nervous, but be sure to *listen*—and to think before responding. And remember to smile! Here are a few questions that interviewers might ask that you can use to practice and build your own list of potential questions:

- Why are you interested in this industry or field?
- What interests you about this specific position?
- What do you know and like about our organization?
- What is your greatest strength? weakness?
- Can you describe a time that you successfully collaborated on a project?

Participating in a video interview. Many employers today use *Skype* or other videoconferencing technologies to conduct interviews. If you're asked to do an interview of this kind, here's some advice:

- Practice speaking over video chat with a friend.
- Dress appropriately and in clothing that is easy to move around in: you may be asked to stand, or sit, or both.
- Avoid using overhead lighting, which can appear harsh on camera; try for natural light if at all possible.
- Make sure that you have a reliable internet connection.
- Remember to look and speak directly into the camera in order to come as close as possible to establishing eye contact with your interviewers.
- Be sure to speak carefully, enunciating each word in case the connection is less than ideal.
- Make sure that the area around you is neat—and that your dog isn't barking!

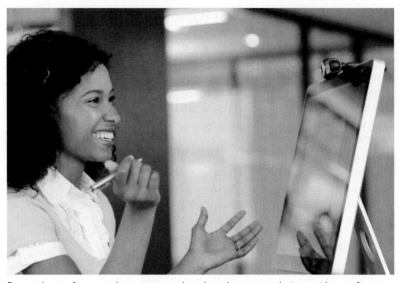

Remember to focus on the camera, rather than the screen, during a videoconference.

Writing on the Job

The fact is that almost any job you take will call for writing—and for speaking and presenting as well. Regardless of what job you do, you will surely be writing email. You will also likely be composing **EVALUATIONS** as well as letters of recommendation for others and carrying out **ANALYSES** of all kinds. Many jobs will call on you to write a whole range of **REPORTS** and to give presentations incorporating handouts or slides.

As rhetorician Deborah Brandt points out, most of those working in the United States today spend part of their day writing:

> A large majority of Americans . . . now make their living in the so-called information economy, people who produce, distribute, process, manipulate or vend mostly written work during a significant percentage of the workday. At the turn of the 20th century, information workers represented 10 percent of all employees. By 1959, they had grown to more than 30 percent; by 1970, they were at 50 percent and now are 75 percent of the employed population. . . . As the nature of work in the

United States has changed—toward making and managing information and knowledge—intense pressure has come to bear on the productive side of literacy, the writing side, made all the more intense . . . with the wide distribution of communication technologies that enable writing, that put keyboards and audiences readily at hand.

—DEBORAH BRANDT, "Writing at Work"

So writing will probably be a key part of your day-to-day work, as well as a key to your future success. And the greatest success comes to those who present themselves effectively, develop a strong work ethic, and seek mentorship and constructive criticism—literally writing and speaking their way to success. Remember that getting—and keeping—a job depends on some basic rhetorical principles that will never go out of style:

- Become a strong and proactive team player who collaborates well with others.

- Know your **AUDIENCE**, and make the effort to meet them more than halfway, with respect and a willingness to listen and learn from them.

- Clarify your goals and **PURPOSES**, and stick to them—but also know when and how to compromise.

- Consider the **RHETORICAL SITUATION** of any task you face, and make sure that what you are doing is appropriate in that context.

- Know your own strengths and weaknesses, and strive to build on the former and minimize the latter.

- Learn from your mistakes.

REFLECT. Think back to the jobs you've held recently. Whether you were a volunteer at your local hospital or animal shelter, a cashier, a barista, a tutor, or a summer intern, chances are that rhetoric, writing, and collaboration played a role in the work you did. Make some notes about how a particular job required you to use writing or rhetorical strategies. How do you think you might use these skills in future jobs or workplaces?

PART II

Reading Processes

DO YOU REMEMBER the first word you learned to read? For many people, that first word is their own name: you learn to print it and you do this over and over again and—suddenly, as if by magic—you can read it! Those first reading moments are miraculous because they open up entire new worlds to us. And as this example suggests, writing and reading are reciprocal processes: writing evokes reading and reading evokes writing, as if they two are intertwined in a seamless dance.

Like writing, many of us take reading for granted: it's something we have been able to do for so long that it seems run-of-the-mill, almost like breathing. But reading turns out to be a complicated process, and one with a long history. The word comes down to us from Old English, *rœdan*: to advise, counsel, guess, learn by reading—and, as early as 1610, "to make out the character of a person." Sojourner Truth, a former slave and abolition advocate who was thought to be illiterate, surely knew this definition of "read" when she said, "I don't read such small things as letters; I read men and nations." This early sense of the word *read* is still with us: we "read" situations, we "read" people, we "read" images, and so on. We also read with eyes, ears, and fingers: those with low vision read by listening or by tracing braille, for example, while people who are hard of hearing use closed captions while watching television.

One aim of the following chapters is to do what ethnographers recommend to spark new ideas: make the familiar strange. We want to make the processes and practices of everyday, commonplace reading "strange" in order to call attention to them, to get you to look at them with fresh and creative eyes, and to think carefully—about what you are doing when you read, about different ways of reading, and about the processes that reading demands of you.

The chapters that follow will introduce you to the concept of reading rhetorically—that is, reading a text with clear intention and attention and putting that text, whether written, oral, visual, or digital, in its context. This kind of reading will help you read and understand the texts you encounter during your college career and well beyond. In addition, we'll focus on particular processes of reading, from annotating and summarizing a text to the point where reading meets writing in the responses you compose to what you have read. And last but certainly not least, we'll focus on drawing careful distinctions among facts, misinformation, and lies—and provide ways in which you can identify, understand, and engage productively with each category, practicing what we call "defensive reading."

Reading is a profoundly social act: it connects us to other people and places and times and at its best can be an act of empathy, helping us to walk in other people's shoes. As novelist Jean Rhys says, "Reading makes immigrants of us all. It takes us away from home, but more important, it finds homes for us everywhere." Or, in the inimitable words of Dr. Seuss: "The more that you read, the more things you will know. The more you learn, the more places you'll go!"

SIX

Reading Rhetorically

CHANCES ARE, YOU READ MORE than you think you do. You read print texts, of course, but you probably also read regularly on a phone, tablet, or computer. Reading is now, as perhaps never before, a basic necessity. In fact, if you think that reading is something you learned once and for all in the first or second grade, think again.

Reading calls for strategic effort. As media critic Howard Rheingold sees it, literacy today involves at least five interlocking abilities: attention, participation, collaboration, network awareness, and critical consumption. Of these, attention is first and foremost. In short, you need to work at paying attention to what you read. In his book *The Economics of Attention*, rhetorician Richard Lanham explains: "We're drowning in information. What we lack is the human attention needed to make sense of it all."

When so many texts are vying for our attention, which ones do we choose? In order to decide what to read, what to pay attention to, we need to practice what Rheingold calls *infotention*, a word he came up with to describe a "mind-machine combination of brain-powered attention skills and computer-powered information filters." Rheingold is talking primarily about reading online, but we think that infotention is important for reading any kind of text because it calls for synthesizing and thinking rhetorically about the enormous amount of information available to us

So many texts vying for our attention!

in both print and digital sources. And while some of us can multitask (fighter pilots are one example Rheingold gives), most of us are not good at it and must learn to focus our attention when we read.

In other words, we need to learn to read rhetorically. Reading rhetorically means attending carefully and intentionally to a text. It means being open-minded to that text. And it means being an active participant in understanding and thinking about and responding to what is in the text. As Nobel laureate Toni Morrison says, "The words on the page are only half the story. The rest is what you bring to the party."

So how do you learn to read rhetorically and to practice infotention? Some steps seem obvious: especially for high-stakes reading, like much of what you do for school, you need to find space and time in which you can really focus—turn off social media and put down your phone. Beyond such obvious steps, though, you can improve your reading by approaching texts systematically. This chapter and the chapter that follows will guide you in doing so, beginning with tips for considering your rhetorical situation and motivating yourself to engage actively with texts.

THINKING ABOUT YOUR RHETORICAL SITUATION

Before jumping into a text, consider your rhetorical situation; doing so will help you get straight where the author—and you—are coming from. Following are some questions to consider when approaching a text:

- What's the **PURPOSE** for your reading? To learn something new? To fulfill an assignment? To prepare for a test?
- Who's the intended **AUDIENCE**? What words or images in the text make you think so? Are you a member of this group? If not, there may be unfamiliar terms or references that you'll need to look up.
- What's the **GENRE**? An argument? Report? Review? Proposal? Knowing the genre will tell you something about what to expect.
- How might the **MEDIUM** affect how you will read the text? Is it a written print text? An oral text? A visual or multimedia text, such as an infographic? How will you go about attending carefully to these different media?
- What do you know about the larger **CONTEXT** of the text? What do you know about the topic? What do you need to find out? What resources can you draw on for the information you will need?
- What is your own **STANCE** on the topic? Are you an advocate? a critic? an impartial observer?

Getting your rhetorical situation straight begins your first job as a reader: making sure you understand what you read. Chapter 7 offers guidance on other essential strategies for understanding texts: previewing, annotating, and summarizing. The rest of this chapter focuses on how to be a motivated, engaged, and persistent reader.

BECOMING AN ACTIVE, ENGAGED READER

"Engagement" is one of the habits of mind scholars see as crucial to success in college, and it's certainly crucial to any reading you do there. You're "engaged" in reading when you are invested in the text. Sounds good in theory, right? But just how can you get yourself "invested" in something you've been assigned to read, especially if it's a text you wouldn't choose to read otherwise? There's no magic wand you can wave to make this happen, but we can offer some advice for staying engaged while reading:

- *Find your comfort zone,* someplace where you're most likely to be able to concentrate. A comfy lounge chair? A desk chair with back support? Starbucks? Some students tell us they like to be a little *uncomfortable* because it keeps them on their mental toes.

- *Choose a device that helps you focus.* Some like print texts best for taking notes, while others like reading on a Kindle or other device without internet distractions.

- *Make it social.* In the case of difficult texts, two heads are usually better than one—and discussing text with someone else will help you both to engage with it. Try to explain something in the text to a friend or classmate; if you can get across the major points, you've surely understood it!

- *Start with what's easy, then tackle what's difficult.* The introduction may be easy to read, so begin there and make sure you understand before moving on to more difficult material. If the text is short, read it all the way through once, marking the hard parts. Then return to the tricky parts without spending too much time; you'll probably find they are easier to understand once you've read through the entire text once.

- *Annotate as you read.* The following chapter will give you guidelines for using annotation to understand, engage, and respond to what you read.

FAST—AND SLOW—READING

Do you feel like you are always rushing? Running to the next thing, and the next, and the next? We seem to like everything fast—fast cars, fast videos, fast food—and often, fast reading. We're not talking about speed reading, which advocates claim can allow you to read up to 1,500 words a minute, but rather about the kind of skimming and scanning that most of us do online.

And there are good reasons to skim texts, particularly when you are looking for specific information. You can skim across passages looking for keywords that signal information you need, or you can read the first sentence of a paragraph to get the gist of whether what follows is relevant for your purposes. Reading expert Louise Rosenblatt calls this kind of reading "efferent," reading that's aimed at getting into a text and extracting key information in the swiftest and most effective way possible. She uses the example of a parent whose child has swallowed a dangerous substance: the parent is looking for the antidote and needs only one piece of information—fast!

The opposite of such fast reading is, logically enough, slow reading. There are lots of "slow" movements with loyal participants today: slow travel, slow media, slow fashion, and even slow reading. Some colleges now offer courses in slow reading; we know of one in a literature department where students are allowed to read only five pages a night. In his book *The Art of Slow Reading*, English professor Tom Newkirk describes six "slow" practices we believe are helpful for the kind of reading you're expected to do in college:

- *Perform.* Imagine the text you're reading is a drama, one that can be played out before an audience. Thinking of the content as a story—a narrative with low points and climaxes—can help you engage with and understand the text.

- *Make a mark.* Annotate what you notice as key parts of a text, what stands out to you as central or important to remember.

- *Find problems.* Stop to note a problem or confusion in the text and try to come up with a strategy for solving it. Such problem finding can work especially well if you are reading with someone else, someone you can talk with about the problem or confusion.

- *Read like a writer,* asking yourself about the decisions or moves the writer is making: Why shift topics here? Why introduce a particular piece of evidence at this point? Why choose this word rather than another?

- *Elaborate,* going beyond the text by comparing and contrasting it with other texts or drawing out unstated implications from the text.

- *Memorize key passages.* Learning key terms and bits of text by heart can help you understand and remember what you are reading. This can be especially helpful for reading literature, though less applicable in other fields and disciplines.

Slow reading, then, doesn't refer simply to speed. Rather it's about attending carefully to the text, taking responsibility for your reading practices.

READING UNFAMILIAR OR DIFFICULT TEXTS

You'll surely encounter subject matter and texts that are hard to understand. Most often these will be texts that you're reading not for pleasure but to learn something. You'll want to slow down with such texts, to stop and think—and you might find this easier to do with print texts, where paragraphs and headings and highlighted features help you see the various parts and find key information. Here are some other tips for making your way through difficult texts:

- On your first reading, read for what you can understand, and simply mark places that are confusing or where you don't understand.
- Then choose a modest amount of material to read—a chapter, say, or even part of a chapter. Look it over to figure out how it is organized and see its main points—look at headings, for example, as well as any **THESIS** and **TOPIC SENTENCES**.
- Check to see if there's a summary at the beginning or end of the text. If so, read it very carefully.
- Re-read the hard parts. Slow down, and focus.
- Try to make sense of the parts: "this part offers evidence," "that paragraph summarizes an alternative view," "here's a signal about what's coming next."
- If the text includes visuals, what do they contribute to the message?
- Resist highlighting: better to take notes in the margins or on digital sticky notes.

READING ON-SCREEN AND OFF

Once upon a time "reading" meant attending to words on paper. But today we often encounter texts that convey information in images and in sound as well—and they may be on- or off-screen. When you approach such texts, think carefully about how the medium of delivery may affect your understanding, engagement, and response.

Researchers have found that we often take shortcuts when we read online, searching and scanning and jumping around in a text or leaping from link to link. This kind of reading is very helpful for finding answers and information quickly, but it can blur our focus and make it difficult to attend to the text carefully and purposefully. Here are a few tips to help you when you're reading on-screen:

- Be clear about your purpose for reading. If you need to understand and remember the text, remind yourself to read carefully and avoid skimming or skipping around.
- Close *YouTube* and other pages that may distract you from reading.
- Learn how to take notes in PDFs and Word documents. Then you can make notes as you read on-screen, just as you would when reading a print text. Or take notes on paper.
- Look up unfamiliar terms as you read, making a note of definitions you may need later.
- For really high-stakes readings, consider printing out the text to read.

The pervasiveness of reading on-screen may suggest that many readers prefer to read that way. But current research suggests that most students still prefer to read print, especially if the reading is important and needs to be internalized and remembered. Print texts, it's worth remembering, are easy to navigate—you can tell at a glance how much you've read and how much you still have to go, and you can move back and forth in the text to find something important.

In addition, researchers have found that students reading on-screen are less likely to reflect on what they read or to make connections and synthesize in ways that bind learning to memory. It's important to note, however, that studies like these almost always end with a caveat: reading practices are changing and technology is making it easier to read on-screen.

It's important to note that online texts often blend written words with audio, video, links, charts and graphs, and other elements that you can attend to in any order you choose. In reading such texts, you'll need to make decisions carefully. When exactly should you click on a link, for example? The first moment it comes up? Or should you make a note to check it out later since doing so now may break your concentration—and you might not be able to get back easily to what you were reading. Links are useful in that they lead to more information, but following them can interrupt your train of thought. In addition, scrolling seems to encourage skimming and to make us read more rapidly. In short, reading on-screen can make it harder to stay on task. So you may well need to make a special effort with digital texts—to read them attentively and to pay close attention to what you're reading.

We are clearly in a time of flux where reading is concerned, so the best advice is for you to think very carefully about why you are reading. If you need to find information quickly, to follow a conversation on *Twitter*, or to look for online sources on a topic you're researching, reading on-screen is the way to go. But if you need to fully comprehend and retain the information in a text, you may want to stick with print.

Reading Visual Texts

Visual texts present their own opportunities and challenges. They have become so familiar and pervasive that "reading" them may seem just natural. But reading visual texts with a critical eye takes time, patience, and attention.

Take a look at the advertisement for a Shinola watch on the next page. You may know that Shinola is a Detroit-based watchmaker proud that its watches are "made in America"; if not, a quick look at the company's website will fill in this part of the ad's **CONTEXT**. But there's a lot more going on in terms of its particular rhetorical situation. The ad first ran in 2015, when it was clearly talking back to smart watches in general and to the launch of the Apple watch in particular, with its full panoply of futuristic bells and whistles. "Hey," the ad writers are saying to the smart watch crowd, "our watch is just smart enough."

Thinking through the rhetorical situation tells you something about the ad's purpose and audience. Of course its major **PURPOSE** is to sell watches, but one other goal seems to be to poke a little fun at all the high-tech, super-smart watches on the market. And what about its **AUDIENCE**: who do you think the ad addresses most directly? Perhaps Americans who think of themselves as solid, "no frills" folks?

Reading a visual begins, then, with studying the purpose, audience, message, and context. But there's a lot more you can do to understand a visual. You can look closely, for instance, at its **DESIGN**. In the Shinola ad, the stark, high-contrast, black-and-white image takes center stage, drawing our eyes to it and its accompanying captions. There are no other distracting elements, no other colors, no glitz. The simplicity gives the watch a retro look, which is emphasized by its sturdy straps, open face, and clear numerals, its old-fashioned wind-up button and second hand.

You'll also want to take a close look at any words. In this case, the Shinola ad includes a large headline centered above the image, three lines of all-caps, sans serif type that match the simplicity and straightforwardness of the image itself. And it's hard to miss the mocking **TONE**: "A WATCH SO SMART THAT IT CAN TELL YOU THE TIME JUST BY LOOKING AT IT." The small caption below the image underscores this message: "THE RUNWELL. IT'S JUST SMART ENOUGH." Take that, Apple!

A WATCH SO SMART
THAT IT CAN TELL YOU THE TIME
JUST BY LOOKING AT IT.

THE RUNWELL. IT'S JUST SMART ENOUGH.™

SMART ENOUGH THAT YOU DON'T NEED TO CHARGE IT AT NIGHT. SMART ENOUGH THAT IT WILL NEVER NEED
A SOFTWARE UPGRADE. SMART ENOUGH THAT VERSION 1.0 WON'T NEED TO BE REPLACED NEXT YEAR,
OR IN THE MANY DECADES THAT FOLLOW. BUILT BY THE WATCHMAKERS OF DETROIT TO LAST
A LIFETIME OR LONGER UNDER THE TERMS AND CONDITIONS OF THE SHINOLA GUARANTEE.

SHINOLA
DETROIT

Where American is made.™

NEW YORK 177 FRANKLIN ST.
DETROIT • MINNEAPOLIS • CHICAGO • WASHINGTON DC • LOS ANGELES • LONDON

SHINOLA.COM

Reading Print Texts

Print texts may consist mostly of sentences and paragraphs that (should) follow logically from one to the next, with a clear beginning, middle, and end. For these texts, the familiar practice of reading left to right, top to bottom (at least in English) will carry you through the text, though you may occasionally need to pause to look up the meaning of a word, to take notes, or just to reflect on what you're reading.

"Reading" Spoken Texts

Spoken texts need to be "read" in a different way, by listening to what speakers are saying while you view images they project on a screen or have put in a handout. If the presentation is a really good one, these elements will complement each other, joining together to get their message across. Still, you may need to learn to split your attention, making sure you are not focusing so much on any slides or handouts that you're missing what the speaker is saying—or vice versa. Remember, too, that you'll be a better audience member if you look at the speaker and any visuals, rather than staring at your laptop or looking down at the desk.

READING ACROSS GENRES

Genres affect how we read and can help guide our reading. Knowing the characteristic features of a genre, therefore, can help you read more attentively and more purposefully. When you read **REPORTS**, for example, you expect information you can trust, and you look for signs that the authors know what they are writing about and have cited authoritative sources. When you read a **REVIEW**, you expect to find some judgment, along with reasons and evidence to support that judgment. And you know to question any **ARGUMENT** that fails to acknowledge likely counterarguments. In other words, what you know about common genres can help you as a reader. Knowing what features to expect will help you read with a critical eye, and just recognizing a genre can help you adjust your reading as need be (reading directions more slowly, for example).

READING ACROSS ACADEMIC DISCIPLINES

Differences in disciplines can make for some very difficult reading tasks, as you encounter texts that seem almost to be written in foreign languages. As with most new things, however, new disciplines and their texts will become familiar to you the more you work with them. So don't be put off by texts in fields like psychology or physics that seem hard to read: the more you read such texts, the more familiar they will become until, eventually, you will be able to "talk the talk" of that discipline yourself.

Pay attention to terminology. It's especially important to read rhetorically when you encounter texts in different academic fields. Take the word *analysis*, for instance. That little word has a wide range of definitions as it moves from one field to another. In philosophy, analysis has traditionally meant breaking down a topic into its constituent parts in order to understand them—and the whole—more completely. In the sciences, analysis often involves the scientific method of observing a phenomenon, formulating a hypothesis about it, and experimenting to see whether the hypothesis holds up. And in business, analysis usually refers to assessing needs and finding ways to meet them. In literary studies, on the other hand, analysis usually calls for close reading in order to interpret a passage of text. When you're assigned to carry out an analysis, then, it's important to know what the particular field of study requires you to do and to ask your instructors if you aren't sure.

Know what counts as evidence. Beyond attending to what particular words mean from field to field, you should note that what counts as effective **EVIDENCE** can differ across academic disciplines. In literature and other fields in the humanities, textual evidence is often the most important: your job as a reader is to focus on the text itself. For the sciences, you'll most often focus on evidence gathered through experimentation, on facts and figures. Some of the social sciences also favor the use of "hard" evidence or data, while others are more likely to use evidence drawn from interviews, oral histories, or even anecdotes. As a strong reader, you'll need to be aware of what counts as credible evidence in the fields you study.

Be aware of how information is presented. Finally, pay attention to the way various disciplines format and present their information. You'll probably find that articles and books in the fields of literature and history present their information in paragraphs, sometimes with illustrations. Physics texts present much important information in equations, while those in psychology and political science rely more on charts and graphs and other visual representations of quantitative data. In art history, you can expect to see extensive use of images, while much of the work in music will rely on notation and sound.

So reading calls for some real effort. Whether you're reading words or images or bar graphs, literary analysis or musical notation, in a print book or on a screen, you need to read rhetorically—attentively and intentionally and with an open mind. And on top of all that, you need to be an active participant with what you read, just as Toni Morrison says: "The words on the page are only half the story. The rest is what you bring to the party."

REFLECT. The next time you're assigned to read a text online, pay attention to your process. Take some notes on just how you read: Do you go straight through, or do you stop often? Do you take notes? Do you take breaks while reading to attend to something else? What do you do if you don't understand a passage? How long can you read at a stretch and maintain full concentration? Then answer the same questions the next time you're assigned to read a print text. What differences do you notice in the way you read each text? What conclusions can you draw about how to be a more effective reader, both on- and off-screen?

SEVEN

Annotating, Summarizing, Responding

OW DO YOU read when the stakes are high, when you really need to understand and remember what you're reading? One student we know, who chooses to read hard copy whenever possible, keeps a highlighter and a stack of sticky notes on hand in order to talk back to the text. Another student makes comments using *Acrobat Reader*. And still another takes photos of lecture slides and annotates them in a *Google Doc* while in class. These students are all using strategies they've developed for reading purposely and attentively, strategies that suit their own needs.

Like these students, you've likely already developed reading strategies that work for you and the kinds of reading you do, and you'll surely be developing new strategies as you encounter new kinds of texts and disciplines, from reports in a plant science course to executive summaries in business management. This chapter offers guidance on three key strategies that will help you engage actively and productively with all kinds of texts. *Annotating*—the process of taking notes, underlining important information, and marking key aspects of a text that strike you as important—helps you focus and attend carefully to what you read. *Summarizing* helps you synthesize the ideas in what you are reading, consolidate your understanding, and remember important points. And *responding* gives you an opportunity to engage the text directly, talking back and joining the conversation.

"We may have the same books, but we highlight entirely different passages."

Each of these strategies marks a point where reading and writing intersect: reading leads to writing (annotating, summarizing, responding), and writing about what you've read often leads you to re-read.

ANNOTATING

Annotating might sound simple: you just mark up the text as you read, right? Keep in mind, however, that what you annotate should be driven by your purpose for reading. Whatever that purpose, annotating will help you read actively—thinking, questioning, and responding as you go. Like Hansel and Gretel sprinkling bread crumbs in the forest, it's also a way of leaving a trail you can revisit later if you need to review concepts for an exam or find a quote for an essay. Taking the following steps will help you annotate purposefully and productively.

Think about your purpose for reading. If you're reading a biology textbook to prepare for an exam, you might highlight key concepts, summarize theories to be sure you understand them, and respond to the chapter's review questions. When reading a treatise by Aristotle to prepare for discussion in a philosophy class, however, you may mark passages that are hard to understand, write out questions to ask in class, and highlight statements to remember. Consider the following questions:

- *Why are you reading this text?* As a model for writing you'll be expected to do? So that you'll learn about a certain topic?

- *What do you need to be able to do with this text?* Apply concepts? Respond to the author's argument? Cite it in something you're writing?

Preview the text. Rather than plunging right in, skim the text first to get a sense of what it's about and how it's organized. Jot down what you notice.

- *What do you already know (and think) about the topic?* Do you have any personal experience with the subject? What do you want or expect to learn?

- *Who are the authors or sponsors?* Where do you think they're coming from? Might they have a particular agenda or purpose?

- *Who published the text,* and what does that tell you about its intended audience and purpose?

- *What does the title tell you?* If there's a subtitle, does it indicate the author's argument or stance?

- *If there's an abstract,* read it. If not, read the introduction. What new information do you learn?

- *Scan any headings* to see what's covered, and look at any text that's highlighted. How will the design help you read the text?

- *What is your initial response* to the text based on your preview of it?

Annotate as you read. Annotate the text as a way of talking back to it— marking *what* the author is saying, *how* the author is getting their message across, and how *you* are reacting to what you're reading.

WHAT'S THE TEXT SAYING?

- What claims does the text make? Underscore the **THESIS** statement. If there's no explicit thesis, what key questions and issues does the text address?

- What **REASONS** and **EVIDENCE** does the author provide? Are they sufficient?

- Does anything surprise you or make you feel skeptical? Mark any facts or statements that seem questionable.

- Note any **COUNTERARGUMENTS**. Does the author represent and respond to them fairly? Are any other perspectives missing?

- Identify any key terms (and look them up if necessary). This can be especially important if you're reading a text in an unfamiliar discipline. Define important terms and concepts in your own words.
- Do you understand graphs, charts, or other visual elements? These often play an important role in the sciences and social sciences.

WHO'S THE INTENDED AUDIENCE?

- Who do you think the author is addressing? Students like you? Other scholars? The general public? Mark words that make you think so. Are you included in that group? If not, does that affect your response?
- What do you know about the audience's values? Highlight words that suggest what the author thinks the audience cares about.

WHAT DO YOU KNOW ABOUT THE AUTHOR?

- Who wrote the text? Is the author credible and reliable? What makes you believe that this is the case? Note places in the text where the author demonstrates **AUTHORITY** to write on the topic. Is the author a scholar? a popular commentator? Do a search to learn what sources you trust say about the author.
- What is the author's **STANCE**? Objective? Passionate? Something else? Mark words that indicate the author's stance.
- How would you describe the author's **STYLE** and **TONE**? Formal? Casual? Serious? Humorous? Mark any words or passages that establish that style and tone.

HOW IS THE TEXT DESIGNED?

- How does the design affect the way you understand the text?
- Note headings, sidebars, or other design features that add emphasis.
- If the text includes visuals, what do they contribute to the message?

WHAT ARE YOUR REACTIONS?

- Mark places in the text where you agree, disagree, or both. Note why.
- Note any claims, facts, or other things you find surprising—and why.
- Note any passages you find confusing or difficult to understand. What questions do you have?

- Jot down any possible counterarguments or conflicting evidence that you need to check out.

- If a passage reminds you of a past experience, memory, or strong emotion, note it.

If you're reading a particularly important text, read it more than once, paying attention to different elements each time. For example, to prepare for a class discussion you might first focus on the argument and then re-read focusing on how the writer supports that argument. With long or dense texts, you may want to annotate by summarizing paragraphs or sections as you go.

Since you likely read on-screen often, take the time to learn one of the many free programs that make it easy to annotate digital texts. *Hypothesis* and *Adobe Acrobat Reader* are two programs that allow you to add notes, highlight, insert URLs and images, and more. In fact, the ebook version of this book includes annotation tools to mark up what you're reading right now!

> ➦ To read—and annotate—a digital version of this book, visit digital.wwnorton.com/everyone3r.

So annotating keeps you active and helps you engage more deeply with what you read. Annotating also helps you approach reading as a social activity, bringing you into conversation with writers, engaging them and their ideas actively. Sometimes, especially for a research project, you'll be assigned to write formal annotations in the form of an **ANNOTATED BIBLIOGRAPHY**. That's a reading (and writing) situation with its own characteristic features. For now, focus on making annotating a habit—especially when you read academic texts.

Online or on a printed page, there are many methods and tools for annotating as you read. Try a few to find the ones that work best for you.

A Sample Annotated Text

Here's the opening of an essay on shopping locally, along with annotations by YULIYA VAYNER, a Hunter College student who read and annotated this piece for a summary/response essay assignment.

AMERICANS TODAY CAN eat pears in the spring in Minnesota, oranges in the summer in Montana, asparagus in the fall in Maine, and cranberries in the winter in Florida. In fact, we can eat pretty much any kind of produce anywhere at any time of the year. But what is the cost of this convenience? In this essay, I will explore some answers to this question and argue that we should give up a little bit of convenience in favor of buying local.

"Buying local" means that consumers choose to buy food that has been grown, raised, or produced as close to their homes as possible ("Buy Local"). Buying local is an important part of the response to many environmental issues we face today (fig. 1). It encourages the development of small farms, which are often more environmentally sustainable than large farms, and thus strengthens local markets and supports small rural economies. By demonstrating a commitment to buying local, Americans could set an example for global environmentalism.

In 2010, the international community is facing many environmental challenges, including global warming, pollution, and dwindling fossil fuel resources. Global warming is attributed to the release of greenhouse gases such as carbon dioxide and methane, most commonly emitted in the burning of fossil fuels. It is such a pressing problem that scientists estimate that in the year 2030, there will be no glaciers left in Glacier National Park ("Global Warming Statistics"). The United States is especially guilty of contributing to the problem, producing about a quarter of all global greenhouse gas emissions, and playing a large part in pollution and shrinking world oil supplies as well ("Record Increase"). According to a CNN article published in 2000, the United States manufactures more than 1.5 billion pounds of chemical pesticides a year that can pollute our water, soil, and air (Baum). Agriculture is particularly interconnected with all of these issues. Almost three-fourths of the pesticides produced in the United States are used in agriculture (Baum). Most produce is

Thesis statement

I wonder what she means exactly by "buying local."

This paragraph states her stance: strongly in favor of sustainable farming and buying local.

But what about people who don't have access to locally produced food or who can't afford to buy it?

Here comes some evidence. Looks like she's done research to inform her argument.

I want to check out this source: I'm a little suspicious of what she says here.

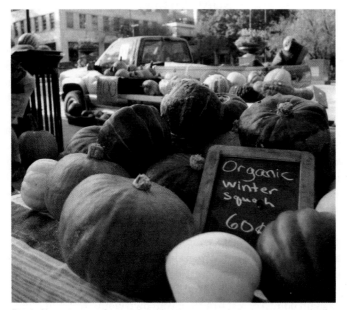

Farmers' markets are expensive. Many people—including me!—can't afford to shop at them.

Fig. 1. Shopping at a farmers' market is one good way to support small farms and strengthen the local economy. Photograph from Alamy.

She's serious about this issue and is making a strong case. Including these researched facts lends credibility, but I'm waiting to see if she acknowledges the fact that many people can't afford or easily get to locally grown food.

shipped many miles before it is sold to consumers, and shipping our food long distances is costly in both the amount of fossil fuel it uses and the greenhouse gases it produces.

REFLECT. *Find something you've read and annotated recently. What kinds of annotations did you make? Calling out keywords, ideas, and claims? Strategies the writer used? Areas of confusion? Points you agree or disagree with? Your own personal connections? Try highlighting your annotations in different colors for a visual breakdown by type. What do these annotations tell you about your reading process? Looking back at the prompts in this section, are there types of annotations that you didn't make but would have proved useful? Re-read the text and add them!*

SUMMARIZING

Summarizing a text helps you understand and engage with it—and internalize and remember what you read. When you summarize, you're boiling a text down to its central ideas, claims, and theories in your own words. One student we know writes summaries in the margins as a strategy for making sure she understands the most important concepts, especially in textbooks. These summaries, along with additional annotations throughout the chapters, help her prepare for exams. Besides helping you understand what you read, summarizing is also essential for weaving the viewpoints of others into your own writing. Both at work and at school, you'll be expected to summarize something—the plot of a short story, the results of a scientific study, takeaways from a meeting. The following advice will help you craft strong summaries in academic and professional writing.

Read the text carefully—and annotate. Read the text to figure out its main message, idea, or argument. Annotate as you read, marking key ideas and claims as well as supporting points such as anecdotes, supporting evidence, and counterarguments. When you identify a sentence or paragraph that states a main point, try restating it in your own words. A pair of highlighters can help; try using different colors to distinguish the main ideas from the supporting points.

When you summarize something other than a printed text—a music video, a printed advertisement, a speech—practice the same careful reading. Observe your subject and take note of the main message as well as the supporting details that lead you to draw this conclusion.

Be brief, stating the main points while leaving out minor supporting details. Summaries are generally brief, stating the main ideas while leaving out the supporting evidence and anecdotes that aren't necessary for understanding. A summary serves as a stand-in for readers who aren't familiar with the full text, so your aim is to get readers up to speed on the main points without getting lost in the details.

Be fair and accurate, using neutral language. Think of a summary as stating the facts, not sharing your opinion. Use neutral language to present the author's main ideas with evenhandedness and respect, not judgment or criticism. Imagine the author reading your summary of their work. Would they find it accurate? Have you left out an important point? Would the writer find it fair? Have your opinions snuck in?

Use SIGNAL PHRASES to present what the author says as distinct from what you say—and use quotations in moderation. Summarizing calls for boiling down information and presenting it in your own words and sentence structure. Use signal phrases such as *she concludes* or *the report states* to indicate that you're summarizing someone else's ideas and claims, not your own. At the start of a summary, state the author's name, credentials, and the title of the work so it's clear what you're referring to. While you may quote notable phrases or key terms, your summary should be made up of mostly your own unique language and sentence structure. And any text you summarize should be documented in a list of works cited or references.

Consider visuals. Not all summaries are written text: summaries can also be presented visually. In scientific, technical, or social science writing, charts and graphs often summarize key information and data from other sources. For example, in the following infographic from a sociology textbook, the author summarizes data from a 2010 study analyzing college students'

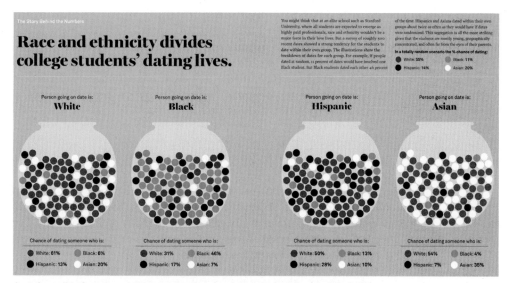

An infographic from a sociology textbook summarizes the results of a Stanford University social science study so that the main takeaway is clear: Stanford students "show a strong tendency to date within their own [racial and ethnic] group."

dating habits by race and ethnicity. The colorful visuals summarize the data so it's easier to understand than if the same results were presented using only words and statistics.

A Sample Summary

Here is a summary of Katherine Spriggs's essay "On Buying Local" (see her full essay on p. 177):

> In her essay "On Buying Local," college student Katherine Spriggs argues that consumers should purchase food grown locally whenever possible. After demonstrating the environmental and practical reasons for doing so, Spriggs shows that buying local can offer an alternative to destructive mass farming, help small farmers and their families, build sustainable agricultural models, reduce the cost of shipping food from faraway places, and avoid the exploitation of workers, especially in third-world countries. In spite of a few drawbacks (local food may be more expensive and seasonal variation may reduce the number of choices available), she concludes that shopping local is an easy lifestyle change that will make a big difference to our environment.

This is a fair and accurate summary of Spriggs's essay. It begins by stating the author's name and the title of the work and includes only the main points of the argument, restated in the writer's own words. This summary serves as the introduction to a summary/response essay (see the full summary/response essay by Yuliya Vayner on p. 93).

RESPONDING

Responding to what you read is nothing new—it's what you do when commenting on a friend's *Instagram* post, replying to an instructor's email, or weighing in on a group text. In college and in many professions, you'll be assigned—or just expected—to respond to what you read, in a written document, a discussion, an exam, or a presentation.

Whenever you read by actively engaging with a text, you are already responding—annotating to talk back to it, question it, assess its claims, and come to conclusions about whether or not you accept them. Looking over your annotations will help you generate ideas when you're assigned to respond formally. Do your annotations reveal any patterns? Maybe you disagreed with many of the author's claims, jotted down a related experience, or noted the author's use of emotional appeals. As you take stock of your annotations, consider which of the following ways you'll respond to what you've read: argue with what the text says, analyze the way it says it, or reflect on its ideas.

Respond to what a text says, agreeing or disagreeing with its position—or both. However you respond, you'll be making an **ARGUMENT** for what you say. Before you come to any final conclusions, keep an open mind by saying "yes," "no," and "maybe" to the text. First say "yes" by making an effort to understand the way the author sees the topic and where they're coming from. Doing so can be especially important if you find yourself strongly disagreeing with the author's position. Then say "maybe" to any passages that seem confusing or poorly supported—and consider why. Finally, look for anything to which you feel obligated to say "no," and think about why it seems unacceptable or just plain wrong. Here are some questions to consider when you're responding to what a text says:

- What does the text **CLAIM**, and what **REASONS** and **EVIDENCE** does the author provide?
- Do you agree or disagree with the author's position? Why?
- Does the author acknowledge any other positions? If so, are they treated fairly? What other perspectives should be addressed?
- Has the author overlooked anything?
- Is it clear why the topic matters, why anyone should care?
- What's the larger **CONTEXT**? How does the text fit into the larger conversation on the topic? Is the author's point corroborated by what others have said, or is it a claim that hardly anyone else agrees with?

Analyze the way a text is written to figure out how it works, what makes it tick. Here are some questions to consider when you're analyzing how a text is written:

- What does the text **CLAIM**? Is it stated explicitly—and if not, should it be? Has it been carefully qualified—and if not, does it need to be?

- Look for and assess the **REASONS** and **EVIDENCE** provided in support of the claim. Are you persuaded? If not, what other kinds of evidence would help?

- Does the author use emotional, ethical, or logical appeals? Do you notice any logical **FALLACIES**?

- Has the writer mentioned any **COUNTERARGUMENTS** or alternative points of view? If so, are they described respectfully and fairly? And how does the writer respond—by acknowledging that other writers have a point? Refuting what they say?

- How has the author established **AUTHORITY** to write on this topic? Do you think the text is trustworthy and fair?

- What design elements help convey the text's main message?

Reflect on a text's ideas by drawing connections to your own personal experiences, beliefs, or ways of thinking. Maybe the text leads you to see a topic in a new light, question your assumptions and biases, or wonder about how your beliefs influenced your reaction. Here are some questions to consider when you're reflecting on a text's ideas:

- What impact has the reading had on you—as a student, scholar, citizen, and researcher? What are the big takeaways for you personally?

- Did any parts of the text make you feel uneasy, laugh, or cry? Investigate why.

- Which past experiences or memories did you recall while reading the text? Can you relate to anything in the text? Why or why not?

- Does the text challenge or uphold any of your beliefs? Or cause you to question some of your assumptions and biases?

- What other texts, images, videos, recordings, etc., does the text remind you of?

- What lessons, insights, or ideas has the text taught you? How might you apply those lessons in your own writing or thinking?

SUMMARY/RESPONSE ESSAYS

A summary/response essay demonstrates that you have engaged with a text, understand its main message, and have something to say as a result. This assignment is common in first-year writing classes because of the focus on critical reading and supporting a position with evidence. Unless the assignment names other requirements, your summary/response should cover the following ground.

A Fair, Accurate, and Concise Summary

A fair and objective summary of the text to which you are responding is essential. To make your subject crystal clear, begin by stating the author, title, and author's credentials. And keep the following points in mind:

- Include the main claims and primary supporting points of the text, and exclude examples or supporting ideas that aren't essential to the text's main message.
- Use an even and objective **TONE**. Would the author of the text find your summary fair and accurate?
- Be concise. Most summaries of full texts are 100 to 125 words, giving readers enough information to understand what you're responding to without unnecessary details.
- Make it clear that you are summarizing someone else's text by using **SIGNAL PHRASES** like "according to X." Words such as "asserts," "argues," and "examines" are also good signals—just be sure they are neutral. Include quotations only when keywords and phrases are central to the overall argument.

A Clear Response, Supported by Evidence

Your response is the meat of a summary/response essay. There's more than one way to respond to a text. See if you're being asked to respond in a particular way—for example, to "assess the author's argument and take a stance" or "analyze how effectively the text addresses its intended audience." If the assignment isn't specific, think about what you're most interested in doing: responding to what the text says, analyzing how the text works, reflecting on the text's ideas, or some combination. No matter how you respond, support your position with evidence.

- If you're responding to what the text says, take a position—agreeing, disagreeing, or both. State your position explicitly in a **THESIS STATEMENT**.

Support your position with evidence from the text and from outside sources, if necessary. Facts, statistics, anecdotal evidence, and textual evidence can serve as support. Think about and address any **COUNTER-ARGUMENTS** to your position.

- If you're analyzing how the text works, you'll describe both what the text is saying and the strategies used to convey the message. You might analyze a text's organization, **DICTION**, use of appeals, design, or other elements. Include evidence from the text to demonstrate the features or strategies you're analyzing. Be sure you state your main takeaway in an explicit thesis statement. Why did you choose to analyze what you did and why does it matter?

- If you're reflecting on the text's ideas, you'll likely explain some way in which the text impacted you personally or evoked a particular emotion, memory, or idea. Passages from the text that prompted your response should be cited as evidence. And your own beliefs, experiences, or emotions might serve to support and explain your personal response. Boil down your main point in a thesis statement—even a reflection should tell readers what you're saying and why it matters.

A Logical Organization

A summary/response can be organized in different ways, and your assignment may ask for a specific structure. Here are some general ways of structuring a summary/response to help you get started:

- Summarize first, and then respond: Introduce and summarize the text first, then state your thesis (this might all fall in the first paragraph). Then respond to the text, providing supporting points for your thesis. End by summing up your response and its implications.

- Summarize and respond point-by-point: Introduce the text and state your thesis. Then summarize a claim or strategy from the text and respond to it. Do this for as many supporting points as you have to develop and defend your thesis. End by summing up your response and its implications.

YULIYA VAYNER, a Hunter College student, summarizes and responds to Katherine Spriggs's essay "On Buying Local" in the following example. You can read Spriggs's full essay on page 177. Vayner primarily responds to what the text says—taking a position that both agrees and disagrees with Spriggs's argument. This essay is organized around several counterarguments that Vayner says Spriggs does not address.

The Higher Price of Buying Local

YULIYA VAYNER

IN HER ESSAY "On Buying Local," Katherine Spriggs argues that consumers should purchase food grown locally whenever possible. After demonstrating the environmental and practical reasons for doing so, Spriggs shows that buying local can offer an alternative to destructive mass farming, help small farmers and their families, build sustainable agricultural models, reduce the cost of shipping food from faraway places, and avoid the exploitation of workers, especially in third-world countries. Though Spriggs acknowledges that buying local can be inconvenient (local food may be more expensive and seasonal variation may reduce the number of choices available), she argues that the benefit outweighs the inconvenience and concludes that shopping local is an easy lifestyle change that will make a big difference to our environment.

Begins with a concise summary

But is buying local truly an "easy step" that "everyone can take"? Is inconvenience the only drawback? There are at least two

Articulates a key question that motivates and grounds the analysis.

A thesis statement offers a clear position.

Agrees with part of Spriggs's argument and explains why.

Summarizes Spriggs's argument in her own words.

Quotes specific details from Spriggs's essay.

Quotes a key term and defines it in her own words.

Notes an argument that Spriggs does not address: how will people who live in food deserts access locally produced foods?

additional challenges to buying local that Spriggs doesn't acknowledge in her analysis: cost and access. It's clear that buying locally grown food benefits the environment, but because cost and access limit some people from being able to buy local, it is not a habit everyone is equally able to practice.

Spriggs makes a convincing argument that giving up a bit of convenience in return for a healthier environment is a worthy trade. In discussing polyculture farming (producing a variety of crops from the same land—an approach small farms tend to prefer), Spriggs juxtaposes personal convenience and environmental benefits. She concedes that being unable to buy whatever produce we want whenever we want is less convenient than most consumers are used to but suggests this sacrifice would allow farmers to harvest from healthier soil and foster a healthier environment. Spriggs explains that while monoculture farms (producing a small number of single crops—the approach large mass-production farms use) provide the convenience of year-round access to produce, they do so by resorting to "modern fertilizers, herbicides, and pesticides [that] allow farmers to harvest crops from even unhealthy land" (154). By giving up the convenience of eating strawberries at any time of year, Americans could begin to rely less on chemical treatments that damage the environment and more on natural resources through what Spriggs calls "dual usage"—like using pigs to plow blueberry fields and putting cows to pasture in last year's cornfields. Considering the environmental damage that large-scale farming causes, sacrificing convenience is a small price to pay for a healthier land and atmosphere.

However, Spriggs doesn't acknowledge that some people would be giving up more than just evergreen strawberries in an attempt to buy local. For many, lack of access to any fresh produce at all is an issue, making the sacrifice of buying produce that's locally sourced unaffordable. According to a recent report by the US Department of Agriculture's Economic Research Service, an estimated 1 in 8 Americans or 40 million people experienced food insecurity, which is defined as "a lack of consistent access to enough food for an active, healthy life" in 2017 ("What Is Food Insecurity?"). So when Spriggs argues that there's little reason to ship strawberries from California all over the United

States when they can easily be grown closer to the customers who want to eat them, she fails to acknowledge that there are areas that can't readily access or grow fresh produce (154). These areas are sometimes called food deserts: areas that have limited access to affordable and nutritious food, forcing residents to rely on food sold at convenience stores or fast-food chains, which is often highly processed and of limited nutritional value ("Why Low-Income People Are Vulnerable"). These food deserts exist overwhelmingly in low-income areas and studies have shown that "both poverty and race matter when it comes to having healthy food options" (Brooks). So, although Spriggs does not mention these issues, buying local is also a question of access—which is impacted by race and income level rather than being purely one about convenience and ease.

Time becomes an issue of access as well: for some a long drive ●— *Here's another argument Spriggs doesn't cover.* to a grocery store is merely inconvenient. For others, there simply aren't enough hours in a day to make an extended trip for fresh, local produce. People living below the poverty line tend to work multiple jobs (Sherman); in addition, they may also be responsible for household errands and family care. Lower-income families are not only less likely to have places nearby that sell locally grown food, they are also less likely to have the time and the means to visit them ("Why Low-Income People Are Vulnerable"). While households with more resources may not have this issue, for families with less resources "transportation costs . . . cut into [their] already limited resources, and these costs plus travel time can be substantial." Even when locally grown food can be found within a reasonable distance, it may still be out of reach for those living on a limited income.

This adds yet another aspect to the challenge of buying local ●— *A third counterargument Spriggs doesn't cover: the financial expense of buying local.* that Spriggs doesn't address: low-income individuals are significantly less likely to be able to afford the extra expense of locally sourced food, which Spriggs explains as only slightly pricier. Yet, "slightly more expensive than 'industrially grown' food" (156) is subjective. Not only would buying local potentially strain the budgets of those struggling to get by, it could also make it more difficult to make use of government assistance, especially since farmers' markets have struggled to obtain the necessary equipment to process SNAP, a government assistance program that provides a monthly supplement for purchasing nutritious foods (Andrews). So for many, buying local is not just an inconvenience, it's not a financial possibility. Furthermore, the price gap seems wider than Spriggs admits; a journalist for *The Washington Post* reports that in 2016 "cage-free eggs, cheese, mushrooms, salad mix and both organic and conventional strawberries" came to be $64.62 at the local market in Richmond, Virginia—"I could have bought them all from Kroger for $31.37" (Hise). At nearly double the price, this difference is far from Spriggs's claim that buying local is only "slightly more expensive." The price increase that comes with buying local is not a mere "inconvenience" but rather a question of affordability for many.

Concludes by summarizing her own argument in response to Spriggs.

While Spriggs succeeds in showing that buying local can contribute to a healthier environment, in addressing the obvious drawback of inconvenience she considers only one aspect of a complex issue involving race, income level, and access. The inconvenience of buying local comes at a much higher price for some people, a fact Spriggs leaves out. People who are struggling to make ends meet cannot always afford this social and economic privilege, nor do they always have access to this privilege. To many, industrially grown food is a necessity rather than, as Spriggs suggests, a convenience.

Works Cited

Andrews, Michelle. "Technical Difficulties May Jeopardize Food
    Stamps at Farmers Markets." NPR, 5 Nov. 2018, www.npr
    .org/sections/thesalt/2018/11/05/662322655/technical
    -difficulties-may-jeopardize-food-stamps-at-farmers
    -markets. Accessed 4 Dec. 2018.
Brooks, Kelly. "Research Shows Food Deserts More Abundant
    in Minority Neighborhoods." The Hub, Johns Hopkins
    University, 10 Mar. 2014, hub.jhu.edu/magazine/2014
    /spring/racial-food-deserts/. Accessed 10 Jan. 2019.
Hise, Phaedra. "Why Does a Strawberry Grown down the Road
    Cost More than One Grown in California?" The Washington
    Post, 21 June 2016, www.washingtonpost.com/lifestyle
    /food/why-local-food-costs-more-a-strawberry-case
    -study/2016/06/20/c7177c56-331f-11e6-8ff7-7b6c1998b7a0
    _story.html?utm_term=.24a56c809026. Accessed
    10 Jan. 2019.
Sherman, Erik. "More People Probably Work Multiple Jobs than
    the Government Realizes." Forbes, 22 July 2018, www
    .forbes.com/sites/eriksherman/2018/07/22/more-people
    -probably-work-multiple-jobs-than-the-government-realizes
    /#3df6ed5a2a21. Accessed 1 Feb. 2019.
"What Is Food Insecurity in America?" Hunger and Health,
    Feeding America, hungerandhealth.feedingamerica.org
    /understand-food-insecurity/. Accessed 8 Jan. 2019.
"Why Low-Income and Food-Insecure People Are Vulnerable to
    Poor Nutrition and Obesity." Food Research & Action Center,
    frac.org/obesity-health/low-income-food-insecure-people
    -vulnerable-poor-nutrition-obesity. Accessed 10 Jan. 2019.

‿◯ REFLECT. *Think about something you were recently assigned to read. What was your purpose for reading? What strategies from this chapter, if any, did you use to achieve that purpose? Re-read the text again, this time preparing to write a brief 250- to 500-word summary/response. Practice annotating, summarizing, and responding using the guidelines in this chapter. How did reading in preparation to respond change your reading process? What did you find challenging—and not so challenging—about writing a brief summary/response?*

EIGHT

Distinguishing Facts from Misinformation

OPE FRANCIS Says 'God Has Instructed Me to Revise the Ten Commandments.'" "Palestinians Recognize Texas as Part of Mexico." "Canada Bans Beyoncé after Her Superbowl Performance." Really? Well, actually, no. While these are actual headlines, none is anywhere near the truth. But being false hasn't kept them from being widely shared—and not as jokes but as facts. With people spreading misinformation, unsubstantiated claims, and even outright lies today, it can be hard to know whom and what to trust or whether to trust anything at all. The good news is that you don't have to be taken in by such misinformation. This chapter provides strategies for navigating today's choppy waters of news and information so that you can make confident decisions about what to trust—and what not to.

Defining Facts and Misinformation

Some say we are living in a "post-truth" era, when the loudest voices take up so much airtime that they can sometimes be seen as telling the truth no matter what they say. A 2018 study by MIT scholars examined tweets about every major contested news story in English across the ten years of *Twitter*'s existence and came to the conclusion that satirist Jonathan Swift was right: "the truth simply can't compete with hoax and rumor."

In fact, the study says, "fake news and false rumors reach more people, penetrate deeper into the social network, and spread much faster than accurate stories."

It's worth asking why misinformation outperforms real news. While it is notoriously difficult to establish airtight cause-and-effect relationships, these researchers suspect that several reasons account for the "success" of false stories. First, they're often outlandish and novel in a way that attracts attention. Second, the content of such stories is often negative and tends to arouse strong emotions. Third, they use language that evokes surprise or disgust, as compared to accurate tweets, which, the researchers found, use words associated with trust or sadness rather than surprise or disgust: as they note, "the truth simply does not compete." For all these reasons, misinformation tends to attract attention and spread quickly.

Lies and misinformation are nothing new. What's new is that anyone with an internet connection can post whatever they think (or want others

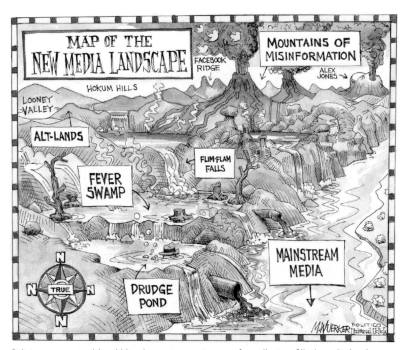

Politico cartoonist Matt Wuerker paints a picture of a pollution-filled media landscape.

to think) online, where it can easily reach a wide audience. And unlike traditional newspapers and other publications, it can go out without being vetted by editors or fact-checkers.

Perhaps it's time to step back, take a deep breath, and attend to some basic definitions. Just what is a "fact"? What's "misinformation"? And what about "fake news"? In the most straightforward terms, *misinformation* is false or inaccurate information that is intended to deceive. *Fake news* is a kind of misinformation made to look like authentic news. Often it's used to spread conspiracy theories or deliberate hoaxes, the more bizarre the better: "Obama Signs Executive Order Banning the Pledge of Allegiance in Schools Nationwide." In addition, some people simply dismiss anything they don't like or agree with as fake news. *Facts*, on the other hand, can be verified and backed up by reliable evidence: Robert F. Kennedy was murdered on June 6, 1968; the Washington Capitals won the 2018 Stanley Cup; consumption of soft drinks in the United States has declined in the last five years. Unlike claims about what God has instructed Pope Francis to do, these statements can be verified and checked; we can then trust them.

Think about Your Own Beliefs

It's one thing to be able to spot unsubstantiated claims and exaggerations in the words of others, but it's another thing entirely to spot them in your own thinking and writing. So you need to take a good look at your own assumptions and biases (we all have them!).

Attribution bias is the tendency to think that your motives for believing, say, that the Environmental Protection Agency (EPA) is crucially important for keeping our air and water clean are objective or good while the motives of those who believe the EPA is not at all necessary are dubious or bad. We all have this kind of bias naturally, tending to believe that what we think must be right. When you're thinking about an argument you strongly disagree with, then, it's a good idea to ask yourself why you disagree—and why you believe you're right. What is that belief based on? Have you considered that your own bias may be keeping you from seeing all sides of the issue fairly, or at all?

Confirmation bias is the tendency to favor and seek out information that confirms what we already believe and to reject and ignore information that contradicts those beliefs. Many studies have documented this phenomenon.

For example, a Stanford University experiment gathered 48 students, half of whom favored capital punishment and thought it was a deterrent to crime and half of whom thought just the opposite. Researchers then asked students to respond to two studies: one provided data that supported capital punishment as a deterrent to crime; the other provided data that called this conclusion into question. Sure enough, the students who were in favor of capital punishment rated the study that showed evidence that it was a deterrent as "more highly credible," while the students who were against capital punishment rated the study that showed evidence that it did not deter crime as "more highly credible"—in spite of the fact that both studies had been made up by the researchers. Moreover, by the end of the experiment, each side had doubled down on its original beliefs.

That's confirmation bias at work, and it works on all of us. It affects the way we search for information and what we pay attention to, how we interpret it, and even what we remember. So don't assume information is trustworthy just because it confirms what you already think. Ask yourself if you're seeing what you want to see. And look for confirmation bias in your sources; do they acknowledge viewpoints other than their own?

Read Defensively and Find the Good Stuff

Well over two thousand years ago, the philosopher Aristotle said that one reason people need rhetoric is self-defense, for making sure that we aren't being deceived, manipulated, or lied to. Today, the need for such caution may be more important than ever when false stories often look authentic and appear right next to accurate, factual information online. These times call, then, for what we think of as defensive reading—the kind of reading that doesn't take things at face value, that questions underlying assumptions, that scrutinizes claims carefully, and that does not rush to judgment. This is the kind of reading that media and technology critic Howard Rheingold calls "crap detection." Crap, he says sardonically, is a "technical term" he uses to describe information "tainted by ignorance or deliberate deception." He warns us not to give in to such misinformation:

> Some critics argue that a tsunami of hogwash has already rendered the web useless. I disagree. We are indeed inundated by online noise pollution, but the problem is soluble. The good stuff is out there if you know how to find and verify it.
>
> —HOWARD RHEINGOLD, "Crap Detection 101"

As Rheingold and many others note, there is no single foolproof way to identify misinformation. But we can offer some advice, along with some specific strategies.

Triangulate—and use your judgment. Find three different ways to check on whether a story can be trusted. Google the author or the sponsor. Check *FactCheck.org* or *Snopes*. Look for other sources that are reporting the same story, especially if you first saw it on social media. If it's true and important, you should find a number of other reputable sources reporting on it. But however carefully you check, and whatever facts and evidence you uncover, it's up to you to sort the accurate information from the misinformation— and to use your own judgment.

Before reading an unfamiliar source, determine whether it's trustworthy. History professor Sam Wineburg and his research team have found that professional fact-checkers don't even start to read an unfamiliar website until they've determined that it's trustworthy. Here are some ways to do so:

- Do a search about the author or sponsor. What's the author's expertise? Be wary if there's no author. Does the author belong to any organizations you don't know or trust? Look up any unfamiliar organizations to see what reliable sources have to say. And do a search about the site's sponsor. If the website is run by an organization you've never heard of, find out what it is—and whether it actually exists. What do reliable sources say about it? Read the site's About page, but check up on what it says. As Wineburg says, "If an organization can game what they are, they can certainly game their About page!"

- Check any links to see who sponsors the site and whether they are trustworthy sources. Do the same for works cited in print sources.

- Be careful of over-the-top headlines, which often serve as clickbait to draw you in. Check to see that the story and the headline actually match. Question any exaggerated words like "amazing," "epic," "incredible," or "unbelievable." (In general, don't believe anything that's said to be unbelievable!)

- Pay attention to design. Be wary if it looks amateurish, but don't assume that a professional-looking design means the source is accurate or trustworthy. Those who create fake news sites often design them to look like real news sites.

- Recognize satire! Remember that some authors make a living by writing satirical fake news articles. Here's one: "China Slaps Two-Thousand-Per-Cent Tariff on Tanning Beds." This comes from Andy Borowitz, who writes political satire in *The New Yorker*, which tips us off not to take it seriously by the label "not the news." *The Onion* is another source that pokes fun at gullible readers. Try this: "Genealogists Find 99% of People Not Related to Anyone Cool." This one's silly enough that it can't possibly be true. But if you're not sure, better check.

Ask questions, and check evidence. Double-check things that too neatly support what you yourself think.

- What's the **CLAIM**, and what **EVIDENCE** is provided? What motivates the author to write, and what's their **PURPOSE**—to provide information? make you laugh? convince you of something?

- Check facts and claims using nonpartisan sites that confirm truths and identify lies. *FactCheck.org*, *Snopes*, and *AllSides* are three such sites. Copy and paste the basics of the statement into the search field; if it's information the site has in its database, you'll find out whether it's a confirmed fact or lie. If you use *Google* to check on a stated fact, keep in mind that you'll need to check on any sources there—and that even if the statement brings up many hits, that doesn't make it accurate.

- If you think a story is too good to be true, you're probably right to be skeptical. And don't assume that it must be true because no one could make up such a story. They can. Do research on stories that are so outrageous that you don't believe them; if they are true, they will be widely reported. On the other hand, double-check stories that confirm your own beliefs; that might well be **CONFIRMATION BIAS** at work.

- Look up any research that's cited. You may find that the research has been taken out of context or misquoted—or that it doesn't actually exist. Is the research itself reliable? Pay close attention to quotations: who said it, and when? Is it believable? If not, copy and paste the quotation into *Google* or check *FactCheck.org* to verify that it's real.

- Check the comments. If several say the article sounds fake, it may well be. But remember that given the presence of trolls and people with malicious intent, comments too can't be taken at face value.

A still from *The Day After Tomorrow* shows fictional tidal waves battering the Statue of Liberty, but when Hurricane Sandy hit in 2012 this image spread as a warning for a real storm's strength. The fake local news banner lends (false) credibility.

Fact-Check Photos and Videos

Is a picture really worth a thousand words? In some cases, yes—but only if the picture is an accurate depiction. It's never been easier to falsify photographs. Take the often repurposed and exaggerated stories of flooding and damage beyond belief whenever a natural disaster strikes like the image on the previous page. When so-called Superstorm Sandy hit New York City in 2012, a photo of waves nearly as tall at the Statue of Liberty—seemingly captured by a live local news broadcast—circulated online. But some were quick to notice a problem. It was an image of Lady Liberty taking on water all right, but one from the science fiction movie *The Day After Tomorrow*, where fictional catastrophic climate events wreak havoc.

And here's one other photo that went viral in 2017, showing President Donald Trump, President Vladimir Putin of Russia, and others in conversation. A little investigation, however, showed that Putin had been photoshopped into the image; he wasn't actually at the table with other world leaders. Again, there are no simple, foolproof ways to identify doctored photos, but experts in digital forensics recommend various steps we can take. Here's advice from Hany Farid, a computer science professor at the University of California at Berkeley:

- Do a reverse image search, using *Google Images* or *Tin Eye* to see if an image has been recirculated or repurposed from another website. Both sites allow you to drag an image or paste a link to an image into a search bar to learn more about the image's source and see where the image appears online.

World leaders gathered during the 2017 G20 leaders' summit. Russian president Vladimir Putin was not in attendance despite what it looks like in the fake photo on the left.

- Check *Snopes*, where altered images are often identified, by typing a brief description of the image into the *Snopes* search box.
- Look carefully at shadows: an image may have been altered if you find shadows where you don't expect them or don't see them where you do expect them.

Farid goes on to say that the best defense against fabricated photos is "to stop and think about the source"—especially before you share it with others. After a shooter killed seventeen people at a Florida school in 2018, an altered photo of Emma González, one student survivor who advocated for stronger gun laws, went viral, showing her tearing up a page of the US Constitution. In fact, she was actually tearing up a shooting target as part of her advocacy for gun control.

The same advice holds true for researching suspicious video, which is also easy to falsify. Videos that flicker constantly or that consist of just one short clip are often questionable, as are videos of famous people doing things that are highly suspicious. How likely is it that NBA all-star Kobe Bryant could jump over a speeding Aston Martin? Not very—but a lot of us were fooled by a fake video made for Nike.

Kobe Bryant is a world-class athlete, but can he really clear a speeding Aston Martin? Nike's ad tries to make us think so.

Such fabricated videos and deepfakes proliferate, especially on *YouTube*. The *Guardian* warns that "advances in artificial intelligence and computer graphics . . . allow for the creation of realistic looking footage of public figures appearing to say, well, anything." Using the fact-finding and defensive-reading strategies described in this chapter, we hope you'll become able to sort out fact from fiction and determine with confidence who and what you can trust in all the kinds of reading you do—from keeping up with the news and scanning your friends' social media posts to conducting research for a project at school or work.

PART III

Writing Processes

IMAGINE THAT YOU are living in the Middle Ages and that you know how to write (a rare skill at that time). Now imagine the processes you have to engage in to do that writing. You might well begin by making the surface you need to write on, probably parchment or vellum made from animal skins—a process that takes several days.

Once you have something to write on, you make lines across the page to "rule" it and guide your writing. When at last you're ready to begin to write, you do so with a quill pen crafted out of a feather that had its end sharpened into a "nib" with a slit in the middle through

The medieval equivalent to a blank *Word* document: writers began by making their own writing surfaces, first soaking animal skins to remove the fur, then stretching and scraping them until they were the right thickness.

which the ink flows onto the parchment. Woe to you if you make a mistake, for correction is exceedingly difficult—or impossible. And once the writing is done, you still might not be finished if you need to illustrate the manuscript, as in the "illuminated" page from *The Canterbury Tales* on the facing page.

Because the process was so complicated, writing often demanded a team approach. In fact, *book* is defined in an early German encyclopedia as a "work of many hands."

With the advent of the printing press and subsequent technological developments, such material aspects of the writing process became easier, so much so that they became somewhat invisible: writers simply *wrote*. The focus, especially in schools, shifted to the final product, one composed by individual students; any concern with the process, as well as with writing's collaborative aspects, disappeared entirely. And so for many years, the emphasis on the final or "published" piece kept us from seeing the many other processes of writing, from generating ideas to hypothesizing, drafting, revising, and more. Writing involves far more than putting words down on

The Knight. An illuminated page from *The Canterbury Tales*, circa 1410.

a page and checking punctuation. For any important piece of writing, the author must think the message through in many ways to understand and communicate it to an audience. As researcher Janet Emig has concluded, writing is a unique form of learning, and understanding it calls for understanding the complex processes involved.

In studying just how those processes work, researchers have lately returned to the medieval notion that a piece of writing is the "work of many hands," recognizing that almost all writing is highly social, created by one or more writers in conversation with many others, from those who have influenced us in the past to those who read and respond to our work. By the end of the twentieth century, the popular image of a writer as a solitary figure (almost always a man) holed up in a tiny room struggling to create an individual work of great genius began to give way to that of a writer as part of an elaborate network, what author Steven Johnson called "connected minds."

The kind of networking now available through the internet and especially through social media surely does involve "connected minds." John Donne's insight that no one "is an island, apart from the main" has never been more true than it is today, as writers around the globe collaborate on everything from a *Google Doc* to a flash mob to a protest movement like Black Lives Matter.

The chapters that follow invite you to think hard about the processes you engage in when you write and about how those processes involve other writers (those you write with and those you write to). We hope that such thinking will not only make you more aware of how, when, and where you write, but also help to make your writing processes more efficient—and more fun!

NINE

Managing the Writing Process

HINK OF SOMETHING YOU LIKE TO DO: ride a bike, play a certain video game, do Sudoku. If you think about it, you'll see that each of these activities involves learning a process that took some effort to get right when you first started doing it. But eventually, the process became familiar, and now you do it almost automatically.

Writing is much the same. It, too, is a process: a series of activities that takes some effort to do well. At some level, everyone who writes knows this—from a child who draws a picture and then erases part of it, thinking, "That tree just doesn't look right," to the college student working over an extended period of time on a research paper.

And as with any process, you can manage the writing process by approaching it in parts. This chapter introduces the various stages of the writing process—from generating ideas and coming up with a topic to drafting and revising—and provides strategies that will help you make the most of the many writing demands you'll encounter at school, at work, and elsewhere.

One important aspect of becoming comfortable with the writing process is figuring out what works best for you. No single process works for every author or every writing task, so work instead to develop a repertoire of strategies that will enable you to become an efficient, productive, and effective writer.

Writing involves complex processes and often the "work of many hands."

Develop writing habits that work for you. Think about how you usually approach a writing task. Do you draw up extensive outlines? Do you organize visually or use note cards? Do you write best at a particular time of the day? Do you write best with solitude and quiet—or do you like to have music playing? Think carefully about what habits seem to help you produce your best work. But be careful: if you think you do your best work while multitasking, think again. Research increasingly challenges that assumption!

WRITING PROCESSES / A Roadmap

Whatever processes you find most productive, following are some tips that provide general guidance. If and when you decide on a particular genre, you'll find genre-specific guidance in the Roadmaps in Chapters 12–17.

Understand your assignment. If you're writing in response to an assignment, make sure you understand what it asks you to do. Does it specify a topic? a theme? a genre? Look for words like *argue, evaluate*, and *analyze*—words that specify a **GENRE** and thus point you to approach your topic in a certain way. An assignment that asks you to analyze, for example, lets you know that you should break down your topic into parts that can then be examined closely. If your assignment doesn't name a genre, think about which genre will best suit your rhetorical situation.

Come up with a topic. If you get to choose your topic, think of things you are particularly interested in and want to know more about—or something that puzzles you or poses a problem you'd like to solve or that gets you fired up. A topic you're passionate about is more likely to interest your audience and to keep you engaged as you research and write. If your topic is assigned, try to find an aspect or angle that interests you. Looking for a particular angle on a topic can help you to narrow your focus, but don't worry if the topic you come up with right now isn't very specific: as you do research, you'll be able to narrow and refine it. Coming up with a broad topic that interests you is just the starting point.

Consider your RHETORICAL SITUATION. Whether you're writing an argument or a narrative, working alone or with a group, you'll have an audience, a purpose, a stance, a genre, a medium and design, and a context—all things that you should be thinking about as you write.

- *Audience.* Whom are you addressing? What do they likely know or believe about your topic? What do you want them to think or do in response to your writing?

- *Purpose.* What is your goal in writing? What has motivated you to write, and what do you wish to accomplish?

- *Stance.* What is your attitude toward your topic? What perspective do you offer on it? What's your relationship with your audience, and how do you want to be seen by them?

- *Genre.* Have you been assigned a specific genre? If not, which genre(s) will best suit your purpose and audience?

- *Medium and design.* What medium or media will best suit your audience, purpose, and message? What design elements are possible (or required) in these media?

- *Context.* Consider the conversation surrounding your argument. What has been said about your topic, and how does that affect what you say? What about your immediate context—when is your writing due, and are there any other requirements or constraints?

Schedule your time. Remember that you must fit any writing project into your schedule, so think about how to use your time most wisely. However you keep yourself on track, taking a series of small steps is easier than doing it all at once. So schedule periodic goals for yourself: meeting them will build your confidence and reinforce good writing habits.

Generate ideas. Most of us find that writing can help us explore a topic and can even lead us to new ideas. Here are some activities that can help you sort out what you already know about your topic—and come up with new ideas about it:

- *Brainstorming* is a way to generate ideas without worrying about whether they're useful or not. Take a few minutes to focus on your topic or thesis (or a broad idea you want to develop into a specific topic or thesis) and list, using words or phrases, everything that occurs to you about this subject. Then review what you have written, looking for ideas that seem promising and relationships that you can develop. Remember: there are no right answers at this point!

- *Clustering* is a strategy for generating and processing ideas visually. Take a sheet of paper and write a word or phrase that best summarizes or evokes your topic. Draw a circle around this word. Now fill in the page by adding related words and ideas, circling them and connecting them to the original word, forming clusters. Then look at all the clusters to see what patterns you can find or where your ideas seem to be leading.

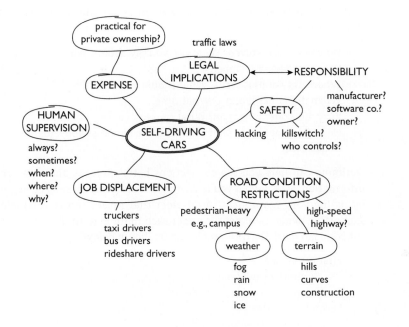

- *Freewriting* is a strategy for writing ideas down quickly, without stopping. To freewrite, simply write about whatever comes into your head in relation to a particular idea or topic for five to ten minutes. Be careful not to censor yourself: let your ideas flow as freely as possible. You may be surprised at the complexity and power of the ideas that you can develop through this process.

- *Looping* is an extended and more focused kind of freewriting. Begin by establishing a subject and then freewrite for five to ten minutes. Look at what you've written. Identify the most important or interesting or promising idea and write a sentence summarizing it. Use this sentence to start another "loop" of freewriting. Repeat this process as many times as necessary.

- *Drawing or sketching a picture of your topic* can help spark and guide your thinking about it. Drawing it may lead to a creative breakthrough. See if creating a series of sketches can help you figure out the structure of an essay you're writing.

- *Questioning* is an especially good way of exploring a topic. Starting with questions can help you discover what you already know about your topic—and, just as importantly, what you don't know and need to learn. Try starting with the questions *Who? What? Where? When? Why? How?*

> Who was / is involved? What can you say about them?
> What happened / happens?
> Where did / does it occur? What should you describe?
> When did / does it occur? What time?
> Why did / does it happen? What caused / causes it to occur?
> How did / does it happen? Was / is there a process you should describe?

- *Outlining* can help you see connections between ideas and organize information, especially if you're writing about a complex subject. Begin by listing your main ideas in an order that makes sense. Then add supporting evidence or details under each main idea, indenting these subpoints to mark the different levels, as shown below:

> First main idea
>   Supporting evidence or detail
>   Supporting evidence or detail
> Second main idea
>   Supporting evidence or detail
>   Supporting evidence or detail

Do some RESEARCH. You may want or need to do some research to better understand your topic, learn more about it, and decide what aspects of it you want to explore further. This could mean reading about your topic, **INTERVIEWING** experts about it, conducting surveys, observing something firsthand, or some combination of those methods. Learning what others have said about a topic is an important step to figuring out what you want to say—and to joining the conversation.

Come up with a tentative THESIS, a statement that identifies your topic and the point you want to make about it. You'll rarely, if ever, have a final thesis when you start writing, but establishing a tentative one will help focus your thinking and any research you may do. Here are some prompts to get you started.

1. ***What point do you want to make about your topic?*** Try writing it out as a promise to your audience: *In this essay, I will present reasons for limiting use of social media.*

2. *Try plotting out a tentative thesis in two parts,* the first stating your topic, the second making some claim about the topic:

    ┌─────── TOPIC ──────────┐┌────────── CLAIM ──────────┐
    Limiting your social media time will improve your concentration, provide

    ┌──┐
    real-life social opportunities, and reduce vulnerability to hacking.

3. *Ask some questions about what you've written.* Will it engage your intended audience? What's your claim? Is it debatable? There's no point in staking a claim that is a fact, or one that no one would disagree with.

4. *Do you need to narrow or* QUALIFY *your thesis?* Can you do what you say you will, given the time and resources available? You don't want to overstate your case—or make a claim that you'll have trouble supporting. Adding words such as *could, might, likely,* or *potentially* can qualify what you say: *Limiting your social media time provide social opportunities will* _likely_ *improve concentration,* _might_, *and* _could potentially_ *reduce vulnerability to hacking.*

5. *Is the thesis clear and focused?* Will it tell readers what's coming? And will it help keep you (and your readers) on track?

Keep in mind that at this point in your process, this is a tentative thesis, one that could change as you research, write, and revise. Continue to explore your topic. Don't stop until you feel you've reached a full understanding of your topic. As you learn more about it, you may well find that you want to revise your thesis.

Once you're satisfied that your thesis makes a clear claim that you can support, and one that will interest your readers, gather together the notes from your research. This is the information you'll draw from as support for your thesis.

ORGANIZE your ideas. Whether you like to write out an outline or prefer to do most of your planning on note cards or sticky notes (or in your head!), you'll want to think about how best to organize your text before beginning to write. Writing about events generally works best when told in CHRONOLOGICAL ORDER. And facts, data, and other EVIDENCE are usually most effective when stated in order of importance, starting with the information that's most crucial to your argument before stating the less important information. If you're describing something, you might organize your information SPATIALLY, beginning at one point and moving from left to right, or top to bottom. As you see, there's no one way to organize your writing; the order in which you present your points will depend on many things, including the topic and what you have to say about it.

Write out a draft. Keep your tentative thesis statement and any other notes and outlines close at hand as you start writing. A complete draft will include an introduction, a body, and a conclusion, though you may not necessarily draft them in that order.

- *The* **INTRODUCTION** is often the most difficult part to write, so much so that some authors decide to write it last. But just as a well-crafted opening can help guide your readers, it can also help you get started writing. A good introduction should grab readers' attention, announce your topic and your claim, and indicate how you plan to proceed. A provocative question, an anecdote, a startling claim: these are some of the ways you might open an essay.

- *The body* of an essay is where you will develop your argument, point by point, paragraph by paragraph. Strategies such as **COMPARISON**, **DESCRIPTION**, **NARRATION**, and others can help you develop paragraphs to present **EVIDENCE** in support of your **THESIS**.

- *The* **CONCLUSION** should sum up your argument in a way that readers will remember. You might end by restating your claim, discussing the implications of your argument, calling for some action, or posing further questions—all ways of highlighting the significance of what you've said.

Be flexible, and make changes if you need to. Even the most well-planned writing doesn't show its true shape until you've written a full draft, so don't be surprised if you find that you need to reorganize, do additional research, or otherwise rethink your argument as you go. Be flexible! Rather than sticking stubbornly to a plan that doesn't seem to be working, use each draft and revision as an opportunity to revisit your plan and to think about how you can strengthen your argument or your appeal.

The ancient Greeks had a word for thinking about the opportunities presented by a particular rhetorical situation. They called it *kairos,* and it referred to the ability to seize an opportune and timely moment. Kairos was the ancient Greek god of opportunity and perfect timing, qualities every author needs. He was often depicted as a young man running, and it was said that you must seize the forelock of his hair as he passes by; once he's passed, there's nothing to cling to because the back of his head is completely bald—you've missed your opportunity.

This is a concept that can be especially helpful when you're drafting—and that can also help you revise. As you work, think of each paragraph and sentence as an opportunity to add (or eliminate) detail, to reorganize, or to improve your point in some other way. Think about how your sentences and paragraphs might be received by your audience—and about how you can get readers to pay attention to and value what you say.

Get response from others—from your instructor, a classmate, a writing center tutor. Be sure to tell them about any questions or concerns you have about the draft, and ask for their advice. But remember: you don't have to take all the advice you get, just what you consider helpful. You're the author!

Kairos

Look at your draft with a critical eye and revise. You'll find genre-specific guidelines for reading a draft carefully and revising in the chapters on **ARGUMENTS**, **NARRATIVES**, **ANALYSES**, **REPORTS**, **REVIEWS**, and **PROPOSALS**. For more general advice, following are some prompts to help you read over a draft, either your own or one you're peer-reviewing for a fellow writer.

- How does the **INTRODUCTION** capture readers' attention and make them want to read on? Does it indicate that (or why) the topic matters? How else might it begin?

- How do you as the author come across—as well-informed? passionate? serious? something else?

- Is it clear what motivated you to write? Consider the larger **CONTEXT**: what else has been said about the topic, and have you considered perspectives other than your own?

- Is there an explicit **THESIS**? If not, does there need to be? If so, does it make clear what you are claiming about the topic?

- Is there sufficient support for the thesis? What **REASONS** and **EVIDENCE** do you provide? Will they be persuasive for the intended audience?

- Is the draft organized in a way that is easy to follow? Check to see how each paragraph supports the thesis, and whether it is developed fully enough to make its point. Are there headings—and if not, should there be? Is there any information that would be easier to follow if set off as a list? Are there explicit **TRANSITIONS** to help readers follow the text—and if not, are they needed?

- How does the text **CONCLUDE**? What does it leave readers thinking? How else might it conclude?

- Is there a title? If so, does it tell readers what your topic is and make them want to read on? If not, think in terms of **KAIROS**: the title is your first opportunity to indicate that this is a text about something that matters and that readers should care about.

Edit and proofread. Now's the time to pay close attention to the details: to check your paragraphs, your sentences, your words, and your punctuation. Think about the **STYLE** of your writing: is it appropriate for your purpose and audience? And don't forget to check for common mistakes. Finally, take the time to proofread. Read with an eye for typos and inconsistencies. Make sure all your sentences are complete. Run a spell checker, but be aware that it is no substitute for careful proofreading.

Approach Your Writing Pragmatically

Even if you have a writing process that works well for you, that doesn't mean you complete all writing tasks the same way—or that you should. It's just common sense that you spend more time and take more care with your writing process for a fifteen-page research paper that counts for 40 percent of your final grade than you do for a much briefer essay that counts for 10 percent of that grade. Approach your writing pragmatically: consider how important your task is, what time constraints you face, what else you may have to do, what the nature of the task itself requires, and how well prepared you feel to complete it. Then, make *realistic* decisions. What do you *need* to do to complete an assignment effectively—and what *can* you do?

REFLECT. Take some time to think about your writing process. What works well? What tends to be a struggle? What do you want to try to do differently? Think about the various ways and places in which you've been able to do good writing. Are you able to make them a regular part of your writing process?

TEN

The Need for Collaboration

"Here Comes Everybody!"

ERE COMES EVERYBODY is the title of NYU professor Clay Shirky's book about "what happens when people are given the tools to do things together, without needing traditional organizational structures" to do them. Put another way, Shirky's book is about how technology has led to connectivity and how connectivity has led to easy and innovative collaborations. Here's what we mean:

- A group of students creates a *Wikipedia* entry devoted to manga, a genre of Japanese comic books. Within hours, others from around the world have joined in, helping to expand and refine the entry.

- A budding essayist uses the blogging platform *Medium* to publish her writing and interact with readers and other writers. She finds that the online community is full of authors who want to collaborate and discuss their ideas.

- Assigned to write an essay about the dangers faced by independent war journalists, a student starts by researching what has been written on this topic (reading current news magazines, online news sites, and *Twitter* feeds and blogs kept by the journalists themselves). When he writes the essay, he weaves the views of others (carefully cited) in with his own, adding his voice to the conversation about that topic.

- Fans of the TV mystery-drama *Veronica Mars* keep the show alive by writing and sharing fanfiction for years after the series ends. The fan base remains so strong that a *Kickstarter* campaign to fund a *Veronica Mars* movie raises over $5 million. The movie hit theaters in 2014, its fans walking down the red carpet alongside the stars.

Even the student mentioned above, researching alone at his computer, depends on others. In short, writers seldom—if ever—write alone. Collaboration has always been inevitable and essential, and our digital connectivity makes working together easier—and more interesting—than ever. This chapter will help you think about the role that collaboration plays in your life, and especially how it affects the work you do as an author and a reader.

In *Powers of Two*, Joshua Wolf Shenk argues that the real genius of the Beatles and their best work grew out of the collaborative nature of the Lennon-McCartney partnership.

REFLECT. Think about reading and writing that you do regularly online—status updates, blog posts, articles, comments—everything. In what ways are you an author, and in what ways are you a member of an audience? To what extent does each activity involve collaboration with others, and how would it be different if there were no collaboration at all?

What Collaboration Means for Authors—and Audiences

The examples above show some of the ways that authors collaborate—and how they sometimes even trade places with their audiences. Readers of the *Wikipedia* entry on manga can take on the role of editors or authors; the student writer using *Medium* becomes an audience for her readers' suggestions and ideas; the student reading and writing about independent war reporters is an audience for those authors whose work he reads and then an author when he responds to their views in his own essay. Authors and audiences shift roles and collaborate constantly—there's hardly any way to avoid doing so.

Once upon a time, newspapers reported information and events; today, they maintain social media accounts and blogs that serve as forums for discussing, challenging, and updating information. Readers who were once passive consumers of the news can now be active participants in responding to and sharing that information with others. As media professor Henry Jenkins puts it, ours is "a world where no one knows everything, but everyone knows something." Putting those somethings together is what happens when we collaborate.

To take another familiar example, players of the first video games were an audience for stories that were written by the games' designers. That's not the case in many of today's games, however, in which the players / audience customize their characters and write their own story—very often in collaboration with other players. Consider, for example, multiplayer online games such as *Fortnite*, in which a large number of people play as a group, or the more serious video game *World without Oil*, in which almost 2,000 individuals from twelve countries collaborated over the course of a month to imagine how to deal with a global oil crisis. Such games don't merely offer opportunities for collaboration; it's actually impossible for any one player to play alone.

Collaboration is an everyday matter. We collaborate for fun, as when a flash mob suddenly appears and starts dancing to Queen or singing the

TAKE A LOOK at some favorite flash mobs at <u>everyonesanauthor.tumblr.com</u>*.
Some promote a cause, others sell a product, still others celebrate something or
someone. The picture above is from a flash mob in the Netherlands to raise awareness
of the exploitation of women. Inspired by One Billion Rising, performances like this
one take place around the world every February to shine light on violence against
women and to demand change. We think you'll agree that in addition to fulfilling
various purposes, flash mobs can be great fun. What ideas do you have for an effective
flash mob? In what ways would a flash mob accomplish your goal better than a piece
of writing?*

"Hallelujah Chorus" and then just as suddenly disappears. And we collaborate for more serious purposes, as when many people contribute over time to develop a *Wikipedia* entry or when people in countries as far-flung as the United States, Malaysia, Germany, Nigeria, and dozens more collaborate on a dance project such as One Billion Rising or when musicians sprinkled throughout the world play together virtually through Playing for Change. In his book *Net Smart*, digital communications scholar Howard Rheingold argues that collaboration is today's tool for social engagement: "Knowing the importance of participation and how to participate has suddenly become not only an individual survival skill but a key to large-scale social change." For these and other purposes, collaboration is a necessity.

What Collaboration Means for You as a Student

As a student, you'll have many occasions to collaborate, from a simple class discussion to a full-fledged team project to research and write a report, carry out and write up an experiment, or build a website.

As a writer, you'll be in constant collaboration with others, from teachers and classmates who read and respond to your drafts to the audience you're addressing—and don't forget those whose work you read and cite. Academic writing in particular calls on you to engage with the ideas of others—to listen to and think about what they say, to respond to views you don't agree with, and to weave the ideas of others (those you agree with and those you don't) into your own arguments. Very often you'll want to present your own views as a direct response to what others say—in fact, when you think about it, the main reason we make arguments at all is because someone has said or done something that we want to respond to. And one reason we make academic arguments is to add our voices to conversations about topics that we're studying, things that matter to us.

And consider your nonacademic writing, particularly the writing you do online. Whether you're posting or following others on *Instagram*, viewing or contributing to *Wikipedia* or *YouTube* these kinds of writing assume and make possible a back-and-forth—a collaboration. You might be an author, an audience, or both. These are all ways that we regularly communicate—and collaborate—with others.

REFLECT. Go to Wikipedia *and work with several classmates to choose an entry that interests you and then revise or add to it. Or, if you don't find what you're looking for, create a new entry yourselves. Revisit in a few days to see what others may have added (or removed). For tips on writing for* Wikipedia, *see pages 785–86.*

Collaboration with a Writing Tutor

Speaking of collaboration in your academic writing, have you heard of your school's writing center? Most schools have one, and it's a place where you can go (online or physically) to consult with a trained tutor on any aspect of a class assignment. All writers need good readers, and a tutor can work with you at any stage of the process—brainstorming ideas, organizing the sequence of information, polishing, clarifying, documenting your sources.

And the good news is that the writing center probably doesn't charge a cent for what it offers. Or rather, you've already paid for it as part of your tuition and fees, so you might as well take advantage.

Here's something we know for sure: the more prepared you are for your writing center session, the more you'll get out of it. First, figure out what you'd like to accomplish in your session and share that information with your tutor early. Discuss your ideas, goals, doubts, and questions. Your tutor may suggest a different focus for your session; be open and flexible to such suggestions and reasoning. Let the session be a collaboration. A lot of ideas and information will be discussed during your session, so it's important that you take good notes in order to be able to remember it all. You may want to sit down immediately after your session and add more details while your memory is still fresh. Finally, write out a plan of action for what you'll do next; this plan will guide you when you get back to your assignment. We also recommend that you schedule your next appointment before leaving the writing center. Doing it promptly will improve your chances of getting a preferred day and time, and having an appointment can be a soft deadline for advancing your project.

Collaboration at Work

Collaboration almost certainly plays a role in your work life. Indeed, teamwork is central to most businesses and industries. Engineers work in teams to design power plants; editors and designers work together to publish books and magazines; businesses from Best Buy to Google rely on teams to develop and market new products. Whatever work you do—whether it is that of an engineer, health-care worker, bookstore owner, chemist, or teacher—you will find yourself continually communicating with others. The effectiveness of these communications will depend to a large extent on your ability to collaborate effectively.

Today's global culture can raise particular challenges for communication. Increasing numbers of workers are telecommuting—spending time working at home rather than at a desk in an office with other workers. Even when they are working from a centralized office, workers often need to communicate with colleagues elsewhere in the world and in other

At public relations agency ID's headquarters in Los Angeles, CEO Kelly Bush Novak leads a videoconference with members of her New York staff.

time zones. Digital humanities professor Cathy Davidson describes how one company holds global conference calls:

> Everyone chats using Sametime, IBM's internal synchronous chat tool, and has a text window open during the conversation. Anyone can be typing in a comment or a question (backchatting) while any other two people are speaking. Participants are both listening to the main conversation between whichever two people happen to be talking while also reading the comments, questions, and answers that any of the other participants might be texting. The conversation continues in response to both the talk and the text.
> —CATHY DAVIDSON, *Now You See It: How the Brain Science of Attention Will Transform the Way We Live, Work, and Learn*

A dizzying scenario to be sure—and an excellent reminder of both the challenges and the opportunities that the future holds for all who wish to make our voices heard in today's global culture. As a student in college, you are well positioned to prepare yourself for this future—which is in fact not the future at all but our present moment. In fact, you're most likely already using remote communication skills by taking courses online. Rather than taking your online writing for granted as "just for fun," learn from it. Take advantage as well of the opportunities that your school provides to learn with and from people with diverse cultural backgrounds. Such collaborative interactions are intrinsically satisfying, and they can also help you practice communicating effectively in the twenty-first century.

Some Tips for Collaborating Effectively

Sometimes your class collaborations will be fleeting and low risk—for example, to work with a group to respond to questions about a reading and then to share the group's ideas with the class. Other collaborations are more extended and high risk, as when you pick lab partners for the whole term or have a major group project that will count for a significant percentage of everyone's final grade.

Extended collaborative assignments can be a challenge. Members of the group may have differing goals—for instance, two members will accept nothing less than an A and others are just hoping for a C. Domineering members of the team may try to run the show; others won't participate at all. And the logistics of collaborating on a major project can be a challenge. Here are some tips that can help ensure efficient, congenial, and productive team relationships when you are working on an extended collaborative project.

- *Find ways of recognizing everyone.* For example, all group members could talk about a strength that they can contribute to the project.

- *Listen carefully*—and respectfully—to every group member.

- *Establish some ground rules.* Whether online or face-to-face, the way your group runs its meetings can make or break your collaborative effort. Spend part of your first meeting exploring your assignment and figuring out how often the group will meet, the responsibilities of each member, and the general expectations you have of each other.

- *Make an effort to develop trust and group identity.* To get started, members could share some pertinent information, such as their favorite spots for writing or their typical writing processes. Remember, too, that socializing can play an important role in the development of group identity. Sharing a pizza while brainstorming can pay off down the road. However, remember to stay focused on the project.

- *Get organized.* Use an agenda to organize your meetings, and be sure that someone takes notes. Don't count on anyone's memory, and don't leave all the note-taking to one person! You may want to take turns developing the agenda, reminding everyone of upcoming meetings via email or text message, maintaining written records, and so on.

- *Develop nonthreatening ways to deal with problems.* Rather than stating that a member's ideas are unclear, for instance, you might say, "I'm having trouble making the connection between your suggestion and my understanding of what we're discussing." Just a simple shift from *your* to *my* can defuse difficult situations. And remember that tact, thoughtfulness, and a sense of humor can go a long way toward resolving any interpersonal issues.

- *Build in regular reality checks* to nip any potential problems in the bud—for example, reserve some time to discuss how the group is working and how it could be better. Try not to criticize anyone; instead, focus on what's working and what could be improved.

- *Encourage the free play of ideas,* one of the most important benefits of working collaboratively. Think carefully about when your group should strive for consensus and when you should not. You want to avoid interpersonal conflicts that slow you down, yet remain open and consider everyone's ideas.

- *Expect the unexpected.* Someone's computer may crash, interlibrary loan materials may arrive later than expected, someone may be sick on the day when she was supposed to write a key section of the text. Try to build in extra time for the unexpected, and help each other out when extra teamwork is needed.

- *Be flexible about how you meet.* If getting together in person poses problems, use video chat or *Google Docs* to meet and work. Use your school's course management system for discussion forums, wikis, and file-sharing folders—all of which will prove helpful for collaborative work.

Remember that when you engage in group work, you need to attend to both the task and the group. And keep in mind that each member of the group should be valued equally and that the process should be satisfying to all.

PART IV

Genres of Writing

WHEN YOU WERE A KID, did you have certain kinds of clothes you liked to wear? Six-year-old Lila describes her wardrobe this way: "I have school clothes—they're okay, I guess. And I have dress-up clothes, like for when I go to the *Nutcracker* or a birthday party. But my favorites are my make-believe clothes: Snow White, Alice in Wonderland, and Princess Anna from *Frozen*. She's my favorite!" What Lila displays here is a fairly sophisticated sense of *genres*, ways that we categorize things. You see genres everywhere—in literature (think poetry, fiction, drama), in movies (Westerns, film noir, documentaries), and in music (rap, country, classical). And when we talk about writing, we often talk in terms of genres too: narratives, lab reports, project proposals, movie reviews, argument essays, and so on. Like all genres, those associated with writing are flexible: they expand and change over time as writers find new ways to communicate and express themselves.

In the ancient world, for example, personal communication involved carving symbols into clay tablets or, a bit later, having a scribe record your message on papyrus. For communicating with speed, couriers memorized letters and raced to deliver them orally. Once paper was available and letters were less costly and easier to produce, they evolved into multiple subgenres: the business letter, the personal letter, the condolence letter, the thank-you letter, and so on. Today, letters have further evolved into electronic forms— emails, *Instagram* messages, texts. It's hard to predict how these genres of communication will evolve in the future, but when they do, we know they will stretch to accommodate new modes and new media, as genres always do. In short, genres reflect current expectations while also shaping—and sometimes even changing—them.

Instructors will often ask you to use particular genres, most likely including the ones taught in this book: arguments, narratives, analyses, reports, reviews, and proposals. You may need to write a rhetorical analysis of a speech, for instance, or to analyze the causes of the increased frequency of wildfires in California. In either case, knowing the characteristic features of an analysis will be helpful. And you may want or need to combine genres—to introduce an analysis with a short narrative or to conclude it with a proposal of some kind.

Of course, you may not always be assigned to write in a particular genre. Your instructor may give you a topic to write about in whatever way you choose. In this case, you'll need to think carefully about what genre will be most appropriate for addressing that topic—and Chapter 11 will help you choose a genre when the choice is yours.

The chapters that follow introduce most of the genres you'll be assigned to do in college. Each chapter explains the genre's characteristic features; discusses how, when, where, and why you might use the genre most appropriately; provides a roadmap to the process of writing in that genre; and includes several example essays. We hope that you'll use these chapters to explore these common academic genres—and to adapt them as needed to your own purposes and goals.

Communication throughout the ages, from clay tablets to couriers delivering messages to tweets and texts.

ELEVEN

Choosing Genres

OMICS HAVE MANGA, superheroes, and fantasy. Music has hip-hop, country, and folk. Video games? Think shooters, simulation, or role-playing. How about restaurants? Try Italian, Vietnamese, Tex-Mex, vegan, or southern soul food. Or movies: sci-fi, thrillers, drama, anime. These are all genres, and they are one important way we structure our world.

Genres are categorizations, ways of classifying things. The genres this book is concerned with are kinds of writing, but you'll find genres everywhere you look.

In fact, rhetorician and researcher Carolyn Miller has been tracking the use of the word *genre* and has found it everywhere, including on many of the sites you visit every day. *Netflix* lists nineteen film genres, from action and drama to sports and thrillers—and many subgenres within each of these. The video game review site *GameSpot* sorts games into sixty-eight genres, and *Spotify* lists forty-three kinds of music and nine categories of podcasts as this book goes to press. You can even see new genres developing on *YouTube*, including microgenres like "cute babies" or "cats being mean." Indeed, there is now such a proliferation of genres that they've become the subject of parody, with comedians mixing musical genres to make new ones, like honky tonk and techno to make "honky techno" or folk and dubstep to make "folk step." To get a sense of the result, just take a look at the cartoon on the next page.

In this cartoon, Roz Chast comes up with her own new movie genres: sci-fi/Western, musical/self-help, sports/horror, and documentary/romance.

What You Need to Know about Genres of Writing

Genres are kinds of writing that you can use to accomplish a certain goal and reach a particular audience. As such, they have well-established features that help guide you in your writing. However, they're not fill-in-the-blank templates; you will adapt them to address your own rhetorical situations.

Genres have features that can guide you as a writer and a reader. Argument essays, for instance, take a position supported by reasons and evidence, consider a range of perspectives, and so on. These features help guide you as an author in what you write—and they also set up expectations for you as a reader, affecting the way you interpret what you read. If something's called a report, for instance, you are likely to assume that it presents information—that it's in some way factual.

This book covers those genres that are most often assigned in school—**ARGUMENTS, ANALYSES, REPORTS, NARRATIVES, REVIEWS, PROPOSALS,** and **ANNOTATED BIBLIOGRAPHIES**—and some subgenres: **VISUAL ANALYSES, PROFILES, LITERACY NARRATIVES, LITERATURE REVIEWS,** and **PROJECT PROPOSALS**. These are kinds of writing that have evolved over the years as a useful means of creating and sharing knowledge. As you advance in a major, you will become familiar with the most important genres and subgenres in that field. Especially when you are new to a genre, its features can serve as a kind of blueprint, helping you know how to approach an assignment. Knowing these features helps you organize a text and guides your choices in terms of content.

Genres are flexible. Keep in mind that genres can be both enabling and constraining. Sometimes you'll have reason to adapt genre features to suit your own goals. One student who was writing an analysis of a sonnet, for example, wanted to bend the analysis genre just a little to include a sonnet of his own. He checked with his teacher, got approval, and it worked. You probably wouldn't want to stretch a lab report in this way, however. Lab reports follow a fairly set template, covering purpose, methods, results, summary, and conclusions to carry out the goals of the scientific fields that use them; they would not be appropriate (or effective) in a creative writing class.

You may also have occasion to combine genres—to tell a story in the course of arguing a position or to conclude a report with a proposal of some kind. If you ever decide to adapt or combine genres, think hard about your rhetorical situation: what genres will help you achieve your purpose? reach the audience you're addressing? work best in the medium you're using?

Genres evolve. While it is relatively easy to identify some characteristic genre features, such features are not universal rules. Genres are flexible, and they evolve across time and in response to shifting cultural contexts. Letters, for example, followed certain conventions in medieval Europe (they were handwritten, of course, and they were highly formal); by the twentieth century, letters had developed dozens of subgenres (thank-you notes, letters to the editor, application letters). Then, in the 1990s, letters began to morph into email, adapting in new ways to online situations. Today, text messages, tweets, and posts to *Instagram* may be seen as offshoots of the letter genre.

And as with all genres and subgenres, letters, email, text messages, and *Instagram* posts have developed their own conventions and features, ones that guide you as a writer and a reader.

REFLECT. Think about a favorite song, movie, or game, and then decide what genre it is. How do you know? List the features that help you identify it as belonging to a particular genre. What do you know about that genre? Name a few other examples of that genre, and then think about what features they have in common.

Deciding Which Genres to Use

Sometimes you'll be assigned to write in a particular genre. If that's the case, think about what you know about the genre, about what it expects of you as a writer, and turn to the appropriate chapter in this book for guidance. But other times your assignments won't make the genre perfectly clear. The following advice can help determine which genre(s) to use when the choice is yours. In all cases, remember to consider your **PURPOSE** for writing and the **AUDIENCE** you want to reach in deciding which genres would be most appropriate.

Look for clues in the assignment. Even without a clearly assigned genre, your assignment should be your starting point. Are there any keywords that suggest one? *Discuss*, for example, could indicate a **REPORT** or an **ANALYSIS**. And you might also need to consider how such a keyword is used in the discipline the assignment comes from—*analyze* in a philosophy assignment doesn't likely mean the same thing as in a literature assignment. In either case, you should ask your instructor for clarification.

Consider this assignment from an introductory communications course: "Look carefully at letters to the editor in one newspaper over a period of two weeks, and write an essay describing what you find. Who are the letter writers? What issues are they writing about? How many different perspectives are represented?" Though this assignment doesn't name a genre, it seems to be asking students for a report: to research a topic and then report on what they find.

But what if this were the assignment: "Look carefully at letters to the editor in one newspaper over a period of two weeks, and write an essay describing what you find. Who are the letter writers? What issues are they writing about? How many different perspectives are represented? What rhetorical strategies do the writers use to get their points across? Draw some conclusions based on what you find." This assignment also asks students to research a topic and report on what they find. But in asking them to draw some conclusions based on their findings, it is also prompting them to do some analysis. As you look at your own assignments, look for words or other clues that will help you identify which genres are expected.

If an assignment doesn't give any clues, here are some questions to ask in thinking about which genre may be most appropriate:

- *What discipline is the assignment for?* Say you're assigned to write about obesity and public health. If you're writing for a journalism course, you might write an op-ed essay ARGUING that high-calorie sodas should not be sold in public schools. If, on the other hand, you're writing for a biology class, you might REPORT on experiments done on eating behaviors and metabolic rates.

- *What is the topic?* Does it call for a specific genre? If you are asked, for example, to write about the campaign speeches of two presidential candidates, that topic suggests that you're being asked to ANALYZE the speeches (and probably COMPARE them). On the other hand, if you're writing about an experiment you conducted, you're probably writing a REPORT and should follow the conventions of that genre.

- *What is your purpose in writing?* If you want to convince your readers that they should "buy local," for example, your purpose will likely call for an ARGUMENT. If, however, you want to explain what buying local means, your purpose will call for a REPORT.

- *Who is the audience?* What interests and expectations might they have? Say you're assigned to write about the collective-bargaining rights of unions for a first-year seminar. There your audience would include other first-year students, and you might choose to write a NARRATIVE about the father of a friend who lost his job as a high school teacher. Imagine, however, writing on the same topic for a public policy course; there you would be more likely to write an essay ANALYZING the costs and benefits of unionized workers in the public sector.

- *What medium will you use?* Are there certain genres that work well— or not—in that medium? If you are assigned to give an oral presentation, for example, you might consider writing a NARRATIVE because listeners can remember stories better than they are able to recall other genres. Even if you decide to write an analysis or a report, you might want to include some narrative.

If the assignment is wide open, draw on what you know about genres. Sometimes you may receive an assignment so broad that not only the genre but even the topic and purpose are left up to you. Consider, for example, a prompt one of the authors of this book encountered in college: in an exam for a drama class, the professor came into the room, wrote "Tragedy!" on the blackboard, and said, "You have an hour and a half to respond." We hope you don't run into such a completely open-ended assignment, especially in a timed exam. But if you do, your knowledge of genre can help out. If this assignment came in a Shakespeare course, for example, you might **ARGUE** that *Hamlet* is Shakespeare's most powerful tragedy. Or you could perhaps **ANALYZE** the role of gender in one of his tragedies.

Luckily, such wide-open assignments are fairly rare. It's more likely that you will encounter an assignment like this one: "Choose a topic related to our course theme and carry out sufficient research on that topic to write an essay of eight to ten pages. Refer to at least six sources and follow MLA citation style." In this instance, you know that the assignment calls for some kind of research-based writing and that you need a topic and thesis that can be dealt with in the length specified. You could write an **ARGUMENT**, taking a position and supporting it with the research you have done. Or you could write a **REPORT** that presents findings from your research. At this point, you would be wise to see your instructor to discuss your choices. Once you have decided on a genre, turn to the appropriate chapter in this book (Chapters 12–17) to guide your research and writing.

When an assignment is wide open, try using what you know about genres as a way to explore your topic:

- What are some of the **POSITIONS** on your topic? What's been said or might be said? What controversies or disagreements exist? What's your own perspective?
- What stories— **NARRATIVES** —could you tell about it?
- How might you **ANALYZE** your topic? What are its parts? What caused it—or what effects might it have? Does it follow a certain process?
- What information might be important or interesting to **REPORT** on?
- How can your topic be evaluated, or **REVIEWED**?
- What problems does your topic present for which you can **PROPOSE** a solution?

REFLECT. Look at three writing assignments you have been given for any of your classes. Did the assignments specify a genre? If so, what was it? If not, what genres would you say you were being asked to use—and how can you tell?

TWELVE

"This Is Where I Stand"
Arguing a Position

O WHAT'S YOUR POSITION ON THAT?" This familiar phrase pops up almost everywhere, from talk radio to social media, from political press conferences to classroom seminars. In fact, much of the work you do as an author responds, in some way, to this question.

After all, taking a position is something you do many times daily: you visit your advisor's office to explain in person your reasons for dropping a course; you text a friend the reasons she should see a certain film with you; in an economics class discussion, you offer your own position on consumer spending patterns in response to someone else's; you survey research on fracking and then write a letter to the editor of your local newspaper advocating (or protesting) a ban on fracking. In all these cases, you're doing what philosopher Kenneth Burke calls "putting in your oar," taking and supporting positions of your own in conversation with others around you.

Look around, and you'll see other positions being articulated all over the place. Here's one we saw recently on a T-shirt:

Work to eat.

Eat to live.

Live to bike.

Bike to work.

The central argument here is clear: bike to work. One of the reasons it's so effective is the clever way that the last sentence isn't quite parallel to the others. (In the first three, *to* can be replaced by *in order to*; in the last case, it can't.) Another reason it works well is the form of the argument, which is a series of short commands, each beginning with the same word that the previous sentence ends with.

This chapter offers guidelines for writing an academic essay that takes a position. While taking a position in an academic context often differs in crucial ways from doing so in other contexts, many of the principles discussed will serve you well when stating a position generally.

REFLECT. Stop for a moment and jot down every time you remember having to take a position on something—anything at all—in the last few days. The list will surely soon grow long if you're like most of us. Then take an informal survey, noting and writing down every time in one day someone around you takes a position. This informal research should convince you that the rhetorical genre of taking a position is central to many of your daily activities.

Across Academic Disciplines

Position papers are written in many fields, and a number of disciplines offer specific guidelines for composing them. In *philosophy*, a position paper is a brief persuasive essay designed to express a precise opinion about some issue or some philosopher's viewpoint. In *computer science*, a position paper considers a number of perspectives on an issue before finally offering the writer's own position. In *political science*, a position paper often critiques a major argument or text, first summarizing and analyzing its main points and then interpreting them in the context of other texts. Many college courses ask students to take a position in response to a course reading, specifying that they state their position clearly, support it with evidence and logical reasons, and cite all sources consulted. So one challenge you'll face when you're asked to write a position paper in various disciplines will be to determine exactly what is expected of you.

Across Media

Different media present different resources and challenges when it comes to presenting your position. Setting up a *website* that encourages people to take action to end animal abuse gives you the ability to link to additional information, whereas writing a traditional *essay* advocating that position for a print magazine requires that you provide all the relevant evidence and reasons on the page. It is very easy to incorporate color images or video clips in the webpage, but the magazine's budget may not allow for color at all. If you make the same argument against animal abuse in an *oral presentation*, you'll mostly be talking, though you may use *PowerPoint* slides to help your listeners follow the structure of your comments, to remind them of your main points, and to show graphs or photos that will appeal to their sense of reason or their emotions. Finally, if your marketing class is designing a fund-raising *TV commercial* for a nonprofit organization that works to stop animal abuse, you'll likely be able to use images and even music to drive home your point, but you might have only thirty seconds to get the message across.

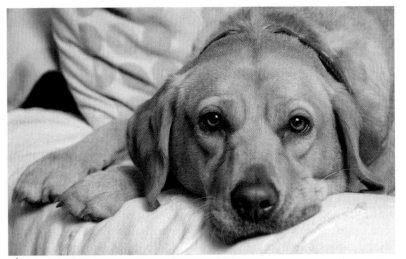

THINK BEYOND WORDS

↪ *TAKE A LOOK at the website of Mutt Love Rescue, a dog adoption organization in Washington, DC, where you can see photos of available dogs, find out about fostering a dog, and more. Click on "Saving a Life" to see the organization's appeal for donations, along with photos of some of the "lucky pups." How compelling do you find the organization's argument? How does the use of words and images contribute to its appeal—is one more important? How would you revise this site to make it more effective—add video? audio? statistics? testimonials? more written information (or less)? Go to* everyonesanauthor.tumblr.com *to access the site.*

Remember that persuasion is always about connecting with an audience, meeting them where they are, and helping them see why your position is one they should take seriously or even adopt. To achieve that goal, you have to convey your position in a medium your audience will be receptive to—and can access. Different media serve different purposes, and you will want to consider your own goals as well as your audience's expectations.

Across Cultures and Communities

Taking a position in cultures or communities other than your own poses special challenges. Advertising—a clear case of taking a position—is full of humorous tales of cross-cultural failure. When Pepsi first sought to break into the Chinese market, for example, its slogan, "Pepsi Brings You Back to Life," got mangled in translation, coming out as "Pepsi Brings Your Ancestors Back from the Grave."

Far more problematic than questions of translation are questions of STANCE. When taking a position in American academic contexts, you're almost always expected to state your position explicitly while showing your awareness of other possible positions. In contrast, in some cultures and communities, you would generally avoid stating your opinion directly; rather, you would hint at it. In yet others, you would be expected to state your mind forthrightly, paying little attention to what others think about the issue or to how your words might make them feel.

Equally important, how people are expected to frame positions they take varies within a community, depending on their place in the social hierarchy as supervisor or employee, teacher or student, ruler or governed. To complicate matters, the expectations with respect to outsiders are almost always different from those for the locals. Most people might be quick to criticize their own government among friends, but they don't necessarily grant outsiders the same privilege. A word to the wise: humility is in order, especially when taking a position in communities or cultures of which you're not a member. Don't assume that what works at home will work elsewhere. A safe first step is to listen and observe carefully when in a new context, paying special attention to how people communicate any positions they are taking.

Across Genres

Arguing a position, as we've pointed out, is something that we do, in small ways or large, almost every day—and even across a range of genres. You might, for instance, write a letter to the editor of your local newspaper lamenting the closure of the local library—and setting forth your **POSITION** that it must be kept open at all costs. Similarly, a company's annual **REPORT** would likely set out its position that collective bargaining with suppliers will improve the company's bottom line. After taking in a highly anticipated film, you might tweet a brief **REVIEW**, arguing that it wasn't as good as you'd expected. In each case, the text states a position.

See how video game publisher Activision-Blizzard states its position on esports in its 2017 annual report. Go to everyonesanauthor .tumblr.com and scroll to p. 15 of the report.

REFLECT. Look to see where and how positions are expressed around you, considering posters, editorials, songs, Instagram postings, blog entries, and so on. Then choose one that most interests you—or that most irritates you—and spend some time thinking about how it presents its position. How does it appeal to you—or why does it fail to appeal? What kinds of words, images, or sounds does it offer as support for its position? If you were going to revise it for a different audience, what would you do? If you were going to create it in another medium, how would it be different?

CHARACTERISTIC FEATURES

Given the many different forms of writing that take a position, no one-size-fits-all approach to composing them is possible. We can, however, identify the following characteristic features common to writing in which the author is arguing a position:

- An explicit position
- A response to what others have said or done
- Appropriate background information
- A clear indication of why the topic matters
- Good reasons and evidence
- Attention to more than one point of view
- An authoritative tone
- An appeal to readers' values

An Explicit Position

Stating a position explicitly is easier said than done, since the complexity of most important issues can make it hard to articulate a position in a crystal-clear way. But it's very important to do so insofar as possible; nothing will lose an audience faster than hemming and hawing or drowning your position in a sea of qualifications. At the same time, in most academic contexts (as well as many others), a position stated baldly with no qualifications or nuances may alienate many readers.

In a syndicated column from 2009, just as the severity of the financial downturn was finally sinking in, *New York Times* columnist Thomas Friedman, writing for an American audience, explained:

> Let's today step out of the normal boundaries of analysis of our economic crisis and ask a radical question: What if the crisis of 2008 represents something much more fundamental than a deep recession? What if it's telling us that the whole growth model we created over the last 50 years is simply unsustainable economically and ecologically and that 2008 was when we hit the wall—when Mother Nature and the market both said: "No more."
>
> We have created a system for growth that depended on our building more and more stores to sell more and more stuff made in more and more factories in China, powered by more and more coal that would cause more and more climate change but earn China more and more dollars to buy more and more U.S. T-bills so Americans would have more and more money to build more and more stores and sell more and more stuff that would employ more and more Chinese. . . .
>
> We can't do this anymore.
>
> —THOMAS FRIEDMAN, "The Inflection Is Near?"

Friedman's position is clear and explicit: Americans' assumptions about their country's economic relationship with China and the behavior growing out of these assumptions must change. Although such a strong position may alienate some readers, all readers have a clear understanding of where Friedman stands.

There are times, however, when you will want to **QUALIFY** your position by using words like *many*, *some*, or *maybe*—or writing *could* rather than *will*. Not every position you take can be stated with absolute certainty, and a qualified claim is generally easier to support than an unqualified one. When LeBron

James announced that he would leave the Cleveland Cavaliers to join the Los Angeles Lakers, many argued that this move would be a great boon to the LA economy. See how one writer for *Fortune* was careful to qualify that position:

> LeBron James' move to Los Angeles is expected to have more than just an impact on the Lakers—a once-dominant team that has sagged in recent years. His move might also boost the local economy. According to a study conducted by legal document website FormSwift in February, LeBron James will likely have a positive economic impact on the food and drink industries in Los Angeles based on data from the previous cities he's called home, including Cleveland and Miami, before and after he left.
>
> —SARAH GRAY, "Why LeBron James' Move to
> Los Angeles Could Boost the City's Economy"

Gray's position is clear—LeBron James's move to Los Angeles will have a positive effect on the economy—but she is careful to qualify that claim so as not to overstate it. Note that she says James's move is *expected* to have an impact, *might* improve the LA economy, and *will likely* add growth to the local food and drink industries.

Keep in mind that while it may be useful, even necessary, to qualify a statement, you should be careful not to overdo it. You don't want to sound unsure of your position.

A Response to What Others Have Said or Done

Crucially, position papers respond to other positions. That is, they are motivated by something that has been said or done by others—and are part of an ongoing conversation. In the *New York Times* example, Thomas Friedman explicitly questions a popular position—namely that despite the current economic downturn, Americans and people around the world will eventually be able to continue the patterns of consumption they have created over the past few decades. His response is a rejection of this position, signaled with his emphatic "we can't do this anymore."

In some cases, the position the author is responding to becomes part of the argument. The music video "Immigrants (We Get the Job Done)," produced by Lin-Manuel Miranda and released in the aftermath of the 2016 presidential election, uses this strategy. Viewed more than

5 million times on *YouTube*, the video features four well-known rappers from around the world responding to the vilification of immigrants by making a case for how much immigrants contribute to the United States. The video begins by acknowledging the debate and the lyrics are punctuated throughout by a chorus with a clear position: "Immigrants, we get the job done. Look how far I come." The video's argument is an explicit response to those who think that *immigrant* is a "bad word." In fact, Lin-Manuel Miranda even described the video as "musical counterweight" to the xenophobia and criticism of immigrants at the time it was written.

Later in this chapter, you will meet Katherine Spriggs, who staked out a position on "buying local" in an essay written for one of her college courses. In this brief excerpt from her essay, she responds directly to those who say buying local will have negative environmental effects:

> It has also been argued that buying locally will be detrimental to the environment because small farms are not as efficient in their use of resources as large farms. This is a common misconception and actually depends on how economists measure efficiency. Small farms are less efficient than large farms in the total output of one crop per acre, but they are more efficient in total output of all crops per acre (McCauley).
>
> —KATHERINE SPRIGGS, "On Buying Local"

In a short space, Spriggs identifies an argument that others have made about the position she is taking and then responds to it explicitly. In academic position papers, authors are expected to acknowledge and address other positions directly in this way. That is often not the case when you take a position in other contexts and in some cultures. In online writing, for instance, it's not unusual for authors to simply provide a brief mention with a link to refer readers to another position within an ongoing conversation.

REFLECT. Think about your writing as part of a larger, ongoing conversation. Examine something that you have recently written—an email, a tweet, an essay for a class—that expresses a position about an issue that matters to you. Check to see whether it makes clear your motivation for writing and the position(s) to which you were responding. If these aren't clear, try revising your text to make them more explicit.

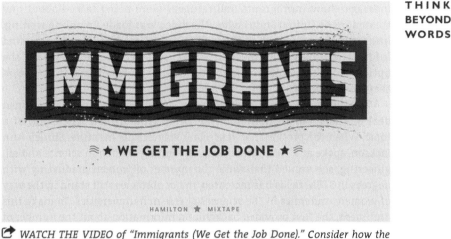

HAMILTON ★ MIXTAPE

🔗 *WATCH THE VIDEO of "Immigrants (We Get the Job Done)." Consider how the medium—video, with the addition of music by diverse performers, a radio voice-over at the start, and images of immigrant experiences—contributes to the power of the argument. Find the link to view the full video at everyonesanauthor.tumblr.com.*

Appropriate Background Information

The amount of background information needed—historical background, definitions, contextual information—will vary widely depending on the scope of your topic, your audience, and your medium. If you are preparing a position paper on the effects of global warming for an environmental group, any background information provided will represent extensive, often detailed, and sometimes highly technical knowledge. If, on the other hand, you are preparing a poster to display on campus that summarizes your position on an increase in tuition, you can probably assume your audience will need little background information—for which you will have only limited space anyway.

The "Immigrants (We Get the Job Done)" video, as a music video partly intended to entertain, provided no background information other than the radio voice-over that sounds like a news broadcast indicating "you know, and it gets into this whole issue of border security" and "we've got the House and the Senate debating this issue." The video's creators assume the viewers will know about the context of the video's message—how immigrants and refugees were being talked about and treated in the United States when the video was made. In online writing, links can often do much of the work of filling readers in on background information; they are especially convenient because readers have the option of clicking on them or not, depending on how much information they need or want.

In academic contexts, writers are generally expected to provide a great deal of background information to firmly ground their discussion of a topic. When the president of Rensselaer Polytechnic Institute, Shirley Ann Jackson, spoke at a 2011 symposium celebrating women in science and engineering, she argued that while the number of women graduating with degrees in STEM fields has increased, major obstacles still stand in the way of women academics in the sciences at research universities. To make this argument, she first provided background information about the number of women PhDs leaving the research science track:

> Writing for the *New York Times*, Steven Greenhouse noted that, based on a University of California, Berkeley, study, "Keeping Women in the Science Pipeline," women are far more likely than men to " 'leak' out of the research science pipeline before obtaining tenure at a college or university." After receiving a PhD, married women with young children are 35 percent less likely to enter a tenure-track position in science than are married men with young children and PhDs in science. According to the report from the University of California, "women who had children after becoming postdoctoral scholars were twice as likely as their male counterparts to shift their career goals away from being professors with a research emphasis—a 41 percent shift for women versus 20 percent for men." And a 2005 report from Virginia Tech found a disproportionate share of women made up "voluntary departures" from the faculty. Although women represented one-fifth of the faculty, they accounted for two-fifths of departures.
>
> At every step along the way—from entering college as a science or engineering major to graduating with a technical degree, from entering graduate school to exiting successfully, to getting a postdoc, to succeeding as faculty, to attaining tenure—we need to provide women with bridges to the next level. As is clear from the studies I mentioned, the unequal burden of family life turns the gaps in the road into chasms. Help

with childcare, which has been provided at MIT, and the establishment of parental childbirth leave, which has been provided at Rensselaer, can help. But there is more to be done.

—SHIRLEY ANN JACKSON, "Leaders in Science
and Engineering: The Women of MIT"

Hearing about specific research studies helps Jackson's audience see that a disproportionately high number of women scientists are "shift[ing] their career goals away from being professors with a research emphasis"—and supports her argument that universities must do more to ease the "unequal burden of family life" that young women scientists bear.

Background information is not always statistical and impersonal, even in academic contexts. In an essay written for *Academe*, a publication of the American Association of University Professors, Randall Hicks, a professor of chemistry at Wheaton College, argues that it is harder for working-class students to become professors than it is for children of

Many women are earning degrees in STEM fields, and universities need to do more to help young women scientists balance the demands of family life and scientific research.

college-educated parents. The background information he provides is startlingly personal:

> "I'll break his goddamned hands," my father said. I wonder if he remembers saying it. Nearly twenty-five years later, his words still linger in my mind. My father had spent the entire day in the auto body shop only to come home and head to the garage for more work on the side. I may have finished my homework, and, tired of roughhousing with my brother, gone out to help him scrape the paint off his current project, some classic car that he was restoring. "It's okay for a hobby, but if somebody tells me that he's thinking of doing it for a living, I'll break his goddamned hands." Although we had no firm plans and little financial means to do so, he was telling me that he expected me to get an education.
>
> —RANDALL HICKS

Note how this story provides readers with important background information for Hicks's argument. Immediately, we learn relevant information about him and the environment that shaped him. Thus, we understand part of his passionate commitment to this topic: he learned, indirectly, from his father to put a high value on education, since doing so in his father's view would allow Hicks to get a job that would be better than something that is just "okay for a hobby."

A Clear Indication of Why the Topic Matters

No matter the topic, one of an author's tasks is to demonstrate that the issue is real and significant—and thus to motivate readers to read on or listeners to keep listening. Rarely can you assume your audience sees why your argument matters.

As a student, you'll sometimes be assigned to write a position paper on a particular topic; in those cases, you may have to find ways to make the topic interesting for you, as the writer, although you can assume the topic matters to the person who assigned it. On other occasions, you may take it upon yourself to write about something you care deeply about, in which case you will need to help your audience understand why they should care as well.

See how Mellody Hobson, president of an investment firm and a board member of Starbucks, JPMorgan Chase, and other prominent companies, begins her 2014 TED talk with a personal story that is meant to illus-

Mellody Hobson calls on businesses "not to be color blind but to be color brave."

trate why Americans need to talk about race—and why that conversation matters:

> So it's 2006. My friend Harold Ford calls me. He's running for U.S. Senate in Tennessee, and he says, "Mellody, I desperately need some national press. Do you have any ideas?" So I had an idea. I called a friend who was in New York at one of the most successful media companies in the world, and she said, "Why don't we host an editorial board lunch for Harold? You come with him."
>
> Harold and I arrive in New York. We are in our best suits. We look like shiny new pennies. And we get to the receptionist, and we say, "We're here for the lunch." She motions for us to follow her. We walk through a series of corridors, and all of a sudden we find ourselves in a stark room, at which point she looks at us and she says, "Where are your uniforms?"
>
> Just as this happens, my friend rushes in. The blood drains from her face. There are literally no words, right? And I look at her, and I say, "Now, don't you think we need more than one black person in the U.S. Senate?"
>
> —MELLODY HOBSON, "Color Blind or Color Brave?"

By sharing this story about how she and Ford were assumed to be kitchen staff on the basis of their race, Hobson establishes in a vivid and distressing way why her topic matters—and she uses the fact that this story makes people uncomfortable to show precisely why it is so important that we talk about race. She then goes on to cite statistics about how few people of color hold board seats in corporate America, driving home for her audience the need for this conversation in concrete terms. Like many writers of academic arguments, Hobson uses personal, statistical, and historical data to demonstrate why her argument matters.

The creators of the "Immigrants (We Get the Job Done)" video certainly believed immigrants matter, as demonstrated in the values they appealed to and the range of people they included in the video. Similarly, Thomas Friedman certainly thinks America's response to the economic downturn that began in 2008 is important. When he writes that the 2008 crisis might be "something much more fundamental than a deep recession" and "the whole growth model . . . is simply unsustainable," his tone in these broad assertions conveys a sense of urgency. In all these cases, the writers share the conviction that what they're writing about matters not just to them but to us all, and they work hard to make that conviction evident.

REFLECT. Examine something you've written that takes a strong position. Catalog the specific ways you make clear to your readers that the topic matters to you—and that it should matter to them.

Good Reasons and Evidence

Positions are only as good as the reasons and evidence that support them, so part of every author's task in arguing a position is to provide the strongest possible reasons for the position, and evidence for those reasons. Evidence may take many forms, but among the most often used, especially in academic contexts, are facts; firsthand material gathered from observations, interviews, or surveys; data from experiments; historical data; examples; expert testimony (often in the form of what scholars have written); precedents; statistics; and personal experience.

In an essay from the *New York Times* op-ed page, Jennifer Delahunty, dean of admissions at Kenyon College, seeks to explain to her own daughter why one of her daughter's college applications had been rejected.

Delahunty's explanation—the position her essay takes—is that the rejection was due at least in part to the fact that young women, even accomplished ones, face particular challenges in getting into prestigious colleges:

> She had not . . . been named a National Merit Finalist, dug a well for a village in Africa or climbed to the top of Mount Rainier. She is a smart, well-meaning, hard-working teenage girl, but in this day and age of swollen applicant pools that are decidedly female, that wasn't enough. . . .
>
> Had she been a male applicant, there would have been little, if any, hesitation to admit. The reality is that because young men are rarer, they're more valued applicants. Today, two-thirds of colleges and universities report that they get more female than male applicants, and more than 56 percent of undergraduates nationwide are women.
>
> —JENNIFER DELAHUNTY, "To All the Girls I've Rejected"

Delahunty offers two related reasons that her daughter had not been admitted. First, for all her daughter's accomplishments, they were not as impressive as those of other applicants. Here she provides specific evidence (her daughter was not a National Merit finalist, nor had she "dug a well for a village in Africa or climbed to the top of Mount Rainier") that makes the reason memorable and convincing.

The second reason focuses on the fact that male applicants in general have a better chance than female applicants of getting into many schools. This time her evidence is of a different sort; she uses statistics to show that "young men are rarer" and therefore "more valued applicants." Note that Delahunty expects readers to share her knowledge that something seen as valuable takes on additional value when it is rare.

The scientific community typically takes the long view in terms of gathering evidence in support of the positions it takes. Certainly that was true in the case of smoking, when decades of research paved the way for a statement on the relationship between smoking and cancer. The 1964 surgeon general's report on the health consequences of smoking notes:

> The U.S. Public Health Service first became officially engaged in an appraisal of the available data on smoking and health in June, 1956, when, under the instigation of the Surgeon General, a scientific Study Group on the subject was established jointly by the National Cancer Institute,

the National Heart Institute, the American Cancer Society, and the American Heart Association. After appraising sixteen independent studies carried on in five countries over a period of eighteen years, this group concluded that there is a causal relationship between excessive smoking of cigarettes and lung cancer.

—*Smoking and Health: Report of the Advisory Committee of the Surgeon General of the Public Health Service*

In this case, the surgeon general's study group analyzed evidence gathered over eighteen years from a range of research conducted by multiple scholars before reaching its conclusion.

Attention to More than One Point of View

Considering multiple, often opposing, points of view is a hallmark of any strong position paper, particularly in an academic context. By showing that you understand and have carefully evaluated other viewpoints, you show respect for the issue's complexity and for your audience, while also showing that you have done your homework on your topic.

In a journal article on human-caused climate change, Naomi Oreskes takes a position based on a careful analysis of 928 scientific articles published in well-known and respected journals. Some people, she says, "suggest that there might be substantive disagreement in the scientific community about the reality of anthropogenic climate change. This is not the case." Yet in spite of the very strong consensus on which Oreskes bases her claim, she still acknowledges other possible viewpoints:

> Admittedly, [some] authors evaluating impacts, developing methods, or studying paleoclimatic change might believe that current climate change is natural. . . . The scientific consensus might, of course, be wrong. If the history of science teaches anything, it is humility, and no one can be faulted for failing to act on what is not known.
>
> —NAOMI ORESKES, "Beyond the Ivory Tower: The Scientific Consensus on Climate Change"

Oreskes acknowledges that the consensus she found in the articles she examined might be challenged by other articles she did not consider and that any consensus, no matter how strong, might ultimately prove to be wrong. Thus does she remain respectful of those members of the scientific community who may hold other views.

Sometimes you'll want to both acknowledge and reply to other viewpoints, especially if you can answer any objections persuasively. Here is college admissions officer Jennifer Delahunty, noting—and ruling out—the possible criticism that college admissions officers do not give careful consideration to all applicants:

> Rest assured that admissions officers are not cavalier in making their decisions. Last week, the 10 officers at my college sat around a table, 12 hours every day, deliberating the applications of hundreds of talented young men and women. While gulping down coffee and poring over statistics, we heard about a young woman from Kentucky we were not yet ready to admit outright. She was the leader/president/editor/captain/ lead actress in every activity in her school. She had taken six advanced placement courses and had been selected for a prestigious state leadership program. In her free time, this whirlwind of achievement had accumulated more than 300 hours of community service in four different organizations.
>
> Few of us sitting around the table were as talented and as directed at age 17 as this young woman. Unfortunately, her test scores and grade point average placed her in the middle of our pool. We had to have a debate before we decided to swallow the middling scores and write "admit" next to her name.
>
> —JENNIFER DELAHUNTY, "To All the Girls I've Rejected"

Delahunty provides evidence from a specific case, demonstrating persuasively that the admissions officers at her college take their job seriously.

Even bumper stickers can subtly acknowledge more than one position, as does this one from late 2008:

> I Support Our Troops / I Question Our Policies

This bumper sticker states two positions that initially might seem contradictory, arguing that supporting the country's troops and questioning our government's foreign policies are not mutually exclusive.

An Authoritative Tone

Particularly in academic contexts, authors make a point of taking an authoritative tone. Even if your goal is to encourage readers to examine a number of alternatives without suggesting which one is best, you should try to do so in a way that shows you know which alternatives are worth examining and why. Likewise, even if you are taking a strong position, you should seek to appear reasonable and rational. The 1964 surgeon general's report on the consequences of smoking does not waver: smoking causes cancer. At the same time, in taking this position, it briefly outlines the history of the issue and the evidence on which the claim is logically based, avoiding emotional language and carefully specifying which forms of smoking ("excessive" cigarettes) and cancer (lung) the claim involves.

Jennifer Delahunty establishes her authority in other ways. Her description of ten admissions officers putting in twelve-hour days going through hundreds of applications and "poring over statistics" backs up her forthright assertion, "Rest assured that admissions officers are not cavalier in making their decisions." Later in the essay, acknowledging her own struggles to weigh issues of fairness to highly qualified young women against the need to maintain gender balance in incoming classes, Delahunty not only demonstrates that she knows what she is writing about but also invites readers to think about the complexity of the situation without offering them any easy answers. In short, she is simultaneously reasonable and authoritative.

An Appeal to Readers' Values

Implicitly or explicitly, authors need to appeal to readers' values, especially when taking a strong position. The creators of the "Immigrants (We Get the Job Done)" video clearly appealed to a number of cultural values Americans hold dear, such as work ethic and opportunity (with references to the demanding kinds of work immigrants do to survive—picking oranges, sewing textiles, nursing the ill, constructing buildings) as well as equality, justice, and hope (depictions of harrowing migration journeys and confrontations with border agents). The refrain "Immigrants, we get the job done" is itself a strong appeal to the audience's sense of fairness and democratic ideals.

Freeman A. Hrabowski III, president of the University of Maryland, Baltimore County, appeals to similar values of opportunity, equality, and democracy in a 2015 essay in *Inside Higher Ed*. His essay responds to the riots in Baltimore that spring, sparked by the death of a black man, Freddie Gray, while in police custody, but which also aired the grievances of a community with a long history of poverty and little opportunity.

> As one of my students said to me recently, the Baltimore story—which is the American story—should remind us that issues related to poverty and inequality, crime and opportunity are not about "those people." They are about us—all of us. How we react to events like those in Baltimore speaks volumes about our values. We know we must do much better, especially for people who have not had a chance to thrive in our society. Americans—not just in Baltimore but across the country—have an opportunity now to ask difficult questions and take long-term action. . . . Historically, one of America's greatest strengths has been our ability to look squarely at our problems and to make hard changes. To do so often requires struggle, and we have a responsibility to embrace that struggle. To do so is a fundamental part of the learning and growing process—and it is fundamental to changing issues of systemic injustice and inequality that are neither new nor isolated.
>
> —FREEMAN A. HRABOWSKI III, "After the Cameras Leave"

Hrabowski appeals to readers' patriotic values of unity and democracy, saying that these issues aren't just about certain communities in Baltimore, but "about us—all of us." He goes on to call for universities to engage with underprivileged communities, upholding the American ideal of hard work and "struggle" that has led the nation to face difficult problems throughout its history. Writing for *Inside Higher Ed*, Hrabowski was addressing a vast audience of educators—and his text appeals to a wide set of values he can assume his readers to hold: the spirit of the American nation.

Online contexts are particularly interesting for considering appeals to values since you can rarely be sure who your actual readers are, and you certainly can't control who will see a text you create. Yet appealing to values is no less important in online situations and may, in fact, take on a greater role in arguing positions effectively. In this case, writers often seek to create their ideal audience through the words and images they choose. Online environments remind us that as writers, we are always imagining who our audience is and appealing to what we imagine their values to be.

RUSSEL HONORÉ wrote this essay for *This I Believe*, a not-for-profit organization that sponsors "a public dialogue about belief, one essay at a time." The essay was later broadcast on *NPR's Weekend Edition* on March 1, 2009. Honoré is a retired lieutenant general in the US Army who has contributed to response efforts to Hurricanes Katrina and Rita in 2005 and other natural disasters.

Work Is a Blessing

RUSSEL HONORÉ

I GREW UP IN Lakeland, Louisiana, one of 12 children. We all lived on my parents' subsistence farm. We grew cotton, sugarcane, corn, hogs, chickens and had a large garden, but it didn't bring in much cash. So when I was 12, I got a part-time job on a dairy farm down the road, helping to milk cows. We milked 65 cows at 5 in the morning and again at 2 in the afternoon, seven days a week.

Background information.

In the kitchen one Saturday before daylight, I remember complaining to my father and grandfather about having to go milk those cows. My father said, "Ya know, boy, to work is a blessing."

A position taken in response to another position.

I looked at those two men who'd worked harder than I ever had—my father eking out a living on that farm and my grandfather farming and working as a carpenter during the Depression. I had a feeling I had been told something really important, but it took many years before it sunk in.

Admitting his own slowness to understand what his father meant contributes to his authoritative tone.

Going to college was a rare privilege for a kid from Lakeland, Louisiana. My father told me if I picked something to study that I liked doing, I'd always look forward to my work. But he also added, "Even having a job you hate is better than not having a job at all." I wanted to be a farmer, but I joined the ROTC program to help pay for college. And what started out as an obligation to the Army became a way of life that I stayed committed to for 37 years, three months and three days.

Citing his father, Honoré shows his attention to more than one point of view about work.

In the late 1980s, during a visit to Bangladesh, I saw a woman with a baby on her back, breaking bricks with a hammer. I asked a Bangladesh military escort why they weren't using a machine, which would have been a lot easier. He told me a machine would put that lady out of work. Breaking those bricks meant she'd earn enough money to feed herself and her baby that day. And as bad as that woman's job was, it was enough to keep a small family alive. It reminded me of my father's words: To work is a blessing.

Reasons and evidence for how the author came to see work as a blessing.

Serving in the United States Army overseas, I saw a lot of people like that woman in Bangladesh. And I have come to believe that people without jobs are not free. They are victims of crime, the ideology of terrorism, poor health, depression and social unrest. These victims become the illegal immigrants, the slaves of human trafficking, the drug dealers, the street gang members. I've seen it over and over again on the U.S. border, in Somalia, the Congo, Afghanistan and in New Orleans. People who have jobs can have a home, send their kids to school, develop a sense of pride, contribute to the good of the community, and even help others. When we can work, we're free. We're blessed.

Specific examples indicate why the topic matters and show the author's awareness of his audience's values.

I don't think I'll ever quit working. I'm retired from the Army, but I'm still working to help people be prepared for disaster. And I may get to do a little farming someday, too. I'm not going to stop. I believe in my father's words. I believe in the blessing of work.

The author concludes by stating his position explicitly.

⮌ Listen to the audio essay at everyonesanauthor .tumblr.com. You'll hear someone who sounds like he grew up on a farm in Louisiana, a fact that contributes to Honoré's authority: this guy knows what he's talking about.

≈⊙ *REFLECT. Choose a short piece of writing on a website such as* Salon *that takes a position on an issue you care about. Look at the list of characteristic features on page 147 and annotate your text to point out the ones that are represented in it, using Honoré's essay as a model. Make a list of any features that are not included as well. (While not every effective position paper will include all of the characteristic features, many of them will.) Then consider whether including those features might have improved the text—and if so, how.*

ARGUING A POSITION / A Roadmap

Choose a topic that matters—to you, and to others

If you get to select your topic, begin by examining your own interests and commitments in light of the context you are writing for. Global warming might be an appropriate topic for a course in the life sciences or social sciences, but it's probably not going to serve you well in a course in medieval history unless you can find a direct link between the two topics. You might consider focusing on some issue that's being debated on campus (Are those new rules for dropping classes fair?), a broader political or ethical issue (Is eating meat by definition unethical?), or an issue in which you have a direct stake (Does early admission penalize those who need financial aid?).

If you've been assigned a topic, do your best to find an aspect of it that interests you. (If you're bored with your subject, you can be sure your readers will be.) If, for example, you're assigned to write about globalization in a required international studies course, you could tailor that topic to your own interests and write about the influence of American hip-hop on world music.

Be sure that your topic is one that is arguable—and that it matters. Short of astounding new evidence, it's no longer worth arguing that there is no link between smoking and lung cancer. It's a fact. But you can argue about what responsibility tobacco companies now have for tobacco-related deaths, as recent court cases demonstrate.

One sure way to find out whether a topic is arguable is to see if it *is* being debated—and that is a good first step as you explore a topic. You can probably assume that any topic that's being widely discussed matters—and of course you'll want to know what's being said about it in order to write about it. Remember that your essay is part of a larger conversation about your topic: you need to become familiar with that conversation in order to contribute to it.

Be careful to keep an open mind. A good, arguable topic will surely trigger at least several different points of view. Keeping an open mind and considering those points of view fairly and carefully at the start is always a good idea. And it will make your argument stronger by showing that you can be trusted to consider all sides of an issue, especially those you may not agree with.

Consider your rhetorical situation

Looking at your audience, your purpose, and other aspects of your rhetorical situation will help you to think carefully about how to achieve your goals.

Focus on your **AUDIENCE**. Who are you trying to reach, and what do you hope to persuade them to think or do?

- What are they likely to know about your topic, and what background information will you need to provide?
- How are they like or unlike you—and one another? Consider such things as age, education, gender, abilities and disabilities, cultural and linguistic heritage, and so on. How will such factors influence the way you make your argument?
- What convictions might they hold about the topic you're addressing— and how sympathetic are they likely to be to your position?

If you're trying to convince your fellow business majors of the virtues of free-market capitalism, your task is quite different than if you're trying to convince members of the campus socialist organization. In the first case, you would almost surely be preaching to the choir, whereas in the second, you would likely face a more skeptical audience.

Keep in mind that there's always danger in speaking only to those who already agree with you; if you keep audiences with differing values and viewpoints in mind, you will be more likely to represent all views fairly and hence encourage others to consider your position seriously. Keeping your audience in mind, then, means thinking in terms of who may respond to your position, how they will likely respond, and why.

Think hard about your **PURPOSE**. Why are you arguing this position? What has motivated you to write on this topic? What do you hope to learn by writing about it? What do you want to convince your audience to think or do? How can you best achieve your purpose or purposes?

Think about your **STANCE**. Start by asking yourself where you are coming from in regard to this topic. What about the topic captured your interest, and how has that interest led you to the position you expect to take on it? Why do you think the topic matters? How would you describe your attitude toward the topic: are you an advocate, a critic, an observer, an apologist, or something else? How do you want to be seen as an author—as forceful? thoughtful? curious? How can you establish your own authority in writing on this topic?

Consider the larger **CONTEXT**. What are the various perspectives on the issue? What have others said about it? If you're writing about the use of ethanol as a fuel source, for instance, you'll need to look at what circumstances led to its use, at who's supported and opposed it (and why), and at the economic ramifications both of producing ethanol for fuel and of not doing so. As you come to understand the larger context, you'll become aware of various positions you'll want to consider, and what factors will be important to consider as you develop your position.

Consider your MEDIUM. Will your writing take the form of a print essay? Will it appear as an editorial in a local paper? on a website? as an audio essay to be broadcast on a local radio station or posted as a podcast? as an oral or multimedia presentation for a class you are taking? The medium you choose should be one that suits both your purpose and your audience.

Consider matters of DESIGN. Think about the "look" you want to achieve and how you can format your text to make it easy to follow. Do you need headings? illustrations? any other graphics? color? Does the discipline you're writing in have any conventions you should follow? Does your medium allow for certain elements such as audio or video links that will help you achieve your purpose?

Research your topic

Begin exploring the topic by looking at it from different points of view. Whatever position you take will ultimately be more credible and persuasive if you can show evidence of having considered other positions.

Begin by assessing what you know—and don't know—about the topic. What interests you about the topic, and why? What more do you want or need to find out about it? What questions do you have about it, and where might you go for answers? To answer these questions, you might try BRAINSTORMING or other activities for GENERATING IDEAS.

What have others said? What are some of the issues that are being debated now about your topic, and what are the various positions on these issues? What other POSITIONS might be taken with respect to the topic? Remember, too, to seek out sources that represent a variety of perspectives.

Where should you start your research? Where you start and what sources you consult depend upon your topic and what questions you have about it. If you are focusing on a current issue, turn to news media and to websites, listservs, *Twitter*, or other online groups devoted to the issue. If you are investigating a topic from the distant past, be sure to look for both older sources and more recent scholarship on the topic. For some issues, you might want to interview experts or conduct other sorts of **FIELD RESEARCH**.

Do you need to cut your topic down to size? Few among us know enough to make strong general claims about global warming. While that fact does not and should not keep us from having opinions about the issue, it suggests that the existence of global warming is much too broad a topic to be appropriate for a five-page essay. Instead, you'll need to focus on some aspect of that topic for your essay. What angle you take will depend on the course you're writing for. For a geology class, you might focus on the effects of rising temperatures on melting glaciers; for an international relations course, you could look at climate shift and national security debates. Just remember that your goal is to take an informed position, one that you can support well.

Formulate an explicit position

Once you have sufficient information about your topic and some understanding of the complexity of the issue, you'll need to formulate a position that you can state explicitly and support fully. Let's say you decide to take a position on a current controversy among scientists about climate change. Here's how one author formulated a position:

> Many scientists have argued that climate change has led to bigger and more destructive hurricanes and typhoons. Other researchers, however, have countered by saying that climate change is not linked causally to an increase in hurricane strength. After reviewing both sides of this debate, I see two strong reasons why changes in our climate have not necessarily led to more severe hurricanes.
> —SOFI MINCEY, "On Climate Change and Hurricanes"

These three sentences articulate a clear position—that climate change is not necessarily to blame for bigger hurricanes—and frame that position as a response to an existing debate. Notice also how the writer qualifies her claim: she does not claim definitively that climate change has not led to bigger hurricanes; rather, she promises to present reasons that argue for this view.

By arguing only that the claims of many scientists *may* be wrong, she greatly increases the likelihood that she can succeed in her argument, setting a reasonable goal for what she must achieve. Note that her position still requires support: she needs to present reasonable evidence to challenge the claim that climate change has "necessarily" led to bigger hurricanes.

State your position as a tentative THESIS. Once you formulate your position, try stating it several different ways and then decide which one is most compelling. Make sure the position is stated explicitly—no beating around the bush. Your statement should let your audience know where you stand and be interesting enough to attract their attention.

Then think about whether you should QUALIFY your position. Should you limit what you claim—is it true only sometimes or under certain circumstances? On the other hand, does it seem too weak or timid and need to be stated more forcefully?

Remember that a good thesis for a position paper should identify your specific topic and make a CLAIM about that topic that is debatable. The thesis should also give your audience some idea of your reasons for making this claim. Consider the following thesis statement from two scholars at a public policy institute:

> The case against raising the minimum wage is straightforward: A higher wage makes it more expensive for firms to hire workers.
>
> —KEVIN A. HASSET AND MICHAEL R. STRAIN,
> "Why We Shouldn't Raise the Minimum Wage"

Hasset and Strain's claim about raising the minimum wage is explicitly stated (they are "against" it), as is a major reason for that position.

Come up with REASONS and EVIDENCE. List all the reasons supporting your position that you discovered in your research. Which ones will be most persuasive to your audience? Then jot down all the evidence you have to support those reasons—facts, quotations, statistics, examples, testimony, visuals, and so on. Remember that what counts as evidence varies across audiences and disciplines. Some are persuaded by testimonials, while others want statistical data. Finally, look for any FALLACIES or weak reasons or evidence, and decide whether you need to do further research.

Identify other positions. Carefully consider COUNTERARGUMENTS and other points of view on the topic and how you will account for them. At the very least, you need to acknowledge other positions that are prominent in the larger conversation about the topic and to treat them fairly. If you disagree with a position, you need to offer reasons why and to do so respectfully.

Organize and start writing

Once you have a fair sense of how you will present your position, it's time to write out a draft. If you have trouble getting started, it might help to think about the larger conversation about the topic that's already going on—and to think of your draft as a moment when you get to say what *you* think.

Be guided by your THESIS. As you begin to organize, type it at the top of your page so that you can keep looking back to it to be sure that each part of your text supports the thesis.

Give REASONS for your position, with supporting EVIDENCE. Determine an order for presenting your reasons, perhaps starting with the one you think will speak most directly to your audience.

Don't forget to consider COUNTERARGUMENTS. Acknowledge positions other than your own, and respond to what they say.

Draft an OPENING. Introduce your topic, and provide any background information your audience may need. State your position clearly, perhaps as a response to what others have said about your topic. Say something about why the issue matters, why your audience should care.

Draft a CONCLUSION. You might want to end by summing up your position and by answering the "so what" question: why does your topic matter—and who cares? Make sure you give a strong takeaway message. What are the implications of your argument? What do you want readers to remember or do as a result of reading what you've written?

Look critically at your draft, get response—and revise

Go through your draft carefully, looking critically at the position you stake out, the reasons and evidence you provide in support of it, and the way you present them to your audience. For this review, play the "doubting game" with yourself by asking "Who says?" and "So what?" and "Can this be done better?" at every point.

Being tough on yourself now will pay off by showing you where you need to shore up your arguments. As you work through your draft, make notes on what you plan to do in your revision.

Next, ask some classmates or friends to read and respond to your draft. Here are some questions that can help you or others read over a draft of writing that takes a position.

- *Is the position stated explicitly?* Is there a clear **THESIS** sentence—and if not, is one needed? Does it need to be qualified, or should it be stated more strongly?

- *What positions are you responding to?* What is the larger conversation?

- *Is it clear why the topic matters?* Why do you care about the topic, and why should your audience care?

- *How effective is the* **OPENING***?* How does it capture your audience's interest? How else might you begin?

- *Is there sufficient background information?* What other information might the audience need?

- *How would you describe the* **STANCE** *and* **TONE** —and are they appropriate to your audience and purpose? Does the tone seem both authoritative and reasonable?

- *What* **REASONS** *do you give for the position, and what* **EVIDENCE** *do you provide for those reasons?* What are the strongest reasons and evidence given? the weakest? What other evidence or reasons are needed to support this position?

- *How trustworthy are the sources you've cited?* Are **QUOTATIONS**, **SUMMARIES**, and **PARAPHRASES** smoothly integrated into the text—and is it clear where you are speaking and where (and why) you are citing others?

- *What other positions do you consider, and do you treat them fairly?* Are there other **COUNTERARGUMENTS** you should address as well? How well do you answer possible objections to your position?

- *How is the draft organized?* Is it easy to follow, with clear **TRANSITIONS** from one point to the next? Are there headings—and if not, would they help? What about the organization could be improved?

- *Is the STYLE appropriate to the audience and purpose?* Could the style—choice of words, kinds of sentences—be improved in any way?

- *How effective is your text DESIGN?* Have you used any visuals to support your position—and if so, have you written captions that explain how they contribute to the argument? If not, what visuals might be appropriate? Is there any information that would be easier to follow if it were presented in a chart or table?

- *How does the draft CONCLUDE?* Is the conclusion forceful and memorable? How else might you conclude?

- *Consider the title.* Does it make clear what the text is about, and does it make a reader want to read on?

- *What is your overall impression of the draft?* Will it persuade your audience to accept the position—and if not, why? Even if they don't accept the position, would they consider it a plausible one?

Revise your draft in light of your own observations and any feedback from others—keeping your audience and purpose firmly in mind, as always.

REFLECT. Once you've completed your essay, let it settle for a while before you look back at it with a critical eye. How well did you argue your point? What additional revisions would you make if you could? Research shows that such reflections help "lock in" what you learn for future use.

Delete Your Social Media Accounts Right Now
JARON LANIER

L ET'S START WITH cats.

Cats are everywhere online. They make the memiest memes and the cutest videos.

Why cats more than dogs?

Dogs didn't come to ancient humans begging to live with us; we domesticated them. They've been bred to be obedient. They take to training and they are predictable. They work for us. That's not to say anything against dogs. It's great that they're loyal and dependable.

Cats are different. They came along and partly domesticated themselves. 5 They are not predictable. Popular dog videos tend to show off training, while the most wildly popular cat videos are the ones that capture weird and surprising behaviors.

Cats are smart, but not a great choice if you want an animal that takes to training reliably. Watch a cat circus online, and what's so touching is that the cats are clearly making their own minds up about whether to do a trick they've learned, or to do nothing, or to wander into the audience.

JARON LANIER, often referred to as the "father of virtual reality," is a scientist, musician, and writer who focuses on virtual reality and advocates for sustainable economics in a digital world. He is the author of *Who Owns the Future* and *You Are Not a Gadget*. His book *Dawn of the New Everything* was named one of the best books of 2017 by the *Wall Street Journal* and the *Economist*. This piece is from his 2018 book, *Ten Arguments for Deleting Your Social Media Accounts Right Now*.

Cats have done the seemingly impossible: They've integrated themselves into the modern high-tech world without giving themselves up. They are still in charge. There is no worry that some stealthy meme crafted by algorithms and paid for by a creepy, hidden oligarch has taken over your cat. No one has taken over your cat; not you, not anyone.

Oh, how we long to have that certainty not just about our cats, but about ourselves! Cats on the internet are our hopes and dreams for the future of people on the internet.

Meanwhile, even though we love dogs, we don't want to *be* dogs, at least in terms of power relationships with people, and we're afraid Facebook and the like are turning us into dogs. When we are triggered to do something crappy online, we might call it a response to a "dog whistle." Dog whistles can only be heard by dogs. We worry that we're falling under stealthy control.

This is about how to be a cat. How can you remain autonomous in a world 10 where you are under constant surveillance and are constantly prodded by algorithms run by some of the richest corporations in history, which have no way of making money except by being paid to manipulate your behavior? How can you be a cat, despite that?

Something entirely new is happening in the world. Just in the last five or ten years, nearly everyone started to carry a little device called a smartphone on their person all the time that's suitable for algorithmic behavior modification. A lot of us are also using related devices called smart speakers on our kitchen counters or in our car dashboards. We're being tracked and measured constantly, and receiving engineered feedback all the time. We're being hypnotized little by little by technicians we can't see, for purposes we don't know. We're all lab animals now.

Algorithms gorge on data about you, every second. What kinds of links do you click on? What videos do you watch all the way through? How quickly are you moving from one thing to the next? Where are you when you do these things? Who are you connecting with in person and online? What facial expressions do you make? How does your skin tone change in different situations? What were you doing just before you decided to buy something or not? Whether to vote or not?

All these measurements and many others have been matched up with similar readings about the lives of multitudes of other people through massive spying. Algorithms correlate what you do with what almost everyone else has done.

The algorithms don't really understand you, but there is power in numbers, especially in large numbers. If a lot of other people who like the foods you like were also more easily put off by pictures of a candidate portrayed in a pink border instead of a blue one, then you *probably* will be too, and no one needs to know why. Statistics are reliable, but only as idiot demons.

Are you sad, lonely, scared? Happy, confident? Getting your period? Experiencing a peak of class anxiety? 15

So-called advertisers can seize the moment when you are perfectly primed and then influence you with messages that have worked on other people who share traits and situations with you.

I say "so-called" because it's just not right to call direct manipulation of people advertising. Advertisers used to have a limited chance to make a pitch, and that pitch might have been sneaky or annoying, but it was fleeting. Furthermore, lots of people saw the same TV or print ad; it wasn't adapted to individuals. The biggest difference was that you weren't monitored and assessed all the time so that you could be fed dynamically optimized stimuli—whether "content" or ad—to engage and alter you.

Now everyone who is on social media is getting individualized, continuously adjusted stimuli, without a break, so long as they use their smartphones. What might once have been called advertising must now be understood as continuous behavior modification on a titanic scale.

Please don't be insulted. Yes, I am suggesting that you might be turning, just a little, into a well-trained dog, or something less pleasant, like a lab rat or a robot. That you're being remote-controlled, just a little, by clients of big corporations. But if I'm right, then becoming aware of it might just free you, so give this a chance, okay?

A scientific movement called behaviorism arose before computers were 20 invented. Behaviorists studied new, more methodical, sterile, and nerdy ways to train animals and humans.

One famous behaviorist was B. F. Skinner. He set up a methodical system, known as a Skinner box, in which caged animals got treats when they did something specific. There wasn't anyone petting or whispering to the animal, just a purely isolated mechanical action—a new kind of training for modern times. Various behaviorists, who often gave off rather ominous vibes, applied this method to people. Behaviorist strategies often worked, which freaked everyone out, eventually leading to a bunch of creepy "mind control" sci-fi and horror movie scripts.

An unfortunate fact is that you can train someone using behaviorist techniques, *and the person doesn't even know it*. Until very recently, this rarely happened unless you signed up to be a test subject in an experiment in the basement of a university's psychology building. Then you'd go into a room and be tested while someone watched you through a one-way mirror. Even though you knew an experiment was going on, you didn't realize *how* you were being manipulated. At least you gave consent to be manipulated in *some* way. (Well, not always. There were all kinds of cruel experiments performed on prisoners, on poor people, and especially on racial targets.)

What has become suddenly normal—pervasive surveillance and constant, subtle manipulation—is unethical, cruel, dangerous, and inhumane. Dangerous? Oh, yes, because who knows who's going to use that power, and for what? . . .

I realize that we live in a world of stunning inequality, and not everyone has the same options. Whoever you are, I hope you have options to explore what your life might be, especially if you are young. You need to make sure your own brain, and your own life, isn't in a rut. Maybe you can go explore wilderness or learn a new skill. Take risks. But whatever form your self-exploration takes, do at least one thing: detach from the behavior-modification empires for a while—six months, say? Note that I didn't name [my] book *Arguments for Deleting Your Social Media Accounts Right Now and Keeping Them Deleted Forever.* After you experiment, you'll know yourself better. Then decide.

➦ See Lanier's TED talk in which he makes a case that we need to remake the internet at everyonesan author.tumblr .com.

Author's Note, March 2018

This book was written primarily during the final months of 2017, but events in 2018 turned out to be explosively relevant. The manuscript was done, done, done—headed to the printer—when the sorry revelations of the Cambridge Analytica scandal fueled a sudden, grassroots movement of people deleting Facebook accounts.

Unfortunately, not all public figures and thought leaders handled the moment with the courage that was required. There were pundits who tried to quit but could not. There were others who pointed out that not everyone is privileged enough to quit, so it felt cruel to leave the less fortunate behind. Others said it was irrelevant to quit because the thing that mattered was pressuring governments to regulate Facebook. Overall, the attitude of professional commentators regarding account deleters was smug and dismissive. And dead wrong.

C'mon people! Yes, being able to quit is a privilege; many genuinely can't. But if you have the latitude to quit and don't, you are not supporting the less fortunate; you are only reinforcing the system in which many people are trapped. I am living proof that you can have a public life in media without social media accounts. Those of us with options must explore those options or they will remain only theoretical. Business follows money, so we who have options have power and responsibility. You, you, you have the affirmative responsibility to invent and demonstrate ways to live without the crap that is destroying society. Quitting is the only way, for now, to learn what can replace our grand mistake.

Thinking about the Text

1. Why does Lanier open his argument with an **ANALOGY** between cats and dogs—and people? How effective do you find this opening strategy and why?

2. Lanier says that he is "living proof that you can have a public life in media without social media accounts." Take a few minutes to look up Lanier and read about his career; do you find that he really has "a public life in media without social media"? How does having a public life, without media, affect his **CREDIBILITY** as an author?

3. Lanier argues that social media train us (like you can train a dog) and that as a result we are losing free will. While Lanier doesn't take up **COUNTERARGUMENTS** in this section of his book, what counterarguments can you offer to his major claim?

4. How would you describe Lanier's **STANCE** and **TONE**? What particular words and phrases lead you to that description?

5. At the end of his book, Lanier makes a final plea: "But whatever form your self-exploration takes, do at least one thing: detach from the behavior-modification empires for a while—six months, say?" Try accepting Lanier's challenge and avoid your accounts—for a week, or even just 24 hours. Then write a few paragraphs describing what you discovered about yourself during this experiment and take a **POSITION** of your own in response in Lanier.

On Buying Local

KATHERINE SPRIGGS

AMERICANS TODAY can eat pears in the spring in Minnesota, oranges in the summer in Montana, asparagus in the fall in Maine, and cranberries in the winter in Florida. In fact, we can eat pretty much any kind of produce anywhere at any time of the year. But what is the cost of this convenience? In this essay, I will explore some answers to this question and argue that we should give up a little bit of convenience in favor of buying local.

"Buying local" means that consumers choose to buy food that has been grown, raised, or produced as close to their homes as possible ("Buy Local"). Buying local is an important part of the response to many environmental issues we face today (fig. I). It encourages the development of small farms, which are often more environmentally sustainable than large farms, and thus strengthens local markets and supports small rural economies. By demonstrating a commitment to buying local, Americans could set an example for global environmentalism.

In 2010, the international community is facing many environmental challenges, including global warming, pollution, and dwindling fossil fuel resources. Global warming is attributed to the release of greenhouse gases such as carbon dioxide and methane, most commonly emitted in the burning of fossil fuels. It is such a pressing problem that scientists estimate that in the year 2030,

KATHERINE SPRIGGS wrote this essay for a writing course she took in her first year at Stanford University.

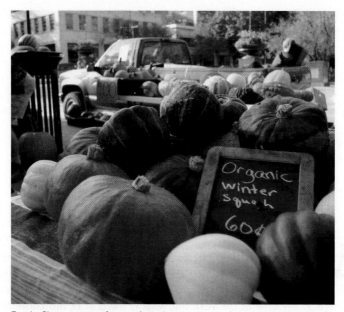

Fig. 1. Shopping at a farmers' market is one good way to support small farms and strengthen the local economy. Photograph from Alamy.

there will be no glaciers left in Glacier National Park ("Global Warming Statistics"). The United States is especially guilty of contributing to the problem, producing about a quarter of all global greenhouse gas emissions, and playing a large part in pollution and shrinking world oil supplies as well ("Record Increase"). According to a CNN article published in 2000, the United States manufactures more than 1.5 billion pounds of chemical pesticides a year that can pollute our water, soil, and air (Baum). Agriculture is particularly interconnected with all of these issues. Almost three-fourths of the pesticides produced in the United States are used in agriculture (Baum). Most produce is shipped many miles before it is sold to consumers, and shipping our food long distances is costly in both the amount of fossil fuel it uses and the greenhouse gases it produces.

A family friend and farmer taught me firsthand about the effects of buying local. Since I was four years old, I have spent every summer on a 150-acre farm in rural Wisconsin, where my family has rented our 75 tillable acres to a farmer who lives nearby. Mr. Lermio comes from a family that has farmed the area for generations. I remember him sitting on our porch at dusk wearing his blue striped overalls and dirty white T-shirt, telling my parents about all of the changes in the area since he was a kid. "Things sure are different around here," he'd say. He told us that all the farms in that region used to milk about 30 head of cattle each. Now he and the other farmers were selling their herds to industrial-scale farms milking 4,000 head each. The shift came when milk started being processed on a large scale rather than at small local cheese factories. Milk is now shipped to just a few large factories where it is either bottled or processed into cheese or other dairy products. The milk and products from these factories are then shipped all across the country. "You see," Mr. Lermio would tell us, "it's just not worth shipping the milk from my 20 cows all the way to Gays Mills. You just can't have a small herd anymore." Farming crops is also different now. Machinery is expensive and hard to pay off with profits from small fields. The Lermio family has been buying and renting fields all around the area, using their tractors to farm hundreds of acres. Because they can no longer sell locally, Mr. Lermio and many other rural farmers have to move towards larger-scale farming to stay afloat.

Buying local could help reverse the trend towards industrial-scale farming, 5 of which the changes in Wisconsin over Mr. Lermio's lifetime are just one

Fig. 2. A small polyculture farm. Photograph from iStockphoto.

example. Buying local benefits small farmers by not forcing them to compete with larger farms across the country. For example, if consumers bought beef locally, beef cattle would be raised in every region and their meat would be sold locally rather than shipped from a small number of big ranches in Texas and Montana. Small farms are often polycultures—they produce many different kinds of products (fig. 2). The Lermios' original farm, for example, grew corn, hay, oats, and alfalfa. They also had milking cattle, chickens, and a few hogs. Large farms are often monocultures—they raise only one kind of crop or animal (fig. 3). The Lermio family has been moving towards becoming a monoculture; they raise only three field crops and they don't have any animals. Buying local, as was common in the first half of the twentieth century, encourages small polyculture farms that sell a variety of products locally (McCauley).

For environmental purposes, the small polyculture farms that buying local encourages have many advantages over industrial-scale monoculture farms because they are more sustainable. The focus of sustainable farming is on minimizing waste, use of chemicals, soil erosion, and pollution ("Sustainable"). Small farmers tend to value local natural resources more than industrial-scale farmers do and are therefore more conscientious in their farming methods. Small farms are also intrinsically more sustainable. As mentioned, small farms

Fig. 3. A large monoculture farm. Photograph from iStockphoto.

are more likely to be polycultures—to do many different things with the land—and using a field for different purposes does not exhaust the soil the way continually farming one crop does. Rotating crops or using a field alternately for pasture and for crops keeps the land "healthy." On small farms, sometimes a farmer will pasture his cattle in the previous year's cornfield; the cattle eat some of the stubble left from last year's crop and fertilize the field. The land isn't wasted or exhausted from continuous production. I've even seen one organic farmer set up his pigpen so that the pigs plow his blueberry field just by walking up around their pen. This kind of dual usage wouldn't be found on a large monoculture farm. Most big farms use their fields exclusively either for crops or for pasture. Modern fertilizers, herbicides, and pesticides allow farmers to harvest crops from even unhealthy land, but this is a highly unsustainable model. Farming chemicals can pollute groundwater and destroy natural ecosystems.

Not only are small farms a more sustainable, eco-friendly model than big commercial farms, but buying local has other advantages as well. Buying local, for example, would reduce the high cost of fuel and energy used to transport food across the world and would bring long-term benefits as well. It is currently estimated that most produce in the United States is shipped about 1,500 miles before it is sold—it travels about the distance from Nebraska to New York ("Why Buy Local?"). Eighty percent of all strawberries grown in the United States are from California ("Strawberry Fruit Facts Page"). They are shipped from California all around the country even though strawberries can be grown in Wisconsin, New York, Tennessee, and most other parts of the United States. No matter how efficient our shipping systems, shipping food thousands of miles is expensive—in dollars, in oil, and in the carbon dioxide it produces (fig. 4). One of the main reasons that produce is shipped long distances is that fruits and vegetables don't grow everywhere all year around. Even though strawberries grow in a lot of places during the early summer, they grow only in Florida in the winter, or in California from spring to fall (Rieger). Americans have become accustomed to being able to buy almost any kind of produce at any time of the year. A true commitment to buying local would accommodate local season and climate. Not everything will grow everywhere, but the goal of buying local should be to eliminate all unnecessary shipping by buying things from as close to home as possible and eating as many things in season as possible.

Some argue that buying local can actually have negative environmental effects; and their arguments add important qualifiers to supporting small local farms. Alex Avery, the director of research and education at the Center for

Fig 4. Interstate trucking is expensive financially and ecologically. Photograph from iStockphoto.

Global Food Issues, has said that we should "buy food from the world region where it grows best" (qtd. in MacDonald). His implication is that it would be more wasteful to try to grow pineapples in the Northeast than to have them shipped from the Caribbean. He makes a good point: trying to grow all kinds of food all over the world would be a waste of time and energy. Buying local should instead focus on buying *as much as possible* from nearby farmers. It has also been argued that buying locally will be detrimental to the environment because small farms are not as efficient in their use of resources as large farms. This is a common misconception and actually depends on how economists measure efficiency. Small farms are less efficient than large farms in the total output of one crop per acre, but they are more efficient in total output of all crops per acre (McCauley). When buying locally, the consumer should try to buy from these more efficient polyculture farms. Skeptics of buying local also say that focusing food cultivation in the United States will be worse for the environment because farmers here use more industrial equipment than farmers in the third world (MacDonald). According to the Progressive Policy Institute, however, only 13 percent of the American diet is imported ("98.7 Percent"). This is a surprisingly small percentage, especially considering that seafood is one of the top imports. It should also be considered that as countries around the world become wealthier, they will industrialize, so exploiting manual labor in the third world would only be a temporary solution (MacDonald). The environmental benefits now, and in the long run, of buying local outweigh any such immediate disadvantages.

Critics have also pointed to negative global effects of buying local, but buying local could have positive global effects too. In the *Christian Science Monitor*, John Clark, author of *Worlds Apart: Civil Society and the Battle for Ethical Globalization*, argues that buying local hurts poor workers in third world countries. He cites the fact that an estimated fifty thousand children in Bangladesh lost their jobs in the garment industry because of the 1996 Western boycott of clothing made in third world sweatshops (qtd. in MacDonald). It cannot be denied that if everyone buys locally, repercussions on the global market seem unavoidable. Nonetheless, if the people of the United States demonstrated their commitment to buying local, it could open up new conversations about environmentalism. Our government lags far behind the European Union in environmental legislation. Through selective shopping, the people of the United States could demonstrate to the world our commitment to environmentalism.

Arguments that decentralizing food production will be bad for the national   10
economy also ignore the positive effects small farms have on local economies. John Tschirhart, a professor of environmental economics at the University of Wyoming, argues that buying locally would be bad for our national economy because food that we buy locally can often be produced cheaper somewhere else in the United States (qtd. in Arias Terry). This seems debatable since most of the locally grown things we buy in grocery stores today aren't much more expensive, if at all, than their counterparts from far away. In New York City, apples from upstate New York are often cheaper than the industrial, waxed Granny Smiths from Washington State or Chile; buying locally should indeed save shipping costs. Nonetheless, it is true that locally grown food can often be slightly more expensive than "industrially grown" food. Probably one of the biggest factors in the difference in price is labor cost. Labor is cheap in third world countries, and large U.S. farms are notorious for hiring immigrant laborers. It is hard to justify the exploitation of such artificially cheap labor. While the case for the economic disadvantages of buying local is dubious, buying local has clear positive economic effects in local communities. Local farms hire local workers and bring profits to small rural communities. One study of pig farmers in Virginia showed that, compared to corporate-owned farms, small farms created 10 percent more permanent local jobs, a 20 percent higher increase in local retail sales, and a 37 percent higher increase in local per capita income (McCauley).

Buying locally grown and produced food has clear environmental, social, and economic advantages. On the surface it seems that buying local could constitute a big personal sacrifice. It may be slightly more expensive, and it wouldn't allow us to buy any kind of produce at any time of the year, a change that would no doubt take getting used to. But perhaps these limitations would actually make food more enjoyable. If strawberries were sold only in the summer, they would be more special and we might even enjoy them more. Food that is naturally grown in season is fresher and also tends to taste better. Fresh summer strawberries are sweeter than their woody winter counterparts. Buying local is an easy step that everyone can take towards "greener" living.

Works Cited

Arias Terry, Ana. "Buying Local vs. Buying Cheap." *Conscious Choice: The Journal of Ecology and Natural Living*, Jan. 2007, Conscious Communications, www.alternet.org/story/342/buying_local_vs._buying_cheap. Accessed 27 Apr. 2011.

Baum, Michele Dula. "U.S. Government Issues Standards on Organic Food." *CNN.com*, 20 Dec. 2000, Turner Broadcasting System, www.cnn.com/FOOD/specials/2000/organic.main/story.html. Accessed 25 Apr. 2011.

"Buy Local." *Sustainable Table*. Grace Communications Foundation, Jan. 2007, www.sustainabletable.org. Accessed 27 Apr. 2011.

"Global Warming Statistics." *Effects of Global Warming*, 2007, www.effectofglobalwarming.com/global-warming-statistics.html. Accessed 25 Apr. 2011.

MacDonald, G. Jeffrey. "Is Buying Local Always Best?" *Christian Science Monitor*, 24 July 2006, pp. 13+.

McCauley, Marika Alena. "Small Farms: The Optimum Sustainable Agriculture Model." *Oxfam America*, 2007, oxfamamerica.org/whatwedo/where_we_work/united_states/news_publications/food_farm/art2570.html. Accessed 27 Apr. 2011.

"98.7 Percent of Imported Food Never Inspected." *Progressive Policy Institute*, 7 Sept. 2007, www.ppionline.org/ppi_ci.cfm?knlgAreaID=85&subsecID=108&contentID. Accessed 25 Apr. 2011.

"Record Increase in U.S. Greenhouse Gas Emissions Reported." *Environment News Service*, 18 Apr. 2006, ens-newsire.com/ens/apr2006/2006-04-18-02.asp. Accessed 25 Apr. 2011.

Rieger, Mark. "Strawberry—*Fragaria X ananassa*." *Mark's Fruit Crops*, 2006, U of Georgia, fruit-crops.com/strawberry-fragaria-x-ananassa. Accessed 25 Apr. 2011.

"Strawberry Fruit Facts Page." Grown in California, Gourmet Shopping Network, growincalifornia.com/fruit-facts/strawberry-facts.html. Accessed 25 Apr. 2011.

"Sustainable." *Paperback Oxford English Dictionary*, 6th ed., Oxford UP, 2001.

"Why Buy Local?" *LocalHarvest*, 2007, localharvest.org/buylocal.jsp. Accessed 23 Apr. 2011.

Thinking about the Text

1. It's clear that this is a topic that matters to Katherine Spriggs. Has she convinced you that it matters—and if so, how? How does Spriggs establish the importance of her topic?

2. What **COUNTERARGUMENTS** or positions other than her own does Spriggs consider—and how does she respond in each case?

3. Choose a section of Spriggs's essay that you find especially effective or ineffective. Referring to the genre features listed on page 147, describe what makes this part of her argument persuasive—or not.

4. Spriggs includes several photos in her essay. How do they contribute to her argument?

5. Consider your own response to Spriggs's position. Write an essay in response to one of the issues she raises. State your **POSITION** explicitly, and be sure to consider arguments other than your own.

THIRTEEN

"Here's What Happened"
Writing a Narrative

SO, TELL ME WHAT HAPPENED." Anytime we ask someone about an incident at work or an event at school, we
are asking for a narrative: tell us about what happened.
Narratives are stories, and they are fundamental parts
of our everyday lives. When we tell someone about a
movie we've seen or a basketball game we played in, we often use narrative. When we want someone to understand something that we did, we
might tell a story that explains our actions. When we post to *Instagram*,
we often write about something we've just done or seen.

If you wrote an essay as part of your college applications, chances
are that you were required to write a narrative. Here, for instance, are
instructions from two colleges' applications:

> Describe a meaningful event or experience and how it has changed or
> affected the person you are today. ——HOFSTRA UNIVERSITY

> Describe a personal moral or ethical dilemma and how it impacted
> your life. ——HAMPTON UNIVERSITY

Each of these prompts asks applicants to write a narrative about some
aspect of their lives. In each case they need to do more than just tell a
good story; they need to make a clear point about why it matters.

Narrative is a powerful way to get an audience's attention. Telling a good story can even help establish your authority as a writer. Take a look, for example, at the opening paragraphs from an obituary for the "Queen of Soul," Aretha Franklin, from the *Guardian*:

> On a crisp, sparkling day in January 2009, Aretha Franklin stood on the steps of the Capitol in Washington, an ample figure swathed in a spectacular ensemble of coat and hat in two shades of grey, singing "My Country, 'Tis of Thee" to her new president. All around her, and down the full length of the National Mall, the vast audience included African Americans with tears in their eyes, celebrating the inauguration of Barack Obama. She was facing west, as hundreds of thousands of slaves had done when they landed on a bitter shore at the conclusion of their portage from Africa. "Let freedom ring," she sang, in the anthem's famous exhortation, and many millions watching on television around the world could not help but share the resonance of a historic moment.
>
> Franklin, who has died aged 76, sounded exalted that day. She almost always did, even when handcuffed to unsympathetic material. Her voice could scald or soothe, singing with equal intimacy and intensity to her God or a faithless lover.
>
> —RICHARD WILLIAMS, "Aretha Franklin Obituary"

Author Richard Williams could have opened this obituary the way he ended it: "Aretha Louise Franklin, singer, pianist and songwriter, born 25 March 1942; died 16 August 2018." However, that statement doesn't draw readers in the way that opening with a story of Franklin singing at Barack Obama's 2009 inauguration does. With vivid and fascinating details, he piques our interest. We want to keep reading about an artist whose "voice could scald and soothe."

Images, too, can tell stories, as the cartoon of Franklin on the following page shows. Artist Jamaal Rolle captures Franklin in mid-song, with eyes closed and microphone in hand, showing us the artist. Surrounding her are the titles of some of her biggest hits. These titles, familiar to Franklin's fans, and the image of a singing Franklin tell the story of the memories her songs invoke, their place in American culture, and the powerful and successful singer that Aretha Franklin was.

Think about some of the powerful personal narratives you've read, perhaps the *Narrative of the Life of Frederick Douglass* or Anne Frank's *Diary of*

One cartoonist's tribute to Aretha Franklin.

a Young Girl. We could, of course, read about their lives on *Wikipedia*, but a good narrative provides more than just the facts; it gives us a well-told story that captures not only our attention but also our imagination.

So what exactly is a narrative? For our purposes, narrative is a kind of writing that presents events in some kind of time sequence with a distinct beginning, middle, and ending (but not necessarily in strict chronological order) and that is written for the purpose of making a point. That is, to write a narrative it is not enough to simply report a sequence of events ("this happened, then that happened"), which is often what children do when they tell stories. Narrative essays, especially in college, are meaningful ways of making sense of our experiences, of what goes on around us—and of illustrating a point, making an argument, or writing about the lives of others.

REFLECT. Think about some stories that are told in your favorite songs or music videos, that you hear in sermons, or that your grandma tells. Make a list of the stories that you hear, read, see, or tell in one day and the subjects of those stories. You'll begin to see how narratives are an important way that we communicate with each other.

Across Academic Disciplines

The narrative essay is a common assignment in the humanities and increasingly in other academic fields as well. In a *composition* class, you may be asked to write a literacy narrative about how you learned to read or write or a personal narrative about an important person or experience in your life. In a *history* class, you may be asked to take data from archives and construct a narrative about a particular historical event. (Some think that historians focus on dates and facts about incidents from the past, but actually they are generally piecing together narratives that provide a context for interpreting what those dates and facts mean.) In *medicine*, patient accounts and medical histories play a key role in diagnosis and treatment and provide important documentation for insurance companies. In the *sciences*, lab reports tell the story of how researchers conducted an experiment and interpreted the data they collected. Since narratives take different forms across disciplines, one challenge you'll face will be to determine which narrative elements are valued or even required in a particular situation.

Visit the Digital Archive of Literacy Narratives (thedaln .org), a site sponsored by Ohio State and Georgia State where you can read literacy narratives as well as post your own.

Across Media

The medium you use makes a big difference in the way you tell a story. *Video*, for example, presents a wide range of possibilities. TV broadcasts of football games cut between shots of players, coaches, and fans. Commentators review key plays in slow motion or from multiple angles, diagram plays on the screen, and pull up player statistics—all of which combine to tell the story of what's happening on the field. These same stories will be told differently in *print*, with written words, still photos, and tables of statistics to show how the players performed.

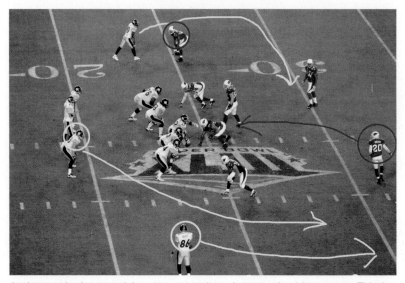

Analysts circle players and draw arrows to show those watching the game on TV what just happened.

When you're writing a narrative, you'll want to think about what media will best suit your audience and purpose. But you won't always have a choice. If you're assigned to work in a specific medium, think about whether a narrative would help get your message across. Well-told stories are a good way to engage your audience's attention in an *oral presentation*, for instance, and to help them remember what you say.

REFLECT. *Compare narratives in different media. From the many kinds of narratives you encounter in one day—in books or magazines, on YouTube or in video games, in textbooks or conversations with friends—choose two narratives on the same topic from different media that you find most interesting. Think about the similarities and differences between the ways the two stories are told. What would change about each narrative if it were presented in a different medium?*

Across Cultures and Communities

What makes a good story often depends on who's telling the story and who's listening. Not only is that the case for individuals, but different communities and cultures also tell stories in unique ways and value particular things in them.

➤ *GO TO itgetsbetter.org, the award-winning site of the It Gets Better Project, begun in 2010 to show LGBTQ+ youths that life will get better "if they can just get through their teen years." There you'll find thousands of videos, including many personal narratives from adults who tell how their lives got better. There's also a button to add your story, in video or writing. Watch some of the videos and read some of the written stories. Which do you find more powerful, and why?*

Many *Native American tribes* consider narrative an important tradition and art form, so much so that storytellers hold a place of honor. In much of *West Africa*, the griots are the official storytellers, entrusted with telling the history of a village or town through recitation and song. And in many *Appalachian communities*, storytelling functions as a way to pass down family and community history. As in West Africa, good storytellers enjoy high status in Appalachia.

In many cultures and communities, stories are the way that history is passed down from generation to generation. Think about the ways that family histories are passed down in your family or community—through oral stories? photo albums? home videos?

Across Genres

Narrative is often a useful strategy for writers working in other genres. For example, in an essay **ARGUING A POSITION**, you may use a narrative example to prove a point. In a **REVIEW** of a film, in which evaluation is the main purpose, you may need to tell a brief story from the plot to demonstrate how the film meets (or does not meet) a specific evaluative criterion. These are only two of the many ways in which narrative can be used as part of a text.

CHARACTERISTIC FEATURES

There is no one way to tell a story. Most written narratives, however, have a number of common features, revolving around the following characteristics and questions:

- A clearly identified event: What happened? Who was involved?
- A clearly described setting: When and where did it happen?
- Vivid, descriptive details: What makes the story come alive?
- A consistent point of view: Who's telling the story?
- A clear point: Why does the story matter?

A Clearly Identified Event:
What Happened? Who Was Involved?

Narratives are based on an event or series of events, presented in a way that makes audiences want to know how the story will turn out. Consider this paragraph by Mike Rose, in which he narrates how he, as a marginal high school student with potential, got into college with the help of his senior-year English teacher, Jack MacFarland:

> My grades stank. I had A's in biology and a handful of B's in a few English and social science classes. All the rest were C's—or worse. MacFarland said I would do well in his class and laid down the law about doing well in others. Still the record for my first three years wouldn't have been acceptable to any four-year school. To nobody's surprise, I was turned down flat by USC and UCLA. But Jack MacFarland was on the case. He had received his bachelor's degree from Loyola, so he made calls to old professors and talked to somebody in admissions and wrote me a strong letter. Loyola finally accepted me as a probationary student. I would be on trial for the first year, and if I did okay, I would be granted regular status. MacFarland also intervened to get me a loan, for I could never have af-

forded a private college without it. Four more years of religion classes and four more years of boys at one school, girls at another. But at least I was going to college. Amazing.

—MIKE ROSE, *Lives on the Boundary*

As inspiring as it is to learn of someone with lots of C's (or worse) getting into college, it's not the actual facts that make this narrative worth reading; rather, it's the way the facts are presented—in other words, the way the story is told.

The narrator grabs our attention with his first sentence ("My grades stank"), then lays out the challenges he faced ("turned down flat by USC and UCLA"), and ends with a flourish ("Amazing"). He could have told us what happened much more briefly—but then it would have been just a sequence of facts; instead, he told us a story. As the author of a narrative, you'll want to be sure to get the facts down, but that won't be enough. Your challenge will be to tell about "what happens" in a way that gets your audience's attention and makes them care enough to keep on reading.

A Clearly Described Setting: When and Where Did It Happen?

Narratives need to be situated clearly within time and space in order for readers to understand what's going on. For that reason, you will generally arrange your story in **CHRONOLOGICAL ORDER** starting at the beginning and moving straight ahead to the end. There are times, though, when you may choose to present a narrative in reverse chronological order, starting at the end and looking back at the events that led up to it—or with a flashback or flash-forward that jumps back to the past or ahead to the future. Whether you tell your story in chronological order or not, the sequence of events needs to be clear to your audience.

Also important is that your audience get a clear idea of the place(s) where the events occur. Time and space work together to create a scene that your audience can visualize and follow, as they do in the following example from student Minh Vu's essay "Dirty Nails," which documents growing up in his family's nail salon.

I was born in my family's nail salon. It was in the waxing room, and my first swaddle was made up of giant waxing strips. Normally, they're used to tear the hair off people. For me, they were warmth and protection.

I was raised within glass doors kept shiny with diluted Windex, among towering boxes of acetone, and atop giant pedicure thrones. Such was my childhood kingdom. Alphabet blocks were replaced by white Arial stickers I used to spell out "JEL MANICURE" and "BIKIKNEE WAX" on the price board. Instead of bicycles I rode bumper cars with the pedicure stools. And the rest of my time I spent trying to fit my toddler toes into the pastel foot separators that looked like mini combs. . . . The pallor of peeling plaster was rolled over with a deep textured azure, like the ocean [my grandma] immigrated across in the 1970s. Dim overhead lights were torn down and replaced with a crystal chandelier that, albeit fake, brought illumination in a time of immigrant loneliness. And red leather diner stools from the space's past life were refurbished into sleek manicure chairs.

The nail salon was my world. It was where all of life existed.

—MINH VU, "Dirty Nails"

Minh Vu establishes the setting by providing vivid, descriptive language of the nail salon that makes up the center of his story. His first statement— "I was born in my family's nail salon"—establishes the setting of the story, but it's the details that come after that that paint a picture for readers: "glass doors kept shiny with diluted Windex," "giant pedicure thrones," "bumper cars with the pedicure stools," "pastel foot separators," and "red leather diner stools . . . refurbished into sleek manicure chairs." These details help readers, especially those who have been to nail salons, visualize where and how the writer grew up.

Vivid, Descriptive Details: What Makes the Story Come Alive?

You may remember English teachers telling you that good writers "show rather than tell." It's an old adage that applies to narratives in particular. Vivid, descriptive detail makes the people, places, and events in a narrative come alive for an audience, helping them see, hear, smell, taste, and feel "what happened." See how the following example from *ESPN Magazine* provides colorful detail that shows us Steph Curry's brilliant technique:

Without ever taking his eyes off the rim, Curry moves to finish his shot. From his toes through his torso to the top of his head, his body is so

Steph Curry elevates for a shot during the 2018 NBA finals.

vertical, he looks as if he's coming down from the ceiling, not jumping toward it. His shooting elbow passes shoulder height, still at a perfect 90-degree angle. And when his arms are straight and extended overhead—elbow over eye, shooters call it—the left hand opens. The path of the ball, like the elbow, stays clean and true, riding the beginning of a Vitruvian arc; it doesn't hitch backward over the crown of his head or veer to the side.

Now the wrist begins its flection. The ball lifts off the tip of his index finger, then off the tip of his middle finger. His palm falls, his fingers now extended to the floor. The left arm stays perfectly still. The head never moves. . . .

Before the game, boyish smile on his face, Curry had laughed, shrugging his shoulders and saying, yeah, he knows the second the ball leaves his hands. As his shot now begins its descent toward the rim, he drops both arms behind his back, palms up, chest out, like a bullfighter. Yeah, he knows. "There's a difference between shooters and shot makers," says [Jerry] West. "This kid is a shot maker."

—DAVID FLEMING, "Sports' Perfect 0.4 Seconds"

Notice how the author slows down the action to show us each step in intricate detail—steps we can't possibly see or understand in the lightning-fast action of real time. With two powerful similes ("his body is so vertical, he looks as if he's coming down from the ceiling," "palms up, chest out, like a bullfighter"), Fleming's text brings Curry to life for readers.

Think about how much detail and what kind of detail your narrative needs to "come to life" for your audience. Remember that you are likely writing for readers (or listeners) unfamiliar with the story you are telling. That means that you need to choose details that help them get a vivid picture of the setting, people, and events in the narrative. When deciding whether to include direct quotations or dialogue, ask yourself if doing so would paint a scene or create a mood more effectively than a summary would.

A Consistent Point of View: Who's Telling the Story?

A good narrative is generally told from one consistent point of view. If you are writing about something that happened to you, then your narrative should be written from the first-person point of view (*I, we*). First person puts the focus on the narrator, as Georgina Kleege does in the following example, which recounts the opening moments of one of her classes:

I tell the class, "I am legally blind." There is a pause, a collective intake of breath. I feel them look away uncertainly and then look back. After all, I just said I couldn't see. Or did I? I had managed to get there on my own—no cane, no dog, none of the usual trappings of blindness. Eyeing me askance now, they might detect that my gaze is not quite focused. My eyes are aimed in the right direction but the gaze seems to stop short of touching anything. But other people do this, sighted people, normal people, especially in an awkward situation like this one, the first day of class. An actress who delivers an aside to the audience, breaking the "fourth wall" of the proscenium, will aim her gaze somewhere above any particular pair of eyes. If I hadn't said anything, my audience might understand my gaze to be like that, a part of the performance. In these few seconds between sentences, their gaze becomes intent. They watch me glance down, or toward the door where someone's coming in late.

I'm just like anyone else. Then what did I actually mean by "legally blind"? They wait. I go on, "Some people would call me 'visually challenged.'" There is a ripple of laughter, an exhalation of relief. I'm making a joke about it. I'm poking fun at something they too find aggravating, the current mania to stick a verbal smiley-face on any human condition which deviates from the status quo. Differently abled. Handicapable. If I ask, I'm sure some of them can tell jokes about it: "Don't say 'bald,' say 'follicularly challenged.'" "He's not dead, he's metabolically stable." Knowing they are at least thinking these things, I conclude, "These are just silly ways of saying I don't see very well."   —GEORGINA KLEEGE, "Call It Blindness"

Notice how the first-person point of view—and the repetition of *I*—keep our attention focused on Kleege. Like the students in her class, we are looking right at her.

If your narrative is about someone else's experience or about events that you have researched but did not witness, then the narrative should probably be written in third person (*he, she, it, they*). Unlike a first-person narrative, a third-person narrative emphasizes someone or something other than the narrator. Historical and medical narratives are usually written in third person, as are newswriting and sportswriting. Look at the following account of the on-field actions leading up to the moment in 1985 when quarterback Joe Theismann was tackled by Lawrence Taylor, suffering a devastating, career-ending broken leg.

From the snap of the ball to the snap of the first bone is closer to four seconds than to five. One Mississippi: The quarterback of the Washington Redskins, Joe Theismann, turns and hands the ball to running back John Riggins. He watches Riggins run two steps forward, turn, and flip the ball back to him. . . . Two Mississippi: Theismann searches for a receiver but instead sees Harry Carson coming straight at him. It's a running down—the start of the second quarter, first and 10 at midfield, with the score tied 7–7—and the New York Giants' linebacker has been so completely suckered by the fake that he's deep in the Redskins' backfield. Carson thinks he's come to tackle Riggins but Riggins is long gone, so Carson just keeps running, toward Theismann. Three Mississippi: Carson now sees that Theismann has the ball. Theismann notices Carson coming straight at him, and so he has time to avoid him. He steps up and to the side and Carson flies right on by and out of the

Athletic trainers surround Joe Theismann after a tackle by Lawrence Taylor broke Theismann's leg.

play. The play is now 3.5 seconds old. Until this moment it has been defined by what the quarterback can see. Now it—and he—is at the mercy of what he can't see.

—MICHAEL LEWIS, *The Blind Side*

The opening sentence takes us right into the game, with "the snap of the ball." The repetition of "one Mississippi . . . two Mississippi . . ." marches us one excruciating second (and sentence) at a time through the actions that led to an injury that became the lead story on every sports broadcast that evening and for days to come. The photograph and caption tell the story of how that play ended for Theismann.

Compare the points of view of Georgina Kleege's first-person narrative and Michael Lewis's third-person one. Notice that there is one consistent point of view in each example. As an author, you will have to determine whether your narrative is most effective told from the first-person or third-person point of view. No matter what you may have been taught in high school, the first person is acceptable in many (though not all) academic contexts. Whatever point of view you use, however, do so consistently. That is, if you refer to yourself in the narrative, do not switch between first (*I, we*) and third (*he, she, they*) person. (Rarely is a narrative told from a second-person—*you*—point of view.)

Part of maintaining a consistent point of view is establishing a clear time frame. Notice Michael Lewis's use of present-tense verbs in the example from *The Blind Side*. By consistently narrating the actions in the game in the present tense, the narrator, much like a play-by-play announcer, places the reader in the moment of the story being told. Using a consistent verb tense situates the actions of the event within a clear time frame.

A clear time frame does not mean that every verb in the narrative has to be in the same tense, only that the writer establishes one primary tense—usually present or past—for the main action of the story. In the example by Mike Rose on page 1015, most of the verbs are in the past tense: *said, made, talked*. But other tenses are used to indicate events that, in relation to the main action of the narrative, occurred earlier (*He had received his bachelor's degree from Loyola*) or might occur later (*I would be granted regular status*).

A Clear Point: Why Does the Story Matter?

Good narratives tell stories that matter. In academic writing in particular, narratives are told to make a point. Whether they begin by stating the point explicitly in a thesis or build toward a point that is expressed at the end, the purpose of the narrative needs to be clear to the audience. Nothing irritates an audience more than reading or listening to a story that has no point. Even if a story is interesting or entertaining, it will most likely be deemed a failure in an academic context if it does not make clear why the events matter. Consider how author and English professor bell hooks makes a point about learning to value work:

> "Work makes life sweet!" I often heard this phrase growing up, mainly from old black folks who did not have jobs in the traditional sense of the word. They were usually self-employed, living off the land, selling fishing worms, picking up an odd job here and there. They were people who had a passion for work. They took pride in a job done well. My Aunt Margaret took in ironing. Folks brought her clothes from miles around because she was such an expert. That was in the days when

using starch was common and she knew how to do an excellent job. Watching her iron with skill and grace was like watching a ballerina dance. Like all the other black girls raised in the fifties that I knew, it was clear to me that I would be a working woman. Even though our mother stayed home, raising her seven children, we saw her constantly at work, washing, ironing, cleaning, and cooking (she was an incredible cook). And she never allowed her six girls to imagine we would not be working women. No, she let us know that we would work and be proud to work.

—BELL HOOKS, "Work Makes Life Sweet"

Hooks opens with her main point, that "work makes life sweet!" In the sentences that follow, she explains how she learned this lesson from "old black folks who did not have jobs in the traditional sense." Through specific examples, she illustrates how they "took pride in a job done well" and passed on this pride in their work to hooks and her sisters. The explicit restatement of the point in the final sentence—that hooks and her six sisters learned from their mother that they would "work and be proud to work"—recasts the notion of "working woman" in a unique and engaging way.

In contrast to bell hooks, author and activist Roxane Gay, in a speech to publishers, withholds her main point even after announcing to the audience that she had anticipated what topic she would be asked to address:

When I received the invitation to speak at Winter Institute, I knew, even before I got the details, that I would be asked to talk about diversity in some form or fashion. This is the state of most industries, and particularly contemporary publishing. People of color are not asked about our areas of expertise as if the only thing we are allowed to be experts on is our marginalization. We are asked about how white people can do better and feel better about diversity or the lack thereof. We are asked to offer "good" white people who "mean well," absolution from the ills of racism.

—ROXANE GAY, speech to *Publishers Weekly*'s Winter Institute, 2017

Rather than announcing her main point right away, Gay provides a bit of context on the word *diversity*, including the current state of discussions about diversity. After giving this background and making a bold admission, she *then* states her main point:

> The word diversity has of late become so overused as to be meaningless. In a 2015 article for *The New York Times Magazine*, Anna Holmes wrote about the dilution of the word diversity, attributing its loss of meaning to "a combination of overuse, imprecision, inertia, and self-serving intentions."
>
> The word diversity is, in its most imprecise uses, a placeholder for issues of inclusion, recruitment, retention and representation. Diversity is a problem, seemingly without solutions. We talk about it and talk about it and talk about it and nothing much ever seems to change. And here we are today, talking about diversity yet again.
>
> I am so very tired of talking about diversity.
>
> Publishing has a diversity problem. This problem extends to absolutely every area of the industry. I mean, look at this room, where I can literally count the number of people of color among some 700 booksellers. There are not enough writers of color being published. When our books are published, we fight, even more than white writers, for publicity and reviews. People of color are underrepresented editorially, in book marketing, publicity, and as literary agents. People of color are underrepresented in bookselling. On and on it goes.

Gay states her main point—"Publishing has a diversity problem"—and provides further clarification and evidence of the problem. She makes the main point even more visible by focusing on the lack of diversity in the audience. In contrast to hooks, Gay moves more slowly toward her main point, describing her reaction both to the speaking invitation and the topic she was asked to cover before offering her main message outright: "People of color are underrepresented in bookselling."

As an author, don't assume that your readers will recognize the point you're trying to make. No matter how interesting you think your story is, they need to know why they should care. Why is the story important? State your main point as bell hooks and Roxane Gay do.

✑ *REFLECT. Look at a narrative in a newspaper or magazine article or on a blog or other website to see what main point it makes and how it does so. Is the main point explicitly stated in a thesis, or is it only implied? Does the narrative make clear to readers why the story is important or why they should care about it?*

WRITING A NARRATIVE / An Annotated Example

RAYA ELFADEL KHEIRBEK is an associate professor at the George Washington University School of Medicine and Health Sciences in Washington, DC, and a physician at the Veterans Affairs (VA) Medical Center in the city. This 2017 essay was originally published in *Health Affairs*, an American journal about national and global health policy and research issues.

The title suggests what the narrative is about: resolving a conflict between doctor and patient.

At the VA, Healing the Doctor-Patient Relationship

RAYA ELFADEL KHEIRBEK

Opens with an attention-grabbing quote and introduction to a central person in the story. And the author sets the scene—the Veterans Affairs (VA) Medical Center.

THE MAN'S VOICE over the phone was angry: "The VA provides terrible care!" I had promised the Veterans Affairs (VA) Medical Center's Patient Advocate office that I would connect with the man, Mr. Davis, who had called three times before to complain about his care. I was warned beforehand that he was displeased, to say the least.

With him on the line, I took a deep breath and began to look up his records. "I am sorry to hear this, Mr. Davis," I said. "Would you please tell me specifically what is bothering you? I am covering for your doctor and will do my best to help."

The author provides details about Mr. Davis's medical condition, necessary background information for readers.

Mr. Davis needed to have an MRI for his right shoulder, as was recommended by his military doctor before he separated from the service. He also was having back pain and wasn't exercising enough. He had gained twenty pounds in six months and asked if we offered liposuction.

He had met his primary care clinician, Dr. Kumar, for the first time a couple of weeks earlier and was very uncomfortable when he saw her. To him, there was great insensitivity in the VA's decision to assign him a doctor who he believed was originally from the Middle East.

"Those people wanted to kill me," he remarked to me on the phone, "and I do not appreciate having a doctor who is one of them."

Even more details that contribute to making Mr. Davis a compelling character.

"If you had a woman who was subjected to repeated rape, would you let her be examined by a male doctor?" he continued.

I knew that our policy would allow him to switch doctors, but I had no idea what to say. I had been practicing medicine for a couple of decades and naturally had encountered many types of unusual behavior. Yet I had never heard this type of comment from a patient. I composed myself and quietly explained to Mr. Davis that Dr. Kumar's family came from India. Dr. Kumar herself was born and raised in Pennsylvania and had no connection to the Middle East whatsoever.

A consistent point of view. The story is told through the author's eyes—with lots of dialogue between her and Mr. Davis.

But Mr. Davis was insistent on having a doctor who looked like him.

And he was angry.

"I am not your typical patient," he fired back. "I am smart, educated, and highly trained. I do not need your opinion. I have lived in my body for three decades. I know what I want, and your job is to deliver."

Direct quotes support the author's claims.

I told him that I wanted to meet with him to help resolve these issues and blocked off an hour the following week to meet during my administrative time. He was excited that I would be able to see him quickly, given what he referred to as the long wait time to get an appointment in the VA. He added that, based on our conversation, I seemed to be a good doctor.

While I was determined to meet and help Mr. Davis, a potential challenge loomed. I am of Middle Eastern origin. I wondered if I should reveal this information after coordinating his care and give him another opportunity to seek a different clinician. My colleagues advised me to stand tall and not give him that choice. To them, his views represented bigotry.

The author provides important details about herself.

A Veteran Affairs health care center in Phoenix, Arizona—similar to the one where Mr. Davis and Dr. Kheirbek met.

Yet Mr. Davis was not the only one struggling with the past. For me, encountering Mr. Davis brought back painful memories and forced me to stop and reflect on my years of service in the VA, my belief system, and my biases. I wondered if his "bigotry" was really so alien to the human nature in us all.

An Occupational Hazard

Details about the author's experience move the story along.

As a primary care physician working in the VA, I have heard countless stories from soldiers reliving their experiences in war zones. As an Arab American immigrant, I had followed the Iraqi war and—later—the promising start of the Arab Spring and then watched them both spiral into the chaos of death and destruction, including a civil war in my native country, Syria. I felt privileged to be a physician and an American, especially as violence took hold overseas. I could have been back home, along with everyone I worried about. I could be dead. Feeling powerless, I forced myself to watch and listen to the news. The least I could do was to be aware.

Meeting Mr. Davis

I introduced myself to Mr. Davis on a Tuesday in March 2017, less than a week after our initial phone conversation. A white man in his early thirties, he was tall and well built, with a rectangular face; a defined, slightly pointed chin; and a sturdy jaw line. He had light brown hair, small blue eyes, and a straight nose. The jacket he wore over his broad shoulders had neatly polished buttons and was slightly frayed in places. Part of his right hand was missing. He glanced at me with a smile. I am a white woman with green eyes and brown hair.

Reestablishing the timeline makes the progression of events clear.

Vivid details paint a picture of Mr. Davis's physical appearance.

"I am very happy you were able to make it to this meeting," I said with a big smile.

He nodded in silence and avoided making eye contact.

"I had a chance to review your chart. I think I can help with your physical needs," I added. "But I am also suspecting there are mental health issues that might need to be addressed."

Given his sentiments about Middle Eastern doctors, I thought he had a plausible PTSD diagnosis. When I began to suggest as much, he cut me off.

"This is all stereotyping," he asserted. "I did what I was supposed to do. I will heal through going back to work and being productive."

Dialogue makes us feel as if we're witnessing the conversation.

I caught him looking at my name badge.

"I understand," I said. "Thank you for clarifying."

I asked how he had ended up in the military. He said he'd signed up simply because college was "so damn expensive." He was not a "military brat" and didn't enlist out of a sense of obligation. He was not angry or in need of some form of revenge. It's not that he felt enlisting was brave or important.

Mr. Davis had been in three combat deployments—Iraq in 2010 and Afghanistan in 2011 and 2013—as a member of the US Army Special Forces. He'd been involved in multiple close-range blasts, traumatic jumps, and firefights. Many of the people he had served with had been killed. Since his return to the United States, he had been having constant pain in his right shoulder. He had nightmares one or two times a week, and recently they'd become more frequent.

Details establish the intensity of Mr. Davis's combat experiences.

"What kept you going during all the deployments?" I asked.

A turning point signals the growing bond between doctor and patient.

"I closed my eyes while hiding from fire and remembered family trips skiing with my little sister and laughing on the slopes of Jackson Hole." He looked up and smiled. I saw a glimpse of the little boy in his face and knew he was in pain. I wanted to reach out and touch his hand, but I was afraid he would not welcome my gesture.

I asked if he'd had any good experiences in Iraq. Yes, he said. It touched him to see families with young children walking for many miles to collect American parachutes to help build houses. The local people found something useful to do with even the trash that Americans had left. All his memories, however, were haunted by the killings he had witnessed and the poverty of the places he had been.

I felt it was then time to address his comments about Dr. Kumar. I said: "You know, Mr. Davis, you are a man of tremendous courage. It is not easy to share your experiences with someone else, especially experiences of this nature."

He looked out the window.

"You mentioned to me in our phone conversation last week that you were uncomfortable with a doctor from the Middle East."

I paused, then continued. "I want you to be comfortable, and I am very happy we met today. I want to thank you for allowing me into your life and for the opportunity to help. I owe to you the knowledge that I was born and raised in Syria."

The few seconds of silence that ensued felt like an eternity.

Then Mr. Davis abruptly got to his feet and raised his severed hand. "I am so sorry I was being a jerk. I would really like you to be my physician—unless you do not feel comfortable caring for me, based on my earlier comments."

I stood up and extended my hand to him. "It was important for us to talk. Please keep doing so, as it's the only way for us to deal with such emotions."

A resolution follows a tense moment.

His face broke out into a wide smile. He was absolutely thrilled at the prospect of us working together. I was, too.

Healing Takes Time

Though I have served in the VA for many years and in different roles, my focus has always been on patients. The sacred time spent with patients in an exam room is the only lasting truth in medicine. In this large bureaucratic system, all else can wait. Yet many priorities compete for our attention during a single visit. It might not be possible to spend the needed time on each important issue. While a slew of mandatory screenings for diseases has improved our medical care, it is equally crucial to take the time to develop a relationship with the patient, exploring his or her service history and the lived experiences that may come with that. It is not always easy. In my work, I know what it is like to be discriminated against, and what it is like to have stereotypes of my own. Yet an admission of our own vulnerability and opening the door to a conversation about self-care, compassion, understanding, and human connection is how we attend to all aspects of our patients' suffering—and perhaps some of our own.

> *The conclusion tells the significance of the two meeting, why the story matters.*

✎ *REFLECT. Analyze a short nonfiction narrative that you find in a magazine or on a website. Look at the list of five characteristic features of narratives on page 192 and annotate the essay to point out these features, using Kheirbek's essay as a model. Then look at your annotations and the parts of the text they refer to and evaluate how well your chosen narrative illustrates the characteristic features. For example, is the setting clearly described? How vivid are the details?*

LITERACY NARRATIVES

Literacy narratives focus on meaningful experiences involving some kind of reading or writing: stories, music, computer code, learning a foreign language, and so on. The focus on learning and literacy makes this sort of narrative a common assignment in first-year writing classes. Professional writers also use the genre to reflect on their craft. Literacy narratives can serve various purposes, but they generally have the following characteristic features.

A Well-Told Story

Whether you're writing about how you learned to do something (or struggled to do so) or why you've always loved a certain book or song, there are some tried-and-true storytelling techniques that can help your literacy narrative interest readers. If you write about something you struggled to learn, for instance, readers will want to know how your struggle turned out, how the story ends. And whatever your topic, make sure your narrative has a clear arc, from a beginning that engages your audience to a conclusion that leaves them understanding why the experience you wrote about matters to you.

A Firsthand Account, Often (but Not Always) about Yourself

You'll want to write about an experience that you know firsthand, not one that you've only read about. Writing about your own experience is the most common way of achieving this close perspective, but you may also reflect on the experiences of others. Perhaps you've observed or had a hand in helping someone else learn to read or write and are able to speak about it firsthand. This, too, could be a productive topic for a literacy narrative.

An Indication of the Narrative's Significance

Readers quickly lose patience with stories that seem to have no point, so you need to make clear what significance your narrative has for those involved. Sometimes you may have an explicit THESIS that makes the point clear from the start; other times, you may prefer to let the narrative play out before explaining its significance.

MELANIE LUKEN was a senior French and English major at The Ohio State University when she wrote this literacy narrative for an English course in which she was being trained to be a writing tutor.

Literacy: A Lineage

MELANIE LUKEN

I**T WOULD BE IMPOSSIBLE** to discuss my path to literacy without talking about my literary guardian, the person who inspired and encouraged my love for reading and writing: my father. I spent a lot of time with my dad as a child, but one of the most important experiences we shared was our Sunday afternoon bike rides. We nearly always took the same route, down to the bike path by the river, circling around, and breaking at Carillon Park under the bell tower. We would just sit, rest, and think under the bells. Etched at the bottom of the bell tower was part of a poem by Henry Wadsworth Longfellow:

> It was as if an earthquake rent
> The hearth-stones of a continent,
> And made forlorn
> The households born
> Of peace on earth, good-will to men!
> And in despair I bowed my head;
> "There is no peace on earth," I said;
> "For hate is strong,

The author makes her point clear from the start: her father played a large role in her love of reading and writing.

And mocks the song
Of peace on earth, good-will to men!"
Then pealed the bells more loud and deep:
"God is not dead; nor doth he sleep;
The Wrong shall fail,
The Right prevail,
With peace on earth, good-will to men." (lines 21–35)

My dad would inevitably read it aloud, but we both knew it by heart; it is one of the many poems that have come to mean something to me. As I got older, my dad didn't come riding as often with me. He was older and more tired, but I still went by myself. Each time I arrived under the bells, I would recite the poem to myself, even when the weather was cold and my breath made the air foggy. It had become part of me, this poem, this tradition of riding and reading and thinking. In the same way, my passion for reading and writing developed in me through the influence of my father who has a deep love of literature himself. For this reason, my definition of literacy involves more than the ability to read and write; for me, it is also a tradition, an inheritance I received from my father, and an ability to appreciate language because of him and because of many other writers who came before me.

Engaging details draw readers into the story.

You could define my dad as a jack-of-all-trades artist. He has dabbled in almost every art: novel-writing, poetry-writing, song-writing, painting, sculpture, and acting. He was originally in graduate school for English with hopes of becoming a professor. After a couple of years, however, he tired of academia. His tendencies towards creativity and individuality did not mix well with the intense analysis and structure of university life. Eventually, he ended up as a stay-at-home dad, *my* stay-at-home dad, who continues to this day to work on his art and writing. Although our relationship has not always been simple and easy, I benefited greatly from having such an intelligent and imaginative father as my primary caretaker.

For my whole life, my father has quoted the "greats," the "classics," or at least the authors that he admired, in normal conversation. It has become a joke among me and my brothers because we can all recite from memory his favorite lines of books and his favorite poems. Because of him I can quote, "If you can keep your

head when all about you / Are losing theirs and blaming it on you"
(Kipling lines 1–2), "And early though the laurel grows / It withers
quicker than the rose" (Housman lines 11–12), "I grow old . . .
I grow old . . . / I shall wear the bottoms of my trousers rolled"
(Eliot lines 120–21), and of course, "Call me Ishmael" (Melville 3),
among many others. Sometimes he will quote things far out of context, and yet I understand and enjoy it because these quotes evoke
intense feelings of tradition and love. My father's love of literature
pervaded my young mind the way it must pervade his own, and it
has stayed with me.

Vivid details and classic lines from literature bring the story to life.

From the time I could read and write, I wrote and acted out princess stories all on my own. I read voraciously and I loved being told
stories. I attribute all of this to my father, who taught me to read and
to write, who put *Little Women* in my hands when I was ten years
old, and who continued to introduce me to his favorite authors as
I got older. The only reason I picked up books like *The Heart Is a
Lonely Hunter* or Capote's *Other Voices, Other Rooms*, is because he
suggested them or handed them to me. I realize that I did not have
a particularly normal American childhood in terms of my relationship with books and literature (most of my friends preferred playing
sports or watching TV to reading), but I am blessed to have a father
who sees art in language and stories and who passed this gift to me.
I have a greater understanding of the diversity of books, authors,
and the ways in which language is used because of my father. He
always pushed me to read literature other than what I read in school
and particularly encouraged me to read female writers like Carson
McCullers, Zora Neale Hurston, and Flannery O'Connor to empower me as a young girl and to expand my perspective. Now, everything I read is within this tradition that he and I have established.

A firsthand account, told from a first-person point of view.

Another thing that I vividly remember as a child is spending quite
a bit of time in public libraries. My brothers, my dad, and I would
visit the library at least once a week, and more often in the summer when we were out of school. We were never allowed to play
video games or watch much TV, so our entertainment consisted of
what we could create ourselves or what we could gain from books.
Our ability to use and understand language proficiently was very
important to my father. Although I am the only child who has displayed a penchant for creative writing, I think my father has always

held on to the hope that each of his children will spring into novel-writers. Since we were about twelve or thirteen, he has consistently demanded that we each write a story for him at Christmastime rather than buy him a gift. His favorite is a story I wrote for him in high school; it was my own personal version of *A Christmas Carol*.

I began seriously writing creatively towards the end of high school. I have kept journals since I was eight or nine, but in high school, I discovered my true capacity for poetry. I wrote poetry for English classes and for our high school literary magazine. When I got to college, I naturally began taking creative writing classes. I have taken Beginning Poetry, Intermediate Poetry twice, and the Honors 598 seminar with a creative writing component. I improve constantly and with each class my relationship to language changes and grows. Anyone who has taken a workshop knows that, in these courses, you have to be able to stand criticism and to pick out which suggestions are beneficial and which are not. It was my father, the constant in my literacy narrative, who encouraged me through all of these classes, telling me that no matter what anybody thought, I was a poet, a better poet than he had ever been.

I believe that my choice to major in French is also rooted in this tradition of language and literature. Studying a foreign language can, at times, be just like learning how to read and write as a child. Studying French intensely became for me the perfect, impossible challenge: to read and write French like I read and write English. However, it seems that as long and hard as I study French, I will never be quite so comfortable nor quite so capable of understanding it or placing it within a context. I believe that this is partially because tradition plays no role in my study of French. It has nothing to do with my family or my background, and it cannot move me emotionally to the extent that English language can. Unlike French, I have a tradition of reading, speaking, and writing English, and I have a much vaster appreciation for English literature in general.

A clear indication of why this story matters to the author.

Because of my father and our shared love of literature, my definition of literacy is intimately linked to the idea of tradition. In a way, my literacy is part of my lineage, part of the legacy of my father. My love for literature and writing, my poetic tendencies, my passion for language are all gifts from him. I think that I tend to have more of an imagination than my peers, and I also love to write and create using words. The reason for these qualities is that my father once inspired in me his own creativity and instructed me on the under-standing of human experience through writing. In turn, this literacy experience is something I want to pass on to my children someday.

Literacy is generally known as the ability to read and write. My definition of literacy is: the ability to read, write, and understand within a tradition. For me, this is a familial tradition that has per-meated my literacy experience. Parents have an incredible power to influence their children through their own behaviors and at-titudes, and it is certainly true that my father has impressed upon me his own attitudes towards literacy and literature. Now, every time we talk he asks me, "What are you reading? What do you think about it?" We talk about what each of us is reading, as well as our thoughts and impressions. In this way, the tradition continues.

Some daughters inherit a certain amount of money from their fathers. Some inherit a car or a house. Others inherit jewelry. My father will never have much money or a nice car or many mate-rial goods at all. I have, however, received something from him that will last my whole life and will continue to give me joy as long as I live. He has passed on to me his love of language and litera-ture. It is within this tradition that I understand literacy, a tradition that causes me to sometimes think "God is not dead; nor doth he sleep" (Longfellow 32) when I hear bells ringing.

The author concludes with a strong statement about why this story is so meaningful.

Works Cited

Eliot, T. S. "The Love Song of J. Alfred Prufrock." *Poets.org*,
     Academy of American Poets, www.poets.org/poetsorg/
     poem/love-song-j-alfred-prufrock. Accessed 12 Oct. 2009.
Housman, A. E. "To an Athlete Dying Young." *Poets.org*,
     Academy of American Poets, www.poets.org/poetsorg/
     poem/athlete-dying-young. Accessed 12 Oct. 2009.
Kipling, Rudyard. "If—." *Poets.org*, Academy of American Poets,
     www.poets.org/poetsorg/poem/if—. Accessed 12 Oct. 2009.
Longfellow, Henry Wadsworth. "Christmas Bells." *Poets.org*,
     Academy of American Poets, www.poets.org/poetsorg/
     poem/christmas-bells. Accessed 12 Oct. 2009.
Melville, Herman. *Moby-Dick*. Penguin Books, 1988.

REFLECT on your own experiences as a writer or reader. Identify one person who played a key role in your developing literacy. What did they teach you, and how? Whatever it was, what impact has it had on your life?

WRITING A NARRATIVE / A Roadmap

Choose a topic that matters—to you, and to others

Whether you write a narrative for personal reasons or in response to an assignment, choose your own topic or work with an assigned topic, try to write about something that matters to you—and try to make sure that it will matter to your audience as well.

If you are writing a personal narrative, choosing a topic can be difficult because you are deciding to share something personal about yourself or someone you know. You will need to choose an experience or event that you feel comfortable sharing, in some detail, with an audience. Be sure that the experience is not only important to you but also of enough general interest to engage your audience.

If your narrative is not a personal one, you still want it to be compelling. Narratives that aren't personal are often part of a larger conversation about an event, or some topic that the event represents, which gives the story significance. For example, if you are writing a narrative about how specific students' academic performances changed when they enrolled in a charter school, you need to recognize that such stories are part of an ongoing educational and political debate about the effectiveness of charter schools as an alternative to traditional public schools. You may need to do some research to understand this debate and how your narrative fits into it.

Consider your rhetorical situation

Whenever you write a narrative (or anything, for that matter), you need to consider the following elements of your rhetorical situation:

Think about your AUDIENCE. Who will be reading what you write, and what's your relationship with them?

- Will your audience have any knowledge about your topic? Will you need to explain anything or provide any background information?
- How are they like or unlike you? Consider age, gender, income, cultural heritage, political beliefs, and so on. How will such factors affect how you tell the story?

- Can you assume they'll be interested in what you write? How can you get them interested?
- How are they likely to react to your narrative? What do you want them to think or do as a result of reading what you say?

Think about your PURPOSE. Why are you writing this narrative? What is the significance of this story, and what do you hope it will demonstrate to your readers? Remember that your narrative needs to do more than just tell an engaging story; it needs to make a point of some kind.

Think about your STANCE. Are you telling a story that is very personal to you, or is it one you have some distance from? How do you want to present yourself as the narrator? Do you want to come across as witty and amusing, if you're telling a humorous family story? As knowledgeable but impersonal, if you're recounting historical events for a political science essay? Whatever your stance, how can you make your writing reflect that stance?

Consider the larger CONTEXT. What broader issues are involved in your narrative? What else has been said and written about this topic? Even if your narrative is personal, how might it speak to some larger topic—perhaps a social or political one? Considering the larger context for your narrative can help you see it from perspectives different from your own and present it in a way that will interest others.

Consider your MEDIUM. If you have a choice, think about which medium best suits your goals and audience. The kinds of details you include, the language you use, the way you present materials from sources, and many other things depend on the medium. The conventions of a print essay, for instance, in which you can use written words and images, differ markedly from those of an audio essay (in which you can use sounds but no written words or images).

Consider matters of DESIGN. Does your narrative need headings? Is there anything in the story that could be conveyed better with a photograph than with words alone? Will embedded audio or video clips help you engage your audience? Often in academic writing, you may be expected to use a specific font and type size or to structure headings a certain way. If you can determine the look of your text, though, remember that design has a powerful impact on the impression your narrative makes.

Explore your topic and do any necessary research

If you are writing a personal narrative, write down all that you remember about your topic. Using **FREEWRITING** or other activities for **GENERATING IDEAS**, write down as many specific details as you can: sounds, smells, textures, colors, and so on. What details will engage your audience? Not all the details that you jot down in this exploratory stage will make it into your essay. You'll need to choose the ones that will engage your audience and support your main point. In addition to sensory details, try to write down direct quotations or dialogue you can remember that will help bring your story to life.

If your narrative is not a personal one, you'll likely need to conduct **RESEARCH** so that you can provide accurate and sufficient details about the topic. Whether your research takes you to sources in the library or online, or into the community to conduct interviews, it's important to get the what, when, and where of the narrative right, and consulting sources will help you do that.

Decide on a point of view

The subject that you choose to write about will usually determine the point of view from which you write. If you're telling a story in which you are a central participant, you will usually use the first person (*I, we*). In some academic disciplines, however, or if you're narrating a story that is not personal, the third person (*he, she, they*) may be more appropriate.

Also think about what verb tense would be most effective for establishing the point of view in your narrative. Most personal narratives that are arranged in chronological order are written in the past tense ("When I *was* twelve, I *discovered* what I *wanted* to do for the rest of my life"). However, if you want readers to feel like they are actually experiencing an event, you may choose to use the present tense, as Georgina Kleege and Michael Lewis do in examples earlier in this chapter.

Organize and start writing

Once you've chosen a subject and identified your main point, considered your rhetorical situation, come up with enough details, and decided on a point of view (not necessarily in this order), it's time to think about how to organize your narrative.

Keep your main point in mind. As you begin to draft, type out that point as a tentative **THESIS** and keep your eye on it as you write; you can decide later whether you want to include it in your text.

Organize your information. What happened? Where? When? Who was there? What details can you describe to make the story come alive? Decide whether to present the narrative in **CHRONOLOGICAL ORDER**, in reverse chronological order, or in some other order.

Draft an OPENING. A good introduction draws your audience into the story and makes them want to know more. Sometimes you'll need to provide a context for your narrative—to describe the setting and introduce some of the people before getting on with what happened. Other times you might start in the middle of your story, or at the end—and then circle back to tell what happened.

Draft a CONCLUSION. If you organize your narrative chronologically, you'll likely conclude by telling how the story ends. But make sure your readers see the point of your story; if you haven't made that clear, you might end by saying something about the story's significance. Why does it matter to you? What do you want readers to take away—and remember?

Look critically at your draft, get response—and revise

Read your draft slowly and carefully. Try to see it as if for the first time: Does the story grab your attention, and can you follow it? Can you tell what the point is, and will your audience care? If possible, get feedback from others. Following are some questions that can help you or others examine a narrative with a critical eye:

- *How does the* **OPENING** *capture the audience's interest?* Is it clear why you're telling the story, and have you given readers reason to want to find out what happened? How else might the narrative begin?

- *Who's telling the story?* Have you maintained a consistent **POINT OF VIEW**?

- *Is the setting of your story clear?* Have you situated the events in a well-described time and place?

- *Is the story easy to follow?* If it's at all confusing, would **TRANSITIONS** help your audience follow the sequence of events? If it's a lengthy or complex narrative, would headings help?

- *Are there enough vivid, concrete details?* Is there an appropriate balance of showing and telling? Have you included any dialogue or direct quotations—and if not, would adding some help the story come alive?

- *Are there any visuals?* If not, would adding some help bring the narrative to life?

- *How do you establish* **AUTHORITY** *and credibility?* How would you describe the **STANCE** and **TONE**—and are they appropriate for your audience and purpose?

- *Does the story have a clear point?* Is the point stated explicitly—and if not, should it be? If the main point is implied rather than stated, is the significance of the narrative still clear?

- *How satisfying is the* **CONCLUSION**? What does it leave the audience thinking? How else might the narrative end?

- *Does the title suggest what the narrative is about,* and will it make an audience want to read on?

Revise your draft in light of any feedback you receive and your own critique, keeping your purpose and especially your audience firmly in mind.

REFLECT. Once you've completed your narrative, let it settle for a while and then take time to reflect. How well did you tell the story? What additional revisions would you make if you could? Research shows that such reflections help "lock in" what you learn for future use.

Bathtime

CONNOR COYNE

THE BATH DELIGHTS her.

When it's 6:45 in the evening—dark or getting darker—and we ask her, "You ready to go night-night?" Ruby toddles over toward the stairs, muttering: "Bobble, Eejee." A bottle of milk. Geegee, her stuffed giraffe. She is one year old.

Her eyes light up when we carry her into the bathroom. We drop the plug and press down the plastic mat—you don't want little babies slipping and banging their heads on the hard porcelain—and fill the small room with the silver sound of falling water.

She gives us a big smile as the lukewarm bath surges up around her sides. She laughs brightly when she sees she can make waves by slapping her hands down against the water. She feels buoyed by the bubbles between her toes, the fine mist that catches in her light, pixie hair. She grabs for floating foam letters, a plastic turtle, a rubber duckie. This is one of the happiest moments of her day, and it's good that she is happy before we ask her to keep calm in the darkness, to let her brain slip into sleep, to stop moving for a while. Bath as benediction. A sacred quietness that slips between the Flinty clatter of distant train wheels rolling. The familiar thrill of train whistles. A reminder of her baptism.

CONNOR COYNE, a fiction writer, grew up in Flint, Michigan. After leaving to attend college in Chicago, Coyne eventually moved back to Flint with his wife to raise a family, and he lives there still. His narrative essay "Bathtime" was originally published in the 2018 edited collection *Voices from the Rust Belt*.

For Ruby, the bath is an immersive experience, and so she tries to dip a 5
plastic cup in the water and take a big gulp. Little kids are immune to parental
squeamishness. They do this all over the world, or at least anywhere little kids
take baths in porcelain bathtubs. Squeamish parents cringe and say, "No, no,
we don't do that. We don't drink water from the tub."

In Flint, though, our reaction is more severe. We lurch forward, our faces
pale. It's like catching your toddler tottering at the top of a flight of stairs. It's like
seeing a preschooler running headlong toward a busy street in pursuit of a plastic ball. You feel it, visceral in your gut, like someone sucker punched you and
you want to puke. They might be making themselves sick from something much
worse than suds and whatever scum has been washed away by the day's play.

* * *

My wife isn't from Flint.

I am.

Well, I grew up in the city until I was twelve, when my parents moved out to
Flushing, a picturesque suburb that finally got its own coffee shop in 1997. That
was the year I graduated high school. But even though I had a Flushing address,
I auditioned for every play at Flint Youth Theatre and went to the Flint Central
High School prom. I always considered myself a Flintstone and spent as much
time as I could in the city. When I went away to college in Chicago, I always
hoped to come back home. To me, Flint was a place of youthful energy and risk,
frisson and connection. I was aware that I was the salmon swimming upstream,
against the current of all the other people eager to leave, but I didn't care.

When I met my eventual wife a few years later, I regaled her with all the 10
stories of my friends and their . . . lives. The insane intensity of life in Flint. The
city had been abandoned, I said. Physically abandoned by the company that
built and nurtured it, and then again by half of its people left struggling in the
wake of deindustrialization . . .

For my wife, practical concerns edged out my visionary rants.

I wanted to go back to the place she said seemed to break everyone I knew. . . .

"I got this," I said.

I actually felt—and I'm not [BSing] here—more able to deliver that happy,
stable childhood in Flint than anywhere else. See, in Flint, I knew the rules. It
isn't chaos. There are rules. There are especially rules if you're 1) middle-class,
2) white, and 3) educated. And the college education supplied by my father's
almost forty years at GM under UAW-earned contracts got me there. My
kids would have friends here. They would live in a stable neighborhood and
go to a good school. They would have educational opportunities, we'd keep

an eye on them, and it wouldn't be any more difficult or risky than a life in Chicago, or New York, or New Orleans, or San Francisco. It would be safer, less risky, because I knew how Flint worked. I didn't know how those other cities worked. I didn't know their rules. I had the tools to control a child's experience of Flint. Anything else, I'd be learning from scratch.

I said this with a lot of arrogance and a fair amount of truth, but hubris 15 always lands the punch line.

When our first daughter was born, we decided to leave Chicago and move to Flint. Because of the fallout from the 2008 housing meltdown, we could afford a house south of Court Street, just east of downtown. When I grew up, this was one of Flint's most exclusive neighborhoods. Now, a family on a single income could land a beautiful 1930s Tudoresque house for a down payment less than that of the tiniest Chicago bungalow, in the middle range of five figures. We could use the money we saved to choose any school for our daughter we wanted. We were close to my parents. We were close to friends. I planted a garden in our backyard and put up a swing set and a fort. The front yard was filled with dappled sunlight that streamed through the maple leaves each summer, enough shade to cool off, and enough sun to nourish the petunias, iridescent in their violet summer glory.

It was cool.

I knew the rules.

* * *

I didn't know the rules.

The rules were [BS].

I was thinking about classroom sizes and museums and violent crime and 20 copper scrappers. I was thinking about street violence and friends from broken homes and arson and unemployment. Too many guns and too little supervision. These were the problems I was trying to puzzle out. Meanwhile, the city went under state receivership and started drawing water from the Flint River instead of the Great Lakes by way of Detroit. The rest is a sad story told across the world by now: the river water wasn't treated properly; it leached lead and other junk from the pipes into tap water. A lot of people drank that water. A lot of people got very sick. Government officials tried to cover up the catastrophe, leading to more sickness, more delays, more damage.

I had never banked on the water going bad.

In all my youthful exuberance, my desire to bring my girls up here, in my community, my pride, my home, I thought I had covered all of the bases, but water is fundamental, the number-two necessity for humans after breathable air. A place that tries to damage you with its water is damaging in the most basic way. And so, I stayed alert each night, watching Ruby bathe, conscious that this isn't right, that this is supposed to be safe, that she would only be safe, for sure, through our unfailing vigilance.

* * *

Ruby doesn't know that the water in this city is bad. Dangerous.

Mary, her five-year-old sister, understands it in a straightforward way, like Darth Vader, like busy traffic, a risk to be avoided. She knows that she shouldn't drink the water just like she shouldn't talk to strangers in strange cars. This loss of innocence and the anonymous lies that prompted it make me sad and angry. Sometimes, it keeps me up at night, thinking of all the injury, the hurt, the real hurt, physical, mental; the loss of trust, the enormity of that loss, the immensity of betrayal; the contempt of those officials who have treated us—treated our children—like expendable animals. Lab rats. Numbers and statistics that might be converted into a political liability, and what a pain in the ass we are for that reason. I've dreamed about it more than once. What if the tests the city conducted on our household water were wrong? What if we didn't act quickly enough? What was this place going to look like in fifteen years? Who was going to be left?

Mary is a bright five-year-old. She is old enough to understand some of this. Not old enough to feel the outrage, but old enough to notice the contradiction and confusion. "It's expensive," we tell her. "Why can't we drink it?" she asks. "Well," I tell her, "you can wash your hands in it, but don't drink it. Don't you drink it. Even if it's the middle of the night and you're thirsty, come and wake me up. I'll get you a glass. You're right. The world isn't right and the world isn't fair."

Some of these are conversations every father expects to have with his child, but not so soon, and certainly not about the unsafe tap water that costs you $130 each month. Not in the first state to light its darkened city streets with streetlamps. Not in the U.S. state that put the world on wheels and taught it to move with speed.

Ruby isn't even two yet. She doesn't see the confusion or the contradiction. For Ruby, the confusion is much simpler: she likes to dip the plastic cup in her bathwater and take a drink when she can. We freak out, lunge forward, snatch up that cup, and toss it to the floor. Ruby yells in surprise and disappointment, at the loud noise, our worried faces, the brief chaos of moving hands and water spray.

She'll relax again, in a few moments, when we soothe her with a song, or give her something else to play with.

We'll relax, too, when the last of the water has finally vanished down 30 the drain.

Thinking about the Text

1. How does Coyne use his daughter's bathtime to make an **EMOTIONAL APPEAL** to his readers? Point to specific words and passages. How effective is this appeal?

2. Coyne's memories of his childhood in Flint help establish the **SETTING**. How else does Coyne set a clear scene?

3. Note how Coyne **COMPARES AND CONTRASTS** his five-year-old daughter Mary's behavior with that of one-year-old Ruby's behavior. How does this comparison contribute to the story? Where else in the story does Coyne compare and contrast people, opinions, and places to make a point?

4. "Bathtime" is about Coyne's fatherhood as much as it is about his daughter's bathtime—his **POINT OF VIEW** as a father is important. How would the story be different if it were told from a different perspective—for example, that of Flint's mayor? A child who's lived through the water crisis? A person who grew up in Flint and didn't move back to raise a family?

5. Coyne's decision to move his family back to Flint is based on his childhood memories and his expectation that Flint would offer his family a good life. His expectations were challenged by the water crisis. Write a **NARRATIVE** about an experience in your life that did not live up to your expectation—describing in detail the anticipated event, the outcome, and why it matters to you and potentially to others, too.

The Look

LARRY LEHNA

I FEAR THAT I CARRY FAR MORE BAGGAGE than the typical college student. Unlike Frank Sinatra, regrets I have more than "a few," and even if I do not mention them they weigh heavily upon me. I sometimes regret my wasted life. Then I stop and wonder if it was really wasted. There are so many things I did not accomplish. However, I helped to raise a fine son and he was almost through college before my downfall. My step-daughters were seven and sixteen when I was sent to prison. Yet they both wrote to me for the full eleven years. At different times they have both told me that I am the only real father they have known. Each of them now has children of her own whom I dote upon. So even among the regrets is a modicum of satisfaction.

Always present are my scars, both physical and mental. Mine was not an easy life. I carry many memories. The burning pain of bullet wounds (they really do burn). The agony of stitches going into a fresh knife wound. The nearly immobilizing ache of broken ribs. But most of all I carry emotions. The anguish of being arrested. The despair over lost loves. The disappointment of unfulfilled dreams. I am an emotional cauldron. There is a reason for this.

LARRY LEHNA is a writer whose work has been published in the *Detroit Metro Times* and *Quail Bell Magazine*, an online feminist magazine that publishes "real and unreal stories." Lehna was a student at University of Michigan–Dearborn at the time that he wrote this essay for a narrative journalism class, and he now volunteers on campus to support nontraditional students striving for a chance through education like he once was.

For eleven years I could not show any emotion. When you go to prison you put on a mask called a "Marquette," the name of Michigan's toughest prison. The look says, "I'm tough, I like to fight, and I would just love to hurt you. So mess with me if you dare." When I was in jail awaiting my sentencing I spent hours glaring into the mirror trying to perfect the look, but what gazed back at me was a look that said instead, "I'm constipated." I concluded I would never achieve that look. Little did I know that it would come naturally.

When I was sentenced to ten to thirty years in prison I was stunned. I wanted to cry. I wanted to be hugged. I wanted my mommy. I wanted to hurt someone, but I knew I should not show any emotion. That is when the look appeared on my face. When I got back to the cell-block I noticed a new-found wariness from the other prisoners. They kept their distance. When I went to the bathroom I glanced in the mirror. There it was: the look I would wear for over eleven years, the look that acted like a stopper in the bottle of my emotions. Nothing could faze me, and nothing did. It was more than a look; it was an attitude that was much more severe than mere stoicism. No emotions in, no emotions out.

Over the course of my first year that attitude became ingrained. Part of it 5 was always expecting the worst. I learned to never anticipate anything good from my fellow prisoners or from the institution. When they denied my first attempt at parole, after ten years, I received the information with the same deadpan expression as if they were handing me a pair of socks.

When I finally received my parole I wore the same look. I assumed they would take my parole away, and they did postpone it six months because I had once assaulted a thieving bunkmate. Another bit of news that had no visible effect. I no longer had to try to hide my feelings; I no longer felt any.

When I was released I was sent to a halfway house in Pontiac, one of the few cities in the country in worse shape than Detroit. There were absolutely no job prospects. Add to this the fact that a minimum of three days a week I had to report to either parole, or one of their programs, such as their Job Shop. What a joke. They acted as if they actually spoke with the people offering the jobs. They never did. They found the ads online and printed them. It did not bother these people to send us miles away to apply only to find out that the employer would not even consider a felon. Meanwhile, the amount they spent on counseling and other programs was enormous. It would have been enough to offer a parolee a fresh start, with a car and an apartment and a little bit of a chance at success. But let's not cloud this issue with logic.

The programs, too, were miles away in different directions. It was winter when I was released. I plodded through the snow wearing my cheap state shoes and the look. Whatever they got, I could take it. I only had 90 days to make something happen, and then I had to leave the halfway house. With less than a week left I told my parole officer that I had nowhere to go. When she suggested the homeless shelter, I took her response with a simple nod of my head and the look. With one day to spare I found a place where I could work for my room and board; I was glad to avoid the shelter, but I don't recall a feeling of happiness.

Once ensconced in my palatial new digs, I found my room was actually smaller than my prison cell, but it was all mine. No bunkie for me, but otherwise I continued on as I had done for the past eleven years. I was existing. I had learned that if I applied for a FAFSA [Free Application for Federal student Aid] educational grant they would pay for my schooling and give me whatever was left over in a check. I applied, was accepted and I made an appointment to see a counselor at Oakland Community College. I expected resistance, having experienced nothing but rejection for the last eleven years. The Secretary of State made it almost impossible to get a driver's license once they saw my prison ID card. Society did not like me; they too had a look when they learned of my past. That was just fine; I didn't like them in return. The pressure was building up like Mount St. Helens.

I arrived for my appointment at OCC less than two weeks before classes 10 were to begin. They ushered me into the office of a woman named Noreen Ruehs. I was fully prepared for her to adopt the look and I was ready to set the counselor straight about how little I cared about her and her fancy college job.

When I told her about my past she raised her eyebrows, nodded and said, "Well, you have some catching up to do. Let's see what kind of degree would suit you best." She proffered a few small pamphlets and suggested I look over the one for General Studies. She asked if I knew about computers. When I admitted my ignorance she recommended a Computer Literacy class. She asked about my typing skills and suggested a keyboarding class. We soon had my whole schedule full and all of it at very convenient times. Her kindness had a remarkable effect. There were times when I had to look at the floor and blink several times before I could speak. Kindness was unexpected and I got choked up. I was starting to believe that I could do this. She asked how I planned to pay for college. I told her about my Pell grant. When she said it could be too late for the summer semester, I know she saw my disappointment.

The counselor picked up the phone. "Have you got a minute or two right now? It's important," she said into the handset. Together we walked to the financial aid office and went straight to the supervisor. Noreen asked the woman if she could rush my paperwork through to get me into the coming semester, adding, "Please do this as a personal favor to me."

"Okay, I will handle this myself," said the supervisor. As we left the office I couldn't speak. I just nodded dumbly. The same thing happened in the enrollment office—straight to the supervisor. The problem was that my financial aid had not been processed and I did not have my transcripts from the 1960's at Henry Ford Community College.

Noreen also asked this woman for a personal favor. "Please, just get him enrolled and make sure he gets these classes," she said. "I guarantee the financial aid will come through and we will have his transcripts in here tomorrow." My eyes were blinking like a strobe light to keep the tears at bay. This woman had spent two hours helping me pick my classes and asking for personal favors on my behalf.

"Well, you're all set. Now it is up to you," she said. I reached out to shake 15 her hand, but she gave me a hug instead and went in to counsel the next student. I was unprepared for a physical demonstration of warmth. I had not been hugged by a woman in eleven years. I walked to the parking structure in a daze. It was darker inside with very few people. By the time I got to my car tears were streaming down my cheeks. When someone walked by I would duck down in the seat. After twenty minutes I managed to slap my mask back on.

But when I walked into my room the mask slipped again. It didn't just slip, the damn thing fell off. This time it was not just tears. My body convulsed in guttural sobs. I fell on the bed, and all of the anguish of the lost years came pouring out. I gagged and gasped and howled. It lasted a good thirty minutes, until I cried myself to sleep. When I woke up an hour later the pillow was wet with tears and drool, and my mustache was stuck to it with dried snot. I got up and washed my face, and afterward I felt remarkably good. I knew I would excel at school. That counselor had given me a new outlook on life. I knew from then on things would change, and they did. But one lingering symptom has refused to go away.

When something good happens to me I get choked up. When someone gives me a compliment I get choked up. While typing this I have used two paper towels just from remembering the counselor's kindness. I blubber through any movie or TV show. It's the same with books. It does not have to be a heart-wrenching scene. If someone succeeds I get tears. If anything good happens I get tears. I sometimes tear up just thinking about good things in my life. There is no returning to what was once my emotional normal. I have turned into a real wuss. Even so, I believe I am a better person now. My look has vanished, but I still get the opposite looks on occasion from people who know about my past. Those looks are the least of my worries; you can't argue with the ignorant.

Noreen Ruehs called Susan Cushner at the University of Michigan–Dearborn and helped me transfer there. I'll graduate in a few weeks with "high distinction" and one of the five Chancellor's Medallions that are awarded to the best in the class. I have tried to thank Noreen but she says that I am the one who did all the work. She has no idea what she did for me. Of course I am wiping tears now.

Thinking about the Text

1. What is Larry Lehna's point in telling this story? Where does he make that point clear?

2. How would you describe the organization of Lehna's narrative? Chronological? Reverse chronological? Some other order? Where does the story start and end, and how effective is this structure?

3. Lehna talks about a look he sometimes receives from "people who know about my past," a look that tells him that "society did not like me" and that people doubted his character. We're willing to bet you feel quite differently after reading his story. How does Lehna connect with his **AUDIENCE** in this piece and establish his **CREDIBILITY**?

4. This essay was written for a course in narrative journalism, a genre that uses individual stories to illuminate public issues. Imagine that Lehna told this story as part of an essay on the need for prison reform for a political science course. How might the essay be different for that **PURPOSE**?

5. Identify an experience from your own life that sheds light on a social, political, cultural, or economic issue. Perhaps you were bullied in middle school, for instance—a deeply personal experience that has broader significance. Write a **NARRATIVE** essay in which you bring your own experience to life while also making the broader significance clear.

FOURTEEN

"Let's Take a Closer Look"
Writing Analytically

NALYSIS IS A NECESSARY STEP in much of the thinking that we do, and something that we do every day. What should you wear today? T-shirt and flip-flops? A sweatshirt? Your new red sweater? You consider the weather forecast, what you will be doing, the people you will be with (and might want to impress, or not), and then decide based on those factors. You may not consciously think of it as analysis, but that's what you've done.

When you analyze something, you break it down into its component parts and think about those parts methodically in order to understand it in some way. Since our world is awash in information, the ability to read it closely, examine it critically, and decide how—or whether—to accept or act on it becomes a survival skill. To navigate this sea of information, we rely on our ability to analyze.

Case in point: you want a new set of headphones, but do you want earbuds? over-the-ear? noise canceling? Bluetooth? wireless? As you consider your options, your analysis will be driven by a number of questions: What's most important to you—sound quality? comfort? price? brand or look? When will you most often be wearing your headphones—at the gym? on your daily bus commute? while playing video games? You could ask your music-loving friends for their opinions, or you might check websites like *CNET*, which provide expert analysis as well as price comparisons. You might test out different styles and designs at your local

Best Buy store. These are some of the ways you might analyze the various options, first to understand what they offer and then to decide which one you want to buy.

You have probably analyzed literary texts in English classes. In many college classes, you'll be expected to conduct different kinds of analyses—of texts, and also of events, issues, arguments, and more. Analysis is critical to every academic discipline, useful in every professional field, and essential to everyday decision making. This chapter provides guidelines for conducting an analysis and writing analytically, with specific advice for rhetorical, causal, discourse, process, data, and visual analysis.

REFLECT. Think about your own use of analysis. How many decisions— large and small—have you made in the last week? in the last month? in the last year? From small (what to have for breakfast) to major (which college to attend), make a chart listing a representative sample of these decisions and what areas of your life they affected. Then note the information you gathered in each case before you came to a final decision. What does this chart tell you about your interests, activities, and priorities? You've just completed an analysis.

Across Academic Disciplines

Some form of analysis can be found in every academic discipline. In a *history* class, you may be asked to analyze how Russia defeated Napoleon's army in 1812. In *biology*, you might analyze how the body responds to exercise. In *economics*, you might analyze the trade-off between unemployment and inflation rates. In a *technical communication* course, you might analyze a corporate website to understand how it appeals to various audiences. In your *composition* course, you'll analyze your own writing for many purposes, from thinking about how you've appealed to your audience to deciding how you need to revise a draft. So many courses require analysis because looking closely and methodically at something—a text, a process, a philosophy— helps you discover connections between ideas and think about how things work, what they mean, and why.

Across Media

Your medium affects the way you present your analysis. In *print*, you'll be writing mostly in paragraphs, and you might include photos, tables, graphs, diagrams, or other images to make your analysis clear. If you're making an *oral presentation*, you might show some information on slides or handouts. A *digital text* allows you to blend words, images, and audio—and you can embed these elements directly in your text or link to more information elsewhere. See how the following analysis from *Examiner.com* links to a *YouTube* video of Serena Williams practicing her serve to let readers see for themselves the process the author is analyzing. Had he been writing for a print publication, he might have included a still image like the one below.

Most casual tennis fans may think Williams simply hits the ball harder than any other female on the planet, but the fact of the matter is that Serena Williams' service mechanics are textbook perfect and allow her to maximize every ounce of energy and power she possesses to its fullest extent—all without trying to bash the felt off the ball.

If you watch Williams' entire service motion from beginning to end, you'll see that she has every part of her body working toward one goal, powering up—and through—the tennis ball.

First, Williams gets that familiar "rocking motion" of hers, shifting back and then forward as she begins her swing take-back. Next, the younger tennis-playing Williams sister begins her service toss motion as

Serena Williams serving at Wimbledon, 2015.

her body weight begins moving toward the net. Williams then brings her feet together and takes a fantastic knee bend that all players need to copy whether male or female. With her weight shifted and her knees bent significantly and left arm still pointing up, Williams literally explodes upward toward the ball while her racquet head drops as her right elbow stretches up toward the heavens.

Now, with her body launched in the air, Williams reaches up for the ball and just before striking it, she pronates her wrist, arm and racquet as she powers through the ball as only she can.

—ERIC WILLIAMS, "Five Things All Tennis Players
Can Learn from Serena Williams"

**THINK
BEYOND
WORDS**

↪ *WATCH THE VIDEO of a TED talk by statistician Nate Silver on whether race affects voting. Silver includes slides with lists, bar graphs, photos, and maps. How do the visuals contribute to his analysis? A space below the posted video invites viewers to comment. Write a comment about something Silver said in his talk that you find thought-provoking: your challenge will be to frame your comment in response to Silver while adding your own perspective. Go to everyonesanauthor.tumblr.com to view the video.*

Across Cultures and Communities

Communicating with people from other communities or cultures challenges us to examine our assumptions and think about our usual ways of operating. Analyzing and understanding beliefs, assumptions, and practices that we are not familiar with may take extra effort. We need to be careful not to look at things only through our own frames of reference.

Sheikh Jamal Rahman, Pastor Don Mackenzie, and Rabbi Ted Falcon put in this extra effort in writing their book, *Getting to the Heart of Interfaith: The Eye-Opening, Hope-Filled Friendship of a Pastor, a Rabbi and a Sheikh*. In this book they take on the challenge of working toward interfaith understanding, saying that religion today "seems to be fueling hatred rather than expanding love" and that in order to heal the divisions between us, we must "find ways of entering into conversation with those different from us." And they say that analysis—what they call "inquiring more deeply"—is essential to their ongoing journey toward understanding issues central to each faith.

All three agree that it is critical to discuss the difficult and contentious ideas in faith. For the minister, one "untruth" is that "Christianity is the only way to God." For the rabbi, it is the notion of Jews as "the chosen people." And for the sheikh, it is the "sword verses" in the Koran, like "kill the unbeliever," which when taken out of context cause misunderstanding.

Their book embodies cultural sensitivity and describes the process of creating a text that's respectful of their different faiths. Reading a sentence that the sheikh had written about the security wall in Israel, the rabbi responded, "If that line is in the book, I'm not in the book." Then they analyzed and discussed the sentence, and Sheikh Rahman revised the wording to be "respectful of [both] their principles."

Having respect for the principles, values, and beliefs of others means recognizing and being sensitive to differences among cultures. The best way to demonstrate cultural sensitivity is to use precise language that avoids negative words or stereotypes about gender, religion, race, ethnicity, and such—in short, by carefully selecting the words you use.

Across Genres

Seldom does any piece of writing consist solely of one genre; in many cases, writers draw on multiple genres as the situation demands. Analysis is a crucial step in writing for many purposes. To **ARGUE A POSITION** on an issue, you'll need to analyze that issue before you can take a stand on it. To compose a **REPORT**, you sometimes have to first analyze the data or the information that the report will be based on. And a **REVIEW** —whether it's of a film, a website, a book, or something else—depends on your analyzing the material before you evaluate it. Likewise, you might use a short **NARRATIVE** as an introductory element in a process or causal analysis.

REFLECT. Look for analysis in everyday use. Find two consumer-oriented websites that analyze something you're interested in—laptops, cell phones, sneakers, places you might like to go, things you might like to do. Study the analyses and decide which one is more useful. Then try to figure out what makes it better. Is it the language? the images? the amount of detail? the format? Keep these observations in mind as you write and design your own analyses.

CHARACTERISTIC FEATURES

While there are nearly as many different kinds of analysis as there are things to be analyzed, we can identify five common elements that analyses share across disciplines, media, cultures, and communities:

- A question that prompts you to take a closer look
- Some description of the subject you are analyzing
- Evidence drawn from close examination of the subject
- Insight gained from your analysis
- Clear, precise language

A Question That Prompts You to Take a Closer Look

If you look at the examples cited earlier in this chapter, you'll note that each is driven by a question that doesn't have a single "right" answer. What should you wear today? Which set of headphones best meets your needs? How can we begin to achieve interfaith understanding? Each question requires some kind of analysis. While an author may not explicitly articulate such a question, it will drive the analysis—and the writing that presents the analysis. In an essay examining our two-party political system, see how *New York Times* journalist David Brooks starts by posing two questions, the second building on the first.

> Is there room for a third party? If some independent mounted a presidential bid, would that person have a chance? . . .
>
> There is no evidence that there are enough centrists or "pragmatists" to threaten the two-party duopoly. To have a chance, the third-party candidate would have to emerge as the most radical person in the race. That person would have to argue that the Republicans and Democrats are just two sides of a Washington-centric power structure that has ground to a halt. That person would have to promise to radically redistribute power across American society . . .
>
> [T]oday, the country is diverse, trust in big institutions is low, the federal government is immobilized by partisanship and debt. Now, state and local governments are more effective across many overlapping domains.
>
> It's no wonder that so many, especially millennials (the most diverse generation of voters in our history), have become disillusioned with federal action. . . .
>
> All recent presidential candidates have run against Washington, but on the premise that they could change Washington. Today, a third-party candidate would have to run on creating different kinds of power structures at different levels.
>
> Across the country, power is being most effectively wielded by civic councils—organically formed groups of local officials, business leaders, neighborhood organizations. The members may have different racial, class and partisan identities, but they have one shared identity—love of their community. My colleague Thomas Friedman wrote about one such council in Lancaster, Pa. If you want to see others you probably don't have to travel far—Winston-Salem, Indianapolis, Detroit, Kalamazoo, Denver, Grand Rapids. Power in these places is not just wielded at the ballot box; it is wielded by movements and collaboratives in a thousand ways. According to a 2015 Heartland Monitor poll, 66 percent of Americans believe that their local area is moving in the right direction. . . . A third-party candidate who shifted attention to local people actually getting stuff done might lose, but he or she would begin to define a new and more plausible version of American greatness.
>
> —DAVID BROOKS, "Third-Party Option"

To answer his opening questions, Brooks lays out the conditions he believes are necessary for a third-party or an independent candidate to get traction. Then he takes a closer look, providing a succinct analysis of those conditions. You might not always start an analytical essay as Brooks does, by asking an explicit question, but your analysis will always be prompted by a question of some kind.

Some Description of the Subject You Are Analyzing

To be sure your audience fully understands your analysis, you need to first describe what you are analyzing. How much description you need depends on your subject, your audience, and the medium in which you present your piece. For example, if you are analyzing tropes in George R. R. Martin's *A Song of Fire and Ice* series for your fantasy literature class, you can assume most of your audience will be familiar with your subject. However, if you are analyzing the success of the TV series based on Martin's novels for your marketing class, you will have to describe the elements that make it HBO's most popular series ever. See how Ken Tucker does so in a piece on the British website *BBC Culture* that tackles that question: "Why is *Game of Thrones* so popular?"

> The return of *Game of Thrones*, back for a fourth season of sword fighting, bed hopping and mud flinging, reminds us once again what a clever gamble HBO took in squeezing this massive production through our TV and laptop screens. Yes, George R. R. Martin's *A Song of Fire and Ice* novels, on which the series is based, were bestsellers. But the size of the audience for epic fantasy fiction is a fraction of what is needed to make a profit on television. Martin's forest-dense family trees of characters—knights in dented armour, damsels in bodice-bursting distress, and a nest of dragons imported from fairy tales—could not have been an easy sell. Legend has it that writer-producer Vince Gilligan sold *Breaking Bad* to TV network AMC with the pithy phrase "Mr. Chips becomes Scarface." One imagines the folks peddling *Game of Thrones* to HBO calling it "The Sopranos with swords."
>
> —KEN TUCKER, "Why Is *Game of Thrones* So Popular?"

Writing for this site, Tucker rightly assumes that some in his audience may know little or nothing about the series and thus he includes descriptions

Daenerys Targaryen, mother of dragons in HBO's *Game of Thrones*.

that help readers understand what the series is about—and what draws so many viewers to it week after week. Vivid language detailing the show's characters ("knights in dented armour, damsels in bodice-bursting distress, and a nest of dragons imported from fairy tales") and typical plotlines ("sword fighting, bed hopping and mud flinging") gives readers a sense of the epic fantasy fiction genre, and does so in a way that highlights the show's most thrilling and scandalous aspects.

In a similar situation, when you're composing a text that will be read by an audience that may not know your topic well, you'll also need to provide necessary description and details. You might also include an image, embed a video, or include a link to a site offering more information on your subject if the medium you're writing in allows it.

Evidence Drawn from Close Examination of the Subject

Examining the subject of your analysis carefully and in detail and then thinking critically about what you find will help you discover key elements, patterns, and relationships in your subject—all of which provide you with the evidence on which to build your analysis. For example, if you are analyzing a poem, you might examine word choice, rhyme scheme, figurative language, repetition, and imagery. If you are analyzing an ad in a magazine, you might look at the use of color, the choice of fonts, and the placement of figures or logos. Each element contributes something significant to the whole; each carries some part of the message being conveyed. The kinds of elements you examine and the evidence you draw from them will depend on the nature of your subject as well as the kind of analysis you are conducting. Following are discussions and examples of five common kinds of analysis: rhetorical analysis, discourse analysis, process analysis, causal analysis, and data analysis.

Rhetorical analysis. This kind of analysis can focus on a written text, a visual text, an audio text, or one that combines words, images, and sound. All of these are rhetorical analyses; that is, they all take a close look at how authors, designers, or artists communicate a message to an audience. Whether they are using words or images, adjusting font sizes or colors, they all are trying to persuade a particular audience to have a particular reaction to a particular message—theirs.

See how the following example from an article published on *Branding Strategy Insider*, a blog about brand strategy and management, analyzes Nike's thirtieth anniversary Just Do It campaign and the company's choice to feature Colin Kaepernick, a former NFL quarterback who sat and knelt during the national anthem at 49ers games in the 2016 season as a protest against the oppression of people of color:

> Is the new Kaepernick 30th Anniversary Just Do It Campaign a smart move for the Nike brand? . . . Perhaps the first question to ask about this campaign from a brand planner's perspective is: *What is it about Colin Kaepernick's character that Nike finds so important to attach it to the Nike brand?*
>
> Developing brand character has many things in common with screenwriting and the attempt to develop relatable characters for film and TV. Relatable characters are . . . sympathetic heroes on a mission to achieve worthy goals. They're often created as original, attractive, intelligent and provocative, and definitely not cliché, predictable or superficial. They have a definite point of view and a convincing way of getting it across. . . . Above all, relatable characters get people talking about them.
>
> In Nike's current campaign, Kaepernick has certainly demonstrated that he has character, conviction about his beliefs, concern for social justice and he certainly has people talking about him. But, is he really

a sympathetic hero? To segments of society struggling with [or sympathetic to] experiences of social injustice he definitely is. . . . [T]o [others] . . . he carries strong and negative emotional associations.

Risk or Reward? In launching this new campaign Nike is risking alienating a huge segment of its U.S. consumer base, perhaps as much as half. Why would they do that? Perhaps they are thinking that it will tighten the tribe with millennials, who tend to be involved in protest movements, particularly when political leaders and other authority figures are not aligned with their feelings and values. They see Kaepernick as a champion of individual rights, fighting for a sense of social justice. . . .

[T]his campaign will [also] scatter parts of the Nike tribe. . . . These people see not standing for the national anthem at a sporting event as an outward sign of disrespect for the idea of America and all the sacrifices made in the name of the nation. They see the gestures taken by Colin Kaepernick as a sign of questionable character. They see his public gestures as inappropriate and out of place.

—JEROME CONLON, "Analyzing Nike's Controversial Just Do It Campaign"

In the rest of the article, Conlon goes on to analyze how two different and opposing audiences are likely to react to the ad: those who will "like that Nike is supporting individual athlete rights, acts of moral conscience, conviction and protest," and those who will see the choice as disrespectful to the American values they embrace. As a former director of marketing for Nike, Conlon also analyzes the advertisement—and its likely impact—by looking at the history of the Just Do It campaign, which was designed to celebrate "the joy of all kinds of sports and fitness activities . . . for everyone, pro sports athletes to fitness amateurs, young and old, men and women, people in America, people around the world. No one was excluded."

To see Nike's Just Do It campaign videos and posters, go to everyonesanauthor .tumblr.com.

Conlon concludes with a prediction and wider implications of the ad: "Short-term pain for Nike's brand, but long-term gain. The social discussion around the campaign will elevate public understanding of the greatness of America and the need for more respect and regard for all people, of all colors and classes." Note how the author begins with a question and then presents evidence by analyzing the ad's tone, stance, context, and how all of these elements will play with two specific audiences.

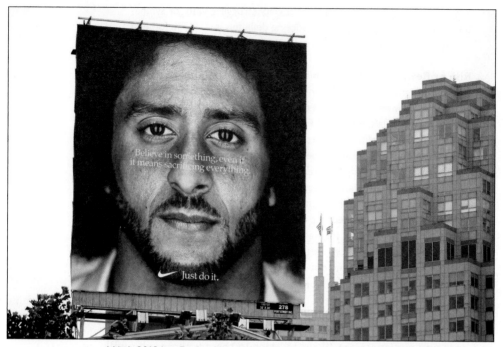

Nike's 2018 Just Do It ad campaign featuring former football quarterback Colin Kaepernick. About his controversial gesture, Kaepernick explained, "I am not going to stand up to show pride in a flag for a country that oppresses black people and people of color."

In the following example from her study of a literacy tradition in African American churches, rhetorician Beverly Moss uses direct quotations from her field notes to illustrate a key rhetorical pattern she noticed in one preacher's sermons.

One of the patterns that leapt out at me as I sat in the pew during all the sermons and as I listened to tapes and reviewed fieldnotes was the high level of participation in the sermons by the congregation. . . . It is a pattern that almost any discussion of African American preaching addresses. Just as in the three churches highlighted [earlier], in this church, the congregation and Reverend M. engaged in a call-and-response dialogue. At times during the revival sermons, the feedback from the congregation was so intense that it was impossible to separate speaker from audience.

Consider the following exchange. . . .

When you shout before the battle is over (Preach!)
It puts things in a proper perspective (Yeah!)
It puts you in a posture of obedience (Yeah!)
And it puts things in a proper perspective
But finally
When you shout before the battle is fought
It puts the enemy in confusion (Yeah! That's right!)

The parenthetical expressions, responses from the congregation, do not appear on separate lines because there was little or no pause between the minister's statement and the congregation's response. Often, the congregation's response overlapped with the minister's statement. This type of feedback was typical in the sermons Reverend M. preached to this congregation, as was applause, people standing, cheering, and so on. Practically every sermon Reverend M. preached ended with the majority of the congregation on their feet clapping and talking back to Reverend M.

—BEVERLY MOSS, *A Community Text Arises*

Members of a congregation move and shout in response to the preacher's words.

Moss analyzes and presents evidence from a spoken text. Because she was writing a print book, she could not include the actual audio of the sermon, but still she presents evidence in a way that demonstrates a key point of her analysis: that the closeness of the preacher's "call" and the congregation's "response" made it almost "impossible to separate speaker from audience." This quoted evidence shows a specific example of how the congregation's response becomes a part of the sermon, filling the church with "applause, people standing, cheering."

Discourse analysis. This kind of analysis can focus on any spoken or written language used in a particular social context. Discourse analysis often entails analyzing the communication practices of a specific community—people who share basic values, beliefs, practices, and goals. For example, a community of scholars such as the teachers at your school all likely value education, believe in helping students grow intellectually, and practice their profession by providing instruction to enable students to learn and achieve their goals. You've probably noticed that most of your teachers—especially those in a particular discipline or department—share a specific vocabulary. This holds true for any field, any profession, any group of people with shared interests; they develop ways of interacting and communicating most effectively with each other. In order to analyze how a specific group communicates, you'll examine that community's values, beliefs, goals, and practices, an effort that requires careful observation and even immersion when possible.

Look at the following example by Alberta Negri, a student at the University of Cincinnati, that analyzes the communication practices of a local group of bikers. Note how the introduction draws you in with a brief narrative and specific sensory details before offering background information. The author moves from common misperceptions of bikers to her specific subject, a group of bikers she refers to as the "Shell Station Squad." Note that Negri gives a rationale for focusing on this specific group; she tells readers why it matters.

> It's 8:56 p.m. on a Tuesday evening, and from my third-floor dorm room, I can once again hear the aggressive growls of 600-pound motorcycles as they roll into the parking lot of the Shell station across the street. The riders meet every night around 9:00 and face the usual apprehensive looks from bystanders. . . . Few investigations have been done from within the

biking community; even fewer have examined the inner workings of the communication among members. In his ethnography *A Brotherhood of Outlaw Bikers*, Daniel Wolf points out the realization that most bike-related media content continues to portray motorcyclists in the same negative light. . . . The following research makes the effort to peek into this unexplored group and discuss the less action-packed qualities, including its status as a discourse community, the process of club enculturation, and how a member's new identity can complicate their previous social roles.

> —ALBERTA NEGRI, "Underneath the Leather Jackets and Chrome Pipes:
> Research into a Community of Local Bikers"

Negri goes on to explain the methods used to conduct her research—including first-hand observation—and then she begins her analysis:

What do these men have in common? The riders of the Shell Station Squad have separate personal lives: full-time gunsmith, engineering firm representative, college student and *Call of Duty* gamer among them, but they all plan to meet every night and anticipate their 9 p.m. ride all day. Their passion to ride is often their only unifying characteristic. There is no need for them to begin each ride with a preface, stating the goals for the ride for the night, or what they hope to accomplish as a team. There is a simple, unspoken understanding that if you pull into that gas station parking lot, you're there for the chance to revel in the thrill of weaving through streets on a motorcycle, while flocking as a group to make the experience a little safer for all involved. . . .

Their primary mode of correspondence is *Facebook*; they use social media to create a private group for discussing matters such as driving routes and safety updates. . . . [T]here is no clear pecking order. The peer-appointed leader never dominated the discourse. More often, he would push for more interaction from those who were recently recruited: addressing questions to them to get individual opinions and inviting them to special weekend rides. [This leader] went as far as directly introducing new riders, saying, "Guys: new kid with us tonight. Thomas is a student at [the university], new rider, let's make sure to make him feel welcome tonight, alrite? Good kid, i think" [sic] (Lucius). His digital diction was a tad gentler in these interactions compared to his brash joking with the more experienced riders.

Visit everyones
anauthor.tumblr
.com for a link to
Negri's complete
analysis.

Negri analyzes the shared motivations and passions that build kinship among the group members—"the thrill of weaving through streets on a motorcycle"—and acknowledges what sets them apart from one another, too: their personal lives outside of biking. She goes on to examine the group's way of communicating and building community, in person and online, in order to understand how the community operates. To conduct her analysis, Negri relies on interviews with group members and a recent recruit as well as "primary texts": texts, *Facebook* group posts, and hand signals.

Process analysis. Analyzing a process requires you to break down a task into individual steps and examine each one to understand how something works or how something is done. Thus there are two kinds of process analyses: **INFORMATIONAL**, showing how something works; and **INSTRUCTIONAL**, telling how something is done. An analysis of the chemistry that makes a cake rise would be informational, whereas an analysis of how to make a cake would be instructional.

The following example analyzes the process of how skaters make high-speed turns. This is the most critical element in speed skating, for being able to consistently make fast turns without slipping and losing ground can be the difference between winning and losing. This analysis from *Science Buddies*, a website for students and parents, closely examines the key steps of the process. Note how the author provides some information about the basic physics of speed and turns and then systematically explains how each element of the action—speed, angle, push-back force from the surface—contributes to the total turn.

Whether it's ice, wood, or a paved surface, the science that governs a skater's ability to turn is essentially the same. It's based on a couple of basic laws of physics that describe speed and the circular motion of turns. The first is Newton's *law of inertia* that says a body in motion will stay in motion unless there is some outside force that changes it. To skaters hoping to make a turn after they speed down the straightaway, that means the force of inertia would tend to keep them going straight ahead if there wasn't a greater force to make them change direction and begin turning.

The force that causes the change in direction comes from the skater's blades or wheels as they cross over at an angle in front of the skater leaning to make a turn. Newton's *law of reaction* explains

Skating for the finish line in the women's 1,000-meter short-track speed skating finals at the 2018 Winter Olympics in Pyeongchang.

that the push from the skater's skates generates an equal but opposite push back from the ice or floor. This push back force draws the skater in towards the track and is described as a "center seeking" or *centripetal* type of force. It's the reason why turns are possible in any sport. The wheels of a bicycle, for example, also angle into the road surface when the cyclist leans to begin a turn. As the road pushes back on both bike and rider, it supplies the inward centripetal force to generate the turning motion.

The more a skater leans into a turn, the more powerful the push from the skate, and the greater centripetal force produced to carry the skater through the turn. Leaning in also creates a smaller arc, or tighter turn, making for a shorter distance and a faster path around the turn. However, there's a catch. As the skater leans more and more into the track, the balancing point of the body, or the skater's *center of gravity*, also shifts more and more to the side. If it shifts too far, the skater no longer can maintain balance and ends up splayed out onto the rink rather than happily heading round the turn to the finishing line.

So success in turns, especially fast ones, means skaters must constantly find their center of gravity while teetering on the edge of their skates. To make the turn at all requires that the skater push the skates against the ice with sufficient power to generate enough inward centripetal force to counter the inertia of skating straight ahead. And to keep up speed in a race, a skater must calculate and execute the shortest, or tightest, turns possible around the track.

—DARLENE JENKINS, "Tightening the Turns in Speed Skating:
Lessons in Centripetal Force and Balance"

To read the full analysis, go to everyonesanauthor.tumblr.com.

This kind of close examination of the subject is the heart of analysis. Darlene Jenkins explains the key elements in the process of making a high-speed turn—speed, angle, push-back force—and also examines the relationships among these elements as she describes what happens in minute detail, revealing how they all combine to create the pattern of movement that leads to a successful high-speed turn. By including a photograph that shows skaters leaning into a turn, blades and bodies angled precariously, Jenkins shows what the process entails, and readers can actually see what's being described.

Causal analysis. Why is the Arctic ice pack decreasing in volume? What causes extreme droughts in California? These and other questions about why something occurs or once occurred call on you to analyze what caused a certain event, but a causal analysis can also investigate the possible effects of an event, or the links in a chain of connected events. Put most simply, causal analyses look at why something happened or will happen as a result of something else.

Go to everyonesanauthor.tumblr.com to link to the full article, "The Cry Embedded within the Purr."

Behavioral ecologist Karen McComb, who studies communication between animals and humans, wanted to understand why cat owners so often respond to purring cats by feeding them. To answer this question, McComb and a team recorded a number of domestic cats in their homes and discovered what the team termed "solicitation purring"—an urgent high-frequency sound, similar to an infant's cry, that is embedded within the cats' more pleasing and low-pitched purring and that apparently triggered an innate nurturing response in their owners. In an article presenting their findings, the team provided quantitative data about the pitch and frequency of different kinds of purring to support their conclusion about what the data showed: that the similarities in pitch and frequency to the cries of human infants "make them very difficult to ignore."

Using data like these to support an analysis is common in science classes, while in the humanities and social sciences, you're more likely to write about causes that are plausible or probable than ones that can be measured. In a literature class, for example, you might be asked to analyze the influences that shaped F. Scott Fitzgerald's creation of Jay Gatsby in *The Great Gatsby*—that is, to try to explain what caused Fitzgerald to develop Gatsby the way he did. In a sociology class, you might be asked to analyze what factors contributed to a population decline in a certain neighborhood. In both cases, these causes are probabilities—plausible but not provable.

Data analysis. Some subjects will require you to examine data. **QUANTITATIVE** analysis looks at numerical data; **QUALITATIVE** analysis looks at data that's not numerical.

When Beverly Moss analyzed the rhetoric of three ministers, she worked with qualitative data: transcripts of sermons, personal testimonies, her own observations from the church pews. Her data came mostly in the forms of words and text, not statistics.

Now see how blogger Will Moller analyzes the performances of ten major-league baseball pitchers using quantitative data—baseball statistics, in this case—to answer the question of whether New York Yankees pitcher Andy Pettitte is likely to get into baseball's Hall of Fame.

I prefer to look at Andy versus his peers, because simply put, it would be very odd for 10 pitchers from the same decade to get in (though this number is rather arbitrary). Along that line, who are the best pitchers of Andy's generation, so we can compare them?

	Wins	Win%	WAR	ERA+	IP	K	K/BB	WAR/9IP
Martinez	219	68.7%	89.4	154	2827	3154	4.15	0.28
Clemens	354	65.8%	145.5	143	4917	4672	2.96	0.27
Johnson	303	64.6%	114.8	136	4135	4875	3.26	0.25
Schilling	216	59.7%	86.1	128	3261	3116	4.38	0.24
Maddux	355	61.0%	120.6	132	5008	3371	3.37	0.22
Mussina	270	63.8%	85.6	123	3563	2813	3.58	0.22
Smoltz	213	57.9%	82.5	125	3473	3084	3.05	0.21
Brown	211	59.4%	77.2	127	3256	2397	2.66	0.21
Pettitte	240	63.5%	66.9	117	3055	2251	2.34	0.20
Glavine	305	60.0%	67.1	118	4413	2607	1.74	*0.14*

The above table tells the story pretty well. I've bolded the numbers that are particularly absurd, and italicized one in particular which should act as a veto. Though I imagine most of the readers of this blog know full well what these statistics mean at this point, for those of you who don't, a primer:

WAR stands for Wins Above Replacement, and is a somewhat complicated equation which estimates the true value of a pitcher, taking into account league, ERA, park effects, etc. For instance, a pitcher that wins a game but gives up 15 earned runs has probably lost value in their career WAR, even though they get the shiny addition to their win-loss record. We like WAR around these parts.

ERA+ is a normalized version of ERA centered on 100, basically showing how much better or worse a pitcher was compared to their league average (by ERA). 110, for example, would indicate that the pitcher's ERA was 10% better than average. 95, on the other hand, would be roughly 5% worse than average. This is a good statistic for comparing pitchers between different time periods—a 4.00 ERA in 2000 doesn't mean the same thing as a 4.00 ERA in 1920, for example.

K/BB is how many strikeouts a pitcher had per walk. More is better, less is worse.

As you can see, the above table doesn't do Andy any favors. He's 6th in wins and 5th in winning percentage, but he's 9th in ERA+ and dead last in WAR. His K/BB beats only Tom Glavine, who comes off looking pretty bad on this list. The only thing he has going for him is his playoff record—and frankly, the team he was on won a whole bunch of playoff games while he was on the team, even when he wasn't pitching. Besides, we're pretty much past the point of taking W/L record as a good indication of pitcher skill—why is it that when we slap the word "postseason" onto the statistic, we suddenly devolve 10 years to when such things seemed to matter?   —WILL MOLLER, "A Painful Posting"

Moller's guiding question, "Should Andy Pettitte be in the Hall of Fame?" is unstated in this excerpt, but it is made clear earlier in the piece. He presents the data in a table for readers to see—and then walks us through his analysis of that data. It's critical when using numerical data like these not only to present the information but also to say what it means. That's a key part of your analysis. Using a table to present data is a good way to include numerical evidence, but be careful that you don't just

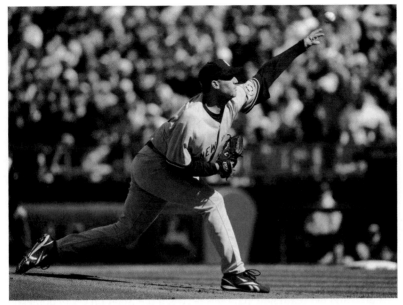

Andy Pettitte pitching against the Kansas City Royals in April 2009.

drop the table in; you need to explain to readers what the data mean and to explain any abbreviations that readers may not know, as Moller does. Though he does not state his conclusions explicitly here, his analysis makes clear what he thinks.

Insight Gained from Your Analysis

One key purpose of an analysis is to offer your audience some insight on the subject you are analyzing. As you examine your subject, you discover patterns, data, specific details, and key information drawn from the subject—which will lead you to some insight, a deeper understanding of the subject you're analyzing. The insight that you gain will lead you to your thesis. When the sheikh, pastor, and rabbi mentioned earlier in this chapter analyzed a sentence in their book that offended the rabbi, each gained insight into the others' principles that led them to further understanding. In "Third-Party Option," David Brooks makes clear the insights he derived from his analysis of the national political climate and especially the community conditions he believes would need to be considered for a third-party option to be viable:

> We also need a national leader to tell a different national story. During the 20th century, a superpower story emerged. In that story, the nation moved as one, and a ridiculous amount of attention got focused on the supposed superhero in the White House. A third-party candidate who shifted attention to local people actually getting stuff done might lose, but he or she would begin to define a new and more plausible version of American greatness.   —DAVID BROOKS, "Third-Party Option"

Brooks makes it clear that the major change represented by a third-party option would require fresh perspectives on the part of both politicians and voters, especially a willingness to shift the focus from what he calls "the supposed superhero in the White House" to one recognizing the importance of accomplishing positive changes in local communities.

Summarizing the study of the way humans react to a cat's purr, Karen McComb and her team note parallels between the isolation cry of domestic cats and the distress cry of human infants as a way of understanding why the "cry embedded within the purr" is so successful in motivating owners to feed their cats. They conclude that the cats have learned to communicate their need for attention in ways that are impossible to ignore, ways that prompt caring responses from people. Thus, their work suggests that much can be learned by studying animal-human communication from both directions, from animals to humans as well as the reverse.

Remember that any analysis you do needs to have a purpose—to discover how cats motivate their owners to provide food on demand, to understand how partisan misperceptions create roadblocks in government, to explain why a favorite baseball player's statistics probably won't get him into the Hall of Fame. In writing up your analysis, your point will be to communicate the insight you gain from the analysis.

Clear, Precise Language

Since the point of an analysis is to help an audience understand something, you need to pay extra attention to the words you use and the way you explain your findings. You want your audience to follow your analysis easily and not get sidetracked. You need to demonstrate that you know what you are talking about. You've studied your subject, looked at it closely, thought about it—*analyzed* it; you know what to say about it and why. Now you have to craft your analysis in such a way that your readers will follow that analysis and understand what it shows. Andy Pettitte doesn't just rank low by his statistics; "he's 9th in ERA+ and dead last in WAR." Political conditions in the United States aren't just in bad shape; "the federal government is immobilized by partisanship and debt." Like Moller and Brooks, you should be precise in your explanations and in your choice of words.

Analyzing an intricate process or a complicated text requires you to use language that your audience will understand. The analysis of speed skating turns earlier in this chapter was written for an audience of young people and their parents. The language used to describe the physics that govern the process of turning is appropriate for such an audience—precise but not technical. When the author refers to Newton's law of inertia, she defines *inertia* and then explains what it means for skaters. The role of centripetal force is explained as "the more a skater leans into a turn, the more powerful the push from the skate." Everything is clear because the writer uses simple, everyday words—"tighter turn," "teetering on the edge of their skates"—to convey complex science.

Look also at the analysis of baseball statistics presented earlier in this chapter; even though it was written for a blog targeting Yankees fans, the author includes a "primer" for those readers who may not understand the kinds of statistics he presents.

You need to consider what your audience knows about your topic and what information you'll need to include to make sure they'll understand what you write. You'll also want to be careful to state your conclusions explicitly—in clear, specific language.

EAMONN FORDE, a British journalist, wrote this article in 2014, analyzing the phenomenal success of "Happy" by Pharrell Williams. It was published in *The Big Issue*, a magazine written by professional journalists and sold by homeless and unemployed people in Great Britain and nine other nations.

"Happy" by Pharrell Williams: Why This Song Has Grabbed the Nation
EAMONN FORDE

In its online version, the article links to a site showing an audience of retirees "clapping and grooving."

YOU KNOW WHEN a song has gone that one step further and connects with people of all ages when it gets the crowd at the World Indoor Bowls Championships in Great Yarmouth clapping and grooving along. "Happy" by Pharrell Williams did exactly that.

The author begins by describing the song's success.

"Happy" has sold more than 650,000 copies so far in the UK, was being played more than 5,500 times a week on British radio at its peak, and has become a viral *YouTube* hit (notably a girl dancing down the street to it like it was a Northern Soul classic), but getting an audience reaction like that at the bowls—that's proper success. It now unashamedly sits in the very heart of the mainstream, capturing the hearts and ears of the nation and making everyone who hears it, well, happy.

Here's the insight that the analysis will explain.

Not bad going for a song that was never supposed to be released as a single. Its history is a curious one and drips in serendipity, showing how something in an age of over-marketing can take on a life of its own and pull off the near impossible by appealing to people of all ages.

Pharrell Williams at the 2015 Pinkpop Festival in the Netherlands.

It was originally released back in June last year, tucked away as track four on the *Despicable Me 2* soundtrack album, released by the Back Lot Music label. Pharrell had signed to Sony Music and the track was considered a "possible" to appear on his new album, which is due out later this year but has no official release date yet. Then dance and urban station Capital Xtra started playing it. Pluggers, as is the norm in radio promotion, had not been knocking on its door. They just decided they liked it and put it on heavy rotation.

This coincided with the DVD release of *Despicable Me 2* and the launch of the 24hoursofhappy.com site that featured, as its name suggests, a 24-hour-long video for the song featuring cameos from Jamie Foxx, Steve Carell and others. RCA hadn't even decided what the lead track from the album would be but quickly swung into action, and it was released as a single by the label.

"Happy" went to number one in the UK at the end of December, selling 107,000 copies in its first week. It dropped to number two the next week but was back at number one the following week, then dipping to number two a week later. RCA is confident it will sell one million copies and has weeks, if not months, in the top 10 to come.

Background information provides context for those unfamiliar with how the music industry works.

A specific question that drives the analysis.

So what is it about the song that has made it so ubiquitous without it becoming irritating?

"It's a very poppy tune and it transcends a few different genres, so maybe people are more open to it," suggests Dr. Lauren Stewart, a reader in psychology at Goldsmiths in London, who has done lengthy research into "earworms"—those songs that burrow into your brain and are difficult to dislodge. "It made me think of that OutKast song 'Hey Ya!,' which had a similar quality to it and seemed to be everywhere."

A precise term, "earworms," is used for a key concept—and carefully defined.

Key to its success is its musical reiteration and the instructional nature of its lyrics, according to Dr. Elizabeth Margulis, director of the Music Cognition Lab at the University of Arkansas and author of *On Repeat: How Music Plays the Mind*. "That's a pretty repetitive song," she says of "Happy." "There is a catchy bit that expressly invites you to clap along. It is literally inviting you." In that sense, "Happy" is basically an update of "If You're Happy and You Know It (Clap Your Hands)" or "Don't Worry, Be Happy."

She adds, "The thing repetition really does is it captures the motor circuitry of the brain, so you have this sense the music is really pulling you along. It can make people feel really happy. There is something about having a song that is literally about being happy that is using this technique that makes people happy. It just feels good."

The author provides evidence for his analysis by quoting experts about some elements that make "Happy" so catchy.

But repetition and irritation are often bedfellows, so it is very tricky to pull off just the right amount of recurrence in a song. "If something is really simple and just does all the ordinary things you'd expect it to do . . . repetition can seem really annoying," says Margulis. "If it has enough sparks of new and interesting things going on in there—and not too many to make it overwhelmingly complex—it can get into that sweet spot where you can just listen to it again and again and again and it doesn't seem to get tired."

Margulis says that listening can be tightly defined by age or subculture, so being appealing to one often means being unappealing to another. "So often music is a marker of group identity," she says. "So when a song can do that [cross age boundaries], that's really powerful and unusual."

Pharrell had, of course, been on the two biggest hits of last year in the UK—"Get Lucky" (1.28 million sales) and "Blurred

Lines" (1.47 million sales), both of which relied heavily on repetition—so things were clearly in place for him with whatever song he put out, allowing him to step up as the focal point rather than play a side role as guest vocalist. "Happy" has gone that bit further and has pan-generational appeal.

"For an artist to sell a significant amount of music in this day and age you need to be applicable to more than one demographic," says Neil Hughes, the director of promotions at RCA. "The most recent one I can think of that worked in this way was 'Get Lucky,' which was also a Pharrell track. 'Get Lucky' was an event record, but the difference with that was there was an awful lot of clever build-up before they launched the project, whereas this is very much a slow-burner."

> *More evidence to explain the song's great success.*

"Happy" is going to be everywhere for months to come, lifting spirits and putting springs in steps. Just as he defined the sound of 2013, Pharrell looks set to provide the soundtrack to 2014—but this time with him in the spotlight and, happily, all on the song's own terms.

REFLECT. *Find a short analytical article in a newspaper or magazine. Look at the list of five characteristic features of analysis on page 234 and, using Forde's essay as a model, annotate the article to point out these features. Then evaluate how successful the article's analysis is. For example, can you identify the question that drove the analysis? Has the author provided enough description for you to follow the analysis? Is the language clear and precise? Has the author clearly stated the insight the analysis led to? Does the author provide evidence to support that insight?*

VISUAL ANALYSIS

Photos, cartoons, ads, movies, *YouTube* videos—all are visual texts, ones that say something and, just like words alone, make some kind of claim that they hope we will accept. When you analyze a visual, you ask the same questions you would of any text: How does it convey its message? How does it appeal to audiences? To answer such questions for a visual text, you'd begin by considering each of its elements—its use of color, light, and shadow; its perspective; any words or symbols; and its overall composition. Visual analysis takes various forms, but it generally includes the following features:

A Description of the Visual

Include an image of the visual in your analysis, but if that's not possible—in a print essay analyzing a video, for instance—you'll need to describe it. Your description should focus on the most important elements and those you'll point to in your analysis. What draws your eye first, and why? What's most interesting or seems most important? Does any use of contrast affect what you see? Consider the cartoon below. Your eyes were probably first drawn to the white speech balloons, because they stand out against the dark background, and they then bring your attention down to the two phones.

Some Contextual Information

You'll need to provide contextual information about your subject. What's its purpose, and who's the target audience? Is there any historical, political, or cultural context that's important to describe? Such factors are important to think about—and to describe in your analysis. The political cartoon about texting, for instance, was published in the *Atlanta Journal-Constitution* in 2009 and made a point about the need for laws prohibiting the use of hand-held cell phones while driving.

Attention to Any Words

If the visual includes any words, what do they add to its message? Whatever the words—the name of a sculpture, a caption beneath a photo, a slogan in an ad, the words in a speech balloon—you'll want to discuss how they affect the way we understand the visual. The same is true of the typography: words in boldface are likely ones the author wants to emphasize; the fonts affect the tone. If you were analyzing the cartoon about texting, for instance, you might point out that the words themselves are in textese ("Im txtng") and that they say something ridiculous (why would the driver send a text saying he's texting?)—demonstrating that texting while driving is not only dangerous but often stupid.

Close Analysis of the Message

What elements are most important in conveying the message? In the cartoon about texting, for instance, the split screen focuses attention on the contrasts between the two sides—bright colors on one side, dark ones on the other; a busy life, the lone figure of Death. And the words make the point clear: when it comes to texting while driving, Death gets the last laugh. Color, contrast, words, focus, the way it's all framed—these are all details that combine to convey a message, ones that you'll want to consider in analyzing what a visual text "says."

Insight into What the Visual "Says"

Your analysis of the visual will lead you to an understanding of what it's saying. The cartoon about texting argues that doing so while driving could be fatal. Athletic shoe ads try to persuade us to buy something—and those featuring stars like Rihanna suggest that we too can be as fierce and cool as a pop music icon: all we need are shoes like hers. How does the photo or painting or whatever you're analyzing make you feel? What does it suggest that you think or do? What techniques does it use to make you feel, think, or act in these ways?

Precise Language

It's especially important to use precise words in writing about a visual. Saying that the cartoonist uses "different colors in the driver's panel than in the one about Death" doesn't say much. Better: "the bright colors of the driver's panel—red and yellow against a purple background—present a vivid contrast to the tan and black in Death's panel." When you write about a visual, you need to use language that will help readers see the things that matter.

THINK BEYOND WORDS

↪ *TAKE A LOOK at "Paradise, Paved," a photo essay about travelers spending the night in Walmart parking lots. Click through the images and read the surrounding text. Then pick one image to analyze. How are the people in the image portrayed? How is the image itself composed? If this photo essay had a thesis, what would it be? Go to* everyonesanauthor.tumblr.com *to access the entire piece.*

VISUAL ANALYSIS / An Annotated Example

SOMINI SENGUPTA writes about technology and the law for the *New York Times*. She posted this article in 2012 on *Bits,* a *Times* blog about the technology industry.

Why Is Everyone Focused on Zuckerberg's Hoodie?
SOMINI SENGUPTA

WHO COULD HAVE THOUGHT a hoodie could mean so much? Over the last two days, there has been a great deal of mudslinging and hand-wringing about the significance of what Mark Zuckerberg, 27, the chief executive of Facebook, wore when he went courting would-be investors in New York.

Contextual information about the subject of the analysis.

On the first stop of the Facebook public offering road show, Mr. Zuckerberg wore a hoodie. The only thing I remember thinking, when I first saw the footage, was that it was not a spring color. It was a dark, drab gray. That made me cringe.

Description of the hoodie that's being analyzed.

Mr. Zuckerberg, of course, often wears a hoodie. Perhaps he thinks it's fetching. Perhaps, he wears it because it is his trademark, much like the Issey Miyake custom-made black turtlenecks that Steve Jobs, one of Mr. Zuckerberg's executive idols, wore during his public appearances. (Mr. Jobs had hundreds of them made, and he told his biographer, Walter Isaacson, that he had enough of them to wear every day for the rest of his life.)

Hoodies, like black turtlenecks, appear casual, like you just threw on the first thing you could find dangling on a hook behind the door. In fact, it carries a lot of meaning. It signifies the opposite of a Hermès tie, the favored accoutrement of Wall Street.

Analysis of what a hoodie signifies, and of the statement that Zuckerberg was making by wearing one when meeting with investors.

[259]

Mark Zuckerberg in New York during Facebook's road show.

It signifies that you're busy making things that are really, really important to the world, which is what Silicon Valley believes, and hey—you don't really care what you look like.

Right.

Mr. Zuckerberg is nothing if not a master of optics. Like Mr. Jobs' black turtleneck, the hoodie is his anti-fashion statement.

The hoodie in Manhattan prompted, as Mr. Zuckerberg may have expected, a gush of approval and disdain. Hoodiegate, it came to be called, and it began to show signs of a culture war between the two coasts—Wall Street versus Silicon Valley.

His critics saw it as a sign of immaturity and disrespect for those whom he expected to finance his company. An equities research analyst, Michael Pachter, said it would have been more fitting had he put on a blazer over a T-shirt. Mr. Pachter, incidentally, is so bullish on Facebook he thinks it's worth more than what the company estimates to be its value. But would Mr. Zuckerberg dress like that at church, Mr. Pachter, wearing a pinstripe suit, wondered aloud on a television program.

Naturally, a Twitter hashtag emerged to take up the cause: #zuckerbergshoodie.

His defenders said the hoodie signified Silicon Valley ethos: a brash, youthful self-confidence.

Clear and precise language presents the two opposing perceptions of the hoodie: as a sign of "immaturity and disrespect" or of "brash, youthful self-confidence."

"Mark Zuckerberg really doesn't give a damn about you," Henry Blodget wrote in *Business Insider.* Mr. Blodget continued, in case New York wanted to listen: "I don't mean to be rude, Wall Street, but Mark Zuckerberg is actually wise not to care much about you. First, as discussed, he controls the company. But second, most of you don't do much to deserve much attention from CEOs."

Quotes from business and technology professionals show what they think of Zuckerberg's hoodie.

Om Malik, founder of the GigaOm technology blog, opined that Mr. Pachter "is smoking stuff that's outside the realm of legality." The dapper blogger went on to conclude: "Now if you were looking for a problem with Zuckerberg's hoodie, then you should see it for what it really is: a fashion abomination."

On Thursday, Mr. Zuckerberg's sister, Randi, posted on Twitter a link to a pinstripe hoodie that a clothing label had unveiled immediately after hoodiegate began. A post in the *Atlantic Wire* surmised that the hoodie gave Mr. Zuckerberg the magical powers that he—and his investors—would need to keep spinning gold.

The to and fro over hoodiegate of course has been largely about what wealthy and, by and large, white men wear in Silicon Valley and on Wall Street.

The author's insight: what she thinks the ruckus about Zuckerberg's hoodie means.

But a hoodie is not just a hoodie, except when it's just a hoodie.

A teenage boy named Trayvon Martin was wearing a hoodie the night that he was killed in a gated townhouse community in Sanford, Fla., outside Orlando. His killer, an armed neighborhood watch volunteer, told police he appeared "real suspicious."

The hoodie became a symbol of solidarity in the days after the boy's death. Many people I know took pictures of themselves wearing hoodies. Naturally, they posted their pictures on *Facebook.*

Trayvon's hoodie is a reminder that neither Wall Street nor Silicon Valley is terribly representative of our country.

An unexpected insight: that those fretting about Zuckerberg's hoodie are focusing on the wrong things.

REFLECT. *How surprised were you by the way Somini Sengupta concluded her post? What do you think her main point was in writing this piece? Look again at her title: what do you think it means? Keeping in mind that she posted this piece on a blog read by people in the technology business, what do you think she was saying to them?*

WRITING ANALYTICALLY / A Roadmap

Find a topic that matters—to you, and to others

Whether you can choose your topic or have to respond to a specific assignment, find an angle that appeals to you—and to your audience. Write about something that you care about, that engages you. No audience will want to hear about something that you are not interested in writing about.

If you can choose your topic, begin by considering your interests. What do you like to do? What issues do you care about? Do you have a favorite book? If you've read and re-read the Harry Potter books, you might analyze J. K. Rowling's storytelling style or the causes behind the books' ongoing popularity. An interest in sports could lead you to analyze statistical data on a favorite athlete (as Will Moller does) or to analyze the process of doing something in a particular sport (as Darlene Jenkins does).

If you've been assigned a topic, say to conduct a rhetorical analysis of the Gettysburg Address, find an angle that interests you. If you're a history buff, you might research the particular occasion on which Lincoln spoke and look at how his words were especially appropriate to that audience and event. Or perhaps your interests lie more in current politics, in which case you might compare Lincoln's address to the speeches politicians make today.

Make your topic matter to your audience. Some topics matter to everyone, or nearly everyone; you might be able to identify such topics by checking the media for what's being debated and discussed. But when you're writing about something that may not automatically appeal to a wide audience, it's your responsibility as the writer to tell them why they should care about it. Somini Sengupta does this in her piece about Mark Zuckerberg's hoodie by showing the powerful assumptions we make about people based on their dress—assumptions that, for a different young man wearing a similar hoodie, determined life and death.

Consider your rhetorical situation

Keep in mind the elements of your particular situation—your audience, your specific purpose, your stance, and so on—and how they will or should influence the choices you make in your writing.

Identify your AUDIENCE. Who do you want to reach, and how can you shape your analysis so that you get through to them? Karen McComb's analysis of cat purring was for an audience of scientific peers, whereas Ken Tucker wrote about *Game of Thrones* for BBC's *Culture* site, which is written for the general public. Very different audiences, very different purposes—very different analyses. You, too, should think carefully about whom you are trying to reach.

- What do you know about them—their age, gender, cultural and linguistic background?
- What are they likely to know about your subject, and what background information will you need to provide?
- How might they benefit from the analysis and insight you offer?
- Will your subject matter to them—and if not, how can you make them care about it?

If you are writing for the internet, you will likely reach a broad audience whose characteristics you can't predict, so you need to assume a range of readers—just as Will Moller does in his blog post about Andy Pettitte. Even though his primary audience is Yankees fans, he knows that some readers won't know much about statistics, so he provides the definitions they need to understand his analysis.

Articulate your PURPOSE. Even if you're writing in response to an assignment, here are some questions that can help you narrow your focus and articulate some more specific purposes:

- What are you analyzing? A text? A community? A process? Causes? Data? A visual?
- What's motivated you to write? Are you responding to some other text or author?
- What do you want to accomplish by analyzing this subject? How can you best achieve your goals?
- What do you want your audience to take away from your analysis?

Think about your STANCE. How do you want to come across as an author? How can your writing reflect that stance? If your subject is surfing and you're writing on a surfers' blog about how to catch a wave for an audience of beginners, your stance might be that of an experienced surfer or a former beginner. Your language would probably be informal, with little or no surfing jargon. If, on the other hand, you're writing an article for *Surfing Magazine* analyzing the process Laird Hamilton developed to ride fifty-foot waves, your stance might be that of an objective reporter, and your language would need to be more technical for that well-informed audience. No matter what your stance or target audience, you need to consider what kind of language is appropriate, what terms need to be defined, and how you can establish your authority as an author.

Consider the larger CONTEXT. If you are analyzing an ad for a composition class, you will want to look at relevant information about its original context. When was the ad created, and who was the target audience? What were the social, economic, and political conditions at the time? All of that is contextual information. If you are preparing a load analysis for an engineering class, you'll need to consider factors such as how, when, and where the structure will be used. Other contextual information comes from what others have said about your subject, and your analysis adds to the conversation.

Consider MEDIA. Will your analysis be delivered in print? on a website? in an oral presentation? Are you writing for an online class? a blog? your campus newspaper? If you get to choose your medium, the choice should depend on how you can best present your subject and reach your intended audience. Do you need to be able to incorporate visuals, or audio or video, or to speak directly to your audience in person? Whether you have a choice or not, the media you use will affect how you design and deliver your analysis.

Consider matters of DESIGN. Think about how to best present your information and whether you need to follow any disciplinary conventions. Does your analysis include data that is easiest to understand in a chart or graph? Would headings help readers follow your analysis? Would illustrations make your point clearer?

Analyze your subject

What kind of analysis is needed for your subject and purpose? You may be assigned to conduct a certain kind of analysis, or you may be inspired by a question, as Will Moller was in analyzing data to determine whether Andy Pettitte is likely to be elected to the Hall of Fame. But sometimes you may be asked simply to "analyze x"—an ad, a game, a historical event, profiles of several companies—in which case you'll need to determine what kind of analysis will work best. The kind of analysis you need to do—*rhetorical analysis, discourse analysis, process analysis, causal analysis, data analysis, visual analysis*—will determine the way you study your subject.

If you're analyzing rhetoric, you need to look at what the text you're examining says and how it supports its claims.

- What question are you asking about this text? What specifically are you looking for?
- What **CLAIM** is the text making—and what **REASONS** and **EVIDENCE** does the author provide for the claim? Do they convince you?
- Does the writer acknowledge or respond to **COUNTERARGUMENTS** or other opinions? If so, are they presented fairly?
- Are there any words that indicate what the author thinks—or wants you to think?
- How does the author establish **AUTHORITY** to address the topic?
- Does the text use any **EMOTIONAL APPEALS**? If so, how?

If you're analyzing a discourse community, you're trying to understand the community whose language practices you are focusing on. And you'll want to be clear about both your reasons for choosing a particular community and the questions you're striving to answer about your subject.

Are you primarily concerned with how a given community creates cohesion through its discourse practices? Or are you interested in narrowing your focus to a particular type of exchange, focusing on vocabulary choices, figurative language, rhetorical elements, or preferred types of argument? Are you interested in understanding how the community establishes its social relationships through language? Or do you want to chart this particular community's similarities to and differences from other groups? Or perhaps you want to focus on how a given individual manages the discourses of multiple communities: an engineering student who is also a birder and a church choir member. Enacting one's identity in multiple communities requires using language at least somewhat differently in each. The following questions can guide your research and analysis:

- Why have you chosen this particular community? Or this specific discourse?

- What questions are you trying to answer about your subject?

- What existing texts—written, visual, recorded—can you draw on for background information?

- What kinds of research will you need to do to observe your subject's communication practices? Textual analysis? Data collection? Interviews?

- Do you observe any patterns or habits? Does what you observe match your expectations or surprise you?

- Can you observe your subject firsthand? Who might help you access the community you're interested in? Will you need permissions from your subjects or your university?

If you're analyzing a process, you'll need to decide whether your analysis will be **INFORMATIONAL** (how something works) or **INSTRUCTIONAL** (how to do something). Writing about how solar panels convert sunshine to energy would be informational, whereas writing about how to install solar panels would be instructional—and would need to explicitly identify all materials needed and then tell readers step-by-step exactly how to carry out the process. Once you've determined the kind of analysis, you might then consider questions like these:

- What question is prompting your analysis?

- If the process is instructional, what materials are needed?

- What are the steps in the process? What does each step accomplish?

- What order do the steps follow? Whether a process follows a set order (throwing a curveball, parallel parking a car) or not (playing sudoku), you'll need to present the steps in some order that makes sense.

If you're analyzing causes, you're looking for answers to why something happened. Why, for instance, have crime rates fallen in a particular city over the past few decades? Is it because police are more actively patrolling neighborhoods? Or because poverty has dropped in some parts of the city? Or because prison programs have expanded?

Questions about causes can rarely be answered definitively, so you'll usually be **ARGUING** that certain causes are the most plausible or the *primary* ones, and that others are less likely or *secondary*. In addition, although an *immediate cause* may be obvious, less obvious *long-term causes* may also have contributed. You'll need to consider all possible causes and provide evidence to support the ones you identify as most plausible.

As you determine which causes are more or less likely, be careful not to confuse coincidence with causation. That two events—such as a new police-patrol policy in a city and a drop in the crime rate—occurred more or less simultaneously, or even that one event preceded the other, does not prove that one *caused* the other.

You'll often need to do some RESEARCH to understand all the possible causes and whether they are primary or contributing, immediate or long-term causes. The following questions can guide your research and analysis:

- What question is prompting your analysis?
- List all the causes you can think of. Which seem to be the primary causes and which are contributing or secondary causes? Which are immediate causes and which are long-term causes?
- Might any of the causes on your list be merely coincidences?
- Which causes seem most plausible—and why?
- What research do you need to do to answer these questions?

If you're analyzing data, you're trying to identify patterns in information that you or someone else has gathered in order to answer a question or make an argument. The information collected by the US Census is data. Social scientists looking for patterns to help them make arguments or predictions about population trends might analyze the data on numbers of families with children in urban areas.

In his blog post on Andy Pettitte, Will Moller provides numerical data on ten pitchers' performances, which he then analyzes to determine whether Pettitte is likely to get into the Hall of Fame. His analysis explicitly states his guiding question—"Should Andy Pettitte be in the Hall of Fame?"—and then answers it by considering each element of the data as it relates to Pettitte's performance.

Although the mathematical nature of analyzing QUANTITATIVE data can often make it more straightforward than other kinds of analysis, identifying statistical patterns and figuring out their significance can be challenging. Finding and interpreting patterns in QUALITATIVE data can also be tricky, especially as the data is more free-form: words, stories, photographs, and so on. Here are some questions to consider when analyzing data:

- What question are you trying to answer?
- Are there any existing data that can help answer your question? If so, will they provide sufficient information, or do you need to conduct any RESEARCH of your own to generate the data you need?
- If you're working with existing data, who collected the data, using what methods, and why? How do the data relate to the analysis you're conducting?
- Do the data show the full picture? Are there other data that tell a different story?
- Can you identify patterns in the data? If so, are they patterns you expected, or are any of them surprising?

If you're analyzing a visual, how do specific visual elements convey a message or create an effect?

- What draws your eye first, and why? What seems most interesting or important?
- What's the PURPOSE of this visual, and who's its target AUDIENCE?
- Is there any larger historical, cultural, or political CONTEXT to consider?
- Are there any words, and what do they tell you about the message?
- What's the overall ARGUMENT or effect? How do you know?

Determine what your analysis shows

Once you've analyzed your subject, you need to figure out what your analysis shows. What was the question that first prompted your analysis, and how can you now answer that question? What have you discovered about your subject? What have you found that interests you—and how can you make it matter to your audience?

State your insight as a tentative THESIS. Once you've determined what insight your analysis has led to, write it out as a tentative thesis, noting what you've analyzed and why and what conclusions or insights you want to share. Your thesis introduces your point, what you want to say about your subject. Let's say you're writing a rhetorical analysis of the Gettysburg Address. Here's how you might introduce an analysis of that speech:

> Following Edward Everett's two-hour oration, President Lincoln spoke eloquently for a mere two minutes, deploying rhetorical devices like repetition, contrast, and rhythm in a way that connected emotionally with his audience.

This sentence tells us that the writer will describe the event, say something about the length of the speech, and explain how specific words and structures resulted in an eloquently simple but profoundly moving speech.

As you formulate your thesis, begin by thinking about your **AUDIENCE** and how you can make your analysis most compelling to them. What aspects of your analysis will they care most about? How might it apply to them? Does your analysis have important implications beyond the immediate subject, as Somini Sengupta's analysis of a simple hoodie does?

Then list the evidence you found that supports your analysis—examples, quotations, significant data points, and so forth. What of all your evidence will best support your point, and what will your audience find most persuasive?

Organize and start writing

Start with your tentative thesis, being sure that it identifies what you're analyzing, what insights you have to offer, and why it is significant. As you write, be sure you're supporting your thesis—and that it's working. That said, don't hesitate to revise it if you have difficulty supporting it.

Give EVIDENCE that supports your thesis. Depending on the kind of analysis, evidence could include examples, statistics, quotations, definitions, and so on.

Cite other sources, but remember that this is *your* analysis. Your audience wants to hear your voice and learn from your insights. At the same time, don't forget to acknowledge other perspectives.

Draft an OPENING. You might begin by describing what you're analyzing and why, explaining what question prompted you to take a closer look at your topic. Provide any background information your audience might need. State your thesis: what are you claiming about your subject?

Draft a **CONCLUSION**. You might reiterate what you've learned from your analysis and what you want your audience to understand about your subject. Make sure they know why your analysis matters, to them and to you.

Look critically at your draft, get response—and revise

Read your draft slowly and carefully to see whether you've made your guiding question clear, described your subject sufficiently, offered enough evidence to support your analysis, and provided your audience with some insight about your subject.

Then ask others to read and respond to your draft. If your school has a writing center, try to meet with a tutor, bringing along any questions you have. Here are some questions that can help you or others read over a draft of analytic writing:

- *Is the question that prompted your analysis clear?* Is it a question worth considering?

- *How does the* **OPENING** *capture the audience's interest?* Does it indicate why this analysis matters? How else might you begin?

- *Is the point of your analysis clear?* Have you stated the point explicitly in a **THESIS** —and if not, do you need to?

- *Is the subject described in enough detail for your audience?* Is there any other information they might need in order to follow your analysis?

- *What* **EVIDENCE** *do you provide to support your point?* Is it sufficient?

- *What insights have you gained from the analysis?* Have you stated them explicitly? How likely is it that readers will accept your conclusions?

- *If you've cited any sources, are they credible and convincing?* Have you integrated them smoothly into your text—is it clear what you are saying yourself and where (and why) you are citing others? And have you **DOCUMENTED** any sources you've cited?

- *Have you addressed other perspectives?* Do you need to acknowledge possible **COUNTERARGUMENTS**?

- *How would you describe the* TONE, and does it accurately convey your STANCE? Is the tone appropriate for your audience and purpose?

- *How is the analysis organized?* Is it easy to follow, with clear TRANSITIONS from one point to the next? Are there headings—and if not, would adding them help? If you're analyzing a process, are the steps in an order that your audience will be able to follow easily?

- *Consider* STYLE. Look at the choice of words and kinds of sentences—are they appropriately formal (or informal) for the audience and purpose? Could the style be improved in any way?

- *How effective is the* DESIGN? Have you included any images or other visual elements—and if so, how do they contribute to the analysis? If not, is there any information that might be easier to understand if presented in a table or chart or accompanied by an image?

- *How does the draft* CONCLUDE? Is the CONCLUSION forceful and memorable? How else might the analysis conclude?

- *Consider the title.* Does it make clear what the analysis is about, and will it make your audience interested in reading on?

Revise your draft in light of your own observations and any feedback you get from others, keeping your audience and purpose firmly in mind. But remember: *you* are the analyst here, so you need to make the decisions.

REFLECT. Once you've completed your analysis, let it settle for a while and then take time to reflect. How well did you analyze your subject? What insights did your analysis lead to? What additional revisions would you make if you could? Research shows that such reflections help "lock in" what you learn for future use.

Google Home vs Alexa:
Two Simple User Experience Design Gestures
That Delighted a Female User

JOHNA PAOLINO

AYEAR AGO, MY BOYFRIEND got an Amazon Echo. I remember first using the product, dazzled at its ability to process requests from across the room. *Alexa, play us some music.*

As the year progressed, the wow factor faded quickly.

The product features continued working to their full effect, but I felt very unsettled. I found myself constantly agitated as I observed my boyfriend bark commands at this black cylinder.

Alexa, turn off the lights. Alexa, set my alarm for 8am.

This declarative speech was so incongruous with how he interacts with me, with how he interacts with any human.

Was it how he was asking? Was it that she was female? Was I jealous?

As a user experience designer, I am constantly questioning the emotional effect technology has on me. Perhaps I was taking too much of my day job into my

JOHNA PAOLINO is a senior product designer at the *New York Times,* where she designs digital tools to make the newsroom more efficient. She also writes about user experience and design. This piece was published on *Medium* in 2017.

personal life. I decided to mute this awareness until this holiday season when I unwrapped my very own Google Home. I configured the device, hesitantly looking forward to some of the features my apartment had been missing over the past year.

Ok Google, play NPR news. Hey Google, set my alarm for 8am.

Why did these interactions suddenly feel so natural? They felt appropriate. In fact, I was delighted by my new Google Home.

Although product features differ slightly, the root cause of my emotional shift had nothing to do with these capabilities. All the feelings I had for Alexa came down to two simplistic user experience design differences.

The Naming of the Products

I've learned throughout my career that the most significant UX performance 5 gains often come down to microcopy. This could not be more true here. Amazon is the name of a pioneering e-commerce platform and revolutionary cloud computing company. Echo is its product name, first to market of its kind. Alexa? Alexa is just the name of a female that performs personal tasks for you in your home.

Apple and Siri set a precedent for this. Was there a need to rename the voice component of these products? Why isn't it Echo or Amazon? Why not Apple? By doing this, we've subconsciously constrained the capabilities of a female. With the Echo, we've even gone as far as to confine her to a home.

The voice component of the Google Home, however, is simply triggered with "Google." Google, a multinational, first-of-its-kind technology company. Suddenly a female's voice represents a lot more. This made me happy.

Conversational Triggers

Alexa responds to her name only. Google's product must be triggered with a "hey Google" or "ok Google." By requiring these introductory words as triggers, Google has forced an element of conversation. The experience difference here is huge! When I return to Alexa now I feel authoritative.

The advancement of feminism requires awareness from both genders. It isn't isolated to how men treat women, but extends to how women treat each other. I am constantly making an effort to change my behaviors towards other women, and in this effort certainly prefer how I am asked to greet Google.

The smallest of user experience details matter. My entire emotional experience   10
between these products can be boiled down to: "Hey," "Ok," and a name. I want to thank Google. Thank you for paying closer attention to the details, and to the female users.

We have a responsibility as designers and technologists. We can make these systems model how we want the world to be—let's take steps forward not backward.

Thinking about the Text

1. With her title, Johna Paolino immediately establishes that this will be a contest: Google Home against Alexa. How does she establish her **AUTHORITY** to write on this topic?

2. Where does Paolino indicate the question driving her analysis?

3. Who is Paolino's **AUDIENCE**? Point to specific places where she uses language to establish a connection with readers. How would you describe her **TONE**?

4. Since Paolino doesn't include any photographs or audio clips (just her own original drawing of her subjects), the analysis largely depends on her **DESCRIPTION** of the two smart speakers. What **EVIDENCE** does Pao-

lino provide to support her stance? What details or evidence might you add to make her argument even stronger?

5. Following the guidelines in this chapter, write an **ANALYSIS** of two competing tech products you have experience using—perhaps an Android phone and an iPhone, two fitness tracking apps, or competing social media platforms. Be sure to state the question you're exploring, the insight you gain, and the evidence supporting your stance.

Advertisements R Us

MELISSA RUBIN

ADVERTISEMENTS ARE WRITTEN to persuade us—to make us want to support a certain cause, buy a particular car, drink a specific kind of soda. But *how* do they do it? How do they persuade us? Since the beginning of modern consumer culture, companies have cleverly tailored advertisements to target specific groups. To do so, they include text and images that reflect and appeal to the ideals, values, and stereotypes held by the consumers they wish to attract. As a result, advertisements reveal a lot about society. We can learn a great deal about the prevailing culture by looking closely at the deliberate ways a company crafts an ad to appeal to particular audiences.

This ad from the August 1950 *Coca-Cola Bottler* magazine, a trade magazine for Coca-Cola bottlers (Fig. 1), features a larger-than-life red Coca-Cola vending machine with the slogan "Drink Coca-Cola—Work *Refreshed*" (Coca-Cola advertisement). Set against a bright blue sky with puffy white clouds, an over-large open bottle of Coke hovers just to the right and slightly above the vending machine, next to the head of "Sprite Boy," a pixie-ish character and onetime Coke symbol, who sports a bottle cap for a hat. Sprite Boy's left hand gestures past the floating Coke bottle and toward a crowd congregating before the vending machine. The group, overwhelmingly male and apparently all white, includes blue-collar workers in casual clothing, servicemen in uniform, and

---

MELISSA RUBIN wrote this analysis when she was a student at Hofstra University using an early draft of this chapter. She now teaches creative writing and composition at Hofstra University and Touro College.

Fig. 1. 1950 ad from *Coca-Cola Bottler* magazine (Coca-Cola advertisement).

businessmen in suits in the foreground; the few women displayed are in the background, wearing dresses. The setting is industrialized and urban, as indicated by the factory and smokestacks on the far left side of the scene and by the skyscrapers and apartment building on the right.

Practically since its invention, Coca-Cola has been identified with mainstream America. Born from curiosity and experimentation in an Atlanta pharmacy in 1886, Coke's phenomenal growth paralleled America's in the industrial age. Benefiting from developments in technology and transportation, by 1895 it was "sold and consumed in every state and territory in the United States" (Coca-Cola Company). In 2010, Diet Coke became the second-most-popular carbonated drink in the world . . . behind Coca-Cola (Esterl). In the immediate post-war world, Coke became identified with American optimism and energy, thanks in part to the company's wartime declaration that "every man in uniform gets a bottle of Coca-Cola for 5 cents, wherever he is, and whatever it costs the Company" (Coca-Cola Company). To meet this dictate, bottling plants were built overseas with the result that many people other than Americans first tasted Coke during this war that America won so decisively, and when peace finally came, "the foundations were laid for Coca-Cola to do business overseas" (Coca-Cola Company).

Given the context, just a few years after World War II and at the beginning of the Korean War, the setting clearly reflects the idea that Americans experienced increased industrialization and urbanization as a result of World War II. Factories had sprung up across the country to aid in the war effort, and many rural and small-town Americans had moved to industrial areas and large cities in search of work. In this advertisement, the buildings surround the people, symbolizing a sense of community and the way Americans had come together in a successful effort to win the war.

The ad suggests that Coca-Cola recognized the patriotism inspired by the 5
war and wanted to inspire similar positive feelings about their product. In the center of the ad, the huge red vending machine looks like the biggest skyscraper of all—the dominant feature of the urban industrial landscape. On the upper right, the floating face of Coca-Cola's Sprite Boy towers above the scene. A pale character with wild white hair, hypnotic eyes, and a mysterious smile, Sprite Boy stares straight at readers, his left hand gesturing toward the red machine. Sprite Boy's size and placement in the ad makes him appear god-like, as if he, the embodiment of Coca-Cola, is a powerful force uniting—and refreshing—hardworking Americans. The placement of the vending machine in the center of the ad and the wording on it evoke the idea that drinking

Coca-Cola will make a hardworking American feel refreshed while he (and apparently it was rarely she) works and becomes part of a larger community. The text at the bottom of the ad, "A welcome host to workers—*Inviting you to the pause that refreshes with ice-cold Coca-Cola*"—sends the same message to consumers: Coke will refresh and unite working America.

The way that Coca-Cola chooses to place the objects and depict men and women in this ad speaks volumes about American society in the middle of the twentieth century: a white, male-dominated society in which servicemen and veterans were a numerous and prominent presence. The clothing that the men in the foreground wear reflects the assumption that the target demographic for the ad—people who worked in Coca-Cola bottling plants—valued hard workers and servicemen during a time of war. White, uniformed men are placed front and center. One man wears an Army uniform, the one next to him wears a Navy uniform, and the next an Air Force uniform. By placing the servicemen so prominently, Coca-Cola emphasizes their important role in society and underscores the value Americans placed on their veterans at a time when almost all male Americans were subject to the draft and most of them could expect to serve in the military or had already done so. The other men in the foreground—one wearing a blue-collar work uniform and the other formal business attire—are placed on either side of and slightly apart from the soldiers, suggesting that civilian workers played a valuable role in society, but one secondary to that of the military. Placing only a few women dressed in casual day wear in the far background of the image represents the assumption that women played a less important role in society—or at least in the war effort and the workforce, including Coke's.

The conspicuous mixture of stereotypical middle-class and working-class attire is noteworthy because in 1950, the U.S. economy had been marked by years of conflict over labor's unionization efforts and management's opposition to them—often culminating in accommodation between the two sides. The ad seems to suggest that such conflict should be seen as a thing of the past, that men with blue-collar jobs and their bosses are all "workers" whom Coca-Cola, a generous "host," is inviting to share in a break for refreshments. Thus all economic classes, together with a strong military, can unite to build a productive industrial future and a pleasant lifestyle for themselves.

From the perspective of the twenty-first century, this ad is especially interesting because it seems to be looking backward instead of forward in significant ways. By 1950, the highly urban view of American society it presents was starting to be challenged by widespread movement out of central cities to the suburbs, but nothing in the ad hints at this profound change. At the time, offices and factories were still located mostly in urban areas and associated in Americans' minds with cities, and the ad clearly reflects this perspective. In addition, it presents smoke pouring from factory smokestacks in a positive light, with no sign of the environmental damage that such emissions cause, and that would become increasingly clear over the next few decades.

Another important factor to consider: everyone in the ad is white. During the 1950s, there was still a great deal of racial prejudice and segregation in the United States. Coca-Cola was attuned to white society's racial intolerance and chose in this ad to depict what they undoubtedly saw as average Americans, the primary demographic of the audience for this publication: Coca-Cola employees. While Coke did feature African Americans in some ads during the late 1940s and early 1950s, they were celebrity musicians like Louis Armstrong, Duke Ellington, Count Basie, or Graham Jackson (the accordion player who was a huge favorite of Franklin Delano Roosevelt) or star athletes like Marion Motley and Bill Willis, the first men to break the color barrier in NFL football ("World of Coca-Cola"). The contrast between these extremes underscores the prejudice: "ordinary" people are represented by whites, while only exceptional African Americans appear in the company's ads.

In 1950, then, the kind of diversity that Coke wanted to highlight and appeal   10
to was economic (middle-class and working-class) and war-related (civilian and military). Today, such an ad would probably represent the ethnic diversity missing from the 1950 version, with smiling young people of diverse skin colors and facial features relaxing with Cokes, probably now in cans rather than bottles. But the differences in economic, employment, or military status or in clothing styles that the 1950 ad highlighted would be unlikely to appear, not because they no longer exist, but because advertisers for products popular with a broad spectrum of society no longer consider them a useful way to appeal to consumers.

While initially the ads for Coca-Cola reflected the values of the time, their enormous success eventually meant that Coke ads helped shape the American identity. In them, Americans always appear smiling, relaxed, carefree, united in their quest for well-deserved relaxation and refreshment. They drive convertibles, play sports, dance, and obviously enjoy life. The message: theirs is a life to be envied and emulated, so drink Coca-Cola and live that life yourself.

Works Cited

Coca-Cola advertisement. *The Coca-Cola Bottler,* vol. 41, no. 6, 1950, www
.vintageadbrowser.com/coke-ads-1950s/6. Accessed 5 May 2011.

Coca-Cola Company. "The Coca-Cola Company Heritage Timeline." *Coca-Cola History,* Coca-Cola Company, www.coca-colacompany.com
/history/. Accessed 26 June 2011.

Esterl, Mike. "Diet Coke Wins Battle in Cola Wars." *The Wall Street Journal,*
17 Mar. 2011, p. B1.

"The World of Coca-Cola Self-Guided Tour for Teachers. Highlights: African American History Month." *World of Coca-Cola,* www.worldofcoca-cola
.com/wp-content/uploads/sites/3/2013/10/aahhighschool.pdf.
Accessed 26 June 2011.

Thinking about the Text

1. What insight does Melissa Rubin offer about the Coca-Cola ad she analyzes, and what **EVIDENCE** does she provide to support her analysis? Has she persuaded you to accept her conclusions? Why or why not?

2. What historical **CONTEXT** does Rubin provide, and what does that information contribute to her analysis?

3. Rubin's analysis is driven by this question: what can we learn about the culture in which a given ad is created by closely examining how that ad appeals to particular audiences? What other questions might you try to answer by analyzing an ad?

4. Rubin looks closely at the men and women in this ad and makes certain assumptions about them. What sorts of details does she point out to identify who these people are? Do you think she's represented them accurately? If not, how might you identify them differently, and why?

5. Write an **ANALYSIS** of a current ad, looking specifically at how it reflects American values in the twenty-first century. Be sure to include the ad in your essay.

FIFTEEN

"Just the Facts"
Reporting Information

SOME **A**MERICANS ASSOCIATE THE LINE "Just the facts, ma'am" with *Dragnet*, a 1950s TV crime drama, and more specifically with Sgt. Joe Friday, played by Jack Webb, who used this phrase when interviewing women during investigations. The first radio show to jump to TV, *Dragnet* was produced in close collaboration with the LAPD. How close? Police Chief William Parker had veto power over every scene in exchange for the use of real LAPD case files. The show was even often filmed in police headquarters. Parker and Webb brought their law-and-order worldview to the series along with its 1950s view of race differences and gender roles.

This story can be seen as a kind of very short report, and it demonstrates an important aspect of reports: they present information to audiences made up of people with varying degrees of knowledge. Perhaps you've heard the phrase "Just the facts, ma'am" but had no idea where it came from. Perhaps you've never heard of *Dragnet*. Now you have, and you know a few things about it. Even if you were familiar with both the program and the expression, you now likely have a new bit of information: the show that defined the genre of police procedurals was a PR vehicle for the LAPD. Thus, this very short report demonstrates how reports are written with a range of readers in mind.

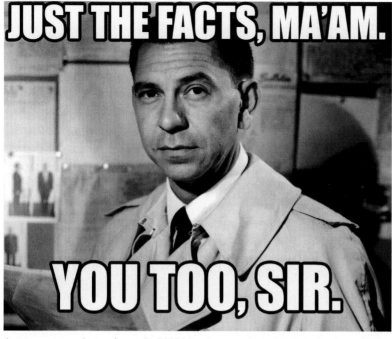

A meme using a photo of actor Jack Webb in his most famous role as Sgt. Joe Friday with his most famous line from the program *Dragnet* at the top, along with a more modern addition below.

Reports are built of information that is factual in some way. As you no doubt realize, separating what is factual from what is opinion can be a challenge, especially when the topic is controversial.

The primary goal of a report is to present factual information to educate an audience in some way. The stance of those who write reports is generally objective rather than argumentative. Thus, newspaper and television reporters—note the word—in the United States have traditionally tried to present news in a neutral way. Writers of lab reports describe as carefully and objectively as they can how they conducted their experiments and what they found. Perhaps even more than authors in other genres, therefore, writers of reports aim to create an **ETHOS** of trustworthiness and reliability.

This chapter offers guidelines for composing reports, including profiles, a kind of report often assigned in college. As you'll see, writing effective reports requires you to pay careful attention to your purpose, audience, and stance as well as to whatever facts you're reporting.

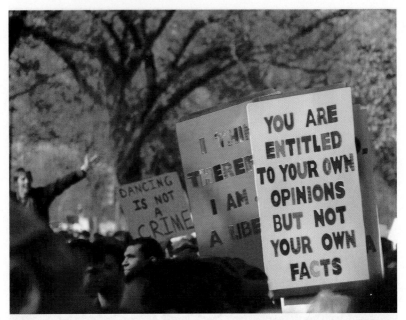

A 2010 rally sign quoting a statement attributed to Daniel Patrick Moynihan (1927–2003), who served as a US senator from New York, advisor to President Richard Nixon, ambassador to India, and UN ambassador.

REFLECT. Think about reports you've read, heard, seen, or written recently, and make a list of them. Your list may include everything from a lab report for a biology class, to a documentary film, to a PowerPoint presentation you and several classmates created for a course. What features do these reports share—and how do they differ?

Across Academic Disciplines

Reports are found everywhere in academic life. You're certainly familiar with book reports, and you're probably familiar with lab reports from science courses. Students and practitioners in most fields in the *physical sciences, social sciences*, and *applied sciences* regularly write reports, generally based on experiments or other kinds of systematic investigation.

Many scientific reports share a common format—often labeled IMRAD (introduction, methods, results, and discussion)—and a common purpose: to convey information. The format mirrors the stages of inquiry: you ask a question, describe the materials and methods you used to try to answer it, report the results you found, and discuss what they mean in light of what you and others already know.

Another kind of report students often write, especially in courses that focus on contemporary society in some way, is the profile, a firsthand report on an individual, a group, an event, or an institution. A profile of a person might be based on an interview, perhaps with an American soldier who served in Afghanistan, for example, or the first female professor to receive tenure in your college's economics department. Similarly, a profile of an institution might report on the congregation of a specific house of worship, an organization, or a company; such reports often have a specific audience in mind, whether it is donors, investors, members, or clients.

Across Media

When reporting information, you'll find that different media offer you radically different resources. Throughout this chapter, we'll refer to reporting by the *New York Times* on the "double-full-full-full," an especially challenging aerial skiing maneuver involving a triple back flip and four body twists. Just before the 2010 Winter Olympics, the *Times* reported on this jump in three media. It was the subject of a *news article* by Henry Fountain that appeared in the Science section in print and online. It was also the basis of a *video* feature on the *Times* website in which Fountain explains the physics of the flip, as demonstrated by US Olympic skier Ryan St. Onge. Finally, it was the focus of part of a science *podcast* featuring interviews with both St. Onge and Fountain. Two of these reports use images, two use spoken words, and one relies primarily on written words.

In studying these three reports, you'll get a clear idea of how medium influences not only how information is reported but also what kinds of information can be covered. For example, consider *Twitter*: imagine what Fountain could have reported about the double-full-full-full in 280 characters.

Across Cultures and Communities

Wherever you find formal organizations, companies, and other institutions, you'll find reports of various kinds. For example, a school board trying to improve safety measures in a time of shrinking budgets will surely rely on information in reports written by *parents' organizations, community groups,*

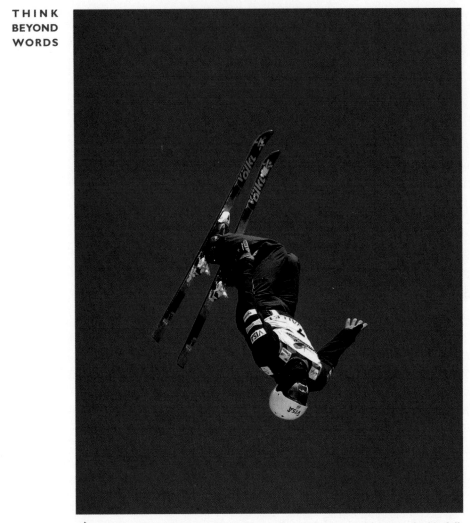

WATCH THE VIDEO of US Olympic skier Ryan St. Onge performing a double-full-full-full, a triple back flip with four body twists. Then read the article on the physics of aerial skiing. Pay attention to how some of the technical terms are defined (and keep in mind that in the video, definitions may include images as well as words). Describe the double-full-full-full using words alone. Then add an image. Do you need to alter your original description once you add the image? Go to everyonesanauthor .tumblr.com to access the video and article.

teachers' unions, or *outside consultants.* Odds are that the reports from each of these groups would differ in focus and tone. Some of these reports might be based primarily on statistical data while others might feature personal testimonies. Those created by outside consultants would likely be very formal and data-driven and might include a *PowerPoint* presentation to the school board followed by a question-and-answer period. In contrast, a report from a parents' group could include a homemade video consisting primarily of conversations with students.

As a student, you'll be working in various academic communities, and you will need to pay attention to the way information is reported across disciplines—and to what is expected of you in any reports that you write.

Across Genres

While reports are a common genre of writing, you'll also have occasion to report information in other genres. **NARRATIVES**, **ANALYSES**, **REVIEWS**, **ARGUMENTS**, and many other kinds of writing contain factual information often presented as neutrally as possible—and you will often report factual evidence to support your claims.

On the other hand, some documents that are called reports present more than "just the facts" and cross the line to **ANALYZE** or interpret the information presented, to make a **PROPOSAL**, and so on. For example, a report on economic development in Austin, Texas, concludes with recommendations for the future. Those recommendations follow many pages of carefully reported information (as well as considerable analysis of that information). When you're assigned to write a report, you will want to determine exactly what the person who assigned it has in mind: a text that only reports information or one that is called a report but that also requires you to analyze the information, make some kind of argument, and so on.

REFLECT. Analyze the purposes of the reports that you listed (see p. 284). Who is the intended audience for each? To what degree does each simply report information, and to what degree does it use information to serve some larger goal, for example, to take a position on an issue? Can you distinguish clearly between a report that only presents information and one that presents information and also argues a point?

CHARACTERISTIC FEATURES

While you can expect differences across media and disciplines, most of the reports you will write share the following characteristics:

- A topic carefully focused for a specific audience
- Definitions of key terms
- Trustworthy information
- Appropriate organization and design
- A confident, informative tone

A Topic Carefully Focused for a Specific Audience

The most effective reports have a focus, a single topic that is limited in scope by what the audience already knows and what the author's purpose is. For example, in 2016, Liveable City, a nonprofit organization that works to protect the quality of life in Austin, Texas, released a report on affordability in Austin. The report's executive summary frames the issue and outlines the organization's activities.

> Austin residents are feeling the burden of rising household costs. Prices for many goods and services . . . are escalating even as incomes for most households remain relatively stagnant. . . . This report examines the seven basic cost categories that significantly impact household budgets. . . . [W]e focus on specific local actions that can influence these [categories] of living costs. We especially emphasize local policy and initiatives that promise to limit cost pressures across multiple elements of household budgets, especially for middle- and lower-income households.
> —LIVEABLE CITY, "Reclaiming Affordability in Today's Austin"

Notice how the authors focus their report on household budgets and issues of affordability, items that, at first glance, may not appear to be local in scope. The authors are careful, however, to emphasize that their recommendations and proposals are intended to be accomplished locally by involved Austin residents along with local government bodies.

Three iconic Austin images from Liveable City's website that depict Austin's vibrant character.

The authors assume that they are writing for people who care about Austin (notice that they refer to specific local actions). The intended readers would have included members of the board of Liveable City as well as individual and corporate donors. Because such reports are often cited in news stories and opinion pieces in the local media, we can assume that the intended readers also included Austinites more broadly. But the authors are also writing for audiences beyond Austin, especially those interested in improving the economic outcomes for working families. Although the report was distributed as a print document, probably to local members of the intended audience, it is also available to anyone with internet access.

In their 2018 annual report for Oakland Promise, a nonprofit group striving to ensure that all children in Oakland, California, graduate from high school with access to the resources required to succeed in college, the authors have a different focus with three clear purposes. First, they aim to showcase the successes over the past year by using attractive infographics detailing the number of children and families served in the organization's programs. Second, the authors inform readers of the short- and medium-range goals of each program through more infographics. Third, the authors demonstrate the ample and enthusiastic community support the initiative receives by including a long list of elected officials, institutions both public and private, and individuals who advise, volunteer, and donate. The report is sprinkled with photos showing the activities and success stories of the programs. These images add life to what might otherwise be a dry recitation of names and numbers; the photos connect to the readers' emotions and ethics in reminding them of Oakland Promise's mission as well as its success.

In composing this report, the authors were obviously thinking about their primary audience: those who have participated in and donated to Oakland Promise in the past and those who might do so in the future, and who want to be informed about the work the initiative does—what it accomplishes and how economically it does so.

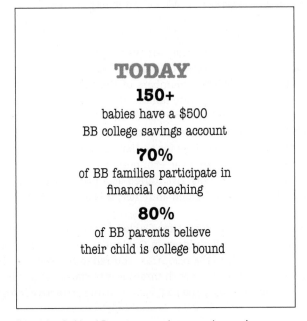

From the Oakland Promise annual report, the year's acccomplishments of the Brilliant Baby (BB) program.

"When we visited UC Berkeley, the whole idea of college became real. We could actually picture the campus and see ourselves there. Everything changed!"
—K2C Parent

From the Oakland Promise annual report, a photo of a college visit (top) and the short- and medium-range goals of the Kindergarten to College (K2C) program (bottom).

In both the Liveable City and Oakland Promise reports, the topic is carefully focused, and the authors approach their task with a keen eye toward the intended audiences and their organization's goals. You'll want to do the same in the reports that you write: to consider carefully whom you're addressing, what they know about your topic, and what information they expect.

Definitions of Key Terms

Effective reports always define key terms explicitly. These definitions serve several functions. Some audience members may not understand some of the technical terms. And even those familiar with the terms pay attention to the definitions for clues about the writer's stance or assumptions. Here's an example of a definition from Liveable City's 2016 report:

> *Support legislation to establish a "circuit breaker" provision for property tax payments.* A circuit breaker provision directs the state to reimburse tax-payers if their total property tax bills exceed a specified percentage of their income. Similar provisions currently exist in 21 states.

Here, the term "circuit breaker" is introduced as a recommendation for change at the state level, where property tax laws are set. Notice how the term is defined in very general terms as soon as it is introduced. Information about other states' use of such a strategy lends authority and confidence to the concept. Another concept in Liveable City's discussion of how affordability is affected by the taxing structure is the term "regressive":

> [T]he chief reason that tax burdens have reduced affordability is that the structure of virtually all taxes paid by residents is highly regressive. Sales taxes, gas taxes, . . . and property taxes are the key revenue sources for state and local governments in Texas. For each of these . . . , the higher your income, the lower share of your income you pay toward these taxes. Conversely, the lower your income, the higher the share of your income you pay. Thus the tax burden hits low- and moderate-income households the hardest, and remains relatively light for the higher-income residents of the city.

Notice how the report doesn't call particular attention to the term "regressive" with italics or any other marking, but the explanation of the term comes immediately along with examples of the relevant tax categories (sales tax, gas tax, etc.) and reasons why such taxes are undesirable.

In the *New York Times* article on aerial skiing mentioned on page 285, Henry Fountain uses a number of strategies to provide readers with definitions they might need. As a newspaper journalist, Fountain writes for a general audience, and he can safely assume that some readers of the Science section will have a great deal of knowledge about physics. He can likewise assume that some readers will know something about aerial skiing, but he also anticipates that other readers will know little about either. Here's one definition Fountain offers:

> The first time you watch skiers hurtle off a curved ramp at 30 miles per hour, soaring six stories in the air while doing three back flips and up to five body twists, you can't help but think: These people are crazy. . . .
>
> Freestyle aerialists, as these athletes are known, are not actually throwing caution, along with themselves, to the wind.
>
> —HENRY FOUNTAIN, "Up in the Air, and Down, with a Twist"

Here the short phrase "as these athletes are known" refers back to the skiers Fountain has described earlier, and this description explains the term "freestyle aerialists."

A few paragraphs later, Fountain explains *torque*, the concept in physics that allows freestyle aerialists to do somersaults, without explicitly defining it:

> "The forces are pretty simple," said Adam Johnston, a physics professor at Weber State University in Ogden, Utah. . . . "There's the force of the ramp on his skis, and the force of gravity on him," Dr. Johnston said, after Ryan St. Onge, the reigning world champion in men's aerials and a member of the Olympic team, zipped down a steep inrun, leaned back as he entered the curved ramp until he was nearly horizontal and flew off at a 70-degree angle. "That's all there is."
>
> But it is enough to create torque that sends Mr. St. Onge somersaulting backward as he takes to the air, arcing toward a landing on a steep downslope that the skiers and coaches have chopped and fluffed for safety.

Later in the article, Fountain writes: "In this training jump, Mr. St. Onge adds a full twist in both the second and third flips—a lay-full-full in the language of the sport." Here Fountain provides a technical term used by experts—a "lay-full-full"—immediately after explaining what the term means. In a subsequent paragraph, Fountain uses another strategy, providing a definition of a "double-full-full-full" in a **SUBORDINATE CLAUSE** (italicized here): "And when doing a double-full-full-full, *which requires four full twists, including two in the first flip,* he will use all three methods at takeoff." Note that none of the definitions shown here quote a dictionary, nor do they use the formula "the definition of X is Y"—and that each of the experts offers memorable examples that help readers understand the subject.

Trustworthy Information

Effective reports present information that readers can trust to be accurate. In some cases, writers provide documentation to demonstrate the verifiability of their information, including citations of published research, the dates of interviews they have conducted, or other details about their sources.

In a report for a writing class at Chapman University, Kelley Fox presents information in ways that lead readers to trust the details she presents and, ultimately, the author herself. The report describes how Griffin, Simon, and Andy, three roommates in Room 115 of her dorm, create their identities. Beginning with Muhammad Ali's line "Float like a butterfly, sting like a bee," which is the caption on a large poster of Ali on Griffin's wall, Fox seeks to characterize Griffin as someone who floats at "the top of the pecking order" and who seems "invincible":

> In a sense, Griffin is just that: socially invincible. A varsity basketball athlete, Griffin has no shortage of friends, or of female followers. People seem to simply gravitate toward him, as if being around him makes all their problems trivial. Teammates can often be found in his room, hanging out on his bed, watching ESPN. Girls are certainly not a rarity, and they usually come bearing gifts: pies, CDs, even homework answers. It happens often, and I have a feeling this "social worship" has been going on for a while, although in myriad other forms. Regardless, the constant and excessive positive attention allows Griffin to never have to think about his own happiness; Griffin always seems happy. And it is because of this that, out of the three roommates, it is easiest to be Griffin.
>
> —KELLEY FOX, "Establishing Identities"

Fox's description demonstrates to readers that she has spent considerable time in or around Room 115 and that she knows what she is writing about. Her use of specific details convinces us that Griffin is real and that the things she describes in fact occur—and on a regular basis.

In a report on early language development in children written for a linguistics class at Portland State University, Katryn Sheppard demonstrates the trustworthiness of her information differently, citing both published research and her own primary research on a speech transcript of one-year-old Allison.

> One feature of Allison's utterances that did adhere to what is expected for a typical child at this age was related to her use of negatives. Although she used only one negative word—"no"—the word was repeated frequently enough to be the fourth most common category in the transcript. Her use of "no" rather than any other negative conformed to Brown's (1973) finding that other forms of negation like "not" and "don't" appear only in later stages (Santelmann, 2014). In Allison's very early stage of linguistic development, the reliance on "no" alone seems typical.
>
> —KATRYN SHEPPARD, "Early Word Production"

By citing both published research and examples from her own primary research, Sheppard demonstrates that she has spent considerable time researching her topic and can thus make informed observations about Allison's speech. These citations not only let readers know that Sheppard can support her claims, they also indicate where readers can go to verify the information if they so choose; both strategies demonstrate trustworthiness.

Although Fox and Sheppard use different techniques, both of them convince readers that the information being presented and the writers themselves can be trusted.

Appropriate Organization and Design

There is no single best strategy for organizing the information you are reporting. In addition to **DEFINING** (as Henry Fountain does), you'll find yourself **DESCRIBING** (as Kelley Fox does), offering specific **EXAMPLES** and data (as the report from Oakland Promise does), **ANALYZING CAUSES AND EFFECTS** (as Liveable City does), and so on. The specific organizational strategies you'll use will depend on the information you want to report.

In many cases, you'll want to include visuals of some sort, whether photographs, charts, figures, or tables. See, for example, the pie chart from the Liveable City annual report. The information conveyed would be harder to understand and thus far less effective if it were presented in a paragraph or even as a table. And as noted on page 290, Oakland Promise also uses color photos to make the report more interesting and appealing. Similarly, see on page 286 the way that Henry Fountain uses images in his discussion of aerial skiing.

Sometimes the way in which you organize and present your information will be prescribed. If you're writing a report following the **IMRAD** format, you will have little choice in how you organize and present information. Everything from the use of headings to the layout of tables to the size of fonts may be dictated.

Some disciplines specify certain format details. Students of *psychology*, for example, are expected to follow **APA STYLE**. On the other hand, a report

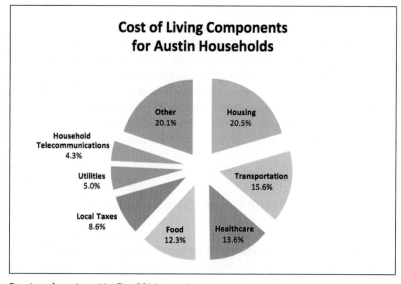

Pie chart from Liveable City 2016 annual report showing the categories of expenditures for Austin households.

for a *composition* class may have fewer constraints. For example, you may get to decide whether you will need headings and whether to use personal examples.

A Confident, Informative Tone

Effective reports have a confident tone that assumes the writer is presenting reliable information rather than arguing or preaching. The authors of the Liveable City report and Henry Fountain both sound like they know what they're writing about. In both these cases, we as readers are by and large getting just "the facts," though it is clear that Liveable City has strong convictions about what the city of Austin should be doing in the future and that Fountain delights in both the beauty and the science of what freestyle aerialists can achieve.

The line between informing and arguing can become fuzzy, however. If you read reports on any number of hot-button issues—climate change, the economy, transgender rights, abortion—you'll find that they often reflect some kind of position or make recommendations that betray a position. But the authors of such reports usually try to create an informative tone that avoids indicating their own opinions.

You may sometimes find yourself struggling with this line, working to present information while stopping short of telling readers what to think about or how to feel about a topic. Here we can offer two pieces of advice. First, keep in mind that you're aiming to explain something to your audience clearly and objectively rather than to persuade them to think about it a certain way. You'll know you've succeeded here if someone reading a draft of your report can't tell exactly what your own opinion about the topic is. Second, pay special attention to word choice because the words you use give subtle and not-so-subtle clues about your stance. Referring to "someone who eats meat" is taking an objective tone; calling that person a "carnivore" is not.

WIKIPEDIA, the free online encyclopedia that "anyone can edit," has become one of the most-visited sites on the internet since its launch in 2001. Like any encyclopedia, the primary purpose of *Wikipedia* is to report information. Below is an example from the entry on gender, as it appeared on July 19, 2018. This article demonstrates how authors negotiate the challenges of reporting information fairly and from an unbiased perspective. *Wikipedia* provides many examples of reporting on controversial topics, and the site has explicit policies and guidelines for authors to follow. Documenting the sources of information is an important tool for maintaining the reliability of information; this lengthy article, for example, has 163 citations, principally from academic journals in the physical and social sciences.

Gender

WIKIPEDIA

A definition of the term followed by several ways that the term may be applied.

GENDER IS THE range of characteristics pertaining to, and differentiating between, masculinity and femininity. Depending on the context, these characteristics may include biological sex (i.e., the state of being male, female, or an intersex variation), sex-based social structures (i.e., gender roles), or gender identity.[1][2][3] People who do not identify as men or women or with masculine or feminine gender pronouns are often grouped under the umbrella terms non-binary or genderqueer. Some cultures have specific gender roles that are distinct from "man" and "woman," such as the hijras of South Asia. These are often referred to as third genders.

The tone is confident and informative and avoids indicating a specific stance or opinion.

Sexologist John Money introduced the terminological distinction between biological sex and gender as a role in 1955. Before his work, it was uncommon to use the word gender to refer to anything but grammatical categories.[1][2] However, Money's meaning of the word did not become widespread until the 1970s, when feminist theory embraced the concept of a distinction between biological sex and the social construct of gender. Today the distinction is strictly followed in some contexts, especially the social sciences[4][5] and documents written by the World Health Organization (WHO).[3]

Underlining signals links to more information in Wikipedia entries.

In other contexts, including some areas of social sciences, gender includes sex or replaces it.[1][2] For instance, in non-human animal research, gender is commonly used to refer to the biological sex of the animals.[2] This change in the meaning of gender can be traced to the 1980s. In 1993, the US Food and Drug Administration (FDA) started to use gender instead of sex.[6] Later, in 2011, the FDA reversed its position and began using sex as the biological classification and gender as "a person's self representation as male or female, or how that person is responded to by social institutions based on the individual's gender presentation."[7] . . .

Notice the overall organization of the entry: definition and explanation first, brief historical context of the term's application, and an amplification of the categories that the term encompasses.

Globally, communities interpret biological differences between men and women to create a set of social expectations that define the behaviors that are "appropriate" for men and women and determine women's and men's different access to rights, resources, power in society and health behaviors.[26] Although the specific nature and degree of these differences vary from one society to the next, they still tend to typically favor men, creating an imbalance in power and gender inequalities within most societies.[27] Many cultures have different systems of norms and beliefs based on gender, but there is no universal standard to a masculine or feminine role across all cultures.[28] Social roles of men and women in relation to each other are based on the cultural norms of that society, which lead to the creation of gender systems. The gender system is the basis of social patterns in many societies, which include the separation of sexes, and the primacy of masculine norms.[27] . . .

Traditionally, most societies have only recognized two distinct, broad classes of gender roles, masculine and feminine, that correspond with the biological sexes of male and female. When a baby is born, society allocates the child to one gender or the other, on the basis of what their genitals resemble.[31] However, some

Go to everyones
anauthor.tumblr
.com to link to
the full *Wikipedia*
article.

Footnotes link to evidence
that demonstrates the
trustworthiness of the
information.

societies explicitly incorporate people who adopt the gender role opposite to their biological sex; for example, the two-spirit people of some indigenous American peoples. Other societies include well-developed roles that are explicitly considered more or less distinct from archetypal female and male roles in those societies. In the language of the sociology of gender, they comprise a third gender,[34] more or less distinct from biological sex (sometimes the basis for the role does include intersexuality or incorporates eunuchs).[35] One such gender role is that adopted by the hijras of India and Pakistan.[36][37] Another example may be the muxe (pronounced ['muʃe]), found in the state of Oaxaca, in southern Mexico.[38] The Bugis people of Sulawesi, Indonesia have a tradition that incorporates all the features above.[39]

REFLECT. *Analyze a* Wikipedia *entry on a topic of your choice to see how focused the information is, how key terms are defined, and how the entry is organized. How trustworthy do you find the information—and what makes you trust it (or not)? How would you characterize the tone—informative? informative but somewhat argumentative? something else? Point to words that convey that tone.*

PROFILES

Profiles provide firsthand accounts of people, places, events, institutions, or other things. Newspapers and magazines publish profiles of interesting subjects; college websites often include profiles of the student body; investors may study profiles of companies before deciding whether or not to buy stock. If you're on *Instagram* or *LinkedIn*, you have likely created a personal profile saying something about who you are and what you do. Profiles take many different forms, but they generally have the following features.

A Firsthand Account

In creating a profile, you're always writing about something you know firsthand, not merely something you've read about. You may do some reading for background, but reading alone won't suffice. You'll also need to talk with people or visit a place or observe an event in some way. Keep in mind, however, that while a profile is a firsthand account, it should not be autobiographical. In other words, you can't profile yourself. In his 2002 *New Yorker* profile of soul singer James Brown, Philip Gourevitch describes Brown's performance as he saw it firsthand as a member of the audience.

> There he is: arms out from his sides as if to welcome an embrace, dentistry blazing in a beatific grin, head turning slowly from side to side, eyes goggle-wide—looking down-right blown away to find himself the focus of such a rite of overwhelming acclamation. He lingers thus for several seconds, then, throwing his head back, he lets out a happy scream and rips into the song "Make It Funky." Within seconds, he has sent his microphone stand toppling toward the first row of orchestra seats, only to snatch the cord and yank it back, while spinning on the ball of one foot in a perfect pirouette, so that his mouth returns to the mike and the mike to his mouth in the same instant. He howls. The crowd howls back.
>
> —PHILIP GOUREVITCH, "Mr. Brown"

Here the author gives readers information about Brown's performance that he could only have gathered from seeing him live, and it's those details of Brown's actions on stage that make the profile come to life.

Detailed Information about the Subject

Profiles are always full of details—background information, descriptive details (sights, sounds, smells), anecdotes, and dialogue. Ideally, these details help bring the subject to life—and persuade your audience that whatever you're writing about is interesting, and worth reading about. What makes the *New Yorker* piece so successful is the kind of details about Brown that the author provides. We can almost see him "spinning on the ball of one foot in a perfect pirouette." Here's another example with different but similarly detailed information about Brown's early musical training (or lack thereof).

> He claims to have mastered the harmonica at the age of five, blowing "Lost John," "Oh, Susannah," and "John Henry," and one afternoon, when he was seven, he taught himself to play the organ by working out the fingering of "Coonshine Baby." Before long, he was picking up guitar licks to such songs as "(Honey) It's Tight Like That" from the great blues-man Tampa Red, who was dating one of Aunt Honey's girls. By the time he was twelve, the young prodigy was fronting his own group.

Much of this information comes from the interviews that Gourevitch conducted while following Brown on tour and visiting his childhood home. The specific details, from the names of songs he sang to the ages when he sang them, go a long way toward establishing Gourevitch's credibility as a writer—and make his profile of Brown even more believable.

Another way that writers of profiles bring their subjects "to life" is by including photos, letting readers see their subjects in action. In the photo on the next page, James Brown seems larger than life, performing with soulful passion, letting us see what Gourevitch describes.

An Interesting Angle

The best profiles present a new or surprising perspective on whatever is being profiled. In other words, a good profile isn't merely a description; rather, it captures something essential about its subject from an interesting angle, much as a memorable photo does. When you plan a profile, try to come up with an angle that will engage readers. That angle will dictate

James Brown performing at the Newport Jazz Festival, 1969.

what information you include. One thing that makes Gourevitch's profile of James Brown so interesting is the angle that he takes on Brown's life and career, starting with his improbable musical genius.

> He was a middle-school dropout, with no formal musical training (he could not read a chart, much less write one), yet from early childhood he had realized in himself an intuitive capacity not only to remember and reproduce any tune or riff he heard but also to hear the underlying structures of music, and to make them his own.

BILL LAITNER covers local news for the *Detroit Free Press*, specializing in social and political issues and human interest stories like the one below. The following profile, published in the *Free Press* in January 2015, inspired a nationwide response.

Heart and Sole:
Detroiter Walks 21 Miles in Work Commute
BILL LAITNER

The profile opens with descriptive details that introduce readers to the subject—and make us want to read on.

LEAVING HOME IN DETROIT at 8 a.m., James Robertson doesn't look like an endurance athlete.

Pudgy of form, shod in heavy work boots, Robertson trudges almost haltingly as he starts another workday.

But as he steps out into the cold, Robertson, 56, is steeled for an Olympic-sized commute. Getting to and from his factory job 23 miles away in Rochester Hills, he'll take a bus partway there and partway home. And he'll also walk an astounding 21 miles.

Five days a week. Monday through Friday.

It's the life Robertson has led for the last decade, ever since his 1988 Honda Accord quit on him.

Every trip is an ordeal of mental and physical toughness for this soft-spoken man with a perfect attendance record at work. And every day is a tribute to how much he cares about his job,

James Robertson commutes 23 miles to and from his job every day—
most of it on foot.

his boss and his coworkers. Robertson's daunting walks and bus
rides, in all kinds of weather, also reflect the challenges some
metro Detroiters face in getting to work in a region of limited
bus service, and where car ownership is priced beyond the reach
of many.

Placing Robertson's challenging commute in the context of the struggles faced by other Detroiters gives it an interesting and meaningful angle.

But you won't hear Robertson complain—nor his boss.

"I set our attendance standard by this man," says Todd Wilson,
plant manager at Schain Mold & Engineering. "I say, if this man can
get here, walking all those miles through snow and rain, well I'll tell
you, I have people in Pontiac 10 minutes away and they say they
can't get here—bull!"

Another interesting angle: Robertson's extraordinary work ethic in spite of the challenging circumstances.

As he speaks of his loyal employee, Wilson leans over his desk
for emphasis, in a sparse office with a view of the factory floor.
Before starting his shift, Robertson stops by the office every day
to talk sports, usually baseball. And during dinnertime each day,
Wilson treats him to fine Southern cooking, compliments of the
plant manager's wife.

Interviews with Robertson and his co-workers provide detailed firsthand information.

"Oh, yes, she takes care of James. And he's a personal favorite of the owners because of his attendance record. He's never

missed a day. I've seen him come in here wringing wet," says Wilson, 53, of Metamora Township.

With a full-time job and marathon commutes, Robertson is clearly sleep deprived, but powers himself by downing 2-liter bottles of Mountain Dew and cans of Coke.

"I sleep a lot on the weekend, yes I do," he says, sounding a little amazed at his schedule. He also catches zzz's on his bus rides. Whatever it takes to get to his job, Robertson does it.

"I can't imagine not working," he says.

"Lord, Keep Me Safe"

The sheer time and effort of getting to work has ruled Robertson's life for more than a decade, ever since his car broke down. He didn't replace it because, he says, "I haven't had a chance to save for it." His job pays $10.55 an hour, well above Michigan's minimum wage of $8.15 an hour but not enough for him to buy, maintain and insure a car in Detroit.

As hard as Robertson's morning commute is, the trip home is even harder.

At the end of his 2-10 p.m. shift as an injection molder at Schain Mold's squeaky-clean factory just south of M-59, and when his coworkers are climbing into their cars, Robertson sets off, on foot—in the dark—for the 23-mile trip to his home off Woodward near Holbrook. None of his coworkers lives anywhere near him, so catching a ride almost never happens.

Instead, he reverses the 7-mile walk he took earlier that day, a stretch between the factory and a bus stop behind Troy's Somerset Collection shopping mall.

"I keep a rhythm in my head," he says of his seemingly mechanical-like pace to the mall.

At Somerset, he catches the last SMART bus of the day, just before 1 a.m. He rides it into Detroit as far it goes, getting off at the State Fairgrounds on Woodward, just south of 8 Mile. By that time, the last inbound Woodward bus has left. So Robertson foots it the rest of the way—about 5 miles—in the cold or rain or the mild summer nights, to the home he shares with his girlfriend.

"I have to go through Highland Park, and you never know what you're going to run into," Robertson says. "It's pretty dangerous. Really, it is dangerous from 8 Mile on down. They're not the type of people you want to run into.

"But I've never had any trouble," he says. Actually, he did get mugged several years ago—"some punks tuned him up pretty good," says Wilson, the plant manager. Robertson chooses not to talk about that.

So, what gets him past dangerous streets, and through the cold and gloom of night and winter winds?

"One word—faith," Robertson says. "I'm not saying I'm a member of some church. But just before I get home, every night, I say, 'Lord, keep me safe.' "

The next day, Robertson adds, "I should've told you there's another thing: determination."

A Land of No Buses

Robertson's 23-mile commute from home takes four hours. It's so time-consuming because he must traverse the no-bus land of rolling Rochester Hills. It's one of scores of tri-county communities (nearly 40 in Oakland County alone) where voters opted not to pay the SMART transit millage. So it has no fixed-route bus service.

Detailed information about Robertson's commute, including a graphic with time stamps, helps readers understand it more clearly—and why it's so incredible.

Buses provide sparse service on Robertson's long work commute, leaving him to walk most of the way on foot.

Once he gets to Troy and Detroit, Robertson is back in bus country. But even there, the bus schedules are thin in a region that is relentlessly auto-centric.

"The last five years been really tough because the buses cut back," Robertson says. Both SMART and DDOT have curtailed service over the last half decade, "and with SMART, it really affected service into Detroit," said Megan Owens, executive director of Transportation Riders United.

The local angle on this story as an example of the struggles many face in Detroit leads Laitner to include information about the city's transportation services.

Detroit's director of transportation said there is a service Robertson may be able to use that's designed to help low-income workers. Job Access and Reverse Commute, paid for in part with federal dollars, provides door-to-door transportation to low-income workers, but at a cost. Robertson said he was not aware of the program.

Still, metro Detroit's lack of accessible mass transit hasn't stopped Robertson from hoofing it along sidewalks—often snow-covered—to get to a job.

At Home at Work

Robertson is proud of all the miles he covers each day. But it's taking a toll, and he's not getting any younger.

"He comes in here looking real tired—his legs, his knees," says coworker Janet Vallardo, 59, of Auburn Hills.

But there's a lot more than a paycheck luring him to make his weekday treks. Robertson looks forward to being around his co-workers, saying, "We're like a family." He also looks forward to the homemade dinners the plant manager's wife whips up for him each day.

"I look at her food, I always say, 'Excellent. No, not excellent. Phenomenal,'" he says, with Wilson sitting across from him, nodding and smiling with affirmation.

Although Robertson eats in a factory lunchroom, his menus sound like something from a Southern café: Turnip greens with smoked pork neck bones, black-eyed peas and carrots in a brown sugar glaze, baby-back ribs, cornbread made from scratch, pinto beans, fried taters, cheesy biscuits. They're the kind of meal that can fuel his daunting commutes back home.

Though his job is clearly part of his social life, when it's time to work this graduate of Northern High School is methodical. He runs an injection-molding machine the size of a small garage, carefully slicing and drilling away waste after removing each finished part, and noting his production in detail on a clipboard.

Strangers Crossing Paths

Robertson has walked the walk so often that drivers wonder: Who is that guy? UBS banker Blake Pollock, 47, of Rochester, wondered. About a year ago, he found out.

Pollock tools up and down Crooks each day in his shiny black 2014 Chrysler 300.

"I saw him so many times, climbing through snow banks. I saw him at all different places on Crooks," Pollock recalls.

Last year, Pollock had just parked at his office space in Troy as Robertson passed. The banker in a suit couldn't keep from asking the factory guy in sweats, what the heck are you doing, walking out here every day? They talked a bit. Robertson walked off and Pollock ruminated.

From then on, Pollock began watching for the factory guy. At first, he'd pick him up occasionally, when he could swing the time. But the generosity became more frequent as winter swept in. Lately, it's several times a week, especially when metro Detroit sees single-digit temperatures and windchills.

"Knowing what I know, I can't drive past him now. I'm in my car with the heat blasting and even then my feet are cold," Pollock says.

Other times, it's 10:30 or 11 p.m., even after midnight, when Pollock, who is divorced, is sitting at home alone or rolling home from a night out, and wondering how the man he knows only as "James" is doing in the frigid darkness.

On those nights, Pollock runs Robertson all the way to his house in Detroit.

"I asked him, why don't you move closer" to work. "He said his girlfriend inherited their house so it's easy to stay there," Pollock said.

On a recent night run, Pollock got his passenger home at 11 p.m. They sat together in the car for a minute, outside Robertson's house.

"So, normally you'd be getting here at 4 o'clock (in the morning), right?" the banker asks. "Yeah," Robertson replies. Pollock flashes a wry smile. "So, you're pretty early, aren't you?" he says. Robertson catches the drift.

"Oh, I'm grateful for the time, believe me," Robertson says, then adds in a voice rising with anticipation: "I'm going to take me a bath!"

After the door shuts and Pollock pulls away, he admits that Robertson mystifies him, yet leaves him stunned with admiration for the man's uncanny work ethic and determination.

"I always say to my friends, I'm not a nice guy. But I find myself helping James," Pollock says with a sheepish laugh. He said he's picked up Robertson several dozen times this winter alone.

Has a Routine

At the plant, coworkers feel odd seeing one of their team numbers always walking, says Charlie Hollis, 63, of Pontiac. "I keep telling him to get him a nice little car," says Hollis, also a machine operator.

Echoes the plant manager Wilson, "We are very much trying to get James a vehicle." But Robertson has a routine now, and he seems to like it, his coworkers say.

"If I can get away, I'll pick him up. But James won't get in just anybody's car. He likes his independence," Wilson says.

Robertson has simple words for why he is what he is, and does what he does. He speaks with pride of his parents, including his father's military service.

"I just get it from my family. It's a lot of walking, I know."

REFLECT. Bill Laitner profiles an ordinary person whose extraordinary commute brought nationwide attention to the challenges of getting to work without a car or public transportation. Think about someone you know whose story might prove significant in this way. If you were to profile this person, what details would bring the person to life and what angle would make their story matter to others?

REPORTING INFORMATION / A Roadmap

Choose a topic that matters—to you, and to others

If you get to select your topic, begin by considering topics that you know something about or are interested in learning more about. Whatever your topic, be sure it's one you find intriguing and can be objective about. If you're a devout Catholic and believe that the church is wrong—or right—in its stance on birth control, you're likely to have trouble maintaining the "just the facts" stance necessary for writing a good report.

The more controversial the topic, the more challenging it may be to report fairly and accurately on it because the facts themselves likely will be the subject of controversy. So if you're going to write about a controversial topic, you might consider reporting on the controversy itself: the major perspectives on the issue, the kinds of evidence cited, and so on.

If you've been assigned a topic, find an aspect of it that is both interesting and focused. Unless you've been specifically instructed to address a broad topic (for example, the consequences of World Bank policies for third-world economies), focus on a narrower aspect of the topic (take a single developing country that interests you and report on the consequences of World Bank policies for that economy). Even when you are asked to report on a broad topic, see if it is possible to start out with a specific case and then move to the broader issue.

Consider your rhetorical situation

Analyzing your audience, purpose, and other elements of your rhetorical situation will help you to make the decisions you'll face as you write.

Address your AUDIENCE appropriately. If you're writing a report for an audience you know—your classmates, your instructor—you can sometimes assume what they will and won't know about your topic. But if you're writing for a broader audience—all students on campus, readers of a blog—you'll probably be addressing people with different levels of knowledge. Your challenge will be to provide enough information without including irrelevant details. For example, Henry Fountain didn't explain what skiing is or waste his readers' time by including information not directly relevant to his topic. Here are some questions that might guide you in considering your audience:

- What do you know about your audience? To what extent are they like or unlike you—or one another?
- What background information will your audience need on your topic? Will their knowledge of it vary?
- What terms need to be defined or illustrated with examples? What sorts of examples will be most effective for your audience?
- What interest does your audience have in your topic? If they're not already interested in it, how can you get them interested—or at least to see that it matters?

Be clear about your PURPOSE. Consider why you are writing a report on this topic for this particular audience. Odds are that you want your report to do more than merely convey information. If you're writing it for a course, you want to learn something and to get a good grade. If the report is part of a large project—a campaign to encourage composting on campus, for example—a lot may be riding on the quality of your work. What short-term goals do you have in writing, and do they relate to any longer-term goals?

Consider your STANCE. Think about your own attitudes toward your topic and your audience: What about this topic captured your interest? Why do you think it matters—or should matter—both in general and to your audience? How can you establish your authority on the topic and get your audience to trust you and the information you provide? How do you want them to see you? As a fair, objective reporter? As thoughtful? serious? curious? something else?

Consider the larger CONTEXT. What are the various perspectives on the topic, and what else has been said about it? What larger conversations, if any, is this topic a part of? For a report that's part of a campaign to encourage composting on campus, for example, you'd need to become familiar with how such programs have been conducted at other schools, and what the main challenges and arguments have been.

Think about MEDIA. As the three reports on aerial skiing make clear, the medium you use to say something plays a big role in determining the message you convey. If you have a choice, will your text be presented in print? online? as an oral report? Which will be most effective for your subject and audience? If you've got audio of an interview, can you embed it in an online report or incorporate it into an oral report? If your report will be in print, can you summarize or quote from the interview? If your report will be oral, should you prepare slides to help your audience follow your main points?

Think about DESIGN. Consider what design elements are available to you and will help you convey your information in the clearest, most memorable way. For example, much of the effectiveness of Oakland Promise's annual report comes from the large color photos and testimonials from students, parents, and teachers. Think about whether your report will include any elements that should be highlighted. Do you need headings? Would photos, charts, tables, or other visuals help you convey information more effectively than words alone? Do you have the option of using color in your text—and if so, what colors will set the right tone?

Research your topic

Your goal in researching your topic is first to get a broad overview of what is known about it and second to develop a deeper understanding of the topic. While most high school reports discuss the research of others, those you write in college may call on you to gather data yourself and then write about the data in light of existing research.

LAB REPORTS, for example, describe the results of experiments in engineering and the natural sciences, and reports based on ethnographic observation are common in the social sciences. And whatever your topic or field, reading SECONDARY SOURCES will help you see how your findings relate to what people already know.

Thus, your first task is to read broadly enough to get a feel for the various issues and perspectives on your topic so that you know what you're talking about and can write about it authoritatively.

Begin by assessing what you know—and don't know—about the topic. What aspects of your topic do you need to learn more about? What questions do you have about it? What questions will your audience have? To answer these questions, you might try BRAINSTORMING or other activities for **GENERATING IDEAS**. Such activities may help you focus your topic and also discover areas you need to research further.

Find out what others say. You can research others' **POSITIONS** and perspectives in many different ways. If your topic is a local one, such as alcohol use at your college, you may want to conduct a student survey, interview administrators or counselors who deal with campus drinking problems, or do a search of local newspapers for articles about alcohol-related incidents. But it would also be a good idea to look beyond your own community, in order to gain perspective on how the situation at your school fits into national patterns. You could consult books and periodicals, databases, websites, or online forums devoted to your topic. If your topic doesn't have a local focus, you will likely start out by consulting sources like these. You may also interview people at your school or in the community who are experts on your topic.

Decide whether you need to narrow your topic. What aspect of your topic most interests you, and how much can you cover given the constraints of your assignment? If your political science professor has assigned a five-minute oral report on climate-change legislation, for example, you will need to find a more specific focus than you would for a twenty-page written report on the same general topic.

Organize and start writing

Once you've narrowed your topic and have some sense of what you want to say about it, you need to think about how you can frame your topic to appeal to your audience and how you can best organize the information you have collected. As you draft, you may discover that you need to do some additional research as new questions and ideas arise. But for now, just get started.

Come up with a tentative thesis. State your topic and the gist of what you have to say about it in a tentative **THESIS** statement, trying to make it broad enough to cover the range of information you want to share with your audience but limited enough to be manageable—and keeping in mind that your goal is to report information, not to argue a position.

Organize your information. Make a list of the information you want to convey, and think about what details you want to include. You'll find that you need various strategies for presenting information—**DESCRIPTION**, **DEFINI-TION**, **ANALYSIS**, **EXAMPLES**, and so on.

Then consider how to arrange your material. Some topics call for a **CHRONOLOGICAL** structure, moving from past to present, maybe even projecting into the future, as the report on economic development in Austin does. Or you may find that a **SPATIAL ORGANIZATION** works well—if you're reporting on the design of a new building, for instance—moving from exterior to interior or from top to bottom. There are any number of ways to organize a report in addition to these; you'll just need to work out a structure that will help your audience understand your topic in a systematic way.

Don't be surprised if you find that you do not need to use all of the information that you have collected. Authors often gather far more information than they finally use; your task is to choose the information that is most relevant to your thesis and present it as effectively as possible.

Draft an **OPENING**. Why do you care about your topic, and how can you get your audience interested in it? You will want to open by announcing your subject in a way that makes your audience want to know more about it. Consider opening with an intriguing example or a provocative question. Perhaps you have a memorable anecdote. It's usually a good idea also to include the thesis somewhere in the introduction so that your audience can follow from the outset where your report is heading and don't have to figure it out for themselves.

Draft a **CONCLUSION**. What do you want your audience to take away from your report? What do you want them to remember? You could end by noting the implications of your report, reminding them why your topic matters. You could summarize your main points. You could even end with a question, leaving them with something to think about.

Look critically at your draft, get response—and revise

Try re-reading your draft several times from different perspectives and imagining how different readers will experience your text. Will readers new to the topic follow what you are saying? Will those who know about the topic think that you have represented it accurately and fairly? If possible, get feedback from a classmate or a tutor at your school's writing center. Following are some questions that can help you and others examine a report with a critical eye:

- *How does the report* **OPEN**? Will it capture your audience's interest? How else might it begin?

- *Is the topic clear and well focused?* Are the scope and structure of the report set out in its opening paragraphs? Is there an explicit **THESIS** statement—and if not, would it help to add one?

- *Is it clear why the topic matters*—why you care about it and why others should?

- *How does the draft appeal to your* **AUDIENCE**? Will they be able to understand what you say, or do you need to provide more background information or define any terms?

- *How do you establish your* **AUTHORITY** *on the topic?* Does the information presented seem trustworthy? Are the sources for your information credible, and have you provided any necessary **DOCUMENTATION**?

- *Is the* **TONE** *appropriate for your audience and purpose?* If it seems tentative or timid, how could you make it more confident? If it comes across as argumentative, how could you make it focus on "just the facts"?

- *How is the information organized?* Past to present? Simple to complex? Some other way? Does the structure suit your topic and **MEDIUM**? What strategies have you used to present information— **COMPARISON**, **DESCRIPTION**, **NARRATION**?

- *What* **MEDIA** *will the report be presented in,* and how does that affect the way it's written? You might consider including photos in a print report, for example, videos and links in an online report, or slides to go along with an oral presentation.

- *Is the report easy to follow?* If not, try adding **TRANSITIONS** or headings. If it's an oral report, you might put your main points on slides.

- *If you've included illustrations,* are there captions that explain how they relate to the written text? Have you referred to the illustration in your text? Is there information in your text that would be easier to follow in a chart or table?

- *Is the* **STYLE** *appropriate for your audience and purpose?* Consider choice of words, level of formality, and so on.

- *How effective is your* **CONCLUSION** *?* How else might you end?

- *Does the title tell readers what the report is about,* and will it make them want to know more?

Revise your draft in response to any feedback you receive and your own analysis, keeping in mind that your goal is to present "just the facts."

REFLECT. Once you've completed your report, let it settle for a while and then take time to reflect. How well did you report on your topic? How successful do you think you were in making the topic interesting to your audience? What additional revisions would you make if you could? Research shows that such reflections help "lock in" what you learn for future use.

Selling the Farm

BARRY ESTABROOK

LAST FRIDAY, for the first time in 144 years, no one at the Borland family farm got out of bed in the pre-dawn hours—rain, shine, searing heat, or blinding blizzard—to milk the cows. A day earlier, all of Ken Borland's cattle and machinery had been auctioned off. After six generations on the same 400 acres of rolling pastures, lush fields, and forested hillsides tucked up close to the Canadian border in Vermont's remote Northeast Kingdom, the Borlands were no longer a farm family.

It was not a decision they wanted to make. A fit, vigorous 62-year-old, Borland could have kept working. His son, who is 35 and has two sons of his own, was once interested in taking over. But the dismal prices that dairy farmers are receiving for their milk forced the Borlands to sell. "We've gone through hard times and low milk prices before," said Borland's wife, Carol, a retired United Methodist minister. "This time there doesn't seem to be any light at the end of the tunnel. There's no sense working that hard when you're 62 just to go into debt."

For several months I'd been reading headlines and following the statistics behind the current nationwide dairy crisis. The math is stark. Prices paid to farmers per hundredweight (about 12 gallons) have fallen from nearly $20 a

---

BARRY ESTABROOK, a journalist who concentrates on food politics, writes for the *New York Times*, the *Washington Post*, and a variety of other publications. This article appeared in *Gourmet* magazine in August 2009.

year ago to less than $11 in June. Earlier this month, the Federal government raised the support price by $1.25, but that is only a drop in the proverbial bucket. It costs a farmer about $18 to produce a hundredweight of milk. In Vermont, where I live, that translates to a loss of $100 per cow per month. So far this year, 33 farms have ceased operation in this one tiny state.

Meanwhile, the price you and I pay for milk in the grocery store has stayed about the same. Someone is clearly pocketing the difference. Perhaps that explains why profits at Dean Foods—the nation's largest processor and ship-per of dairy products, with more than 50 regional brands—have skyrocketed. The company announced earnings of $75.3 million in the first quarter of 2009, more than twice the amount it made during the same quarter last year ($30.8 million). (Dean countered that "current supply and demand is contributing to the low price environment.")

But rote statistics have a way of masking reality. So last week, I drove up to   5 the village of West Glover for a firsthand look at the human side of the dairy crisis by attending the Borland auction. "You will be witnessing what is going to be the fate of all heritage farms," Carol Borland told me.

It was a breathtakingly clear morning in one of the most stunning settings imaginable. The Northeast Kingdom is an undulating patchwork of fields, woodlots, streams, lakes, barns, and white clapboard houses, set against the jagged, blue-gray backdrop of distant mountaintops. I didn't need a sign to direct me to the Borland place: For more than a mile before I crested a hill and saw the barns and silos, the gravel road leading to the farm was lined with dusty, mud-splattered pickup trucks. A crowd of close to 900 had gathered, in part because a country auction is always a major social event, a festive excuse for bone-weary farmers to take a day off, bring the kids, catch up with the gossip, and grumble about the weather, costs, and prices. That made it easy to overlook the sad, serious nature of the business at hand: selling off every last item there (and with any luck, providing the Borlands with a retirement nest egg). Among other things to go on the auction block was a massive amount of equipment, much of which had been shared with neighbors in loose, mutu-ally beneficial arrangements stretching back generations. The demise of one family farm can affect similar small operators for miles in all directions. The auctioneer had to sell a half-dozen tractors, a dump truck, a couple of pickup trucks, manure spreaders, hay balers, wagons, seeders, mowers, milking ma-chines, and assorted antique farm implements. There was feed that Borland had harvested but would no longer have any use for, 50 tons of shelled corn, 800 bales of hay. And, last in the photocopied catalogue, 140 prime Holsteins,

Nearly 900 farmers attended the auction that marked the end of the 144-year-old Borland family farm.

a herd known for its excellence, having earned Borland 16 quality awards over the previous two decades. Unlike the cows that pass their lives in complete confinement on the factory farms that are replacing farms like his, Borland's cows went out on those hilly pastures every day, strengthening their bodies and feeding on grass. Borland worried that with most other farmers as financially strapped as he was, or worse, the cows might not sell. "I didn't spend my whole life breeding up a good herd to see them beefed" (meaning slaughtered for hamburger meat), he said.

Items were sold at a nerve-rattling pace as the auctioneer chanted his frenzied, mesmerizing, "I've got five. Give me ten, ten, ten. Five, gimme ten, ten, ten. A ten dollar bill. Five gimme ten, ten ten." Three "ringmen" worked the crowd, waving their canes to cajole bids, and whooping when the price rose. A John Deere tractor started at $25,000 and was dizzily bid up to $30,000, $40,000, $50,000, and finally $60,000, in a matter of three minutes. Lesser machines sometimes sold in half that time. All morning long, there was no let-up.

Just after the Deere was sold, I asked Borland's son Nathan how he thought things were going. "Online, that tractor would be listed for $75,000, if you can find one half that good, which you can't," he said. "But I guess you can't complain, given how hard it is for everybody."

Making maple syrup a century ago at the sugarhouse built by Ken Borland's great-grandfather in 1898.

After attending college and working out of state for a few years, Nathan came home and joined his father on the farm. But he left to become a paramedic. "I like the work, but it got so bad financially that I felt guilty taking a paycheck," he said. "My sons, they're young. It'd be nice if they wanted to farm one day, but there's not a living to be made in dairy farming."

Carol, who was beside us, added, "The reality of farming is that as a parent, even if you'd like to and they want to, you can't encourage a child to go into something where he won't be able to earn a decent living."   10

Once the last piece of machinery was gone, the throng moved to folding chairs set up around a fenced ring inside the barn. Borland, who had been taciturn and shy most of the day, stood before the crowd to deliver a short speech. After thanking everybody for coming and expressing his gratitude for the efforts of the auction crew, he said, "I just want to say that these are a good bunch of cows. This auction wasn't their fault. They've always done their part. They have produced well."

Then he told a sad joke. "There was this farmer's son who left the farm and found work as a longshoreman in the city. The first ship that came in carried a cargo of anvils. To impress his new workmates, the boy picked up two anvils, one under each arm. But the gangplank snapped under the weight. He fell

The Borlands still sugar the old-fashioned way, insisting it makes for better-tasting maple syrup.

into the water and sank. He came up one time and shouted for help. No one moved. He went down and came up a second time. Still no help. The third time he came up he hollered, 'If you guys don't help me soon, I'm going to have to let go of one of these anvils.' "

There was nervous laughter. Borland went on, "That's what farming's been these last six months, trying to stay afloat with anvils. This is the day that I let go of mine."

The herd sold well. As an emotional bonus, 20 went to local farmers and would still be grazing on nearby pastures. Borland and Carol were pleased with the overall proceeds of the auction, and doubly pleased because they had been fortunate enough to find a buyer for the property and buildings who would take good care of the land that had supported their family through the generations. The Borlands severed off a piece of land where they will build a house. In the spring, they still plan to tap some maples. The sap will be boiled in the sugarhouse that Borland's great-grandfather built in 1898.

Before the auction, Borland had told his son that he planned to sleep until noon the day afterwards. Fat chance. He was up at 3:30 in the morning, as always. A few cows that had been sold had yet to be picked up, and cows, even ones that now belong to another man, need to be milked. He finished   15 that chore and drove the full milk cans over to a neighbor who was still in the business and had a cooling tank. Borland offered him a lift back to a hayfield he wanted to cut that day. As they rode along in the cab of the truck with the early morning sun streaming over the mountains, the neighbor said, "Ken, do you know how many farmers around here would give anything to be in your shoes? We have to keep struggling. You had a way out."

Thinking about the Text

1. How does Barry Estabrook make this profile of the Borland auction interesting? What details does he provide to show the "human side of the dairy crisis"?

2. "Selling the Farm" is a profile, a firsthand account written for *Gourmet* magazine. How would Estabrook's **AUDIENCE**, readers interested in food and wine, have affected the details he included?

3. How does Estabrook establish his **AUTHORITY** to write on this topic? How does he convince readers that the information he's providing is trustworthy?

4. Imagine Estabrook had written about the Borland auction for a newspaper, as an objective **REPORT** rather than a profile. How would it have been different?

5. Write a **PROFILE** of a person or event, following the guidelines on pages 301–03. To come up with an interesting angle for your profile, it might help to identify the audience you want to reach: what angle would probably interest them?

The Right to Preach on a College Campus

RYAN JOY

FREE SPEECH ON college campuses has recently become a hotly contested issue in both the popular press and academic circles. The question of whether incendiary speech abides by university guidelines and constitutional protections raises important and fraught questions for both students and the administrators who arbitrate disputes over what qualifies as protected free expression.

Last month, in an area of campus on Park Avenue called the Park Blocks, a street preacher aggressively ministered to the students of Portland State University (PSU) in service to his religious beliefs. On a number of occasions over about a week, he harangued passersby, even instigating verbal altercations with students. The man seems to have been unaffiliated with any student group or organization.

In seeking to understand the significance of such an event, we come to a better comprehension of the larger issue of how college administrators seek to foster a safe and secure environment for students without running afoul of laws protecting the right to freedom of expression.

The question of whether informal public preaching falls within the First

RYAN JOY graduated from Lewis and Clark College with a degree in religious studies and went on to study economics at Portland State University. A version of this article was first published in 2015 in the *Portland Spectrum*, a student magazine at Portland State.

Amendment's definition of protected religious speech becomes more complicated when considering a few of the comments this preacher made to specific
people. For example, he is purported to have called one woman a "slut" and
to have asked others intrusive, personal questions.

When deciding on issues of free speech, administrators must balance the   5
competing interests of a student's right to attend class free of harassment with
someone else's right to voice his or her views unimpeded. Indeed, it is often the
most objectionable views that require the most steadfast protection. Generally,
the Supreme Court disallows speech restrictions that discriminate on the basis
of content, and religious speech has been notoriously difficult to proscribe.

Legal precedent has something to say on the subject: in *McGlone v. University of Tennessee*, a 6th U.S. Circuit Court of Appeals decided against the
school after the administration sought to bar an itinerant preacher from speaking publicly on campus. Although the preacher, John McGlone, appears to have
been moderately respected in the community (the PSU preacher struck many
observers as unstable at best), the precedent set by the *McGlone* decision
starkly illustrates how our courts balance rival interests in such disputes.

In *McGlone*, the preacher successfully reversed a lower court ruling and
affirmed his right to preach on the basis of a rule known as the "vagueness
doctrine," a legal test founded in the due process clause of the Fifth and Four-
teenth Amendments which requires that laws must be clearly comprehensible
and allow for uniform enforcement ("Vagueness Doctrine"). The judge who
wrote the opinion in *McGlone* remarked that First Amendment cases must
apply the vagueness doctrine stringently. Thus, since John McGlone contends
that the university gave him conflicting information about his right to preach
on campus, the 6th Circuit Court overturned the lower court's decision to
uphold the university's rule barring public speech absent formal permission
from a registered student organization or a current student.

Extrapolating from this court's decision, one may wonder whether a clear,
unambiguous rule banning unaffiliated speakers would pass constitutional mus-
ter if instituted at PSU. As it stands, the university has no restrictions against
people wandering onto campus and expounding on their topic of choice. While
it is true that PSU has instituted and assiduously promoted its safety guidelines,
PSU's codes of conduct stay largely silent on the type of on-campus conflicts
that might occur between a student and those unaffiliated with the university—
the types of conflicts that are abundant on a downtown college campus.

In response to an emailed list of questions concerning whether PSU might
successfully restrict the presence of such visitors, Phillip Zerzan, PSU's Chief

of Campus Public Safety, confirmed that "the ability to regulate or control speech in the Park Blocks is guided by the First Amendment" and that while the preacher appears to have harassed students, such "non-physical, generally directed harassment speech is still protected speech."

"There is much case law confirming [that the regulation of speech] must be content neutral," Zerzan added, recognizing that speech restrictions are difficult if not impossible to institute when they restrict speech on a certain topic, especially religion. Even religiously motivated hate-speech enjoys the same protections as more benign forms of expression. "The preachers are a common event on campus, and we encourage students to engage in this conversation in a constructive manner, or otherwise ignore the speech," Zerzan concluded.

David Johns, a PSU professor of political science, corroborates this reading of the law as it applies to the preacher, who technically was preaching on public, city-owned property. According to Johns, as long as someone in the Park Blocks is not drawing noise complaints, engaging in disorderly conduct, or specifically threatening students, "they can pretty much say what they want."

To be sure, there are categories of speech that courts have exempted from First Amendment protections. Speech that presents an imminent danger to public health, for instance, and that which intends to do harm enjoy no legal immunity. In the landmark 1942 Supreme Court case *Chaplinsky v. New Hampshire*, the "fighting words" doctrine limited the First Amendment's protection of certain types of speech, including "the lewd and obscene, the profane, the libelous, and the insulting or 'fighting' words—those which by their very utterance inflict injury or tend to incite an immediate breach of the peace" (*Chaplinsky*).

This category may not apply to street preachers, however, regardless of the illicit questions they might pose to students. And while the courts may have once been sympathetic to the notion that large categories of speech deserved little in the way of First Amendment protections, as of the late twentieth century, courts have begun to roll back such exemptions and have granted First Amendment protection to all types of speech. As Johns notes, "although *Chaplinsky* has never been overturned directly . . . its effect has been considerably reduced."

The current Supreme Court seems more inclined than ever to give preference to those claiming immunity under the First Amendment, often invoking the reasoning that more speech equals more freedom. PSU, for one, is in no danger of stifling freedom of expression. Recently, PSU has witnessed a flourishing display of ideas, and while certain visitors may strike some as unworthy of careful consideration, it is the principle that allows them to continue that many consider worthy of protection.

Works Cited

Chaplinsky v. State of New Hampshire. The Oyez Project at IIT Chicago-Kent College of Law, today.oyez.org/cases/1940-1949/1941/1941_255. Accessed 24 Aug. 2015.

McGlone v. University of Tennessee at Knoxville. U.S. Court of Appeals for the Sixth Circuit, 2012. National Association of College and University Attorneys, 2 Aug. 2013, www.nacua.org/documents/McGlone_v_UTennessee.pdf. Accessed 24 Aug. 2015.

"Vagueness Doctrine." Legal Information Inst., Cornell U Law School, www.law.cornell.edu/wex/vagueness_doctrine. Accessed 24 Aug. 2015.

Thinking about the Text

1. A good report generally does not take sides on an issue and instead presents a balanced discussion of the major viewpoints in play. What key positions does Ryan Joy identify in the controversy over the rights of the campus preacher? How fairly does he represent each side?

2. Examine the way that Joy introduces the issue in the first few paragraphs of his report. What kind of background information does he provide? Do you think he should have provided any additional background information or definitions—and if so, why?

3. Joy wrote this report for the *Portland Spectrum*, a student publication about campus issues, yet he addresses a controversy that has wide significance. How does Joy make his report applicable to **AUDIENCES** beyond the Portland State community?

4. What types of **EVIDENCE** does Joy rely on to develop his discussion of the two sides of this issue? How does the range of evidence affect Joy's **CREDIBILITY** as an author?

5. Choose an important campus issue that you want to explore. Research the issue by reading what others have written, speaking to people in your campus community, conducting a survey, or some other method of gathering information. Write a **REPORT** that presents a balanced view of all sides of the issue. Consider submitting the report to a school publication.

SIXTEEN

"Two Thumbs Up"
Writing a Review

ESTAURANTS, CELL PHONES, BOOKS, movies, TV shows, cars, toaster ovens, employees—just about anything can be reviewed. Many people don't buy a new product or try a new restaurant without first checking to see what others have said about it online—and even posting their own thoughts on it afterward.

You've probably given casual reviews of this sort yourself. If a friend asks what you think of the TV series *The Handmaid's Tale*, your response would probably constitute a brief review: "It mostly lived up to the hype. The acting was really impressive, but sometimes the plot lagged. I guess I'll keep watching since so many people are talking about it." Even this offhand opinion includes two basic elements of all reviews: a judgment ("impressive," "lagged") and the criteria you used to arrive at that judgment, in this case the quality of the performances, the script, and the show's popularity.

Reviews can vary a good deal, however, as you can see in these examples from other reviews of *The Handmaid's Tale*.

Gilead may be the creation of religious patriarchy grown monstrous, but "The Handmaid's Tale" is a creation shaped by the female gaze. Reed Morano, who directed the first three episodes, establishes

A still from *The Handmaid's Tale*.

a visual language that plays as important a role in this series as the dialogue. Her lush cinematography latches onto the hazy nightmarishness of Offred's tenuous existence.

Gilead is a place of shadowed interiors, where costume designer Ane Crabtree's creations remind us with elegant subtlety of the place's sinister caste system. The aquamarine dress of the commander's wife pops into the fore in dim hallways, the dove gray worn by the Marthas and Aunts demarcates the border between light and shadow, and the handmaids' scarlet dresses mark them as targets as well as silent, compliant objects of desire. . . .

And [Elizabeth] Moss' acting style works in concert with Morano's direction. She devastatingly conveys Offred's seething exasperation with shock darting through slightly widened eyes or tiny curls of defiance dancing around the edge of her lips. Those milliseconds of honesty make the viewer's adrenaline spike along with the character's.

—MELANIE McFARLAND, "'The Handmaid's Tale': A Dystopian Tale of
Female Subjugation That Hits Close to Home"

Melanie McFarland's review, published on *Salon*, makes clear her criteria: the show's cinematic qualities, on the one hand, and its actors' performances, on the other. McFarland is able to elaborate on these criteria with vivid examples like the costumes and acting methods she describes above.

On the other hand, *Metacritic.com* gives ratings by gathering numerical scores from multiple sources and calculating an average—92 out of 100 in the case of this series, on the high end of "Universal Acclaim." The site also provides excerpts and links to full reviews, and lets visitors add their own reviews. On *Metacritic.com*, everyone can be a reviewer.

This chapter provides guidelines for writing reviews—whether an academic book review for a political science class, a product review on *Amazon*, or a review of the literature on a topic you're researching.

REFLECT. Think about reviews you've read. All reviews evaluate something and they do so using relevant criteria. Someone reviewing a movie, for instance, would generally consider such factors as the quality of the script, acting, directing, and cinematography. Think about a product you are familiar with or a performance you have recently seen. Develop a list of criteria for evaluating it, and then write an explanation of why these criteria are appropriate for your subject. What does this exercise help you understand about the process of reviewing?

Across Academic Disciplines

Reviews are a common genre in all academic disciplines. As a student, you will often be assigned to write a review of something—a book, a work of art, a musical performance—as a way of engaging critically with the work. While students in the *humanities* and *social sciences* are often asked to write book reviews, students in the *performing arts* may review a performance. In a *business* course, you may be asked to review products or business plans.

In each of these cases, you'll need to develop appropriate criteria for your evaluation and to support that evaluation with substantial evidence. The kind of evidence you show will vary across disciplines. If you're evaluating a literary work, you'll need to show evidence from the text (quotations, for example), whereas if you are evaluating a proposed tax policy for an economics class, you're probably going to be required to show numerical data demonstrating projected outcomes.

➦ *LOOK AT this photo of artist Alex Da Corte's* Rubber Pencil Devil, *an art installation that features videos playing inside the neon-lit frame of a house. The photo was included in an online review of the 57th Carnegie International, an exhibition held at Pittsburgh's Carnegie Museum of Art in 2018. The review, which you can see at* everyonesanauthor.tumblr.com, *includes a digital gallery of art from the exhibit. How else could a review designed specifically for the internet take advantage of the medium—with maps? music? video? interviews? What else?*

Across Media

Reviews can appear in many media—from print to digital, online to television and radio. Each medium offers different resources and challenges. A *television* film critic reviewing a new movie can intersperse clips from the film to back up her points, but her own comments will likely be brief. A different critic, writing about the same film for a *print magazine*, can develop a fuller, more carefully reasoned review, but will be limited to still images rather than video clips.

The same choices may be available to you when you are assigned to review something. For instance, if you give an *oral presentation* reviewing an art show, you might create slides that show some of the art you discuss.

Perhaps your review could be a *video* that includes not only images of the art but also footage of viewers interacting with it. If you get to choose media, you'll need to think about which one(s) will allow you to best cover your subject and reach your audience.

Across Cultures and Communities

Conventions for reviewing vary across communities and cultures. In most US academic contexts, reviews are quite direct, explicitly stating whether something is successful or unsuccessful and why. Especially on the internet, reviews are often very honest, even brutal. In other contexts, reviewers have reason to be more guarded. When the *Detroit News* reviews a new car, for instance, its writers have to keep in mind the sensitivities of the community, many of whom work in the auto industry, and of the company that produces that car, which may be a major advertiser in the newspaper. *Consumer Reports* might review the same car very differently, since it is supported not by advertisers but by subscribers who want impartial data and information that will help them decide whether or not to purchase that car.

A very different sort of review occurs in most workplaces, where employees receive annual performance reviews by their supervisors. There are often explicit criteria for evaluating workers, but these vary across professional communities and institutions: the criteria for someone who works at a hospital (a *medical community*) will be different from those for college instructors (an *academic community*).

Across Genres

Evaluation is often used as a strategy in other genres. **PROPOSALS** offer solutions to problems, for example, and in that process they must consider—and review—various other solutions. Evaluation and **ANALYSIS** often go hand in hand as well, as when *Consumer Reports* analyzes a series of smartphones in order to evaluate and rank them for its readers.

REFLECT. *Look for several reviews of a favorite movie. You're likely to find many reviews online, but try also to find reviews in print sources or online versions of print publications. How do the reviews differ from one medium to the next? What, if anything, do the online reviews have that the print versions do not? Then check out some fan sites or* Twitter *about the same movie. How does the medium affect the decisions that a reviewer makes about content, length, style, and design?*

CHARACTERISTIC FEATURES

Whatever the audience and medium, the most successful reviews share most of the following features:

- Relevant information about the subject
- Criteria for the evaluation
- A well-supported evaluation
- Attention to the audience's needs and expectations
- An authoritative tone
- Awareness of the ethics of reviewing

Relevant Information about the Subject

The background information needed in a review may entail anything from items on a restaurant menu to a description of the graphics of a video game to the plot summary of a novel or movie. What information to include—and how much—depends on your rhetorical situation. In the case of an academic review, your instructor may specify a length, which will affect how much information you can provide. What's needed in nonacademic reviews varies depending on the audience and publication. Someone reviewing a new album by an indie group for *Rolling Stone* may not need to provide much background information since readers are already likely to be familiar with the group. This would not be the case, however, if the same author were writing a review for a more general-interest magazine, such as *Time*.

See how a review of the Nintendo Switch device opens with background information to help readers appreciate its portability and convenience:

Nintendo Switch

> When you're deep in a video game, the last thing you want to do is leave home. If only you could take the game with you for your commute to work or your bus ride to school, or to liven up your lunch hour.
>
> Nintendo's new Switch console tries to address that by letting you play it anywhere. You simply yank the Switch out of its docking station. It functions as a tablet with a built-in display, so you don't have to worry about finding a TV. Games typically work without a persistent internet connection. Once you're back home, just slide it back into the docking station to play games on a big-screen TV.
>
> The Switch works like a traditional game console when you want that; it offers portability when you need that. Over the past week, I've played the new "Legend of Zelda" game at home, outside, in a laundromat and in a mechanic's waiting room. The game picks right up wherever I left off.
>
> The big question, as it so often is with Nintendo, is whether it will be able to deliver enough games.
>
> —LOU KESTEN, "Review: Nintendo Switch Is Impressive,
> but Needs More Games"

This example comes from a 2017 review written for the *Associated Press News*; the author assumes that his readers have some familiarity with video games but that they may not have paid much attention to the particulars of gaming consoles.

Reviews of films (and other narratives) often provide background information about the story, as does the following example from a newspaper review of *Walk the Line*, the film about the singer Johnny Cash:

> Arkansas, 1944. Two brothers walk the long, flat corridor of earth between one corn field and another. Jack Cash, the elder, is memorizing the Bible. His little brother prefers the music of the hymnals and worries that Jack's talent for stories is the nobler enterprise. Jack wants to be a preacher. "You can't help nobody," he explains, "if you don't tell them the right story." Yet we already know it is his little brother, Johnny, who will grow up to tell the memorable stories, the kind you sing, the kind that matter most. In their own generic way, musical biopics are always the right story: the struggle towards self-actualization. With songs. They

Joaquin Phoenix as Johnny Cash in *Walk the Line* (2005).

are as predictable and joyful as Bible stories: the Passion of Tina Turner, the Ascension of Billie Holiday. It is a very hard-hearted atheist indeed who does not believe that Music Saves.   —ZADIE SMITH

This review was written for the *Daily Telegraph*, a British newspaper, by the novelist Zadie Smith. She opens with a summary of the story as the film begins and quotes some dialogue that catches our interest—but she also tells us something about "biopics," the film's genre. In short, this review's opening gives us information we will need, and that makes us want to read on.

Criteria for the Evaluation

Underlying all good reviews are clear criteria. As an author, then, you'll need to establish the criteria for any review you write. Sometimes, the criteria are obvious or can be assumed: criteria for reviewing cars, for example, would almost assuredly include price, style, comfort, performance, safety, gas mileage, and so on. Often, however, you may want to shape the criteria for specific purposes and audiences. See how a reviewer of a performance of Handel's vocal music focuses on two criteria as the basis for her evaluation: expressive and technical abilities.

> Forsythe was unquestionably the star of the evening. Her tone was like toasted caramel and her expressiveness and vocal control were astounding. Her embellishments sounded spontaneous and effortless, pinpoint clear and fiendishly twisty but never gratuitous; every display of vocal fireworks had an expressive purpose. I've heard coloratura sopranos with expressive or technical abilities equal to Forsythe's, but almost none so rich in both.   —KATIE TAYLOR, "Handel in Good Hands"

If you were posting a quick review of the same concert on *Twitter*, you might be able to assume that your followers are familiar with these criteria and skip straight to the evaluation. In fact, one tweet about this concert said it simply: "Heart-stopping Handel." No need to name criteria—the author assumed her followers know what it takes for a soprano to stop hearts.

Many reviews combine both **QUANTITATIVE** and **QUALITATIVE** criteria. For example, one well-known source for evaluating colleges and universities is the annual rankings published by *U.S. News & World*

Report, whose criteria are mostly quantitative. Here's how Texas A&M University, College Station fared in this ranking system in 2019, coming in at number 66:

Tuition	Total Enrollment Fall 2019	Acceptance Rate	6-year Graduation
In-state: $10,968 Out of state: $36,636	67,580	70%	80%

In addition, *U.S. News & World Report* often includes brief reviews written by students that rely on qualitative criteria:

> I love Texas A&M for all of its quirks and traditions. There is no other school this large where you will not feel like just another number to the faculty and staff. In fact, I rarely notice that the school is big at all. I love that everything seems to have a tradition to go along with it. While it takes a while to learn them all, and a lot of them seem kind of hokey, the traditions will enrich your college experience, and make you feel a kinship with your fellow schoolmates. Everyone you meet on campus is not a stranger, but merely a friend you've yet to meet! It's so true. Aggies are the friendliest bunch you will encounter.   —K'LEE, senior at Texas A&M

K'Lee uses qualitative criteria such as the campus atmosphere ("you will not feel like just another number") and values ("everything seems to have a tradition to go along with it") to give readers a sense of the school that they don't get from just seeing the numbers.

A Well-Supported Evaluation

The foundation of every review is a clear evaluation, a claim that something is good or bad, right or wrong, useful or not. Whatever you're reviewing, you need to give reasons for what you claim and sufficient evidence to support those reasons. And because rarely is anything all good or all bad, you also need to acknowledge any weaknesses in things you praise and any positives in things you criticize. Also, remember to anticipate and acknowledge reasons that others might evaluate your subject differently than you do. In other words, you need to consider other possible perspectives on whatever you're reviewing.

Journalist Amy Goldwasser approached a number of passengers on a New York subway and asked them for impromptu reviews of what they were reading. She then collaborated with the illustrator Peter Arkle to compose graphic reviews for the *New York Times Book Review*. Here's what two readers had to say:

MARIAH ANTHONY, 18, high school senior, on p.133 of THE KITE RUNNER, by Khaled Hosseini (paperback)

I read every day. Every. Day. I'm not a novel-reader. I'm more self-help and psychology. But this is an *amazing* book. You should read it. The author went way into depth. Where I'm at, the main character's 18. He and his father moved to San Francisco from Kabul...they were refugees who had to be smuggled into the States. He had to travel *inside an oil tank* to be here. I don't think I can exactly relate, but it's about how people go through things. It's beautiful.

DON SHEA, 70, fiction writer, on p. 214 of LIT, by Mary Karr (paperback)

This is her third book. I've read the first two. She's a poet.... I've been struck by the **wonderful** metaphors. I'm always surprised when poets really write superb prose. It gets a little **draggy** in the rehab part. She just keeps **slipping and slipping**. But it's good—all her stuff is good.

Both readers clearly stated what they thought of the books they were reading ("an amazing book," "it's good"). And then they gave reasons ("the author went way into depth," "all her stuff is good") and evidence to support those reasons ("he had to travel *inside an oil tank* to be here," "wonderful metaphors"). Note as well that one of the readers, Don Shea, acknowledges one weakness in Mary Karr's book ("It gets a little draggy in the rehab part").

When you're writing a review for a college class, you'll need to be more systematic and organized than these off-the-cuff reviews—with an explicitly stated evaluation, for one thing. See how a more formal review opens with a clear evaluation of a documentary film about a cave in southern France that contains paintings thought to have been done more than 30,000 years ago:

> What a gift Werner Herzog offers with *Cave of Forgotten Dreams*, an inside look at the Cave of Chauvet-Pont d'Arc—and in 3-D too.
> —MANOHLA DARGIS, "Herzog Finds His Inner Man"

The reviewer states her evaluation explicitly: the film is so good it is "a gift." As the review continues, she gives her readers background information on the cave and provides good reasons for her evaluation: "It's a blast . . . to see these images, within 3-D grabbing reach"; "Herzog is an agreeable, sometimes . . . funny guide, whether showing you the paintings or talking with

A still from *Cave of Forgotten Dreams* (2010).

the men and women who study them"; and he "also has a talent for tapping into the poetry of the human soul." At the same time, she acknowledges that the film has some shortcomings, though nothing that changes her overall assessment:

> *Cave of Forgotten Dreams* is . . . an imperfect reverie. The 3-D is some-
> times less than transporting, and the chanting voices in the composer
> Ernst Reijseger's new-agey score tended to remind me of my last spa
> massage. Yet what a small price to pay for such time traveling!

In addition, the reviewer provides an image from the film, visual evidence of the "inside look" *Cave of Forgotten Dreams* offers. This review appeared in the *New York Times*; the print version includes the photo shown here, but the online version also includes four video clips from the film, along with several reviews posted by readers.

Attention to the Audience's Needs and Expectations

All authors need to consider what their audience expects from them. But this consideration plays a particularly important role in the case of reviews. In many situations, some audience members will be familiar with what you're reviewing, whereas others will need a detailed sum-mary or description; some will need an explicit statement of the criteria for the evaluation, while others will know what the criteria are without being told.

Audience considerations can also influence the criteria that reviewers identify as most crucial for their evaluation. Consider, for instance, reviews of video games. Gamers might expect one set of criteria, perhaps focusing on the games' playability and entertainment value. Parents and teachers might want entirely different criteria, ones that call attention instead to any violence and strong language.

Here, for instance, is the introduction to a review of *Minecraft: PlayStation 4 Edition* from *GameSpot*, a website for news and reviews serving the gaming community. This review was clearly written for an audience concerned with what this game lets them explore and create.

> To say that *Minecraft* is a game about digging and building huts to protect you from zombie attacks is to only scratch the surface of its immense depth. *Minecraft* has evolved considerably since its release to PC more than five years ago. Its boundaries have been tested by its community, which has birthed stunning castles and cities, as well as music machines, calculators, and tender homages to popular television shows and film. While the game eventually made a home on consoles, the aging hardware of the Xbox 360 and PlayStation 3 kept *Minecraft*'s voxel world restrained by an invisible border.
>
> *Minecraft: PlayStation 4 Edition* shatters that barrier, allowing you to fully experience seemingly endless worlds in which to explore and create. The stretching horizon, combined with better performance and sharper aesthetics, do not only make this version of *Minecraft* the best you can find on modern consoles. The boundless delight in creation, coupled by challenging exploration, all shouldered by supreme accessibility, makes *Minecraft: PlayStation 4 Edition* one of the best games to own on PlayStation 4.   —CAMERON WOOLSEY, "Blocky Empires"

Woolsey also assumes his readers are familiar with other gaming systems (Xbox 360, PlayStation 3) and know the language of gamers; later in this review he uses terms like "tooltips" and "four-player cooperative split-screen play" without taking the time to define them. More general audiences would have appreciated it if he had paused to explain, but defining terms his audience already knows would position him as an outsider to the gaming community and thus diminish his credibility with readers of *GameSpot*. Instead, he signals respect for his readers by addressing them as knowledgeable gamers and focusing on issues they will care about.

⟨⟨◎ REFLECT. *Find two reviews of the same subject (a movie, a band, whatever) from two different sources:* Yelp *and* Travel + Leisure, *perhaps, or* Salon *and* Time. *Look over each source, considering both articles and ads, and decide what kind of audience each one addresses. Young? Affluent? Intellectual? A general audience? Then study each review. How much prior knowledge does each one expect of its readers? How much space is devoted to describing the subject and how much to evaluating it? Do the two reviews use the same criteria—and if not, what might account for the difference? What does this analysis suggest about the role that audience plays in the way reviews are written?*

An Authoritative Tone

Authors of reviews have multiple ways of establishing their authority and credibility, and introductions are often crucial to doing so. Here, for instance, is the first paragraph of a lengthy review of several histories of American whaling that appeared in the *New Yorker*:

> If, under the spell of *Moby-Dick*, you decided to run away to the modern equivalent of whaling, where would you go? Because petroleum displaced whale oil as a source of light and lubrication more than a century ago, it might seem logical to join workers in Arabian oil fields or on drilling platforms at sea. On the other hand, firemen, like whalers, are united by their care for one another and for the vehicle that bears them, and the fireman's alacrity with ladders and hoses resembles the whaler's with masts and ropes. Then, there are the armed forces, which, like a nineteenth-century whaleship, can take you around the world in the company of people from ethnic and social backgrounds unfamiliar to you. All these lines of work are dangerous but indispensable, as whaling once was, but none seems perfectly analogous. Ultimately, there is nothing like rowing a little boat up to a sixty-ton mammal that swims, stabbing it, and hoping that it dies a relatively well-mannered death.
>
> —CALEB CRAIN, "There She Blew: The History of American Whaling"

"Moby Dick swam swiftly round and round the wrecked crew."

The series of arresting examples not only captures readers' attention but also demonstrates how thoroughly and carefully the reviewer knows his subject, thus making readers trust him and want to hear what he has to say.

Here is the introduction to an essay published in *Harper's Magazine* reviewing a number of works by Egyptian novelists Albert Cossery and Sonallah Ibrahim:

> Egypt is hard on its novelists. Their audience is tiny, their rewards few, their risks considerable. This is true in most if not all Arab countries, but Egypt is notable in having a long and astonishingly varied novelistic tradition, some of which is now becoming available in translation.
>
> —ROBYN CRESWELL, "Undelivered"

The broad generalizations at the start of this review make clear that this reviewer has considerable knowledge about Egyptian novels and Arabic literature more generally.

Finally, here is the introduction to a review of *Spider-Man: Into the Spider-Verse* written by Orange Coast College student Areyon Jolivette and published in the *Daily Californian*, the independent student-run newspaper of the University of California, Berkeley.

> Sony's most recent production of Spider-Man, *Spider-Man: Into the Spider-Verse*, is a dramatic departure from the Spider-Man audiences have seen time and time again. If you've ever rolled your eyes at the massive catalog of Spider-Men on screen, this one's for you. The film is incredibly self-aware, making a point to acknowledge some of the most infamous moments cemented in the canon of the superhero. *Spider-Verse* doesn't shy away from making fun of itself; instead, the animated feature embraces the multitude of memes and pop culture tropes to come out of the superhero's long run both on-screen and off.
>
> —AREYON JOLIVETTE, "*Spider-Man: Into the Spider-Verse* Is as Extraordinary as It Allows Its Audience to Be"

This introduction shows that the reviewer is knowledgeable about previous Spider-Man movies and also about the conventions of the superhero genre.

If you get to choose your subject, be sure to select a topic that you know (and care) about, and share some of what you know in your introduction. Telling your audience something interesting about your subject and giving some sense that it matters will help establish your credibility and make them want to know more.

The many faces of the iconic superhero in *Spider-Man: Into the Spider-Verse* (2018).

Awareness of the Ethics of Reviewing

Depending on context and purpose, a review can have substantial—or minimal—consequences. When the late, widely syndicated film reviewer Roger Ebert gave a Hollywood movie a thumbs-up or thumbs-down, his judgment influenced whether the movie was shown in theaters across America or went immediately to DVD. Those reviewing Broadway plays for publications like the *New York Times* hold similar powers. And reviews in *Consumers Reports* significantly influence the sale of the products they evaluate.

By comparison, a review of a local high school musical will not determine how long the musical will run or how much money it will make, but an especially negative review, particularly if it is unjustified, will certainly wound the feelings of those involved in the production. And a movie review on the *Internet Movie Database* (*IMDb*) that gives away key elements of a plot without including a "spoiler alert" will ruin the film for some of the audience. So an ethical reviewer will always keep in mind that a review has power—whether economic, emotional, or some other kind—and take care to exercise that power responsibly.

Considering the likely effect of your review on those who created whatever you're reviewing is part of the ethics of reviewing as well. It's one thing to criticize the latest episode of *The Handmaid's Tale* (the creators of that series can likely afford to laugh all the way to the bank) but quite another when you're reviewing a new restaurant in town. It's not that you should hold back criticism (or praise) that you think the subject deserves, but you do need to think about the effect of your judgments before you express them.

How you express them is also important. In academic contexts, remember this responsibility especially when reviewing other students' drafts. Don't avoid mentioning problems just because you might make the writer feel bad, but be sure that any criticisms are constructive. Be sure to mention strengths as well as weaknesses and offer suggestions and encouragement for overcoming those weaknesses if you can.

TIM ALAMENCIAK is studying ecological restoration at the University of Waterloo. He previously wrote for the *Toronto Star*, Canada's most widely read newspaper, where this book review was published in 2015.

Monopoly: The Scandal Behind the World's Favorite Board Game

TIM ALAMENCIAK

SOMETIMES THE IRONIES OF THE WORLD are stranger than fiction. That a game based on wheeling and dealing was born of wheeling and dealing writ large is a prime example of this.

Mary Pilon's *The Monopolists* unearths and charts the fascinating history of the popular board game Monopoly and the court battle fought by Ralph Anspach, a quixotic professor trying to save his own game. It's a story rife with controversy and scandal.

The book hitches its narrative on the tale of Anspach, the professor who took umbrage with Monopoly's capitalist focus and created Anti-Monopoly. His move so rankled Parker Brothers, the then-owner of the original game, they started a legal action that unfolded over decades of hearings and appeals.

Once thought to be the brainchild of a man named Charles Darrow, who profited immensely from the game's success, the history is much more complicated than that.

A woman named Elizabeth Magie originally invented "The Landlord's Game" to teach students about Henry George's "single tax" concept—a notion that all land should be owned by

Opening with a mysterious but clever statement that turns out to be about a game many readers will know establishes an authoritative tone; the promise of a good story makes us want to read on.

the public and simply rented by the occupants. She patented it in 1903—three decades before Darrow attempted to sell the game.

Magie was a prolific advocate for the rights of women but remained hidden for decades—overshadowed by the story Parker Brothers included with every game about Darrow, a down-on-his-luck man during the depression who invented a game for his kids.

Alamenciak summarizes the history told in Pilon's book (without giving too much away) and provides relevant background information.

Magie made waves in other ways after inventing the game. Finding it difficult to support herself on a stenographer's wage and frustrated with the way things were, she took out an ad in the paper offering herself for sale as a "young woman American slave." The satirical ad spread like wildfire and Magie was eventually hired as a newspaper reporter.

Meanwhile, her game had taken on a life of its own and was being passed around from family to family across the country. While still obscure, its fans were devoted and eager to teach it to others.

Words like "meticulously" and "compelling" (in the following paragraph) establish Alamenciak's criteria for evaluation.

The board went through some transformations as others picked up the game and copied it for themselves. The original game was anti-capitalist, with an alternate set of rules to teach the difference. Pilon meticulously charts the path the design took from Magie's hands to Atlantic City, where Quakers penned the famous street names that exist to this day, then to the living room of Darrow.

The book is a compelling look at history through the lens of Monopoly. Pilon paints Magie as a heroine long forgotten who contributed more than just a game but also then-rebellious writing that advanced the cause of women.

Pilon's book is full of interesting historical info, but rather than unfolding as a cohesive narrative that follows Anspach's quest to keep Anti-Monopoly alive, it reads more like a book divided into two parts. The reader is provided the true biography of Monopoly and then is asked to accompany Anspach as he uncovers the revelations that were just delivered.

Alamenciak acknowledges the book's limitations, but he also notes its strengths. In considering both and phrasing his criticisms fairly, he shows he is aware of the ethics of reviewing.

More could have been done to weave the two together and bring the reader with Anspach throughout the text.

An explicit statement of another criterion for evaluation.

That said, Pilon's writing is on-point and the historical information she's uncovered is fascinating. She is not writing about Monopoly; she is writing about American history intertwined with games.

"Games aren't just relics of their makers—their history is also told through their players," writes Pilon. "And like Lizzie's original innovative board, circular and never-ending, the balance between winners and losers is constantly in flux."

Quotes and specific examples from the book provide evidence for Alamenciak's claims.

This is not just a book for Monopoly fans. It's a great read for anyone who likes to know the quirky, interesting history of board games in twentieth century America. Even discussions on trademarks and brands—which are frequent in the book—are made interesting by Pilon's well-reported examples.

She chronicles the fight by Parker Brothers to keep the sport of ping-pong known as Ping-Pong, their brand name, rather than table tennis. In 1933, the United States Table Tennis Association was formed to oversee the sport.

"It's hard to say just how much money Parker Brothers lost after control of the game slipped out of its grasp, meaning it now produced the game alongside a fleet of competitors," writes Pilon.

This is a great book for anyone who likes a good historical read. It moves quickly and provides lots of interesting bits of history, wrapped together in a fascinating package that tells the true story of Monopoly.

Alamenciak concludes by stating his overall evaluation of the book in a way that is useful to his audience.

REFLECT. *Study a review on a subject that interests you and evaluate it, using the list of characteristic features of reviews on page 333. Annotate the text you have chosen, noting which of the features are included and which are not. For any features you find missing, consider whether including them might have improved the review.*

LITERATURE REVIEWS

When instructors refer to "the literature" on a certain topic, they probably aren't talking about poetry or other literary texts. Rather, "literature" in this case means published research on a given topic, and a literature review is a common assignment that asks you to survey, synthesize, and evaluate that research. You may be assigned to write a full essay reviewing a body of research, or to write a literature review as part of a report on research you've conducted. In either case, a literature review contains these features.

A Survey of Relevant Research on a Carefully Focused Topic

The literature you review should be credible, relevant academic sources related to your topic. When the choice is yours, a narrower topic is best: a review of what historians have learned about colonies and postcolonialism could easily run to thirty or more pages, whereas a review of what's been said about just one aspect of one of those topics would be more manageable. If your review is part of a research report, the literature you review will be guided by your **RESEARCH QUESTION** and should cover all the sources your study is based on. In some fields, you may be expected to cite only the most recent research, while in others you would likely begin with foundational studies and then trace the research that's followed. Keep in mind your assignment and the discipline you're working in to determine what kinds of sources are appropriate and how many are required in your review.

An Objective Summary of the Literature

Once you've collected the sources you'll review, you'll need to **SYNTHESIZE** them, looking for significant connections, trends, and themes that have emerged in the scholarship over time. Summarizing the themes and trends shows that you understand how the pieces in your review relate to one another and provides readers with an overview of their significance. In addition, you'll want to look for any ways that sources diverge or disagree. A synthesis of important trends might begin something like this: "Researchers writing about X have generally taken one of three perspectives on it," followed by a section discussing each perspective and what it has contributed to our understanding of the topic.

An Evaluation of the Literature

Like all reviews, literature reviews include an evaluation. The criteria for your evaluation will depend on your purpose for reviewing and the discipline you're writing in. If you're reviewing research as background for a report, its relevance to your project will be a key criterion. In all cases, you will also be looking at whether the research considers important questions and offers new insights—and at the **EVIDENCE** it provides. Your evaluation might point out strengths and weaknesses, as well as any limitations in what the research covers. Are there any important questions that are ignored? Claims for which little evidence exists? Gaps that future research might address?

An Appropriate Organization

It may be easiest to march through your sources one by one, but this sort of organization is hardly the most effective—and may end up reading like an annotated bibliography. When organizing sources for a literature review, think about how the sources relate to one another logically. Do they follow a clear progression that makes a chronological organization the most logical? Do they group by theme? by the authors' perspectives? by research methods? by trends in the results? Looking for ways in which your sources connect with one another will help you both synthesize the information and organize it in a way that helps readers see any significant patterns and trends.

Careful, Accurate Documentation

Be sure to follow carefully any disciplinary conventions for **CITING** and **DOCUMENTING** sources. For guidelines on following MLA and APA style, see Chapters 28 and 29.

CRYSTAL AYMELEK wrote the following literature review as part of a research report for a course in experimental psychology at Portland State University. To frame her research question, she first reviews literature on the nature of memory, then hones in on her topic with research on the effects of stress on memory, on mindfulness meditation and its potential benefits, and on the reported benefits of exercise. Evaluating this literature helps establish how her study attempts to add to our present knowledge of the topic. Her review includes a long list of the sources she reviews, which we've abbreviated here to save space.

The Effects of Mindfulness Meditation and Exercise on Memory

CRYSTAL AYMELEK

ACCORDING TO INFORMATION PROCESSING THEORY (Atkinson & Shiffrin, 1968; Baddeley & Hitch, 1974), human memory comprises three interconnected systems: sensory, working, and long-term memory. Information is initially detected and processed by sensory memory. The quality or quantity of information processed by the senses is determined by one's level of attention. Once information enters the working memory, its ability to be encoded and stored in long-term memory depends on the efficiency by which initial connections are made. Together these systems process information in response to stimuli through encoding, storage, and retrieval.

The opening paragraph establishes the research topic and gives background information about the workings of human memory.

Research has shown that high levels of stress both impede the ability to focus attention and interfere with working memory during the acquisition of information (Al'Absi et al., 2002; Aronen et al., 2005; Hadwin et al., 2005; Owens et al., 2012). The effects of stress on brain structure have been connected to decreases in gray matter similar to those typically associated with age (Hedden & Gabrieli, 2004). Such changes occur when an excess of cortisol inhibits the production of neurotrophic proteins responsible for the growth of new neurons and synapses. Consequently, this process prevents regions of the brain associated with memory, such as the hippocampus and amygdala, from modulating effectively (Cahill & McGaugh, 1996; Roozendaal et al., 2009).

Summarizes a major research finding and cites the relevant sources. Parenthetical citations follow APA style.

Over the last 30 years, mindfulness meditation has acquired popularity in the West thanks to its success in effectively reducing stress (Grossman et al., 2004). Moreover, it is increasingly applied in psychotherapeutic programs for the treatment of anxiety and depression (Hofmann et al., 2010; Salmon et al., 1998). Meditation is the practice of training mental attention to achieve a state of mindfulness. Mindfulness is commonly defined as "paying attention in a particular way: on purpose, in the present moment, and non-judgmentally" (Kabat-Zinn, 1994, p. 4). It is cultivated during meditation and extends beyond the time of formal practice. The major components of mindfulness, awareness and acceptance of both internal (e.g., cognitive-affective-sensory) and external (e.g., social-environmental) experiences in the present moment, are considered effective agents against psychological malaise (Keng et al., 2011). The benefits of meditation for anxiety and depression are thought to depend partially on the development of greater attentional control and executive functioning (Baer, 2003). That is, attention and energy previously allocated towards negative stimuli are redirected to more neutral or positive stimuli. The most well known meditation treatment program is Mindfulness-Based Stress Reduction (MBSR; Kabat-Zinn, 1990), which provides comprehensive training in mindfulness meditation.

Aymelek organizes her literature review by topic; here she surveys literature on mindfulness and meditation.

Such a statement, along with the numerous citations, helps demonstrate Aymelek's awareness of the relevant research literature.

Recently, meditation has been correlated with improvements in memory, cognition, and brain composition (Jha et al., 2007, 2010; Ortner et al., 2007; Slagter et al., 2007; Zeidan et al., 2010). A study by Hölzel et al. (2011) used the Five Facet Mindfulness Question-naire (FFMQ; Baer et al., 2006) and magnetic resonance imaging (MRI) to measure subjective mindfulness and neurological chang-es in participants of the MBSR program. They found that partici-pation in MBSR was associated with increased concentrations of gray matter in the left hippocampus and other regions of the brain connected to learning and memory processes as well as emotion regulation. Regular meditation has also been shown to strengthen one's ability to control impulses and maintain attention with less utilization of the brain's resources (Kozasa et al., 2012). In addition, Pagnoni and Cekic (2007) used voxel-based morphometry (VBM; Ashburner & Friston, 2000) and a computerized neuropsycholog-ical test to determine if gray matter in older populations would be more substantial in experienced meditators versus inexperienced meditators. They discovered increases in gray matter volume in the putamen, an area of the brain implicated in attentional pro-cesses, in experienced meditators but not in controls.

Summarizes a recurring research finding, citing the findings of several studies.

The benefits of exercise for physical health and stress manage-ment have been well documented (Penedo & Dahn, 2005). Cur-rent research suggests that frequent exercise may also enhance brain structure and cognition (Griffin et al., 2011; Hillman et al., 2008). A controlled, longitudinal study by Erickson et al. (2011) aimed to determine if aerobic exercise could promote growth in the hippocampus of healthy older adults. They used an MRI to measure volume in the hippocampus at baseline, at 6 months, and at 1 year, and found that the exercise group demonstrated an increase in the left and right hippocampus by 2.12% and 1.97%, re-spectively, while the control group showed a 1.40% and 1.43% de-crease in hippocampal volume. Furthermore, physical activity has been reported potentially to enhance cognitive capacity through the production of brain-derived neurotrophic factors (BDNF), which support the growth of neurons and synapses (Tyler et al., 2002). Griffin et al. (2011) measured cognition and blood levels of BDNF in sedentary young males following acute and chronic ex-ercise. To assess cognition, they used a face-name task previously demonstrated by MRI to engage the hippocampus and medial-temporal lobes. Griffin et al. found increases in BDNF concentration in both acute and chronic exercise groups that corresponded with improved scores on the face-name task.

Although both meditation and exercise have been associated with enhancements in cognition and memory, it is important to note some of the limitations of past research. For example, many studies on meditation did not randomly assign participants and/ or used small sample sizes (Eberth & Sedlmeier, 2012). In addition, studies frequently used clinical populations, and participants with prior interest in or experience with meditation (Chiesa et al., 2011; Hofmann et al., 2010). Likewise, many previous studies on exercise have not controlled and/or randomized designs. Additionally, subjects have often been limited to animals, human adult males, and older populations (Lambourne & Tomporowski, 2010; Smith et al., 2010).

Evaluates earlier research, acknowledging some of its limitations.

Despite these limitations, the above findings provide evidence that prolonged practice of tasks such as meditation and exercise induce positive changes in anatomical plasticity reflected in both subjective and objective measures of cognition. Based on the success of meditation and exercise in decreasing inhibitory stress levels that interfere with cognition and thus memory function, I hypothesize that: (1) practicing mindfulness meditation over not practicing mindfulness meditation will improve memory function; (2) practicing exercise over not practicing exercise will improve memory function; (3) the effects of mindfulness meditation on memory function will be greater in the exercise group versus the non-exercise group as measured by the Wechsler Memory Scale, fourth edition, adult version (WMS-IV; Wechsler, 2009).

Aymelek concludes by stating her hypotheses, which represent the research questions she will investigate and are clearly based on her review of existing research.

References

Al'Absi, M., Hugdahl, K., & Lovallo, W. R. (2002). Adrenocortical stress responses and altered working memory performance. *Psychophysiology, 39*(1), 95–99. https://doi.org/cjz8bh

Aronen, E. T., Vuontela, V., Steenari, M. R., Salmi, J., & Carlson, S. (2005). Working memory, psychiatric symptoms, and academic performance at school. *Neurobiology of Learning and Memory, 83*(1), 33–42. https://doi.org/dpwf55

Ashburner, J., & Friston, K. J. (2000). Voxel-based morphometry: The methods. *Neuroimage, 11*(6), 805–821. https://doi.org/brt2cb

Atkinson, R. C., & Shiffrin, R. M. (1968). Human memory: A proposed system and its control processes. *The Psychology of Learning and Motivation: Advances in Research and Theory, 2,* 89–195. https://doi.org/dnbb7v

Baddeley, A. D., & Hitch, G. J. (1974). Working memory. *The Psychology of Learning and Motivation, 8,* 47–89. https://doi.org/d4vgnk

Baer, R. A. (2003). Mindfulness training as a clinical intervention: A conceptual and empirical review. *Clinical Psychology: Science and Practice, 10*(2), 125–143. https://doi.org/fjq9qc

Baer, R. A., Smith, G. T., Hopkins, J., Krietemeyer, J., & Toney, L. (2006). Using self-report assessment methods to explore facets of mindfulness. *Assessment, 13*(1), 27–45. https://doi.org/dj5sc9

Cahill, L., & McGaugh, J. L. (1996). Modulation of memory storage. *Current Opinion in Neurobiology, 6*(2), 237–242. https://doi.org/bqn28r

Chiesa, A., Calati, R., & Serretti, A. (2011). Does mindfulness training improve cognitive abilities? A systematic review of neuropsychological findings. *Clinical Psychology Review, 31*(3), 449–464. https://doi.org/fhj9jp

. . .

Penedo, F. J., & Dahn, J. R. (2005). Exercise and well-being: A review of mental and physical health benefits associated with physical activity. *Current Opinion in Psychiatry, 18*(2), 189–193. https://doi.org/cfcxb2.

Roozendaal, B., McEwen, B. S., & Chattarji, S. (2009). Stress, memory and the amygdala. *Nature Reviews Neuroscience, 10*(6), 423–433. https://doi.org/b95m9c

Salmon, P. G., Santorelli, S. F., & Kabat-Zinn, J. (1998). Intervention elements promoting high adherence to mindfulness-based stress reduction programs in the clinical behavioral medicine setting. In S. A. Shumaker, E. B. Schron, J. K. Ockene, & W. L. McBee (Eds.), *Handbook of health behavior change* (2nd ed., pp. 239–266). Springer.

Slagter, H. A., Lutz, A., Greischar, L. L., Francis, A. D., Nieuwenhuis, S., Davis, J. M., & Davidson, R. J. (2007). Mental training affects distribution of limited brain resources. *PLOS Biology, 5*(6), e138. https://doi.org/cw46zf

Smith, P. J., Blumenthal, J. A., Hoffman, B. M., Cooper, H., Strauman, T. A., Welsh-Bohmer, K., Browndyke, J. N., & Sherwood, A. (2010). Aerobic exercise and neurocognitive performance: A meta-analytic review of randomized controlled trials. *Psychosomatic Medicine, 72*(3), 239–252. https://doi.org/d7vvcj

Tyler, W. J., Alonso, M., Bramham, C. R., & Pozzo-Miller, L. D. (2002). From acquisition to consolidation: On the role of brain-derived neurotrophic factor signaling in hippocampal-dependent learning. *Learning & Memory, 9*(5), 224–237. https://doi.org/cdnzhq

Wechsler, D. (2009). *WMS-IV: Wechsler Memory Scale administration and scoring manual* (4th ed). Pearson.

Zeidan, F., Johnson, S. K., Diamond, B. J., David, Z., & Goolkasian, P. (2010). Mindfulness meditation improves cognition: Evidence of brief mental training. *Consciousness and Cognition, 19*(2), 597–605. https://doi.org/fdvb4r

REFLECT. Find an article in a scholarly journal in a field you're interested in, perhaps your major. Locate the literature review section of the article (it may or may not be explicitly labeled as such) and analyze it in terms of the genre features on page 333. What kinds of sources does the author review? What aspects are discussed? How is the review organized? What is the author's evaluation of the literature, and how does that set up the rest of the article?

WRITING A REVIEW / A Roadmap

Choose something to review and find an interesting angle

If you get to choose your topic, pick a subject you're interested in and know something about. Perhaps you're an avid fan of Harry Potter. Reviewing the final novel in the series might be a good choice. Or maybe you love mountain biking: you could review three best-selling bikes. Remember that many things can be reviewed—shoes, appliances, restaurants, books, music. Choose a topic you want to learn more about.

If your topic is assigned, try to tailor it to your interests and to find an angle that will engage your audience. For instance, if your assignment is to review a specific art exhibit, see if you can focus on some aspect of the work that intrigues you, such as the use of color or the way the artist represents nature. If you are assigned to review a particular book, try to center your review on themes that you find compelling and that might interest your audience.

Consider your rhetorical situation

Once you have a tentative topic, thinking about your audience and the rest of your rhetorical situation will help you focus on how you can best address it.

Think about what your AUDIENCE knows and expects. If your review is for an assignment, consider your instructor to be your primary audience (unless they specifies otherwise) and know what's expected of a review in your discipline. If, however, you're writing for a specific publication or another audience, you'll have to think about what's appropriate or expected in that situation. Here are some things to consider:

- Who are you trying to reach, and why?
- In what ways are they like or unlike you? Are they likely to agree with you?
- What do they probably know about your subject? What background information will you need to provide?
- Will the subject matter to your audience? If not, how can you persuade them that it matters?
- What will they be expecting to learn from your review? What criteria will they value?

Think about your **PURPOSE**. Why are you writing this review? If it's for a class, what motivations do you have beyond getting a good grade? To recommend a book or film? evaluate the latest smart device? introduce your classmates to a new musical group? What do you expect your audience to do with the information in your review? Do you want them to go see something? buy something (or not)? just appreciate something? How can you best achieve your purpose?

Consider your **STANCE**. Think about your overall attitude about the subject and how you want to come across as an author. Are you extremely enthusiastic about your subject? firmly opposed to it? skeptical? lukewarm? How can you communicate your feelings? Think also about how you want your audience to see you as author. As well informed? thoughtful? witty? How can your review reflect that stance?

Think about the larger **CONTEXT**. What, if any, background information about your subject should you consider—other books on the same subject or by the same author? movies in the same genre? similar products made by different companies? What else has been said about your subject, and how will you respond to it in your review?

Consider **MEDIA**. Whether or not you have a choice of medium—print, spoken, or electronic—you need to think about how your medium will affect what you can do in your review. If you're presenting it online or to a live audience, you may be able to incorporate video and audio clips of a film or a concert. If your review will appear in print, can you include still photos? And most important of all: if you get to choose your medium, which one will best reach your audience?

Consider matters of **DESIGN**. If you are writing for an academic assignment, be sure to follow the format requirements of the discipline you're writing in. If you're writing for a particular publication, you'll need to find out what design options you have. But if you have the option of designing your text yourself, think about what will help readers understand your message. Should you include illustrations? Are you including any information that would be best presented in a list or a graph? Product reviews, for example, often display data in a table so that readers can compare several products.

Evaluate your subject

Think about your own first impressions. What about the subject got your interest? What was your first reaction, and why? What is the first thing you would tell someone who asked your opinion on this subject?

Examine your subject closely. If you're reviewing a performance, take notes as you're watching it; if you're reviewing a book, read it more than once. Look for parts of your subject that are especially powerful, or weak, or unexpected to mention in your review.

Do any necessary RESEARCH. Your subject will be your primary source of information, though you may need to consult other sources to find background information or to become aware of what else has been written about your subject. Would learning more about a book's author or a film's director help you evaluate your subject? If you're writing an academic review, do you need to find out what else has been said about your subject?

Determine the CRITERIA for your evaluation. Sometimes these are obvious: film reviews, for instance, tend to focus on criteria like acting, directing, script, and so forth. At other times, you'll need to establish the criteria that will guide your review. If you're unsure what criteria are most appropriate for your subject, look up reviews others have written on a similar topic. What criteria do those models use effectively?

Make a judgment about your subject. Based on the criteria you've established, evaluate your subject. Remember that few things are all good or all bad; you will likely find some things to praise, and others to criticize. Whatever you decide, use your criteria to examine your subject carefully, and look for specific EVIDENCE you can cite—lines or scenes from a movie, particular features of a product, and so on.

Anticipate other points of view. Not everyone is going to agree with your evaluation, and you need to acknowledge COUNTERARGUMENTS to what you think. Even if you don't persuade everyone in your audience to accept your judgment, you can demonstrate that your opinion is worth taking seriously by acknowledging and responding respectfully to those other perspectives.

Think about your mix of DESCRIPTION or SUMMARY and EVALUATION.
You need to describe or summarize your subject enough so that readers will
understand it, but remember that your primary goal is to evaluate it. The
balance will depend on your purpose. Some reviews are expected to give a
simple star rating, or a thumbs-up (or down). Others require more complex
judgments.

Organize and start writing

Once you've determined your overall evaluation of your subject, compiled a
list of its strengths and weaknesses, and assembled EVIDENCE you can draw
upon to support that evaluation, it's time to organize your materials and
start writing. To organize your review, think about what you want to tell
readers about your subject, what your evaluation of it is, and why.

Come up with a tentative THESIS. What major point do you want to make
about your subject? Try writing this point out as a tentative thesis. Then
think about whether the thesis should be stated explicitly or not. Also consider whether to put the thesis toward the end of your introduction or save
it for the conclusion.

DESCRIBE or SUMMARIZE the subject you're reviewing, and provide any
background information your audience may need.

Evaluate your subject. Using the CRITERIA you identified for your review,
present your subject's strengths and weaknesses, generally in order of importance. Provide REASONS and specific EVIDENCE to back them up. Don't
forget to acknowledge other points of view.

Draft an OPENING. Introduce your subject in a way that makes clear what
you're reviewing and why your audience should care about it—and shows
that you know what you're talking about!

Draft a CONCLUSION. Wrap up your review by summarizing your evaluation. If you have any recommendations, here's where to make them
known.

Look critically at your draft, get response—and revise

Once you have a complete draft, read it over carefully, focusing on your evaluation, the reasons and evidence you provide as support, and the way you appeal to your audience. If possible, ask others—a writing center tutor, classmate, or friend—for feedback. Be sure to give your readers a clear sense of your assignment or purpose and your intended audience. Here are some questions that can help you or others respond:

- *Is the evaluation stated explicitly?* Is there a clear THESIS —and if not, is one needed?

- *How well does the introduction capture the audience's interest?* How well does it establish your AUTHORITY as a reviewer? Does it make clear what the review is about? How will it engage your audience's interest? How else might it begin?

- *Is the subject* DESCRIBED *or* SUMMARIZED *sufficiently* for your audience? Is any additional description or background information needed?

- *How much of the review is* DESCRIPTION *and how much is* EVALUATION —and does the balance seem right for the subject and purpose?

- *What are the* CRITERIA *for the evaluation?* Are they stated explicitly— and if not, should they be? Do the criteria seem appropriate for the subject and audience? Are there other criteria that should be considered?

- *What good* REASONS *and* EVIDENCE *support the evaluation?* Will your audience be persuaded?

- *What other viewpoints do you consider,* and how well do you respond to these views? Are there other views you should consider?

- *How would you describe the* STANCE *and* TONE *?* Are they appropriate and authoritative? What words or details create that impression?

- *How is the draft organized?* Is it easy to follow, with clear TRANSITIONS from one point to the next?

- *What about* DESIGN *?* Should any material be set off as a list or chart or table? Are there any illustrations—and if not, should there be?

- *Is the* STYLE —choice of words, kinds of sentences, level of formality— appropriate for the intended audience?

- *How does the draft* CONCLUDE*?* Is the conclusion decisive and satisfying? How else might it conclude?

- *Is this a fair review?* Even if readers do not agree with the evaluation, will they consider it fair?

REFLECT. Once you've completed your review, let it settle for a while and then take time to reflect. How well did you argue for your evaluation? How persuasive do you think your readers will find your review? Will those who do not agree with your evaluation consider it fair? What additional revisions would you make if you could? Research shows that such reflections help "lock in" what you learn for future use.

Black Panther Gets So Much Right and One Crucial Thing Wrong

MARC BERNARDIN

THERE'S A MOMENT early on in *Black Panther* that took my breath away. T'Challa (Chadwick Boseman), not yet a king, is riding in his hovercraft shuttle with spy and former paramour Nakia (Lupita Nyong'o) and General Okoye (Danai Gurira), leader of the Dora Milaje, the Panther's personal honor guard. We follow the craft as it makes its way through the holographic barrier that conceals Wakanda from the outside world, and you can see the thrusters that propel it—and in the energy bloom, you can make out African symbols, shifting, pulsing, morphing.

Someone had to design that (namely, production designer Hannah Beachler). Someone had to approve it. Hundreds of thousands of dollars had to be spent to render something that, in any other movie, would just be "space blue."

It's as if everyone enlisted to bring the project to life understood the magnitude of what *Black Panther*, the first comic-based studio movie with a black hero at the center since 1998's *Blade*, would represent: The chance to fill every corner of their fictional Wakanda with the same level of craft and detail

MARC BERNARDIN, former film critic for the *L.A. Times*, has written comic books, television shows, and podcasts in addition to his work for *Entertainment Weekly* and the *Hollywood Reporter*. In 2018, Bernardin won a Comic-Con Ink Pot award for those who make a significant contribution to the worlds of "comics, science fiction/ fantasy, film, television, animation, and fandom services." This review appeared on *Nerdist.com* in 2018.

usually reserved for British-star-studded period pieces; an opportunity to tell a story about black lives, which matter and are not defined by their pain but, instead, by their glory; an answer to a culture's question, "When will it be our time in the sun?"

As such, it can be hard to separate what *Black Panther* means from what it is. What it means is *everything*, especially to any kid who has never put the words "African" and "king" together in the same sentence. Or to any young woman who was ever discouraged from chasing a life in science and technology. To anyone who was ever told "you fight like a girl."

As for what it is? *Black Panther* is like the most delicious cake you've ever 5 tasted in your entire life, but which isn't quite cooked all the way through.

Black Panther picks up where *Captain America: Civil War* left off: With T'Challa still grieving the death of his father, even on the eve of his ascendance to the throne. In short order, we see the web of relationships that bind T'Challa to Wakanda. His love for his widowed mother, Queen Ramonda (the resplendent Angela Bassett), who invests in her son all the dreams of a happy future curtailed. His respect for Zuri (Forest Whitaker), his father's boon companion and Wakanda's spiritual leader. His playful bond with his younger sister Shuri (Letitia Wright), a tech wizard whose inventions kick Tony Stark's and James Bond's to a distant curb. His trust in Okoye, who has the rare

A still shows Black Panther T'Challa with two characters who support his fight to hold onto power—Nakia, a Wakandan spy, and Okoye, head of the Wakandan special forces.

Shuri, T'Challa's sister, engineers an arsenal of gadgets to protect and equip her brother.

pleasure of both serving the throne of Wakanda and liking the man who sits upon it. And his affection for Nakia, one of Wakanda's spies-at-large who thinks it might be time for her nation to share its tremendous gifts with a world that needs them.

Into that web wanders Ulysses Klaue (Andy Serkis), a South African arms dealer and mercenary who has been caught and branded for stealing the miraculous metal Vibranium from Wakanda, the only place in the world it can be mined.

And then there's the sinewy Erik Killmonger (Michael B. Jordan), an American veteran who is crazy about Wakanda, Wakandans, and the new King T'Challa. The minute he strides on screen, you can't take your eyes off of him—partially because he's played by the unfairly charismatic Jordan, partially because his attire is all Dwyane Wade-meets-Big Boi funky. As his story develops and deepens, we understand why he's a villain, what broke him as a child, and how he never healed right. We understand who he is and exactly what he wants.

In fact, every character's wants and needs are clearly defined, with one exception: T'Challa's. When the film opens, he wants to be king. Ten minutes and one ceremonial duel with rival tribe-leader M'Baku (Winston Duke) later, he's king. After that, he wants to maintain the status quo: Preserve the Wakandan way of life. But the status quo, by definition, is static, and stasis isn't drama. His romance with Nakia never exceeds nascence; by the time the film ends, you might've forgotten they had ever been "a thing." For too much of *Black Panther*, the Black Panther has everything he wants.

Chadwick Boseman as King T'Challa in *Black Panther*.

On top of this, he is also almost entirely devoid of flaws. He's a deadly 10 martial artist, a stalwart friend, well-educated, even-tempered, quick to smile, and, despite all that, he's humble. Flaws are the grooves, the nocks that add depth. Perfection in fiction, unlike in life, can be boring. I mean, even Indiana Jones was afraid of snakes.

The movie leaps to its feet when T'Challa, Nakia, and Okoye find themselves in Busan, South Korea, hot on the heels of the criminal Klaue. For a hot 15 minutes, *Black Panther* becomes the best Bond movie you'll ever see, partially because, here, the Panther wants something—to kill or capture Klaue. But this can also be thanked to the bone-crushing, wall-smashing action executed to perfection by director Ryan Coogler, who takes to it like an artist in love with the ways human bodies can cause destruction. Quickly, the sequence morphs into a car chase that feels as inspired by anime as it does by John Frankenheimer's *Ronin*.

Then, *Black Panther* settles back into its groove, in which everything on the periphery is awesome (especially the Dora Milaje . . . my gods, the Dora Milaje), but the center does not hold. Though Boseman pivots from dignity to delight on a dime, the screenplay (by Coogler and Joe Robert Cole) has trouble finding ways to emotionally engage with the character, all the way through to an action climax whose humanity is outweighed by its CGI.

The film does deal head-on with issues of race, subjugation, and oppression in ways both heartbreaking and hilarious. The final coda is as direct an address to the xenophobia at home in our current administration as that which you'll find in any film this year, let alone any giant Marvel movie. As a nerd and as a black man, I've been waiting for this movie for my entire life, whether I knew it or not. The fact that *Black Panther* gets so much right, but one crucial thing wrong, is both thrilling and maddening.

What it is. And what it means.

There are a few scenes set in Oakland, California—Coogler's hometown.   15 At one point, a young black boy in a rundown apartment dismisses the idea of Wakanda itself: What good is "a kid in Oakland, running around believing in fairy tales"? Coogler is that kid and this is his fairy tale—a fairy tale for other kids who rarely get them, and never like this.

What it means.

Thinking about the Text

1. Write a one-paragraph **SUMMARY** of Bernardin's review, being sure to identify his criteria for evaluation and the extent to which he claims the movie did or did not satisfy them.

2. Do you find Bernardin's **TONE** authoritative? Why or why not? How does Bernardin establish his own **AUTHORITY** and **CREDIBILITY**—or fail to do so? Point to specific parts of the text to support your response.

3. What assumptions does Bernardin make about his **AUDIENCE** and the things they are familiar with? How do you know? You might start by considering the vocabulary he uses and the topics he mentions as he discusses the film.

4. How does Bernardin frame his review? In other words, how does the review open, and how does Bernardin use this **OPENING** to make a crucial point about the significant achievement of *Black Panther*?

5. Bernardin states that he has two main criteria for reviewing *Black Panther*: "what it is" and "what it means." Think of a movie, book, television show, concert—anything—that represents an important milestone, either for you personally or to the larger culture it impacted. Write a **REVIEW** in which you evaluate not just what this significant thing "is" but also what it "means." Be sure to state your **CRITERIA** clearly and use **EVIDENCE** to support your claims.

Indie Gem *Please Knock on My Door* Expertly Captures Mental Illness

MANISHA UMMADI

FOR SOMEONE WHO NEVER personally experienced the crippling effects of mental illness, the idea of climbing into the complex mind of an afflicted individual may seem like a daunting experience. But as Swedish indie developer Michael Levall proves through his new story-driven, top-down adventure game *Please Knock on My Door*, investigating depression and anxiety at a personal level may be the key to understanding the inner mechanisms of our own minds.

Built around Levall's own experiences with depression, *Please Knock on My Door* gives the player control over the daily life of an individual navigating depression and social anxiety—the player takes on the responsibility of getting the unnamed protagonist through the routine of eating, working, sleeping, and tending to his other needs as he progresses through the workweek. Yet what begins as an inconsequential life simulator quickly escalates to an emotionally grueling daily battle against both time and the darker voices in the protagonist's head.

MANISHA UMMADI is an undergraduate student at the University of California, Berkeley, where she is studying molecular and cell biology. Ummadi is also a staff writer for the *Daily Californian,* an independent, student-run newspaper, for which she wrote this review in 2017.

Please Knock on My Door features a thoughtfully minimalistic art style reminiscent of an old-school, two-dimensional, top-down game—even the game's protagonist is depicted as a simple Minecraft-esque being, devoid of any detail except for his expressive eyes. Yet the game uses extensive narration and written text in the form of text boxes and journal entries to construct a thorough narrative that delves into the deep roots of the protagonist's most vulnerable feelings.

Consistent with its art style, most of the game takes place in the protagonist's darkened apartment, which contains only a limited number of objects, such as his bed or computer, that can be interacted with. Throughout the game, the player is also led to make decisions that determine the protagonist's interpersonal relationships and job performance each workday.

But embedded in these deceivingly simple daily interactions is a robust system 5 of rewards and consequences that factors the player's every decision into the protagonist's mental well-being and physical health—making the decision to forsake sleep or work in order to appease the protagonist's all-encompassing thoughts affect his emotional engagement and the end result of his journey.

As the game progresses and the protagonist increasingly falls victim to his own headspace, completing even the simplest sequence of tasks within the limited time frame each day becomes a near-impossible challenge. Learning from the player's decisions, the game attempts to push and pull the protagonist against the will of the player, leaving the player to painfully fight the game itself to just survive through each increasingly difficult day.

Yet despite the inevitably heavy subject matter that *Please Knock on My Door* tackles, the game manages to approach mental illness with a sense of realistic optimism—for every isolating interaction the protagonist experiences within his own headspace, the game presents a support system in the form of friends and coworkers, each with a particular personality, that reminds both the protagonist and the player that healing is as much an aspect of mental illness as the symptoms themselves. In fact, Levall adds an utterly human dimension to the gameplay by using the game's unique endings to explore the direct effects of reaching out and seeking help in the face of even the most debilitating mental challenges.

A unique experience from start to finish, *Please Knock on My Door* uses its quirky gameplay to masterfully radiate an unwavering sense of authenticity as it conducts an exploration into the emotions associated with mental illness. The game's basis in Levall's own struggle with depression undoubtedly feeds into its hauntingly realistic nature, developing the game itself into an extremely personal journey of varying interpretation depending on the player. Indeed, no two playthroughs of the game are remotely identical to one another, adding to the game's replay value.

As the protagonist perpetually struggles through the symptoms of depression and anxiety that cloud his days, the player cannot help but reciprocate his raw feelings of helplessness and frailty. Placing the player in the darkest corner of the protagonist's mind, *Please Knock on My Door* manages to do the unthinkable and force the player into not just observing but experiencing the indescribable effects of mental illness. Through every aspect of the game, Levall showcases his prowess as an interactive storyteller, affirming that video games as a genre can be used to tell rich stories that carry emotional weight, rather than being confined to a series of mind-numbing shooters. *Please Knock on My Door* undeniably cements itself as an indie gem bent on changing the way in which narratives are delivered to the player, making the experience of interacting with a game a highly personal matter.

While the player's takeaway from the taxing journey of *Please Knock on My* 10 *Door* ultimately depends on the real-life experiences that the player enters with, the game undoubtedly bestows a level of profound insight upon all— some may experience a mind-shattering introspective epiphany by the end of the game, some may not—but at the very least, the player will walk away with a more nuanced understanding of mental illness.

Thinking about the Text

1. How does Manisha Ummadi establish her **AUTHORITY** and credibility as a reviewer? How does her **INTRODUCTION**, for instance, contribute to her credibility? How would you describe her **TONE**? Point to specific words and passages that contribute to that tone.

2. What is Ummadi's **EVALUATION** of this video game, and what evidence does she offer in support of her views? How persuasive do you find her evaluation? What **CRITERIA** do Ummadi use as a basis for her evaluation? How does she make these criteria clear? Point out specific passages from the text that support your response.

3. Mental illness is an unusual subject for a video game to address, and it poses challenges for those reviewing the video game as well. What strikes you as particularly helpful and relevant in Ummadi's comments

on mental illness in the review? How does Ummadi work to build her **AUDIENCE**'s interest on this topic?

4. Imagine that you, like Ummadi, wanted to tell your classmates about a book, performance, game, podcast, or artist that you like—or don't like—in a piece that will be published in your campus newspaper. Write a **REVIEW** to persuade other students to check it out—or not. Take care to introduce your subject, establish criteria for your evaluation, and show evidence from the subject to support what you say.

SEVENTEEN

"Here's What I Recommend"
Making a Proposal

ILL YOU MARRY ME? There is no clearer proposal than the one this question represents. It proposes something that at least one person thinks ought to occur. Proposals are just that: recommendations that something be done, often to bring about some kind of change or to solve a problem. You'll likely have occasion to write proposals for various purposes; and if you're reading this chapter now, you've probably been assigned to write one for a composition class.

You might propose better financial aid options, a new way of disposing of excess cafeteria food, a possible solution to the childhood obesity crisis. Like a marriage proposal, each suggests change; unlike a marriage proposal, however, each of these cases addresses a problem and calls for careful analysis of several possible courses of action. While it may be obvious to your beloved that you are the one, it's less obvious how a more flexible borrowing plan can ease the burden of student debt, how composting can create a more sustainable food system, or how school lunch programs can help end childhood obesity. Proposals of this kind argue for clear solutions to specific problems; and as with any argument, they build a convincing case that what they recommend should be considered—and even acted on.

This chapter provides guidelines for writing proposals that will be taken seriously, ones that say, "Here's what I recommend—and why you should take my advice."

REFLECT. Proposals are part of daily life, but some are more compelling than others. Find a proposal that interests you, perhaps an op-ed on a social issue such as homelessness or inequality or a GoFundMe *campaign. How does the proposal convince or fail to convince you that it's important and that the recommended solution is worth your support?*

Across Academic Disciplines

If you've been assigned to write a research paper, chances are your instructor has asked you to present a proposal before you begin researching and drafting the paper. Such proposals ensure that your topic and plan of action are appropriate for the assignment. You'll likely have occasion to write these and other kinds of proposals in many courses. For a *biology* course, you may be asked to propose an experiment, explaining why it's important and hypothesizing what you expect to find. In a *public policy* course, you might work with a group to analyze a specific policy—perhaps your city's policy of providing incentives to encourage the use of solar power—and to propose changes. In each case, you'll need to think about what's expected, given the topic and the discipline.

Across Media

Authors of proposals often use multiple media to present their recommendations. Crowdfunding sites like *Kickstarter* may use *video* to show their projects in action or bring audiences face-to-face with their cause. Op-ed columnists writing for *print* newspapers rely on carefully crafted words to make their points, but online versions of the papers include links to supporting materials. If you're presenting a proposal in an *oral presentation*, slides can help illustrate what you're recommending—and you may be asked to provide a print document to elaborate on what you propose.

Across Cultures and Communities

Proposals of various sorts are common in the United States. At your school, for example, students might band together to propose more effective campus

➤ *CROWDFUNDING SITES are filled with proposals. Take a look at the proposal that former flight attendant Robin Wearly created on* Kickstarter *for a disabled passenger transfer sling (ADAPTS) that permits air travelers who use wheelchairs to get off the plane quickly and safely in case of evacuation. It states a problem and proposed a solution. Go to* everyonesanauthor.tumblr.com *to see the full proposal. Note how the campaign page uses written text, images, and videos. Imagine how Wearly might present this proposal in a meeting with potential investors. What information would be best presented as speech, on slides, as an embedded video, or in a handout? What additional information might investors want that the website does not contain?*

policies to prevent sexual assault. In business, many companies encourage employees at all levels to share ideas for improving the company's products or services. And in many states, voters can propose a ballot initiative to change existing laws.

Proposals are common in cultures and industries that thrive on open discussion and innovation, but not every community is receptive to input from just anyone. Many governments, organizations, and households around the world value the judgment of authorities and community leaders, and proposals from others may be seen as disrespectful. So be aware of the situation you're writing in and the audience you are speaking to, not just to avoid offending someone but to determine how best to present your ideas.

Across Genres

Proposals occur in many kinds of writing. **REVIEWS** sometimes end with proposals for how something could be improved, and many **REPORTS**, especially those on pressing social issues, conclude by proposing a course of action to address the issue.

A fully developed proposal is based on an **ANALYSIS** of a problem or situation in great detail. It requires **REPORTING** trustworthy information, and often involves **NARRATING** one or more past events as part of that reporting.

REFLECT. Find two proposals that address the same issue, perhaps one students are currently debating on your campus. How does each proposal define the issue, what solutions does each of them offer, and what evidence does each provide to show that its solutions will work? Which of the two proposals do you find more persuasive, and why?

CHARACTERISTIC FEATURES

Although there will be variation depending on the topic, you'll find that nearly all strong proposals share the following characteristics:

- A precise description of the problem
- A clear and compelling solution to the problem
- Evidence that your solution will address the problem
- Acknowledgment of other possible solutions
- A statement of what your proposal will accomplish

A Precise Description of the Problem

The goal of all proposals is to offer a solution for some problem, so most of them begin by explicitly stating the problem and establishing that it is serious enough that it needs a solution. Some problems are obvious—that there's a water shortage in California, for instance, or few women majoring in engineering—so you won't have to say much to convince your audience that they matter. In other cases, though, you'll need to describe the problem in detail and provide data, examples, and other evidence to convince readers that it's serious enough to require a solution.

The title of a controversial article by journalist David Freedman identifies a problem and proposes a possible solution: "How Junk Food Can End Obesity." But in the following passage from that article, Freedman describes a specific problem in the wide debate about obesity that his proposal then responds to.

> If the most-influential voices in our food culture today get their way, we will achieve a genuine food revolution. Too bad it would be one tailored to the dubious health fantasies of a small, elite minority. And too bad it would largely exclude the obese masses, who would continue to sicken and die early. Despite the best efforts of a small army of wholesome-food heroes, there is no reasonable scenario under which these foods could become cheap and plentiful enough to serve as the core diet for most of the obese population—even in the unlikely case that your typical junk-food eater would be willing and able to break lifelong habits to embrace kale and yellow beets. And many of the dishes glorified by the wholesome-food movement are, in any case, as caloric . . . as anything served in a Burger King.
>
> Through its growing sway over health-conscious consumers and policy makers, the wholesome-food movement is impeding the progress of the one segment of the food world that is actually positioned to take effective, near-term steps to reverse the obesity trend: the processed-food industry.   —DAVID FREEDMAN, "How Junk Food Can End Obesity"

Not only does Freedman say that the views of many well-known food writers are wrong (that there wouldn't be so much obesity if only we all ate more "wholesome food"); he also argues that their "growing sway" over consumers and policy makers is actually "impeding the progress" of one group that might be able to do something to "reverse the obesity trend." In other words, he identifies them as part of the problem.

Robin Wearly, author of the *Kickstarter* proposal illustrated on page 373, begins her proposal by stating the problem in terms that appeal to readers' emotions and logic in a culture that values individual responsibility and thinking ahead: "Emergencies happen. What if you or a loved one rely on a wheelchair? What's the plan?" She then provides a series of brief but vivid scenarios that confront readers with the reality of the problem:

> Wheelchairs are checked in cargo on airplanes. Elevators are shut down in hotel emergencies. So did you ever wonder how wheelchair travelers escape a burning airplane, a derailed train, a bus accident, a cruise ship disaster, or hotel room when told to evacuate? What if they can't wait for rescue personnel and their only hope is the crew or kindness of strangers? What if you have less than 90 seconds to make it to an emergency exit? Will a trapped person leave both your lives in peril? Here's how ADAPTS comes to the rescue!
> —"ADAPTS, the First Evacuation Sling for Wheelchair Users"

These descriptions remind readers, especially able-bodied ones, of things that can go wrong and the consequences of such situations for wheel-chair users. These high-stakes scenarios define the problem that the proposal will then address.

In any proposal, it's important to identify the problem clearly and in a way that sets up the solution you'll be recommending. Defining the problem precisely can also help make your solution realistic: preventing emergencies that endanger individuals with various mobility impairments is a tall order, while creating a tool that helps people with physical disabilities get to safety more easily in an emergency seems doable.

A Clear and Compelling Solution to the Problem

Successful proposals offer a compelling solution to the problem at hand. That is, it isn't sufficient merely to have a good idea; in a proposal, you'll have to convince readers that your idea squarely addresses the problem as you've defined it.

You'll want to explain the solution succinctly but in enough detail to make a clear and confident case for it. See how the Interdisciplinary Group on Preventing School and Community Violence offers a research-based proposal to respond to gun violence in schools and communities. While acknowledging the need for security measures—a common response to such acts of violence, the group proposes a more focused solution: "a change in mindset and policy," that is, focusing on preventing such events in the first place. They frame the issue as a public health problem and detail specific steps to achieve the needed shift in mindset and policy:

> A public health approach to protecting children as well as adults from gun violence involves three levels of prevention: (1) universal approaches promoting safety and well-being for everyone; (2) practices for reducing risk and promoting protective factors for persons experiencing difficulties; and (3) interventions for individuals where violence is present or appears imminent.
> —INTERDISCIPLINARY GROUP ON PREVENTING SCHOOL AND
> COMMUNITY VIOLENCE, "Call to Action to Prevent Gun Violences"

In the paragraphs that follow, the group then explains what each level of prevention would require of various stakeholders—from Congress and social service agencies to students and parents. The number and detail of the proposed actions along with logical appeals make a strong and clear case why, if the country carried out these actions, gun violence in schools and communities would be greatly reduced.

Now consider a proposal for a policy that would provide more affordable housing in Portland, Oregon, from an article by a member of that city's city council written for *Street Roots*, a weekly newspaper often sold by people who are experiencing homelessness:

> We can't require developers to build affordable housing; state law prevents it. But we can encourage those who want to build here to be part of the solution. . . . The city currently provides "density bonuses" to developers for including certain public benefits in their projects— meaning they can build taller buildings or get more floor space than would normally be allowed in exchange for including features like eco-roofs or bicycle parking.
>
> Now is the time to restructure our density bonus regulations to prioritize affordable housing development. . . .
>
> Under a proposal that will go before the council on July 9, developers seeking a density bonus must either provide affordable housing within their development or pay a fee into a fund for the creation and preservation of affordable housing. This proposal . . . would require them to contribute to the creation of affordable housing in order to receive the maximum density that our zoning currently allows.
> —DAN SALTZMAN, "Incentive for Developers
> Would Spur Affordable Housing"

Saltzman's proposal describes a solution that addresses the problem clearly: to build the largest permissible buildings (and hence make more money), developers will have to include affordable units in the development *or* contribute to a fund for creating affordable housing. In return for something a developer wants, the city gets something it wants: more affordable housing.

Evidence That Your Solution Will Address the Problem

A proposal is convincing when the evidence it provides shows that the solution being proposed will, in fact, address the problem. The kind of evidence that will be convincing will vary depending on what it is you're proposing and to whom. If you're pitching a new business venture to potential investors, your evidence would include numbers showing the projected returns on investment. If you're proposing a new honor code at your school, your evidence would likely include testimonies and examples of how it would improve the learning environment. In his article on the Portland affordable housing proposal, Dan Saltzman provides data projecting what the proposal could accomplish:

> This "affordable housing incentive zoning proposal" could result in as many as 60 additional units of affordable housing a year on top of those already being developed by the city, or it could mean an additional $120 million to $200 million in funds for affordable housing over the next 20 years.
>
> This proposal alone will not solve our affordable-housing crisis but is a critical step to ensuring more affordable housing in our city.

By acknowledging that this proposal will not totally solve the problem of affordable housing but demonstrating its potential benefits—more affordable housing or funds to create such housing—Saltzman limits his solution to one that Portland will be able to address at the time, thus making a persuasive case that what he is suggesting is feasible.

Another example comes from Appleton, Wisconsin, a city facing the challenge of redesigning its streets and transit systems to accommodate pedestrians and bicyclists. In an eighty-page proposal laying out a twenty-year plan to improve such access, the city's designers offer plenty of evidence to support their ideas: diagrams showing how specific roads will be reconfigured to include bike lanes, charts of costs and funding sources,

and a timetable for completing the project over the twenty-year construction period. Some of this evidence illustrates that the proposed changes will
achieve the city's goal; other evidence shows that they will do so in a feasible manner.

Acknowledgment of Other Possible Solutions

Part of crafting a persuasive proposal is making it clear that your solution is
the best course of action—and hence better than other options. To do so, you
need to account for other possible solutions and demonstrate the compara-
tive advantages of the solution you're suggesting.

In his article proposing that junk food has the best potential to end
obesity, David Freedman describes in detail what those in the "wholesome
food" camp suggest—and then points out why what they advocate is not
so good after all. Here he visits his local Whole Foods store, where he finds
many "wholesome" items:

> One that catches my eye . . . is Vegan Cheesy Salad Booster . . . whose
> package emphasizes the fact that it is enhanced with spirulina, chlorella,
> and sea vegetables. The label also proudly lets me know that the con-
> tents are raw—no processing!—and that they don't contain any geneti-
> cally modified ingredients. What it does contain, though, is more than
> three times the fat content per ounce as the beef patty in a Big Mac . . .
> and four times the sodium.
>
> —DAVID FREEDMAN, "How Junk Food Can End Obesity"

Later in his article, he does acknowledge that some of the arguments on
behalf of "wholesome food" are accurate:

> For the purpose of this article, let's simply stipulate that wholesome foods
> are environmentally superior. But let's also agree that when it comes to
> prioritizing among food-related public-policy goals, we are likely to save
> and improve many more lives by focusing on cutting obesity—through
> any available means—than by trying to convert all of industrialized agri-
> culture into . . . small organic farms.

Notice that in each case Freedman first describes something others have
proposed (or might propose)—and then points out its shortcomings.

Other situations call for proposals that consider several possible solutions at the same time, as in the case of the one for creating bicycle and pedestrian access in Appleton, Wisconsin. Because there's no one-size-fits-all solution that will work for every street in the city, the authors of this proposal suggest several possible configurations, including those shown on the following page in Figures 17.a and 17.b.

Bike lanes, which are meant only for cyclists, and shared lanes, which are shared by bicycles and cars, are two of the possible road configurations the authors explore. They provide detailed information about each option, describing its purpose, listing its advantages and disadvantages, and including a diagram. By presenting multiple design options, the authors address the full range of situations that exist. In situations that call for multiple solutions, considering all possibilities shows that you have fully considered the problems' complexity.

A Statement of What Your Proposal Will Accomplish

So what if readers decide to follow your proposal? What can they expect it to accomplish? The strongest proposals answer that question explicitly. Given that your goal is to persuade readers to agree with what you suggest and perhaps to take some kind of action, you need to help them understand the likely outcomes. Many proposals end by making clear what's to be gained, what outcomes large and small they might bring about.

Megan Hopkins, a former teacher with Teach For America (TFA), concludes her proposal calling for changes in that program by making clear how her suggestions—a longer commitment period, a full year of training, more incentives to continue teaching—will help TFA realize its mission.

> While these proposals would require substantial redesign of the TFA model, the results are likely to be worth the investment. Teach For America has the potential to effect large-scale change in the field of education. It recruits highly qualified, motivated corps members who appreciate the importance of equal education opportunities, and many go on to devote their lives to this mission. However, these bright individuals are not as effective in the classroom as they could be, and their students do not perform as well as students in classrooms where teachers have more formal training. Corps members who are given a full year to learn effective instructional practices and to fully prepare to work

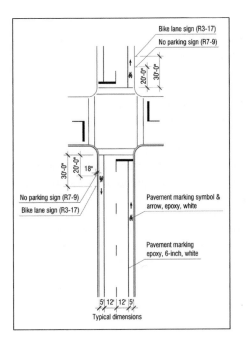

Fig. 17.a BIKE LANE

Description/Purpose: Marked space along length of roadway for exclusive use of cyclists. Bike lanes create separation between cyclists and automobiles.

Advantages
- Provides bicycle access on major through streets
- Clarifies lane use for motorists and cyclists
- Increases cyclists' comfort through visual separation

Disadvantages
- Space requirements may preclude other possible uses like parking or excess travel lane width

Fig. 17.b SHARED LANE

Description/Purpose: Shared roadway pavement markings, or "sharrows," are markings used to indicate a shared lane environment for bicycles and automobiles. Sharrows identify to all road users where bicycles should operate on a street where a separated facility is not feasible.

Advantages
- Helps cyclists position themselves in lanes too narrow for a motor vehicle and a bicycle to travel side by side
- Provides pavement markings where bike lanes are not possible

Disadvantages
- Maintenance requirements
- Not as effective as a separated bicycle facility

—WISCONSIN DEPARTMENT OF TRANSPORTATION, *City of Appleton On-Street Bike Plan* within the context of their placement sites will be better prepared to enter their classrooms as skilled teachers. If TFA can prepare its recruits to be more successful in their classrooms from the beginning of their service, it may be able to achieve its vision more effectively, so that, as the TFA mission states, "One day, all children in this nation will have the opportunity to attain an excellent education."

—MEGAN HOPKINS, "Training the Next Teachers for America"

Hopkins states one immediate result of the reforms she's suggesting, namely that corps members will be "better prepared to enter their classrooms." However, to highlight the true impact that her proposal would have, she starts and ends her summary of results by explaining how these adjustments would help TFA realize its "potential to effect large-scale change in the field of education" and thereby "achieve its vision" of providing every child in America with a good education—an inspiring outcome most audiences would happily stand behind, and one that shows persuasively why this proposal matters.

WRITING A PROPOSAL / An Annotated Example

In response to the deadly 2018 shooting at Marjory Stoneman Douglas High School in Parkland, Florida, this proposal was issued by a group of nationally recognized experts across fields whose research focuses on violence prevention. More than 4,000 individuals, 80 national organizations, and 170 other state and local organizations signed in support. This proposal relies on the credibility of the authors instead of a great deal of documented evidence for the claims presented. This approach keeps the proposal brief—one page exactly in the version posted online—and therefore more likely to be read, understood, and ultimately enacted by a wide general audience.

↗ See the complete list of authors and signatories by visiting everyonesanauthor.tumblr.com.

Call for Action to Prevent Gun Violence in the United States of America

INTERDISCIPLINARY GROUP ON PREVENTING SCHOOL AND COMMUNITY VIOLENCE

SCHOOL SHOOTINGS AND widespread community gun violence are far greater in the United States than other nations. America cannot be great and realize its promise of life, liberty, and the pursuit of happiness if our children are not safe from gun violence.

Although security measures are important, a focus on simply preparing for shootings is insufficient. We need a change in mindset and policy from reaction to prevention. Prevention entails more than security measures and begins long before a gunman comes to school. We need a comprehensive public health approach to gun violence that is informed by scientific evidence and free from partisan politics.

A public health approach to protecting children as well as adults from gun violence involves three levels of prevention: (1) universal approaches promoting safety and well-being for everyone; (2) practices for reducing risk and promoting protective factors for persons experiencing difficulties; and (3) interventions for individuals where violence is present or appears imminent.

A direct statement of the problem. Words from the Declaration of Independence establish a serious tone.

Acknowledgement of a common response—and an argument why it's inadequate.

The authors are clear about what kinds of evidence their solution is based on: scientific evidence unaffected by political affiliation.

A proposed three-point solution to the problem.

[383]

Clear, detailed actions for each "level" of the solution are evidence that the proposal will address the problem.

On the first level we need:

1. A national requirement for all schools to assess school climate and maintain physically and emotionally safe conditions and positive school environments that protect all students and adults from bullying, discrimination, harassment, and assault;

2. A ban on assault-style weapons, high-capacity ammunition clips, and products that modify semi-automatic firearms to enable them to function like automatic firearms.

On the second level we need:

3. Adequate staffing (such as counselors, psychiatrists, psychologists, and social workers) of coordinated school- and community-based mental health services for individuals with risk factors for violence, recognizing that violence is not intrinsically a product of mental illness;

4. Reform of school discipline to reduce exclusionary practices and foster positive social, behavioral, emotional, and academic success for students;

5. Universal background checks to screen out violent offenders, persons who have been hospitalized for violence towards self or others, and persons on no-fly, terrorist watch lists.

On the third level we need:

6. A national program to train and maintain school- and community-based threat assessment teams that include mental health and law enforcement partners. Threat assessment programs should include practical channels of communication for persons to report potential threats as well as interventions to resolve conflicts and assist troubled individuals;

7. Removal of legal barriers to sharing safety-related information among educational, mental health, and law enforcement agencies in cases where a person has threatened violence;

8. Laws establishing Gun Violence Protection Orders that allow courts to issue time-limited restraining orders requiring that firearms be recovered by law enforcement when there is evidence that an individual is planning to carry out acts against others or against themselves.

Congress and the executive branch must remove barriers to gun violence research and institute a program of scientific research on gun violence that encompasses all levels of prevention. We contend that well-executed laws can reduce gun violence while protecting all Constitutional rights.

Response to major barriers and potential objections to acting on these proposals.

Reiterating what the proposed solutions can accomplish.

It's time for federal and state authorities to take immediate action to enact these proposals and provide adequate resources for effective implementation. We call on law enforcement, mental health, and educational agencies to begin actions supporting these prevention efforts. We ask all parents and youth to join efforts advocating for these changes, and we urge voters to elect representatives who will take effective action to prevent gun violence in our nation.

A call to action that proposes everyone can—and should—be a part of the solution.

REFLECT. *Find a proposal in a campus publication or local newspaper. Read it first to see if you find it persuasive. If not, why not? Then annotate it as we've done with the proposal of the Interdisciplinary Group on Preventing School and Community Violence to see if it includes all the features listed on page 374. If not, would it be improved by adding any of the features it's lacking or by elaborating on any it doesn't demonstrate well?*

PROJECT PROPOSALS

You may be asked to write a project proposal to explain your plans for a large or long-term assignment: what you intend to do, how you'll go about doing it, and why the project is important. Like any proposal, a project proposal makes an argument, demonstrating that the project is worth doing and feasible given the available time and resources. Unless the assignment names other requirements, your proposal should cover the following ground:

An Indication of Your Topic and Focus

Explain what your topic is, giving any necessary background information. In some cases, you might be required to do some background research and to include a **LITERATURE REVIEW** summarizing what you find, including any issues or controversies you want to investigate. Say what your research focus will be, with the **RESEARCH QUESTION** you plan to pursue and a tentative **THESIS**. Finally, say why the topic matters—so what, and who cares?

An Explanation of Why You're Interested in the Topic

Briefly explain what you already know about your topic and why you've chosen to pursue this line of inquiry. You might describe any coursework, reading, or experience that contributes to your knowledge and interest. Also note what you don't yet know but intend to find out.

A Plan

Explain how you will investigate your research question. What types of sources will you need, and what will your research methods be? If you plan to do **FIELD RESEARCH**, how will you conduct your study? And what **GENRE** and **MEDIUM** will you use to present your findings? What steps will be required to bring it all together into the final document?

A Schedule

Break your project into tasks and make a schedule, taking into account all the research, reading, and writing you'll need to do. Include any specific tasks your instructor requires, such as handing in a draft or an **ANNOTATED BIBLIOGRAPHY**. Be sure also to leave yourself time to get feedback and revise.

DAVID PASINI, wrote this project proposal for a first-year writing course at The Ohio State University on the theme of sports in contemporary American society.

The Economic Impact of Investing Public Funds in Sports Franchises

DAVID PASINI

SINCE THE 1960S, local governments have provided increased funding and subsidies for professional sports franchises. Taxpayer money has gone toward facilities like stadiums and arenas, and many cities have offered tax exemptions and other financial incentives to keep a team in town that has threatened to relocate. Proponents of public funding for privately owned sports franchises argue that cities gain more from the arrangement—namely jobs, status, and tourist dollars—than they lose. Opponents argue that using public funds for these purposes results in long-term financial drains on local governments and point out that many communities have been abandoned by teams even after providing substantial benefits, leaving the city or state holding the proverbial debt-heavy bag.

The introduction announces the topic and summarizes a controversy the project will focus on.

Writing in the *New York Times*, Ken Belson gives an example of one such government-funded project: "The old Giants Stadium, demolished to make way for New Meadowlands Stadium, still carries about $110 million in debt, or nearly $13 for every New Jersey resident, even though it is now a parking lot" (Belson). The image

Fig. 1. Left to right: The governor of New Jersey, William T. Cahill; the owner of the Giants, Wellington Mara; and chairman of the New Jersey sports authority, Sonny Werblin, admire a drawing of Giants Stadium. Photo by Neal Boenzi. (Belson A1)

included here shows the governor of New Jersey looking over a drawing of the Giants Stadium, which was completed in 1976 and destroyed in 2010 (fig. 1).

An explicit statement of his research questions.

Given the high stakes involved—and particularly the use of taxpayer dollars—it seems important, then, to ask what these sports franchises contribute (or do not contribute) to their cities and wider metropolitan areas. Do these teams "generate positive net economic benefits for their cities," or do they "absorb scarce government funds" that would be better spent on programs that have "higher social or economic payoff" (Noll and Zimbalist 55)? My research project will investigate these questions.

A statement of why this topic matters, and to whom.

Pasini explains his interest in the topic and his current knowledge of it.

The question of public funding for sports is important to any resident of a community that has a professional sports franchise or is trying to lure one, as well as to any citizen, sports fan or not, who is interested in the economic and political issues surrounding this topic. I am in the latter group, a nonfan who is simply interested in how public monies are being used to support sports, and whose knowledge about the issues is primarily in the economic domain. At this point in the research process, I am neither a proponent nor an opponent of investing in sports, but I think that it's important to consider just how—and how much—professional sports contribute to the economic well-being of the government that funds them. How much of the money that teams generate supports local businesses, school districts, or other important entities that benefit all citizens? How much of it stays in the owners' pockets? Do the franchises "give back" to their communities in any other tangible or intangible ways? The franchises themselves should consider these questions, since the communities that helped to provide them with the amenities they require to be successful sports teams have a right to expect something in return.

More focused research questions, leading to a tentative thesis statement.

To learn more about investment in sports teams and the teams' economic impact, I will consult business and sports management journals and appropriate news sources, both print and digital. I will also interview stakeholders on both sides of the debate as well as experts on this topic. In my research, I will consider the many factors that must be taken into account, such as the benefits of tourism and the costs of "creating extra demand on local services" (Crompton 33). As a result of my research, I hope to offer insight on whether public funds are in fact put to good use when they are invested in major sports franchises.

A research plan, including kinds of sources he'll consult and field research he plans to conduct.

The conclusion restates why this research matters.

Proposed Schedule

Do library and internet research	April 6–20
Submit annotated bibliography	April 20
Schedule and conduct interviews	April 21–25
Turn in first draft	May 10
Turn in second draft	May 18
Turn in final draft	May 25

A schedule that allows time for research, writing, and revising—and lists assignment deadlines.

Preliminary Works Consulted

Belson, Ken. "As Stadiums Vanish, Their Debt Lives On." *The New York Times*, 8 Sept. 2010, p. A1.

Crompton, John L. "Economic Impact Analysis of Sports Facilities and Events: Eleven Sources of Misapplication." *Journal of Sport Management*, vol. 9, no. 1, 1995, pp. 14–35.

Pasini uses MLA style for a preliminary list of works consulted.

Noll, Roger G., and Andrew Zimbalist, editors. *Sports, Jobs, and Taxes: The Economic Impact of Sports Teams and Stadiums.* Brookings Institution, 1997.

Robertson, Robby. "The Economic Impact of Sports Facilities." *The Sport Digest,* vol. 16, no. 1, 2008, www.thesportdigest .com/archive/article/economic-impact-sports-facilities. Accessed 1 Apr. 2011.

REFLECT. If you're reading about project proposals, you've probably been assigned to write one. Analyze what your assignment is asking for, comparing it with the features listed on page 374. What does this exercise help you appreciate about how such a proposal works? What you can learn from doing one?

WRITING A PROPOSAL / A Roadmap

Think of a problem you can help solve

If you get to select the topic, identify an issue you know something about. You'll find it easiest—and most rewarding—to tackle an issue on which you can have some real impact. Try choosing a topic you have authority to speak on and one that is narrowly focused or local enough that your suggestions may be heard. You can't expect to solve all the problems of America's food system, but you may well be able to propose a more healthy and sustainable campus dining option.

If you've been assigned a topic, consider ways that you can make it interesting to you and your readers. This may mean finding an interesting angle on the topic you've been assigned, or, if the assignment is framed in general terms, finding a specific aspect that you can address with a specific solution.

Consider your rhetorical situation

Once you have a topic, thinking about your rhetorical situation will help you focus on how to proceed.

Think about your AUDIENCE. Who do you want your proposal to reach, and why? If you're proposing changes to a campus policy, you would do so differently if you're writing to school administrators in charge of that policy than if you're writing a piece for the newspaper. Here are some things to consider:

- What do you know about your audience? In what ways are they like or unlike you—and one another?
- What will they likely know about your topic? What background information will you have to provide?
- What interest or stake are they likely to have in the situation you're addressing? Will you need to convince them that the problem matters—and if you do, how can you do so?
- What sorts of evidence will they find most convincing?
- How likely are they to agree with what you propose?

Be clear about your **PURPOSE**. Odds are that you'll have multiple purposes—everything from getting a good grade to demonstrating your understanding of a situation to making your community a better place for everyone. The more you understand your own motivations, the clearer you can be with your audience about what is at stake.

Be aware of your **STANCE**. What is your attitude about your topic, and how do you want to come across to your audience? How can your choice of words help convey that stance? When David Freedman refers to those he disagrees with as the "let-them-eat-kale" crowd, his dismissive language tells us as much about him as it does about those he is criticizing.

Examine the larger **CONTEXT**. What do you know about the problem you're tackling? What might you need to learn? How have others addressed it? What solutions have they proposed and how well have they worked?

Think about **MEDIA**. If the choice is yours, what medium will best reach your audience and suit your purpose? If you're assigned to use a particular medium, how can you use it best? If, for example, you're giving an oral presentation, *PowerPoint* slides can help your audience follow the main points of your proposal, especially if you're presenting quantitative data.

Think about **DESIGN**. If you have the option of designing your proposal, think about what it needs. If it's lengthy or complex, should you use headings? Is there anything in your proposal that would be hard to follow in a paragraph—and easier to read in a chart or a graph?

Study the situation

Whatever the problem, you have to understand it in all its complexity and think about the many ways different parties will likely understand it.

Begin by thinking about what you know about the situation. What interests you about the issue, and why do you care? What more do you need to find out about it? To answer these questions, try **BRAINSTORMING** or other activities for **GENERATING IDEAS**.

Be sure you understand the problem. To do so, you'll surely need to do some **RESEARCH**. What **CAUSED** this problem, and what are its **EFFECTS**?

How serious is it? Who cares about it? What's been said about it? What efforts have already been made to address the problem, and how have they succeeded? How have similar problems been handled, and what insights can you gain from studying them?

Consider how you can best present the problem for your AUDIENCE. If they're aware of the problem, how much do they care about it? Does it affect them? If they're not aware of it, how can you make them aware? What kind of evidence can you provide to make them recognize the potential consequences? Why do you think the issue matters, and how can you persuade others to take it seriously?

For example, if you were writing about the need for a program to raise awareness of the effects of hate speech on campus, you might open with an anecdote about hateful things that have been said about others to make those not otherwise concerned with the topic aware of the issue. And you could then appeal to their goodwill and concern for fellow students to understand why it's a problem that needs to be tackled.

Determine a course of action

Once you've got a thorough understanding of the problem and what others think about it, you can start thinking about possible solutions.

Come up with some possible solutions. Start by making a list of options. Which ones seem most feasible and most likely to solve the problem? Is there one that seems like the best approach? Why? Will it solve the problem entirely, or just part of it?

If, for example, you're proposing a program to raise awareness about hate speech on campus, what are the options? You could suggest an open forum, or a teach-in. Maybe you could get an outside speaker to visit campus.

Decide on the best solution. Determine which of the options would be feasible and would work the best. Then think about how far it would go toward actually solving the problem. Hate speech is not easily solved, so this might well be a case when you can realistically only raise awareness of the problem.

These are some of the questions you'll need to ask and answer as you determine the best solution to propose.

Organize and start writing

Once you've clearly defined the problem, figured out a viable solution, and identified evidence to support your proposal, it's time to organize your materials and start drafting.

Come up with a tentative THESIS that identifies the problem that it proposes a solution. Use this statement to guide you as you write.

Provide EVIDENCE showing that the problem in fact exists, that it is serious enough to demand a solution, and that your proposed solution is feasible and the best among various options.

Acknowledge other possible solutions. Decide how and at what point in your proposal you will address other options. You might start with them and explain their shortcomings, as David Freedman does in "How Junk Food Can End Obesity." Or you could raise them after presenting your own solution, comparing your solution with the others as a way of showing that yours is the most feasible or the most likely to solve the problem.

Draft an OPENING. Identify and describe the problem, making clear why the issue matters—and why the problem needs a solution.

Draft a CONCLUSION. Reiterate the nature of the problem and the solution you're proposing. Summarize the benefits your proposal offers. Most of all, remind readers why the issue matters, why they should care, and why they should take your proposal seriously (and perhaps take action).

Look critically at your draft, get response—and revise

Once you have a complete draft, read it over carefully, focusing on how you define the problem and support the solution you propose—and the way you appeal to your audience. If possible, ask others to read it over as well. Here are some questions to help you or others read over the draft with a critical eye:

- *How does the proposal* OPEN*?* Will it capture readers' interest? Does it make clear what problem will be addressed and give some sense of why it matters? How else might it begin? Does the title tell readers what the proposal is about, and will it make them want to know more?

- *Is the problem* DESCRIBED *in enough detail?* Will any readers need more information to understand that it's a problem that matters? Have you said anything about its CAUSES and consequences—and if not, do you need to?

- *Is the proposed solution explicit and compelling?* Have you provided enough EVIDENCE to show that it's feasible and will address the problem—and that it's better than other possible solutions? Is there an explicit statement of what it will accomplish?

- *Have other possible solutions been acknowledged fairly?* How well have you responded to them? Are there any other solutions to be considered?

- *Is the proposal easy to follow?* If not, try adding TRANSITIONS or headings.

- *How have you established your* AUTHORITY *to write on this topic?* Does the information seem trustworthy? How do you come across as an author—passionate? serious? sarcastic?—and how does this tone affect the way the proposal comes across to readers?

- *How would you characterize the* STYLE*?* Is it appropriate for your intended audience? Consider the choice of words, the level of formality, and so on.

- *How about* DESIGN*?* Are there any illustrations—and if so, how do they contribute to the proposal? If not, is there any information that would be easier to show with a photo or in a chart? What about the font: is it appropriate for a proposal of this kind? Is the design appropriate for the MEDIUM?

- *How does the proposal* CONCLUDE*?* Will it inspire the change or action you're calling for? How else might it conclude?

Revise your draft in response to any feedback you receive and your own analysis.

REFLECT. Once you've completed your proposal, let it settle for a while and take time to reflect. How well did you define the problem? How thoroughly did you support your proposed solution? How persuasively have you demonstrated the feasibility of your solution? How fairly did you acknowledge and respond to other possible solutions? Research shows that such reflections help "lock in" what you learn for future use.

Speaking While Female
SHERYL SANDBERG AND ADAM GRANT

YEARS AGO, while producing the hit TV series *The Shield*, Glen Mazzara noticed that two young female writers were quiet during story meetings. He pulled them aside and encouraged them to speak up more.

Watch what happens when we do, they replied.

Almost every time they started to speak, they were interrupted or shot down before finishing their pitch. When one had a good idea, a male writer would jump in and run with it before she could complete her thought.

Sadly, their experience is not unusual.

We've both seen it happen again and again. When a woman speaks in a pro-   5
fessional setting, she walks a tightrope. Either she's barely heard or she's judged as too aggressive. When a man says virtually the same thing, heads nod in appreciation for his fine idea. As a result, women often decide that saying less is more.

Some new studies support our observations. A study by a Yale psychologist, Victoria L. Brescoll, found that male senators with more power

SHERYL SANDBERG serves as the chief operating officer of *Facebook*; she is also founder of *LeanIn.org*, inspired by her bestselling book of the same name. ADAM GRANT teaches at the Wharton School of Business at the University of Pennsylvania; he is the author of *Originals: How Non-Conformists Move the World* (2016). This essay was the second in a series of four on women in the workplace that Sandberg and Grant wrote for the *New York Times* in 2015. Go to everyones anauthor.tumblr.com to access the links (underscored here) as you read.

(as measured by tenure, leadership positions and track record of legislation passed) spoke more on the Senate floor than their junior colleagues. But for female senators, power was not linked to significantly more speaking time.

Suspecting that powerful women stayed quiet because they feared a backlash, Professor Brescoll looked deeper. She asked professional men and women to evaluate the competence of chief executives who voiced their opinions more or less frequently. Male executives who spoke more often than their peers were rewarded with 10 percent higher ratings of competence. When female executives spoke more than their peers, both men and women punished them with 14 percent lower ratings. As this and other research shows, women who worry that talking "too much" will cause them to be disliked are not paranoid; they are often right.

One of us, Adam, was dismayed to find similar patterns when studying a health care company and advising an international bank. When male employees contributed ideas that brought in new revenue, they got significantly higher performance evaluations. But female employees who spoke up with equally valuable ideas did not improve their managers' perception of their performance. Also, the more the men spoke up, the more helpful their managers believed them to be. But when women spoke up more, there was no increase in their perceived helpfulness.

This speaking-up double bind harms organizations by depriving them of valuable ideas. A University of Texas researcher, Ethan Burris, conducted an experiment in which he asked teams to make strategic decisions for a bookstore. He randomly informed one member that the bookstore's inventory system was flawed and gave that person data about a better approach. In subsequent analyses, he found that when women challenged the old system and suggested a new one, team leaders viewed them as less loyal and were less likely to act on their suggestions. Even when all team members were informed that one member possessed unique information that would benefit the group, suggestions from women with inside knowledge were discounted.

Obviously, businesses need to find ways to interrupt this gender bias. Just 10 as orchestras that use blind auditions increase the number of women who are selected, organizations can increase women's contributions by adopting practices that focus less on the speaker and more on the idea. For example, in innovation tournaments, employees submit suggestions and solutions to problems anonymously. Experts evaluate the proposals, give feedback to all participants and then implement the best plans.

Since most work cannot be done anonymously, leaders must also take steps to encourage women to speak and be heard. At *The Shield*, Mr. Mazzara, the show runner, found a clever way to change the dynamics that were holding those two female employees back. He announced to the writers that he was instituting a no-interruption rule while anyone—male or female—was pitching. It worked, and he later observed that it made the entire team more effective.

The long-term solution to the double bind of speaking while female is to increase the number of women in leadership roles. (As we noted in our previous article, research shows that when it comes to leadership skills, although men are more confident, women are more competent.) As more women enter the upper echelons of organizations, people become more accustomed to women's contributing and leading. Professor Burris and his colleagues studied a credit union where women made up 74 percent of supervisors and 84 percent of front-line employees. Sure enough, when women spoke up there, they were more likely to be heard than men. When President Obama held his last news conference of 2014, he called on eight reporters—all women. It made headlines worldwide. Had a politician given only men a chance to ask questions, it would not have been news; it would have been a regular day.

As 2015 starts, we wonder what would happen if we all held Obama-style meetings, offering women the floor whenever possible. Doing this for even a day or two might be a powerful bias interrupter, demonstrating to our teams and colleagues that speaking while female is still quite difficult. We're going to try it to see what we learn. We hope you will, too—and then share your experiences with us all on Facebook or in the comments section.

Thinking about the Text

1. What specific problem do Sheryl Sandberg and Adam Grant seek to solve in this essay? What sorts of EVIDENCE do they offer to show that the problem exists?

2. What specific solutions do they suggest? Consider both the short- and long-term solutions that they raise. How practical or compelling do you find these solutions?

3. The problem Sandberg and Grant describe extends beyond women's frustrations in their workplaces. What is the ultimate significance of the problem, and how do these authors make it clear? In other words, what meaningful outcomes do they argue their proposal can ultimately bring about?

4. How did the AUDIENCE for this piece, the readers of a major US newspaper, likely affect this essay? How might it have been different had it been written for an audience of male executives? of female employees?

5. Sandberg and Grant tackle a persistent problem of some magnitude, one that is clearly important to them. Choose a problem that matters to you and offer a PROPOSAL that addresses some aspect of that problem. You might start by observing issues you see around you, but you'll likely find that you need to do some research to precisely define the problem and propose a solution. Use the genre features listed on page 374 as a guide as you construct your proposal.

Snowflakes and Free Speech on Campuses

SHAWNA SHAPIRO

O VER THE PAST FEW YEARS, we have seen a <u>growing concern in public discourse</u> about free speech on college campuses in the United States. The familiar narrative labels college-aged students "snowflakes" who <u>don't like discomfort</u> and therefore expect colleges to be intellectual "safe spaces" in which their <u>ideological bubbles</u> are left intact.

This, the story goes, is creating a <u>crisis of free speech</u> in American higher education. The proposed solution for that crisis, according to many critics, is to bring <u>high-profile, controversial speakers to campuses</u> to somehow break through the echo chambers—an ideological "exposure therapy" of sorts.

Often missing in that narrative are the voices of students themselves. That absence became increasingly salient for me after <u>Charles Murray's visit to my campus last year</u>.* As I spoke with my students in the fallout from those events,

SHAWNA SHAPIRO teaches writing and linguistics at Middlebury College, directs the college's Writing & Rhetoric Program, and has published and edited works focused on international student success. This essay was published in *Inside Higher Ed,* an online publication about issues related to colleges and universities, in 2018. Go to <u>every onesanauthor.tumblr.com</u> to access the links underscored in the version printed here.

*Charles Murray, a political scientist and writer whose work has been accused of scientific racism, was invited to speak on Middlebury's campus by a student-run club. Prior to Murray's lecture, college administrators reminded students they were permitted to protest but not to disrupt a campus event. Yet more than 100 students began chanting during the talk, causing Murray and the moderating professor to relocate their discussion to a private studio. The college disciplined sixty-seven students for disruptive behavior, but several masked individuals who assaulted Murray and the faculty moderator outside the lecture hall were not identified.

I found that many of them had complex reactions that didn't fit the simplistic "free speech vs. inclusion/diversity" dichotomy that has become dominant in such discussions.

In response, since last summer, I have been working with undergraduate researchers on a study entitled "Middlebury Students Engaging Across Difference." We developed an online survey that was completed by 80 undergraduates, from first years through seniors. We then drew from those findings to develop a protocol for more in-depth, one-on-one interviews with 19 students.

Here's some of what we've found thus far: 5

Students want to engage with ideological difference. As many as 89 percent of all survey participants, including 83 percent of left-leaning students (who made up 71 percent of the sample), said that it was "important" or "very important" to them to have conversations about controversial issues with people who have a viewpoint distinct from their own. A number of participants talked about the relationship between engaging across difference and their personal growth. As one explained, "It's important to value putting in the effort to know someone whose values are different from yours. If you are stuck in a bubble, there is no room to grow as a person." Students who were "neutral" about the importance of such conversations cited concerns about lack of purpose or productivity for the conversation rather than a disinterest in engaging other viewpoints.

Many students (58 percent) are having such conversations on at least a weekly basis. We asked those we surveyed to note all of the locations where such interactions tend to occur. They reported that they are more prevalent over a meal (78 percent) or in the residence halls (65 percent) than in classrooms (53 percent) or at public lectures (38 percent).

The majority (almost 80 percent) reported that such conversations, when they do occur, can be difficult to navigate. Many survey participants said the discussion too quickly devolves into a debate where, as one put it, "We're talking *at* people instead of *with* them." An interviewee said it's easy to forget to "see the person as a person and not just a clump of ideas." Students expressed a keen desire for interactions centered on empathy—not just "being right." Many said they don't feel heard, but they also admitted that they struggle to listen fully to others as well.

One prevalent barrier to productive interaction is confusion about goals and responsibilities. Many students indicated that they have absorbed some confusing messages about speaking and silence. They have been taught that in some situations—for instance, as a bystander to bullying—silence equals complicity. As a result, they worry that simply listening, without offering a rebuttal, might be interpreted as tacit support for a particular viewpoint. Hence, while they may want to "just listen," they feel tremendous pressure to "speak out."

Some participants acknowledged that this pressure to speak hinders empathy and understanding. One admitted that at times, feeling empathy with someone who has a view that is "crazy, absurd, mean or hateful . . . scares me because I feel like I am agreeing with this hateful thing." Another said, "Calling people out does need to happen, but [I'm] also realizing that that's not the solution every time."

A further complication is that fear of social marginalization is pervasive, particularly on a small, residential campus like ours. "The fear of ostracization is terrifying . . . of being the only one and a social outcast," one interviewee explained. Some students claimed that this fear created a dynamic of "bandwagoning" in which "many people just seem to agree with one another for the sake of having the correct opinion." One student framed the situation as "rhetorical gymnastics."

Unsurprisingly, some students decide only to engage in these conversations with close friends, recognizing that probably limits the range of perspectives represented since "friend groups . . . often have similar ideas and opinions [as] mine." Others feel differently: "I do not want to create a conflict with friends," one said, adding, "It is also difficult to be in a relationship with someone when you disagree on most things political." Students in this latter group expressed a preference for conversations in a more structured environment like the classroom.

Perhaps some readers will see these findings as nothing more than a confirmation of the "snowflake" narrative. But I see much more going on: students want to engage deeply and productively with ideological difference, and many are aware of the barriers to that sort of engagement. Our first step as educators must be to acknowledge that these challenges exist and to talk about them openly with students and colleagues. 10

What else can be done? This research suggests that our institutional resources should be invested not just in the *what* of ideological difference but in the *how*. Perhaps some of the money and energy spent on bringing high-profile speakers to campus should be devoted to creating opportunities for more small-group dialogue about those speakers' ideas and students' reactions to them. We also need to see empathetic listening as a skill set to be taught, not just as a disposition students are expected to develop on their own. One central component of that skill set is the capacity for self-questioning: What do I hope to gain from this conversation? What assumptions am I bringing? How can I respect the humanity of the people with whom I am in dialogue? Of course, we as educators are often lacking in this area, as can be attested by anyone who has taken part in a highly contentious faculty meeting. Faculty members need not only professional development in how to create the conditions for productive dialogue: we also need to consider how we might engage differing viewpoints more productively among ourselves.

In recent years, my institution has been piloting a number of initiatives aimed at cultivating the skills necessary for engaging across difference. All our first-year students are required to attend <u>a daylong workshop</u> in which they discuss "race and other difficult topics." We have begun offering occasional meals in which students, staff and faculty engage in "<u>deliberative dialogue</u>." We are also exploring ways to bring <u>restorative practices</u> into student life.

Those efforts have not yet been integrated systematically into the classroom, however—nor are they prioritized (yet) in the academic curriculum. We need a comprehensive approach to creating a community of thoughtful listeners who are willing and prepared to engage productively with ideological difference. That could include courses or workshops on topics such as civil dialogue, empathetic listening and intercultural competence. Faculty members could form professional learning communities in which they share strategies and resources for engaging students in difficult conversations. The administration could request—or even require—that major co-curricular events (keynotes, symposia and the like) be accompanied by opportunities for small-group discussion and/or personal reflection before or after the event.

Of course, our students will also be able to tell us what they need, if given the opportunity. We must make "engaging across difference" an explicit pedagogical focus, if we wish to achieve the ideal of free speech in higher education.

Thinking about the Text

1. What problem has Shapiro defined, and what solutions does she **PROPOSE** to solve that problem? What specific actions does Shapiro propose be taken on college campuses as part of the solution?

2. Shapiro's **AUDIENCE** is college and university faculty and administrators. How does Shapiro establish her **CREDIBILITY** and tailor her proposal for her audience? How might this proposal be different if it were written instead for a student newspaper?

3. What **COUNTERARGUMENTS** does Shapiro acknowledge? What other objections could she address to make her proposal more convincing? Raise and respond to additional objections you come up with yourself.

4. What **EVIDENCE** does Shapiro offer to demonstrate that her proposal will address the actual problem she defines? Why is it important to her to avoid the common "free speech vs. inclusion/diversity" dichotomy that frames most discussions of these issues?

5. What's your reaction to Shapiro's proposal? Write an essay to respond—agreeing, disagreeing, or both, raising any questions you think need to be considered or offering suggestions about how to carry out or adapt Shapiro's proposal on your campus.

PART V

The Centrality of Argument

CHANCES ARE THAT your first attempt to communicate was an argument. Your first cry, that is, argued that you were hungry or sleepy or wanted to be held. Later, you could use words to say what you wanted: "More!" "No!" "Candy!" All arguments. So if you think that argument is just about disputes or disagreements, think again. In rhetorical terms, argument refers to any way that human beings express themselves to try to achieve a particular purpose—which, many would say, means any way that people express themselves at all.

If you think about the kinds of writing covered in this book, for example, it is easy to understand that an op-ed taking a position on a political issue or a TV critic's rave review of a new series is "arguing" for or against something. An editorial cartoon about the issue or an ad for the movie is making an obvious argument, too. But even when you post on *Instagram* about something you just did, you're implicitly arguing that it will be intriguing or important or perhaps amusing to your audience, those who follow you on *Instagram*. Even when you write a lab report, you'll describe and interpret the results of an experiment, arguing that your findings have certain implications.

In fact, you are immersed in argument. Try counting the number of arguments you either make or encounter in just one day, starting with the argument you have with yourself over what to wear, moving on to the barrage of posters asking you to support certain causes or attend various concerts, to a biology lecture where the professor explains the conflicting arguments about climate change, then the flood of claims and arguments you scroll through in your social media feed, and ending only when you and a friend agree to disagree about who's better, Michael Jordan or LeBron James. We bet you'll be surprised by how many arguments you encounter in a day.

The point we want to make is simple: you are the author of many arguments and the target of many more—and you'll be a better reader and writer of your own arguments if you understand how they work.

It's important to mention as well that arguments today most often consist of more than just words, from the signs admonishing you to fasten your seat belt, to a big "thumbs up," to an ad for McDonald's. These familiar images demonstrate how words and images can make strong visual arguments.

Words, graphics, and images can be combined to make strong visual arguments.

It's also worth noting that arguments today are more seductive than ever. A fifteen-second sound bite sways millions of voters; a song you loved as a twelve-year-old now boosts sales of soft drinks; celebrities write op-ed essays on issues they care about. Even your school mounts arguments intended to attract prospective students—and, later, to motivate alumni to give generously. Check out your school's homepage, and you'll find appeals intended to attract applications and contributions.

Perhaps you think that such arguments are somewhat manipulative, intended to trick you into buying a product or contributing to a cause. But arguments are always trying to achieve some purpose, so it is up to you both as a reader and as a writer to distinguish the good from the bad. And arguments can, of course, be used for good (think of the powerful arguments for human rights) or ill (think of Hitler's hypnotic arguments). They can be deceptive, even silly—does that gorgeous woman holding a can of cleanser really mean to claim that if you buy the cleanser, you'll look just like her?

In fact, argument is about many things and has many purposes. Of the many purposes we might name, here are just a few:

to explore

to understand

to find consensus

to make decisions

to convince or persuade

Keep in mind, however, that arguments are always embedded in particular contexts—and that what is persuasive can vary from one context to another, or from one culture to another. The most persuasive evidence in one community might come from religious texts; in another, from personal testimony; in another, from facts or statistics. Especially now that arguments so often take place online, reaching people all around the world, it's important to be aware of such differences.

When two brothers attacked the Paris offices of the satiric journal *Charlie Hebdo* in 2015, leaving twelve people dead and eleven others wounded, the entire world was caught up in the story. Why attack a journal that publishes satirical comics? As we later learned, the brothers were acting on their belief that the artists at *Charlie Hebdo* were guilty of (mis)representing the Prophet Mohammed in cartoons and thus of violating the traditions of Islam as they understood them. Condemnations of the attacks echoed around the world, from Europe to Australia and Japan, arguing that murder is never an appropriate act and that the brothers had struck not only at *Charlie Hebdo* but at a bedrock principle of the Western world: freedom of speech. Yet others disagreed, arguing that the cartoonists' satires had gone too far, that their work was insulting and destructive of another culture's beliefs; while they did not condone the bloodshed, these critics argued that the cartoonists' work had been deliberately inflammatory. Still others argued that the attack was justified, that the brothers were heroes and martyrs to their faith. Not surprisingly, these opinions varied from culture to culture. Especially when their message spreads online, writers, speakers, cartoonists, and activists must remember that their intended arguments will be interpreted variably, depending on audience and context. The poster below illustrates a French-language slogan, "I am Charlie," that quickly spread around the world as supporters of free speech rallied. Clearly, not everyone who saw the poster agreed with its sentiments.

Posters often make powerful arguments—and those who disagree sometimes argue back on the poster itself.

During his lifetime, Martin Luther King Jr. did not have the benefit of the internet, but the arguments he made eventually reverberated around the world. In his "Letter from Birmingham Jail," King was responding to a statement written in 1963 by eight white Alabama clergymen who had urged him to stop his campaign of civil disobedience to protest racial discrimination. This particular context—the US South at the height of the civil rights struggle—informs his argument throughout. And while King's argument remains the same, having been republished countless times, its interpretation varies across time and cultures. When the letter first appeared, it responded point by

Martin Luther King Jr. in a jail cell in Birmingham, Alabama.

point to the statement by the eight clergymen, and it was read as an answer to their particular charges. Today, however, it is read as a much more general statement about the importance of civil rights for all people. King's famous conclusion to this letter sums up his argument and consciously addresses an audience that extends far beyond the eight clergymen:

> Let us all hope that the dark clouds of racial prejudice will soon pass away
> and the deep fog of misunderstanding will be lifted from our fear-drenched
> communities, and in some not too distant tomorrow the radiant stars of
> love and brotherhood will shine over our great nation with all their scintil-
> lating beauty.   —MARTIN LUTHER KING JR., "Letter from Birmingham Jail"

As with all arguments, the effectiveness of King's letter has always varied
according to the context in which it is read and, especially, the audience that
is reading it. In most of his letter, King addresses eight specific people, and
they are clearly part of his primary audience. But his use of "us" and "our"
in the passage above works to broaden that audience and reaches beyond
that time and place to many other readers and listeners.

Because arguments are so central to our lives, it's important to
understand how they work—and to learn how to make effective arguments
of your own, remembering that you can do so only by paying very careful
attention to your purpose, your intended audience, and the rest of your
rhetorical situation. The next two chapters focus on how good arguments
work and on strategies for supporting the arguments that you make.

EIGHTEEN

Analyzing and Constructing Arguments
Those You Read, Those You Write

HE CLOTHES YOU CHOOSE TO WEAR argue for your own sense of style; the courses your college requires argue for what educators consider important; the kind of transportation you take, the food you eat (or don't eat)— almost everything represents some kind of argument. So it is important to understand all these arguments, those you encounter and those you create. Consider a couple of everyday examples.

What's in a social media handle? An email address? You may not have thought much about the argument that these chosen titles make, but they certainly do make a statement about you. One student we know chose the email address 2hot2handl@gmail.com. But when it came time to look for meaningful employment, he began to think about what that address said about him. As a result, he chose an address he felt was more appropriate to the image he wanted to convey: DavidLopez494@gmail.com.

If you need to think about what arguments you may be making yourself, it's also important to understand the arguments that come from others. Take a look, for example, at the two images on the next page, both of which appeared after the 2012 shootings at Sandy Hook Elementary School. The first image shows signs that make the argument that gun control will protect our loved ones; the second takes a very different approach, showing gun rights activists invoking their constitutional right to bear arms. These two images make radically different arguments

Protesters' signs make decidedly different arguments about guns in America.

about the role guns should play in US society, arguments that call on us to think very carefully before we respond. Crucially, they demonstrate that arguments always exist in a larger context, that they always involve more than just the person or group making the argument.

Arguments, in short, don't appear out of thin air: every argument begins as a response to some other argument—a statement, an event, an image, or something else. From these images we see how important it is to analyze any argument you encounter—and consider the other side—before deciding where you yourself stand. That goes for arguments you read and for ones you write. Either way, all arguments are part of a larger conversation. Whether you're responding to something you've read, discussing a film you've seen, or writing an essay that argues a position, you enter into a dialogue with the arguments of others.

This chapter will help you analyze the arguments you encounter and compose arguments of your own.

WHERE'S THE ARGUMENT COMING FROM?

As a reader, you need to pay special attention to the source of an argument— literally to where it is coming from. It makes a difference whether an argument appears in the *New York Times* or a school newspaper, in *Physics Review* or on someone's *Twitter* feed you know nothing about, in an impromptu speech by a candidate seeking your vote or in an analysis of that speech done by the nonpartisan website *FactCheck.org*. And even when you know who's putting forward the argument, you need to dig deeper to find out where—what view of the world—that source itself is "coming from."

For example, here's the homepage of the website of Public Citizen, a nonprofit organization founded in 1971 by consumer advocate and social critic Ralph Nader. So what can we tell about where this argument is coming from? We might start with the image in the upper-left corner of Lady Liberty holding up her torch right next to the headline "PUBLIC CITIZEN Protecting Health, Safety and Democracy." Below that is the menu bar and an example of the kind of analysis Public Citizen is known for:

> As Medicare-for-all gains popularity with the public and lawmakers, opponents like Big Pharma are already pushing false claims. What's fact and what's fiction?

Based on its website and its stated goal of "defending democracy and resisting corporate power," we can surmise, then, that Public Citizen supports the rights of ordinary citizens and liberal democratic values and opposes the

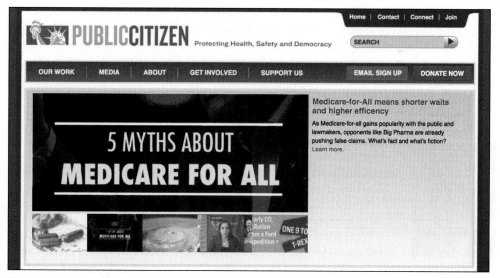

The homepage of Public Citizen's website.

influence of corporations on government. Indeed, if we look a bit further, to
the About page, we will find the following statement:

> Public Citizen is a nonprofit consumer advocacy organization that cham-
> pions the public interest—your interests—in the halls of power. Since
> our founding in 1971, we have defended democracy, resisted corporate
> power and worked to ensure that government works for the people—
> not for big corporations.

Together, these images and statements tell us a lot about Public Citizen's
stance, where the organization is coming from. And other trustworthy
sources confirm it, calling Public Citizen a "progressive" and "liberal" organization that practices "lobbying and advocacy." As savvy readers, we then
have to assess the claims Public Citizen makes on its website and elsewhere
in light of this knowledge: knowing where an organization is coming from
and how it is seen by others affects how willing or skeptical we are to accept
what it says.

Or consider a more lighthearted example, this time from political
pundit David Brooks:

> We now have to work under the assumption that every American has a
> tattoo. Whether we are at a formal dinner, at a professional luncheon,
> at a sales conference or arguing before the Supreme Court, we have to
> assume that everyone in the room is fully tatted up—that under each
> suit, dress or blouse, there is at least a set of angel wings, a barbed wire
> armband, a Chinese character or maybe even a fully inked body suit. We
> have to assume that any casual anti-tattoo remark will cause offense,
> even to those we least suspect of self-marking.
>
> —DAVID BROOKS, "Nonconformity Is Skin Deep"

David Brooks

What can we know about where Brooks is coming from? For starters, it's
easy to find out that he is a conservative journalist whose work appears in
many publications across the political spectrum and who often appears as
a television commentator on the *PBS NewsHour*. We also know that this passage comes from one of his op-ed columns for the *New York Times*. His photo
on the *Times* website presents him as a professional, in jacket and tie.

What more can we tell about where he's coming from in the passage
itself? Probably first is that Brooks is representing himself here as somewhat old-fashioned, as someone who's clearly an adult and a member of

what might be called "the establishment" in the United States (note his off-handed assumption that "we" might be "at a formal dinner" or "arguing before the Supreme Court"). He's someone who almost certainly does not have a tattoo himself. He's also comfortable using a little sarcasm ("everyone in the room is fully tatted up") and exaggeration ("every American has a tattoo") to make a humorous point. Finally, we can tell that he is a self-confident—and persuasive—author and that we'll need to be on our toes to understand the argument that he's actually making.

As an author, you should always think hard about where *you* are coming from in the arguments you make. What's your STANCE, and why? How do you want your audience to perceive you? As reasonable? knowledgeable? opinionated? curious? something else?

How can you convey your stance? Through your choice of words, of course—both *what* you say and *how* you say it—but also through any images you include and the way you design your text. The words you choose not only convey your meaning, they reveal a lot about your attitude—toward your subject and your audience. Introducing a quotation with the words "she insists" indicates a different attitude than the more neutral "she says."

WHAT'S THE CLAIM?

You run into dozens of claims every day. Your brother says the latest Spiderman film is the best one ever; your news feed says that Kentucky will be in the Final Four; a friend texts to say it's a waste of time and money to eat at Power Pizza. Each of these statements makes a claim and argues implicitly for you to agree. The arguments you read and write in college often begin with a claim, an arguable statement that must then be supported with good reasons and evidence.

The *New Yorker* cover on the next page titled "Moment of Joy" shows *Sesame Street* character Bert with his arm around Ernie's shoulder as they watch the 2013 Supreme Court ruling overturning the Defense of Marriage Act, which had denied federal benefits to same-sex couples. The cover immediately sparked debate. The creator of the image saw it as portraying a celebratory moment, saying, "It's amazing to witness how attitudes on gay rights have evolved in my lifetime. This is great for our kids, a moment we can all celebrate." But others read the image differently, saying that using puppets rather than actual people trivialized the issue; still others claimed

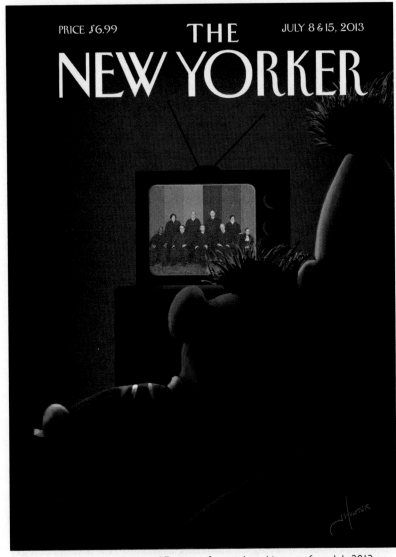

Sesame Street characters Bert and Ernie are featured on this cover from July 2013 marking the Supreme Court's decision to grant federal benefits to same-sex couples.

that the image inappropriately sexualized the much-loved children's show. Images can make powerful arguments that often spark debate.

The easiest claims to identify are those that are stated directly as an explicit **THESIS**. Look, for instance, at the following paragraph from a journal article by civil rights activist W. E. B. Du Bois in 1922. As you read each sentence, ask yourself what Du Bois's claim is.

> Abraham Lincoln was a Southern poor white, . . . poorly educated and unusually ugly, awkward, ill-dressed. He liked smutty stories and was a politician down to his toes. Aristocrats—Jeff Davis, Seward and their ilk—despised him, and indeed he had little outwardly that compelled respect. But in that curious human way he was big inside. He had reserves and depths and when habit and convention were torn away there was something left to Lincoln—nothing to most of his contemners. There was something left, so that at the crisis he was big enough to be inconsistent—cruel, merciful; peace-loving, a fighter; despising Negroes and letting them fight and vote; protecting slavery and freeing slaves. He was a man—a big, inconsistent, brave man.
>
> —W. E. B. DU BOIS, "Abraham Lincoln"

We think you'll find that the claim is difficult to make out until the last sentence, which lets us know in an explicit thesis that the contradictions Du Bois has been detailing are part of Lincoln's greatness, part of what made him "big" and "brave." Take note as well of where the thesis appears in the text. Du Bois holds his claim for the very end.

Here is a very different example, from a newspaper column about legendary dancer Judith Jamison. Note that it begins with an explicit thesis stating a claim that the rest of the passage expands on—and supports:

> Judith Jamison is my kind of American cultural icon. . . . She has many accolades and awards—among them the National Medal of Arts, the Kennedy Center Honors and an Emmy. . . .
>
> But when I met her . . . she said with a huge smile, "Yes, honey, but you know I still have to do the laundry myself, and no one in New York parts the sidewalk 'cause I am comin' through!"
>
> I like icons who are authentic and accessible. I think our country benefits from that. It can only serve to inspire others to believe that they can try to do the same thing.
>
> —MARIA HINOJOSA, "Dancing Past the Boundaries"

Judith Jamison dancing with the Alvin Ailey Dance Theater.

Notice that although Hinojosa's claim is related to her own personal taste in American cultural icons, it is not actually about her taste itself. Her argument is not about her preference for cultural icons to be "authentic and accessible." Instead, she's arguing that given this criterion, Judith Jamison is a perfect example.

As an author making an argument of your own, remember that a claim shouldn't simply express a personal taste: if you say that you feel lousy or that you hate the New York Yankees, no one could reasonably argue that you don't feel that way. For a claim to be *arguable*—worth arguing—it has to take a **POSITION** that others can logically have different perspectives on. Likewise, an arguable claim can't simply be a statement of fact that no one would disagree with ("Violent video games earn millions of dollars every year"). And remember that in most academic contexts, claims based on religious faith alone often cannot be argued since there are no agreed-upon standards of proof or evidence.

In most academic writing, you'll be expected to state your CLAIM explicitly as a THESIS, announcing your topic and the main point(s) you are going to make about that topic. Your thesis should help readers follow your train of thought, so it's important that it state your point clearly. A good thesis will also engage your audience's interest—and make them want to read on.

Be careful, however, not to overstate your thesis: you may need to QUALIFY it with words like *some*, *might*, or *possible*—for example, that "Recent studies have shown that exercise has a *limited* effect on a person's weight, so eating less *may be* a better strategy for losing weight than exercising more." By saying that dieting "may be" more effective than exercise, the author of this thesis has limited her claim to one she will be able to support.

In most US academic contexts, authors are expected to make claims directly and get to the point fairly quickly, so you may want to position the thesis near the beginning of your text, often at the end of the introduction or the first paragraph. When your claim is likely to challenge or surprise your audience, though, you may want to build support for it more gradually and hold off stating it explicitly until later in your argument, as Du Bois does. In other situations, you may not need to make a direct statement of your claim at all. But always make sure in such cases that your audience has a clear understanding of what the claim is.

WHAT'S AT STAKE?

Figuring out the answer to this question takes you to the heart of the argument. Rhetoricians in ancient Rome developed what they called *stasis theory*, a simple system for identifying the crux of an argument—what's at stake in it—by asking four questions in sequence:

1. What are the facts?
2. How can the issue be defined?
3. How much does the issue matter, and why?
4. What actions should be taken as a result?

Together these questions help determine the basic issues at stake in an argument. A look at the arguments that swirled around Hurricane Katrina and its effects can illustrate how these questions work.

What are the facts? Certainly the hurricane hit the Gulf Coast squarely, resulting in almost unimaginable damage and loss of life, especially in New Orleans, where levees failed along with the city's evacuation plan. Many arguments about the disaster had their crux (or stasis) here, claiming that the most important aspect of "what happened" was not the hurricane itself but the lack of preparation for it and the response to it.

How can the issue be defined? In the case of Katrina, the question of definition turned out to be crucial for many arguments about the event: it was easy enough to define the storm itself as a "category 4 hurricane" but much more difficult to classify the disaster beyond that simple scientific tag. To what extent was it a national disaster or a local one? A natural disaster or a man-made one? Was it proof of corruption and incompetence on the part of local and state officials? of FEMA and the Bush administration? Something else?

How much does the issue matter, and why? In addition to questions of fact and definition, ones about how serious the event was also produced many arguments in the wake of Katrina. In the first week or so after the storm hit, the mayor of New Orleans argued that it was the most serious disaster ever to strike that city and that up to 10,000 lives would be lost. Others argued that while the storm represented a huge setback to the people of the region, they could and would overcome their losses and rebuild their cities and towns.

What actions should be taken as a result? Of all the stasis questions, this one was the basis for the greatest number of arguments. From those arguing that the federal government should be responsible for funding reconstruction, to those arguing that the government should work with insurance agencies and local and state officials, to those arguing that the most damaged neighborhoods should not be rebuilt, thousands of proposals were offered and debated.

Such questions can help you understand what's at stake in an argument—to help you figure out and assess the arguments put forth by others, to identify which stasis question lies at the heart of an argument—and then to decide whether or not the argument answers the question satisfactorily.

As an author, you can use these questions to identify the main point you want to make in an argument of your own. In the Katrina example, for instance, working through the four stasis questions would help you see the disaster from a number of different perspectives and then develop a cogent argument related to them. In addition, these questions may help you decide just what **GENRE** of argument you want to make: a question of fact might lead you to write a **NARRATIVE**, explaining what happened, while the question of what action(s) should be taken might lead you to compose a **PROPOSAL**.

MEANS OF PERSUASION: EMOTIONAL, ETHICAL, AND LOGICAL APPEALS

Aristotle wrote that good arguments should make use of "all the available means" of persuading an audience and named three in particular, which he labeled *emotional* appeals (to the heart), *ethical* appeals (about credibility or character), and *logical* appeals (to the mind).

Emotional Appeals

Emotional appeals (also referred to as *pathos*) stir feelings and often invoke values that the audience is assumed to hold. The paragraph on Lincoln on page 417, for example, offers a strong appeal to readers' emotions when it represents Lincoln as "big" and "brave," invoking two qualities Americans traditionally value. Images can make especially powerful appeals to our emotions, such as the ones below from the Ebola outbreak in West Africa.

These images pull at our heartstrings, leading us both to empathize with the plight of children facing Ebola and to support efforts to end the epidemic.

The first image appeals directly to our hearts, showing a young boy suspected of having Ebola, a table of medications on one side and a healthcare worker in full protective gear on the other. In the second image, from the international relief agency CARE, the message is clear and simple: donate now and help halt the outbreak. As the first example shows, images can appeal very strongly to emotions. But words too can make a powerful emotional appeal, as in the second example. As a reader, you'll want to consider how any such emotional appeals support an author's claim.

As an author, you should consider how you can appeal to your audience's emotions and whether such appeals are appropriate to your claim, your purpose, and your audience. And whatever you decide, be careful not to overdo emotional appeals, pulling at the heartstrings so hard that your audience feels manipulated.

Ethical Appeals

Ethical appeals (also referred to as *ethos*) invoke the credibility and good character of whoever is making the argument. See how the website for the Interfaith Youth Core, a nonprofit organization building common ground between people with different beliefs, includes information intended to establish founder Eboo Patel's credibility and integrity. Here is part of Patel's "bio" page from the site:

> [Eboo] is inspired to build this bridge by his identity as an American Muslim navigating a religiously diverse social landscape.
>
> For over 15 years he has worked with governments, social sector organizations, and college and university campuses to help make interfaith cooperation a social norm. Named by *U.S. News & World Report* as one of America's Best Leaders of 2009, Eboo served on President Obama's Inaugural Faith Council and is the author of *Acts of Faith, Sacred Ground, Interfaith Leadership: A Primer,* and *Out of Many Faiths: Religious Diversity and the American Promise.* He holds a doctorate in the sociology of religion from Oxford University, where he studied on a Rhodes scholarship.
>
> These days, Eboo spends most of his time on the road, doing what he loves: meeting students, educators, and community leaders to talk about the complex landscape of religious diversity and the power of interfaith cooperation in the 21st century.   —INTERFAITH YOUTH CORE, "Eboo Patel"

Interfaith leader Eboo Patel delivering a talk on religious diversity and the American promise at Dickinson University.

All of this information, including Patel's numerous degrees and publications and his position advising the US president helps establish his credibility and helps readers decide how much stock they can put in his words and the work of the organization he founded.

Citing scholarly achievements and national positions of influence is only one way of establishing credibility. Here Patel uses another approach during a *PBS NewsHour* interview when he responds to a question about "hostile racial divisions" on campus:

> I'm on 25 college campuses a year. I have probably visited something like 130 in the past eight or 10 years. It's not like things don't ever get tense, but what I read about in the news on college campuses is foreign to me, right, which is to say it is by definition sensational.
>
> How am I not going to be optimistic, really? . . . The beautiful thing is, there's lots of us that feel this way. There's this whole growing network of college student interfaith leaders on American campuses basically saying, where's the divide? Let me bridge it. That's the future of America, or we have no future at all.
>
> —EBOO PATEL, *PBS NewsHour* Interview, "To Narrow Toxic Divides, Students Build Bridges between Faiths"

In his comments, Patel lets listeners know that he is basing his claim on a lot of personal experience. And his informal tone suggests that he has a simple, direct message to give to his audience. His extensive experience gives him confidence to talk with conviction about why he's optimistic in the face of deep differences.

Building common ground. Patel's use of simple, everyday language helps establish credibility in another way: by building common ground with his audience. He is not "putting on airs" but speaking directly to them; the concerns so many feel, he seems to say, are his concerns. He also uses **ANALOGIES**, invoking universally respected figures, that few people will disagree with: "I think that the great lesson of Lincoln and Jane Addams and King and Mandela is, for every stitch of hate or distrust that you put into the fabric now, you're going to have to unstitch at a later point." Given Patel's goals and the aims of the organization he founded, it's no surprise that he seeks to build common ground with his audience.

Visit everyones anauthor.tumblr .com to find Patel's full interview.

While building common ground cannot ensure that your audience is "on your side," it does show that you respect your audience and their views and that you've established, with them, a mutual interest in the topic. Both parties care about the issues that you are addressing. Thus, building common ground is a particularly important part of creating an effective argument. Especially if you are addressing an audience unlikely to agree with your position, finding some area of agreement with them, some common ground you can all stand on, can help give the argument a chance of being heard.

No global leader in recent history has been more successful in building common ground than Nelson Mandela, who became the first black president of South Africa in 1994 after the country's harsh apartheid system of racial segregation ended. In *Playing the Enemy: Nelson Mandela and the Game That Made a Nation*, the basis for the 2009 film *Invictus*, author John Carlin recounts hearing Mandela say that "sport has the power to change the world . . . the power to unite people in a way that little else does" and that "It is more powerful than governments in breaking down racial barriers." Carlin uses this quotation as an example of Mandela's singular ability to "walk in another person's shoes" and to build common ground even where none seems possible. He goes on to detail the ways in which Mandela used white South Africans' love of rugby to build common ground between them and the country's black majority, which had long seen the almost all-white national rugby team, the Springboks, as a symbol of white supremacy:

> He explained how he had . . . used the 1995 Rugby World Cup as an instrument in the grand strategic purpose he set for himself during his five years as South Africa's first democratically elected president: to reconcile blacks and whites and create the conditions for a lasting peace. . . . He told me, with a chuckle or two, about the trouble he had persuading his own people to back the rugby team. . . . Having won over his own people, he went out and won over the enemy.
>
> —JOHN CARLIN, *Playing the Enemy*

Mandela understood, in short, that when people were as far apart in their thinking as black and white South Africans were when apartheid ended, the only way to move forward, to make arguments for the country's future that both groups would listen to, was to discover something that could bring them together. For Mandela—and for South Africa—rugby provided the common ground. His personal meetings with the Springboks players and his support for the team paid off to such an extent that when they won a stunning upset victory in the 1995 World Cup final in Johannesburg, the multiracial crowd chanted his name and the country united in celebration. And establishing that common ground contributed to Mandela's extraordinary ethical appeal—which he put to good use in the difficult arguments he had to make in the transition to a post-apartheid South Africa.

In all the arguments you encounter, you'll want to consider how much you can trust the author. Do they seem knowledgeable? represent opposing positions fairly (or at all)? do anything to build common ground?

As an author, you need to establish your own **AUTHORITY** : to show that you know what you're talking about by citing trustworthy sources; to demonstrate that you're fair by representing other positions even-handedly and accurately; and to establish some kind of common ground with your audience.

Logical Appeals

Appeals to logic (also referred to as *logos*) have long been regarded as the most important of all the appeals, following Aristotle's definition of humans as rational animals. Recent research has made it increasingly clear, however, that people seldom make decisions based on logic alone and that emotion often plays a larger role in our decision making than does logic. Nevertheless, in academic contexts, logical appeals count for a lot. When we

President Nelson Mandela, wearing a Springboks cap and shirt, presents the Rugby World Cup to South African captain Francois Pienaar in June 1995.

make an argument, we need to provide **REASONS** and **EVIDENCE** to support our claims. Such evidence may include facts and statistics, data from surveys and questionnaires, direct observations, interviews, testimony, experiments, personal experience, visuals, and more.

Facts and statistics. Facts and statistics are two of the most commonly used kinds of evidence. Facts are claims that have been proven to be true—and that an audience is likely accept without further proof. Statistics are research-based numerical data. Here *Men's Health* editor David Zinczenko offers facts and statistics as support for an argument in the *New York Times* about the effects of fast foods on Americans:

> Before 1994, diabetes in children was generally caused by a genetic disorder—only about 5 percent of childhood cases were obesity-related, or Type 2 diabetes. Today, according to the National Institutes of Health, Type 2 diabetes accounts for at least 30 percent of all new childhood cases of diabetes in this country.
>
> Not surprisingly, money spent to treat diabetes has skyrocketed, too. The Centers for Disease Control and Prevention estimate that diabetes accounted for $2.6 billion in health care costs in 1969. Today's number is an unbelievable $100 billion a year.
>
> Shouldn't we know better than to eat two meals a day in fast-food restaurants? That's one argument. But where, exactly, are consumers—particularly teenagers—supposed to find alternatives? Drive down any thoroughfare in America, and I guarantee you'll see one of our country's more than 13,000 McDonald's restaurants. Now, drive back up the block and try to find someplace to buy a grapefruit.
>
> —DAVID ZINCZENKO, "Don't Blame the Eater"

The facts about the proliferation of fast-food chains compared to the relative lack of healthier options will be obvious to Zinczenko's readers, and most of his statistics come from respected health organizations whose authority adds to the credibility of his argument. Statistics can provide powerful support for an argument, but be sure they're accurate, current, from reliable sources—and relevant. And if you base an argument on facts, be sure to take into account all the relevant information. Realistically, that's hard to do—but be careful not to ignore any important available facts. The advice in chapter 8 will further help you distinguish facts from misinformation.

Surveys and questionnaires. You have probably responded to a number of surveys or questionnaires, and you will often find them used as evidence in support of arguments. When a college student wondered about the kinds of reading for pleasure her dormmates were doing, she decided to gather information through a survey and to present it in a pie chart.

What Genres Students Are Reading

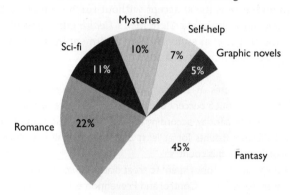

The information displayed in the chart offers evidence that fantasy is the most-read genre, followed by romance, sci-fi, mysteries, self-help, and graphic novels. Before accepting such evidence, however, readers might want to ask some key questions: How many people were surveyed? What methods of analysis did the student use? How were particular works classified? (For example, how did she decide whether a particular book was a "romance" or a "mystery"?) Whether you're reacting to survey data in an essay or a lecture, or conducting a survey of your own, you need to scrutinize the methods used and findings. Who conducted the survey, and why? (And yes, you need to think about that even if you conducted it.) Who are the respondents, how were they chosen, and are they representative? What do the results show?

Observations. A 2011 study reported in *Science News* demonstrates the way direct observations can form the basis for an argument. In this study, researchers in Uganda observed the way young chimpanzees play, and their findings support arguments about the relative importance of biology and socialization on the way boys and girls play.

A young chimp holds a stick in imitation of a mother caring for her child.

A new study finds that young females in one group of African chimpanzees use sticks as dolls more than their male peers do, often treating pieces of wood like a mother chimp caring for an infant. . . .

Ape observations, collected over 14 years of field work with the Kanyawara chimp community in Kibale National Park, provide the first evidence of a nonhuman animal in the wild that exhibits sex differences in how it plays, two primatologists report in the Dec. 21 *Current Biology*. This finding supports a controversial view that biology as well as society underlies boys' and girls' contrasting toy preferences.

—BRUCE BOWER, "Female Chimps Play with 'Dolls' "

As this study suggests, observations carried out over time are particularly useful as evidence since they show that something is not just a onetime event but a persistent pattern. As a college student, you probably won't have occasion to spend 14 years observing something, but in most cases you'll need to observe your subject more than once.

Interviews. Reporters often use information drawn from interviews to add authenticity and credibility to their articles. For an article on the danger concussions cause to athletes and the number of such unreported injuries, Kristin Sainani, a professor of health policy, interviewed Stanford neuroscientists conducting research on concussions as well as one athlete who had suffered several. Here is basketball star Toni Kokenis describing the effects her concussions had on her:

> I felt withdrawn from everything. It was like I was there, but in slow motion. I didn't feel comfortable shooting three-pointers because I couldn't focus on the basket long enough to know that the ball was actually going to go near the hoop.   —KRISTIN SAINANI, "Damage Control"

Sainani also cites information she learned from researcher David Camarillo, whose lab is at work on understanding concussions—a science, he says, that is still in its infancy. Preventing concussions won't be possible, he tells us, until we understand them. Camarillo then goes on to describe, in everyday language, what happens during a concussion: "You've got this kind of gelatinous blob in a fluid floating in a sealed pressure vessel. A concussion occurs when the brain is sloshed and bounced around in this fluid."

Unfortunately, he tells Sainani, wearing a helmet does little to prevent concussions, and so his lab is conducting research to "change the industry standards" for protective equipment.

Throughout this article, Sainani uses evidence drawn from interviews to engage readers and convince them that equipment to protect against concussions "needs to be better." As an author, be sure that anyone you interview is an authority on your subject whom your audience will consider trustworthy.

Testimony. Most of us depend on reliable testimony to help us accept or reject arguments: a friend tells us that *This Is Us* is a great TV show, and likely as not we'll watch it at least once. Testimony is especially persuasive evidence when it comes from experts and authorities on a topic. When you cite authorities to support an argument, you build your own credibility as an author; readers know that you've done your homework and are aware of the different perspectives on your topic. In the example on pages 428–29 about gender-linked behavior among chimpanzees, for example, the *Science News* report notes testimony from the two scientists who conducted the research.

Experiments. Evidence based on experiments is especially important in the sciences and social sciences, where data is often the basis for supporting a claim. In arguing that multitaskers pay a high mental price, Clifford Nass, a professor of communications, based his claims on a series of empirical studies of college students who were divided into two groups, those identified as "high multitaskers" and those identified as "low multitaskers." In the first studies, which measured attention and memory, Nass and his fellow researchers were surprised to find that the low multitaskers outperformed high multitaskers in statistically significant ways. Still not satisfied that low multitaskers were more productive learners, the researchers designed another test, hypothesizing that if high multitaskers couldn't do well in the earlier studies on attention and memory, maybe they would be better at shifting from task to task more quickly and effectively than low multitaskers.

> Wrong again, the study found.
>
> The subjects were shown images of letters and numbers at the same time and instructed what to focus on. When they were told to pay attention to numbers, they had to determine if the digits were even or odd. When told to concentrate on letters, they had to say whether they were vowels or consonants.
>
> Again, the heavy multitaskers underperformed the light multitaskers.
>
> "They couldn't help thinking about the task they weren't doing," the researchers reported. "The high multitaskers are always drawing from all the information in front of them. They can't keep things separate in their minds." —ADAM GORLICK, "Media Multitaskers Pay Mental Price"

As Gorlick notes, these researchers had evidence to support their hypothesis. Nevertheless, they realized the dangers of generalizing from one set of students to all students. Whenever you use data drawn from experiments, you need to be similarly cautious not to overgeneralize.

Personal experience can provide powerful support for an argument since it brings "eyewitness" evidence, which can establish a connection between author and audience. In an *Atlantic* article about Cesar Chavez, Caitlin Flanagan—who grew up where Chavez's United Farm Workers movement began—recounts her mother's personal experience to support the argument that Chavez had a "singular and almost mystical way of eliciting not just fealty but a kind of awe."

Cesar Chavez

> Of course, it had all started with Mom. Somewhere along the way, she had met Cesar Chavez, or at least attended a rally where he had spoken,

and that was it. Like almost everyone else who ever encountered him, she was spellbound. "This wonderful, wonderful man," she would call him, and off we went to collect clothes for the farmworkers' children, and to sell red-and-black UFW buttons and collect signatures.

—CAITLIN FLANAGAN, "The Madness of Cesar Chavez"

In your own writing, make sure that any personal experience you cite is pertinent to your argument and will be appropriate to your purpose.

Charts, images, and other visuals. Visuals of various kinds often provide valuable evidence to support an argument. Pie charts like the one showing the literary genres favored in a college dorm, photographs like the one of the female chimpanzee cradling a stick, and many other kinds of visuals—including drawings, bar and line graphs, cartoons, screenshots, videos, and advertisements—can often make it easier for an audience to see certain kinds of evidence. Imagine how much more difficult it would be to take in the information shown in the pie chart about the genres read by students in the dorm had the data been presented in a paragraph. Remember, though, that visual evidence usually needs to be explained—photos need captions, and any visuals need to be referenced in the accompanying text.

As an author, keep in mind that the **MEDIUM** you're using affects the kind of **EVIDENCE** you choose and how you present it. In a print text, evidence has to be in the text itself; in a digital medium, you can link directly to statistics, images, and other information. In a spoken text, any evidence needs to be said or shown on a slide or a handout—and anything you say should be simple, direct, and memorable (your audience can't rewind what you say). In every case, any evidence drawn from sources needs to be fully **DOCUMENTED**.

Are There Any Problems with the Reasoning?

Some kinds of appeals use faulty reasoning, or reasoning that some may consider unfair, unsound, or demonstrating lazy or simpleminded thinking. Such appeals are called *fallacies*, and because they can often be very powerful and persuasive, it's important to be alert for them in arguments you encounter—and in your own writing. Here are some of the most common fallacies.

Begging the question tries to support an argument by simply restating it in other language, so that the reasoning goes around in circles. For example, the statement "We need to reduce the national debt because the government owes too much money" begs the question of whether the debt is actually too large, because what comes before and after *because* say essentially the same thing.

Either-or arguments, also called *false dilemmas,* argue that only two alternatives are possible in a situation that actually is more complex. A candidate who declares, "I will not allow the United States to become a defenseless, bankrupt nation—it must remain the military and economic superpower of the world," ignores the many possibilities in between.

Ad hominem (Latin for "to the man") arguments make personal attacks on those who support an opposing position rather than address the position itself: "Of course council member Acevedo doesn't want to build a new high school; she doesn't have any children herself." The council member's childlessness may not be the reason for her opposition to a new high school, and even if it is, such an attack doesn't provide any argument for building the school.

Faulty causality, the mistaken assumption that because one event followed another, the first event caused the second, is also called *post hoc, ergo propter hoc* (Latin for "after this, therefore because of this"). For example, a mayor running for reelection may boast that a year after her administration began having the police patrol neighborhoods more frequently, the city's crime rate has dropped significantly. But there might be many other possible causes for the drop, so considerable evidence would be needed to establish such a causal connection.

Bandwagon appeals simply urge the audience to go along with the crowd: "Join the millions who've found pain relief through Weleda Migraine Remedy." "Everybody knows you shouldn't major in a subject that doesn't lead to a job." Such appeals often flatter the audience by implying that making the popular choice means they are smart, attractive, sophisticated, and so on.

Slippery slope arguments contend that if a certain event occurs, it will (or at least might) set in motion a chain of events that will end in disaster, like a minor misstep at the top of a slick incline that causes you to slip and then slide all the way to the bottom. For example, opponents of physician-assisted suicide often warn that making it legal for doctors to help people end their lives would eventually lead to an increase in the suicide rate, as people who would not otherwise kill themselves find it easier to do so, and even to an increase in murders disguised as suicide. Slippery slope arguments are not always wrong—an increasingly catastrophic chain reaction does sometimes grow out of a seemingly small beginning. But the greater the difference is between the initial event and the predicted final outcome, the more evidence is needed that the situation will actually play out in this way.

Setting up a straw man misrepresents an opposing argument, character-izing it as more extreme or otherwise different than it actually is, in order to attack it more easily. The misrepresentation is like an artificial figure made of straw that's easier to knock down than a real person would be. For example, critics of the 2010 Affordable Care Act often attacked it as a "federal takeover of health care" or a "government-run system." In fact, although the legislation increased the government's role in the health-care system, it still relied primarily on private systems of insurance and health-care providers.

Hasty generalizations draw sweeping conclusions on the basis of too little evidence: "Both of the political science classes I took were deadly dull, so it must be a completely boring subject." "You shouldn't drink so much coffee—that study that NPR reported on today said it causes cancer." Many hasty generalizations take the form of stereotypes about groups of people, such as men and women, gays and straights, and ethnic or religious groups. It's difficult to make arguments without generalizing, but they always need to be based on sufficient evidence and appropriately qualified with words like *most, in many cases, usually, in this state, in recent years*, and so on.

Faulty analogies are comparisons that do not hold up in some way crucial to the argument at hand. Accusing parents who homeschool their children of "educational malpractice" by saying that parents who aren't doctors wouldn't be allowed to perform surgery on their children, so parents who aren't trained to teach shouldn't be allowed to teach their children makes a false analogy. Teaching and surgery aren't alike enough to support an argument that what's required for one is needed for the other.

WHAT ABOUT OTHER PERSPECTIVES?

In any argument, it's important to consider perspectives other than those of the author, especially those that would not support the claim or would argue it very differently. As a reader, you should question any arguments

Camels ad, 1946.

that don't acknowledge other positions, and as a writer, you'll want to be sure that you represent—and respond to—perspectives other than your own. Acknowledging other arguments, in fact, is another way of demonstrating that you're fair and of establishing your credibility—whereas failing to consider other views can make you seem close-minded or lazy, unfair or manipulative. Think of any advertisements you've seen that claim, "Doctors recommend drug X."

The cigarette ad included here is one of the most infamous of such advertising arguments. Of course, this ad doesn't claim that all doctors smoke Camels, but it implies that plenty of them do and that what's good for a doctor is good for other consumers. But what if the ad had been required to consider other viewpoints? The result would have been a more honest and more informative, though perhaps a less successful, argument. Today, cigarette ads are required to carry another point of view: a warning about the adverse effects of smoking. So if an argument does not take other points of view into consideration, you will be right to question it, asking yourself what those other viewpoints might be and why they were not taken into account.

Compare the misleading Camels ad to the following discussion of contemporary seismology:

> Jian Lin was 14 years old in 1973, when the Chinese government under Mao Zedong recruited him for a student science team called "the earthquake watchers." After a series of earthquakes that had killed thousands in northern China, the country's seismologists thought that if they augmented their own research by having observers keep an eye out for anomalies like snakes bolting early from their winter dens and erratic well-water levels, they might be able to do what no scientific body had managed before: issue an earthquake warning that would save thousands of lives.
>
> In the winter of 1974, the earthquake watchers were picking up some suspicious signals near the city of Haicheng. Panicked chickens were squalling and trying to escape their pens; water levels were falling in wells. Seismologists had also begun noticing a telltale pattern of small quakes. "They were like popcorn kernels," Lin tells me, "popping up all over the general area." Then, suddenly, the popping stopped, just as it had before a catastrophic earthquake some years earlier that killed more than 8,000. "Like 'the calm before the storm,' " Lin says. "We have the exact same phrase in Chinese." On the morning of February 4, 1975, the seismology bureau issued a warning: Haicheng should expect a big earthquake, and people should move outdoors.
>
> At 7:36 p.m., a magnitude 7.0 quake struck. The city was nearly leveled, but only about 2,000 people were killed. Without the warning, easily 150,000 would have died. "And so you finally had an earthquake forecast that did indeed save lives," Lin recalls. . . .
>
> Lin is now a senior scientist of geophysics at Woods Hole Oceanographic Institution, in Massachusetts, where he spends his time studying not the scurrying of small animals and fluctuating electrical current between trees (another fabled warning sign), but seismometer readings, GPS coordinates, and global earthquake-notification reports. He and his longtime collaborator, Ross Stein of the U.S. Geological Survey, are champions of a theory that could enable scientists to forecast earthquakes with more precision and speed.

Some established geophysicists insist that all earthquakes are random, yet everyone agrees that aftershocks are not. Instead, they follow certain empirical laws. Stein, Lin, and their collaborators hypothesized that many earthquakes classified as main shocks are actually aftershocks, and they went looking for the forces that cause faults to fail.

Their work was in some ways heretical: For a long time, earthquakes were thought to release only the stress immediately around them; an earthquake that happened in one place would decrease the possibility of another happening nearby. But that didn't explain earthquake sequences like the one that rumbled through the desert and mountains east of Los Angeles in 1992. . . .

Lin and Stein both admit that [their theory] doesn't explain all earthquakes. Indeed, some geophysicists, like Karen Felzer, of the U.S. Geological Survey, think their hypothesis gives short shrift to the impact that dynamic stress—the actual rattling of a quake in motion—has on neighboring faults.

—JUDITH LEWIS MERNIT, "Seismology: Is San Francisco Next?"

As this excerpt shows, Lin and Stein's research supports the claim that earthquakes can be predicted some of the time, but they—and the author of the article about them—are careful not to overstate their argument or to ignore those who disagree. The author responds to other perspectives in three ways. She *acknowledges* the "all random" theory held by "[s]ome established geophysicists"; she provides evidence (not shown here) to *refute* the idea that "earthquakes release only the stress immediately around them." And in the last paragraph she *accommodates* other perspectives by qualifying Lin and Stein's claim and mentioning what some critics see as a weakness in it.

As an author, remember to consider what other perspectives exist on your topic—and what **COUNTERARGUMENTS** someone might have to your position. You may not agree with them, but they might lead you to **QUALIFY** your thesis—or even change your position. Whatever you think about other viewpoints, be sure to **ACKNOWLEDGE** them fairly and respectfully—and to accommodate or refute them as possible. And carefully investigate your reactions to opposing positions to be sure you aren't falling prey to **CONFIRMATION BIAS** or **ATTRIBUTION BIAS**. They will help you to sharpen your own thinking, and your writing can only improve as a result.

WAYS OF STRUCTURING ARGUMENTS

You can organize arguments in several ways. You may decide to approach a controversial or surprising argument slowly, *building up to the claim* but withholding it until you have established plenty of evidence to support it, as in this introductory paragraph from an essay about sports injuries:

> The flood of media attention highlighting damaged brains, dementia, and suicides in retired NFL players has made concussions synonymous with football. That attention was greatly needed: the debilitating consequences of brain injuries in football players of all ages has been severely overlooked. But the focus of this controversy has been far too narrow. It's true that young players need better equipment and stricter safety standards on the gridiron. But in many of the most popular sports, boys aren't the ones most likely to be afflicted by concussions. Girls are.
>
> —MARJORIE A. SNYDER, "Girls Suffer Sports Concussions at a Higher Rate than Boys. Why Is That Overlooked?"

On the other hand, you may choose to *start right off with the claim* and then build support for it piece by piece by piece, as in this opening from a 2011 essay in *Wired* on the power of product tie-ins.

> Cartoon characters permeate every aspect of our children's existences. We serve them Transformers Lunchables and have them brush with SpongeBob-branded toothpaste. We tuck them in on branded sheets, fix their owies with branded bandages, and change their branded diapers because we know, or at least we think, that the characters will make them happy. Whether our kids are sleeping, bleeding, or pooping, Spider-Man is there. Even if you operate one of those rarefied TV-free households, the brands will penetrate, assuming your children go to preschool, have friends, or eat food.
>
> —NEAL POLLACK, "Why Your Kids Are Addicted to *Cars*"

Another common way to begin is to *note what others have said* about your topic and then to present your own ideas—your claim—as a response. Whether you agree, disagree, or both, this is a way of adding your voice to the larger conversation. See how libertarian journalist Radley Balko uses this technique to begin an essay on government policies on obesity:

This toy store display argues that if you loved the movies, you should buy Minions-themed products.

This June, *Time* magazine and ABC News will host a three-day summit on obesity [that] promises to be a pep rally for media, nutrition activists, and policy makers—all agitating for a panoply of government anti-obesity initiatives. . . . In other words, bringing government between you and your waistline. . . .

    This is the wrong way to fight obesity. Instead of manipulating or intervening in the array of food options available to American consumers, our government ought to be working to foster a sense of responsibility in and ownership of our own health and well-being.

—RADLEY BALKO, "What You Eat Is Your Business"

Whatever the approach, arguments are inherently social, involving an author and an audience. They always have certain purpose(s) and make of debatable claims that the author presents as true or beneficial. In addition, they all provide reasons and evidence as support for their claims, though what counts as good evidence varies across fields and communities. And finally, arguments almost always rely on assumptions that may not be explicitly stated but that the audience must agree with in order to accept the argument. For example:

> *Claim*: Colleges should not rely on standardized tests for admission.
>
> *Reason*: Such tests are socioeconomically biased.
>
> *Evidence*: The disparity in test scores among various groups has been linked to cultural biases in the types of questions posed on such tests.
>
> *Assumption*: Questions that favor any group are inherently unfair.

Now let's consider four ways of approaching and structuring an argument: **CLASSICAL**, **TOULMIN**, **ROGERIAN**, and **INVITATIONAL**.

Classical Arguments

Originating in the ancient Greek law courts and later refined by Roman rhetoricians, the classical system of argumentation is still favored by writers in different fields. Throughout a classically structured argument, you'll rely on **ETHICAL**, **EMOTIONAL**, and **LOGICAL** appeals to your audience. Ethical appeals (those that build your credibility) are especially effective in the introduction, while logical and emotional appeals are useful anywhere.

The introduction engages the interest and attention of its audience by establishing the importance of the issue, establishing **COMMON GROUND** with the audience and showing how they are affected by the argument, and establishing the author's **CREDIBILITY**. To engage the audience, you might begin with an anecdote, ask a provocative question, or state the issue explicitly. Most writers taking a classical approach state the **CLAIM** in the introduction; students making an academic argument do so in an explicit **THESIS** statement.

The body of the argument provides any necessary background information, followed by **REASONS** and **EVIDENCE** in support of the claim. In addition, this section should make clear how the argument you're making is in the best interests of the audience. Finally, it should acknowledge possible **COUNTERARGUMENTS** and alternative points of view, presenting them fairly and respectfully and showing how your own argument is preferable.

The conclusion may summarize your argument, elaborate on its implications, and make clear what you want those in your audience to do in response. Just as it's important to open in a way that will engage their attention, you'll want to close with something that will make them remember your argument—and act on it in some way.

Let's suppose you've been assigned the topic of free speech on campus, and you believe that free speech must always be protected. That's a fairly broad topic, so eventually you decide to focus on the trend at many colleges to withdraw invitations to speakers holding controversial viewpoints. You might begin your introduction with a provocative statement, followed by some facts that will get your readers' attention (both ways of appealing to emotions) and culminating in a statement of your claim:

> Our most cherished American freedom is under attack—and not from abroad. On numerous campuses in recent years, an increasing number of invited speakers have been disinvited or driven to decline because various members of the campus community find it offensive to hear from people who hold beliefs or positions that they or others disagree with. However, true freedom of speech requires us to encounter ideas and even language we don't like, don't agree with, or find offensive. As students, we need to wrestle with ideas that challenge us, that make us think beyond our personal beliefs and experiences, and that educate us in and out of the classroom.

You might then introduce some background information about this issue, identifying points you'll develop later as support for your claim. Here you might note examples of disinvitation campaigns. Using specific examples will make your argument more credible:

> According to the Foundation for Individual Rights in Education (FIRE), 192 college campus speakers have been disinvited between 1999 and 2014, and most often conservative speakers. As noted by Isaac Chotiner in the New Republic, such campaigns indicate "rising levels of liberal intolerance, which is good for neither university campuses nor the truly shun-worthy people in our midst."

And then you might provide support for your claim by noting specific instances when invitations to speak have been withdrawn or speeches have been derailed by hecklers and giving reasons that free speech applies to everyone:

Former Secretary of State Condoleezza Rice, Director of the International Monetary Fund Christine Lagarde, New York Police Commissioner Ray Kelly, and former U.C. Berkeley Chancellor Robert Birgeneau: each was silenced by hecklers as they attempted to speak or even before they had the opportunity to speak on campus. If we accept only speakers whose political philosophies are ones no one would disagree with, free speech becomes "free only if you agree with me" speech. And then we may as well give up the notion of independent thought.

Acknowledging and responding to counterarguments or other viewpoints strengthens your argument by showing you to be well informed, fair, and open-minded:

> On the other hand, some resistance may well be justified, as when some students and faculty at Brown University protested a speech by Ray Kelly, arguing that it took such a "disruption" to have their voices heard.

And then in your conclusion you might reiterate the major points of your argument and rephrase your claim:

> We should strive to accept diverse voices and viewpoints on campus. Our conversations should challenge us to question our own long-held beliefs and closely examine those of others. We can do so only if we protect and truly embrace the right to freedom of speech—for one and all.

Toulmin Arguments

Philosopher Stephen Toulmin developed a detailed model for analyzing arguments, one that has been widely used for writing arguments as well.

The introduction presents a CLAIM, one that others will find debatable. If need be, you'll want to carefully QUALIFY this claim using words like *often* or *it may be* that limit your argument to one you'll be able to support.

The body of the argument presents good REASONS and EVIDENCE (which Toulmin calls "grounds") in support of the claim and explains any underlying assumptions (Toulmin calls these "warrants") that your audience needs to agree with in order to accept your argument. You may need to provide further evidence (which Toulmin calls "backing") to illustrate the assumptions. Finally, you'd acknowledge and respond to any **COUNTERARGUMENTS**.

The conclusion restates the argument as strongly and memorably as possible. You might conclude by discussing the implications of your argument, saying why it matters. And you'll want to be clear about what you want readers to think (or do).

For example:

> *Claim*: Our college should ban the smoking of e-cigarettes.
>
> *Qualification*: The ban should be limited to public places on campus.
>
> *Good reasons and evidence*: E-cigarettes contain some of the same toxins as cigarettes; research shows that they are a hazard to health.
>
> *Underlying assumptions*: Those who work and study here are entitled to protection from the harmful acts of others; the US Constitution calls for promoting "the general welfare" of all citizens.
>
> *Backing for the assumptions*: Other colleges and even some cities have banned e-cigarettes; highly respected public health advocates have testified about their ill effects.
>
> *Counterarguments*: E-cigarettes are less harmful than traditional cigarettes; smokers have rights too. However, this argument limits the ban to public spaces, which means smokers can still use e-cigarettes in their homes and other private places.
>
> *Conclusion*: Our school should ban the use of e-cigarettes in public places to protect the health of all who work and study here.

Now let's see how an argument about free speech on campus would work using Toulmin's model. You'd begin with your claim, carefully qualified if need be. The italicized words in the following example are qualifiers:

> To be successful as college students, to truly develop into independent thinkers, we need to wrestle with ideas that challenge us and that make us think beyond our personal beliefs and experiences, both in and out of the classroom. Such intellectual challenges are being diminished at *many* colleges as *some* on campus decide that ideas they or others disagree

with are more threatening than educational. On numerous campuses in recent years, a number of invited speakers have been disinvited or driven to decline because some on campus find it offensive to hear from those who hold beliefs different from theirs.

You would then follow that claim with the reasons and evidence that support your claim:

Education requires exposure to multiple points of view, at least according to Aristotle and Martin Luther King Jr. Aristotle notes in his Metaphysics that "It is the mark of an educated mind to be able to entertain a thought without accepting it." More than two thousand years later, King defined the purpose of education as enabling a person to "think incisively and to think for one's self . . . [and not to] let our mental life become invaded by legions of half truths, prejudices, and propaganda."

Then you would make clear the assumptions on which you base your claim:

Considering a variety of viewpoints is a hallmark of intelligent thinking. Freedom of speech is the right of every American.

And you'd add backing to support your assumptions:

Freedom of speech requires us to encounter ideas, language, or words we don't like, don't agree with, or find offensive. To truly protect our own right to free speech, we need to protect those rights for everyone.

Next you'd acknowledge and respond to counterarguments and other views, showing yourself to be well-informed, fair, and open-minded:

Sometimes, supporting free speech calls for just the kind of protests that have led to disinviting speakers. For example, students and faculty at Brown University protested a speech by New York Police Commissioner Ray Kelly, arguing that it took a disruption to have their voices heard.

Finally, in your conclusion you'd remind your readers of your claim, reiterate why it matters, and let them know what you want them to think or do.

Free speech is a bedrock value of American life. It's up to all of us to protect it—for ourselves as well as for others.

Rogerian Arguments

Noting that people are more likely to listen to you if you show that you are really listening to them, psychologist Carl Rogers developed a series of nonconfrontational strategies to help people involved in a dispute listen carefully and respectfully to one another. Rhetoricians Richard Young, Alton Becker, and Kenneth Pike developed an approach to argument based on Rogers's work as a way to resolve conflict by coming to understand alternative points of view. Rogerian argument aims to persuade by respectfully considering other positions, establishing **COMMON GROUND**, encouraging discussion and an open exchange of ideas, and seeking mutually beneficial compromise. Success depends on a willingness to listen and to try to understand where others are coming from.

The introduction identifies the issue and **DESCRIBES** it as fully and fairly as possible. It then acknowledges the various viewpoints on the issue, using nonjudgmental language to show that you respect the views of others.

The body of the argument discusses the various **POSITIONS** respectfully and in neutral language, presenting **REASONS** and **EVIDENCE** showing how each position might be acceptable in certain circumstances. Then state your own position, also using neutral language. You'll want to focus on the commonalities among the various positions—and if at all possible, show how those who hold other positions might benefit from the one you propose.

The conclusion proposes some kind of resolution, including a compromise if possible and demonstrating how it would benefit all parties.

Now let's take a look at how you'd approach the topic of free speech on campus using Rogerian methods. You could begin by identifying the issue, noting that there are a number of different viewpoints, and describing them respectfully:

> On many campuses today, reasonable people are becoming increasingly concerned about the unwillingness of some students and others to listen to people with viewpoints they disagree with—or even to let them speak. As Americans, we can all agree that our right to speak freely is guaranteed by the US Constitution. Yet this principle is being tested at

many colleges. Some say that controversial figures should not be invited to speak on campus; others have even argued that certain people who've been invited to speak should be disinivited.

Next you'd discuss each position, showing how it might be reasonable. Then explain your position, being careful to use neutral language and to avoid seeming to claim the moral high ground:

> Some speakers may bring messages based on untruths or lies or hate. If such speakers represent a threat to campus life and safety, it seems reasonable that they be disinvited or simply not invited in the first place. Others feel that speakers who hold extreme or radical positions— on either the right or the left—should not be invited to speak on our campuses. In some cases, this position might be justified, especially if the speaker's position is irrelevant to higher education. Except in such extreme circumstances, however, a very important part of a college education involves exposure to multiple points of view. Such great thinkers as Aristotle and Martin Luther King Jr. have expressed this better than I can: in the *Metaphysics*, Aristotle notes that "It is the mark of an educated mind to be able to entertain a thought without accepting it," and more than two thousand years later, King defined the purpose of education as enabling a person to "think incisively and to think for one's self."

Try to conclude by suggesting a compromise:

> Speakers who threaten campus life or safety may be best left uninvited. But while controversial figures may sometimes cause disruption, our community can learn from them even if we disagree with them. Rather than disinviting such speakers, let's invite discussion after they speak— and make it open to all of the interested parties.

Invitational Arguments

Feminist scholars Sonja Foss and Cindy Griffin have developed what they call "invitational" arguments, using an approach that aims to foster conversation instead of confrontation. Rather than trying to convince an audience to accept a position, invitational argument aims to get people to work together toward understanding. This approach begins with demonstrating to your audience that you understand and respect their position, setting the stage for discussion and collaboration in which all parties can benefit.

As you can see, invitational arguments have much in common with the Rogerian approach. One important difference, however, lies in the emphasis on openness and the focus on a shared goal. Rather than presenting the audience with a predetermined position that you then attempt to convince them to accept, an invitational argument starts out by assuming that both author and audience are open to changing their minds.

The introduction presents the topic, acknowledges that there are various **POSITIONS** and perspectives on it, and makes clear that the goal is to understand each viewpoint so that readers can decide what they think.

In the body of the argument, you'd **DESCRIBE** each perspective fairly and respectfully. If you can, **QUOTE** those who favor each viewpoint—a way of letting them speak for themselves.

The conclusion looks for **COMMON GROUND** among the various perspectives, calling on readers to consider each carefully before making up their minds.

Using an invitational approach to the subject of disinvitations and free speech on campus, you could begin by focusing on the complexity of the issue, noting the ways that well-meaning people can have strong differences of opinion but still aim for a common goal:

> On many campuses today, well-meaning people are increasingly concerned about a tendency to reject others' viewpoints out of hand, without even listening to them. This trend has led to such acts as disinviting speakers to campus or preventing them from speaking, once there. This issue might seem to pit freedom of speech against the right to resist speakers whose views may be harmful in certain ways. Yet looking only at this dichotomy ignores the many other possible perspectives people hold on this issue. The goal of this essay is to bring the major perspectives on free speech on campus together in order to understand each one thoroughly, to identify any common ground that exists among the perspectives, and to provide readers with the information they need to make informed decisions of their own.

Next, you would discuss each perspective fairly and openly, showing its strengths and weaknesses.

There seem to be at least four perspectives on the issue of free speech on our campus. First, there are those who believe that the principle of free speech is absolute and that anyone should be able to speak on any issue—period. A second perspective holds that free speech is "free" in context; that is, the right to free speech goes only so far and when it verges on harming others, it is "free" no more. Still a third perspective argues that universities must accept the role of "in loco parentis" and protect students from speech that is offensive, even if it potentially offends only a small group of students. Finally, some hold that universities are indeed responsible for maintaining a safe environment—physically, mentally, and emotionally—and that they can do so while still honoring free speech in most circumstances.

You could then look in detail at the four perspectives, allowing proponents of each to speak for themselves when possible (through quoted and cited passages) and exploring each respectfully and fairly. Following this discussion, you could identify any commonalities among the perspectives:

Each perspective on this issue has good intentions. Let us use that common ground as the starting point for further exploration, seeing if we can develop guidelines for protecting free speech on campus while also keeping our campus safe. It may well be that considering these perspectives carefully, honestly, and fairly will lead some to change their minds or to come together in certain areas of agreement. I hope that readers of this essay will do just that before taking a position on this issue.

REFLECT. Look for an argument you've read recently that caught your attention and re-read it with an eye for the argumentative strategies it uses. Does it use one particular approach—classical? Toulmin? Rogerian? invitational?—or does it mix strategies from more than one approach? Is the argument persuasive? If not, try revising it using strategies from one of these approaches.

MATTERS OF STYLE

An argument's style usually reinforces its message in as many ways as possible. The ancient Roman orator Cicero identified three basic styles, which he termed "high," "middle," and "low." Today, we can see a wider range of styles, from the highly formal language of US Supreme Court opinions to the informal style of everyday written communication such as memos and email, to the colloquial style of spoken language and the casual shorthand of texts and tweets.

You can learn a lot by looking closely at the stylistic choices in an argument—the use of individual words and figurative language, of personal pronouns (or not), of vivid images (verbal and visual), of design and format. In 2005, the *Los Angeles Times* announced an experiment it called its "Wikitorial," in which the newspaper cautiously invited readers to log on to its website and rewrite editorials:

> Plenty of skeptics are predicting embarrassment; like an arthritic old lady who takes to the dance floor, they say, the *Los Angeles Times* is more likely to break a hip than to be hip. We acknowledge that possibility.

The skeptics turned out to be right, and after three days the paper ended the experiment, saying:

> Unfortunately, we have had to remove this feature, at least temporarily, because a few readers were flooding the site with inappropriate material. Thanks and apologies to the thousands of people who logged on in the right spirit.

Savvy readers will be alert to the power of stylistic choices in these messages. The description of closing down "Wikitorial" as "unfortunate" and the equally careful choice of "a few readers," "flooding," and "inappropriate material" mark this as a formal and judicious message that stands in sharp contrast to the slightly self-deprecating style of the first announcement, with its casual use of "plenty of " and its play on "hip." How does the sober style of the second announcement influence your response? How different might your response be if the paper had declared, "We're pulling the plug on this page since a few creeps loaded it with a bunch of crap"?

Now let's look at a visual argument. The spoof ad on the next page was created by Adbusters, whose website identifies it as a "global network of artists, activists, writers, pranksters, students, educators and entrepreneurs" whose aim is "to topple existing power structures and forge a major shift in the way we will live in the twenty-first century." The ad satirizes the assumption that drugs can simply "wash your blues away," like laundry

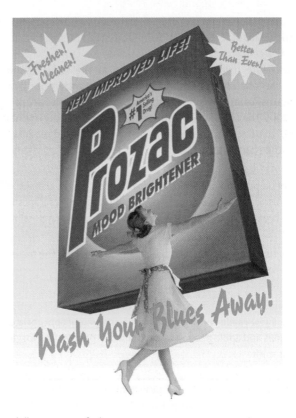

Adbusters spoof ad.

detergent. Note especially the retro style, which evokes the "happy house-wife" of the 1950s.

As an author, you will need to make such important stylistic choices, beginning—as is almost always the case—with the overall effect you want to create. Try to identify that overall effect in a word or phrase (for instance, concern, outrage, sympathy, or direct action), and then use it to help you choose specific words, images, and design elements that will create that effect and convey it most powerfully to your audience.

NINETEEN

Strategies for Supporting an Argument

RGUMENTS ARE ONLY AS STRONG as the evidence that supports them. Just as a house built on weak foundations is likely to crumble, so it is with arguments. As an author arguing a point, then, you will need to provide good, strong, reliable evidence to support your position. Ancient Greek rhetoricians developed strategies for finding such support, strategies that continue to serve us well today. This chapter introduces you to those strategies, arranged alphabetically from analogy to reiteration.

Analogy

Analogies are comparisons that point out similarities between things that are otherwise very different. Authors often use them to create vivid pictures in a reader's mind and make abstract ideas more concrete. Analogies can be especially powerful in an **ARGUMENT**, demonstrating that what is true in one case is true in another, usually more complicated, case. Here Annie Dillard draws an analogy between a writer's words and various tools:

> When you write, you lay out a line of words. The line of words is a miner's pick, a wood-carver's gouge, a surgeon's probe. You wield it, and it digs a path you follow. Soon you find yourself deep in new

territory. Is it a dead end, or have you located the real subject? You will
know tomorrow, or this time next year.

—ANNIE DILLARD, *A Writing Life*

Dillard uses this analogy to suggest that writers can use words as tools for
exploring a topic—to "probe" or "dig a path" into their subject.

Now see how Malala Yousafzai uses an analogy in a speech to the
United Nations to support her argument that education is the best means of
overcoming poverty and injustice:

> We will continue our journey to our destination of peace and education
> for everyone. No one can stop us. We will speak for our rights and we
> will bring change through our voice. We must believe in the power and
> the strength of our words. Our words can change the world because
> we are all together, united for the cause of education. And if we want
> to achieve our goal, then let us empower ourselves with the weapon of
> knowledge and let us shield ourselves with unity and togetherness.
>
> Dear brothers and sisters, we must not forget that millions of people
> are suffering from poverty, injustice, and ignorance. We must not forget
> that millions of children are out of schools. We must not forget that our
> sisters and brothers are waiting for a bright, peaceful future.

Malala Yousafzai addressing the United Nations in 2013.

> So let us wage a global struggle against illiteracy, poverty, and terror-
> ism and let us pick up our books and pens. They are our most powerful
> weapons.   —MALALA YOUSAFZAI, 2013 Speech at the United Nations

Yousafzai, a Pakistani activist for girls' education and Nobel Prize winner, builds her argument on an analogy that compares "the power and strength of our words" to the power of weapons used by the Taliban and others who would deny women education. She draws this analogy throughout her speech, calling upon us to use knowledge to "empower," unity to "shield," and books and pens to "wage a global struggle" against illiteracy, poverty, and terrorism. If these are our weapons, she says, then "no one can stop us." As an author, when you use an analogy, check to be sure it isn't a faulty analogy. In other words, compare things that are alike enough to support your claim; compare apples to apples, not apples to oranges.

Cause / Effect

When we analyze causes, we're trying to understand and explain why something happened. Why did the Virgin Galactic spaceship come apart in midair seconds after its launch? Why has there been so much extreme weather in recent years? Why did your chocolate chip cookies all run together on the cookie sheet? And when we think about effects, we speculate about what might happen. How will recent weather patterns affect crop yields? Will the cookies still run if you let the cookie sheet cool between batches?

Authors of **LITERARY NARRATIVES** could focus on teachers or books that caused them to love (or hate) reading, whereas someone writing a **PROPOSAL** may argue that a specific solution will have a particular effect. And in a **NARRATIVE**, you might use cause-and-effect reasoning to explain an event.

Arguing about causes and effects can be tricky, because often it's almost impossible to link a specific cause to one specific effect. That's why it took decades of research to establish a strong enough link between cigarette smoking and cancer to label tobacco products with a warning: researchers had to be able to discount many other possible causes. For the past several decades, astrophysicists have tried to photograph the black hole at the center of the Milky Way in order to test two dominant (but thought to be conflicting) theories of the nature of matter. Using data recently collected with an Event Horizon Telescope, they believe they will be able to support one theory or the other—or to reconcile the two.

Given the many variables involved, the researchers will likely discuss the behavior of the black hole in terms of *probable* or *possible* causes of observed phenomena. Claiming definite causes will take much longer, and it may never be possible to do so.

Exact effects are similarly difficult to determine. In 2014, the United Nations released a report on climate change, stating the possible environmental effects if we continue to burn fossil fuels. Notice how the report's authors qualify their statements by noting what effects greenhouse emissions "could" cause to happen:

- The risks of climate change could reverse years of progress against poverty and hunger if greenhouse emissions continue at their present pace.
- The emission of greenhouse gases could cause dangerous warming and long-lasting changes in the climate system, severely impacting people and ecosystems.
- Failure to reduce emissions . . . could cause food shortages, flooding of cities and even nations and a dangerous climate during the hottest times of the year.

— *Climate Change 2014: Synthesis Report*

A map showing Minard's analysis of Napoleon's failed invasion of Russia in 1812.

Often when you write about causes and effects, then, you can only argue that they are likely or probable, not proven. This is just one reason that you'll want to **QUALIFY** what you say: to add words like "might" or "should" that limit your claim.

Causal analysis can sometimes be easier to understand in a chart or graph than in words alone. See an especially famous example in the history of information graphics on the facing page, a map created in 1869. It depicts the horrific loss of life resulting from Napoleon's decision to march on Moscow in 1812. Its creator, Charles Joseph Minard, plotted information about troop numbers and locations, dates, direction and distances traveled, longitude and latitude, and the temperatures as soldiers retreated from Moscow. He used the width of the tan line to show the troops going into Russia (initially 680,000) and the much narrower black line to show those retreating (27,000). His causal argument was clear as he linked the dropping temperatures to the retreat: the colder the temperature, the fewer soldiers who survived.

Classification

When you classify, you group items into categories according to similarities. Tomatoes, for example, can be classified according to their varieties: cherry, plum, grape, heirloom, and so on. Authors frequently turn to classification in order to organize and elaborate on a topic. Writers of **REVIEWS** often use classification when focusing on more than one work, as Adam Gopnik does in evaluating a number of books about the internet by categorizing the authors into groups.

> The Never-Betters believe that we're on the brink of a new utopia, where information will be free and democratic, news will be made from the bottom up, love will reign, and cookies will bake themselves. The Better-Nevers think that we would have been better off if the whole thing had never happened, that the world that is coming to an end is superior to the one that is taking its place, and that, at a minimum, books and magazines create private space for minds in ways that twenty-second bursts of information don't. The Ever-Wasers insist that at any moment in modernity something like this is going on, and that a new way of organizing data and connecting users is always thrilling to some and chilling to others—that something like this is going on is exactly what makes it a modern moment. One's hopes rest with the Never-Betters; one's head

with the Ever-Wasers; and one's heart? Well, twenty or so books in, one's heart tends to move toward the Better-Nevers, and then bounce back toward someplace that looks more like home.

                    —ADAM GOPNIK, "How the Internet Gets Inside Us"

Classification is an essential feature of all websites, one that makes accessible the enormous amount of information available on a site. Take a look at the homepage on the National Weather Service site at weather.gov and you'll find various kinds of classification, starting with the horizontal menu bar at the top that categorizes the information on the site into commonly consulted topics: Forecast, Safety, News, and so on. Hovering your mouse over "Forecast" opens a drop-down menu that classifies forecasts into various categories: Aviation, Marine, Hurricanes, Fire Weather, and so on.

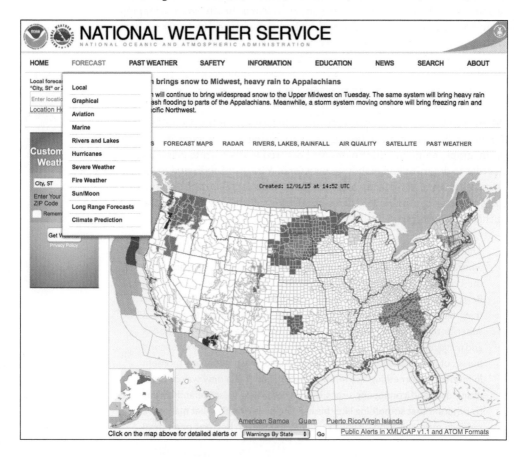

Comparison / Contrast

When you compare things, you focus on their similarities, and when you contrast them, you look at their differences. Both strategies can be very useful in developing an argument, helping to explain something that is unfamiliar by comparing (or contrasting) it with something more familiar. In a book **REVIEW**, for example, you might compare the Hunger Games trilogy to the Harry Potter series, or in a **REPORT** on Brexit, the prespectives of those who support it with those opposing it.

There are two ways you can organize a comparison: block and point by point. Using the *block* method, you present the subjects you're comparing one at a time, as in the following paragraphs:

> Most men, I believe, think of themselves as average-looking. Men will think this even if their faces cause heart failure in cattle at a range of 300 yards. Being average does not bother them; average is fine, for men. This is why men never ask anybody how they look. Their primary form of beauty care is to shave themselves, which is essentially the same form of beauty care that they give to their lawns. If, at the end of his four-minute daily beauty regimen, a man has managed to wipe most of the shaving cream out of his hair and is not bleeding too badly, he feels that he has done all he can, so he stops thinking about his appearance and devotes his mind to more critical issues, such as the Super Bowl.
>
> Women do not look at themselves this way. If I had to express, in three words, what I believe most women think about their appearance, those words would be: "not good enough." No matter how attractive a woman may appear to be to others, when she looks at herself in the mirror, she thinks: woof. She thinks that at any moment a municipal animal-control officer is going to throw a net over her and haul her off to the shelter.   —DAVE BARRY, "Beauty and the Beast"

Or you can organize your comparison *point by point*, discussing your subjects together, one point at a time, as David Sedaris does in the following paragraph comparing his own childhood in Raleigh, North Carolina, with that of his partner Hugh, a diplomat's son who grew up in Africa:

> Certain events are parallel, but compared with Hugh's, my childhood was unspeakably dull. When I was seven years old, my family moved to North Carolina. When he was seven years old, Hugh's family moved to the Congo. We had a collie and a house cat. They had a monkey and

two horses named Charlie Brown and Satan. I threw stones at stop signs. Hugh threw stones at crocodiles. The verbs are the same, but he definitely wins the prize when it comes to nouns and objects. An eventful day for my mother might have involved a trip to the dry cleaner or a conversation with the potato-chip deliveryman. Asked one ordinary Congo afternoon what she'd done with her day, Hugh's mother answered that she and a fellow member of the Ladies' Club had visited a leper colony on the outskirts of Kinshasa. No reason was given for the expedition, though chances are she was staking it out for a future field trip.

—DAVID SEDARIS, "Remembering My Childhood on the Continent of Africa"

Here's Ashley Highfield, managing director of Microsoft UK, drawing a comparison in a 2005 speech to the Royal Television Society of Britain to illuminate an argument that the "digital revolution is only just beginning":

I was reading an article the other day called "The Dangers of Wired Love," about a teenage girl called Maggie, who helped her dad run a newspaper stand in Brooklyn. Business was booming, so Maggie's dad, George McCutcheon, decided to get wired up, to help him process electronic orders. Being a total technophobe, Mr. McCutcheon got Maggie to operate the thing, but soon found out she was using it to flirt with a number of men, particularly one married man she had met online called Frank. Breaking all the known rules of cyber dating, she invited Frank to visit her in the real world, and of course he accepted. McCutcheon found out, went mad and forbade his daughter to meet up with Frank. But Maggie nevertheless continued to meet him in secret. Her furious father found out and one day followed her to one of the couple's rendezvous. He threatened to blow her brains out. She later had him arrested and charged with threatening behaviour.

An everyday story of modern times maybe? McCutcheon's fathering skills perhaps a bit severe, and Maggie perhaps a little naive? The striking thing about this story is that it was published in a magazine called *Electrical World* in 1886. The Victorian network that McCutcheon got wired to, and Maggie got hooked on, was of course the telegraph.

Those of us in technology like to think we're breaking new ground, that we're creating history through the latest revolution, when we're quite clearly not, as the very modern Maggie McCutcheon illustrates. The telegraph and the internet are perhaps more evolution than revolution: but in a way that means the seismic shifts in society that they cause creep up on us unnoticed. But these cycles of change come round again and again—and people tend to see them as momentous and more often than not scary.   —ASHLEY HIGHFIELD, "Why the Digital Revolution Is Only Just Beginning"

Comparisons of data can often be easier to understand in a chart or graph than in paragraphs. Why spend pages describing changes in demographics over the last fifty years, for example, when a bar graph can make the comparison in a half page? See how the graph below, from an article in the *Atlantic*, compares the number of college graduates in fourteen American cities, helping to support the article's argument that "America's educated elite is clustering in a few cities—and leaving the rest of the country behind."

The Uneven Fortunes of America's Cities

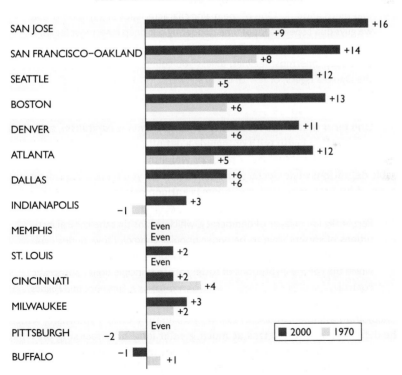

Number of college graduates per 100 people, relative to the national average.
        —RICHARD FLORIDA, "Where the Brains Are"

Definition

Definitions often lie at the heart of an argument: if readers don't agree with your definition of "the good life," for example, they aren't likely to take your advice on how to achieve one. As such, definitions themselves are rhetorical choices, especially in the case of controversial topics. Whether you're writing an **ANALYSIS**, a **REPORT**, or using some other genre, you'll often have reason to include definitions. Good definitions provide clear explanations of a word, concept, or idea, often by listing its characteristic features, noting distinguishing details, and perhaps providing an illustration as well. A good definition tells readers what something is—and sometimes what it is not.

In a humorous essay about what it means to be a guy, Dave Barry starts out by noting one thing that guys are not:

> And what, exactly, do I mean by "guys"? I don't know. I haven't thought that much about it. One of the major characteristics of guyhood is that we guys don't spend a lot of time pondering our deep innermost feelings. There is a serious question in my mind about whether most guys actually have deep innermost feelings, unless you count, for example, loyalty to the Detroit Tigers, or fear of bridal showers.
>
> —DAVE BARRY, "Guys vs. Men"

One term that is the focus of many arguments is *capitalism*, and such arguments often begin with or include a definition of the word. Here is linguist and social critic Noam Chomsky weighing in with brief but memorable definitions of *democracy* and *capitalism*. As you'll note, his definitions support his argument that capitalism is antidemocratic:

> Personally I'm in favor of democracy, which means that the central institutions of society have to be under popular control. Now, under capitalism, we can't have democracy by definition. Capitalism is a system in which the central institutions of society are in principle under autocratic control.
>
> —NOAM CHOMSKY, *Language and Politics*

Theologian Michael Novak takes a very different view of capitalism, which he defines in glowing terms at much greater length by focusing on what capitalism *does*, in a keynote address to an international conference on economies and nation-states in 2004:

Finally, capitalism instills in tradition-bound populations a new and in some respects a higher personal morality. It demands transparency and honest accounts. It insists upon the rule of law and strict observance of contracts. It teaches hard work, inventiveness, initiative, and a spirit of responsibility. It teaches patience with small gains, incremental but steady and insistent progress. During the 19th century, Great Britain achieved an average of one-and-a-half percent of GDP growth every year, with the happy result that the average income of the ordinary laborer in Britain quadrupled in a single century. The moral habits of invention, discovery, hard work, persistence, saving, investment, and moral seriousness brought about the single greatest transformation in the condition of the poor of all time—the greatest advances in hygiene, medicine, longevity, and physical well-being in all recorded history.

Capitalism brings in its train immense transformation, and the root of this transformation is moral. Those peoples and nations that neglect the moral ecology of their own cultures will not enjoy the fruits of such a transformation—or, having tasted them, will fall into rapid decline.

—MICHAEL NOVAK, "The Spirit of Capitalism"

Visuals can help in making arguments that hinge on definition. Below is a case in which the way the word *capitalism* is designed argues for yet another definition of that word. What argument(s) do you find in this illustration?

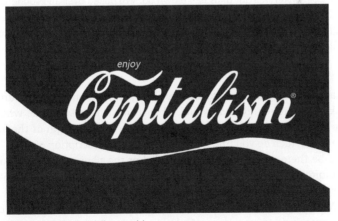

Image from *Daily Wallpapers* blog.

Description

When you describe something, you explain how it looks (or sounds, smells, tastes, or feels). Good descriptions focus on distinctive features and concrete details that add up to some **DOMINANT IMPRESSION** and help readers or listeners imagine what you are describing. You'll have occasion to use description in most of the writing you do—in a **PROFILE** of a neighborhood, you might describe the buildings and people; in a **NARRATIVE**, you'll likely describe people, places, and events.

In writing about atomic testing in Utah in her 1991 book *Refuge: An Unnatural History of Family and Place*, writer and activist Terry Tempest Williams uses description to set the scene for the facts she then presents about the high incidence of breast cancer there. She tells her father of a recurring dream she has, of a flash of light in the desert. Hearing this story, he has a sudden realization:

> "You did see it," he said.
> "Saw what?"
> "The bomb. The cloud. We were driving home from Riverside, California. You were sitting on [your mother's] lap. . . . In fact, I remember the day, September 7, 1957. We had just gotten out of the Service. We were driving north, past Las Vegas. It was an hour or so before dawn, when this explosion went off. We not only heard it, but felt it. I thought the oil tanker in front of us had blown up. We pulled over and suddenly, rising from the desert floor, we saw it, clearly, this golden-stemmed cloud, the mushroom. The sky seemed to vibrate with an eerie pink glow. Within a few minutes, a light ash was raining on the car."
> —TERRY TEMPEST WILLIAMS, "The Clan of One-Breasted Women"

Williams's description lets readers see the "golden-stemmed cloud" and feel the sky "vibrate"—and understand what it must have been like when the bomb exploded. Compare her description with a photograph of the atomic bomb test. Which do you find more powerful—the description of what it was like to be there when the bomb exploded or the photograph of the actual explosion? Would adding the photo have made Williams's description—and her argument—even more forceful?

Williams eventually testified before Congress about the effects of nuclear testing and has also worked as an environmental advocate. In 1995, aghast at a federal wilderness bill that would protect only a tiny fraction of

Utah's wilderness areas, she spoke at a public hearing. In this passage from an interview, see how her description of the hearing helps her make the case that the governmental officials were openly dismissive of her arguments:

> Congressman Jim Hansen and his colleagues sat on a riser above us. I remember how his glasses were perched on the end of his nose, how when I began to speak he was shuffling his papers, yawning, coughing, anything to show his boredom and displeasure. I was half-way through reading the citizens' testimonies—speaking on behalf of those who were at the Indian Walk-In Center the night before. He wasn't even listening—that was clear. Finally, I stopped mid-sentence and said something to the effect, "Congressman Hansen, I have been a resident of Utah all of my life. Is there anything I could say to you that will in some way alter your perspective so that you might consider wilderness in another way?"
>
> What I remember is how he leaned over his elbows and looked down on me over the tops of his glasses and said simply, "I'm sorry, Ms. Williams, there is something about your voice I cannot hear." It was chilling—personal. I don't think he was referring to the quality of the microphone. And then, it was over.
>
> —TERRY TEMPEST WILLIAMS, interview with David Sumner

Fiery mushroom cloud rising above Nevada atomic bomb test site, 1957.

Williams could have simply told us who said what and what was decided, but her description helps us picture the congressman "shuffling his papers" and "yawning," hear him "coughing," and sense "his boredom and displeasure."

Examples

If a picture is sometimes worth a thousand words, then a good example runs a close second: examples can make abstract ideas concrete and provide specific instances to back up a claim. See how novelist Gretel Ehrlich uses two examples to support her **ANALYSIS** of courage in a cowboy context:

> In a rancher's world, courage has less to do with facing danger than with acting spontaneously—usually on behalf of an animal or another rider. If a cow is stuck in a boghole, he throws a loop around her neck, takes his dally (a half hitch around the saddle horn), and pulls her out with horse-power. If a calf is born sick, he may take her home, warm her in front of the kitchen fire, and massage her legs until dawn.
>
> —GRETEL EHRLICH, "About Men"

You can sometimes draw on personal experience for powerful examples, provided that the experience you cite is pertinent to your point. In a commencement address to Stanford University's graduating class of 2005, Apple founder Steve Jobs used the example of his own experience with cancer in **ARGUING** that the graduates should make the most of every moment:

Steve Jobs

> About a year ago I was diagnosed with cancer. . . . The doctors told me this was almost certainly a type of cancer that is incurable, and that I should expect to live no longer than three to six months. My doctor advised me to go home and get my affairs in order, which is doctor's code for prepare to die. . . .
>
> I lived with that diagnosis all day. Later that evening I had a biopsy. . . . I was sedated, but my wife, who was there, told me that when they viewed the cells under a microscope the doctors started crying because it turned out to be a very rare form of pancreatic cancer that is curable with surgery. . . .

Your time is limited, so don't waste it living someone else's life. Don't be trapped by dogma—which is living with the results of other people's thinking. Don't let the noise of others' opinions drown out your own inner voice. And most important, have the courage to follow your heart and intuition. They somehow already know what you truly want to become. Everything else is secondary.

—STEVE JOBS, Stanford University commencement address

Examples can also be presented visually. See how the following *Twitter* post from someone who attended Fyre Festival includes a minimum of words but uses an image to show what the event really amounted to.

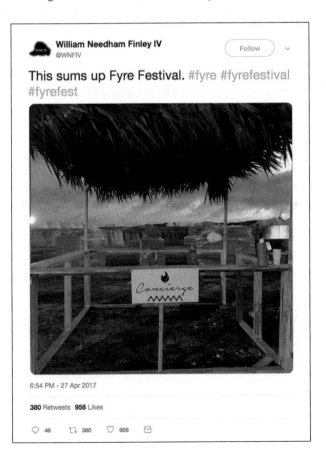

William Needham Finley IV
@WNFIV

Follow

This sums up Fyre Festival. #fyre #fyrefestival #fyrefest

Concierge

6:54 PM - 27 Apr 2017

380 Retweets **958** Likes

♡ 46   ↻ 380   ♡ 958   ✉

Humor

Comedian John Oliver uses humor to stake his claims. See an example by visiting everyones anauthor.tumblr .com.

Humor can often be used to good effect to support an argument—as long as the humor is appropriate to the context and audience. Of course, humor comes in many forms, from a self-deprecating story to a gentle parody or satire, from biting ridicule to a tired joke. While few of us are talented enough to write an argument based entirely on humor, it's possible to learn to use it judiciously. Doing so can help you to connect with your audience, provide some relief from a serious topic, or just vary the tone of your argument.

In today's world, however, you'll want to make sure that most members of your audience will understand the humor. Jokes are notoriously difficult to translate, and what's funny in one language rarely comes through the same way in another. Sometimes attempts to translate advertisements into various languages are a source of humor themselves, as when Kentucky Fried Chicken's "finger lickin' good" came out in Chinese as "eat your fingers off"! And cultural context can also determine if something will be funny at all—if it will fall flat, or worse, offend. For example, a story beginning "two cows walked into a bar" might seem like a humorous way to introduce an argument about overproduction of beef in the United States, but it probably wouldn't sit too well in India, where cows are sacred.

The late journalist Molly Ivins was famous for using humor in arguing serious positions. In the following interview on *Nightline*, Ivins is arguing in favor of gun regulation, but she uses humorous exaggeration—and a bit of real silliness—to help make her point:

> I think that's what we need: more people carrying weapons. I support the [concealed gun] legislation but I'd like to propose one small amendment. Everyone should be able to carry a concealed weapon. But everyone who carries a weapon should be required to wear one of those little beanies on their heads with a little propeller on it so the rest of us can see them coming.   —MOLLY IVINS

We're all familiar with the way cartoons use humor to make arguments—as in the one on the facing page, which argues that perhaps airport security has gone just a little overboard.

The 5th Wave By Rich Tennant

©RICHTENNANT

AIRPORT SECURITY

"They won't let me through security until I remove the bullets from my Word document."

The Onion is a satirical news website that regularly uses humor to make its arguments. This article makes an indirect argument that at too many colleges and universities, athletics outweigh academics:

SARASOTA, FL—Bowing to pressure from alumni, students, and a majority of teaching professors of Florida State University, athletic director Dave Hart Jr. announced yesterday that FSU would completely phase out all academic operations by the end of the 2010 school year in order to make athletics the school's No. 1 priority. "It's been clear for a while that Florida State's mission is to provide the young men and women enrolled here with a world-class football program, and this is the best way to cut the fat and really focus on making us No. 1 every year," Hart said. "While it's certainly possible for an academic subsidiary to bring a certain amount of prestige to an athletic program, the national polls have made it clear that our non-athletic operations have become a major distraction." FSU's restructuring program will begin with the elimination of the College of Arts and Sciences, effective October 15.

—*THE ONION*, "Florida State University to Phase Out Academic Operations"

Narration

A good story well-told can engage your audience and help to support an argument. Both writers and speakers use narratives often—in **REPORTS**, **MEMOIRS**, and many other genres. Be sure, however, that any story you tell supports your point and that it is not the only evidence you offer. In most academic contexts, you shouldn't rely only on stories to support an argument, especially personal stories.

In the following example, author Bich Minh Nguyen writes about her experiences becoming "the good immigrant student." In this essay, she uses narration to capture the tension she felt between wishing to fit in and wanting to rebel as well as to document the racist behavior she endured.

> More than once, I was given the assignment of writing a report about my family history. I loathed this task, for I was dreadfully aware that my history could not be faked: it already showed on my face. When my turn came to read out loud the teacher had to ask me several times to speak louder. Some kids, a few of them older, in different classes, took to pressing back the corners of their eyes with the heels of their palms while they chanted, "Ching-chong, ching-chong!" during recess. This continued until Anh [Nguyen's sister], who was far tougher than me, threatened to beat them up.
>
> I have no way of telling what tortured me more: the actual snickers and remarks and watchfulness of my classmates, or my own imagination, conjuring disdain. My own sense of shame. At times I felt sickened by my obedience, my accumulation of gold stickers, my every effort to be invisible.   —BICH MINH NGUYEN, "The Good Immigrant Student"

Advertisements use narrative to appeal to viewers, as in this ad campaign for animal adoption. With three frames and eight words, the cartoon below tells a story to make an argument.

Narrative is often used to **OPEN** an argument. A good story can get an audience's attention and make them interested in the argument that follows. In arguing for the need to take global warming seriously by rethinking our dependence on fossil fuels, Naomi Klein opens with this narrative:

> A voice came over the intercom: would the passengers of Flight 3935, scheduled to depart Washington, D.C., for Charleston, South Carolina, kindly collect their carry-on luggage and get off the plane.
>
> They went down the stairs and gathered on the hot tarmac. There they saw something unusual: the wheels of the US Airways jet had sunk into the black pavement as if it were wet cement. The wheels were lodged so deep, in fact, that the truck that came to tow the plane away couldn't pry it loose. . . . Someone posted a picture: "Why is my flight cancelled? Because DC is so damn hot that our plane sank 4 inches into the pavement." —NAOMI KLEIN, *Capitalism vs. the Climate*

Problem / Solution

Most **PROPOSALS** articulate a problem and then offer a solution that addresses that problem. The following passage from a National Institutes of Health press release sets out a clear problem (drinking among college students) and identifies three elements that must be addressed in any solution:

> The consequences of college drinking are larger and more destructive than commonly realized, according to a new study supported by the National Institute on Alcohol Abuse and Alcoholism (NIAAA). Commissioned by the NIAAA Task Force on College Drinking, the study reveals that drinking by college students age 18–24 contributes to an estimated 1,400 student deaths, 500,000 injuries, and 70,000 cases of sexual assault or date rape each year. It also estimates that more than one-fourth of college students that age have driven in the past year while under the influence of alcohol. . . .
>
> "Prevention strategies must simultaneously target three constituencies: the student population as a whole; the college and its surrounding environment; and the individual at-risk or alcohol-dependent drinker," says [task force co-chair Dr. Mark] Goldman. "Research strongly supports strategies that target each of these factors."
> —"College Drinking Hazardous to Campus Communities: Task Force Calls for Research-Based Prevention Programs"

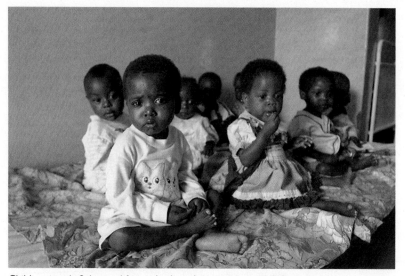

Children in sub-Saharan Africa who have lost parents to AIDS.

Often writers open with a statement of the problem, as Rhoi Wangila and Chinua Akukwe do in their article on HIV and AIDS in sub-Saharan Africa:

> Simply stated, Africans living with H.I.V./AIDS and the millions of others at high risk of contracting H.I.V. are not benefiting significantly from current domestic, regional, and international high profile remedial efforts.
>
> —RHOI WANGILA AND CHINUA AKUKWE,
> "H.I.V. and AIDS in Africa: Ten Lessons from the Field"

Wangila and Akukwe's article includes a photograph of African children affected by AIDS, which enhances their statement of the problem. The remainder of their essay then tackles the staggering complexities involved in responding to this problem.

Infographics are often used to present problems and solutions. Here's the final panel of an infographic that Chloe Colberg created about saving rhinos from illegal poaching. It identifies three ways of helping solve the problem: "get informed," "spread the word," and "support a campaign." The same information could be communicated in a paragraph or a bulleted list, but the large bold type makes the message much more visible.

What can you do to make a difference?
There are a number of different ways to get involved.

1

GET INFORMED

Continue to educate yourself on this issue. Visit the WWF website to learn more specifics and details about the rhino crisis.

2

SPREAD THE WORD

The more people that know about this issue, the better! Let your colleagues, friends and families know about this serious problem.

3

SUPPORT A CAMPAIGN

Support the WWF and other organizations' campaigns by learning about their efforts and considering a financial contribution.

SOURCES:
http://www.bbc.co.uk/news/uk-england-11477508
http://www.cites.org/eng/news/pr/2013/20131106_forensics.php
http://www.savetherhino.org/rhino_info/poaching_statistics
http://www.savetherhino.org/rhino_info/thorny_issues/
http://www.worldwildlife.org/species/rhino

DESIGNED FOR:
World Wildlife Fund
Chloe Colberg
December 2013

Reiteration

A form of repetition, reiteration helps support an argument through emphasis: like a drumbeat, the repetition of a keyword, phrase, image, or theme can help drive home a point, often in very memorable ways. Reiterating is especially powerful in presentations and other spoken texts—think "Yes, we can!" and Sojourner Truth's "Ain't I a Woman?" Martin Luther King Jr. was a master of effective repetition, as is evident in the famous speech he delivered on the steps of the Lincoln Memorial in 1963. Just think for a moment what would be lost in this speech without the power of that repeated phrase, "I have a dream."

> I have a dream that one day this nation will rise up and live out the true meaning of its creed: "We hold these truths to be self-evident, that all men are created equal." I have a dream that one day on the red hills of Georgia, the sons of former slaves and the sons of former slave owners will be able to sit down together at the table of brotherhood. I have

a dream that one day even the state of Mississippi, a state sweltering with the heat of injustice, sweltering with the heat of oppression, will be transformed into an oasis of freedom and justice. I have a dream that my four little children will one day live in a nation where they will not be judged by the color of their skin but by the content of their character.

I have a dream today!

I have a dream that one day, down in Alabama, with its vicious racists, with its governor having his lips dripping with the words of "interposition" and "nullification"—one day right there in Alabama little black boys and black girls will be able to join hands with little white boys and white girls as sisters and brothers.

I have a *dream* today!

I have a dream that one day every valley shall be exalted, and every hill and mountain shall be made low, the rough places will be made plain, and the crooked places will be made straight; "and the glory of the Lord shall be revealed and all flesh shall see it together."

This is our hope, and this is the faith that I go back to the South with.

—MARTIN LUTHER KING JR., "I Have a Dream"

Reiteration also works in visual texts and is a hallmark of graphic novelist Marjane Satrapi's work. Born and raised in Iran before being sent abroad in 1984 to escape what became the country's Islamic revolution, Satrapi recounts her childhood in *Persepolis I*, arguing implicitly that repressive regimes squelch individuality. In the frame shown here, Satrapi depicts a class of female students, using reiteration to make her point: all these girls are dressed exactly the same.

Part of a frame from *Persepolis*.

A little reiteration can go a long way. In an article published in *Ebony* magazine about the future of Chicago, see how it drives an argument that Chicago is still a home of black innovation and creativity:

> [Chicago]'s the place where organized Black history was born, where gospel music was born, where jazz and the blues were reborn, where the Beatles and the Rolling Stones went up to the mountaintop to get the new musical commandments from Chuck Berry and the rock 'n' roll apostles.   —LERONE BENNETT JR., "Blacks in Chicago"

Here the reiteration of "where" and the parallel clauses help establish a rhythm of forward movement that drives the argument.

REFLECT. Choose an example in this chapter that's all words. Think about whether the same argument could be made visually—in a chart, with a photo and caption, and so on. If that doesn't seem possible, how might you illustrate the example?

PART VI

Research

RESEARCH IS AN EVERYDAY MATTER. You gather information from reliable sources all the time to help you make decisions, support arguments, solve problems, become more informed, and for a host of other reasons. Filling out a March Madness basketball bracket? You probably review team records, player profiles, and statistics to help decide which teams you think will win. Going out for dinner and a movie? You probably look up reviews on *Yelp* and the *Internet Movie Database* before deciding where to go. Need directions to the theater? Arguing that this film is better and more critically acclaimed than another? In each case you'd probably do some research—to know what route to take, to locate information, to support an argument. Research helps you do all those things, and you do them all the time.

When you do research, you engage in a process of inquiry: that is, you are guided by questions for which you want answers. You might use a variety of methods—fieldwork, lab experiments, *Google* searches; and you'll find information in a variety of sources—books, articles, news reports, databases, websites, letters, photographs, historical records. However you approach it, research is more than simply a matter of compiling information; the most meaningful research is a process of discovery and learning.

As a student, you'll engage in research in many of the courses you take and in a variety of disciplines. Research is likely to be part of your work life as well. People working in business, government, and industry all need to follow research in order to make important decisions and keep up with new developments in their fields. Restaurant owners need to do research, for instance, to discover how to maximize profits from menu options and portion sizes. Engineers constantly do research to find equipment and suppliers. When a group of US senators argued for a federal ban on texting while driving, they cited research from a Virginia Tech study as evidence showing the dangers of allowing distracted drivers on the road.

Artists too rely on research for inspiration and also to gather information and materials to use in their artwork. As photographer Laurie Simmons said, "Artists are always doing research on their own behalf and for their work. For some artists, it's reading. For some, it's shopping. For some, it's traveling. And I think that there's always this kind of seeking quality that artists have where they're looking for things that will jog them and move them in one direction or another."

When you do academic research, you'll likely be studying a topic that scholars before you have examined. You'll want to start by learning what has been written about your topic and then thinking carefully about questions you want to pursue. In this way, you'll be engaging with the ideas of others and participating in discussions about topics that matter—and adding your own insights and discoveries. You'll be joining the larger academic conversation. The following chapters can help you do so.

REFLECT. Think about questions you've had in the past few weeks that have led you to do research to find an answer. List the different kinds of information you've sought and the ways you went about finding it. How did you then use the information or data that you gathered?

TWENTY

Starting Your Research

Joining the Conversation

HAT DO YOU FIND MOST DIFFCULT about doing research? Gathering data? Writing it up? Documenting sources? For most students, the hardest part is just getting started. Researchers from Project Information Literacy, a nonprofit research institute conducting ongoing national studies of college learning practices in the digital age, report that US students doing course-related research have the most difficulty with three things: getting started, defining a topic, and narrowing a topic. This chapter will help you tackle these tricky first steps, identify specific questions that will drive your research, and make a schedule to manage the many tasks involved in a research project.

At the same time, we aim to show you that doing research means more than just finding sources. College-level research is a discovery process: it's as much about the search for knowledge and answers as it is about managing sources. When we search, we go down expected and unexpected paths to answer interesting questions, to discover solutions to problems, and to come to new perspectives on old issues. Doing research means learning about something you want to know more about. It means finding out what's been said about that topic, listening to the variety of perspectives (including those that differ from your own)—and then adding your own ideas to that larger conversation when you write about that topic.

While this chapter suggests a sequence of activities for doing research, from finding a topic to coming up with a research question to establishing a schedule, keep in mind that you won't necessarily move through these stages in a fixed order. As you learn more about your topic, you may want to reexamine or change your focus. But first, you have to get started.

Find a Topic That Fascinates You

At its best, research begins as a kind of treasure hunt, an opportunity for you to investigate a subject that you care or wonder about. So finding that topic might be the single most important part of the process.

If you've been assigned a topic, study the instructions carefully so that you understand exactly what you are required to do. Does the assignment give you a list of specific topics to choose from or a general topic or theme to address? Does it specify the research methods? number and kinds of sources? a GENRE in which to write up your findings? Even if you've been assigned a particular topic and told how to go about researching it, you'll still need to decide what aspect of the topic you'll focus on. Consider the following assignment:

> Identify a current language issue that's being discussed and debated nationally or in your local community. Learn as much as you can about this issue by consulting reliable print and online sources. You may also want to interview experts on the issue. Then write a 5- to 7-page informative essay following MLA documentation style. And remember, your task is to report on the issue, not to pick one side over others.

This assignment identifies a genre (a report), research methods (interviews and published sources), a documentation style (MLA), and a general topic (a current language issue), but it leaves the specific issue up to the author. You might investigate how your local school district handles bilingual education for immigrants, for example, or you could research the debate about how texting and social media affect writing habits.

While this particular assignment is broad enough to allow you to choose a particular issue that interests you, even assignments that are more specific can be approached in a way that will make them interesting to you.

Is there some aspect of the topic related to your major that you'd like to look into? For example, a political science major might research court cases about the issue.

If you get to choose your topic, think of it as an opportunity to learn about something that intrigues you. Consider topics related to your major, or to personal or professional interests. Are you a hunter who is concerned about legislation that impacts gun rights in your hometown? Are you into binge-watching *Netflix* or *Hulu* shows, but frustrated by streaming services' restrictions and limitations so you want to learn why and how they operate? Maybe you're an environmentalist interested in your state's policies on fracking.

    In addition to finding a topic that interests you, try to pick one that has not been overdone. Chances are, if you're tired of hearing about an issue—and if you've heard the same things said repeatedly—it's not going to be a good topic to research. Instead, pick a topic that is still being debated: the fact that people are talking about it will ensure that it's something others care about as well.

    Think about doing research as an invitation to explore a topic that really matters to you. If you're excited about your topic, that excitement will take you somewhere interesting and lead you to ideas that will in turn inform what you know and think.

> ↪ For ideas and inspiration, visit TED.com, a site devoted to "ideas worth spreading." While there, check out Steven Johnson's talk, "Where Good Ideas Come From."

Consider Your Rhetorical Situation

As you get started, think about your rhetorical situation, starting with the requirements of the assignment. You may not yet know your genre, and you surely won't know your stance, but thinking about those things now will help you when you're narrowing your topic and figuring out a research question.

- **AUDIENCE**. Who will be reading what you write? What expectations might they have, and what are they likely to know about your topic? What kinds of sources will they consider credible?

- **PURPOSE**. What do you hope to accomplish by doing this research? Are you trying to report on the topic? argue a position? analyze the causes of something? something else?

- **GENRE**. Have you been assigned to write in a particular genre? Will you **ARGUE A POSITION**? **NARRATE** a historical event? **ANALYZE** some kind of data? **REPORT** information? something else?

- **STANCE**. What is your attitude toward the topic—and toward your audience? How can you establish your authority with them, and how do you want them to see you? As a neutral researcher? an advocate for a cause? something else? Check your biases—is **CONFIRMATION** or **ATTRIBUTION BIAS** keeping you from considering all sides fairly?

- **CONTEXT**. Does the assignment have any length requirements? When is the due date? What other research has been done on your topic, and how does that affect the direction your research takes?

- **MEDIA**. Are you required to use a certain medium? If not, what media will be most appropriate for your audience, your topic, and what you have to say about it? Will you want or need to include links to other information? audio? video?

- **DESIGN**. Will you include photographs or other illustrations? present any data in charts or graphs? highlight any parts of the text? use headings or lists? Are you working in a discipline with specific format requirements?

Don't worry if you can't answer all of these questions at this point or if some elements change along the way. Just remember to keep these questions in mind as you work.

Narrow Your Topic

A good academic research topic needs to be substantive enough that you can find adequate information but not so broad that you become overwhelmed by the number of sources you find. The topic "women in sports," for example, is too general; a quick search on *Google* will display hundreds of subtopics, from "Title IX" to "women's sports injuries." One way to find an aspect of a topic that interests you is to scan the subtopics listed in online search results. Additionally, online news sites like *Google News* and *NPR Research News* can give you a sense of current conversations related to your topic. Your goal is to move from a too-general topic to a manageable one, as shown on the facing page:

General topic: women in sports

Narrower topic: injuries among women athletes

Still narrower: injuries among women basketball players

Even narrower: patterns of injuries among collegiate women basketball players compared with their male counterparts

Notice how the movement from a broad topic to one with a much narrower focus makes the number of sources you will consult more manageable. But just as a topic that is too broad will yield an overwhelming number of sources, one that is too narrow will yield too little information. The topic "shin splints among women basketball players at the University of Tennessee," for example, is so narrow that there is probably not enough information available.

Another way of narrowing a topic is to think about what you already know. Have you had any experiences related to your topic? read about it? heard about it? talked with friends about it? Suppose you have been asked to investigate a current health debate for a public health class. You think of the US opioid crisis that's affected families in your hometown. Maybe you've seen news stories in which doctors explained the positive pain management provided by opioids but caution about the addiction potential, while law enforcement officials and the families of people who suffer from addiction attest to the human cost. These are all things that can help you to narrow a topic.

Whatever your topic, write down what you know about it and what you think. Do some **BRAINSTORMING** or some of the other activities for **GENERATING IDEAS**. And if it's an issue that's being debated, you could search online to find out what's being said—just be sure to analyze what you find to ensure it's not **MISINFORMATION**. Exploring your topic in this way can give you an overview of the issue and help you find a focus that you'd like to pursue.

REFLECT. Review your research assignment. Make a list of three topics that you're considering and jot down what you already know about each. Review those notes. What do they suggest to you about your interest in these topics? Finally, narrow each one to a specific, manageable research topic. Which of the three now seems most promising?

Do Some Background Research

Becoming familiar with some existing research on your topic can provide valuable background information and give you an overview of the topic before you dive into more specialized sources. It can also help you discover issues that have not been researched—or perhaps even identified. At this point, your goal should be to see your topic in a larger context and to begin formulating questions to guide the rest of your research.

You may want to take a look at some encyclopedias, almanacs, and other **REFERENCE WORKS**, which can provide an overview of your topic and point you toward specific areas where you might want to follow up. Subject-specific encyclopedias provide more detail, including information about scholarly books to check out.

If you don't have access to a university library, see what information you can find online. Though free online encyclopedias such as *Wikipedia* may not be considered appropriate to cite as authoritative sources, such sites can be helpful in the early stages of research because they link to additional sources and will often summarize any controversies around a topic.

Finally, you might begin your background research by reading articles in popular newsmagazines or newspapers to get a sense of who's talking about the topic and what they're saying.

Articulate a Question Your Research Will Answer

Once you have sufficiently narrowed your topic, you will need to turn it into a question that will guide your research. Start by asking yourself what you'd like to know about your topic. A good research question should be simple and focused, but require more than a "yes" or "no" answer. "Yes" or "no" questions are not likely to lead you anywhere—and often obscure the complexity of an issue. Instead, ask an open-ended question that will lead you to gather more information and explore multiple perspectives on your topic. For example:

Topic: injuries among women soccer players

What you'd like to know: What are the current trends in injuries among women soccer players, and how are athletic trainers responding?

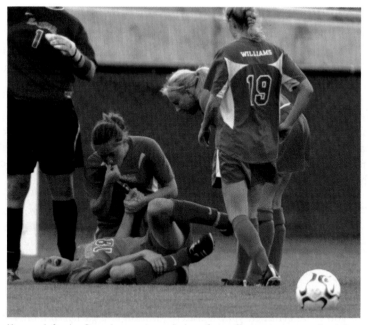

Kansas defender Stacy Leeper is tended to after suffering a game-ending injury.

This is a question that's focused, complex, and meaningful. Before settling on a research question, you should consider why the answer to that question matters. Why is it worth looking into and writing about? And why will others want to read about it? Answering the above question, for instance, can help athletic trainers see if their approach can be improved.

Keep your rhetorical **CONTEXT** in mind as you work to be sure your research question is manageable in the time you have and narrow or open enough to address in the number of pages you plan to write. Consider also any **GENRE** requirements. If you're assigned to argue a position, for example, be sure your research question is one that will lead to an argument. Notice how each question below suggests a different genre:

A question that would lead to a **REPORT**: What are the current trends in injuries among women soccer players?

A question that would lead to an **ANALYSIS** : Why do women soccer players suffer specific types of injuries during training?

A question that would lead to an **ARGUMENT** : At what age should young girls interested in soccer begin serious athletic training to minimize the chance of injury?

Once you've settled on a research question, your next step is to do some more research. Keeping your question in mind will help you stay focused. Your goal at this point is to look for possible answers to your question—to get a sense of the various perspectives on the issue and to start thinking about where you yourself stand.

REFLECT. Write a research question for your narrowed topic that would lead to a report, one that would lead to an analysis, and one that would lead to an argument. Remember, try to avoid "yes" or "no" questions.

Plot Out a Working Thesis

Once you've determined your research question and gathered more information, you should begin to think about what answers are emerging—in sources you consult and in your own mind. When you think you've found the best possible answer, the next step is to turn it into a working thesis. Basically, a working thesis is your hypothesis, your best guess about the claim you will make based on your research thus far.

Your working thesis will not necessarily be your final thesis. As you conduct more research, you may find more support for it or new information that prompts you to rethink your position. Consider one working thesis on the question about why women soccer players experience so many injuries during training:

> Female soccer players sustain more injuries than their male counterparts during training because they use training methods that were developed for men; developing training methods to suit female physiology would reduce the incidence of injuries.

This working thesis makes a clear, arguable claim and provides reasons for that position.

Keep in mind that your working thesis may well change as you learn more about your topic; stay flexible—and expect to revise it as your ideas develop. The more open your mind, the more you'll learn.

Establish a Schedule

A research project can seem daunting if you think of it as one big undertaking, rather than as a series of gradual tasks. Establishing a schedule will help you break your research into manageable steps, stay organized, and focus on the task at hand. The following template can help you make a plan:

Working title:

Working thesis:

	Due date
Choose a topic.	_____
Analyze your rhetorical situation.	_____
Do some preliminary research.	_____
Narrow your topic and decide on a research question.	_____
Plot out a working thesis.	_____
Do library and web research.	_____
Start a working bibliography.	_____
Turn in your research proposal and annotated bibliography.	_____
Plan and schedule any field research.	_____
Do any field research.	_____
Draft a thesis statement.	_____
Write out a draft.	_____
Get response.	_____
Do additional research, if needed.	_____
Revise.	_____
Prepare your list of works cited.	_____
Edit.	_____
Write your final draft.	_____
Proofread.	_____
Turn in the final draft.	_____

TWENTY-ONE

Finding Sources

Online, at the Library, in the Field

IF YOU'VE SEEN *The Amazing Race*, a reality show that sends teams of contestants to overcome challenges as they race around the world, then you know what has kept it winning Emmys for more than a decade. Each season, we see the teams learning about cultural traditions in small Italian villages, famous art in German museums, and social practices in little-known regions of the world—all during their wild race to the finish line.

What we don't see is the research on those locations and cultures conducted by the 2,000 crew members who explore potential sites, interview residents and town officials, read histories, pore over maps, and seek information from as many sources as they can before sending the contestants out on their quests.

Like the *Amazing Race* crew, student researchers today have access to a vast number of resources. And with so much information out there, housed in libraries, archives, museums, and online, you too face the challenge of sifting through a lot of information to find the sources you're looking for. A daunting task, perhaps, but much like finding your way to an unfamiliar location, finding sources is a process of exploration that will lead to new discoveries.

Luckily, you have access to a number of resources to ease the journey.

This chapter will teach you how to use these resources, from library catalogs and reference works to online search engines and social media as research tools. The following sections introduce you to different types of sources by explaining what's out there, where to find it, how to access it, and how to use it. Finally, this chapter teaches methods of conducting field research firsthand, for examining uncharted territory.

Starting with *Wikipedia* or Social Media

You've probably been told you must use reliable sources, and you may have been steered away from *Wikipedia* or *Google*. But today, these and other casual sources like *YouTube* can offer good starting points for your research. Indeed, you might even begin with social media. Of course, whenever you use online sources like these, it's crucial to read defensively—checking out the information you find to be sure it's trustworthy.

One student we know saw a *YouTube* review of a video game developed by Native Alaskans. Curious, she googled the game and found links to information about its origins and artwork, along with a statement about the purpose of the project: "We want to take back our culture out of the museum . . . to share who we are with the world." This statement got our student thinking about how Native Alaskans were representing their own culture in this game compared to how museums were representing it in exhibitions. So she searched the internet for more information about the game, visited her campus library for books and articles on Native Alaskan culture, and perused museum websites to investigate their presentation of it. She checked out her sources along the way, especially those turned up by *Google* searches. A *YouTube* video led this student all the way to the Smithsonian! That's how research often develops: curiosity and the questions that grow out of it lead to valuable and relevant sources.

As this example also demonstrates, the questions that emerge as you examine sources will determine the kinds of information you will seek out. Do you need to learn the history of a group of people or an event? Do you need to research different perspectives on an issue? Do you need statistical data? personal narratives? Once you've determined the types of information that will best address your questions, you will need to figure out where to find this information—what sources you will need to locate or what studies you will need to conduct.

WHAT KIND OF SOURCES DO YOU NEED?

The decisions you make about what types of sources you seek, where you look for them, and how authoritative you need them to be will be guided not only by the requirements of your assignment, but also by your **PUR-POSE**, **AUDIENCE**, and other elements of the **RHETORICAL SITUATION**. For the research you do in college, an important part of that rhetorical situation may be the discipline you are working in; for example, scientists tend to value research done through observation and experimentation whereas historians tend to value research done in libraries and archives.

You may not always be able to anticipate who will read your writing, especially if you're posting online, but you can analyze other aspects of your rhetorical situation to determine what types of sources you'll need. For instance, if your purpose is to convince voters of a political candidate's honesty, what information will be most persuasive and where will you find it? If you're writing about this candidate for a website, what kinds of sources do other writers cite on that site? Who's the site's primary audience? Will you find what you need in the library, online, or will you need to go out and talk to voters? Or will you need to use a variety of sources?

For academic research, you'll also want to keep several other distinctions in mind: the differences between primary and secondary sources, scholarly and popular sources, and older and more current sources.

Primary and secondary sources. Primary sources are original documents or materials, firsthand accounts, or field research like interviews or observations. Secondary sources are texts that analyze and interpret primary sources; they offer background and context that can help you gain perspective on your topic. Secondary sources on a subject might include scholarly books and journal articles about the topic, magazine and newspaper reviews, government research reports, or annotated bibliographies. The student who researched the video game that drew on Native Alaskan culture conducted primary research when she analyzed the game itself and secondary research when she turned to articles about the game's development and books about the politics surrounding the representation of Native Alaskans.

Whether a particular source is considered primary or secondary often depends on what the topic is. If you are analyzing an artistic work, say a film, then the film itself is a primary source, while A. O. Scott's review of the

Research sources vary by topic and discipline: interviews, observations (both in the outdoors and in the lab), library databases and printed resources, and archives can all prove valuable to your research project.

film is a secondary source. But if you are researching Scott's work as a critic, then his review would be a primary source.

Scholarly and popular sources. For most academic assignments, you'll want to consult scholarly sources: articles, books, conference papers, and websites written by authorities in a given field. Such sources have usually been peer-reviewed, evaluated by experts in the field before publication. Because they are written for a knowledgeable audience, scholarly texts go into more depth than popular sources do, citing research and including detailed documentation.

Popular sources, by contrast, are written by journalists and writers for a general audience. They may be fact-checked, but they are not likely to be evaluated by experts before publication. Popular magazine articles and websites can play an important role at the start of a research project. Popular magazines can be a good source of information on current issues since they're published so frequently. Like scholarly sources, they often cite research, but rarely do they document those citations. Make sure that any such sources you use serve your subject and purpose. If, for instance, you're writing about fashion, *Vogue* might be a useful source—but its brief reviews of new books would not be appropriate sources in a literary analysis.

DETERMINING IF A SOURCE IS SCHOLARLY

- *What are the author's credentials* to write on the topic? Look authors up to confirm they are who they say they are.

- *Who's the publisher or sponsor?* Look for academic presses, professional or academic organizations, or government sources. And see what others say about the source to ensure it's legitimate.

- *What's the URL,* if it's an online source? Colleges and universities use *edu,* and government agencies use *gov.*

- *Does the source include original research* or interpret research by others that it cites?

- *Does it provide documentation?* Look for a list of works cited or references at the end and parenthetical documentation within the text. Check out a few cited sources to see that they're reputable.

- *Does the text seem authoritative?* Most scholarly texts use **FORMAL** language and provide evidence that shows the author can be trusted.

- *Does the text* look *academic?* Scholarly texts tend to use conservative fonts and often include tables and charts. Popular texts are more likely to include color photos and to highlight certain things in sidebars.

- *Are there ads?* Scholarly texts have few, if any, ads; popular articles and sites have many ads.

Considering these questions can help you distinguish between sources such as the two on the following page, one from the popular magazine *National Geographic*, the other from the scholarly *American Journal of Human Genetics*. While both sources address the legacy of Genghis Khan, note the differences in focus and design. Famous for its photographs, *National Geographic* displays on its cover a striking image of the Khan's face; the article's first pages feature large and colorful photographs, and the typography and layout include some decorative elements. The visuals attract readers' attention. In contrast, the journal's cover includes only its name (which tells us it's a *journal*) and publication information and a picture of a former president of the American Society of Human Genetics. The article looks like serious scholarship; the first page includes its genre (report), its title ("The Genetic Legacy of the Mongols"), the authors' names and credentials, and an abstract.

While the questions above can help you judge whether a source is scholarly and appropriate for your research project, keep in mind that some sources are designed to look, act, and feel scholarly, but aren't. You'll need to be vigilant about checking out all the sources you consult—even those that seem scholarly—to ensure you aren't relying on **MISINFORMATION**. For example, some predatory publishers pose as legitimate even while they publish anything someone pays to have published—without conducting any peer review. These predatory journals have names, websites, and published works that look and seem scholarly. **READING DEFENSIVELY** by checking out what others say about the source will help you steer clear of these unreliable sources.

Older and more current sources. You will need to determine whether older or more current sources are most appropriate for your topic, purpose, and

Popular source

Scholarly source

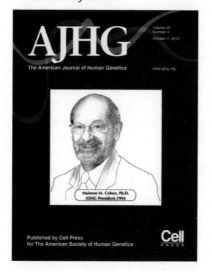

audience. Although you will always want to investigate the latest news and research about your topic, sometimes older works will serve as sources of essential information. Your research question and your discipline may dictate the balance between using older or more current sources. In scientific and technological fields, the most current scholarly sources are usually favored, since change is occurring so rapidly, while in history or literature, older sources that have stood the test of time may offer the best and most appropriate information.

Remember that your professors may expect—or require—certain kinds of sources. They may, for instance, want you to use only scholarly books and articles. Most projects, however, call for information drawn from many types of sources. For a report on the impact of recent floods on small local farms, for example, you may need to conduct primary research by interviewing local farmers affected; carry out secondary research online for news reports, photographs, and videos that document the floods; and use library sources to document flood conditions in the past.

TYPES OF SOURCES—AND WHERE TO FIND THEM

Reference Works

General reference sources include general encyclopedias (*Encyclopaedia Britannica, Columbia Encyclopedia*), dictionaries (*Merriam-Webster's, Oxford English Dictionary*), almanacs (*The World Almanac and Book of Facts*), and atlases (*The National Atlas of Canada*), among others. Besides brief overviews of your topic, such sources can be helpful for gathering background information, defining core concepts and terms, and understanding the larger context of your topic—or narrowing it if need be—as well as for getting leads to more specific sources. Your library may have print versions of some of these resources and online subscriptions to others. Still other dictionaries and encyclopedias, such as *Wikipedia*, are online only and free to access.

Specialized encyclopedias and wikis can give information that is more specifically related to your topic or discipline than general reference works. Through your library or the library website you'll find subject-specific resources ranging from the *Encyclopedia of Ethics* to the *Encyclopedia Latina* and many more. Specialized wikis put similar information online in groups of pages about health and medicine, or philosophy, or comic book superheroes of the Marvel universe. Wikis can connect you to information and communities online, but keep in mind that their open, collaborative authoring policy means that anyone can edit the information on a page.

So be sure to evaluate the source carefully and use the information only as a starting point.

Bibliographies, also called references or works cited, are lists of publications that appear at the end of books or scholarly articles and can lead you to further sources on a topic. If you've located a useful source, check its bibliography to find additional sources related to your topic. Your library may also have compiled longer, standalone bibliographies for popular or widely researched subjects; ask your librarian about availability. Many bibliographies also include descriptive annotations for sources that can help you determine if a source will be useful to you.

Books

If you're looking for a print book, the first place you think to go is probably the library. But before you venture into the library stacks, you'll want to search a topic or title in the library catalog, accessible through the library website, to see what your library has in its holdings and where a book you're looking for is physically located. The catalog can also tell you if a title is available as an ebook.

In addition to the thousands of print books available through your campus library, you can also access many books online. *Project Gutenberg* makes freely available over 57,000 ebooks and digitized texts that are in the public domain. *Google Books* also provides free digital access to books in the public domain, and it makes these texts searchable.

Rarely will an entire book be relevant to your specific topic, so you'll need to be selective. Reading the table of contents, skimming chapter headings and sections, and examining the list of keywords and topics in the book's catalog or database entry can tell you whether all or part of a book is relevant to your research.

Periodicals

Articles from newspapers, magazines, and scholarly journals are available online through news sites, academic search engines, journal websites, and open-access databases. In addition to these, many more articles may be available to you in your library in print or online or both, depending on the library and the periodical; you can locate such articles through indexes and databases to which the library subscribes. If you can't access an index electronically through your library, ask a reference librarian to help you locate the print version on the library shelves.

Journal articles can be found online through academic search engines such as *Google Scholar* and *JURN*, which yield results from electronic journals and works from academic publishers. *Google Scholar* tends to produce more results in the sciences than in the humanities, while *JURN* focuses on humanities and the arts. You may come across a site that offers an abstract but charges to unlock the full text. In such cases, see whether your library gives you access to the journal. Your campus library may also give you access to subscription-only articles that simply don't turn up on *Google Scholar* and *JURN*, which find a portion of the scholarly texts available online but can miss content held behind paywalls. For this reason, library databases are a good place to go when searching for articles from scholarly journals.

Magazine and news articles are available online through news organizations' websites that provide searchable access to current and archived articles, photos, podcasts, videos, and streaming broadcasts. Some sites, like that of the *New York Times*, provide only limited access or require subscriptions, but much is available for free online. News aggregators like *Google News* are also useful for searching news on specific subjects, turning up articles from a range of international or local news sources; often you can personalize such aggregators to track news on specific subjects.

For newspapers that do not archive their articles online, and for older or historical articles that have not been digitized, you can turn to your library's indexes and databases. To find articles published before 1980, you'll most likely need to search print indexes such as *The Readers' Guide to Periodical Literature*, *Magazine Index*, and *National Newspaper Index*. Like the index of this book, print indexes list articles by topic and point you to issues and pages where relevant articles can be found. Many databases also include newspaper as well as journal articles and might give you access to articles not openly available online. Remember to carefully scrutinize and evaluate news sources you encounter so that you aren't duped by FAKE NEWS or material that seems trustworthy but isn't based on facts.

Government and Legal Documents

Official reports, legislative records, laws, maps and photos, census data, and other information from federal, state, and local governments are available for free online. Check the websites of government departments and agencies for these resources; you can access such resources for the US government through *USA.gov*. The Library of Congress website provides a large archive of photographs, maps, and other US historical and cultural materials.

Primary and Historical Documents

Most university libraries include among their holdings rare and unique materials—books, photographs, fine art, cultural artifacts, maps, and other material—held in the library's archives or special collections. These materials are usually searchable through the library's main catalog, but because the items are often rare and hard, if not impossible, to replace, you'll need to contact your library for access.

Some libraries also house digital images of rare documents in online archives; this is one way of viewing documents held by another institution

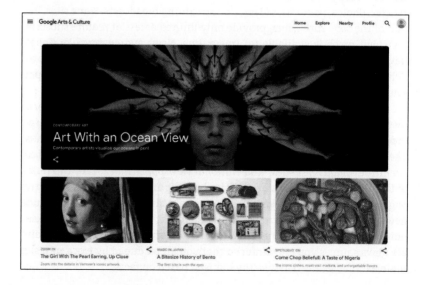

that you cannot access in person. Many museums, cultural institutions, and historical societies also make their holdings available for viewing through their own online archives—you can explore many rooms of the Smithsonian this way—or through open-access archives like *Google Arts and Culture*.

RESEARCH SITES:
ON THE INTERNET, IN THE LIBRARY

Many researchers turn to the internet first for answers to all sorts of questions, and understandably so; you can quickly and easily use it to locate an array of sources. Convenient and powerful the internet may be, but given the prevalence of false and misleading information, using this vast resource requires extra caution in order to verify the accuracy of what you uncover. At the same time, academic libraries still provide access to a wealth of reliable resources, from reference works to bibliographies to **PRIMARY SOURCES** and **SECONDARY SOURCES**. Most college libraries provide online access to electronic resources such as indexes, databases, and the library catalog remotely. The following sections introduce you to some tools for finding sources on the internet and in the library; knowing how to use these tools effectively will help you take advantage of all that these sites have to offer.

Search sites. You're likely already familiar with search engines like *Google* and *Bing*. These powerful tools help you locate information on general sites like *Wikipedia*, government information sites like the Library of Congress, and social media sites like *Twitter* or *Instagram*, as well as public sites for colleges and professional organizations. Through them, you can also access local, national, and international news sites, though some will require you to subscribe in order to access their materials. One drawback to reading information on public sites found from an internet search is that you'll often need to disregard distracting advertisements and pop-ups.

General search sites like these are a good starting point, but you can find more specialized sources on your topic by identifying which sites will be most relevant to your search. For academic searches, try *Google Scholar* or *JURN*. *Google Scholar* locates peer-reviewed articles, books, abstracts, and technical reports by searching the websites of academic publishers, professional societies, and universities. A variety of search sites are useful for specific types of searches, including those devoted to maps or image searches (*Google Maps, Flickr*), news aggregators (*Google News, NewsNow*), and so on.

As you use search terms to further your research, move from general concepts to more specific ones by configuring short, increasingly narrowed combinations of keywords. Most search sites also allow advanced searches that help you limit results by date, type of source, or other criteria; check the site's search tips for guidelines that are specific to the search engine you're using.

Keep in mind that some search sites allow websites to pay for higher placement or ranking in search results, which means that what comes up first in a search may not be the most useful or relevant to your topic. And we know that many search engines collect information on us each time we search, which impacts what we see in future searches. So don't take search results at face value—go beyond the first few results and see what multiple search engines produce, not just one. You can also seek out search engines that don't track users, like *DuckDuckGo*.

Social media may be something you search unconsciously as you scroll through your personal feeds. Sites like *Twitter, Instagram, YouTube,* and *Facebook* are useful as "sources of sources," where you can connect with people who share your interests to find and share information and sources about those interests. *Twitter* especially has become a popular site for sharing information, following other people, and staying on top of the latest news and trends. Many journalists break big stories on *Twitter* before they reach official news sites. With so many prominent people tweeting, the site can also provide you with primary source material. By following experts in the field you're researching, you can find relevant quotes or introductions to a larger discussion.

Online forums, groups, and discussion lists can also connect you with people who share an interest or expertise in specific topics. Many forums and discussion lists archive past posts and threads that you can search to see if your topic has come up in the discussion before; you can also join current discussions and post questions or requests for information.

While social media let you see what others are reading and allow them to recommend sources you might otherwise miss, recent research tells us that people tend to follow like-minded individuals from similar social circles; that is, the view from your feed may not be truly representative of a larger reality. And we know that social media sites are where FAKE NEWS and MISINFORMATION spread most quickly. So be sure to evaluate every source: Is the person you are quoting actually an expert? Can you confirm the information in the tweet and follow it to a larger discussion? Have you checked sites like *Snopes* and *FactCheck.org* to be sure you aren't relying on something phony?

Libraries. College libraries are often large and spread across many wings, so it's a good idea to sign up to take a tour of yours. You'll learn the location of key materials and spaces, including the library stacks, special collections, computer rooms, computers designated for searching databases or the catalog, screening and other media rooms, study areas, meeting rooms, and so on. If there are no guided tours available, pick up a library map at the information desk and spend a little time exploring on your own.

Librarians are especially valuable resources. All college libraries are staffed with reference librarians whose major responsibility is to help faculty and students with their research inquiries. While they will not do the research for you, reference librarians can be enormously helpful in showing you where you can find materials specific to your research question or topic and how you can search for them most efficiently. Their advice can save you considerable time and frustration.

In addition to reference librarians, many libraries have specialists in specific academic disciplines. Discipline (or subject) librarians work closely with academic departments to make sure that the relevant journals, databases, and books for that discipline are available to students and faculty.

Schedule a meeting with a reference or discipline librarian, and come to the meeting prepared to discuss your research question or topic. This is also your chance to ask about library resources available on your topic or any specific kinds of sources you're looking for.

Library websites. In addition to information about hours, location, and holdings, library websites often provide useful guides or tutorials to using the library. College libraries often provide online research guides that list databases, references, websites, organizations, and other discipline- or subject-specific resources. The image on the following page shows the homepage of the College of Southern Nevada library. Note the links that allow you to search in various ways and access specific services, including getting help from research librarians. In addition to multiple libraries on campus and special collections, many universities offer research guides

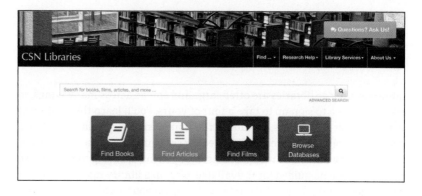

by discipline. If you're conducting research in a particular discipline, these guides can help you understand conventions and search for books, journals, and articles in that field.

Library catalogs. Most libraries have electronic catalogs that account for all their holdings. Searching the catalog is the best method for locating books and other materials, such as audio and video recordings, that you can access through the library. The record for each item includes the author, title, and publication information; a physical description of the item; and sometimes a summary or overview of the contents. The electronic catalog also provides a call number that tells you where the item is physically located in the library stacks (or a networked library), and whether or not it is currently available.

You can search a library catalog by author, title, series, subject, or keyword—or some combination of those in an advanced search. The image on the following page shows the initial search terms for a paper in an introduction to biology course. The student researcher, intrigued by the conflicting stories they had heard about the impact of caffeine on the human body, searched by selecting filters (subject terms include "caffeine," "effects," and "humans"), limited the type of source (articles only), selected a specific language (English), and specified a date range (the last 10 years).

These search criteria turned up 184 results in the College of Southern Nevada library catalog. All the results yielded peer-reviewed articles, so the student knows they can trust them. Analyzing the results reveals a variety of ways the researcher could narrow their focus. For example, several of the articles examine the effects of combining caffeine with energy drinks or alcohol or high-calorie foods; others look at behavioral effects at a variety of consumption levels. The point is that doing the initial search of a library's full catalog, depending on your findings, can help you focus—or broaden—your scope and identify more specific databases that include works relevant to your topic.

Databases organize and provide access not only to listings (bibliographic citations) of journal and news articles but also, in many cases, to abstracts and full texts. A variety of open-access databases, such as the *Directory of Open Access Journals*, allow you to search research journals that are freely available online. Your library probably also has subscriptions to a number of databases that you can access through its website.

General databases that cover a range of disciplines and topics and include scholarly articles, popular magazines, and news stories may be a good place to start. Here are a few that are widely used:

- *Academic Search Complete* (EBSCO) includes the full text of many periodicals from the humanities, arts, and sciences—the majority of which are peer-reviewed—and provides abstracts for others.

- *JSTOR* makes available scanned copies of scholarly journals from many disciplines. It includes issues from further back in time than most other scholarly databases.

- *Nexis Uni* collects full-text documents from news, government, business, and legal sources. This database includes transcripts of broadcast news sources.

- *ProQuest One* provides full-text articles from journals, periodicals, dissertations, newspapers, and video broadcasts.

Subject-specific databases are useful when you have a focused topic and research question. For example, if you are conducting research on sustainable farming efforts in urban areas, you might begin by searching databases that focus on food and nutrition, such as the *Food Science and Technology Abstracts*. If you are searching for information on trends in sports injuries among soccer players, you might search a sports research database like *SPORTDiscus*. Below are some examples of subject-specific databases; ask a subject or reference librarian to direct you to those most relevant to your topic.

- *CAB Abstracts* provides bibliographic information, abstracts, and some limited full text for a range of agricultural sources including peer-reviewed journals, technical reports, and conference proceedings.

- *IEEE Xplore* provides access to full-text documents in computer science, electronics, and electrical engineering.

- *PsycINFO* provides indexes and abstracts for peer-reviewed sources in psychology and the behavioral sciences.

- *MLA International Bibliography* indexes scholarly books and articles on literature, languages, linguistics, and folklore from around the world.

- *ERIC* (Educational Resources Information Center) provides bibliographies for journal articles, books, and other materials related to education.

- *SocINDEX*, a sociology-specific research database provided by EBSCO, includes bibliographic records, a sociology-specific thesaurus, author profiles, indexing, and abstracts of journal articles.

RUNNING SEARCHES

Whether you're looking for sources online or in the library, the search typically starts with a website and an open search bar. Most academic libraries offer multiple options for searches available through the library's website. Remember to meet the reference/research librarians—they are an invaluable resource as you search for sources. The following sections cover some basic tips for using search sites, library catalogs, and electronic databases.

Keyword Searches

Keyword searches allow you to use words and phrases, including author names, titles, and descriptions, to locate sources—but keep in mind that you may need to adjust your keywords or use synonyms if your initial searches don't yield useful results. If searching for *women's sports injuries* doesn't yield much, try *female athlete injuries*. You may also need to try broader keywords (*women sports medicine*). If your search returns too many results, try narrowing your term (*women's sports injuries soccer*).

Following are some advanced search techniques that can help you focus your search. *Google* and many search sites provide their own advanced search options—allowing you to limit searches, for example, to items published only during a particular time period.

Quotation marks can be used around terms to search for an exact phrase, such as "International Monetary Fund" or "obesity in American high schools." Using quotation marks may exclude useful results, however—for example, searching for "factory farms" may omit results with "factory farming" in a library search.

Wildcard searches allow you to insert a special symbol (usually ? or *) in the middle or at the end of a word to retrieve multiple forms of that word. For example, typing in *wom?n* would retrieve both *woman* and *women*.

Truncation allows the symbols ? or * to stand in for one or more missing letters at the end of a word; for example, typing in *ethnograph** would retrieve *ethnography*, *ethnographic*, *ethnographer*, and so on.

Boolean operators (AND, OR, and NOT) let you refine your search by combining keywords in different ways to include or exclude certain terms. Using AND narrows a search to include all terms joined by AND; using OR broadens a search to include items with any of the terms joined by OR; and using NOT limits a search to exclude items with any term preceded by NOT. For example, if you're researching solar energy, typing in *alternative energy* will bring up many more options than *alternative energy AND solar*, which reduces the number to only those that include the term *solar*. Typing in *alternative energy NOT wind* narrows the search to results that exclude the term *wind*.

Parentheses allow you to combine Boolean searches in a more complex way. For example, a search for *alternative energy AND (solar OR wind)* yields only those items that contain both *alternative energy* and *solar* or both *alternative energy* and *wind*. *Alternative energy NOT (solar OR wind)* yields only items that contain *alternative energy* but do not contain either *solar* or *wind*; this kind of search might be useful, for example, if you are specifically researching forms of alternative energy other than solar or wind energy.

Plus and minus signs are used by some search sites instead of AND and NOT. Using a plus sign (+) in front of words and phrases indicates that those exact words must appear, so *+"alternative energy" +solar* will bring up results that include both terms. The minus sign (a hyphen) excludes results, so *+"alternative energy" -solar* brings up sources in which *alternative energy* is included but *solar* is not. Searching for *+"alternative energy" -solar -biofuel* excludes results with both *solar* and *biofuel*.

Author, Title, and Subject Searches

Most library catalogs and many databases are searchable by author, title, and subject as well as by keyword. Using the author and title fields allows you to go directly to a source when you know its title or author. Subject searches allow an overview of your library's holdings on a topic. To do an effective subject search, it helps to know what cataloging system the library uses—most commonly the Library of Congress Subject Headings (LCSH) or the National Library of Medicine's Medical Subject Headings (MeSH). Subject heading searches use what is called "left-hand truncation," which means that you can access a list of headings by entering the first term. These types of searches require terms that are specific to their lists. For example, if you're searching for material on the American Civil War, and you search for the subject *civil war*, you'll get a long list that begins with your term and branches to the right, like this:

Num	Mark	Subjects (1-50 of 870)	Year	Entries 10000 Found
1		Civil War -- See Also the narrower term Insurgency		1
2	☐	Civil War		41
3	☐	Civil War 43 31 B C Rome History		5
4	☐	Civil War 43 31 B C Rome History Drama		7
5	☐	Civil War 49 45 B C Rome History		12
6	☐	Civil War 49 45 B C Rome History Literature And The War		4
7	☐	Civil War 68 69 Rome History		2

These results are not on your topic. If you then go back to the subject search page and type in *American Civil War*, you'll get this suggestion:

American Civil War 1861 1865 is not used in this library's catalog. *United States History Civil War, 1861-1865* is used instead.

Try a search for United States History Civil War, 1861-1865

Once you know that the LCSH list uses "United States History Civil War 1861–1865" to begin subject headings on this topic, you'll be on the right track and will get the following search result:

Num	Mark	Subjects (1–50 of 432)	Year	Entries 10000 Found
1		United States History Civil War 1861 1865 -- 2 Related Subjects		2
2	☐	United States History Civil War 1861 1865		1079
3	☐	United States History Civil War 1861 1865 19th Century		3
4	☐	United States History Civil War 1861 1865 Abstracts Periodicals	1984 -	1
5	☐	United States History Civil War 1861 1865 Aerial Operations		2
6	☐	United States History Civil War 1861 1865 Aerial Operations Juvenile Fiction		2
7	☐	United States History Civil War 1861 1865 Aerial Operations Juvenile Literature : Jarrow, Gail.	2010	1

CONDUCTING FIELD RESEARCH

Journalists who interview eyewitnesses, researchers who spend months observing the behavior of a particular population, historians who gather oral histories, and pollsters who conduct surveys on the general public's attitudes about current government policies are all engaging in field research. Depending on your research question, you may need to go "into the field" to conduct research, using data-gathering methods that rely on firsthand accounts. The three most common discovery methods for field research are observation, interviews, and surveys or questionnaires.

Keep in mind that conducting field research on human subjects may require prior approval from your college's Institutional Review Board, a group responsible for making sure that a study will not harm research participants. Observing what kinds of clothing people wear to the mall may not need permission, but observing interactions in a private space like a doctor's office or doing any kind of field research with children probably will. Check with your instructor to find out if your project requires approval. If it does, be sure you understand the approval process and the time required to complete it.

Observations

Observation as a field research method calls for a lot more than casual "people watching." It involves taking careful notice of environments and behaviors, with a clear sense of your purpose and of how your observations will help you answer your research question. Many disciplines use observation to collect data about individuals and communities in order to answer questions about how and why they organize, relate to, or interact with one another and the world around them. In many cases, observation is the best and often the only means of gathering field data.

When reference librarian Linda Bedwell and graduate student Caitlin Banks wanted to find out how the study areas in Canada's Dalhousie University Library were being used, they observed students there, noting behaviors and paying attention to how they themselves used the spaces. Bedwell and Banks were conducting **PARTICIPANT OBSERVATION**, which operates on the principle that researchers can learn by doing as well as by watching. In non-participant observation, on the other hand, researchers focus on the actions of others but do not participate in the situations they're observing.

The process (and resulting information) will differ significantly depending on the type of observation, and you should choose the type most appropriate to the situation and for addressing your research topic and question. If you're studying the winning strategies of video gamers, you might choose to do participant observation if you're an expert gamer yourself and if playing the games would result in more insightful data. If you are researching careers in medicine and want to learn about the typical day of a nurse, participant observation would not be an option—unless you have the credentials, training, and legal standing to provide patient care.

Keep your research question clearly in mind when conducting observations and carefully record what you see. Following are some additional tips for conducting effective observations.

- *Determine your purpose and method for observing.* Is participant observation the appropriate method to pursue your research question? Or do you need to focus only on the actions of others—and not to participate yourself? How do you expect to use the data?

- *Plan ahead.* Decide where you will observe and what materials you'll need—and make sure your equipment is ready and working. Determine whether you'll need permission to observe, photograph, and/or record; if so, secure appropriate permissions ahead of time. Keep in mind that it may not be appropriate to take photographs or record video in some sites—at a church service, for instance.

- *Record your observations.* Take detailed descriptive notes, even if you are also recording audio or video; your notes will add necessary texture. Note who is present, the activities they engage in, where they're situated, and pertinent details about the setting such as the physical design of the space. Be sure to record the date, time, and location. As you observe, focus on recording and describing; save the interpretation and analysis for later, when you review your notes and recordings.

- *Be guided by your purpose for observing,* but don't let that purpose restrain you. Be open to whatever you see. Sometimes in the process of looking for one thing, you may find something else that is equally interesting or important. And don't look only for extraordinary behavior. The goal of observation is generally to look for the routine and for patterns, things that are important because they happen regularly.

- *After your observation,* take a moment to flesh out what you've recorded with notes about any additional thoughts or reflections you have.

- *Review your observation notes* and any audio or videotapes, looking for patterns that emerge. Look for actions that recur, for topics that are repeatedly addressed, for individual participants who seem to play important roles. Also note when deviations from patterns occur and what seems to prompt the deviation. You should also consider whether those you observe have changed their behavior because they are being observed and, if so, how these changes may affect your data. You won't be able to correct for these effects, but you can consider and acknowledge them in your analysis. Your goal at this point is to start to analyze and look for an answer to your research question.

Interviews

You may find that the best way to answer your research question is to interview people who have a valuable perspective on your topic, such as experts, witnesses, or key participants in an event. Interviews can provide information that may not be available elsewhere; they can also complement other research and data-gathering methods, such as observations and library research. Just as with observations, you'll need to consider your purpose for conducting an interview and how the information you gain from it will speak to your research question.

You'll also need to decide who to interview. Will one interview provide the needed information, or will you need several? And how qualified are those you're considering to address your research question? As a veteran of the war in Afghanistan, a friend may not be the most credible source for a detailed analysis of the history of US involvement in the region; print sources may be a better starting place for that type of background information. But your friend or relative probably *would* be a valuable, reliable source for a firsthand account of the combat experience and could probably provide details that you would never get from a book.

In any case, remember to ask your interviewees for their written consent to the interview, especially if your work will be published online or elsewhere. Following are additional tips for conducting successful interviews.

- *Plan to conduct your interviews early in your research* in case you have to do follow-up interviews. Contact interviewees well before your research project is due to set up appointments.

- *Do some background research* on your topic before the interview so that you can ask informed questions.

- *Write out a list of questions* that you will ask in the interview. These questions should be directly related to your research. Avoid questions that are too general that lead to one-word answers like "yes" or "no." For example, don't ask, "Do you like music?" when you want specific details. Try asking "What kind of music do you like?" instead. Also avoid leading questions, ones that prompt answers that you want. The question "Don't you think his campaign tactics were dishonest?" allows the interviewee to disagree, but it still suggests a particular response. A better question would be "What is your opinion on the candidate's campaigning methods?" This question is specific enough to provide a focus yet open enough to let the interviewee answer freely.

- *Decide how you'll record the interview.* Will you rely solely on note taking, or will you combine it with audio or video recording? Remember to ask permission before you tape any part of an interview.

- *If your interview requires any electronic equipment,* test it before the interview to make sure that it is working. And have a back-up plan; there's nothing more frustrating than finding out that you've lost the data from a wonderful interview because batteries died.

- *Be polite.* Remember that the person you're interviewing is doing you a favor by agreeing to speak with you.

- *Record the date, time, and location* of every interview that you conduct, and write down contact information for the interviewee.

- *Send a thank-you note* to anyone you interview.

- *Check facts, dates, and other information* the interviewee provides, especially about anything controversial. If any of the information seems questionable, try to interview others who can corroborate it or provide another perspective.

Surveys and Questionnaires

You've probably been asked to participate in marketing surveys that review products or services, or maybe you've completed questionnaires for course evaluations. Such surveys and questionnaires can be useful in soliciting information from a large number of people. Most often they aren't meant to poll an entire population; rather, they usually target a *representative sample*, a selected subset of a group that accurately reflects the characteristics of the whole group. The most reliable way to select such a group is by *random sampling*. A true random sample is one in which every member of the target population has the same chance of being selected to participate. Say you want to survey the first-year students in your school. You could try to track down each one—not a problem in a tiny school, but what if there are 5,000? Not feasible. Or you could acquire a list of names from the registrar, assign each name a number (you can use Excel to assign random numbers), and then select a certain percentage of these people.

Unlike interviews, most surveys or questionnaires do not solicit detailed information; generally, researchers use them to gauge trends and opinions on a rather narrow topic. Following are some tips for deciding when to use surveys and how to design and administer them.

Consider your PURPOSE. Will a survey be an effective way to collect the information you need to address your research question? If you are trying to find out how first-year medical residents negotiate the challenges of their demanding schedule, a survey is not likely to provide you with the level of detail you will need; interviews might be more effective. However, if you are researching how the residents account for their time in a typical day, a survey would likely be your best method.

Once you've decided that a survey is the practical way to proceed, think about how you will use the results. Will the results provide essential support for your argument or anecdotal details to make your discussion more interesting and concrete? These considerations will determine the number of people you survey and what sorts of questions you ask them.

Determine your sample. Unless you are only after anecdotal information, you should aim to survey a representative sample, a randomly selected subset of a group that reflects the characteristics of the whole group. If you want to discover your college community's level of satisfaction with campus dining services, for example, you'll need to solicit a sample that represents all those who use the services—students, faculty, administrative staff, and visitors—and also reflects the range of ages, genders, ethnicities, and so on. Including only students who eat breakfast in the dining halls on weekends is not likely to give you a viable sample. Most important, decide how many people you will contact; generally, the more of the target population you sample, the more reliably you will be able to claim that your results represent trends in that population.

Choose your distribution method. Will you administer the survey over the phone or face-to-face? send a written survey through email? Or will you use an online service like *Qualtrics*, *SurveyMonkey*, or *Google Forms*? Most universities provide access to one of these tools; check with the Office of Research on campus. And don't expect a 100 percent response rate. Researchers often distribute surveys multiple times to get as many people in their targeted population to respond as they can.

Write the questions and an introduction, and test the survey. Respondents tend not to complete long or complicated surveys, so the best surveys include only a few questions and are easy to understand. Sequence questions from simple to complex unless there is a good reason not to do so. Also decide what kinds of questions are most likely to yield the information you're after. Here are examples of four common kinds of survey questions: open-ended, multiple-choice, agreement scale, and rating scale.

Open-ended

What genre of books do you like to read?

Where is your favorite place to read?

Multiple-choice

Please select your favorite genre of book (check all that apply):
__ fiction __ autobiography __ self-help __ histories __ biography

Please indicate your favorite location for reading (check one):
__ coffee shop __ library __ home __ office __ other

Agreement scale

Indicate your level of agreement with the following statements:

	Strongly Agree	Agree	Strongly Disagree	Disagree
The library should provide both ebooks and print books.	☐	☐	☐	☐

Rating scale

How would you rate your campus library?
__ Excellent __ Good __ Fair __ Poor

Your questions should focus on specific topics related to your research question. For example, undergraduate researcher Steven Leone believed that solar energy provided by thin-film solar cells could be an alternative to fossil fuels as an energy source, but he knew many homeowners resist expensive solar installations. His project, "The Likelihood of Homeowners to Implement Thin-Film Solar Cells," was designed to discover the relationship between homeowners' socioeconomic status and their attitudes about alternative energy sources in order to gauge how likely they are to adopt this new technology. These are the questions he asked in a survey of homeowners. Notice that some call for short answers while others ask for detailed responses.

1. What is your combined annual household income?

2. What is the highest level of education you have completed?
   __ high school __ some college __ college __ graduate school

3. How is your home currently heated?

4. How much are you currently spending each year on home energy costs?

5. Which is more important to you—saving money or going green? Why?

6. Have you considered using solar energy as your home energy source? Why or why not?

7. Thin-film solar cells cost significantly less than conventional solar installations and offer an energy-cost payback that is twice as fast. How much more likely does this information make it that you will implement this technology?
   __ very likely   __ somewhat likely
   __ somewhat unlikely   __ very unlikely

8. Thin-film solar cells will increase the resale value of your home. How much more likely does this information make it that you will implement the technology?
   __ very likely   __ somewhat likely
   __ somewhat unlikely   __ very unlikely

Leone's questions provided him with data that he then analyzed to determine patterns (education, income, lifestyle) of attitudes on his topic.

Once you're satisfied with your questions, write a brief introductory statement that will let participants know the purpose of the survey and what they can expect, including an estimate of how long it will take to complete.

Manage your results. When you are done collecting data, be sure to carefully record and store your responses. If you are using a print survey, one simple method is to use a blank survey and tally responses next to each question. You can also use a spreadsheet to track your findings. If your survey includes open-ended questions, you may want to choose some responses to quote from when you present your results.

ANALYZE your results. After you have tallied up the results, you need to analyze them, looking for patterns that reveal trends and explaining what those trends may mean. Data from survey results do not speak for themselves. You need to analyze the data by looking for similar responses to questions you've asked. Group those that are similar, and label them accordingly. What does that pattern or trend in responses indicate about your research question? When you move from describing the patterns and trends to discussing what they mean, you are interpreting your results. For example, suppose you survey 200 classmates about a recent increase in student fees for using the on-campus fitness center and find that the students, by a significant majority, think the fees are cost-prohibitive. Based on your survey results, your interpretation is that the fee increase is likely to lead to decreased use of the fitness center. You didn't just report the results; you interpreted them as well.

REFLECT on how well the survey worked. When you present your results, be sure to acknowledge any limitations of your survey. What topics were not covered? What populations were not surveyed? Was your sample truly representative?

Information today lives everywhere: in traditional libraries, on the internet, and out "in the field." Your research question and your rhetorical situation—including who will read your research—dictate what kinds of sources you consult and cite. But ultimately, research should be a voyage of discovery, driven by *your* questions based on *your* desire to find out something you didn't know before.

REFLECT. Now that you have thought more about your topic and questions, done some preliminary research, decided on methods, and located some sources, review the types of sources that you've consulted. How did each of those sources help you answer your research question? What other sources do you still need to consult?

TWENTY-TWO

Keeping Track

Managing Information Overload

ESEARCH HAS ALWAYS been a complex, often messy process, but in an age of information overload, it can spiral out of control. Where did you save those notes you took? Did that piece of information come from the book you read or somewhere online? Researchers today have so much information at their fingertips that just managing it has become tough. This chapter aims to help you organize potential chaos by offering tips for keeping track of your sources, taking notes, and maintaining a working bibliography.

Keep Track of Your Sources

The easiest way to keep track of your sources is to save a copy of each one. Especially when your research is spread out over several days or weeks, and when it turns up dozens of potential sources, don't rely on your memory.

Electronic sources. Download and save files, or print them out. Make copies of materials on the web, which can change or even disappear: print out what you might use, or take a screenshot and save the image. Some subscription database services let you save, email, or print citations and articles. You might also want to use one of the free online tools, like

Zotero or *Mendeley*, that allow you to organize, store, analyze, and share articles, images, and even audio/video files.

Once you've got copies of your sources, the challenge is to keep them all organized and easy to find. Store all the files for a single project together in one folder, and use a consistent file-naming system so each item is easy to identify. The following example uses the author's last name and keywords from the source's title. All of the sources are saved in a folder under the course title and assignment.

> ENG1102_ResearchProject
>   Ehrenreich_ServingFL
>   hooks_TouchingEarth
>   Kohls_CleanSweep
>   McMillanCottom_LogicOfPoor

You should note the author(s), title, URL, and date of access on each item—and record all the other information needed in a **WORKING BIBLIOGRAPHY**. And be sure to back up your files regularly.

Print sources. Make photocopies, printouts, or scans of everything you think will be useful to your research. Keep a copy of the title and copyright pages of books and of the table of contents or front page of periodicals. Label everything with the author(s), title, and page numbers, and file related materials together in a clearly marked folder.

Take Notes

We cannot stress enough the importance of taking notes systematically *as you go*. But this doesn't mean you should write down everything; carefully select what details you note to be sure they are pertinent to your project. **ANNOTATING** as you read sources will help you understand and synthesize important information.

Take notes in your own words, and be sure to enclose any words taken directly from a source in quotes. Label anything you **QUOTE**, **PARAPHRASE**, or **SUMMARIZE** as such so that you'll remember to acknowledge and document the original source if you use it—and so that you don't accidentally **PLAGIARIZE**. Consider this example:

Lyon, G. Reid. "Learning Disabilities." *The Future of Children: Special Education for Children with Disabilities*, vol. 6, no. 1, Spring 1996, pp. 54-76, futureofchildren.org/publications/journals/article/index. xml?journalid=57&articleid=340. Accessed 1 June 2019.

Summary: Focuses on problems with reading skills but cautions that early intervention with reading won't address all manifestations of LD.

- Lyon is chief of Child Development and Behavior in the National Institute of Child Health and Human Development at the NIH.
- LD is several overlapping disorders related to reading, language, and math (paraphrase, p. 54).
- Lyon: "[L]earning disability is not a single disorder, but is a general category of special education composed of disabilities in any of seven specific areas: (1) receptive language (listening), (2) expressive language (speaking), (3) basic reading skills, (4) reading comprehension, (5) written expression, (6) mathematics calculation, and (7) mathematical reasoning" (direct quotation, p. 55).

Comment: Lyon breaks down LD into more precise categories. Defines each category. Will help me define LD.

Notice the specific information included in these notes—all details that will help the researcher later on if she decides to reference this article in her own writing: a full MLA-style citation, a brief summary of the article, and notes about how the source might relate to her research. And notice too that she's indicated when she's paraphrased and quoted from the text, with page numbers in each case. If she does end up citing this source in her own work, she'll already have all the documentation information she'll need.

Label notes with full citation information—the author(s) and title, publication information, page numbers, date of access, and URL.

SUMMARIZE the main point and any other important points you want to remember in a sentence or two. Be very careful to write your summary using your own words and sentence patterns.

If you copy any passages by hand, take care to do so accurately, paying attention to both words and punctuation and enclosing the entire passage in quotation marks. If you cut and paste any text from electronic sources, put quotation marks around it.

Record your own questions or reactions as you go. Do you see anything that addresses your research question? anything you want to know more about? Consider what role this source might play in your own writing. Does it provide evidence? represent perspectives show why the topic matters?

Maintain a Working Bibliography

It might seem easiest to keep track only of the sources that you know you will cite. But what if your research takes an interesting twist and you need to include some of the sources that you discarded earlier? Rather than having to stop and search for those earlier sources, you could access the source information right away if you keep a working bibliography—a list of all the sources that you consult.

Unlike a final works cited or reference page, a working bibliography constantly changes as you find more sources to add to it. Keep it on a computer or individual note cards for easy updating. As you update, note for each source whether you have already used it, rejected it, or are still thinking about it. You may even want to annotate your working bibliography with a summary of each source. Eventually this information will become your list of works cited or references, so follow whatever **DOCUMENTATION** style you plan to use. See Chapters 28 and 29 for information on **MLA** and **APA** style.

Consider the working bibliography entries below:

Ellcessor, Elizabeth. *Restricted Access: Media, Disability*, and *the Politics of Participation*. NYU P, 2016.

Drawing on multiple examples from participant observation in blogs and websites, Ellcessor exposes the myth of digital media accessibility to the disabled. Support for my central claim re: "participatory culture"?

Brueggemann, Brenda. Personal interview. 10 July 2019.

Professor Brueggemann is one of the world's leading scholars in the field of disability studies. This interview focused on the growth of that field.

WHAT TO PUT IN YOUR WORKING BIBLIOGRAPHY

For books

- Author(s), editors, or translators
- Title
- Edition or volume number
- Publisher, year published

For periodicals

- Author(s)
- Title and subtitle of article
- Name of periodical
- Volume and issue numbers, date
- Page numbers
- URL and date accessed (for online sources)

Additional items for articles accessed via database

- Name of database
- DOI, if there is one, or URL if not

For web sources

- Author(s) and any editors
- Title and subtitle of source
- Name of site
- Date published, posted, or last updated
- Publisher or sponsor of site (if different from name or site)
- Page or paragraph numbers, if any
- URL
- Date accessed

REFLECT. Review your system for organizing and tracking your sources. Are your sources organized in a way that lets you go back to them easily? Have you recorded the necessary bibliographic information? If you answered "no," take the time now to set up a system that helps you keep track of your sources.

TWENTY-THREE

Evaluating Sources

OUR RESEARCH QUESTION: Is it important to address the loss of sea ice in the Arctic? If so, what actions should be taken? To research this topic, rather than merely giving your opinion, you would need to consult reliable sources. Which do you trust more: official reports from the National Aeronautics and Space Administration (NASA), the *Wikipedia* page on the issue, or a post on the website *JunkScience.com*? Is it possible that they could all be useful? How will you know?

Your integrity as an author rests to some degree on the quality of the sources you cite, so your sources need to be appropriate and reliable. You can probably trust that an article or website recommended by a known expert on your topic is a credible source of information.

But in the absence of such advice, and given the overwhelming amount of information available—not to mention *mis*information, it can be difficult to know which sources will be useful, appropriate, and relevant. Or, as media expert Howard Rheingold puts it, the unending stream of information on the internet calls for some serious "crap detection": we have to know how to separate the credible sources from the questionable ones. This chapter provides advice for determining which sources are appropriate for your purposes and then for reviewing those sources with a critical eye.

Is the Source Worth Your Attention?

A database search turns up fifty articles on your topic. The library catalog shows hundreds. *Google*? Thousands. So how do you decide which sources are both reliable and worth your time and attention? Professional fact-checkers don't start to read a new source and judge its relevance until they've determined it's trustworthy—so the two processes should go hand-in-hand. Being a skeptical, defensive reader is never a bad idea, but it's most important when sifting through sources from an internet search. Sources you uncover in library catalogs or databases, on the other hand, are generally already vetted for credibility. Here are some questions to consider as you first scan your search results.

What's the title? Does it sound relevant to your topic? Does it sound serious? humorous? Is it too good to be true or extreme? Do the title and the content of the source match up? What does the title tell you about the source's purpose?

Who are the authors? Do a search to check that they are who they say they are. Are they experts on your topic? journalists? staff writers? Are they affiliated with any institution that would indicate their expertise—or affect their viewpoints? Check the source for biographical information, and confirm any pertinent information you find there by looking elsewhere—at other reliable sources.

If, for example, you were researching brain injuries among NFL players, you might run across the opinions of two medical experts, Dr. Ann McKee and Dr. Elliott Pellman, each offering very different evidence about the long-term effects of concussions. Looking into their credentials and affiliations, you'd learn that McKee is a neurologist who specializes in brain injuries, while Pellman is a rheumatologist who specializes in the body more than the brain—and chairs a medical committee in the NFL—information that tells you something about each one's **STANCE**.

Who's the publisher or sponsor? Is it an academic press? a news organization? a government agency or nonprofit? a business or individual? What do other reliable sources say about it? Read the source's "about" page online and follow up on what you find to confirm it's accurate. Knowing the publisher or sponsor can tell you whether the content has been peer-reviewed by experts, as is typical for scholarly works and government publications, or fact-checked,

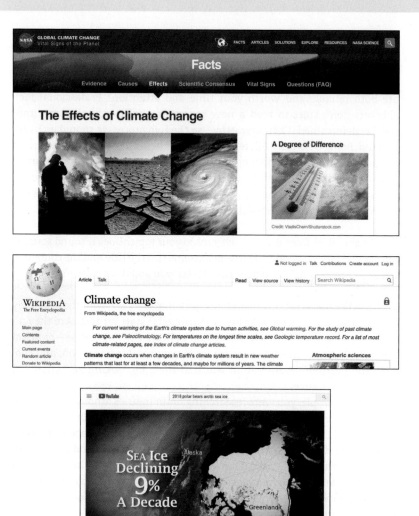

Which would you trust more: official reports with data from NASA, the *Wikipedia* page on the issue, or a clip from ABC's *Nightline* found on *YouTube*?

"On the Internet, nobody knows you're a dog."

as news organizations typically require. Consider also whether the publication or its sponsor has a particular agenda, especially if it presents the opinions of an individual.

What's the URL? A site's URL can tell you something about what kind of organization is sponsoring the site: generally, *com* is used by commercial organizations, *edu* by colleges and universities, *org* by nonprofits, *gov* by government agencies. If it's a site you've never heard of, do an internet search of the source's URL to be sure it checks out.

When was it published or last updated? Does your topic call for the most current sources or for older historical ones? Even if you're researching a current issue, you may still want to consult older sources to get a sense of the larger context. Likewise, if your topic calls for older sources, you may also want to read the current research on it. And if your source is on a website, check to see that the site itself and any links are still active.

What's the genre? Pay particular attention to whether it's REPORTING information or ARGUING some kind of claim. You'll have reason to look for both, but for those that make an argument, you'll need to find multiple sources expressing a number of different perspectives. And double-check facts, claims, and evidence that too neatly support what you already think or seem too good to be true. Sites like *Snopes* and *FactCheck.org* can help.

Is it cited in other works? Are there links to it in other online sources? Has it been referenced or reposted? You can determine this by searching for the author and title using *Google Scholar.* For instance, if you enter *Susan Miller "Textual Carnivals,"* the search page returns information letting you know the work has been cited in 541 related articles. If many other writers refer or respond to this author's work, you can probably assume they find it credible.

Let's say you are conducting preliminary research on climate change and a *Google* search turns up an article titled "On the Linearity of Local and Regional Temperature Changes from 1.5°C to 2°C of Global Warming." You've heard that small temperature increases are significant and the title uses academic language, so this article sounds promising. Following the guidelines above will help you determine whether it'll be worth your attention.

Before you read the article itself, check out the author and source to be sure they're reliable. Written by seven international scholars, this report is hosted on the American Meteorological Society's page and was published in the *Journal of Climate.* Clicking on each author's name provides their individual publishing history which helps verify their expertise. Googling each of the authors' names plus "climate science" further confirms their identities and expertise by uncovering university faculty bios and *Google Scholar* pages listing when their works have been cited by others. Now look at the source itself; the American Meteorological Society's "about" page says it was established in 1919, has more than 13,000 members, and "is the nation's premier scientific and professional organization promoting and disseminating information about the atmospheric, oceanic, and hydrologic sciences." This information paints a picture of a trustworthy source, but don't stop there. Doing an internet search of the society's name turns up other trustworthy sources (such as *Forbes* and *JSTOR*) that confirm its mission and stature.

Now that you've confirmed the report comes from a credible source, look more closely to see if it is relevant to your research topic. While the title suggests the article will focus on local and regional temperature change, the abstract gives a summary of why the research was conducted, what research methods were used, and the implications of the findings—all important moves for laying out a researched argument. Given your topic, you're likely to encounter many more research reports, so this one seems like a good start for understanding how to read and analyze them. In addition, it lists keywords that seem relevant to your research ("climate models," "temperature") and lists of additional scholarly articles. Finally, note that the date of publication is September 2018, so it's recent enough to be useful.

Given all that you know about this source, is it worth your attention? We would say so. The report seems to provide valuable information in addition to giving you an example of how climate science research is conducted and analyzed. And even if you don't end up citing the findings of this paper, it still offers links to additional related research published in a source you've already verified as reliable.

That said, you should be mindful to research other relevant perspectives on your topic—especially those outside of the sources that confirm what you already think. In this case, clicking on the keyword "climate change" at the end of the abstract turns up a list of additional papers, including one offering a different point of view titled "'We Have Seen It with Our Own Eyes': Why We Disagree about Climate Change Visibility." The title indicates this article will present opposing positions on something called "climate change visibility." In the abstract and article that follow, the author summarizes and investigates positions held by opposing sides in the debate on whether climate change can be witnessed firsthand. Now things are getting interesting; this article introduces a more human, even personal, element to the debate, suggesting that even scientists disagree on how— even if—people experience climate change firsthand. If this human element sparks your interest, then this article is definitely relevant to your research and worth your attention. It might even help you focus your research question. As you go further in your research, you should seek out other credible sources arguing from different sides of the issue.

REFLECT. Read the Popular Science *article titled "What you should know about the new climate change report" on* everyonesanauthor.tumblr.com. *Underlined words are linked to sources—open a few of these sources and evaluate them, using the questions earlier in this chapter, to determine if they would be credible sources for research on this topic. What are the sources' strengths and weaknesses?*

Reading Sources with a Critical Eye

Once you've determined that a source is credible and appropriate, you'll need to read it closely, thinking carefully about the author's position, how (and how well) it's supported, and how it affects your understanding of the topic as a whole. As you read your sources, approach each one with a critical eye and practice READING DEFENSIVELY. The following questions can help you do so.

Consider your own RHETORICAL SITUATION. Will the source help you achieve your PURPOSE? Look at the preface, abstract, or table of contents to determine how extensively and directly it addresses your topic. Will your AUDIENCE consider the source reliable and credible? Are they expecting you to cite certain kinds of materials, such as historical documents or academic journals? Does the source confirm what you already believe or expose you to new considerations?

What is the author's STANCE? Does the title indicate a certain attitude or perspective? How would you characterize the TONE? Is it objective? argumentative? sarcastic? How does the author's stance affect its usefulness for your project?

Who is the AUDIENCE for this work? Is it aimed at the general public? members of a field? policy makers? Sources written for a general audience may provide useful overviews or explanations. Sources aimed at experts may be more authoritative and provide more detail—but they can be challenging to understand.

What is the main point, and what has motivated the author to write? Is the author responding to some other argument? What's the larger conversation on this issue? Is it clear why the topic matters?

What REASONS and EVIDENCE does the author provide as support? Are the reasons fair, relevant, and sound? Is the evidence drawn from credible sources? Is the kind of evidence (statistics, facts, examples, expert testimony, and so on) appropriate to the point it's supporting? How persuasive do you find the argument? Check facts and claims you're skeptical of by using nonpartisan sites (*Snopes* and *FactCheck.org*) that confirm truths and identify lies or misinformation.

Does the author acknowledge and respond to other viewpoints? Look for mention of multiple perspectives, not just the author's own view. And be sure to consider how fairly any **COUNTERARGUMENTS** are represented. The most trustworthy sources represent other views and information fairly and accurately, even (especially) those that challenge their own. Check out the people and ideas cited to be sure they are reliable themselves. The sources and ideas an author is in conversation with can help you uncover more information about the author's own purpose, stance, and bias.

Have you seen ideas given in this source in any other sources? Information found in multiple sources is more reliable than information you can find in only one place. Do other credible sources challenge this information? If so, is

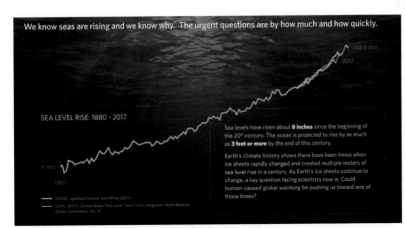

THINK BEYOND WORDS

↪ *SUPPOSE YOU'RE RESEARCHING climate change and come across NASA's site sealevel.nasa.gov. Checking out what others say about the source tells you that NASA stands for* National Aeronautics and Space Administration, *and it is an agency of the US government that employs thousands of scientists and publishes information on natural-science topics. If you were writing an essay about how climate change impacts coastal communities, what kinds of information from this site would you consider citing? How does the way information is presented make it seem more or less credible? For instance, compare the site's report "Melting Ice, Warming Ocean" with the infographic shown above. Is one source easier to vet than the other? Does one seem more appropriate to cite than the other—and if so, why?*

what's said in this source controversial or is it flat out false? Copy and paste the basics of the questionable statement into a search engine and see what reliable sources say. Even if a search brings up many hits, that doesn't make the information accurate—look for sources you trust to weigh in.

How might you use this source? Source materials can serve a variety of purposes in both your research and your writing. You might consult some sources for background information or to get a sense of the larger context for your topic. Other sources may provide support for your claims—or for your credibility as an author. Still others will provide other viewpoints, ones that challenge yours or that provoke you to respond. Most of all, they'll give you some sense of what's been said about your topic. Then, in writing up your research, you'll get your chance to say what *you* think—and to add your voice to the conversation.

REFLECT. Choose three or four different sources on your chosen topic—possibly one from a government source, one from an academic journal, one from a popular source, and one from a website. Evaluate each of the sources according to the guidelines laid out in this chapter. Explain what makes each source credible (or not).

TWENTY-FOUR

Annotating a Bibliography

WHEN WE ASSIGN RESEARCH PROJECTS, we often require our students to annotate a bibliography as part of the research process. Instructors do this for a variety of reasons: to ensure that you read sources carefully and critically, summarize useful information about them, and think about how and why you expect to use particular ones. The rhetorical purpose of the annotated bibliography is to inform—and you are part of the audience. Conscientiously done, annotating a bibliography will help you gain a sense of the larger conversation about your topic and think about how your work fits into that conversation.

In a formal annotated bibliography, you **DESCRIBE** each of the sources you expect to consult and state what role each will play in your research. Sometimes you will be asked to **EVALUATE** sources as well—to assess their strengths and weaknesses in one or two sentences.

Characteristic Features

Annotations should be brief, but they can vary in length from a sentence or two to a few paragraphs. They also vary in terms of style: some are written in complete sentences; others consist of short phrases. And like a works cited or references page, an annotated bibliography is arranged in alphabetical order. You'll want to find out exactly what your instructor expects, but most annotated bibliographies include the following features.

Complete bibliographic information, following whatever documentation style you'll use in your essay— MLA, APA, or another style. This information will enable readers to locate your sources—and can also form the basis for your final list of works cited or references.

A brief SUMMARY or DESCRIPTION of each work, noting its topic, scope, and STANCE. If a source reports on research, the research methods may also be important to summarize. Other details you include will depend on your own goals for your project. Whatever you choose to describe, however, be sure that it represents the source accurately and objectively.

Evaluative comments. If you're required to write evaluative annotations, you might consider how AUTHORITATIVE the source is, how up-to-date, whether it addresses multiple perspectives, and so on. Consider both its strengths and its limitations.

Some indication of how each source will inform your research. Explain how you expect to use each source. Does it present a certain perspective you need to consider? report on important new research? include a thorough bibliography that might alert you to other sources? How does each source relate to the others? How does each source contribute to your understanding of the topic and to your research goals? Or if you find that it isn't helpful to your project, explain why you won't use it.

A consistent and concise presentation. Annotations should be presented consistently in all entries: if one is written in complete sentences, they all should be. The amount of information and the way you structure it should also be the same throughout. And that information should be written concisely, summarizing just the main points and key details relevant to your purpose.

Following are two annotated bibliographies, the first descriptive and the second evaluative.

A Descriptive Annotated Bibliography

Renewable and Sustainable Energy in Rural India

SAURABH VAISH

Germany, German Energy Agency. "Renewable Energies." Deutsche Energie-Agentur GmbH (dena), www.dena.de/en/topics/renewable-energy.html. Accessed 12 Apr. 2011.

Complete bibliographic information for this source, following MLA style.

The German Energy Agency provides information on energy efficiency, renewable energy sources, and intelligent energy systems. The website contains some useful databases, including ones of energy projects in Germany and of recent publications. It is a useful source of information on the manufacturing and production of alternative energy systems.

Summarizes and describes the source.

Though this site does not provide statistical data and covers only a limited number of projects and publications, it includes links to much useful information. It's a great source of publications and projects in both Germany and Russia, and so it will help me broaden my research beyond the borders of the United States.

Explains how this source will inform his project.

SAURABH VAISH was a management and entrepreneurship major at Hofstra University when he wrote this descriptive annotated bibliography for a research project on renewable and sustainable energy in rural India. We then adapted two entries to demonstrate evaluative annotations.

Moner-Girona, Magda, editor. "A New Scheme for the
    Promotion of Renewable Energies in Developing
    Countries: The Renewable Energy Regulated Purchase
    Tariff." European Commission Joint Research Centre
    Publications Repository, 2008, www.energy.eu/publications/
    LDNA23284ENC_002.pdf. Accessed 12 Apr. 2011.

This report on a study by the PhotoVoltaic Technology Platform
discusses how to promote the use of renewable energy in
developing countries. The report proposes a new tariff scheme
to increase the flow of money where it is most needed, suggests
several business models, and estimates the potential success
or failure of each. The detailed information it provides about
business models, supply-chain setups, and financial calculations
will be useful in my analysis, especially in the part of my project
that deals with photovoltaic cells.

United States, Energy Information Administration. Renewable &
    Alternative Fuels Analysis Reports. 1998–2010, U.S. Dept.
    of Energy, www.eia.gov/renewable/reports.cfm. Accessed
    2 Feb. 2012.

This site reports statistical and graphical data on energy
production and consumption, including all major alternative
energies. It provides access to numerous databases on energy
consumption across the world. This website provides most of
the statistical data I will need to formulate conclusions about the
efficiency of alternative energies. Its data are reliable, current,
and easy to understand.

An Evaluative Annotated Bibliography

Moner-Girona, Magda, editor. "A New Scheme for the
　　　Promotion of Renewable Energies in Developing
　　　Countries: The Renewable Energy Regulated Purchase
　　　Tariff." *European Commission Joint Research Centre
　　　Publications Repository*, 2008, www.energy.eu/publications/
　　　LDNA23284ENC_002.pdf. Accessed 12 Apr. 2011.
This report on a study by the PhotoVoltaic Technology Platform
discusses how to promote renewable energy in developing
countries. The report proposes a new tariff scheme to increase
the flow of money where it is needed, suggests several business
models, and estimates the potential success or failure of each.

　　　The detailed information about business models, supply-
chain setups, and financial calculations will be useful, especially in the
part of my project that deals with photovoltaic cells. One potential
drawback is that this report makes premature assumptions: the
proposed business plan is probably not implementable for 20 years.
Even so, this report contains useful data and models, including
graphs and charts, that will support my claims.

Evaluates the source, acknowledging a potential weakness—but explains why it is still useful.

United States, Energy Information Administration. Renewable &
　　　Alternative Fuels Analysis Reports. 1998–2010, U.S. Dept.
　　　of Energy, www.eia.gov/renewable/reports.cfm. Accessed
　　　2 Feb. 2012.
This website reports statistical and graphical data on energy
production and consumption, including all major alternative
energies. It provides access to numerous databases on energy
consumption across the world.

　　　This site provides most of the statistical data I will need
to formulate conclusions about the efficiency of alternative
energies. Its data are reliable, current, and easy to understand.
I see no potential weakness in this source because the data
it presents are non-biased statistics and supporting graphics
pertaining to alternative energies. Using such data will allow me
to shape my own opinions regarding the research I undertake.

TWENTY-FIVE

Synthesizing Ideas

Moving from What Your Sources Say to What You Say

T'S SUPER BOWL SUNDAY, just before kickoff and just after the teams have been introduced. The broadcast cuts back from a commercial set to DJ Schmolli's "Super Bowl Anthem" and returns to the stadium where Idina Menzel is singing "The Star-Spangled Banner." So you've just heard two anthems. But what else, if anything, do these tunes have in common? Answer: each is a mash-up—a combination of material from a number of different sources. "The Star-Spangled Banner" combines a poem written by Francis Scott Key with the music of an old British drinking song. DJ Schmolli's effort combines clips from more than a dozen popular stadium anthems, from Madonna's "Celebration" to Queen's "We Will Rock You." And each smoothly integrates its sources into one seamless whole. In academic terms, the authors of these mash-ups have effectively engaged in **SYNTHESIS**, bringing together material from various sources to create something new.

Like a good mash-up artist, you don't just patch together ideas from various sources when you do research. Instead, you synthesize what they say to help you think about and understand the topic you're researching—to identify connections among them and blend them into a coherent whole that at the same time articulates *ideas of your own*. This chapter will help you blend ideas from sources with your own ideas smoothly and effectively—just like a really great mash-up.

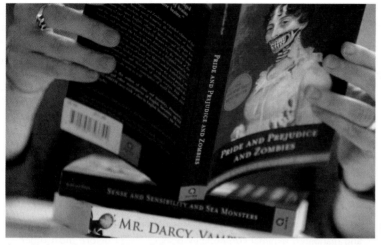

An unlikely mash-up: Jane Austen's *Pride and Prejudice* and . . . zombies! With 85 percent Austen's original text and 15 percent zombie gore, *Pride and Prejudice and Zombies* became an instant best-seller, setting off a slew of literary monster mash-ups.

Synthesizing the Ideas in Your Sources

Here are some questions to help you synthesize information as you work with your sources. Try **ANNOTATING** sources with these questions in mind:

- What issues, problems, or controversies do your sources address?

- What else do your sources have in common? Any ideas? facts? examples? statistics? Are any people or works cited in more than one source?

- What significant differences do you find among sources? Different stances? positions? purposes? kinds of evidence? conclusions?

- Do any of your sources cite or refer to one another? Does one source provide details, examples, or explanations that build on something said in another? Does any source respond specifically to something said in another?

Your goal is to get a sense of how the information from your various sources fits together—how the sources speak to one another and what's being said about your topic.

One function of a synthesis is to establish **CONTEXT** and set the scene for what you yourself have to say. See how the following example from an academic article on high-stakes testing brings together information from a number of sources about the history of testing as context for the discussion of trends in school testing today.

> Although the practice of high-stakes testing gained a prominent position in educational reform with the passage of the No Child Left Behind Act (NCLB) of 2002, its use as a lever for school change preceded NCLB. Tests have been used to distribute rewards and sanctions to teachers in urban schools since the mid 1800s (Tyack, 1974) and for most schools throughout the United States since at least the 1970s (Haertel & Herman, 2005). New York state in particular has led the United States in test-based accountability efforts, "implementing state-developed (1965) and mandated minimal competency testing (MCT) before most other states (1978) and disseminating information to the media about local district performance on the state assessments before it became routinely popular (1985)" (Allington & McGill-Franzen, 1992, p. 398).
>
> —SHARON NICHOLS, GENE GLASS, AND DAVID BERLINER,
> "High-stakes Testing and Student Achievement"

Look now at this dramatic opening to a magazine article on actor-comedian Robin Williams's death by suicide:

> If you were keeping an eye on Robin Williams' *Twitter* feed these past few months—along with his 875,000 followers—you would have noticed nothing the least bit worrying about the 63-year-old actor-comedian's state of mind. On June 6, he uploaded a photo of himself visiting the San Francisco Zoo, where one of the monkeys had been named after him ("What an honor!"). On July 30, he posted a plug for his December movie, *Night at the Museum: Secret of the Tomb* ("I hope you enjoy it!"). And then, on July 31, in what would turn out to be his last public comment, he tweeted his daughter Zelda a birthday message ("Quarter of a century old today but always my baby girl").
>
> Eleven days later, he was discovered dead at his home in Marin County, California.—BENJAMIN SVETKEY, "Robin Williams Remembered by Critics, Close Friends"

By synthesizing multiple sources—in this case, Williams's *Twitter* posts—and presenting them as one cohesive whole, Svetkey paints a picture of a seemingly happy man.

While these two examples are quite different—one cites academic sources in an academic publication, the other cites social media sources in a popular magazine—they both synthesize information to give readers context for what the authors go on to say. For all writers, including you, that's the next step.

REFLECT. Try your hand at synthesizing the sources you've consulted so far for something you're writing. What patterns do you see? What's being said about your topic?

Moving from What Your Sources Say to What You Say

As a researcher, you'll always be working to synthesize the ideas and information you find in your research, to see the big picture and make sense of it all. At the same time, you'll be striving to connect the data you gather to your own ideas and to your research goals. You'll be learning a lot about what many others have discovered or said about your topic, and that will surely affect what you yourself think—and write—about it. Here are some questions that can help you move from the ideas you find in your sources to the ideas that you'll then write about:

- How do the ideas and information in your sources address your **RESEARCH QUESTION**? What answers do they give? What information do you find the most relevant, useful, and persuasive?

- How do they support your tentative **THESIS**? Do they suggest reasons or ways that you should expand, qualify, or otherwise revise it?

- What viewpoints in your sources do you most agree with? disagree with? Why?

- What conclusions can you draw from the ideas and information you've learned from your sources? What discoveries have you made in studying these sources, and what new ideas have they led you to?

- Has your research changed your own views on your topic? Do any of your sources raise questions that you can pursue further?

- Have you encountered any ideas that you would like to build on— or challenge?

- From everything you've read, what is the significance of the topic you're researching? Who cares, and why does it matter?

When you work with your sources in this way, you can count on your ideas to grow and change. As we've been saying, research is an act of learning and inquiry, and you never know where it will lead. But as soon as you sit down and write, no matter what you say or how you say it, you will be, as Kenneth Burke says, "putting in your oar," adding your voice *and your ideas* to the very conversation you've been researching.

THINK BEYOND WORDS

↪ *WATCH* Cause/Effect: The Unexpected Origins of Terrible Things, *a video essay by Adam Westbrook that makes a fascinating argument about what caused World War I. (You'll find it at* everyonesanauthor.tumblr.com.*) As you'll see, Westbrook synthesizes many kinds of sources and information—history books, maps, cartoons, newspapers, archival photographs and video, data from public records, and more—to build a case for his argument. How does he synthesize all these sources in a video? How does he go about introducing each one and weaving them together with his own ideas?*

Entering the Conversation You've Been Researching

Once you've thought carefully about what others have said about your topic, you can add your own voice to the conversation. Look at the following example from the introduction to an essay tracing the changes in political cartoons in the United States between World War II and the Iraq War. See how the writer synthesized ideas from her research into her writing in a way that set up her own questions and thoughts.

> A cartoon shows carolers at the White House door making a choral argument to then president George W. Bush that "we gotta get out of this place," referring to America's involvement in the war in Iraq (fig. 1). Bush appears completely oblivious to their message.
>
> First published in 2006, this cartoon offered a critique of America's continued presence in Iraq by criticizing the president's actions and attitudes towards the war, exemplifying how political cartoons have long been, and continue to be, a prominent part of wartime propaganda.

Combining eye-catching illustrations with textual critique, such cartoons do more than merely convey messages about current events. Rather, political cartoons serve as a tool for shaping public opinion. In fact, since the 1500s, political cartoons have used satirical critiques to persuade the general public about matters large and small (McCloud 16–17).

In the United States, the political (or editorial) cartoon is a form of editorializing that began as "scurrilous caricatures," according to Stephen Becker, author of *Comic Art in America*. His book looks, in part, at the social history of political cartoons and states that it was only after "newspapers and magazines came to be published regularly . . . that caricatures, visual allegories, and the art of design were combined to form . . . modern editorial art" (15). As all-encompassing as that description of "modern editorial art" seems to be, it suggests several questions that remain unanswered: Do cartoonists use common themes to send their critical messages? As society and regulations change from generation to generation, do the style and content of political cartoons change as well? Have political cartoons become "modernized" since World War II? The essay that follows aims to answer as well as draw out the implications of these questions.   —JULIA LANDAUER, "War, Cartoons, and Society: Changes in Political Cartoons between World War II and the Iraq War"

Landauer begins with a cartoon (a primary source) that illustrates a point she is making—that editorial cartoons are known for stinging political critiques. She then refers to a source (McCloud) to provide some background information and then another (Becker) to provide additional commentary on the "modern editorial art" she intends to examine in her essay. At that point, she raises questions "that remain unaddressed"—and says that answering them will be the work of her essay. Thus she uses ideas drawn from her sources to introduce her own ideas—and weave them all together into a strong introduction to her essay.

In your college writing, you will have the opportunity to come up with a research question and to dig in and do some research in order to answer it. That digging in will lead you to identify key sources already in conversation about your topic, to read and analyze those sources, and to begin synthesizing them with your own ideas. Before you know it, you won't be just listening in on the conversation: you'll be an active participant in it.

TWENTY-SIX

Quoting, Paraphrasing, Summarizing

 HEN YOU'RE TEXTING or talking with friends, you don't usually need to be explicit about where you got your information; your friends trust what you say because they know you. In academic writing, however, it's important to establish your credibility, and one way to do so is by consulting authoritative sources. Doing so shows that you've done your homework on your topic, gives credit to those whose ideas you've relied on, and helps demonstrate your own authority as an author.

Your challenge in much academic writing is to integrate other voices with your own. How do you let your audience hear from expert sources while ensuring that their words don't eclipse yours? How do you pick and choose brief segments from long passages of text—or condense those passages into much briefer statements—without misrepresenting someone's ideas? How do you then introduce these segments and integrate them with your own words and ideas? This chapter provides guidelines on the three ways you can incorporate sources into your writing: quoting, paraphrasing, and summarizing.

A **QUOTATION** consists of someone's exact words, enclosed in quotation marks or set off as a block from the rest of your text. A **PARAPHRASE** includes the details of a passage in your own words and syntax. A **SUMMARY** contains the points of a passage that are important to your purpose, leaving out the other details.

Deciding Whether to Quote, Paraphrase, or Summarize

Quote

- Something that is said so well that it's worth repeating
- Complex ideas that are expressed so clearly that paraphrasing or summarizing could distort or oversimplify them
- Experts whose opinions and exact words help to establish your own **CREDIBILITY** and **AUTHORITY** to write on the topic
- Passages that you yourself are analyzing
- Those who disagree or offer **COUNTERARGUMENTS** —quoting their exact words is a way to be sure you represent their opinions fairly

Paraphrase

- Passages where the details matter, but not the exact words
- Passages that are either too technical or too complicated for your readers to understand

Summarize

- Lengthy passages when the main point is important to your argument but the details are not

Whatever method you use for incorporating the words and ideas of others into your own writing, be sure that they work to support what *you* want to say. You're the author—and whatever your sources say needs to connect to what you say—so be sure to make that connection clear. Don't assume that sources speak for themselves. Introduce any source that you cite, naming the authors and identifying them in some way if your audience won't know who they are. In addition, be sure to follow quotations with a comment that explains how they relate to your point.

And regardless of whether you decide to quote, paraphrase, or summarize, you'll need to credit each source. Even if what you include is not a direct quotation, the ideas are still someone else's, and failing to credit your source can result in plagiarism. Indicate the source in a **SIGNAL PHRASE** and include in-text documentation.

Quoting

When you include a direct quotation, be sure to use the exact words of the original source. And while you don't want to include too many quotations—you are the author, after all—using the exact words from a source is sometimes the best way to ensure that you accurately represent what was said. Original quotations can also be an effective way of presenting a point, by letting other people speak in their own words. But be sure to frame any quotation you include, introducing it and then explaining why it's important to the point that you are making.

Enclose short quotations in quotation marks within your main text. Such quotations should be no longer than four typed lines (in MLA style) or forty words (in APA style).

> Programmer and digital media pioneer Jaron Lanier describes the problems resulting from "lock-in" (in which software becomes difficult to change because it has been engineered to work with existing programs), arguing that lock-in "is an absolute tyrant in the digital world" (8). He means that "lock-in" inhibits creativity as new development is constrained by old software.

In MLA style, short quotations of poetry—no more than three lines—should also be enclosed in quotation marks within the main text. Include slashes (with a space on either side) between each line of verse.

> In "When You are Old," poet William Butler Yeats advises Maud Gonne, the radical Irish nationalist, that when she looks back on her youth from old age, she should consider "How many loved your moments of glad grace, / And loved your beauty with love false or true, / But one man loved the pilgrim soul in you." Yeats thus suggests that he is the "one man" who truly loved her so sincerely all these years.

Set off long quotations as a block by indenting them from the left margin. No need to enclose them in quotation marks, but do indent five spaces (or one-half inch) if you are using either MLA or APA style. Use this method for quotations that are more than four lines of prose or three lines of poetry (in MLA) or longer than forty words (in APA).

> In her 1976 keynote address to the Democratic National Convention, Texas congresswoman Barbara Jordan reflects on the occasion:
>
>> Now that I have this grand distinction, what in the world am I supposed to say? . . . I could list the problems which cause people to feel cynical, angry, frustrated: problems which include lack of integrity in government; the feeling that the individual no longer counts; the reality of material and spiritual poverty; the feeling that the grand American experiment is failing or has failed. I could recite these problems, and then I could sit down and offer no solutions. But I don't choose to do that either. The citizens of America expect more. (189)
>
> In this passage, Jordan resists the opportunity to attack the opposing party, preferring instead to offer positive solutions rather than simply a list of criticisms and problems.

Go to every onesanauthor .tumblr.com to listen to the full text of Barbara Jordan's speech.

Notice that with block quotations, the parenthetical citation falls *after* the period at the end of the quotation.

Indicate changes to the text within a quotation by using brackets to enclose text that you add or change and ellipses to indicate text that you omit.

Use brackets to indicate that you have altered the original wording to fit grammatically within your text or have added or changed wording to clarify something that might otherwise be unclear. In this example, the author changed the verb *had* to *should have*:

> John Maeda, president of the Rhode Island School of Design, reacts to America's current emphasis on STEM education with the proposal that "just like STEM is made up of science, technology, engineering and math, we [should have] IDEA, made up of intuition, design, emotion and art—all the things that make us humans feel, well, human" ("On Meaningful Observation").

Use ellipsis marks in place of words, phrases, or sentences that you leave out because they aren't crucial or relevant for your purpose. Use three dots, with a space before each one and after the last, when you omit only words and phrases within a sentence. If you leave out the end of a sentence or a whole sentence or more, put a period after the last word before the ellipsis mark. Note how a writer does both in the example below.

> Warning of the effects of GPS on our relationship to the world around us, Nicholas Carr concludes that "the automation of wayfinding . . . encourages us to observe and manipulate symbols on screens rather than attend to real things in real places. . . . What we should be asking ourselves is, *How far from the world do we want to retreat?*" (137)

When you use brackets or ellipses, make sure your changes don't end up misrepresenting the author's original point, which would damage your own credibility. Mark Twain once joked that "nearly any invented quotation, played with confidence, stands a good chance to deceive." Twain was probably right—it's quite easy to "invent" quotations or twist their meaning by taking them out of context or changing some keyword. You don't want to be guilty of this!

Set off a quotation within a quotation with single quotation marks. In the following passage, the author quotes Nicholas Carr, who himself quotes the writing of anthropologist Tim Ingold:

Nicholas Carr sums up the difference between navigating with and without a GPS device using two terms borrowed from Scottish anthropologist Tim Ingold. As Carr explains, Ingold "draws a distinction between two very different modes of travel: wayfaring and transport. Wayfaring, he explains, is 'our most fundamental way of being in the world'" (132). It is navigating by our observations and mental maps of the world around us, as opposed to blindly following GPS-generated directions from point A to point B—the mode Ingold and Carr call "transport."

Punctuate quotations carefully. Parenthetical documentation comes after the closing quotation mark, and any punctuation that is part of your sentence comes after the parentheses (except in the case of a block quote, where the parenthetical documentation goes at the very end).

- *Commas and periods* always go inside the closing quotation marks. If there's parenthetical documentation, however, the period goes after the parentheses.

  "Everybody worships," said David Foster Wallace in a 2005 commencement speech. "There is no such thing as not worshipping" (8).

- *Colons and semicolons* always go outside closing quotation marks.

  Wallace warned as well that there are "whole parts of adult American life that nobody talks about in commencement speeches": sometimes, he says, we'll be bored (4).

  He also once noted that when a lobster is put in a kettle of boiling water, it "behaves very much as you or I would behave if we were plunged into boiling water"; in other words, it acts as if it's in terrible pain (10).

- *Question marks and exclamation points* go inside closing quotation marks if they are part of the original quotation, but outside the quotation marks if they are part of your sentence.

Wallace opened his speech with a now famous joke about how natural it is to be unaware of the world: an old fish swims by two young fish and says, "Morning, boys. How's the water?" They swim on, and after a while one young fish turns to the other and asks, "What the hell is water?" (1)

So what, according to David Foster Wallace, is the "capital-T Truth about life" (9)?

Paraphrasing

When you paraphrase, you restate information or ideas from a source using your words, your sentence structure, your style. A paraphrase should cover the same points that the original source does, so it's usually about the same length—but sticking too closely to the sentence structures in your source could be plagiarizing. And even though you're using your own words, don't forget where the ideas came from: you should always name the author and include parenthetical documentation.

Here is a paragraph about the search for other life-forms similar to our own in the universe, followed by three paraphrases.

Original source

As the romance of manned space exploration has waned, the drive today is to find our living, thinking counterparts in the universe. For all the excitement, however, the search betrays a profound melancholy—a lonely species in a merciless universe anxiously awaits an answering voice amid utter silence. That silence is maddening. Not just because it compounds our feeling of cosmic isolation, but because it makes no sense. As we inevitably find more and more exo-planets where intelligent life *can* exist, why have we found no evidence—no signals, no radio waves—that intelligent life *does* exist?

  —CHARLES KRAUTHAMMER, "Are We Alone in the Universe?"

As the underlined words show, the following paraphrase uses too many words from the original.

Unacceptable paraphrase: wording too close to the original

Charles Krauthammer argues that finding our intelligent counterparts in the universe has become more important as the romance of manned space exploration has declined. Even so, the hunt for similar beings also suggests our sadness as a species waiting in vain for an acknowledgment that we aren't alone in a merciless universe. The lack of response, he says, just doesn't make sense because if we keep finding planets that *could* support life, then we should find evidence—like radio waves or signals—of intelligent life out there (A19).

While the next version uses original language, the sentence structures are much too similar to the original.

Unacceptable paraphrase: sentence structures too close to original

As the allure of adventuring into the unknown cosmos has diminished, the desire to discover beings like us out there has grown. There is a sadness to the search though—the calling out into empty space that brings no response. Nothing. Only a vast silence that not only emphasizes our solitary existence but increases our frustration. How can we continue to discover potentially hospitable planets that could sustain life like ours, yet find no evidence—no signs, no data—that such life exists (Krauthammer A19)?

When you paraphrase, be careful not to simply substitute words and phrases while replicating the same sentence structure. And while it may be necessary to use some of the key terms from the original in order to convey the same concepts, be sure to put them in quotation marks—and not to use too many (which would result in plagiarism).

Acceptable paraphrase

Syndicated columnist Charles Krauthammer observes that our current quest to discover other "intelligent life" in the universe comes just as the allure of exploring outer space is dimming. It's a search, he says, that reveals a deep sadness (that we may in fact be living in "cosmic isolation") and a growing frustration: if scientists continue to discover more planets where life like ours can be sustainable, why do we find no actual signs of life (A19)?

Summarizing

Like a paraphrase, a summary presents the source information in your words. However, a summary dramatically condenses the information, covering only the most important points and leaving out the details. Summaries are therefore much briefer than the original texts, though they vary in length depending on the size of the original and your purpose for summarizing; you may need only a sentence or two to summarize an essay, or you may need several paragraphs. In any case, you should always name the author and document the source. The following example appropriately summarizes Krauthammer's passage in one sentence:

> Charles Krauthammer questions whether we will ever find other
> "intelligent life" in the universe—or whether we'll instead discover that
> we do in fact live in "cosmic isolation" (A19).

This summary tells readers Krauthammer's main point and includes in quotation marks two key phrases borrowed from the original source. If we were to work the summary into an essay, it might look like this:

> Many scientists believe that there is a strong probability—given the
> vastness of the universe and how much of it we have yet to explore,
> even with advances like the Hubble telescope—that there is life
> like ours somewhere out there. In a 2011 opinion piece, however,
> syndicated columnist Charles Krauthammer questions whether we
> will ever find other "intelligent life" in the universe—or whether we'll
> instead discover that we do in fact live in "cosmic isolation" (A19).

Three ways a summary can go wrong are if it represents inaccurately the point of the original source, provides so many details that the summary is too long, or is so general that readers are left wondering what the source is about. Consider the following unsuccessful summaries of Krauthammer's passage:

Unacceptable summary: misrepresents the source

Pulitzer Prize–winning columnist Charles Krauthammer extols the
virtues of space exploration.

This summary both misses the point of Krauthammer's questioning our
troubled search for "intelligent life" beyond Earth and claims that the author praises space exploration when at no point in the passage does he
do so.

Unacceptable summary: provides too many details

Award-winning columnist Charles Krauthammer suggests that while
sending people into space is no longer as exciting to us as it once was,
we are interested in finding out if there is life in the universe beyond
Earth. He laments the feeling of being alone in the universe given
that all signs point to the very real possibility that intelligent life exists
elsewhere. Krauthammer wonders "why we have no evidence . . . of
intelligent life" on other habitable planets. He finds this lack of proof
confounding.

This summary is almost as long as the original passage and includes as
many details. As a summary, it doesn't let readers know what points are
most important.

Unacceptable summary: too general

Charles Krauthammer is concerned about the search for life on other
planets.

While the statement above is not false, it does not adequately reflect Krauthammer's main point in a way that will help the reader get the gist of the
original passage. A better summary would tell readers what precisely about
the search for life concerns Krauthammer.

*REFLECT. Return to the quotation from Barbara Jordan on page 544.
First, write an appropriate paraphrase of the quotation; then write an appropriate
summary.*

Incorporating Source Material

Whether you quote, paraphrase, or summarize source material, you need to be careful to distinguish what you say from what your sources say, while at the same time weaving the two together smoothly in your writing. That is, you must make clear how the ideas you're quoting, paraphrasing, or summarizing relate to your own—why you're bringing them into your text.

Use signal phrases to introduce source materials, telling readers who said what and providing some context if need be. Don't just drop in a quotation or paraphrase or summary; you need to introduce it. And while you can always use a neutral signal phrase such as "he says" or "she claims," try to choose verbs that reflect the **STANCE** of those you're citing. In some cases, a simple "she says" does reflect that stance, but usually you can make your writing livelier and more accurate with a more specific signal verb.

Use a **SIGNAL PHRASE** and parenthetical documentation to clearly distinguish your own words and ideas from those of others. The following paraphrase introduces source material with a signal phrase that includes the author's name and closes with documentation giving the page number from which the information is taken.

> As Ernst Mayr explains, Darwin's theory of evolution presented a significant challenge to then-prevalent beliefs about humanity's centrality in the world (9).

If you do not give the author's name in a signal phrase, include it in the parenthetical documentation.

> Darwin's theory of evolution presented a significant challenge to then-prevalent beliefs about humanity's centrality in the world (Mayr 9).

Sometimes you'll want or need to state the author's authority or credentials in the signal phrase, lending credibility to your own use of that source.

> According to music historian Ted Gioia, record sales declined sharply during the Great Depression, dropping by almost 90 percent between 1927 and 1932 (127).

Choose verbs that reflect the author's stance toward the material—or your own stance in including it. Saying "she notes" means something different than saying "she insists" or "she implies."

> Because almost anyone can create a blog, most people assume that blogs give average citizens a greater voice in public dialogue. Political scientist Matthew Hindman questions this assumption: "Though millions of Americans now maintain a blog, only a few dozen political bloggers get as many readers as a typical college newspaper" (103).

Signal phrases do not have to come first. To add variety to your writing, try positioning them in the middle or at the end of a sentence.

> "Attracting attention," observes Richard Lanham, "is what style is all about" (xi).

> "We've got to stop the debates! Enough with the debates!" pleaded John McCain last Sunday on *Meet the Press* (31).

SOME USEFUL SIGNAL VERBS

acknowledges	concludes	observes
adds	declares	reports
asserts	implies	responds
claims	objects	suggests

Verb tenses. The verb tense you use when referring to a text or researcher in a signal phrase will depend on your documentation style. MLA style requires the present tense (*argues*) or the present perfect (*has argued*). Using MLA style, you might write, "In *Rhetoric*, Aristotle argues" or "In commenting on Aristotle's *Rhetoric*, scholars have argued." An exception involves sentences that include specific dates in the past. In this case, the past tense is acceptable: "In his introduction to the 1960 edition of Aristotle's *Rhetoric*, Lane Cooper argued."

The past tense is conventional in APA style, as is the present perfect. You might write, "In *Rhetoric*, Aristotle argued" or "In commenting on Aristotle's *Rhetoric*, scholars have argued." However, use the present tense when you refer to the results of a study ("the results of Conrad (2012) demonstrate") or when you make a generalization ("writing researchers agree").

Parenthetical documentation. If you're following **MLA**, you'll need to include page numbers for all quotations, paraphrases, and summaries from print sources in your parenthetical documentation. If you're using **APA**, page numbers are required for quotations; for paraphrases and summaries, they're optional—but it's always a good idea to include them whenever you can do so.

Incorporating Visual and Audio Sources

Sometimes you will want to incorporate visual or audio elements from sources that you cannot write into a paragraph. For example, you may include charts, photographs, or audio/video clips. Remember that any such materials that come from sources need to be introduced, explained, and documented just as you would a quotation. If you're following MLA or APA style, refer to Chapters 28 and 29 for specific requirements.

Tables. Label anything that contains facts or figures displayed in columns as a table. Number all tables in sequence, and provide a descriptive title for each one. Supply source information immediately below the table; credit your data source even if you've created the table yourself. If any information within the table requires further explanation (abbreviations, for example), include a note below the source citation.

Figures. Number and label everything that is not a table (photos, graphs, drawings, maps, and so on) as a figure and include a caption letting readers know what the image illustrates. Unless the visual is a photograph or drawing you created yourself, provide appropriate source information after the caption; graphs, maps, and other figures you produce based on information from other sources should still include a full credit. If the visual is discussed in detail within your text, you can use an abbreviated citation and include full documentation in your list of **WORKS CITED** or **REFERENCES**.

Audio and video recordings. If your medium allows it, provide a link to any recorded element or embed a media player into the text. If you're working

Fig. 1: The Guggenheim Museum, Spain.

in a medium that won't allow linking or embedding, discuss the recording in your text and provide a full citation in your list of **WORKS CITED** or **REFERENCES** so your readers can track down the recording themselves.

Captions. Create a clear, succinct caption for each visual or recording: "Fig. 1: The Guggenheim Museum, Spain." The caption should identify and explain the visual—and should reflect your purpose. In an essay about contemporary architecture in Spain, your caption might say "Fig. 1: The Guggenheim Museum, Bilbao. Designed by Frank Gehry."

Sizing and positioning visuals and recordings. Refer to every visual or embedded recording in your text: "(see fig. 1)," "as shown in Table 3," "in the *YouTube* video below." The element may be on the page where it's discussed, but it should not come before you introduce it to your readers. Think carefully about how you will size and position each visual to be most effective: you want to make sure that your visuals are legible and that they support rather than disrupt the text.

TWENTY-SEVEN

Giving Credit, Avoiding Plagiarism

HO OWNS WORDS AND IDEAS? Answers to this question differ from culture to culture. In some societies, they are shared resources, not the property of individuals. In others, using another person's words or ideas may be seen as a tribute or compliment that doesn't require specific acknowledgment. In the United States, however (as in much of the Western world), elaborate systems of copyright and patent law have grown up to protect the intellectual property (including words, images, voices, and ideas) of individuals and corporations. This system forms the foundation of the documentation conventions currently followed in US schools. And while these conventions are being challenged today by the open-source movement and others who argue that "information wants to be free," the conventions still hold sway in the academy and in the law. As a researcher, you will need to understand these conventions and to practice them in your own writing. Put simply, these conventions allow you to give credit where credit is due and thereby avoid plagiarism (the use of the words and ideas of others as if they were your own work).

But acknowledging your sources is not simply about avoiding charges of plagiarism (although you would be doing that too). Rather, it helps establish your own CREDIBILITY as a researcher and an author. It shows that you have consulted other sources of information about your topic and can engage with them in your own work. Additionally, citing and documenting your sources allows readers to locate them for their own purposes if they wish; in effect, it anticipates the needs of your audience.

There are some cases, however, in which you do not need to provide citations for information that you incorporate—for example, if the information is common knowledge. This chapter will help you identify which sources you must acknowledge, explain the basics of documenting your sources, and provide strategies for avoiding plagiarism.

Knowing What You Must Acknowledge

As a general rule, material taken from specific outside sources—whether ideas, texts, images, or sounds—should be CITED and DOCUMENTED. But there are some exceptions.

INFORMATION THAT DOES NOT NEED TO BE ACKNOWLEDGED

- *Information that is "common knowledge."* Uncontroversial information ("People today get most of their news and information from the internet"), well-known historical events ("Neil Armstrong was the first person to walk on the moon"), facts ("All mammals are warm-blooded"), and quotations (Armstrong's "That's one small step for man, one giant leap for mankind") that are widely available in general reference sources do not need to be cited.

- *Information well known to your audience.* Keep in mind that what is common knowledge varies depending on your audience. While an audience of pulmonary oncologists would be familiar with the names of researchers who established that smoking is linked to lung cancer, for a general audience you might need to cite a source if you give the names.

- *Information from well-known, easily accessible documents.* You do not need to include the specific location where you accessed texts that are available from a variety of public sources and are widely familiar, such as the United States Constitution.

- *Your own work.* If you've gathered data, come up with an idea, or generated a text (including images, multimedia texts, and so on) entirely on your own, you should indicate that to your readers in some way—but it's not necessary to include a formal citation, unless the material has been previously published elsewhere.

INFORMATION THAT MUST BE ACKNOWLEDGED

- *Direct quotations, paraphrases, and summaries.* Exact wording should always be enclosed in quotation marks and cited. And always cite specific ideas taken from another source, even when you present them using your own words.

- *Controversial information.* If there is some debate over the information you're including, cite the source so readers know whose version or interpretation of the facts you're using.

- *Information given in only a few sources.* If only one or two sources make this information available (that is, it isn't common knowledge widely accessible in general sources), include a citation.

- *Any materials that you did not create yourself*—including tables, charts, images, and audio or video segments. Even if you create a table or chart yourself, if it presents information from an outside source, that's someone else's work that needs to be acknowledged.

A word to the wise: it's always better to cite any information that you've taken from another source than to guess wrong and unintentionally plagiarize. If in doubt, err on the safe side and include a citation.

Fair Use and the Internet

In general, principles of fair use apply to the writing you do for your college classes. These principles allow you to use passages and images from the copyrighted work of others without their explicit permission as long as you do so for educational purposes and you fully cite what you use. When you publish your writing online, however, where that material can be seen by all, then you must have permission from the copyright owner in order to post it.

Students across the country have learned about this limitation on fair use the hard way. One student we know won a prize for an essay she wrote, which was then posted on the writing prize website. In the essay, she included a cartoon that was copyrighted by the cartoonist. Soon after the essay was posted, she received a letter from the copyright holder, demanding that she remove the image and threatening her with a lawsuit. Another student, whose essay was published on a class website, was stunned when his instructor got an angry email from a professor at another university, saying that the student writer had used too much of her work in the essay and that, furthermore, it had not been fully and properly cited. The student, who had intended no dishonesty at all, was embarrassed, to say the least.

Many legal scholars and activists believe that fair use policies and laws should be relaxed and that making these laws more restrictive undermines creativity. While these issues get debated in public forums and legal courts, however, you are well advised to be careful not only in citing and documenting all your sources thoroughly but in getting permission in writing to use any copyrighted text or image in anything you plan to post or publish online.

Avoiding Plagiarism

In US academic culture, incorporating the words, ideas, or materials of others into your own work without giving credit through appropriate citations and documentation is viewed as unethical and is considered plagiarism. The consequences of such unacknowledged borrowing are serious: students who plagiarize may receive failing grades for assignments or courses, be subjected to an administrative review for academic misconduct, or even be dismissed from school.

Certainly, the deliberate and obvious effort to pass off someone else's work as your own, such as by handing in a paper purchased online or written by someone else, is plagiarism and can easily be spotted and punished. More troublesome and problematic, however, is the difficulty some students have using the words and ideas of others fairly and acknowledging them fully. Especially when you're new to a field or writing about unfamiliar ideas, incorporating sources without plagiarizing can be challenging.

In fact, researcher Rebecca Moore Howard has found that even expert writers have difficulty incorporating the words and ideas of others acceptably when they are working with material outside their comfort zone or field of expertise. Such difficulty can often lead to what Howard calls PATCHWRITING: restating material from sources in ways that stick too closely to the original language or syntax.

But patchwriting can help you work with sources. Some call patchwriting plagiarism, even when it's documented, but we believe that it can be a step in the process of learning how to weave the words and thoughts of others into your own work. Assume, for example, that you want to summarize ideas from the following passage:

> Over the past few decades, scholars from a variety of disciplines have devoted considerable attention toward studying evolving public attitudes toward a whole range of LGBT civil rights issues including support for open service in the military, same-sex parent adoption, employment non-discrimination, civil unions, and marriage equality. In the last 10 years in particular, the emphasis has shifted toward studying the various factors that best explain variation in support for same-sex marriage including demographic considerations, religious and ideological predispositions, attitudes toward marriage and family, and social contact (Baunach 2011, 2012; Becker, 2012a, 2012b; Becker & Scheufele, 2009, 2011; Becker & Todd, 2013; Brewer, 2008; Brewer & Wilcox, 2005; Lewis, 2005, 2011; Lewis & Gossett, 2008; Lewis & Oh, 2008).
>
> —AMY BECKER, "Employment Discrimination, Local School Boards, and LGBT Civil Rights: Reviewing 25 Years of Public Opinion Data"

This passage includes a lot of detailed information in complex sentences that can be hard to process. See how one student first summarized it, and why this summary would be unacceptable in an essay of his own:

A patchwritten summary

For more than 20 years, scholars from many disciplines have committed their energies to examining changing public attitudes toward a variety of LGBT civil rights issues. These encompass things like open military service, same-sex parent adoption, equal employment opportunities, civil unions, and marriage equality. Since 2004, focus has moved toward examining those elements that best account for differences in public support for same-sex marriage like demographic considerations, religious and ideological predispositions, attitudes toward marriage and family, and social contact (Baunach 2011, 2012; Becker, 2012a, 2012b; Becker & Scheufele, 2009, 2011; Becker & Todd, 2013; Brewer, 2008; Brewer & Wilcox, 2005; Lewis, 2005, 2011; Lewis & Gossett, 2008; Lewis & Oh, 2008).

This is a classic case of patchwriting that would be considered plagiarism. The sentence structure looks very much like Becker's, and even some of the language is taken straight from the original article. While such a summary would not be acceptable in any writing you turn in, this sort of patchwriting can help you understand what a difficult source is saying.

And once you understand the source, writing an acceptable summary gets a lot easier. In the acceptable summary below, the writer focuses on the ideas in the long second sentence of the original passage, turning those ideas into two simpler sentences and using a direct quotation from the original.

Acceptable summary

Scholars studying changes in public opinion on LGBT issues have increasingly focused on the growing support for same-sex marriage. In looking at the question of why opinions on this issue differ, these scholars have considered factors such as "demographic considerations, religious and ideological predispositions, attitudes toward marriage and family, and social contact" (Becker 342).

An acceptable summary uses the writer's own language and sentence structures, and quotation marks to indicate any borrowed language. To write a summary like this one, you would need to be able to restate the source's main point (that same-sex marriage has gotten greater scholarly attention lately than other LGBTQ issues) and decide what information is most important for your purposes—what details are worth emphasizing with a quotation or a longer summary. Finally, notice that the citation credits Becker's article, because that is the source this writer consulted, not the research Becker cites. Chapter 26 offers you more guidelines on **QUOTING**, **PARAPHRASING**, and **SUMMARIZING** appropriately.

STEPS YOU CAN TAKE TO AVOID PLAGIARISM

Understand what constitutes plagiarism. Plagiarism includes any unacknowledged use of material from another source that isn't considered common knowledge; this includes phrases, ideas, and materials such as graphs, charts, images, videos, and so on. In a written text, it includes neglecting to put someone else's exact wording in quotation marks; leaving out in-text documentation for sources that you **QUOTE**, **PARAPHRASE**, or **SUMMARIZE**; and borrowing too many of the original sources' words and sentence structures in paraphrases or summaries. Check to see if your school has any explicit guidelines for what constitutes plagiarism.

Take notes carefully and conscientiously. If you can't locate the source of words or ideas that you've copied down, you may neglect to cite them properly. Technology makes it easy to copy and paste text and materials from electronic sources directly into your own work—and then to move on and forget to put such material in quotation marks or record the source. So keep copies of sources, note documentation information, and be sure to put any borrowed language in quotation marks and to clearly distinguish your own ideas from those of others.

Know where your information comes from. Because information passes quickly and often anonymously through the internet grapevine, you may not always be able to determine the origin of a text or image you find online. If you don't know where something came from, don't include it. Not only would you be unable to write a proper citation, chances are you haven't been able to verify the information either.

DOCUMENT sources carefully. Below you'll find an overview of the basics of documenting sources. More detail on using MLA and APA documentation is given in the next two chapters.

Plan ahead. Work can pile up in a high-pressure academic environment. Stay on top of your projects by scheduling your work and sticking to the deadlines you set. This way, you'll avoid taking shortcuts that could lead to inadvertent plagiarism.

Consult your instructor if necessary. If you're uncertain about how to acknowledge sources properly or are struggling with a project, talk with your instructor about finding a solution. Even taking a penalty for submitting an assignment late is better than being caught cheating or being accused of plagiarism that you didn't intend to commit.

Documenting Sources

When you document sources, you identify the ones you've used and give information about their authors, titles, and publication. Documenting your sources allows you to show evidence of the research you've done and enables your readers to find those sources if they wish to. Most academic documentation systems include two parts: **IN-TEXT DOCUMENTATION**, which you insert in your text after the specific information you have borrowed, and an end-of-text list of **WORKS CITED** or **REFERENCES**, which provides complete bibliographic information for every work you've cited.

This book covers two documentation systems—those of the Modern Language Association (**MLA**) and the American Psychological Association (**APA**). MLA style is used primarily in English and other humanities subjects, and APA is used mostly in psychology and other social sciences. Chances are that you will be required to use either MLA or APA style or both in your college courses. Note that some disciplines may require other documentation systems, such as CSE (Council of Science Editors) or *Chicago Manual of Style*.

MLA and APA both call for the same basic information; you'll need to give the author's name (or sometimes the editor's name or the title) in the in-text citation, and your end-of-text list should provide the author, title, and publication information for each source that you cite. But the two systems differ in some ways. In APA, for example, your in-text documentation always includes the date of publication, but that is not generally done in MLA. You'll find detailed guidance on the specifics of MLA in Chapter 28 and of APA in Chapter 29, with color-coded examples to help you easily distinguish where the author and editor, title, and publication information appear for each type of work you document. Each of these chapters also includes a student paper that uses that style of documentation.

REFLECT. Think about the kinds of information you'll need to give when writing about your research. For your topic and your intended audience, what would be considered common knowledge? What might not be common knowledge for a different audience? What do you know about your audience that can help you make that decision?

TWENTY-EIGHT

MLA Style

 LA STYLE CALLS for (1) brief in-text documentation and (2) complete bibliographic information in a list of works cited at the end of your text. The models and examples in this chapter draw on the eighth edition of the *MLA Handbook*, published by the Modern Language Association in 2016. For additional information, visit style.mla.org.

A DIRECTORY TO MLA STYLE

In-Text Documentation   565

1. Author named in a signal phrase 566
2. Author named in parentheses 566
3. Two or more works by the same author 566
4. Authors with the same last name 567
5. Two or more authors 567
6. Organization or government as author 567
7. Author unknown 567
8. Literary works 568
9. Work in an anthology 568
10. Encyclopedia or dictionary 569
11. Legal and historical documents 569
12. Sacred text 569
13. Multivolume work 570
14. Two or more works cited together 570
15. Source quoted in another source 570
16. Work without page numbers 570
17. An entire work or a one-page article 571

Notes   571

List of Works Cited   572

Core Elements   572

Authors and Other Contributors 572

Titles 572

Publisher 573

Dates 573

Location 573

Punctuation 574

Authors and Other Contributors   574

1. One author 575
2. Two authors 575
3. Three or more authors 575
4. Two or more works by the same author 575
5. Author and editor or translator 576
6. No author or editor 576
7. Organization or government as author 576

Articles and Other Short Works   577

Documentation Map: Article in a Print Journal   579

Documentation Map: Article in an Online Magazine   581

Documentation Map: Article Accessed through a Database   582

8. Article in a journal 577
9. Article in a magazine 577
10. Article in a newspaper 578
11. Article accessed through a database 578
12. Entry in a reference work 580
13. Editorial 580
14. Letter to the editor 583
15. Review 583
16. Comment on an online article 583

Books and Parts of Books   584

Documentation Map: Print Book   586

17. Basic entries for a book 584
18. Anthology 584
19. Work in an anthology 585
20. Multivolume work 585
21. Book in a series 587
22. Graphic narrative 587
23. Sacred text 587
24. Edition other than the first 587
25. Republished work 588
26. Foreword, introduction, preface, or afterword 588
27. Published letter 588
28. Paper at a conference 588
29. Dissertation 589

author   title   publication

Websites   589

Documentation Map: Work on a Website   590

30. Entire website 589
31. Work on a website 591
32. Blog entry 591
33. Wiki 591

Personal Communication and Social Media   591

34. Personal letter 591
35. Email 592
36. Text message 592
37. Post to an online forum 592
38. Post to *Twitter, Facebook*, or other social media 592

Audio, Visual, and Other Sources   593

39. Advertisement 593
40. Art 593
41. Cartoon 594
42. Supreme Court case 594
43. Film 594
44. Interview 595
45. Map 595
46. Musical score 596
47. Online video 596
48. Oral presentation 596
49. Podcast 596
50. Radio program 597
51. Sound recording 597
52. TV show 597
53. Video game 598

Formatting a Research Paper   598

Sample Research Paper   600

Throughout this chapter, you'll find models and examples that are color coded to help you see how writers include source information in their texts and in their lists of works cited: tan for author, editor, translator, and other contributors; yellow for titles; gray for publication information — publisher, date of publication, page number(s) or other location information, and so on.

IN-TEXT DOCUMENTATION

Brief documentation in your text makes clear to your reader what you took from a source and where in the source you found the information.

In your text, you have three options for citing a source: **QUOTING**, **PARAPHRASING**, and **SUMMARIZING**. As you cite each source, you will need to decide whether or not to name the author in a signal phrase—"as Toni Morrison writes"—or in parentheses—(Morrison 24).

The first examples below show basic in-text documentation of a work by one author. Variations on those examples follow. The examples illustrate the MLA style of using quotation marks around titles of short works and italicizing titles of long works.

1. Author named in a signal phrase

If you mention the author in a **SIGNAL PHRASE**, put only the page number(s) in parentheses. Do not write *page* or *p.*

> McCullough describes John Adams's hands as those of someone used to manual labor (18).

2. Author named in parentheses

If you do not mention the author in a signal phrase, put the last name in parentheses along with the page number(s). Do not use punctuation between the name and the page number(s).

> Adams is said to have had "the hands of a man accustomed to pruning his own trees, cutting his own hay, and splitting his own firewood" (McCullough 18).

Whether you use a signal phrase and parentheses or parentheses only, try to put the parenthetical documentation at the end of the sentence or as close as possible to the material you've cited — without awkwardly interrupting the sentence. Notice that in the example above, the parenthetical reference comes after the closing quotation marks but before the period at the end of the sentence.

3. Two or more works by the same author

If you cite multiple works by one author, include the title of the work you are citing either in the signal phrase or in parentheses. Give the full title if it's brief; otherwise, give a short version.

> Kaplan insists that understanding power in the Near East requires "Western leaders who know when to intervene, and do so without illusions" (*Eastward* 330).

author   title   publication

Put a comma between author and title if both are in the parentheses.

> Understanding power in the Near East requires "Western leaders
> who know when to intervene, and do so without illusions"
> (Kaplan, *Eastward* 330).

4. Authors with the same last name

Give the author's first and last names in any signal phrase, or add the author's first initial in the parenthetical reference.

> *Imaginative* applies not only to modern literature but also to writing of
> all periods, whereas *magical* is often used in writing about Arthurian
> romances (A. Wilson 25).

5. Two or more authors

For a work with two authors, name both, either in a signal phrase or in parentheses.

> Carlson and Ventura's stated goal is to introduce Julio Cortázar,
> Marjorie Agosín, and other Latin American writers to an audience of
> English-speaking adolescents (v).

For a work by three or more authors, name the first author followed by *et al.*

> One popular survey of American literature breaks the contents into
> sixteen thematic groupings (Anderson et al. A19-24).

6. Organization or government as author

Acknowledge the organization either in a signal phrase or in parentheses. It's acceptable to shorten long names.

> The US government warns, "If you are overpaid, we will recover any
> payments not due you" (Social Security Administration 12).

7. Author unknown

If you don't know the author, use the work's title or a shortened version of the title in the parenthetical reference.

A powerful editorial in last week's paper asserts that healthy liver donor Mike Hurewitz died because of "frightening" faulty postoperative care ("Every Patient's Nightmare").

8. Literary works

When referring to literary works that are available in many different editions, give the page numbers from the edition you are using, followed by information that will let readers of any edition locate the text you are citing.

Novels. Give the page and chapter number, separated by a semicolon.

In *Pride and Prejudice*, Mrs. Bennet shows no warmth toward Jane and Elizabeth when they return from Netherfield (105; ch. 12).

Verse plays. Give act, scene, and line numbers, separated by periods.

Macbeth continues the vision theme when he says, "Thou hast no speculation in those eyes / Which thou dost glare with" (3.3.96-97).

Poems. Give the part and the line numbers (separated by periods). If a poem has only line numbers, use the word *line(s)* only in the first reference.

Whitman sets up not only opposing adjectives but also opposing nouns in "Song of Myself" when he says, "I am of old and young, of the foolish as much as the wise, / . . . a child as well as a man" (16.330-32).

One description of the mere in *Beowulf* is "not a pleasant place" (line 1372). Later, it is labeled "the awful place" (1378).

9. Work in an anthology

Name the author(s) of the work, not the editor of the anthology— either in a signal phrase or in parentheses.

"It is the teapots that truly shock," according to Cynthia Ozick in her essay on teapots as metaphor (70).

In *In Short: A Collection of Creative Nonfiction*, readers will find both an essay on Scottish tea (Hiestand) and a piece on teapots as metaphors (Ozick).

author   title   publication

10. Encyclopedia or dictionary

For an entry in an encyclopedia or dictionary, give the author's name, if available. For an entry without an author, give the entry's title in parentheses. If entries are arranged alphabetically, no page number is needed.

> According to *Funk & Wagnall's New World Encyclopedia*, early in his career Kubrick's main source of income came from "hustling chess games in Washington Square Park" ("Kubrick, Stanley").

11. Legal and historical documents

For legal cases and acts of law, name the case or act in a signal phrase or in parentheses. Italicize the name of a legal case.

> In 2005, the Supreme Court confirmed in *MGM Studios, Inc. v. Grokster, Ltd.* that peer-to-peer file sharing is copyright infringement.

Do not italicize the titles of laws, acts, or well-known historical documents such as the Declaration of Independence. Give the title and any relevant articles and sections in parentheses. It's fine to use common abbreviations such as *art.* or *sec.* and to abbreviate well-known titles.

> The president is also granted the right to make recess appointments (US Const., art. 2, sec. 2).

12. Sacred text

When citing a sacred text such as the Bible or the Qur'an for the first time, give the title of the edition, and in parentheses give the book, chapter, and verse (or their equivalent), separated by periods. MLA recommends abbreviating the names of the books of the Bible in parenthetical references. Later citations from the same edition do not have to repeat its title.

> The wording from *The New English Bible* follows: "In the beginning of creation, when God made heaven and earth, the earth was without form and void, with darkness over the face of the abyss, and a mighty wind that swept over the surface of the waters" (Gen. 1.1-2).

13. Multivolume work

If you cite more than one volume of a multivolume work, each time you cite one of the volumes, give the volume *and* the page number(s) in parentheses, separated by a colon and a space.

> Sandburg concludes with the following sentence about those paying last respects to Lincoln: "All day long and through the night the unbroken line moved, the home town having its farewell" (4: 413).

If your works cited list includes only a single volume of a multivolume work, give just the page number in parentheses.

14. Two or more works cited together

If you're citing two or more works closely together, you will sometimes need to provide a parenthetical reference for each one.

> Tanner (7) and Smith (viii) have looked at works from a cultural perspective.

If you include both in the same parentheses, separate the references with a semicolon.

> Critics have looked at both *Pride and Prejudice* and *Frankenstein* from a cultural perspective (Tanner 7; Smith viii).

15. Source quoted in another source

When you are quoting text that you found quoted in another source, use the abbreviation *qtd. in* in the parenthetical reference.

> Charlotte Brontë wrote to G. H. Lewes: "Why do you like Miss Austen so very much? I am puzzled on that point" (qtd. in Tanner 7).

16. Work without page numbers

For works without page numbers, including many online sources, identify the source using the author or other information either in a signal phrase or in parentheses.

author   title   publication

> Studies show that music training helps children to be better at
> multitasking later in life ("Hearing the Music").

If the source has chapter, paragraph, or section numbers, use them with the abbreviations *ch., par.,* or *sec.* ("Hearing the Music," par. 2). Alternatively, you can refer to a heading on a screen to help readers locate text.

> Under the heading "The Impact of the Railroad," Rawls notes that the
> transcontinental railroad was called an iron horse and a greedy octopus.

For an audio or a video recording, give the hours, minutes, and seconds (separated by colons) as shown on the player: (00:05-08:30).

17. An entire work or a one-page article

If you cite an entire work rather than a part of it, or if you cite a single-page article, there's no need to include page numbers.

> Throughout life, John Adams strove to succeed (McCullough).

NOTES

Sometimes you may need to give information that doesn't fit into the text itself — to thank people who helped you, to provide additional details, to refer readers to other sources, or to add comments about sources. Such information can be given in a *footnote* (at the bottom of the page) or an *endnote* (on a separate page with the heading *Notes* just before your works cited list). Put a superscript number at the appropriate point in your text, signaling to readers to look for the note with the corresponding number. If you have multiple notes, number them consecutively throughout your paper.

Text
> This essay will argue that small liberal arts colleges should not recruit
> athletes and, more specifically, that giving student athletes preferential
> treatment undermines the larger educational goals.[1]

Note
> 1. I want to thank all those who have contributed to my thinking
> on this topic, especially my classmates and my teacher Marian Johnson.

LIST OF WORKS CITED

A works cited list provides full bibliographic information for every source cited in your text. See page 600 for guidelines on formatting this list and page 617 for a sample works cited list.

Core Elements

MLA style provides a list of "core elements" for documenting sources, advising writers to list as many of them as possible in the order that MLA specifies. We've used these general principles to provide templates and examples for documenting 53 kinds of sources college writers most often need to cite. The following general guidelines explain how to treat each of the core elements.

Authors and Other Contributors

- If there is one author, list the last name first: Morrison, Toni.
- If there are two authors, list the first author last name first and the second one first name first: Lunsford, Andrea, and Lisa Ede. Put their names in the order given in the work.
- If there are three or more authors, give the first author's name followed by *et al.*: Rose, Mike, et al.
- Include any middle names or initials: Heath, Shirley Brice; Toklas, Alice B.
- If you're citing an editor, translator, or others who are not authors, specify their role. For works with multiple contributors, put the one whose work you wish to highlight before the title, and list any others you want to mention after the title. For contributors named before the title, put the label after the name: Fincher, David, director. For those named after the title, specify their role first: directed by David Fincher.

Titles

- Include any subtitles and capitalize all the words in titles and subtitles except for articles (*a, an, the*), prepositions (*to, at, from,* and so on), and coordinating conjunctions (*and, but, for, or, nor, yet*) — unless they are the first or last word of a title or subtitle.

- Italicize the titles of books, periodicals, and other long whole works (*Pride and Prejudice, Wired*), even if they are part of a larger work.
- Enclose in quotation marks the titles of short works and sources that are part of larger works: "Letter from Birmingham Jail."
- To document a source that has no title, describe it without italics or quotation marks: Letter to the author, Review of doo wop concert.

Publisher

- Write most publishers' names in full, but omit words like *Company* or *Inc.*
- For university presses, use *U* for "University" and *P* for "Press": Princeton UP, U of California P.

Dates

- Whether to give just the year or to include the month and day depends on the source. Give the full date that you find there.
- For books, give the year of publication: 1948. If a book lists more than one date, use the most recent one.
- Periodicals may be published annually, monthly, seasonally, weekly, or daily. Give the full date that you find in the periodical: 2019, Apr. 2019, Spring 2019, 16 Apr. 2019.
- Abbreviate the months except for May, June, and July: Jan., Feb., Mar., Apr., Aug., Sept., Oct., Nov., Dec.
- Because online sources often change or even disappear, provide the date on which you accessed them: Accessed 6 June 2015.
- If an online source includes the time when it was posted or modified, include the time along with the date: 18 Oct. 2015, 9:20 a.m.

Location

- For most print articles and other short works, give a page number or range of pages: p. 24, pp. 24-35. For those that are not on consecutive pages, give the first page number with a plus sign: pp. 24+.
- For online sources, give the URL, omitting *http://* or *https://*. If a source has a permalink, give that.

- For sources found in a database, give the DOI for any source that has one. Otherwise, give the URL.
- For physical objects that you find in a museum, archive, or some other place, give the name of the place and its city: Menil Collection, Houston. Omit the city if it's part of the place's name: Boston Public Library.
- For performances or other live presentations, name the venue and its city: Mark Taper Forum, Los Angeles. Omit the city if it's part of the venue's name: Berkeley Repertory Theatre.

Punctuation

- Use a period after the author name(s) that start an entry (Morrison, Toni.) and the title of the source you're documenting (*Beloved*.).
- Use a comma between the author's last and first names: Morrison, Toni.
- Sometimes you'll need to provide information about more than one work for a single source — for instance, when you cite an article from a periodical that you access through a database. MLA refers to the periodical and database (or any other entity that holds a source) as "containers." Use commas between elements within each container and put a period at the end of each container. For example:

> Semuels, Alana. "The Future Will Be Quiet." *The Atlantic*, Apr. 2016, pp. 19-20. *ProQuest*, search.proquest.com/docview/ 1777443553?accountid+42654. Accessed 5 Apr. 2016.

The guidelines below should help you document kinds of sources you're likely to use. The first section shows how to acknowledge authors and other contributors and applies to all kinds of sources — print, online, or others. Later sections show how to treat titles, publication information, location, and access information for many specific kinds of sources. In general, provide as much information as possible for each source — enough to tell readers how to find a source if they wish to access it themselves.

Authors and Other Contributors

When you name authors and other contributors in your citations, you are crediting them for their work and letting readers know who's in on the

conversation. The following guidelines for citing authors and other contributors apply to all sources you cite: in print, online, or in some other
medium.

1. One author

Author's Last Name, First Name. *Title*. Publisher, Date.

Anderson, Curtis. *The Long Tail: Why the Future of Business Is Selling Less
of More*. Hyperion, 2006.

2. Two authors

1st Author's Last Name, First Name, and 2nd Author's First and Last
Names. *Title*. Publisher, Date.

Lunsford, Andrea, and Lisa Ede. *Singular Texts/Plural Authors: Perspectives
on Collaborative Writing*. Southern Illinois UP, 1990.

3. Three or more authors

1st Author's Last Name, First Name, et al. *Title*. Publisher, Date.

Sebranek, Patrick, et al. *Writers INC: A Guide to Writing, Thinking, and
Learning*. Write Source, 1990.

4. Two or more works by the same author

Give the author's name in the first entry, and then use three hyphens in the
author slot for each of the subsequent works, listing them alphabetically by
the first important word of each title.

Author's Last Name, First Name. *Title That Comes First Alphabetically*.
Publisher, Date.

---. *Title That Comes Next Alphabetically*. Publisher, Date.

Kaplan, Robert D. *The Coming Anarchy: Shattering the Dreams of the Post
Cold War*. Random House, 2000.

---. *Eastward to Tartary: Travels in the Balkans, the Middle East, and the
Caucasus*. Random House, 2000.

5. Author and editor or translator

> Author's Last Name, First Name. *Title*. Role by First and Last Names, Publisher, Date.

> Austen, Jane. *Emma*. Edited by Stephen M. Parrish, W. W. Norton, 2000.
> Dostoevsky, Fyodor. *Crime and Punishment*. Translated by Richard Pevear and Larissa Volokhonsky, Vintage Books, 1993.

Start with the editor or translator if you are focusing on their contribution rather than the author's.

> Pevear, Richard, and Larissa Volokhonsky, translators. *Crime and Punishment*. By Fyodor Dostoevsky, Vintage Books, 1993.

6. No author or editor

When there's no known author or editor, start with the title.

> *The Turner Collection in the Clore Gallery*. Tate Publications, 1987.

> "Being Invisible Closer to Reality." *The Atlanta Journal-Constitution*, 11 Aug. 2008, p. A3.

7. Organization or government as author

> Organization Name. *Title*. Publisher, Date.

> Diagram Group. *The Macmillan Visual Desk Reference*. Macmillan, 1993.

For a government publication, give the name of the government first, followed by the names of any department and agency.

> United States, Department of Health and Human Services, National Institute of Mental Health. *Autism Spectrum Disorders*. Government Printing Office, 2004.

When the organization is both author and publisher, start with the title and list the organization only as the publisher.

> *Stylebook on Religion 2000: A Reference Guide and Usage Manual*. Catholic News Service, 2002.

Articles and Other Short Works

Articles, essays, reviews, and other short works are found in journals, magazines, newspapers, other periodicals, and books — all of which you may find in print, online, or in a database. For most short works, you'll need to provide information about the author, the titles of both the short work and the longer work, any page numbers, and various kinds of publication information, all explained below.

8. Article in a journal

Print

Author's Last Name, First Name. "Title of Article." *Name of Journal,* Volume, Issue, Date, Pages.

Cooney, Brian C. "Considering *Robinson Crusoe*'s 'Liberty of Conscience' in an Age of Terror." *College English,* vol. 69, no. 3, Jan. 2007, pp. 197-215.

Online

Author's Last Name, First Name. "Title of Article." *Name of Journal,* Volume, Issue, Date, Pages (if any), URL. Accessed Day Month Year.

Gleckman, Jason. "Shakespeare as Poet or Playwright? The Player's Speech in *Hamlet*." *Early Modern Literary Studies,* vol. 11, no. 3, Jan. 2006, purl.oclc.org/emls/11-3/glechaml.htm. Accessed 31 Mar. 2015.

9. Article in a magazine

Print

Author's Last Name, First Name. "Title of Article." *Name of Magazine,* Date, Pages.

Neyfakh, Leon. "The Future of Getting Arrested." *The Atlantic,* Jan.-Feb. 2015, pp. 26+.

Online

Author's Last Name, First Name. "Title of Article." *Name of Magazine,*
    Date on web, Pages (if any), URL. Accessed Day Month Year.

Khazan, Olga. "Forgetting and Remembering Your First Language."
    The Atlantic, 24 July 2014, www.theatlantic.com/international/
    archive/2014/07/learning-forgetting-and-remembering-your-first
    -language/374906/. Accessed 2 Apr. 2015.

10. Article in a newspaper

Print

Author's Last Name, First Name. "Title of Article." *Name of Newspaper,*
    Date, Pages.

Saulny, Susan, and Jacques Steinberg. "On College Forms, a Question of
    Race Can Perplex." *The New York Times,* 14 June 2011, p. A1.

To document a particular edition of a newspaper, list the edition (*late ed.,
natl. ed.,* and so on) after the date. If a section of the newspaper is numbered,
put that detail after the edition information.

Burns, John F., and Miguel Helft. "Under Pressure, YouTube Withdraws
    Muslim Cleric's Videos." *The New York Times,* 4 Nov. 2010, late ed.,
    sec. 1, p. 13.

Online

Author's Last Name, First Name. "Title of Article." *Name of Newspaper,*
    Date on web, URL. Accessed Day Month Year.

Banerjee, Neela. "Proposed Religion-Based Program for Federal Inmates
    Is Canceled." *The New York Times,* 28 Oct. 2006, www.nytimes
    .com/2006/10/28/us/28prison.html?_r=0. Accessed 4 Apr. 2015.

11. Article accessed through a database

Author's Last Name, First Name. "Title of Article." *Name of Periodical,*
    Volume, Issue, Date, Pages. *Name of Database,* DOI or URL.
    Accessed Day Month Year.

author   title   publication

Documentation Map (MLA) / Article in a Print Journal

Marge Simpson, Blue-Haired Housewife: ◄------- **Title of Article**
Defining Domesticity on *The Simpsons*

JESSAMYN NEUHAUS ◄---------------------------- **Author**

MORE THAN TWENTY SEASONS AFTER ITS DEBUT AS A SHORT ON *THE Tracy Ullman Show* in 1989, pundits, politicians, scholars, journalists, and critics continue to discuss and debate the meaning and relevance of *The Simpsons* to American society. For academics and educators, the show offers an especially dense pop culture text, inspiring articles and anthologies examining *The Simpsons* in light of American religious life, the representation of homosexuality in cartoons, and the use of pop culture in the classroom, among many other topics (Dennis; Frank; Henry "The Whole World's Gone Gay"; Hobbs; Kristiansen). Philosophers and literary theorists in particular are intrigued by the quintessentially postmodern self-aware form and content of *The Simpsons* and the questions about identity, spectatorship, and consumer culture it raises (Alberti; Bybee and Overbeck; Glynn; Henry "The Triumph of Popular Culture"; Herron; Hull; Irwin et al.; Ott; Parisi).

Simpsons observers frequently note that this TV show begs one of the fundamental questions in cultural studies: can pop culture ever provide a site of individual or collective resistance or must it always ultimately function in the interests of the capitalist dominant ideology? Is *The Simpsons* a brilliant satire of virtually every cherished American myth about public and private life, offering dissatisfied Americans the opportunity to critically reflect on contemporary issues (Turner 435)? Or is it simply another TV show making money for the Fox Network? Is *The Simpsons* an empty, cynical, even nihilistic view of the world, lulling its viewers into laughing hopelessly at the pointless futility of

Volume   **Issue**

Name of Journal -----► *The Journal of Popular Culture*, Vol. 43, No. 4, 2010 ◄---------------- **Year**
© 2010, Wiley Periodicals, Inc.

761

Neuhaus, Jessamyn. "Marge Simpson, Blue-Haired Housewife: Defining Domesticity on *The Simpsons*." *The Journal of Popular Culture*, vol. 43, no. 4, 2010, pp. 761-81.

Stalter, Sunny. "Subway Ride and Subway System in Hart Crane's 'The
Tunnel.'" *Journal of Modern Literature,* vol. 33, no. 2, Jan. 2010, pp.
70-91. *JSTOR,* doi:10.2979/jml.2010.33.2.70. Accessed 30 Mar. 2015.

12. Entry in a reference work

Print

Author's Last Name, First Name (if any). "Title of Entry." *Title of
Reference Book,* edited by Editor's First and Last Names (if any),
Edition number, Publisher, Date, Pages.

"California." *The New Columbia Encyclopedia,* edited by William H. Harris
and Judith S. Levey, 4th ed., Columbia UP, 1975, pp. 423-24.

"Feminism." *Longman Dictionary of American English,* Longman, 1983, p. 252.

Online

Document online reference works the same as print ones, adding the URL
and access date after the date of publication.

"Baseball." *The Columbia Electronic Encyclopedia,* edited by Paul Lagassé,
6th ed., Columbia UP, 2012, www.infoplease.com/encyclopedia.
Accessed 25 May 2016.

13. Editorial

Print

"Title of Editorial." Editorial. *Name of Periodical,* Date, Page.

"Gas, Cigarettes Are Safe to Tax." Editorial. *The Lakeville Journal,* 17 Feb.
2005, p. A10.

Online

"Title of Editorial." Editorial. *Name of Periodical,* Date on web, URL.
Accessed Day Month Year.

"Keep the Drinking Age at 21." Editorial. *Chicago Tribune,* 28 Aug. 2008,
articles.chicagotribune.com/2008-08-26/news/0808250487_1
_binge-drinking-drinking-age-alcohol-related-crashes. Accessed
26 Apr. 2015.

Documentation Map (MLA) /
Article in an Online Magazine

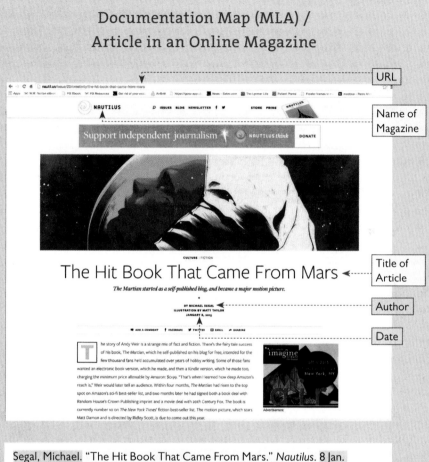

URL

Name of Magazine

Title of Article

Author

Date

Segal, Michael. "The Hit Book That Came From Mars." *Nautilus*. 8 Jan.
2015, nautil.us/issue/20/creativity/the-hit-book-that-came-from
-mars. Accessed 10 Oct. 2016.

Documentation Map (MLA) /
Article Accessed through a Database

URL

Name of Database

Title of Article

Author

Pages

Name of Periodical

Volume, Issue, Date

Neuhaus, Jessamyn. "Marge Simpson, Blue-Haired Housewife: Defining
 Domesticity on *The Simpsons*." *Journal of Popular Culture,* vol. 43,
 no. 4, Aug. 2010, pp. 761-81. *SportsDiscus with Full Text,* ezproxy
 .libraries.wright.edu/login?url=http://search.ebscohost.com/login
 .aspx?direct=true&db=a9h&AN=52300944&site=ehost-live.
 Accessed 24 Mar. 2016.

14. Letter to the editor

Author's Last Name, First Name. "Title of Letter (if any)." Letter. *Name of Periodical,* Date on web, URL. Accessed Day Month Year.

Pinker, Steven. "Language Arts." Letter. *The New Yorker,* 4 June 2012, www .newyorker.com/magazine/2012/06/04/language-arts-2. Accessed 6 Apr. 2015.

15. Review

Print

Reviewer's Last Name, First Name. "Title of Review." Review of *Title,* by Author's First and Last Names. *Name of Periodical,* Date, Pages.

Frank, Jeffrey. "Body Count." Review of *The Exception,* by Christian Jungersen. *The New Yorker,* 30 July 2007, pp. 86-87.

If a review has no author or title, start with what's being reviewed:

Review of *Ways to Disappear,* by Idra Novey. *The New Yorker,* 28 Mar. 2016, p. 79.

Online

Reviewer's Last Name, First Name. "Title of Review." Review of *Title,* by Author's First and Last Names. *Name of Periodical,* Date, URL. Accessed Day Month Year.

Donadio, Rachel. "Italy's Great, Mysterious Storyteller." Review of *My Brilliant Friend,* by Elena Ferrante. *The New York Review of Books,* 18 Dec. 2014, www.nybooks.com/articles/2014/ 12/18/italys-great-mysterious-storyteller. Accessed 28 Sept. 2015.

16. Comment on an online article

Commenter. Comment on "Title of Article." *Name of Periodical,* Date posted, Time posted, URL. Accessed Day Month Year.

Nick. Comment on "The Case for Reparations." *The Atlantic,* 22 May 2014, 3:04 p.m., www.theatlantic.com/business/archive/2014/05/how-to-comment -on-reparations/371422/#article-comments. Accessed 8 May 2015.

Books and Parts of Books

For most books, you'll need to provide information about the author, the title, the publisher, and the year of publication. If you found the book inside a larger volume, a database, or some other work, be sure to specify that as well.

17. Basic entries for a book

Print

Author's Last Name, First Name. *Title*. Publisher, Year of publication.

Watson, Brad. *Miss Jane*. W. W. Norton, 2016.

Ebook

Document an ebook as you would a print book, but add information about the ebook—or the type of ebook if you know it.

Watson, Brad. *Miss Jane*. Ebook, W. W. Norton, 2016.

Watson, Brad. *Miss Jane*. Kindle ed., W. W. Norton, 2016.

In a database

Author's Last Name, First Name. *Title*. Publisher, Year of publication. *Name of Database*, DOI or URL. Accessed Day Month Year.

Anderson, Sherwood. *Winesburg, Ohio*. B. W. Huebsch, 1919. *Bartleby.com*, www.bartleby.com/156/. Accessed 8 Apr. 2015.

18. Anthology

Last Name, First Name, editor. *Title*. Publisher, Year of publication.

Hall, Donald, editor. *The Oxford Book of Children's Verse in America*. Oxford UP, 1985.

Kitchen, Judith, and Mary Paumier Jones, editors. *In Short: A Collection of Brief Creative Nonfiction*. W. W. Norton, 1996.

author   title   publication

19. Work in an anthology

Author's Last Name, First Name. "Title of Work." *Title of Anthology,* edited
by First and Last Names, Publisher, Year of publication, Pages.

Achebe, Chinua. "Uncle Ben's Choice." *The Seagull Reader: Literature,*
edited by Joseph Kelly, W. W. Norton, 2005, pp. 23-27.

Two or more works from one anthology

Prepare an entry for each selection by author and title, followed by the anthology editors' last names and the pages of the selection. Then include an
entry for the anthology itself (see no. 18).

Author's Last Name, First Name. "Title of Work." Anthology Editors'
Last Names, Pages.

Hiestand, Emily. "Afternoon Tea." Kitchen and Jones, pp. 65-67.

Ozick, Cynthia. "The Shock of Teapots." Kitchen and Jones, pp. 68-71.

20. Multivolume work

All volumes

Author's Last Name, First Name. *Title of Work.* Publisher, Year(s) of
publication. Number of vols.

Churchill, Winston. *The Second World War.* Houghton Mifflin, 1948-53.
6 vols.

Single volume

Author's Last Name, First Name. *Title of Work.* Vol. number, Publisher,
Year of publication. Number of vols.

Sandburg, Carl. *Abraham Lincoln: The War Years.* Vol. 2, Harcourt, Brace &
World, 1939. 4 vols.

Documentation Map (MLA) / Print Book

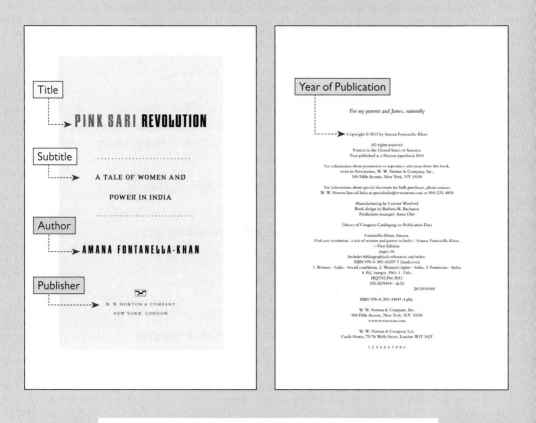

Title

→ PINK SARI REVOLUTION

Subtitle

→ A TALE OF WOMEN AND
POWER IN INDIA

Author

→ AMANA FONTANELLA-KHAN

Publisher

→ W. W. NORTON & COMPANY
NEW YORK LONDON

Year of Publication

For my parents and James, naturally

→ Copyright © 2013 by Amana Fontanella-Khan

All rights reserved
Printed in the United States of America
First published as a Norton paperback 2014

For information about permission to reproduce selections from this book,
write to Permissions, W. W. Norton & Company, Inc.,
500 Fifth Avenue, New York, NY 10110

For information about special discounts for bulk purchases, please contact
W. W. Norton Special Sales at specialsales@wwnorton.com or 800-233-4830

Manufacturing by Courier Westford
Book design by Barbara M. Bachman
Production manager: Anna Oler

Library of Congress Cataloging-in-Publication Data

Fontanella-Khan, Amana.
Pink sari revolution : a tale of women and power in India / Amana Fontanella-Khan.
—First Edition.
pages cm
Includes bibliographical references and index.
ISBN 978-0-393-06297-7 (hardcover)
1. Women—India—Social conditions. 2. Women's rights—India. 3. Feminism—India.
4. Pal, Sampat, 1961– I. Title.
HQ1743.F66 2013
305.4209594—dc23
2013018948

ISBN 978-0-393-34947-4 pbk.

W. W. Norton & Company, Inc.
500 Fifth Avenue, New York, N.Y. 10110
www.wwnorton.com

W. W. Norton & Company Ltd.
Castle House, 75/76 Wells Street, London W1T 3QT

1 2 3 4 5 6 7 8 9 0

Fontanella-Khan, Amana. *Pink Sari Revolution: A Tale of Women
and Power in India.* W. W. Norton, 2013.

21. Book in a series

Author's Last Name, First Name. *Title of Book.* Edited by First and Last
    Names, Publisher, Year of publication. Series Title.

Walker, Alice. *Everyday Use.* Edited by Barbara T. Christian, Rutgers UP,
    1994. Women Writers: Texts and Contexts.

22. Graphic narrative

Author's Last Name, First Name. *Title.* Publisher, Year of publication.

Bechdel, Alison. *Fun Home: A Family Tragicomedy.* Houghton Mifflin, 2006.

If the work has both an author and an illustrator, start with the one whose
work is more relevant to your research, and label the role of anyone who's
not an author.

Pekar, Harvey. *Bob & Harv's Comics.* Illustrated by R. Crumb, Running
    Press, 1996.

Crumb, R., illustrator. *Bob & Harv's Comics.* By Harvey Pekar, Running
    Press, 1996.

23. Sacred text

If you cite a specific edition of a religious text, you need to include it in your
works cited list.

The New English Bible with the Apocrypha. Oxford UP, 1971.

The Torah: A Modern Commentary. Edited by W. Gunther Plaut, Union of
    American Hebrew Congregations, 1981.

24. Edition other than the first

Author's Last Name, First Name. *Title.* Name or number of edition,
    Publisher, Year of publication.

Fowler, H. W. *A Dictionary of Modern English.* 2nd ed., Oxford UP,
    1965.

25. Republished work

Author's Last Name, First Name. *Title.* Year of original publication. Current publisher, Year of republication.

Bierce, Ambrose. *Civil War Stories.* 1909. Dover, 1994.

26. Foreword, introduction, preface, or afterword

Part Author's Last Name, First Name. Name of Part. *Title of Book,* by Author's First and Last Names, Publisher, Year of publication, Pages.

Tanner, Tony. Introduction. *Pride and Prejudice*, by Jane Austen, Penguin, 1972, pp. 7-46.

27. Published letter

Letter Writer's Last Name, First Name. Letter to First and Last Names. Day Month Year. *Title of Book,* edited by First and Last Names, Publisher, Year of publication, Pages.

White, E. B. Letter to Carol Angell. 28 May 1970. *Letters of E. B. White*, edited by Dorothy Lobarno Guth, Harper & Row, 1976, p. 600.

28. Paper at a conference

Paper published in conference proceedings

Author's Last Name, First Name. "Title of Paper." *Title of Published Conference Proceedings,* edited by First and Last Names, Publisher, Year of publication, Pages.

Flower, Linda. "Literate Action." *Composition in the Twenty-first Century: Crisis and Change*, edited by Lynn Z. Bloom, et al., Southern Illinois UP, 1996, pp. 249-60.

Paper heard at a conference

Author's Last Name, First Name. "Title of Paper." Title of Conference, Day Month Year, Venue, City.

author | title | publication

Hern, Katie. "Inside an Accelerated Reading and Writing Classroom."
Conference on Acceleration in Developmental Education, 15 June
2016, Sheraton Inner Harbor Hotel, Baltimore.

29. Dissertation

Author's Last Name, First Name. *Title.* Diss. Institution, Year,
Publisher, Year of publication.

Goggin, Peter N. *A New Literacy Map of Research and Scholarship in
Computers and Writing.* Diss. Indiana U of Pennsylvania, 2000,
University Microfilms International, 2001.

For an unpublished dissertation, put the title in quotation marks, and end
with the institution and the year.

Kim, Loel. "Students Respond to Teacher Comments: A Comparison of
Online Written and Voice Modalities." Diss. Carnegie Mellon U,
1998.

Websites

Many sources are available in multiple media — for example, a print periodical
that is also on the web and contained in digital databases — but some are published only on websites. This section covers the latter.

30. Entire website

Last Name, First Name, role. *Title of Site.* Publisher, Date, URL.
Accessed Day Month Year.

Zalta, Edward N., principal editor. *Stanford Encyclopedia of Philosophy.*
Metaphysics Research Lab, Center for the Study of Language,
Stanford U, 1995-2015, plato.stanford.edu/index.html. Accessed
21 Apr. 2015.

Personal website

Author's Last Name, First Name. *Title of Site.* Date, URL. Accessed
Day Month Year.

Documentation Map (MLA) / Work on a Website

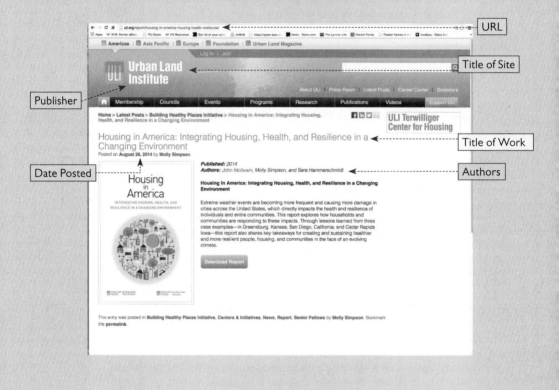

Labels on the image: URL, Title of Site, Publisher, Title of Work, Date Posted, Authors

McIlwain, John, et al. "Housing in America: Integrating Housing, Health,
and Resilience in a Changing Environment." *Urban Land Institute*,
28 Aug. 2014, uli.org/report/housing-in-america-housing-health
-resilience. Accessed 17 Sept. 2015.

Heath, Shirley Brice. *Shirley Brice Heath*. 2015, shirleybriceheath.net.
Accessed 6 June 2015.

31. Work on a website

Author's Last Name, First Name (if any). "Title of Work." *Title of Site*,
Publisher, Date, URL. Accessed Day Month Year.

"Global Minnesota: Immigrants Past and Present." *Immigration History
Research Center*, U of Minnesota, 2015, cla.umn.edu.ihrc. Accessed
25 May 2016.

32. Blog entry

Author's Last Name, First Name. "Title of Blog Entry." *Title of
Blog*, Date, URL. Accessed Day Month Year.

Hollmichel, Stefanie. "Bringing Up the Bodies." *So Many Books*, 10 Feb.
2014, somanybooksblog.com/2014/02/10/bring-up-the-bodies/.
Accessed 12 Feb. 2014.

Document a whole blog as you would an entire website (no. 30) and a
comment on a blog as you would a comment on an online article (no. 16).

33. Wiki

"Title of Entry." *Title of Wiki*, Publisher, Date, URL. Accessed Day
Month Year.

"Pi." *Wikipedia*, Wikimedia Foundation, 28 Aug. 2013, en.wikipedia.org/
wiki/Pi. Accessed 25 Oct. 2013.

Personal Communication and Social Media

34. Personal letter

Sender's Last Name, First Name. Letter to the author. Day Month Year.

Quindlen, Anna. Letter to the author. 11 Apr. 2013.

35. Email

Sender's Last Name, First Name. "Subject Line." Received by First and Last Names, Day Month Year.

Smith, William. "Teaching Grammar—Some Thoughts." Received by Richard Bullock, 19 Nov. 2013.

36. Text message

Sender's Last Name, First Name. Text message. Received by First and Last Names, Day Month Year.

Douglass, Joanne. Text message. Received by Kim Yi, 4 June 2015.

37. Post to an online forum

Author. "Subject line" or "Full text of short untitled post." *Name of Forum,* Day Month Year, URL.

@somekiryu. "What's the hardest part about writing for you?" *Reddit,* 22 Apr. 2016, redd.it/4fyni0.

38. Post to *Twitter, Facebook,* or other social media

Author. "Full text of short untitled post" or "Title" or Descriptive label. *Name of Site,* Day Month Year, Time, URL.

@POTUS44 (Barack Obama). "I'm proud of the @NBA for taking a stand against gun violence. Sympathy for victims isn't enough—change requires all of us speaking up." *Twitter,* 23 Dec. 2015, 1:21 p.m., twitter.com/POTUS44/status/679773729749078016.

Black Lives Matter. "Rise and Grind! Did you sign this petition yet? We now have a sign on for ORGANIZATIONS to lend their support." *Facebook,* 23 Oct. 2015, 11:30 a.m., www.facebook.com/BlackLivesMatter/photos/a.294807204023865.1073741829.180212755483311/504711973033386/?type=3&theater.

@quarterlifepoetry. Illustrated poem about girl at Target. *Instagram*,
22 Jan. 2015, www.instagram.com/p/yLO6fSurRH/.

Audio, Visual, and Other Sources

39. Advertisement

Print

Name of Product or Company. Advertisement or Description of it.
Name of Periodical, Date, Page.

Cal Alumni Association. Sports merchandise ad. *California*, Spring
2016, p. 3.

Audio or video

Name of Product or Company. Advertisement or Description of it.
Date. *Name of Host Site,* URL. Accessed Day Month Year.

Chrysler. Super Bowl commercial. 6 Feb. 2011. *YouTube*, www.youtube
.com/watch?v=SKLZ254Y_jtc. Accessed 1 May 2015.

40. Art

Original

Artist's Last Name, First Name. *Title of Art.* Year created, Venue, City.

Van Gogh, Vincent. *The Potato Eaters.* 1885, Van Gogh Museum,
Amsterdam.

Reproduction

Artist's Last Name, First Name. *Title of Art.* Year created.
Title of Book, by First and Last Names, Publisher, Year of
publication, Page.

Van Gogh, Vincent. *The Potato Eaters.* 1885. *History of Art: A Survey
of the Major Visual Arts from the Dawn of History to the Present
Day,* by H. W. Janson, Prentice-Hall/Harry N. Abrams, 1969,
p. 508.

Online

Artist's Last Name, First Name. *Title of Art.* Year created. *Name of Site,* URL. Accessed Day Month Year.

Warhol, Andy. *Self-portrait.* 1979. *J. Paul Getty Museum,* www
.getty.edu/art/collection/objects/106971/andy-warhol-self
-portrait-american-1979/. Accessed 20 Jan. 2015.

41. Cartoon

Print

Author's Last Name, First Name. "Title of Cartoon." *Name of Periodical,* Date, Page.

Chast, Roz. "The Three Wise Men of Thanksgiving." *The New Yorker,* 1 Dec. 2003, p. 174.

Online

Author's Last Name, First Name. "Title of Cartoon." *Title of Site,* Date, URL. Accessed Day Month Year.

Munroe, Randall. "Up Goer Five." *xkcd,* 12 Nov. 2012, xkcd.com/1133/. Accessed 22 Apr. 2015.

42. Supreme Court case

Name of court. *First Defendant v. Second Defendant.* Date of decision. *Name of Source Site,* Publisher, URL. Access Day Month Year.

United States, Supreme Court. *District of Columbia v. Heller.* 26 June 2008. *Legal Information Institute,* Cornell U Law School, www.law .cornell.edu/supct/html/07-290.ZS.html. Accessed 25 Feb. 2020.

43. Film

Name individuals based on the focus of your project — the director, the screenwriter, the cinematographer, or someone else.

Title of Film. Role by First and Last Names, Production Studio, Date.

Breakfast at Tiffany's. Directed by Blake Edwards, Paramount, 1961.

Streaming

Title of Film. Role by First and Last Names, Production Studio,
   Date. *Streaming Service,* URL. Accessed Day Month Year.

Interstellar. Directed by Christopher Nolan, Paramount, 2014. *Amazon
   Prime Video,* www.amazon.com/Interstellar-Matthew
   -McConaughey/dp/B00TU9UFTS. Accessed 2 May 2015.

44. Interview

If the interview has a title, put it in quotation marks following the subject's
name.

Broadcast

Subject's Last Name, First Name. Interview or "Title of Interview." *Title
   of Program,* Network, Day Month Year.

Gates, Henry Louis, Jr. Interview. *Fresh Air,* NPR, 9 Apr. 2002.

Published

Subject's Last Name, First Name. Interview or "Title of Interview."
   Name of Publication, Date, Pages.

Stone, Oliver. Interview. *Esquire,* Nov. 2004, pp. 170-71.

Personal

Subject's Last Name, First Name. Personal interview. Day Month Year.

Abrams, Stacey. Personal interview. 17 Aug. 2018.

45. Map

"Title of Map." Publisher, URL. Accessed Day Month Year.

"National Highway System." US Department of Transportation Federal
   Highway Administration, www.fhwa.dot.gov/planning/images/
   nhs.pdf. Accessed 10 May 2015.

46. Musical score

Composer's Last Name, First Name. *Title of Composition.* Year of composition. Publisher, Year of publication.

Stravinsky, Igor. *Petrushka.* 1911. W. W. Norton, 1967.

47. Online video

Author's Last Name, First Name. *Title. Name of Host Site,* Date, URL. Accessed Day Month Year.

Westbrook, Adam. *Cause/Effect: The Unexpected Origins of Terrible Things. Vimeo,* 9 Sept. 2014, vimeo.com/105681474. Accessed 20 Dec. 2015.

48. Oral presentation

Presenter's Last Name, First Name. "Title of Presentation." Sponsoring Institution, Date, Location.

Cassin, Michael. "Nature in the Raw — The Art of Landscape Painting." Berkshire Institute for Lifelong Learning, 24 Mar. 2005, Clark Art Institute, Williamstown.

49. Podcast

If you accessed a podcast online, give the URL and date of access; if you accessed it through a service such as *iTunes* or *Spotify,* indicate that instead.

Last Name, First Name, role. "Title of Episode." *Title of Program,* season, episode, Sponsor, Date, URL. Accessed Day Month Year.

Koenig, Sarah, host. "DUSTWUN." *Serial,* season 2, episode 1, WBEZ, 10 Dec. 2015, serialpodcast.org/season-two/1/dustwun. Accessed 23 Apr. 2016.

Foss, Gilad, writer and performer. "Aquaman's Brother-in-Law." *Superhero Temp Agency,* season 1, episode 1, 16 Apr. 2015. *iTunes.*

author   title   publication

50. Radio program

Last Name, First Name, role. "Title of Episode." *Title of Program*, Station, Day Month Year of broadcast, URL. Accessed Day Month Year.

Glass, Ira, host. "In Defense of Ignorance." *This American Life*, WBEZ, 22 Apr. 2016, thisamericanlife.org/radio-archives/episode/585/ in-defense-of-ignorance. Accessed 2 May 2016.

51. Sound recording

Online

Last Name, First Name. "Title of Work." *Title of Album*, Distributor, Date. *Name of Audio Service*.

Simone, Nina. "To Be Young, Gifted and Black." *Black Gold*, RCA Records, 1969. *Spotify*.

CD

Last Name, First Name. "Title of Work." *Title of Album*, Distributor, Date.

Brown, Greg. "Canned Goods." *The Live One*, Red House, 1995.

52. TV show

Original Broadcast

"Title of Episode." *Title of Show*, role by First and Last Names, season, episode, Network, Day Month Year.

"The Silencer." *Criminal Minds*, written by Erica Messer, season 8, episode 1, NBC, 26 Sept. 2012.

DVD

"Title of Episode." Broadcast Year. *Title of DVD*, role by First and Last Names, season, episode, Production Studio, Release Year, disc number.

"The Pants Tent." 2003. *Curb Your Enthusiasm: Season One*, performance by Larry David, season 1, episode 1, HBO Video, 2006, disc 1.

Online

"Title of Episode." *Title of Show,* role by First and Last Names (if any),
    season, episode, Production Studio, Day Month Year. *Name of
    Host Site,* URL. Accessed Day Month Year.

"Shadows in the Glass." *Marvel's Daredevil,* season 1, episode 8, Netflix,
    10 Apr. 2015. *Netflix,* www.netflix.com/watch/80018198?trackId
    =13752289&tctx=0%2C7%2Cbcfd6259-6e64-4d51-95ab-2a9f747e
    abf0-158552415. Accessed 3 Nov. 2015.

53. Video game

Last name, First name, role. *Title of Game.* Distributor, Date of release.
    Gaming System or Platform.

Metzen, Chris, and James Waugh, writers. *StarCraft II: Legacy of the Void.*
    Blizzard Entertainment, 2015. OS X.

FORMATTING A RESEARCH PAPER

Name, course, title. MLA does not require a separate title page. In the upper
left-hand corner of your first page, include your name, your professor's
name, the name of the course, and the date. Center the title of your paper on
the line after the date; capitalize it as you would a book title.

Page numbers. In the upper right-hand corner of each page, one-half inch
below the top of the page, include your last name and the page number.
Number pages consecutively throughout your paper.

Font, spacing, margins, and indents. Choose a font that is easy to read (such
as Times New Roman) and that provides a clear contrast between regular
and italic text. Double-space the entire paper, including your works cited
list. Set one-inch margins at the top, bottom, and sides of your text; do not
justify your text. The first line of each paragraph should be indented one-
half inch from the left margin.

Long quotations. When quoting more than three lines of poetry, more than four lines of prose, or dialogue between characters in a drama, set off the quotation from the rest of your text, indenting it one-half inch (or five spaces) from the left margin. Do not use quotation marks, and put any parenthetical documentation *after* the final punctuation.

> In *Eastward to Tartary*, Kaplan captures ancient and contemporary
> Antioch for us:
>> At the height of its glory in the Roman-Byzantine age, when it
>> had an amphitheater, public baths, aqueducts, and sewage pipes,
>> half a million people lived in Antioch. Today the population is
>> only 125,000. With sour relations between Turkey and Syria, and
>> unstable politics throughout the Middle East, Antioch is now a
>> backwater—seedy and tumbledown, with relatively few tourists. I
>> found it altogether charming. (123)

> In the first stanza of Arnold's "Dover Beach," the exclamations make
> clear that the speaker is addressing someone who is also present in the
> scene:
>> Come to the window, sweet is the night air!
>> Only, from the long line of spray
>> Where the sea meets the moon-blanched land,
>> Listen! You hear the grating roar
>> Of pebbles which the waves draw back, and fling. (6-10)

Be careful to maintain the poet's line breaks. If a line does not fit on one line of your paper, put the extra words on the next line. Indent that line an additional quarter inch (or two spaces).

Illustrations. Insert illustrations close to the text that discusses them. For tables, provide a number (*Table 1*) and a title on separate lines above the table. Below the table, provide a caption and information about the source. For graphs, photos, and other figures, provide a figure number (*Fig. 1*), caption, and source information below the figure. If you give only brief source information (such as a parenthetical note), or if the source is cited elsewhere in your text, include it in your list of works cited. Be sure to make clear how any illustrations relate to your point.

List of Works Cited. Start your list on a new page, following any notes. Center the title and double-space the entire list. Begin each entry at the left margin, and indent subsequent lines one-half inch (or five spaces). Alphabetize the list by authors' last names (or by editors' or translators' names, if appropriate). Alphabetize works with no author or editor by title, disregarding *A*, *An*, and *The*. To cite more than one work by a single author, list them as in no. 4 on page 575.

SAMPLE RESEARCH PAPER

Walter Przybylowski wrote the following analysis, "Holding Up the Hollywood Stagecoach: The European Take on the Western," for a first-year writing course. It is formatted according to the guidelines of the MLA (style.mla.org).

author   title   publication

1"

½"

Walter Przybylowski

Professor Matin

English 102, Section 3

4 May 2019

Put your last name
and the page num-
ber in the upper-right
corner of each page.

Center the title.

Holding Up the Hollywood Stagecoach:

The European Take on the Western

Double-space
throughout.

The Western film has long been considered by film scholars and

enthusiasts to be a distinctly American genre. Not only its subject

matter but its characteristic themes originate in America's own violent

and exciting past. For many years, Hollywood sold images of hard men

fighting savages on the plains to the worldwide public; by ignoring

the more complicated aspects of "how the West was won" and the true

nature of relations between Native Americans and whites, filmmakers

were able to reap great financial and professional rewards. In particular,

1"

the huge success of John Ford's 1939 film *Stagecoach* brought about

1"

countless imitations that led over the next few decades to American

Westerns playing in a sort of loop, which reinforced the same ideas and

myths in film after film.

Indent paragraphs
5 spaces or ½".

After the success of German-made Westerns in the 1950s, though,

a new take on Westerns was ushered in by other European countries.

Leading the Euro-Western charge, so to speak, were the Italians, whose

cynical, often politically pointed Westerns left a permanent impact

on an American-based genre. Europeans, particularly the Italians,

challenged the dominant conventions of the American Western by

complicating the morality of the characters, blurring the lines between

1"

good and evil, and also by complicating the traditional narrative, visual, and aural structures of Westerns. In this way, the genre motifs that *Stagecoach* initiated are explored in the European Westerns of the 1950s, 1960s, and early 1970s, yet with a striking difference in style. Specifically, Sergio Leone's 1968 film *Once Upon a Time in the West* broke many of the rules set by the Hollywood Western and in the process created a new visual language for the Western. Deconstructing key scenes from this film reveals the demythologization at work in many of the Euro-Westerns, which led to a genre enriched by its presentation of a more complicated American West.

 Stagecoach is a perfect example of almost all the visual, sound, and plot motifs that would populate "classic" Hollywood Westerns for the next few decades. The story concerns a group of people, confined for most of the movie inside a stagecoach, who are attempting to cross a stretch of land made dangerous by Apache Indians on the warpath. Little effort is made to develop the characters of the Indians, who appear mainly as a narrative device, adversaries that the heroes must overcome in order to maintain their peaceful existence. This plot, with minor changes, could be used as a general description for countless Westerns. In his book *The Crowded Prairie: American National Identity in the Hollywood Western*, Michael Coyne explains the significance of *Stagecoach* to the Western genre and its influence in solidifying the genre's archetypes:

> [I]t was *Stagecoach* which . . . redefined the contours of the myth. The good outlaw, the whore with a heart of gold, the Madonna/Magdalene dichotomy between opposing female

Quotations of more than 4 lines are indented ½" (5 spaces) and double-spaced.

Przybylowski   3

leads, the drunken philosopher, the last-minute cavalry rescue,
the lonely walk down Main Street—all became stereotypes
from *Stagecoach*'s archetypes. *Stagecoach* quickly became the
model against which other "A" Westerns would be measured.
(18-19)

Coyne is not exaggerating when he calls it "the model": in fact, all of
these stereotypes became a sort of checklist of things that audiences
expected to see. The reliance on a preconceived way to sell Western films
to the public—where you could always tell the good characters from the
bad and knew before the film ended how each character would end up—
led to certain genre expectations that the directors of the Euro-Westerns
would later knowingly reconfigure. As the influential critic Pauline Kael
wrote in her 1965 book *Kiss Kiss Bang Bang*, "The original *Stagecoach* had
a mixture of reverie and reverence about the American past that made
the picture seem almost folk art; we wanted to believe in it even if we
didn't" (52).

    There seemed to be a need not just in Americans but in moviegoers
around the world to believe that there was (or had been) a great untamed
land out there just waiting to be cultivated. More important, as Kael
pointed out, Americans wanted to believe that the building of America
was a wholly righteous endeavor wherein the land was free for the
taking—the very myth that Europeans later debunked through parody
and subversive filmmaking techniques. According to Theresa Harlan,
author of works on Native American art, the myth was based on the need
of early white settlers to make their elimination of American Indians

For a set-off quotation, the parenthetical reference follows the closing punctuation.

Verb in signal phrase is past tense because date of source is mentioned.

Parenthetical reference following a quotation within the main text goes before the closing punctuation of the sentence.

more palatable in light of the settlers' professed Christian beliefs. In her
article "Adjusting the Focus for an Indigenous Presence," Harlan writes
that

> Eurocentric frontier ideology and the representations of indigenous
> people it produced were used to convince many American settlers
> that indigenous people were incapable of discerning the difference
> between a presumed civilized existence and their own "primitive"
> state. (6)

Although this myth had its genesis long before the advent of
motion pictures, the Hollywood Western drew inspiration from it and
continued to legitimize and reinforce its message. *Stagecoach*, with its
high level of technical skill and artistry, redefined the contours of the
myth, and a close look at the elements that made the film the "classic"
model of the Western is imperative in order to truly understand its
influence.

The musical themes that underscore the actions of the characters
are especially powerful in this regard and can be as powerful as the
characters' visual representation on screen. In *Stagecoach*, an Apache
does not appear until more than halfway through the movie, but
whenever one is mentioned, the soundtrack fills with sinister and
foreboding drumbeats. The first appearance of Indians is a scene without
dialogue, in which the camera pans between the stagecoach crossing
through the land and Apaches watching from afar. The music that
accompanies this scene is particularly telling, since as the camera pans
between stagecoach and Apaches, the music shifts in tone dramatically

from a pleasant melody to a score filled with dread. When the heroes shoot and kill the Apaches, then, the viewer has already been subjected to specific film techniques to give the stagecoach riders moral certitude in their annihilation of the alien menace. To emphasize this point, the music swells victoriously every time an Apache is shown falling from a horse. This kind of score is powerful stuff to accompany an image and does its best to tell the viewers how they should react. When Europeans start to make Westerns, the line of moral certitude will become less distinct.

In her essay "Of Mother Nature and Marlboro Men: An Inquiry into the Cultural Meanings of Landscape Photography," Deborah Bright argues that landscape photography has reinforced certain formulaic myths about landscape, and the same can be said of the Hollywood Western during the 1940s and 1950s. For example, in *Stagecoach*, when the stagecoach finally sets out for its journey through Apache territory, a fence is juxtaposed against the vast wide-open country in the foreground. The meaning is clear—the stagecoach is leaving civilized society to venture into the wilds of the West, and music swells as the coach crosses into that vast landscape (fig. 1). Ford uses landscape in this way to engender in the audience the desired response of longing for a time gone past, where there was land free for the taking and plenty to go around. Yet Bright suggests that "[i]f we are to redeem landscape photography from its narrow self-reflexive project, why not openly question the assumptions about nature and culture that it has traditionally served and use our practice instead to criticize them?" (141).

Figure number calls readers' attention to illustration.

Brackets show that the writer has changed a capital letter to lowercase to make the quotation fit smoothly into his own sentence.

Fig. 1. In *Stagecoach*, swelling music signals the coach's passage through the western landscape. Photograph from *Internet Movie Database*, www.imdb.com.

Documentation of image source given after the caption.

This is exactly what Europeans, and Italians in particular, seem to have done with the Western. When Europeans started to make their own Westerns, they took advantage of their outsider status in relation to an American genre by openly questioning the myths that have been established by *Stagecoach* and its cinematic brethren.

Sergio Leone's *Once Upon a Time in the West* is a superior example of a European artist's take on the art form of the American Western. The title alone signals the element of storytelling: in a sublime stroke of titling, Leone makes the connection between Western films and fairy tales and announces that the genre myths that *Stagecoach* presented for audiences to revel in will now be questioned. In his book *Spaghetti Westerns*, Christopher Frayling observes that *"Once Upon a Time* is concerned with the 'language' and 'syntax' of the Western . . . an unmasking or 'display' of the terminology of the genre" (213). The "plot" of the film is flimsy, driven by the efforts of a mysterious character played by Charles Bronson to avenge himself against Henry Fonda's character, a lowdown gunfighter trying to become a legitimate businessman. Claudia Cardinale plays a prostitute who is trying to put her past behind her. All of these classic types from countless American Westerns are integrated into the "Iron Horse" plotline, wherein the coming of the railroad signifies great changes in the West. The similarities to American Westerns, on paper at least, seem to be so great as to make *Once Upon a Tim*e almost a copy of what had long been done in Hollywood, but a closer look at European Westerns and at this film in particular shows that Leone is consciously sending up the stereotypes. After all, he needs to work within the genre's language if he is to adequately challenge it.

The opening scene of *Once Upon a Time* runs roughly ten minutes and provides an introduction to many of the aesthetic and ideological changes made by the European Western to the American model. The viewer quickly notices how little dialogue is spoken during the whole ten minutes, since the requirements of post-synchronization (the

rerecording of the movie's dialogue after filming in order to produce
a clearer soundtrack) and country-specific dubbing into multiple
languages resulted in a reliance on strong visual storytelling. Financial
reasons made English the default language for most Euro-Westerns since
it produced the largest market and, consequently, the greatest monetary
rewards. Even cast members who could not speak it would sometimes
mouth the words in English. However, the use of post-synchronization
has an unsettling effect on any viewer, even an English-speaking one,
who is used to the polished soundtracks of a Hollywood film. When
viewers experience a post-synchronized film, the result is a distancing
from the material; certain characters match the words coming out of
their mouths better than others, so the movie takes on a surreal edge.
This visual touch perfectly complements Leone's goal—to divorce the
reality of the West from the myths encouraged by American Westerns.

 During the opening of *Once Upon a Time in the West*, the viewer
is given a kind of audio and visual tour of Euro-Western aesthetics.
Leone introduces three gunmen in typical Italian Western style, with
the first presented by a cut to a dusty boot heel from which the camera
slowly pans up until it reaches the top of the character's cowboy hat.
During this pan, the gunman's gear and its authenticity—a major aspect
of the Italian Western—can be taken in by the audience. A broader
examination of the genre would show that many Euro-Westerns use this
tactic of hyperrealistic attention to costuming and weaponry, which
Ignacio Ramonet argues is intended to distract the viewer from the
unreality of the landscape:

Przybylowski   9

Extreme realism of bodies (hairy, greasy, foul-smelling), clothes or
objects (including mania for weapons) in Italian films is above all
intended to compensate for the complete fraud of the space and
origins. The green pastures, farms and cattle of American Westerns
are replaced by large, deserted canyons. (32)

   In the opening scene, the other two gunfighters are introduced by
a camera panning across the room, allowing characters to materialize
seemingly out of nowhere. Roger Ebert notes that Leone

> established a rule that he follows throughout . . . that the ability
> to see is limited by the sides of the frame. At important moments
> in the film, what the camera cannot see, the characters cannot
> see, and that gives Leone the freedom to surprise us with
> entrances that cannot be explained by the practical geography of
> his shots.

It is these aesthetic touches created to compensate for a fraudulent
landscape that ushered in a new visual language for the Western. The
opening of *Once Upon a Time in the West* undercuts any preconceived
notion of how a Western should be filmed, and this is exactly Leone's
intention: "The director had obviously enjoyed dilating the audience's
sense of time, exploiting, in his ostentatious way, the rhetoric of the
Western, and dwelling on the tiniest details to fulfill his intention"
(Frayling 197). By using jarring edits with amplified sounds, Leone
informs the audience not only that he has seen all the popular
Hollywood Westerns, but that he is purposely not going to give them
that kind of movie. The opening ten-minute scene would be considered

No page number given for online source.

When no signal phrase is used to introduce a quotation, the author's name is included in the parenthetical citation.

needlessly long in a typical Hollywood Western, but Leone is not making a copy of a Hollywood Western, and the length of such scenes allows for more meditation on the styling of the genre. In fact, it is this reliance on the audience's previously established knowledge of Westerns that allows Euro-Westerns to subvert the genre. Barry Langford, writing for *Film & History*, claims that

> *Once Upon a Time* strips bare the form's claims on historical verisimilitude and pushes its innately ritualized and stylized aspects to near-parodic extremes that evacuate the film of narrative credibility and psychological realism alike. (31)

Leone and other directors of Euro-Westerns are asking the public to open their eyes, to not believe what is shown; they are attempting to take the camera's power away by parodying its effect. When Leone has characters magically appear in the frame, or amplifies the squeaking of a door hinge on a soundtrack, he is ridiculing the basic laws that govern American Westerns. The opening of *Once Upon a Time* can be read as a sort of primer for what is about to come for the rest of the film, and its power leaves viewers more attuned to what they are watching.

Leone's casting also works to heighten the film's subversive effect. Henry Fonda, the quintessential good guy in classic Hollywood Westerns like *My Darling Clementine*, is cast as the ruthless Frank, a gunman shown murdering a small child early in the film. In a 1966 article on Italian Westerns in the *Saturday Evening Post*, Italian director Maurizio Lucidi gave some insight into the European perspective that lay behind such choices:

Przybylowski   11

We're adding the Italian concept of realism to an old American
myth, and it's working. Look at Jesse James. In your country he's
a saint. Over here we play him as a gangster. That's what he was.
Europeans today are too sophisticated to believe in the honest
gunman movie anymore. They want the truth and that's what we're
giving them. (qtd. in Fox 55)

Leone knew exactly what he was doing, and his casting of Fonda went a
long way toward confusing the audience's sympathies and complicating
the simple good guy versus bad guy model of Hollywood films. For this
reason, Fonda's entrance in the film is worth noting. The scene begins
with a close-up of a shotgun barrel, which quickly explodes in a series
of (gun)shots that establish a scene of a father and son out hunting near
their homestead. Here, Leone starts to move the camera more, with pans
from father to son and a crane shot of their house as they return home
to a picnic table with an abundance of food: the family is apparently
about to celebrate something. Throughout this scene, crickets chirp on the
soundtrack—until Leone abruptly cuts them off, the sudden silence quickly
followed by close-ups of the uneasy faces of three family members. Leone
is teasing the audience: he puts the crickets back on the soundtrack until
out of nowhere we hear a gunshot. Instead of then focusing on the source
or the target of the gunshot, the camera pans off to the sky, and for a
moment the viewer thinks the shot is from a hunter. We next see a close-up
of the father's face as he looks off into the distance, then is rattled when he
sees his daughter grasping the air, obviously shot. As he runs toward her,
tracked by the camera in a startling way, he is quickly shot down himself.

*A citation of a source
the writer found
quoted in another
source.*

The family has been attacked seemingly out of nowhere, with only a young boy still alive. During the massacre, there is no musical score, just the abstract brutality of the slayings. Then Leone gives us a long camera shot of men appearing out of dust-blown winds, from nearby brush. It is obvious to the viewer that these men are the killers, but there is no clear sight of their faces: Leone uses long camera shots of their backs and an overhead shot as they converge on the young boy. This is the moment when Leone introduces Henry Fonda; he starts with the camera on the back of Fonda's head and then does a slow track around until his face is visible. At this point, audience members around the world would still have a hard time believing Fonda was a killer of these innocent people. Through crosscutting between the young boy's confused face and Fonda's smiling eyes, Leone builds a doubt in the audience—maybe he will not kill the boy. Then the crosscutting is interrupted with a close-up of Fonda's large Colt coming out of its holster, and Ennio Morricone's score, full of sadness, becomes audible. The audience's fears are realized: Fonda is indeed the killer. This scene is a clear parody of Hollywood casting stereotypes, and Leone toys with audience expectations by turning upside down the myth of the noble outlaw as portrayed by John Wayne in *Stagecoach*.

During the late 1960s and the early 1970s, Europeans were at odds with many of the foreign policies of the United States, a hostility expressed in Ramonet's characterization of this period as one "when American imperialism in Latin America and Southeast Asia was showing itself to be particularly brutal" (33). Morton, the railroad baron who is Frank's unscrupulous employer in *Once Upon a Time in the West*, can easily be read as a critique of the sometimes misguided ways Americans went about bringing their way of life to other countries. Morton represents the bringer of civilization, usually a good thing in the classic Western genre, where civilization meant doctors, schools, homes for everyone. But the Europeans question how this civilization was built. Leone, in a telling quotation, gives his perspective: "I see the history of the West as really the reign of violence by violence" (qtd. in Frayling 134).

Leone's critique of the "civilizing" of the American West becomes apparent in his depiction of Morton's demise at the hands of a bandit gang that Frank has tried to frame for the murder of the family. As Frank returns to Morton's train, wheezing and gasping resonates from the track. In a long, one-take shot, the camera follows Frank as he looks for Morton, and in the process dead and dying bodies in various poses are revealed strewn about the ground. Many people have died for the dream of "civilizing" the West, and there is nothing noble in their deaths. Frank finally finds Morton crawling along outside the train in mud, striving to reach a puddle; as he dies, the lapping waves of the Pacific Ocean—the goal toward which the civilizing of the West always pushes—can be heard.

Instead of the civilizing myth and its representations, the concern of *Once Upon a Time*—and the Euro-Western in general—is to give voice to the perspective of the marginal characters: the Native Americans, Mexicans, and Chinese who rarely rated a position of significance in a Hollywood Western. In *Once Upon a Time*, Bronson's character, Harmonica, pushes the plot forward with his need to avenge. Harmonica can be

seen as either Mexican or Native American, though it matters little
since his character stands in for all the racial stereotypes that populated
the American Western genre. When he and Frank meet in the movie's
climactic duel, Frank is clearly perplexed about why this man wants
to fight him, but his ego makes it impossible for him to refuse. They
meet in an abandoned yard, with Frank in the extreme foreground
and Harmonica in the extreme background (fig. 2). The difference

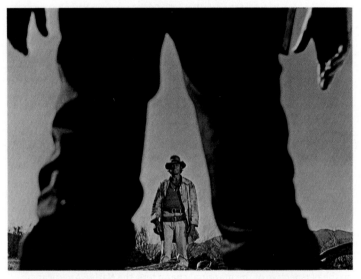

Fig. 2. The climactic duel in *Once Upon a Time in the West* challenges
the casting and costuming stereotypes of the Hollywood Western.
Photograph from *Internet Movie Database*, www.imdb.com.

between the two is thus presented from both physical and ideological standpoints: Frank guns down settlers to make way for the railroad (and its owner), whereas Harmonica helps people to fend for themselves. Morricone's score dominates the soundtrack during this final scene, with a harmonica blaring away throughout. The costuming of Frank in black and Harmonica in white is an ironic throwback to classic Hollywood costuming and one that suggests Harmonica is prevailing over the racial stereotypes of American Westerns. Leone milks the scene for all it's worth, with the camera circling Harmonica as Frank looks for a perfect point to start the duel. Harmonica never moves, his face steadily framed in a close-up. Meanwhile, Frank is shown in mostly long shots; his body language shows that he is uncertain about the outcome of the duel, while Harmonica knows the ending.

As the two seem about to draw, the camera pushes into Harmonica's eyes, and there is a flashback to a younger Frank walking toward the camera, putting a harmonica into the mouth of a boy (the young Harmonica), and forcing him to participate in Frank's hanging of the boy's older brother. This brutal scene, in which Frank unknowingly seals his own destiny, is set in actual American locations and is taken directly from John Ford Westerns; Leone is literally bringing home the violence dealt to minorities in America's past. As soon as the brother is hanged, the scene returns to the present, and Frank is shot through the heart. As he lies dying, we see a look of utter disbelief on his face as he asks Harmonica, "Who are you?" At this moment, a harmonica is shoved into his mouth. Only then does recognition play over Frank's face; as he falls to the ground, his face in close-up is a grotesque death-mask not unlike the massacred victims of Morton's train. The idea of past misdeeds coming back to haunt characters in the present is a clear attempt to challenge the idea that the settlers had a moral right to conquer and destroy indigenous people in order to "win" the West.

The tremendous success of *Stagecoach* was both a blessing and curse for the Western genre. Without it, the genre would surely never have gained the success it did, but this success came with ideological and creative limitations. Both the popularity and the limitations of the American Western may have inspired European directors to attempt something new with the genre, and unlike American filmmakers, they could look more objectively at our history and our myths. Leone's demythologization of the American Western has proved a valuable addition to the Western genre. The effect of the Euro-Western can be seen in American cinema as early as *The Wild Bunch* in 1969—and as recently as the attention in *Brokeback Mountain* to types of Western characters usually marginalized. In this way, Italian Westerns forced a new level of viewing of the Western tradition that made it impossible to ever return to the previous Hollywood model.

List of works cited begins on a new page. Heading is centered.

Works Cited

Bright, Deborah. "Of Mother Nature and Marlboro Men: An Inquiry into the Cultural Meanings of Landscape Photography." *The Contest of Meaning: Critical Histories of Photography*, edited by Richard Bolton, MIT P, 1993, pp. 125-43.

Coyne, Michael. *The Crowded Prairie: American National Identity in the Hollywood Western*. I. B. Tauris, 1997.

Ebert, Roger. "The Good, the Bad and the Ugly." *Chicago Sun-Times*, 3 Aug. 2003, www.rogerebert.com/reviews/great-movie-the-good-the-bad -and-the-ugly-1968. Accessed 25 Jan. 2019.

Fox, William. "Wild Westerns, Italian Style." *The Saturday Evening Post*, 6 Apr. 1968, pp. 50-55.

Frayling, Christopher. *Spaghetti Westerns: Cowboys and Europeans from Karl May to Sergio Leone*. St. Martin's Press, 1981.

Harlan, Theresa. "Adjusting the Focus for an Indigenous Presence." *Overexposed: Essays on Contemporary Photography*, edited by Carol Squiers, New Press, 1999.

Kael, Pauline. *Kiss Kiss Bang Bang*. Bantam Books, 1965.

Langford, Barry. "Revisiting the 'Revisionist' Western." *Film & History*, vol. 33, no. 2, 2003, pp. 26-35. *Project Muse*, muse.jhu.edu /article/396082/pdf. Accessed 2 Feb. 2019.

Once Upon a Time in the West. Directed by Sergio Leone, performances by Henry Fonda and Charles Bronson. Paramount, 1968.

Ramonet, Ignacio. "Italian Westerns as Political Parables." *Cineaste,* vol. 15, no. 1, 1986, pp. 30-35. *JSTOR*, www.jstor.org/stable/41686858. Accessed 2 Feb. 2019.

Stagecoach. Directed by John Ford. United Artists, 1939.

Each entry begins at the left margin, with subsequent lines indented.

List is alphabetized by authors' last names or by title for works with no author.

TWENTY-NINE

APA Style

AMERICAN PSYCHOLOGICAL ASSOCIATION (APA) style calls for (1) brief documentation in parentheses near each in-text citation and (2) complete documentation in a list of references at the end of your text. The models in this chapter draw on the *Publication Manual of the American Psychological Association*, 7th edition (2020). Additional information is available at www.apastyle.org.

A DIRECTORY TO APA STYLE

In-Text Documentation 620

1. Author named in a signal phrase 621
2. Author named in parentheses 621
3. Authors with the same last name 622
4. Two authors 622
5. Three or more authors 622
6. Organization or government as author 622
7. Author unknown 623
8. Two or more works together 623
9. Two or more works by one author in the same year 623
10. Source quoted in another source 623
11. Work without page numbers 624
12. An entire work 624
13. Personal communication 624

Notes   625

Reference List   625

Key Elements for Documenting Sources   625

Authors and Other Contributors   626

1. One author 626
2. Two authors 627
3. Three or more authors 627
4. Two or more works by the same author 627
5. Author and editor 628
6. Author and translator 628
7. Editor 628
8. Unknown or no author or editor 629
9. Organization or government as author 629

Articles and Other Short Works   629

Documentation Map: Article in a Journal with DOI 631
Documentation Map: Webpage on a Website 634

10. Article in a journal 629
11. Article in a magazine 630
12. Article in a newspaper 630
13. Article on a news website 630
14. Editorial 632
15. Review 632
16. Comment on an online article or post 632
17. Webpage on a website 633

Books, Parts of Books, and Reports   633

Documentation Map: Book 635

18. Basic entry for a book 633
19. Edition other than the first 636
20. Edited collection or anthology 636
21. Work in an edited collection or anthology 636
22. Entry in a reference work (dictionary, thesaurus, or encyclopedia) 636
23. Book in a language other than English 637
24. One volume of a multivolume work 637
25. Ancient Greek, Roman, or other classical work 637
26. Work by Shakespeare or other classical literature in English 637
27. Religious work 638
28. Report by a government agency or other organization 638
29. Published dissertation 638
30. Paper or poster presented at a conference 639

Audio, Visual, and Other Sources 639

31. *Wikipedia* entry 639
32. Online forum post 640
33. Blog post 640
34. Online streaming video 640
35. Podcast episode 640
36. Film 641
37. Television series episode 641
38. Song 641
39. Software, computer program, or mobile app 642

40. *PowerPoint* slides or lecture notes 642
41. Recording of a speech or webinar 642
42. Map 642
43. Social media posts 643
44. Data set 644

Sources Not Covered by APA 644

Formatting a Research Essay 644

Sample Research Essay 646

Throughout this chapter, you'll find models and examples that are color-coded to help you see how writers include source information in their texts and reference lists: tan for author or editor, yellow for title, gray for publication information—publisher, date of publication, page number(s), DOI or URL, and so on.

IN-TEXT DOCUMENTATION

Brief documentation in your text makes clear to your readers precisely what you took from a source. If you are quoting, provide the page number(s) or other information that will help readers locate the quotation in the source. You are not required to give the page number(s) with a paraphrase or summary, but you may want to do so if you are citing a long or complex work.

PARAPHRASES and SUMMARIES are more common than QUOTATIONS in APA-style projects. See Chapter 26 for more on all three kinds of citation. As

author   title   publication

you cite each source, you will need to decide whether to name the author in a signal phrase—"as McCullough (2001) wrote"—or in parentheses—"(McCullough, 2001)." Note that APA requires you to use the past tense or present perfect tense for verbs in SIGNAL PHRASES: "Moss (2003) argued," "Moss (2003) has argued."

1. Author named in a signal phrase

Put the date in parentheses after the author's last name, unless the year is mentioned in the sentence. If you are including the page number, put it in parentheses after the quotation, paraphrase, or summary. Documentation information in parentheses should come *before* the period at the end of the sentence and *outside* quotation marks.

> McCullough (2001) described John Adams as having "the hands of a man accustomed to pruning his own trees, cutting his own hay, and splitting his own firewood" (p. 18).

> In 2001, McCullough noted that John Adams's hands were those of a laborer (p. 18).

> John Adams had "the hands of a man accustomed to pruning his own trees," according to McCullough (2001, p. 18).

If the author is named after a quotation, as in this last example, put the page number(s) after the date within the parentheses.

2. Author named in parentheses

If you do not mention an author in a signal phrase, put the name, a comma, and the year of publication in parentheses at the end of the sentence or right after the quotation, paraphrase, or summary.

> John Adams had "the hands of a man accustomed to pruning his own trees, cutting his own hay, and splitting his own firewood" (McCullough, 2001, p. 18).

3. Authors with the same last name

If your reference list includes more than one person with the same last name, include initials in all documentation to distinguish the authors from one another.

> Eclecticism is common in modern criticism (J. M. Smith, 1992, p. vii).

4. Two authors

Always mention both authors. Use *and* in a signal phrase, but use an ampersand (&) in parentheses.

> Carlson and Ventura (1990) wanted to introduce Julio Cortázar,
> Marjorie Agosín, and other Latin American writers to an audience of
> English-speaking adolescents (p. v).

> According to the Peter Principle, "In a hierarchy, every employee tends
> to rise to his level of incompetence" (Peter & Hull, 1969, p. 26).

5. Three or more authors

When you refer to a work by three or more contributors, name only the first author followed by "et al.," Latin for "and others."

> Peilen et al. (1990) supported their claims about corporate corruption
> with startling anecdotal evidence (p. 75).

6. Organization or government as author

If an organization name is recognizable by its abbreviation, give the full name and the abbreviation in brackets the first time you cite the source. In subsequent references, use only the abbreviation. If the organization does not have a familiar abbreviation, always use its full name.

> **First reference**
>
> (American Psychological Association [APA], 2020)

> **Subsequent references**
>
> (APA, 2020)

7. Author unknown

Use the complete title if it's short; if it's long, use the first few words of the title under which the work appears in the reference list. Italicize the title if it's italicized in the reference list; if it isn't italicized there, enclose the title in quotation marks.

> *Webster's New Biographical Dictionary* (1988) identifies William James as "American psychologist and philosopher" (p. 520).

> The article noted that one healthy liver donor died because of "frightening" postoperative care ("Every Patient's Nightmare," 2007).

8. Two or more works together

If you document multiple works in the same parentheses, place the source information in alphabetical order, separated by semicolons.

> Many researchers have argued that what counts as "literacy" is not necessarily learned at school (Heath, 1983; Moss, 2003).

9. Two or more works by one author in the same year

If your list of references includes more than one work by the same author published in the same year, order them alphabetically by title, adding lowercase letters ("a," "b," and so on) to the year.

> Kaplan (2000a) described orderly shantytowns in Turkey that did not resemble the other slums he visited.

10. Source quoted in another source

When you cite a source that was quoted in another source, add the words *as cited in.*

> Thus, Modern Standard Arabic was expected to serve as the "moral glue" holding the Arab world together (Choueri, 2000, as cited in Walters, 2019, p. 475).

11. Work without page numbers

Instead of page numbers, some works have paragraph numbers, which you should include (preceded by the abbreviation *para.*) if you are referring to a specific part of such a source. In sources with neither page nor paragraph numbers (e.g., many online journals), refer readers to a particular part of the source if possible, perhaps indicating a heading and the paragraph under the heading.

> Russell's dismissals from Trinity College at Cambridge and from
> City College in New York City have been seen as examples of the
> controversy that marked his life (Irvine, 2006, para. 2).

12. An entire work

You do not need to give a page number if you are directing readers' attention to an entire work.

> Kaplan (2000) considered Turkey and Central Asia explosive.

When you are citing an entire website, give the URL in the text. You do not need to include the website in your reference list. To cite a webpage on a website, see no. 17 on page 633.

> Beyond providing diagnostic information, the website for the
> Alzheimer's Association (http://www.alz.org) includes a variety of
> resources for family and community support of patients suffering from
> Alzheimer's disease.

13. Personal communication

Document emails, telephone conversations, interviews, personal letters, messages from nonarchived electronic discussion sources, and other personal texts as *personal communication*, along with the person's initial(s), last name, and the date. You do not need to include such personal communications in your reference list.

> L. Strauss (personal communication, December 6, 2013) told about
> visiting Yogi Berra when they both lived in Montclair, New Jersey.

NOTES

You may need to use footnotes to give an explanation or information that doesn't fit into your text. To signal a content footnote, place a superscript numeral at the appropriate point in your text. Include this information in a footnote, either at the bottom of that page or on a separate page with the heading "Footnotes" in bold, after your reference list. If you have multiple notes, number them consecutively throughout your text. Here is an example from *In Search of Solutions: A New Direction in Psychotherapy* (2003).

Text with superscript

An important part of working with teams and one-way mirrors is taking the consultation break, as at Milan, BFTC, and MRI.[1]

Footnote

[1] It is crucial to note here that while working within a team is fun, stimulating, and revitalizing, it is not necessary for successful outcomes. Solution-oriented therapy works equally well when working solo.

REFERENCE LIST

A reference list provides full bibliographic information for every source cited in your text with the exception of entire websites, common computer software and mobile apps, and personal communications. See page 645 for guidelines on preparing such a list; for a sample reference list, see page 660.

Key Elements for Documenting Sources

APA style provides a list of four elements that should be used to document a source: author, date, title, and source. The kind of information that makes up each element can change slightly depending on the type of source. The following guidelines explain how to handle each of the key elements generally; refer to these guidelines and the section on "Authors and Other Contributors" if your specific kind of source isn't covered in the examples provided.

AUTHOR: Use the author's last name, but replace the first and middle names with initials and invert the order: Kinder, D. R. for Donald R. Kinder.

DATE: Include the date of publication, which will vary based on the type of work you are citing.

TITLE: Capitalize only the first word and proper nouns and adjectives in the title and subtitle of the work you are citing. Titles of periodicals and websites are capitalized differently, so refer to an example for specifics.

SOURCE: The source indicates where the work can be found. It includes the publisher, any additional information about the source (e.g., volume number, issue number, pages), and the DOI or URL if applicable.

DOI OR URL: Include a DOI (digital object identifier, a string of letters and numbers that identifies an online document) for any work that has one, regardless of whether you accessed the source in print or online. For a print work with no DOI, do not include a URL. For an online work with no DOI, include a URL unless the URL is no longer working or unless the work is from an academic database.

Authors and Other Contributors

This section provides general guidelines for documenting authors and other contributors across sources and in various kinds of media (in print, online, and in other media). Note that most of the examples in this section are books. If you are documenting a different kind of source, follow the appropriate formatting guidelines.

1. One author

> Author's Last Name, Initials. (Year of publication). *Title of book.*
> Publisher. DOI *or* URL

> Lewis, M. (2003). *Moneyball: The art of winning an unfair game.* W. W. Norton.

This book does not have a DOI, so that element does not appear in the reference entry.

author   title   publication

2. Two authors

First Author's Last Name, Initials, & Second Author's Last Name, Initials. (Year of publication). *Title of book.* Publisher. DOI *or* URL

Montefiore, S., & Montefiore, S. S. (2016). *The royal rabbits of London.* Aladdin.

3. Three or more authors

For three to 20 authors, include all names.

First Author's Last Name, Initials, Next Author's Last Name, Initials, & Final Author's Last Name, Initials. (Year of publication). *Title of book.* Publisher. DOI *or* URL

Greig, A., Taylor, J., & MacKay, T. (2013). *Doing research with children: A practical guide* (3rd ed.). Sage.

For a work by 21 or more authors, name the first 19 authors, followed by three ellipsis points, and end with the final author.

Gao, R., Asano, S. M., Upadhyayula, S., Pisarev, I., Milkie, D. E., Liu, T.-L., Singh, V., Graves, A., Huynh, G. H., Zhao, Y., Bogovic, J., Colonell, J., Ott, C. M., Zugates, C., Tappan, S., Rodriguez, A., Mosaliganti, K. R., Sheu, S.-H., Pasolli, H. A., . . . Betzig, E. (2019, January 18). Cortical column and whole-brain imaging with molecular contrast and nanoscale resolution. *Science, 363*(6424). https://doi.org/10.1126/science.aau8302

4. Two or more works by the same author

If the works were published in different years, list them chronologically.

Lewis, B. (1995). *The Middle East: A brief history of the last 2,000 years.* Scribner.

Lewis, B. (2003). *The crisis of Islam: Holy war and unholy terror.* Modern Library.

If the works were published in the same year, list them alphabetically by title, adding "a," "b," and so on to the year.

> Kaplan, R. D. (2000a). *The coming anarchy: Shattering the dreams of the post cold war.* Random House.
> Kaplan, R. D. (2000b). *Eastward to Tartary: Travels in the Balkans, the Middle East, and the Caucasus.* Random House.

5. Author and editor

If a book has an author and an editor who is credited on the cover, include the editor in parentheses after the title. If the book is a republished version of an earlier book, include the year of publication of the version you are using as the date and the original publication year at the end.

> Author's Last Name, Initials. (Year of publication). *Title of book* (Editor's Initials Last Name, Ed.). Publisher. DOI *or* URL (Original work published Year)

> Dick, P. F. (2008). *Five novels of the 1960s and 70s* (J. Lethem, Ed.). Library of America. (Original works published 1964–1977)

6. Author and translator

> Author's Last Name, Initials. (Year of publication). *Title of book* (Translator's Initials Last Name, Trans.). Publisher. DOI *or* URL (Original work published Year)

> Hugo, V. (2008). *Les misérables* (J. Rose, Trans.). Modern Library. (Original work published 1862)

7. Editor

> Editor's Last Name, Initials (Ed.). (Year of publication). *Title of book.* Publisher. DOI *or* URL

> Jones, D. (Ed.). (2007). *Modern love: 50 true and extraordinary tales of desire, deceit, and devotion.* Three Rivers Press.

author   title   publication

8. Unknown or no author or editor

When there's no known author or editor, start with the title.

> *Title of book.* (Year of Publication). Publisher. DOI *or* URL

> *Webster's new biographical dictionary.* (1988). Merriam-Webster.

> Hot property: From carriage house to family compound. (2004, December). *Berkshire Living, 1*(1), 99.

> Clues in salmonella outbreak. (2008, June 21). *The New York Times,* A13.

If the author is listed as *Anonymous,* treat the reference list entry as if the author's name were Anonymous.

9. Organization or government as author

Sometimes an organization or a government agency is both author and publisher. If so, omit the publisher.

> Organization Name *or* Government Agency. (Year of publication). *Title of book.* DOI *or* URL

> Catholic News Service. (2002). *Stylebook on religion 2000: A reference guide.*

Articles and Other Short Works

Articles, essays, reviews, and other short works are found in periodicals and books—in print, online, or in a database. For most short works, provide information about the author, the titles of both the short work and the longer work, any volume and issue numbers, any page numbers, various kinds of publication information, and a DOI or URL if applicable.

10. Article in a journal

> Author's Last Name, Initials. (Year). Title of article. *Title of Journal, volume*(issue), page(s). DOI *or* URL

> Gremer, J. R., Sala, A., & Crone, E. E. (2010). Disappearing plants: Why they hide and how they return. *Ecology, 91*(11), 3407–3413. https://doi.org/10.1890/09-1864.1

If a DOI is long or complicated, it's acceptable to use a shortDOI. Create one by entering the DOI into the shortDOI service (https://shortdoi.org/). A URL can also be shortened using any online URL shortener, as long as the shorter URL leads to the correct work.

11. Article in a magazine

If a magazine is published weekly, include the day and the month. Include the volume number and issue number after the magazine title.

> Author's Last Name, Initials. (Year, Month Day). Title of article. *Title of Magazine, volume*(issue), page(s). DOI *or* URL

> Klump, B. (2019, November 22). Of crows and tools. *Science, 366*(6468), 965. https://doi.org/10.1126/science.aaz7775

12. Article in a newspaper

If page numbers are consecutive, separate them with an en dash. If not, separate them with a comma.

> Author's Last Name, Initials. (Year, Month Day). Title of article. *Title of Newspaper,* page(s). URL

> Schneider, G. (2005, March 13). Fashion sense on wheels. *The Washington Post,* F1, F6.

13. Article on a news website

Articles on CNN, HuffPost, Salon, Vox, and other news websites are documented differently from articles published in online newspapers and magazines. If an article is published in an online news source that is not a periodical or a blog, the article is treated as a stand-alone work, and the title should be italicized. Do not italicize the name of the website.

> Author's Last Name, Initials. (Year, Month Day). *Title of article.* Title of Site. URL

> Travers, C. (2019, December 3). *Here's why you keep waking up at the same time every night.* HuffPost. https://bit.ly/3drSwAR

Documentation Map (APA) / Article in a Journal with DOI

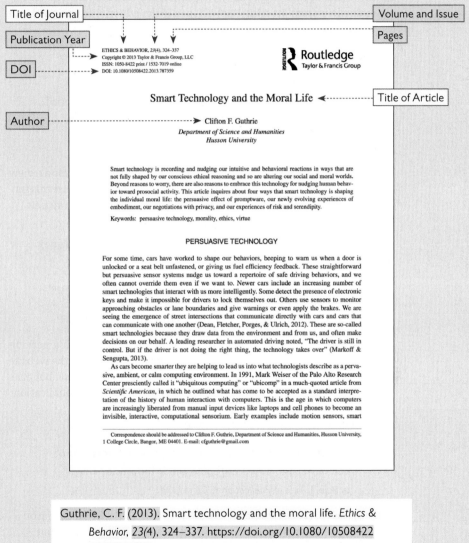

Title of Journal

Volume and Issue

Publication Year

Pages

DOI

Title of Article

Author

ETHICS & BEHAVIOR, 23(4), 324–337
Copyright © 2013 Taylor & Francis Group, LLC
ISSN: 1050-8422 print / 1532-7019 online
DOI: 10.1080/10508422.2013.787359

Routledge
Taylor & Francis Group

Smart Technology and the Moral Life

Clifton F. Guthrie
Department of Science and Humanities
Husson University

Smart technology is recording and nudging our intuitive and behavioral reactions in ways that are not fully shaped by our conscious ethical reasoning and so are altering our social and moral worlds. Beyond reasons to worry, there are also reasons to embrace this technology for nudging human behavior toward prosocial activity. This article inquires about four ways that smart technology is shaping the individual moral life: the persuasive effect of promptware, our newly evolving experiences of embodiment, our negotiations with privacy, and our experiences of risk and serendipity.

Keywords: persuasive technology, morality, ethics, virtue

PERSUASIVE TECHNOLOGY

For some time, cars have worked to shape our behaviors, beeping to warn us when a door is unlocked or a seat belt unfastened, or giving us fuel efficiency feedback. These straightforward but persuasive sensor systems nudge us toward a repertoire of safe driving behaviors, and we often cannot override them even if we want to. Newer cars include an increasing number of smart technologies that interact with us more intelligently. Some detect the presence of electronic keys and make it impossible for drivers to lock themselves out. Others use sensors to monitor approaching obstacles or lane boundaries and give warnings or even apply the brakes. We are seeing the emergence of street intersections that communicate directly with cars and cars that can communicate with one another (Dean, Fletcher, Porges, & Ulrich, 2012). These are so-called smart technologies because they draw data from the environment and from us, and often make decisions on our behalf. A leading researcher in automated driving noted, "The driver is still in control. But if the driver is not doing the right thing, the technology takes over" (Markoff & Sengupta, 2013).

As cars become smarter they are helping to lead us into what technologists describe as a pervasive, ambient, or calm computing environment. In 1991, Mark Weiser of the Palo Alto Research Center presciently called it "ubiquitous computing" or "ubicomp" in a much-quoted article from *Scientific American*, in which he outlined what has come to be accepted as a standard interpretation of the history of human interaction with computers. This is the age in which computers are increasingly liberated from manual input devices like laptops and cell phones to become an invisible, interactive, computational sensorium. Early examples include motion sensors, smart

Correspondence should be addressed to Clifton F. Guthrie, Department of Science and Humanities, Husson University, 1 College Circle, Bangor, ME 04401. E-mail: cfguthrie@gmail.com

Guthrie, C. F. (2013). Smart technology and the moral life. *Ethics & Behavior, 23*(4), 324–337. https://doi.org/10.1080/10508422 .2013.787359

14. Editorial

Editorials can appear in journals, magazines, and newspapers. The follow-ing example is from an online newspaper. If the editorial is unsigned, put the title of the editorial in the author position.

> Author's Last Name, Initials. (Year, Month Day). Title of editorial
>   [Editorial]. *Title of Newspaper.* URL

> *The Guardian* view on local theatres: The shows must go on [Editorial].
>   (2019, December 6). *The Guardian.* https://bit.ly/2VZHIUg

15. Review

The following example is a book review in a newspaper; if you are citing a review that appears in print or online in a journal, magazine, or newspaper, use this gen-eral format, indicating in brackets what is being reviewed (a film, an app, etc.)

> Reviewer's Last Name, Initials. (Year, Month Day). Title of review
>   [Review of the book *Title of book*, by Author's Initials Last Name].
>   *Title of Newspaper.* DOI or URL

> Joinson, S. (2017, December 15). Mysteries unfold in a land of minarets
>   and magic carpets [Review of the book *The city of brass*, by S. A.
>   Chakraborty]. *The New York Times.* https://nyti.ms/2kvwHFP

For a review published on a website that is not associated with a periodi-cal or a blog, italicize the title of the review and do not italicize the website name. If the review does not have a title, include the information about the work being reviewed in brackets immediately after the date of publication.

16. Comment on an online article or post

> Author's Last Name, Initials [username]. (Year, Month Day). Text of
>   comment up to 20 words [Comment on the article "Title of
>   article"]. *Title of Publication.* DOI or URL

> PhillyTheKid. (2019, November 24). "NEXT MAN UP!" – SB 52 Champion
>   Eagles [Comment on the article "Injuries are never an excuse, but
>   oh boy…"]. *The Philadelphia Inquirer.* http://disq.us/p/25r5mpu

Include a link to the comment if possible; if not, include the URL of the article.

17. Webpage on a website

Author's Last Name, Initials. (Year, Month Day). *Title of work*. Title of
Site. URL

Pleasant, B. (n.d.). *Annual bluegrass*. The National Gardening Association.
https://garden.org/learn/articles/view/2936/

Centers for Disease Control and Prevention. (2019, December 2). *When
and how to wash your hands*. https://www.cdc.gov/handwashing
/when-how-handwashing.html

Worldometer. (n.d.). *World population*. Retrieved February 2, 2020, from
https://www.worldometers.info/world-population/

If the author and the website name are the same, use the website name as
the author. If the content of the webpage is intended to change over time
and no archived version exists, use "n.d." as the date and include a retrieval
date.

Books, Parts of Books, and Reports

18. Basic entry for a book

Author's Last Name, Initials. (Year of publication). *Title of book*.
Publisher. DOI *or* URL

Print book

Schwab, V. E. (2018). *Vengeful*. Tor Books.

Ebook

Jemisin, N. K. (2017). *The stone sky*. Orbit. https://bit.ly/2DrGzKR

A print book and an ebook are documented in the same way. For an ebook,
do not include the format or platform you used (e.g., Kindle).

Documentation Map (APA) / Webpage on a Website

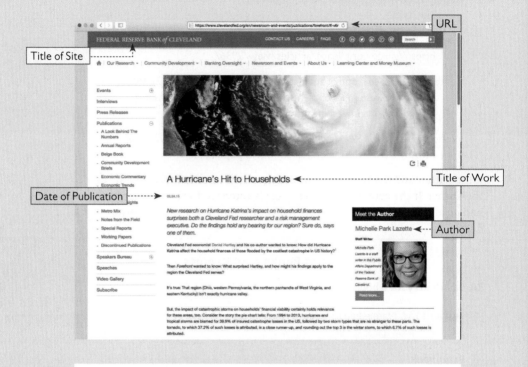

Title of Site

URL

Title of Work

Date of Publication

Author

Lazette, M. P. (2015, February 24). *A hurricane's hit to households*. Federal
Reserve Bank of Cleveland. https://www.clevelandfed.org
/en/newsroom-and-events/publications/forefront/ff-v6n01/ff
-20150224-v6n0107-a-hurricanes-hit-to-households.aspx

Documentation Map (APA) / Book

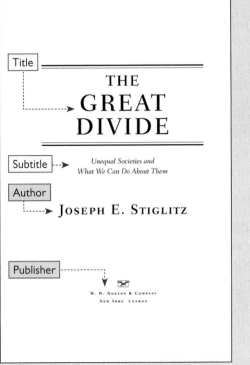

Title

THE
GREAT
DIVIDE

Subtitle

*Unequal Societies and
What We Can Do About Them*

Author

JOSEPH E. STIGLITZ

Publisher

W. W. NORTON & COMPANY
NEW YORK LONDON

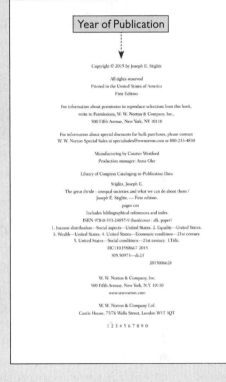

Year of Publication

Copyright © 2015 by Joseph E. Stiglitz

All rights reserved
Printed in the United States of America
First Edition

For information about permission to reproduce selections from this book,
write to Permissions, W. W. Norton & Company, Inc.,
500 Fifth Avenue, New York, NY 10110

For information about special discounts for bulk purchases, please contact
W. W. Norton Special Sales at specialsales@wwnorton.com or 800-233-4830

Manufacturing by Courier Westford
Production manager: Anna Oler

Library of Congress Cataloging-in-Publication Data

Stiglitz, Joseph E.
The great divide : unequal societies and what we can do about them /
Joseph E. Stiglitz. — First edition.
pages cm
Includes bibliographical references and index.
ISBN 978-0-393-24857-9 (hardcover : alk. paper)
1. Income distribution—Social aspects—United States. 2. Equality—United States.
3. Wealth—United States. 4. United States—Economic conditions—21st century.
5. United States—Social conditions—21st century. I. Title.
HC110.I5S8667 2015
305.50973—dc23
2015006628

W. W. Norton & Company, Inc.
500 Fifth Avenue, New York, N.Y. 10110
www.wwnorton.com

W. W. Norton & Company Ltd.
Castle House, 75/76 Wells Street, London W1T 3QT

1 2 3 4 5 6 7 8 9 0

Stiglitz, J. E. (2015). *The great divide: Unequal societies and what
we can do about them.* W. W. Norton.

19. Edition other than the first

Author's Last Name, Initials. (Year). *Title of book* (Name or number ed.). Publisher. DOI or URL

Burch, D. (2008). *Emergency navigation: Find your position and shape your course at sea even if your instruments fail* (2nd ed.). International Marine/McGraw-Hill.

20. Edited collection or anthology

Editor's Last Name, Initials (Ed.). (Year of edited edition). *Title of anthology* (number ed., Vol. number). Publisher. DOI or URL

Raviv, A., Oppenheimer, L., & Bar-Tal, D. (Eds.). (1999). *How children understand war and peace: A call for international peace education.* Jossey-Bass.

21. Work in an edited collection or anthology

Author's Last Name, Initials. (Year). Title of work. In Editor's Initials Last Name (Ed.), *Title of anthology* (number ed., Vol. number, pp. pages). Publisher. DOI or URL (Original work published Year)

Baldwin, J. (2018). Notes of a native son. In M. Puchner, S. Akbari, W. Denecke, B. Fuchs, C. Levine, P. Lewis, & E. Wilson (Eds.), *The Norton anthology of world literature* (4th ed., Vol. F, pp. 728–743). W. W. Norton. (Original work published 1955)

22. Entry in a reference work (dictionary, thesaurus, or encyclopedia)

If the entry has no author, use the name of the publisher as the author. If the reference work has no editor, do not include an editor. If the entry is archived or is not intended to change, use the publication date and do not include a retrieval date.

Author's Last Name, Initials. (Year). Title of entry. In Editor's Initials Last Name (Ed.), *Title of reference book* (Name or number ed., Vol. number, pp. pages). Publisher. URL

Merriam-Webster. (n.d.). Epoxy. In *Merriam-Webster.com dictionary*.
Retrieved January 29, 2020, from https://www.merriam-webster
.com/dictionary/epoxy

23. Book in a language other than English

Author's Last Name, Initials. (Year). *Title of book* [English translation of
title]. Publisher. DOI *or* URL

Ferrante, E. (2011). *L'amica geniale* [My brilliant friend]. Edizione E/O.

24. One volume of a multivolume work

If the volume does not have a separate title, include the volume number in
parentheses after the title.

Author's Last Name, Initials. (Year). *Title of entire work* (Vol. number).
Publisher. DOI *or* URL

Spiegelman, A. (1986). *Maus* (Vol. 1). Random House.

If the volume does have a separate title, include the volume number and
title in italics after the main title (see no. 27 for an example from a religious
work).

25. Ancient Greek, Roman, or other classical work

Author's Name. (Year of publication). *Title of work* (Translator's Initials
Last Name, Trans.). Publisher. URL (Original work published Year)

Aristotle. (1994). *Nichomachean ethics* (W. D. Ross, Trans.). The Internet
Classics Archive. http://classics.mit.edu/index.html (Original
work published ca. 350 B.C.E.)

If the exact date is unknown, use "ca.," which stands for "circa."

26. Work by Shakespeare or other classical literature in English

Author's Last Name, Initials. (Year of publication). *Title of work* (Editor's Initials
Last Name, Ed.). Publisher. URL (Original work published Year)

Shakespeare, W. (2009). *Macbeth* (S. Barnes & A. Coleman, Eds.).
Insight Publications. (Original work published 1606)

27. Religious work

Do not include an author for most religious works. If you are citing an annotated version, include the editor and/or translator. If the date of original publication is known, include it at the end.

Unannotated

Title of work. (Year of publication). Publisher. URL (Original work published Year)

The New American Bible. (2002). United States Conference of Catholic Bishops. http://www.vatican.va/archive/ENG0839/_INDEX.HTM (Original work published 1970)

Annotated

Editor's Last Name, Initials (Ed.). (Year of publication). *Title of work.* Publisher. URL (Original work published Year)

Marks, H. (Ed.). (2012). *The English Bible, The King James Version: Vol. 1. The Old Testament.* W. W. Norton. (Original work published 1611)

28. Report by a government agency or other organization

Author's Last Name, Initials. (Year, Month Day). *Title of report* (Report No. number). Publisher. DOI *or* URL

Centers for Disease Control and Prevention. (2009). *Fourth national report on human exposure to environmental chemicals.* US Department of Health and Human Services. https://www.cdc.gov/exposurereport/pdf/fourthreport.pdf

Omit the report number if one is not given. If more than one government department is listed as the publisher, list the most specific department as the author and the larger department as the publisher.

29. Published dissertation

Author's Last Name, Initials. (Year). *Title of dissertation* (Publication No. number) [Doctoral dissertation, Name of School]. Database *or* Archive Name. DOI *or* URL

Solomon, M. (2016). *Social media and self-examination: The examination of
social media use on identity, social comparison, and self-esteem in young
female adults* (Publication No. 10188962) [Doctoral dissertation,
William James College]. ProQuest Dissertations and Theses Global.

If the thesis or dissertation is in a database, do not include a URL. Include a
URL if the thesis or dissertation is published elsewhere online. If the dissertation is unpublished, use the name of the school as the source.

30. Paper or poster presented at a conference

Presenter's Last Name, Initials. (Year, Month First Day–Last Day).
Title of paper or *poster* [Paper or Poster presentation]. Name of
Conference, City, State, Country. URL

Dolatian, H., & Heinz, J. (2018, May 25–27). *Reduplication and finite-state
technology* [Paper presentation]. The 53rd Annual Meeting of the
Chicago Linguistic Society, Chicago, IL, United States. http://
chicagolinguisticsociety.org/public/CLS53_Booklet.pdf

Audio, Visual, and Other Sources

If you are referring to an entire website, do not include the website in your reference list; simply mention the website's name in the body of your paper and
include the URL in parentheses. Do not include email, personal communication,
or other unarchived discussions in your list of references.

31. *Wikipedia* entry

Because *Wikipedia* has archived versions of its pages, give the date on which
you accessed the page and the permanent URL of the archived page, which
is found by clicking "View history."

Title of entry. (Year, Month Day). In *Wikipedia*. URL

List of sheep breeds. (2019, September 9). In *Wikipedia*. https://en.wikipedia
.org/w/index.php?title=List_of_sheep_breeds&oldid=914884262

For a wiki that doesn't have permanent links to archived versions of its
pages, include a retrieval date before the URL.

32. Online forum post

Author's Last Name, Initials [username]. (Year, Month Day). *Content of the post up to 20 words* [Online forum post]. Title of Site. URL

Hanzus, D. [DanHanzus]. (2019, October 23). *GETCHA DAN HANZUS. ASK ME ANYTHING!* [Online forum post]. Reddit. https://bit.ly /38WgmSF

33. Blog post

Author's Last Name, Initials [username]. (Year, Month Day). Title of post. *Title of Blog.* URL

gcrepps. (2017, March 28). Shania Sanders. *Women@NASA.* https:// blogs.nasa.gov/womenatnasa/2017/03/28/shania-sanders/

If only the username is known, do not use brackets.

34. Online streaming video

Uploader's Last Name, Initials [username]. (Year, Month Day). *Title of video* [Video]. Name of Video Platform. URL

CinemaSins. (2014, August 21). *Everything wrong with* National Treasure in 13 minutes or less [Video]. YouTube. https://www.youtube.com /watch?v=1ul-_ZWvXTs

The person or group that uploaded the video is considered the author, even if someone else created the content. If only the username is known, do not use brackets. If there is another title within a title, put that other title in reverse italics.

35. Podcast episode

Host's Last Name, Initials (Host). (Year, Month Day). Episode title (No. episode number) [Audio podcast episode]. In *Podcast name.* Production Company. URL

Tamposi, E., & Samocki, E. (Hosts). (2020, January 8). The year of the broads [Audio podcast episode]. In *The broadcast podcast.* Podcast One. https://podcastone.com/episode/the-year-of-the-broads

The host of the podcast, or the executive producer if known, is considered the author. Do not include an episode number if one isn't given.

36. Film

Director's Last Name, Initials (Director). (Year). *Title of film* [Film]. Production Company. URL

Jenkins, B. (Director). (2016). *Moonlight* [Film]. A24; Plan B; PASTEL.

Cuarón, A. (Director). (2016). *Harry Potter and the prisoner of Azkaban* [Film; two-disc special ed. on DVD]. Warner Bros.

List the director as the author of the film. Indicate how you watched the film only if the format is important to the content.

37. Television series episode

Writer's Last Name, Initials (Writer), & Director's Last Name, Initials (Director). (Year, Month Day). Title of episode (Season number, Episode number) [TV series episode]. In Executive Producer's Initials Last Name (Executive Producer), *Title of series*. Production Company. URL

Siegal, J. (Writer), Morgan, D. (Writer), & Sackett, M. (Director). (2018, December 6). Janet(s) (Season 3, Episode 10) [TV series episode]. In M. Schur, D. Miner, M. Sackett, & D. Goddard (Executive Producers), *The good place*. Fremulon; 3 Arts Entertainment; Universal Television.

To document an entire series, use the executive producer as the author.

38. Song

Artist's Last Name, Initials. (Year). Title of song [Song]. On *Title of album*. Label. URL

Giddens, R. (2015). Shake sugaree [Song]. On *Tomorrow is my turn*. Nonesuch.

The recording artist or group is considered the author. Do not include a URL unless the song can be accessed only on one specific online platform.

39. Software, computer program, or mobile app

Include entries for software, programs, or mobile apps only if they are un-common or will not be known by your audience. If they are common or will be known to your audience, just include the name (not italicized) and version number in the body of your text. Include a description of the content in brackets after the version number.

> Last Name, Initials. (Year). *Name of program* (Version number) [Computer software]. Publisher. URL

> Blount, K. (2018). *Scrivener for Windows* (Version 1.9.9.0) [Computer software]. Literature & Latte. https://www.literatureandlatte.com/scrivener

For a mobile app, use "App Store" or wherever you accessed the app as the publisher. Use the year of publication of the version you accessed as the date.

40. *PowerPoint* slides or lecture notes

> Author's Last Name, Initials. (Year, Month Day). *Title of presentation* [Description of content]. Publisher. URL

> Pavliscak, P. (2016, February 21). *Finding our happy place in the internet of things* [PowerPoint slides]. Slideshare. https://bit.ly/3aOcfs7

If the lecture notes or slides do not have a title, describe the contents in brackets after the date.

41. Recording of a speech or webinar

> Author's Last Name, Initials. (Year, Month Day). *Title of speech* [Speech audio recording]. Publisher. URL

> Kennedy, J. F. (1961, January 20). *Inaugural address* [Speech audio recording]. American Rhetoric. https://bit.ly/339Gc3e

42. Map

> Mapmaker's Last Name, Initials. (Year). *Title of map* [Map]. Publisher. URL

> Daniels, M. (2018). *Human terrain: Visualizing the world's population, in 3D* [Map]. The Pudding. https://pudding.cool/2018/10/city_3d/

author   title   publication

Google. (n.d.). [Google Maps directions for biking from Las Vegas,
    Nevada, to Los Angeles, California]. Retrieved January 30, 2020,
    from https://goo.gle/maps/9NdekwAkHeo4HM4N7

To cite a dynamic map, such as a map from *Google Maps*, use "n.d." for the
date and include a retrieval date. For the title, include a description of the
map in brackets.

43. Social media posts

Use the author's real name and include the social media handle in brackets.
If only the handle is known, do not use brackets. If the post contains any
added content (e.g., a video, an image, a thumbnail with link attached), indicate that in brackets after the content of the post. Replicate emoji if possible;
if not, include a bracketed description.

Author's Last Name, Initials [@username]. (Year, Month Day). *Content*
    of post up to 20 words [Description of multimedia content] [Type of
    post]. Platform. URL

Tweet

Baron, D. [@DrGrammar]. (2019, November 11). *Gender conceal: Did*
    you know that pronouns can also hide someone's gender? [Thumbnail
    with link attached] [Tweet]. Twitter. https://bit.ly/2vaCcDc

Instagram photograph or video

Jamil, J. [@jameelajamilofficial]. (2018, July 18). *Happy Birthday to our*
    leader. I steal all my acting faces from you. @kristenanniebell [Face
    with smile and sunglasses emoji] [Photograph]. Instagram. https://
    www.instagram.com/p/BIYX5F9FuGL/

Facebook post

Philadelphia Eagles. (2019, December 3). *"'We control our own destiny.'*
    That's going to be the message moving forward to this football team."
    #FlyEaglesFly [Thumbnail with link attached] [Status update].
    Facebook. https://bit.ly/39Ghjil

44. Data set

Author's Last Name, Initials. (Year). *Title of data set* (Version number) [Data set]. Publisher. DOI *or* URL

Pew Research Center. (2019). *Core trends survey* [Data set]. https://www.pewresearch.org/internet/dataset/core-trends-survey/

If the name of the author is the same as the name of the publisher, omit the publisher.

Sources Not Covered by APA

To document a source for which APA does not provide guidelines, look at models similar to the source you have cited. Give any information readers will need in order to find it themselves—author; date of publication; title; source, including DOI or URL (if applicable); and any other pertinent information. You might want to test your reference note to be sure it will lead others to your source.

FORMATTING A RESEARCH ESSAY

Title page. APA generally requires a title page. The page number should go in the upper right-hand corner. Center the full title of the paper in bold in the top half of the page. Center your name, the name of your department and school, the course number and name, the instructor's name, and the due date on separate lines below the title. Leave one line between the title and your name.

Page numbers. Place the page number in the upper right-hand corner. Number pages consecutively throughout.

Fonts, spacing, margins, and indents. Use a legible font that will be accessible to everyone, either a serif font (such as Times New Roman or Bookman) or a sans serif font (such as Calibri or Verdana). Use a sans serif font within figure images. Double-space the entire paper, including any notes and your list of references; the only exception is footnotes at the bottom of a page, which should be single-spaced. Leave one-inch margins at the top, bottom, and sides of your text; do not justify the text. The first line of each paragraph should be indented one-half inch (or five to seven spaces) from the left margin. APA recommends using one space after end-of-sentence punctuation.

Headings. Though they are not required in APA style, headings can help readers follow your text. The first level of heading should be bold, centered, and capitalized as you would any other title; the second level of heading should be bold and flush with the left margin; the third level should be bold, italicized, and flush left.

First Level Heading

Second Level Heading

Third Level Heading

Abstract. An abstract is a concise summary of your paper that introduces readers to your topic and main points. Most scholarly journals require an abstract; an abstract is not typically required for student papers, so check your instructor's preference. Put your abstract on the second page, with the word "Abstract" centered and in bold at the top. Unless your instructor specifies a length, limit your abstract to 250 words or fewer.

Long quotations. Indent quotations of forty or more words one-half inch (or five to seven spaces) from the left margin. Do not use quotation marks, and place the page number(s) or documentation information in parentheses *after* the end punctuation. If there are paragraphs in the quotation, indent the first line of each paragraph another one-half inch.

> Kaplan (2000) captured ancient and contemporary Antioch:
>
> > At the height of its glory in the Roman-Byzantine age, when it had an amphitheater, public baths, aqueducts, and sewage pipes, half a million people lived in Antioch. Today the population is only 125,000. With sour relations between Turkey and Syria, and unstable politics throughout the Middle East, Antioch is now a backwater—seedy and tumbledown, with relatively few tourists. (p. 123)
>
> Antioch's decline serves as a reminder that the fortunes of cities can change drastically over time.

List of references. Start your list on a new page after the text but before any endnotes. Title the page "References," centered and in bold, and double-space the entire list. Each entry should begin at the left margin, and subsequent lines should be indented one-half inch (or five to seven spaces). Alphabetize the list by authors' last names (or by editors' names, if appropriate). Alphabetize works that have no author or editor by title, disregarding *A, An,* and *The.* Be sure every source listed is cited in the text; do not include sources that you consulted but did not cite.

Tables and figures. Above each table or figure (charts, diagrams, graphs, photos, and so on), provide the word "Table" or "Figure" and a number, flush left and in bold (e.g., **Table 1**). On the following line, give a descriptive title, flush left and italicized. Below the table or figure, include a note with any necessary explanation and source information. Number tables and figures separately, and be sure to discuss them in your text so that readers know how they relate.

Table 1
Hours of Instruction Delivered per Week

	American classrooms	Japanese classrooms	Chinese classrooms
First grade			
Language arts	10.5	8.7	10.4
Mathematics	2.7	5.8	4.0
Fifth grade			
Language arts	7.9	8.0	11.1
Mathematics	3.4	7.8	11.7

Note. Adapted from "Peeking Out from Under the Blinders: Some Factors We Shouldn't Forget in Studying Writing," by J. R. Hayes, 1991, National Center for the Study of Writing and Literacy (Occasional Paper No. 25). National Writing Project website: http://www.nwp.org/

SAMPLE RESEARCH ESSAY

Katryn Sheppard wrote the following paper, "Early Word Production: A Study of One Child's Word Productions," for a linguistics course. It is formatted according to the guidelines of the *Publication Manual of the American Psychological Association,* 7th edition (2020).

1 •——— Page numbers appear in the upper right corner.

Early Word Production: A Study of One Child's Word Productions

e title is bold, ntered, and placed the upper half of e page.

Katryn Sheppard

Department of Applied Linguistics, Portland State University

LING 437: First Language Acquisition

Dr. Lynn Santelmann

October 31, 2019

Your name is centered below the title, with one double-spaced line in between.

The school name and department, course number and name, professor's name, and due date of the paper are centered below your name.

Abstract

Early word production, one of the initial stages of language development in children, plays an important role in the development of later language skills. This study identifies the word classes and number of words spoken in a recorded interaction (Bloom, 1973) by one normally developing child of sixteen months and analyzes aspects of the child's speech, with the goal of noting if the characteristics observed were supported by the existing research on early word production or if they deviated from those findings. The words that I analyzed fell into six categories: nouns, spatial terms, adjectives, negatives, social phrases, and verbs. Although the frequency with which the child used words from some of these categories reflected the expectations established by previous research, her use of words in other categories was less predictable. Noting word usage in the six categories led to an analysis of the functions that those categories served in the child's semantic communication at this early stage of language development.

Abstract begins on a new page. Heading is centered and bold. An abstract is not generally required for a student paper, so check with your professor.

Abstract text does not need a paragraph indent.

Use one space after each sentence.

250 words or fewer.

3

Early Word Production: A Study of One Child's Word Productions ●————— *Text starts on a new page. Title is centered and bold.*

 Each step in the course of language development and acquisition in children provides a foundation for later skills and eventual mastery of the language. Early word production, a stage of language development in ●————— *Essay is double-spaced.* which children have only a few words in their vocabularies, provides the foundation for later vocabulary building and language production and has been shown to be closely linked to later language performance skills (Walker et al., 1994). The early word production stage is therefore worthy ●————— *Because this source has more than two authors, the in-text documentation begins with the first author's name followed by et al. The year of publication is included in the reference.* of examination, as it "signals that children have a new tool that will enable them to learn about and participate more fully in their society" (Uccelli & Pan, 2013, p. 95).

 Because so few words are produced by children in this early stage, the analysis of their word production focuses on the frequency of particular word classes in speech. When examining typically developing English-speaking children who have few words in their productive vocabulary, Bates et al. (1994) found that the words produced were most ●————— *The signal phrase uses past tense, and the year of publication is given in parentheses.* often nouns, while other categories more seldom appeared. These less frequent categories included verbs and closed-class words. *Closed-class* words are function words, categories to which new members cannot be added: articles, conjunctions, numbers, pronouns, and prepositions.

 Reporting on the most common kinds of the nouns uttered in ●————— *Indent each paragraph ½" (5–7 spaces).* early vocabularies, Nelson (1973) found that children "began by naming objects exhibiting salient properties of change whether as the result of the child's own action . . . or independent of it" (p. 1). In other words,

1" margins

4

nouns that point to consistent, concrete objects are most prevalent in early speech because "children learn to name and understand categories that are functionally relevant to them" (Anglin, 1995, p. 165)—they learn to name the objects they see and interact with day to day.

The author, year, and page number are given in parentheses right after a quotation.

Although nouns make up the largest percentage of the words produced by children in the earlier stages of language acquisition, other word classes also appear. While occurring in children's first fifty words, "verbs, adjectives, and function words each account for less than 10 percent" of total utterances (Uccelli & Pan, 2013, p. 96). Infrequent use of these categories supports the idea that, while all word classes are represented, nouns are expected to occur most often.

Because the authors are not named in a signal phrase, their names are given in parentheses, with an ampersand rather than and between them. A page number is provided for a direct quotation.

1" margins

Other lexical items found in the speech of children with limited vocabulary are words indicating spatial relationships, how things relate to one another in physical space. According to Bowerman (2007), "children's earliest spatial words are topological forms like 'in' and 'on'" (p. 177). This observation supports the hypothesis that those prepositions are among the first lexical items acquired (Brown, 1973; Zukowski, 2013).

The page number is provided in parentheses for a direct quotation when the author and year of the work are given earlier in the signal phrase.

Multiple sources documented in the same parentheses are ordered alphabetically and separated by a semicolon.

Overall, the research on early word production in children just beginning to acquire their first language has found that the majority of words produced will be nouns that refer to concrete objects. According to Pine (1992), children frequently use their early words to describe or label or to do both. Pine concluded that "children are making referential statements about the world with the kind of vocabulary items which they . . . have available to them" (p. 53). That is, children try to comment on referents

1" margins

1" margins

5

(the things that words stand for) in various ways using just the limited language skills that they possess in their early stage of development.

Taking into account prior research on the early words children produce, I analyzed the classes and categories of words appearing in a transcript of a young child speaking. I wanted to compare this particular child's speech with what is expected during this early stage of language development, knowing that research predicts a higher number of nouns than other word classes. I was interested to know whether nouns occur as frequently as the literature would have me believe and whether or not spatial terms appear in such early speech. Furthermore, I wanted to note whether verbs occur as infrequently as expected and, if so, what words the child used instead of verbs to convey action.

The first person is used when describing your own actions.

Method

First-level headings are centered, bold, and capitalized.

The transcript that I chose to analyze is one sample from a series of six recordings by Bloom (1973) of her daughter, Allison, a normally developing, English-speaking child. Allison's age in the samples ranged from 1 year 4 months and 21 days to 2 years and 10 months. The transcript that I analyzed was the earliest of these. Information about the socioeconomic status of Allison and her family was not available in the transcript or the North American English manual of the CHILDES database (MacWhinney, 2000), from which the transcript came. However, we can assume the family was from the professional class, as Bloom was a professor at Columbia University.

According to information in the CHILDES manual, the recordings occurred in the Audio-Visual Studio at Teachers College, Columbia

6

University, in a room containing some furniture and toys. The sessions were conducted with audio-recording devices alone; as a result, no videos were available. Each recording session lasted 40 minutes, for a total of four hours of recording. Bloom (1973) described her role as "more investigator than mother" (p. 11), but the interactions seem to have been more relaxed than one associates with investigators and not structured according to a test or other prearranged activity. Rather, the interactions were led by the child's actions in relation to her mother and objects in the room.

The data are organized in six separate transcripts, arranged chronologically. They contain the actual utterances and morphological notation indicating the parts of speech being used. Bloom initially transcribed the recordings; later, Lois Hood, a fellow researcher, revised the transcript, which was revised again by a larger group of researchers. Each time, the researchers added notes to provide situational context. Each line of the transcript is numbered, and there was an attempt to divide the data to reflect "shift[s] in topic or focus" (Bloom, 1973, p. 11).

Results

During the 40-minute exchange between Bloom and Allison, Allison produced a total of 362 occurrences of identifiable words. I did not distinguish between single- and multi-word utterances because that distinction was not relevant to the purpose of this study. Not all of Allison's turns in the conversation were intelligible; only intelligible words were included in my analysis. Altogether, I identified 27 different words (types) used by the subject, although there were many repetitions

The date is placed right after the author's name; the page number in parentheses is as close to the quotation as possible.

Data is treated as a plural noun; therefore, the verb (are) is plural.

The past tense is used to discuss the results of a study.

7

(tokens) of words. I assigned the 27 words to six categories: nouns, spatial terms, adjectives, negatives, social phrases, and verbs.

The category of nouns contained the largest number of distinct types as well as the largest number of tokens, as shown in Figure 1. Allison used a total of 12 nouns, and all reflected concrete concepts. These included household objects, nouns that referenced people, and the names of animals referring to toys in the recording room. The most frequently used noun was "baby" (n=25); "chair" was second (n=24). The total number of nouns represented 122 occurrences, or 34% of the total words uttered.

Figure I is referred to in the text.

Figure number is bold and flush left

Figure 1

Categories of Words Uttered by the Subject

Descriptive figure title is italicized and appears below the figure number.

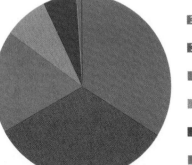

- 34% Nouns
- 33% Spatial Terms
- 18% Adjectives
- 8% Negatives
- 6% Social Phrases
- 1% Verbs

Legend explains what each section of the pie chart represents.

Description and source information are given in the figure note.

Words uttered by the subject, by word category (n=362), are shown. Data recorded in transcripts by L. Bloom (1973), accessed through the CHILDES database (MacWhinney, 2000).

The second most frequent category of words found in Allison's utterances was spatial terms. Five different spatial terms, or types, occurred, with "up" being the most common (n=48). All of the spatial terms Allison used referred to her immediate surroundings—for example, the chair that she wanted to climb "up" on or "down" from. Altogether, 120 of Allison's words were spatial words, accounting for 33% of her speech by word count.

The third most frequently used category of words in the data was adjectives, of which there were three types. Although "more" was the most frequently occurring adjective, "gone" was also often repeated. I will elaborate on the special role that adjectives played in Allison's speech in the discussion and conclusion section.

Negatives also appeared with some frequency in Allison's speech, although the category comprised only one type: "no." The word occurred 28 times (n=28). Sometimes it referred back to and negated other words that she had previously spoken; at other times it negated the word or words that followed. The level of emphasis Allison placed on the word varied. Sometimes her utterance was transcribed as "no"; at other times it was transcribed more emphatically, with an exclamation point, as "no!" This negative term accounted for 8% of her total words.

The remaining categories, social phrases and verbs, occurred less frequently. Social phrases—utterances that are appropriately used in specific social contexts—were present in the transcript in two different words: "uhoh" (n=20), and "oh" (n=3). Together, these add up to a total of 23 words.

9

The category of verbs was by far the least common in the subject's production. Four different verbs were used, three of which occurred only a single time. "Stop" was used twice, while "turn," "climb," and "sit" were used once each. A total of five tokens (n=5) were identified as verbs.

Discussion and Conclusion

Allison's single-word utterances fell into six identifiable categories, the frequency of which varied considerably. Some categories contained only a few items that were not repeated often while other words and categories of words showed up repeatedly. Allison's tendency to use words in certain categories matches the findings of the existing research literature on child language production. In other instances, Allison's use of words differed slightly from what might be expected.

As predicted, nouns made up a large portion of Allison's speech. Since researchers have found the majority of early words to be nouns, it was not surprising that Allison used the greatest number of different words within the noun category and likewise showed the greatest number of repeated tokens in this category. Furthermore, the kinds of nouns Allison used are also in line with the finding that children in the early stages of language acquisition focus on concrete concepts. All the nouns that Allison used referred to things in the recording room, mostly common objects that she could draw attention to. For instance, Allison used the noun "baby" when she wanted to communicate something to her mother about a doll she wanted to play with.

The category of spatial terms also accounted for a large percentage of the words Allison produced. The most frequently uttered word in any category in the transcript was "up." That word, like other spatial terms, was often repeated and sometimes took the place of a more complex construction, as when the subject said "up" as she struggled to get up onto the chair and "down" when she wished to get back down. Allison's choice of words fits with the descriptions by Bowerman (2007) of children's first spatial terms: "early acquired spatial words revolve around relationships of . . . verticality (up, down)" (p. 180). This use of spatial terms contrasts with more complex spatial terms that appear in later development. However, the fact that Allison used five different words in the spatial word category could suggest that those terms play several important roles in her communication at this early stage.

Only the first author's last name included in the sig phrase.

As noted, adjectives like "gone" and "more" played important roles in Allison's speech when she wanted to convey something to her mother, as when she finished eating a cookie and repeatedly told her mother "more." This single word seemed to stand in for a more elaborate question or request Allison could not produce at this stage, such as "Give me more." "Gone" was also used repeatedly in the same context to refer to the cookie. The use of "gone" to describe what had happened to the cookie might be seen as evidence of the observation by Pine (1992) that children's early words are used to label and describe objects around them.

While the category of adjectives formed a smaller portion of Allison's speech than nouns or spatial words, adjectives composed a surprising 18% of total words in the transcript. Generally, adjectives and other word classes that are not nouns are expected to account for a much smaller percentage of words spoken in early word production (Bates et al., 1994).

11

One feature of Allison's utterances that adhered to what is expected for a typical child at this age was her use of negatives. Although she used only one negative word—"no"—it was repeated frequently enough to be the fourth most common category. Her use of "no" rather than any other negative conformed to Brown's (1973) finding that forms of negation like "not" and "don't" appear only in later stages of development. In this very early stage, Allison's reliance on "no" alone seems typical.

Allison used "no" in varied contexts. In some cases, the word seemed to convey a lack of something, as when she uttered "cookie," looked around for the cookies, and then said "no." This sequence of events might indicate that Allison was conveying the lack of cookies to her mother. A similar exchange involved a picture of a girl: when Allison turned the picture over and found the other side blank, she said "no," evidently trying to convey that there was nothing on that side of the picture. On other occasions, "no" was produced as an answer to a question. In one example, Bloom asked Allison if the cup was for her (i.e., Bloom), to which the girl replied "no" and took the cup back. While adhering to the use of the single, simple form of negation that might be expected, Allison's utterances of "no" were varied in purpose and effective in communicating a range of ideas.

The remaining categories, social phrases and verbs, made up only a small percentage of Allison's words. Social words appeared infrequently and were sometimes attached to other words, as when the subject said "uhoh there." The infrequency of social phrases in Allison's speech reflects typical aspects of early vocabulary development. As

12

Because this source is a personal communication, it is cited in the text only and not documented in the list of references.

L. Santelmann (personal communication, 2014) explained, at this stage in a child's development, nearly all lexical items will be nouns and adjectives, with a limited number of social phrases.

True to previous research findings, verbs formed the least frequently used category in Allison's speech. Allison used four different verbs to describe what something was in the act of doing or what she intended to do. For example, she used "stop" to describe a toy car coming to a stop. The remaining three verbs were produced when Allison was performing an action herself, as when she said "turn" when turning the pages of a book, "climb" when trying to climb up onto the chair, and "sit" when going to sit on the chair. Although four different verbs showed up in Allison's speech, the total number of tokens from the verb category was much lower than for any other word category. This follows what researchers generally expect of children's early speech, which includes only a small percentage of verbs (Uccelli & Pan, 2013).

While Allison used these four verbs to communicate action, she often used other words to convey the same meaning. For example, Allison used "up" in two different contexts. The first was narrating an action she was performing, as when she said "up" while trying to get up onto the chair. The second was a request to Bloom to help her up. Allison also used the spatial term "down" to indicate similar intentions.

When not using spatial terms in place of more specific verbs, Allison used nouns to communicate intention and action. For example, one instance of her uttering "cookie" was to tell her mother that she wanted a cookie, indicating intention without using a verb. This

13

pattern occurred in other contexts, as when she used the concrete noun "chair" but not the verb "sit" to indicate that she wanted to get onto the chair. The use of nouns instead of verbs when communicating certain concepts is perhaps expected, given the established preponderance of nouns in early word production. It also supports the idea that children communicate using the tools at hand (Pine, 1992): since Allison frequently employed nouns and spatial terms, those are the tools that she had to rely on to convey whole hosts of meaning.

The results of my analysis of the transcript of Allison interacting with Bloom revealed aspects of the child's speech that were mostly in line with the established features of early word production. The frequency of the use of different word classes conformed to previous findings that concrete nouns are most common. Her choice of the spatial terms "up" and "down" and the simple negative "no" is also typical of children at this age. However, the uncommon frequency of adjectives in her speech indicates that they are important to how she communicated certain meanings; like spatial terms, they often filled in for verbs in cases where the actual verb was beyond her vocabulary. Her use of verbs, while predictably limited, showed how she conveyed meaning when she did not have the precise verbs available to her. Overall, Allison used a somewhat varied set of words to communicate a wide range of meanings even though she had only a limited vocabulary.

14

References

Anglin, J. M. (1995). Classifying the world through language: Functional relevance, cultural significance, and category name learning. *International Journal of Intercultural Relations, 19*(2), 161–181. http://doi.org/bg4cz3

Bates, E., Marchman, V., Thal, D., Fenson, L., Dale, P., Reznick, J. S., & Hartung, J. (1994). Developmental and stylistic variation in the composition of early vocabulary. *Journal of Child Language, 21*(1), 85–123. http://doi.org/fbjfz6

Bloom, L. (1973). *One word at a time: The use of single-word utterances before syntax.* Mouton.

Bowerman, M. (2007). Containment, support, and beyond: Constructing topological spatial categories in first language acquisition. In M. Aurnague, M. Hickmann, & L. Vieu (Eds.), *The categorization of spatial entities in language and cognition* (pp. 177–203). John Benjamins. http://doi.org/dffs

Brown, R. (1973). *A first language: The early stages.* Harvard University Press.

MacWhinney, B. (2000). *The CHILDES Project: Tools for analyzing talk* (3rd ed.). Lawrence Erlbaum Associates.

Nelson, K. (1973). Structure and strategy in learning to talk. *Monographs of the Society for Research in Child Development, 38*(1), 1–135. http://doi.org/fpfm6f

List of references begins on a new page. Heading is centered and bold.

All entries are double-spaced, and all lines except the first are indented ½" (5–7 spaces).

Entries are arranged alphabetically.

DOI given when one is available. Do not add a period at the end of a DOI or a URL.

Entry for a work found in an edited collection includes the editors' names, first initial followed by last name.

15

Pine, J. M. (1992). The functional basis of referentiality: Evidence from children's spontaneous speech. *First Language, 12*(1), 39–55. http://doi.org/d3769w

Uccelli, P., & Pan, B. A. (2013). Semantic development. In J. Berko Gleason & N. Bernstein Ratner (Eds.), *The development of language* (pp. 89–112). Pearson.

Walker, D., Greenwood, C., Hart, B., & Carta, J. (1994). Prediction of school outcomes based on early language production and socioeconomic factors. *Child Development, 65*(2), 606–621. http://doi.org/cb8pjs

Zukowski, A. (2013). Putting words together. In J. Berko Gleason & N. Bernstein Ratner (Eds.), *The development of language* (pp. 120–156). Pearson.

PART VII

Style

"How to Get and Hold Attention"

ONCE UPON A time—and for a very long time too—style in writing and speaking meant ornamentation, "dressing up" your language the way you might dress yourself up for a fancy party. In fact, ancient images often show rhetoric as a woman, Dame Rhetorica, in a gaudy, flowing gown covered with figures of speech—metaphors, similes, alliteration, hyperbole, and so on: her "stylish" ornaments. The influence of this view eventually led many writers to set aside issues of style, preferring to focus on substance, getting to the point and not worrying about making it fancy or pretty.

But not today. Not in a time of instant communication, of being inundated with notifications, news, advertisements—all of them coming at us with the force of a fire hose. In such

Dame Rhetorica, from Gregor Reisch's *Margarita Philosophica* (1504).

a time, scholars like Richard Lanham and Howard Rheingold argue, the most important task facing writers and speakers is making our messages so compelling that they will stand out from all the others. While pundits often claim we live in an information society, Lanham insists that, instead, "we're drowning in information" and that what we "lack is the human attention to make sense of it all." We would add, too, that we're missing the critical ability to know what to pay attention to and what to ignore.

How can we achieve this goal of getting and managing attention? Both Lanham and Rheingold, among others, answer with one word: **STYLE**. Just what do we mean by this simple-sounding word? When it comes to writing, most dictionaries offer something about word choice and how it differs from field to field or they will define style as "distinctiveness of expression." But style is not so much about *what* a message says as about *how* a message is presented—whether the message is in writing, in speech, includes (or is made up of) visuals, is delivered using formal language, and many more possibilities.

Wow. So style turns out to be all the elements that go into making a message (in any form) effective, memorable, compelling. Think, for instance, of a movie you really admire and that you think has real "style." Then make a list of all the things that go into creating its particular style: the "how" of its acting, directing, musical score, camera angles, editing, and so on. All these elements are at work in the film's style.

Style and substance are inseparable, and style is more crucially important to writers and speakers than ever before. Without close attention to style, to how our messages are presented, we are unlikely to attract an audience, much less hold its attention.

How can you create your own particular, powerful style in writing, speaking, and presenting? The chapters that follow aim to guide you in this task. But what we can say now is that you already have the primary tools that writers and speakers have always had for creating style: words—words that can create spellbinding images, rouse deep emotions, hammer home points, seize and hold attention. Choosing words (**DICTION**) and putting them in the best places (**SYNTAX**) still matter a lot in developing your style. But today you also have many other tools—visuals, video, sound, color, and more. All these elements are available as you choreograph the dance of your message, as you develop its style.

Getting and holding an audience's attention, however, is not the one single thing that matters when it comes to style. You want to get that attention in ways that are *appropriate* to your entire rhetorical situation. If you're dressing for an important job interview, you will probably choose clothes that are pleasing in a businesslike way (unless you're applying to be a lifeguard); if you're dressing for a championship basketball game or a religious service, however, you'll dress very differently.

It's hard (maybe impossible) to set hard-and-fast rules to be sure you're making the best choice for a particular situation. Consider a fascinating analogy from rhetorician Brent Simoneaux about the calculated choices baseball players have to make and the choices we as authors have to make:

> Imagine . . . the relationship between the pitcher and the batter. It's a complicated relationship forged in a complex calculus of the probable, yet unknown. I love those close-up shots on television of the batter studying the pitcher, waiting for the ball. The batter is poised, bat over shoulder, feet planted just so, ready to nimbly meet whatever comes. In that moment, the batter is both *at the mercy of* the pitcher, the rules of the game, the equipment, the umpire and also a *participant* and a *creator* of the game.
>
> The ball leaves the pitcher's hand.
>
> In that moment, the coach can't tell the batter exactly what to do at the plate. There's absolutely no way of knowing exactly where that ball is going to go. . . . The only thing the batter can do is to arrive at the plate poised and remain sensitive to the game unfolding.
>
> Of course, the coach can make a pretty good guess about what will happen. . . . The batter can guess as well. And they can both prepare accordingly. But in that utterly kairotic moment when the ball is flying through the air, everything is in flux. . . . And the coach's line has to be: *do the right thing.*
>
> That doesn't mean do whatever you want. It doesn't mean anything goes. Rather, it's an acknowledgment that . . . the terms of "rightness" are always shifting. . . . Do the *right* thing.
>
> —BRENT SIMONEAUX, "Do the Right Thing"

The same goes for authors. But that's part of the fun of writing with style. You get to analyze the situation before you and to think about how to seize the moment in order to get and hold the attention of your audience in the most appropriate ways. You even get something that the batter and pitcher don't have: you can take time to make your rhetorical decisions. The chapters that follow aim to help you achieve that goal.

THIRTY

What's Your Style?

"Style is all that matters."

—VLADIMIR NABOKOV

AKE A LOOK at the image on the following page: row after row of construction workers in identical outfits, interrupted by a stately figure—the queen of England—in bright turquoise. Our eyes are drawn to the queen because of her ensemble—hat, dress, and stockings—against a sea of men in orange jumpsuits: she stands out. This image could be captioned "Got style?" because it demonstrates that being like everyone or everything around you doesn't add up to a style that can get and hold attention. The same is true for writing; style helps you get readers to take notice—and listen—to what you have to say.

But style isn't just about getting attention: it's also about making choices that are appropriate to your particular situation, and all in an effort to achieve your purpose. You might wear shorts and running shoes to the gym but not to a job interview, a bathing suit to the beach but not to class. It's a delicate balance. Style in writing works the same way. How can the words, images, and sentence structures you use stand out (like the queen) while at the same time meeting your intended audience's expectations and giving you credibility? This chapter offers strategies for achieving this balance and shaping your own flexible style of writing.

Queen Elizabeth II of the United Kingdom sits for a photo with construction workers at the opening of a new rail station in Reading, England.

Appropriateness and Correctness

Making good stylistic choices, ones that strike the balance between getting attention and keeping readers with you, calls for considering what's appropriate to your particular situation. In the simplest terms, an "appropriate" writing style is one in which your words and the way you arrange them suits your topic, your purpose, and your audience. But making stylistic choices in writing can be tricky, especially because we don't have a set of hard-and-fast rules to follow. You may have "learned" that it isn't appropriate to start a sentence with *and* or *but* and never to end a sentence with a preposition. But those "rules" are far from universal, and they change over time. In fact, a lot of fine writing today bends and breaks these rules to good effect.

So it won't work to think about style simply as a matter of following rules. In fact, if you have to choose between being "correct" and being "appropriate," being appropriate almost always wins out. In 1966, in the original *Star Trek*, when Captain Kirk of the starship *Enterprise* announced

The crew of the USS *Enterprise* split infinitives boldly, and with emphasis.

its mission "to boldly go where no man has gone before," that split infinitive ("boldly" splits the two words of the infinitive "to go") wasn't absolutely "correct," but it created just the emphasis the writers were after. Moreover, it was an appropriate choice for the time (the 1960s) and place (a TV show). One mark of its stylistic appropriateness and effectiveness: it's still quoted, even in textbooks like this one. Making appropriate stylistic choices, then, will almost always depend on your **RHETORICAL SITUATION**.

Some contexts already have a defined style of communicating or a specific dialect that's considered most appropriate. In those situations, being aware of the conventional style will help guide your style decisions. For example, what some refer to as "edited academic English" is the **DIALECT** often thought of as appropriate for writing done in most school, government, and professional contexts. But like any other "standard," it has changed across time and will continue to change. If you read the stories of Flannery O'Connor, a twentieth-century American fiction writer and essayist, you'll notice she uses the words *man* and *he* to refer to people in general. Stylistic choices like this were completely appropriate at the time. But when many criticized the use of "he" to refer to all people—including women—conventions changed, and writers looked for more appropriate choices, including alternatives to the designation of all people as either male or female, *he and she,* or even *they,* the increasingly preferred option. Were O'Connor, who died in 1964, writing today, it's very likely she would make different choices when using personal pronouns.

But the fact that academic dialects of languages emerge and change over time and that the appropriate use of a language most often depends on context doesn't mean that stylistic choices are without any boundaries at all. Audiences often expect that writers will follow accepted conventions, and choosing to do so—or not—has consequences. When the choices you make ignore or defy audience expectations or when they push the envelope, you may be able to get an audience's attention, but you may not hold it for very long.

Take a look, for instance, at how linguist Geneva Smitherman pushes against the traditional "rules" of academic English and does so brilliantly. In fact, had she stuck to the traditional rules, the following paragraph would have been far less effective than it is.

> Before about 1959 (when the first study was done to change black speech patterns), Black English had been primarily the interest of university academics, particularly the historical linguists and cultural anthropologists. In recent years, though, the issue has become a very hot controversy, and there have been articles on Black Dialect in the national press as well as in the educational research literature. We have had pronouncements on black speech from the NAACP and the Black Panthers, from highly publicized scholars of the Arthur Jensen–William Shockley bent, from executives of national corporations such as Greyhound, and from housewives and community folk. I mean, really, it seem like everybody and they momma done had something to say on the subject!
>
> —GENEVA SMITHERMAN, *Talkin and Testifyin:*
> *The Language of Black America*

Geneva
Smitherman

Smitherman obviously knows the rules of edited academic English but breaks them to support her point and also to create a clear rhetorical stance, as a scholar, a skilled writer, and a proud African American. Writing in the late 1970s, she could assume that her readers would know that the NAACP is the National Association for the Advancement of Colored People, that the Black Panthers were a revolutionary social action group in the 1960s and 1970s, and that Arthur Jensen and William Shockley had made controversial claims about relationships between race and intelligence. She could also assume that readers of her book would expect her to write in edited academic English since the volume was published by a mainstream publisher and treated its subject from an academic perspective.

But Smitherman wasn't interested in writing a book about the language of African Americans using only edited academic English. After all, one of her claims was that the language practices of African Americans were influencing American culture and language in many ways. Notice how her stylistic choices support that claim. She not only talks the talk of edited academic English but walks the walk of African American English as well. When she switches in her final sentence from edited academic English to African American English, she simultaneously drives home her point—that everyone at that time seemed to have an opinion about the language of African Americans—while demonstrating membership in that community by using the language variety associated with it. In short, she makes sound and appropriate stylistic choices.

You'll find more on mixing dialects and languages in the following chapter. For now, remember that your style should be appropriate to your purpose, audience, and rhetorical situation, even—and especially—when you bend the rules.

Connecting with Audiences

In all your writing, you'll want to have a reasonably good sense of your intended **AUDIENCE** in order to make effective stylistic choices. Take a look at the image on the following page; it's the webpage for a supermarket in a small town in California that appeals directly to its local community. The writers set a friendly, informal tone right away, announcing that "we love good food" and appealing to their audience to "SHOP LOCAL." The emphasis on the local continues as they note that they've been "serving our community" for decades. They also invite readers to visit their *Facebook* page—and learn about "our sustainable fish program." The use of "our" emphasizes the community and establishes **COMMON GROUND** with readers. The bright colors and simple design add to the warm, inviting tone that underscores the overall message.

A student writing about this same topic for a class project must be more formal and would need to include the background and contextual information that an academic audience expects. For example, here is Katherine Spriggs arguing for the importance of "buying local":

est 1956

SURF
MARKET
we love good food!

SHOP LOCAL
Mendonoma Coast

Winter Hours: 7:30am - 8pm Daily

Upcoming Events Calendar 2015

Visit us on Facebook

PROUDLY SERVING OUR COMMUNITY SINCE 1956

We are committed to offering the highest quality food and excellent customer service. Environmental responsibility is one of our highest priorities.

Learn about FishWise, our sustainable fish program.

Come visit our store in Gualala, on the ocean side of Highway 1.

The Surf Market in Gualala, California, welcomes customers to its webpage with a friendly, informal tone.

> "Buying local" means that consumers choose to buy food that has been grown, raised, or produced as close to their home as possible. Buying local is an important part of the response to many environmental issues we face today. It encourages the development of small farms, which are often more environmentally sustainable than large farms, and thus strengthens local markets and supports small rural economies. By demonstrating a commitment to buying local, Americans could set an example for global environmentalism.
>
> —KATHERINE SPRIGGS, "On Buying Local"

Rather than assuming that her audience already knows what "buying local" means, Spriggs begins with a careful definition—something the Surf Market webpage doesn't need to do—as a way of laying the groundwork for her argument and demonstrating that she is knowledgeable about her topic. She then starts to build her argument by linking the idea of buying local to environmental issues and community values. Her tone is serious; she gives practical reasons for why buying local is "important," noting that it "encourages the development of small farms" and "supports small rural economies." Like Surf Market and Spriggs do, you'll want to think about who will read what you write and make stylistic choices that help you connect with them.

Levels of Formality

Being appropriate also calls on writers to pay attention to the level of formality they use. In ancient Rome, Cicero identified three levels of style: low or plain style, used to teach or explain something; middle style, used to please an audience; and high or grand style, used to move or persuade an audience. Note that these classifications link style with a specific purpose and a likely audience.

On August 27, 2018, an aide to Senator John McCain shared a farewell statement McCain had written to America before his death two days earlier. Here is the opening of that letter:

> My fellow Americans, whom I have gratefully served for sixty years, and especially my fellow Arizonans,
>
> Thank you for the privilege of serving you and for the rewarding life that service in uniform and in public office has allowed me to lead. I have tried to serve our country honorably. I have made mistakes, but I hope my love for America will be weighed favorably against them.
>
> I have often observed that I am the luckiest person on earth. . . . Like most people, I have regrets. But I would not trade a day of my life, in good or bad times, for the best day of anyone else's.
>
> I owe that satisfaction to the love of my family. No man ever had a more loving wife or children he was prouder of than I am of mine. And I owe it to America. To be connected to America's causes—liberty, equal justice, respect for the dignity of all people—brings happiness more sublime than life's fleeting pleasures. Our identities and sense of worth are not circumscribed but enlarged by serving good causes bigger than ourselves.
>
> —JOHN MCCAIN, "Farewell Letter to America"

Writing in full awareness of his imminent death, McCain uses a solemn, deliberate, formal tone, writing in the grand style that seeks to inspire by both word and deed. Twice he uses balanced phrases to acknowledge weaknesses as well as strengths ("I have made mistakes, but I hope my love of America . . . " and "I have regrets. But I would not trade a day . . . "). And he expresses deep satisfaction at his connection to "America's causes—liberty, equal justice, respect for the dignity of all people," saying that this connection brings him happiness "more sublime than life's fleeting pleasures." In concluding his letter, McCain uses repetition and very brief sentences to punctuate this final message:

> Do not despair of our present difficulties but believe always in the promise and greatness of America, because nothing is inevitable here. Americans never quit. We never surrender. We never hide from history. We make history. Farewell, fellow Americans. God bless you, and God bless America.

The four short sentences that follow the longer opening sentence are like drumbeats, with their use of the repeated "we," calling Americans to attend to McCain and to be inspired by his example. McCain's style choices match his unique **RHETORICAL SITUATION**—and help his message land with impact.

Stance

Stance refers to the attitude authors take toward their topic and audience. For example, you might write about immigration as an impassioned advocate or critic, someone with strong opinions about the inherent good or evil of immigration. Or you might write as a dispassionate analyst, someone trying to weigh carefully the pros and cons of the arguments for and against a particular proposal. Either stance—and any possible stances in between—will affect what style you use.

If your audience changes, your language will likely shift, too. Debating immigration issues with close friends whose opinions you're fairly sure of will differ in crucial ways from debating them with people you know less well or not at all because you'll be able to take less for granted. That you will likely shift all aspects of your message—from word choice and sentence structure to amount of background information and choice of examples—doesn't make you a hypocrite or a flip-flopper; instead, it demonstrates your skill at finding the most effective rhetorical resources to make your point.

In a posting titled "Same Food Planet, Different Food Worlds," blogger Rod Dreher calls attention to the drastically different stances taken by two restaurant reviewers. Here's an excerpt from one, a review of a new Olive Garden restaurant in Grand Forks, North Dakota, by eighty-five-year-old Marilyn Hagerty:

It had been a few years since I ate at the older Olive Garden in Fargo, so I studied the two manageable menus offering appetizers, soups and salads, grilled sandwiches, pizza, classic dishes, chicken and seafood and filled pastas.

At length, I asked my server what she would recommend. She suggested chicken Alfredo, and I went with that. Instead of the raspberry lemonade she suggested, I drank water.

She first brought me the familiar Olive Garden salad bowl with crisp greens, peppers, onion rings and yes—several black olives. Along with it came a plate with two long, warm breadsticks.

The chicken Alfredo ($10.95) was warm and comforting on a cold day. The portion was generous. My server was ready with Parmesan cheese. . . .

All in all, it is the largest and most beautiful restaurant now operating in Grand Forks. It attracts visitors from out of town as well as people who live here.   —MARILYN HAGERTY, "Long-awaited Olive Garden Receives Warm Welcome"

Hagerty's polite, unpretentious stance is evident in this review—and as it happens, the style of her writing attracted much attention when it went viral, with readers both celebrating and bashing that style.

Dreher contrasts Hagerty's stance with that of Dive Bar Girl (DBG), who writes for a newsletter in Baton Rouge, Louisiana. In fact, DBG starts right out by announcing her stance—she's going to be "mean," not "informative"—and so after saying "a few nice things" about her topic, a restaurant called Twin Peaks, she writes the review that she assumes her readers "want to read":

Marilyn Hagerty. Read the *Los Angeles Times*' take on the controversy—and Hagerty's son's response in the *Wall Street Journal*—at everyones anauthor .tumblr.com.

Admit it, you like it when DBG is mean. You only send her fan mail when she's mean. She never gets mail for being informative. . . . So she is going to write about the positive things first and then write the review you want to read. The smokehouse burger was above average. The patio was a nice space. The staff, while scantily clad, was professional. The salads even looked good. The place was miles above Hooters.

Here is the review you want: Twin Peaks has to be the brainchild of two 14-year-old boys who recently cracked the parental controls on the home computer. Waitresses are known as "Lumber Jills." In case you are missing the imagery—each Lumber Jill has been endowed with an epic pair of Twin Peaks.   —CHERRYTHEDIVEBARGIRL

These two reviews could hardly be more different in stance: the first is low key and even-handed, well suited to Hagerty's stance as a modest and sincere reviewer. The second is highly opinionated and sarcastic, true to the brash, in-your-face stance of Dive Bar Girl. So both are written in styles that suit (and reflect) their respective stances.

But what happens when that stance doesn't fit well with a particular audience? That's what happened when Hagerty's review went viral: some writers immediately began making fun of her as inept and hopelessly out of it; others jumped in just as quickly to defend Hagerty's review, while still others read her review as an indirect parody of local restaurant reviews. Now imagine that Dive Bar Girl's review appeared in Hagerty's hometown newspaper. Chances are it would attract some hefty criticism as well.

The takeaway lesson here: as a writer, you need to consider whether your **STANCE** is appropriate not only to your topic and audience but also to your **MODE** of distribution.

Tone

All the writing you do, regardless of stance or level of formality, has a particular **TONE**. You may not think consciously about how to establish that tone, especially when commenting on a friend's *Instagram* post or writing a text message, but even in social media writing you are making choices about whether you want to convey a serious tone, a humorous tone, an exasperated tone. When you know that your readers are friends and family, your tone can probably be pretty casual, like this *Facebook* update posted by a student in Washington, DC, which is playful, critical, reasoned, and ironic:

> Note to self: avoid union station on weekday mornings. Hordes of angry commuters make getting to the train impossible? #notfun #DCMetro #rushhour #istheworst

Here the tone is one of frustration and exasperation, expressed in the hashtags the writer adds (#notfun, etc.). She is assuming her readers will not only know what she is talking about but also appreciate her playful tone.

For a report on commuters in Union Station for an urban studies class, the author establishes the more serious tone of a reporter or researcher:

> Walking into Union Station on a weekday morning can be like going against a herd of stampeding cattle. Riders rush from the trains, swinging briefcases and computer bags, knocking over anything or anyone in the way. Rush hour in this station, one of the busiest train stations in the country, is not enjoyable. Looking at some usage statistics and videos will show just how unpleasant this experience is and how it affects those who regularly ride the metro.

Here the tone is studied and serious. The writer opens by describing the scene in the congested station and then moves to introduce an analysis of usage statistics and videos. But even a serious tone doesn't need to result in a dull, boring style: note the lively description ("stampeding cattle"; "swinging briefcases"; "knocking over everything or anyone in the way"). Your **PURPOSE**, **AUDIENCE**, **STANCE**, and even **MEDIUM** will help determine an appropriate and effective tone.

Style across Media

You probably already find yourself using a variety of media to communicate every day and making intuitive choices about style: you post a message on *Twitter*, you make an oral presentation using *Prezi* for a class, you conduct research for an article that you submit in print and then "remediate" as part of a website. Each of these tasks calls for an appropriate medium, whether written, oral, or electronic. In each case, you have a good sense of your purpose and audience, and you use that knowledge to establish an appropriate style and choose the best medium to deliver your message. This is the same kind of rhetorical thinking you need to be doing consciously and analytically for the writing you do in school or work. So in all your writing across media—at home, at work, at school, wherever—you will want to make stylistic choices that are appropriate for your rhetorical situation, your audience, and your purpose.

You are no doubt familiar with the hashtag #BlackLivesMatter, which has generated over 50 million tweets since Alicia Garza, grieving over the death of Trayvon Martin and astonished that his killer was not convicted of any crime, logged onto *Facebook* in July 2013 and wrote "Black people, I love you. I love us. Our lives matter," and her good friend Patrissa Cullors wrote back, closing her post with "#blacklivesmatter." Note the stylistic choices that make these messages memorable: very short sentences; repetition; a serious and urgent tone. Garza, Cullors, and Opal Tometi—cofounders of the Black Lives Matter movement—used those same choices as they went on to create pages on *Tumblr*, *Twitter*, and *Facebook* to launch a rallying cry across the country.

Some writers post images to get their message across, such as this tweet which includes a photo taken after a protest against the separation of immigrant children from their parents during the summer of 2019:

How would you describe the style and tone of this message and its accompanying images? How might the author adjust the style in writing an op-ed in the local newspaper instead? Or creating a *YouTube* video or brief podcast describing and analyzing the issue? Different media and platforms call for different style choices in order to grab attention and get your message across. And remember that grabbing attention is only half the battle—making sure your style is appropriate and effective is just as important. Especially online, it can be easy and tempting to use an over-the-top title or a startling image to grab attention (it's how clickbait works, after all), but they won't keep your readers with you beyond a flashy opening, so stick to style choices that strike the right balance.

REFLECT. Take some time to look carefully at some of your posts on social media. How informal or formal are they? What do they assume your audience will know about your topic? What are your purposes for writing—to share information? To ask for advice? What else? What kind of style does your audience respond best to? Do you use a mix of media—words, images, video? Then write a few sentences describing what you've noticed about your writing style on social media and how it differs from the other kinds of writing you do—at school, at work, at home.

Style across Disciplines

Making good choices is especially important when writing in different disciplines, where what's appropriate and effective often varies from field to field or workplace to workplace. Many fields have established conventions—reading published writing in a field or discipline can help you see what stylistic features are most common. Look for patterns—do writers use a particular verb tense? Active voice instead of passive voice? A specific organization or style of headings? Identifying what other successful writers have done in a field that's new to you is a good way to figure out what you'll try in order to be effective and appropriate.

One notable stylistic difference between fields is favoring the **ACTIVE VOICE** or the **PASSIVE VOICE**. For example, reports in the sciences usually call for the passive voice. Take a look at this passage from a 2017 article on whether long-distance running affects runners' ankles and feet in a way that's detectable by MRI (magnetic resonance imaging). The authors explain what methods they used to review existing research on their topic; notice that most of the verbs are passive:

> **Methods:** Scopus, Web of Science, Embase and Ovid Medline *were searched* using key terms in relation to MRI findings of the ankle and foot in response to long-distance running, published between 1990 and 2016. The final search *was conducted* on 19 September, 2016. Studies *were identified* using inclusion and exclusion criteria. Methodological quality *was assessed* using a modified Quality Index.

In scientific writing the passive is generally favored because it shouldn't matter who searched for the articles, applied the criteria, or assessed the quality using the stated criteria; in the end, the results should be the same. The passive voice also focuses the reader's attention on what was done, not on who did it. So although you may have been instructed in your writing classes to "avoid the passive," it is often the appropriate and effective choice in the sciences.

At the same time, there are many occasions when writers avoid the passive voice for good reason. For example, engineers often rely on information gathered by other firms or information they gather themselves from interviews. In contexts where they need to make clear who is responsible for observations, recommendations, or judgments, engineers use the active voice to locate responsibility. Thus, engineers would write "Our firm hired ABC Tech to conduct a geotechnical evaluation" rather than "A geotechnical evaluation was conducted" so that readers know the source of the data presented and analyzed. Voice is just one example of how style changes between disciplines—the point is you'll want to seek out reliable examples to learn what style works and is expected of you in a new field.

Thinking about Your Own Style

As you've seen, style is all about making appropriate choices, choices that inevitably depend on your topic and all the elements of your rhetorical situation, especially your **STANCE**, your **PURPOSE**, your **GENRE**, and your **AUDIENCE**. Have you written a review of something—a restaurant for the campus newspaper? a book on *Amazon*? your instructor on ratemyprofessor.com? If so, take a look at the choices you made in the review, and then compare them to those you made in an essay you wrote for class. You'll see right away that you have instinctively used different styles for these different occasions.

For an example of what we mean about making appropriate stylistic choices, take a look at a paragraph from this book, first as it appears on page 663 and then as it is revised as a tweet, a report, and a flyer.

Original text

Once upon a time—and for a very long time too—style in writing and speaking meant ornamentation, "dressing up" your language the way you might dress yourself up for a fancy party. In fact, ancient images often show rhetoric as a woman, Dame Rhetorica, in a gaudy, flowing gown covered with figures of speech—metaphors, similes, alliteration, hyperbole, and so on: her "stylish" ornaments.

Revised as a tweet

Writing style used to mean dressing up your words, like Cinderella getting ready for the ball. Not anymore. #rhetorictoday

Revised as a report

For more than 500 years, the definition of "style" held relatively stable. Style was a form of ornamentation that was added to texts in order to make them more pleasing or accessible to an audience. In ancient depictions, Rhetoric is often shown as a woman dressed in elegant attire and "ornamented" with dozens of stylish figures of speech.

Revised as a flyer

Once upon a time . . .

writing style was all about ornamentation.

ℬ *Language* ℛ

in fancy dress

What do you know about writing style?

Join us in the Writing Center to learn how style has changed over time

and how your style can be *in* style.

Sterling C. Evans Library

Room 214

Note how the style changes to match each genre and audience: the tweet is short, of course, and very informal; it uses a sentence fragment and then uses a hashtag to link readers with others talking about rhetoric today. The report is much more formal and is written in edited academic English. The flyer uses a much more conversational style—ellipses to signal a pause, a sentence fragment, a question, and italics for emphasis—and announces an event (the purpose of a flyer).

We've tried in this chapter to emphasize how important the stylistic choices you make are to getting the attention of your audiences—and holding it; style really is the key to achieving that goal. And remember that, as an author, you get to call a lot of the stylistic shots. As you do so, of course, you'll want to think carefully about what styles are appropriate in particular situations and how you can meet an audience's expectations without "painting by the numbers" or writing dull, predictable prose. You're a lot better than that: you've got **STYLE**.

REFLECT. Think about a person who you think has style (a friend or family member, a public figure, a boss or teacher): how would you describe that style? What about this person and their style appeals to you—or doesn't? What choices has the person made that contribute to this particular style? If you can, look at a few examples of the person's style in language and writing (social media posts, for example, or captions on a T-shirt). How does their writing style align (or not) with the other parts of the person's style?

Now think about you: how would you describe your own style? What makes up your style? Finally, look at a few recent pieces of writing you've done for school or for your job: how well do they represent you? Do they align (or not) with your style? Do these pieces of writing sound like you—does your voice come through? What about these pieces of writing is memorable or vivid, and what makes them so? What is their level of formality? What is your stance in them and what tone do you take? How would you describe your writing style?

THIRTY-ONE

Mixing Languages
and Dialects

OW MANY LANGUAGES do you know well enough to speak or write? Which languages would you like to know? The United States is often referred to as a monolingual country, one where English is the only language needed to get along. But that characterization has never been accurate. Languages other than English have always been present here. Today, the US Census Bureau estimates that approximately 20 percent of Americans report speaking a language other than English at home—Spanish, Chinese, and Tagalog are the three most common. And American Sign Language is probably the third most commonly used language (after Spanish), although the census doesn't ask about signed languages.

So the United States is a country of many languages. It is also a country of multiple dialects and, again, it always has been. *Dialects* are varieties of language that are spoken by people in a particular region, social class, or ethnic group—like the English spoken by residents of Appalachia or the Spanish spoken in Texas. *Registers* are varieties of language associated not with particular people but with a particular activity or occupation—like soccer or chemical engineering. Just listen closely to people you know or see on *YouTube*, and you will surely hear various dialects and registers, as well as distinctive vocabularies, at work.

Spend a day taking notice of all the languages, dialects, and registers you encounter around you—from conversations on campus to signs, billboards, and texts that convey information.

The languages, dialects, and registers you use make up your own unique way of speaking—a sort of linguistic fingerprint, called an *idiolect*. One of our grandmothers, who lived in the foothills of Tennessee's Smoky Mountains, referred to kitchen cabinets as "the upper division"—something we've never heard said by anyone else, in Tennessee or elsewhere! She also drew out the sound of vowels in words like "broil" so that the word sounded as if it had several syllables rather than one. These quirks—among others—made up her idiolect.

No matter how many languages you speak, you probably use a number of different dialects and registers. Is the way you speak at the dinner table different from the way you speak in class or at work? Is the way you write an *Instagram* post different from an email to an instructor? We bet that it is.

We also bet that you probably mix whatever languages, dialects, and registers you use, consciously or unconsciously. Language scholars have identified two ways in particular that people do so. **CODE-SWITCHING** is the practice of shifting from one language or dialect to another, whereas **CODE-MESHING** is a way of weaving together languages and dialects. Both are ways of mixing varieties of language for various purposes—to reflect a particular **STANCE**, for example, or to establish a connection with certain **AUDIENCES**. This chapter provides examples and guidelines to help you mix languages, dialects, and registers for various rhetorical situations.

〰◎ *REFLECT. Think for a few minutes about the varieties of language spoken where you grew up. What features of pronunciation and vocabulary can you identify? What groups do you belong to now that have a specialized way of communicating? Fans of one type of music? A religious community? An athletic team or social club? Write a paragraph describing what influences the way you speak; include specific examples.*

Using Edited Academic English and Other Dialects

What some call **EDITED ACADEMIC ENGLISH** is actually a dialect—one that's used both in formal and informal contexts. For example, during a heated discussion about jobs and automation with a friend, you may say things in informal but effective ways that wouldn't work as well if you were writing up the same point in a formal report. Even within a single dialect there's almost always more than one appropriate way to say or write something; your audience and purpose inform your choices.

That is not to say that all dialects are regarded as equals. What we are calling edited academic English—and some have called "standard" English—has long held a prestigious position in the United States. But so-called standard languages have been challenged for centuries by vernacular dialects and languages. After all, English once challenged Latin and Greek as the languages of power, notably in Chaucer's *Canterbury Tales*. So it's no surprise that in the United States, many writers have challenged or even rejected the privileged dialect of edited academic English. This chapter provides a number of examples of writers mixing varieties of language—often beyond edited academic English—in ways that speak powerfully to their audiences. Such moves are increasingly common, but doing so doesn't always come risk-free. Keep your rhetorical situation front and center—what's your purpose? what's at stake? what does your audience consider appropriate?—when you make language choices that push against readers' expectations.

Connecting with Audiences

If you're a fan of popular music today, you can probably come up with examples of lyricists mixing languages to craft powerful messages. Here is the opening of Kenyan rapper Bamboo's remix of the song "Mama Africa," first written and sung by Jamaican reggae artist Peter Tosh. A love song to the African continent, which has in Bamboo's view too often been represented negatively, his remix connects to his international audience of hip-hop and pop music fans by moving between Swahili and English:

> *tunaishi vizuri*
> check out the way we be livin
> *na tunakula vizuri*
> we always eating the best
> *poteza yako kwa nini*
> why should you settle for less
> *TV haiwezi kuambia*
> they never show on your screen
> *kwa hivyo mi ntawaambia*
> so you can see what I mean
> *Africa maridadi*
> Africa's beautiful baby
> —BAMBOO, "Mama Africa"

Bamboo uses hip-hop rhythms and dialect to connect with the listeners he wants to reach. By using both Swahili and English, he reaches more people than if he'd used just one language—and exposes those who speak just one of these languages to the other.

Sandra Cisneros, a Mexican American writer who's fluent in both English and Spanish, makes similar choices in a collection of short stories inspired by her experience growing up in the United States surrounded by Mexican culture. See how she mixes languages to speak to an audience that's likely to include both English and Spanish speakers:

> "¡Ay!" The true test of a native Spanish speaker. ¡Ay! To make love in Spanish, in a manner as intricate and devout as la Alhambra. To have a lover sigh *mi vida, mi preciosa, mi chiquitita,* and whisper things in that

language crooned to babies, that language murmured by grandmothers, those words that smelled like your house, like flour tortillas.
—SANDRA CISNEROS, *Woman Hollering Creek and Other Stories*

As writers and speakers, we have to think carefully about when mixing languages or dialects will help us connect with our audiences—and when it won't. In most cases, authors have a kind of informal contract with readers: while readers may need to work some to understand what a writer is saying, the writer in turn promises to consider the audience's expectations and abilities. The end goal is usually accessibility: will your message be understood by those you are trying to reach? If some members of your audience aren't likely to understand, should you provide a translation? Are you choosing not to translate so that readers experience what it's like to *not* understand?

Providing Translation

One way to stay true to a language or dialect you identify with while still reaching readers who may not understand is to provide a translation. Bamboo's example, which invites English-speaking listeners to think about Africa's rich culture in part by including Swahili, demonstrates how translation helps when you're mixing languages. When including translations, you will usually want to introduce the term that is being translated in its original language, followed by the translation, as in the poster on the following page announcing a conference taking place in the Navajo Nation.

Note that the designer places the Navajo title first—and in slightly larger and bolder text—to underscore the importance of the Navajo language at this conference.

For another example, see how sociolinguist Guadalupe Valdés uses translation in an ethnographic study of a family of Mexican origin that included a young boy named Saúl:

> During his kindergarten year, . . . winning was important to Saúl. Of all the cousins who played together, it was he who ran the fastest and pushed the hardest. "*Yo gané, yo gané*" (I won, I won), he would say enthusiastically. . . . Saúl's mother, Velma, wished that he would win just a bit more quietly. . . . "*No seas peleonero*" (Don't be so quarrelsome),

Conference poster announcing—in both Navajo and English—
a gathering of writers in Window Rock, the capital of Navajo
Nation.

she would say. "*Es importante llevarse bien con todos*" (It's important to
get along with everyone).
— GUADALUPE VALDÉS, *Con Respeto: Bridging the Distances Between
Culturally Diverse Families and Schools*

Note especially that Valdés always puts the Spanish words first, as they were
spoken, and only then gives the English translation. She could have chosen
to put the English translation first, or to write only in English, but giving the
Spanish first puts the spotlight on her subjects' voices and their own words.
By including the English translation at all, Valdés acknowledges readers

who don't speak Spanish and makes sure they can understand what she's written. Like Bamboo and the Navajo writing conference poster, she translates to make sure her message is accessible to as many people as possible. Notice, too, that Valdés italicizes words in a language other than English, which is a common academic convention when mixing languages.

Illustrating a Point

Professional groups have their own specialized ways of speaking: people in economics and finance will have different vocabulary and style at work from people in medicine, engineering, or food service. Much has been written about what is often called "valley speak," a common way of speaking in Silicon Valley where tech giants like Google, Apple, and Twitter reside. In a book that aims to be a definitive guide to the language of Silicon Valley, authors Rochelle Kopp and Steven Ganz incorporate examples to illustrate their point:

> When we moved to Silicon Valley, we found it challenging to pick up the lingo. . . . Around here, people toss off sentences like "Everyone thought that [the] *semantic search startup* launched by those Stanford *whiz kids* was going to be the next *unicorn*, but now they are doing a *down round* and it's looking like they are candidates for an *acqui-hire*." It can be awkward if you're the only one who doesn't understand what people here are saying.
> —ROCHELLE KOPP AND STEVEN GANZ, *Valley Speak:*
> *Deciphering the Jargon of Silicon Valley*

By mixing in phrases like *semantic search startups* and *down round*, Kopp and Ganz illustrate valley speak while suggesting that the vocabulary of Silicon Valley startups may alienate any people who don't want to take the time to penetrate the jargon.

Professor Jamila Lyiscott mixes dialects to illustrate her point in a spoken-word essay called "Broken English" in which she "celebrates—and challenges—the three distinct flavors of English she speaks." Prompted by a "baffled lady" who seemed surprised to find that Lyiscott is "articulate," Lyiscott says:

> Pay attention
> 'Cause I'm "articulate"
> So when my father asks, "Wha' kinda ting is dis?"

My "articulate" answer never goes amiss
I say "Father, this is the impending problem at hand"
And when I'm on the block I switch it up just because I can
So when my boy says, "What's good with you son?"
I just say, "I jus' fall out wit dem people but I done!"
And sometimes in class
I might pause the intellectual sounding flow to ask
"Yo! Why dese books neva be about my peoples"
Yes, I have decided to treat all three of my languages as equals
Because I'm "articulate"

—JAMILA LYISCOTT, "Broken English"

In her performance, which has more than four million views online, Lyiscott uses what she calls "three tongues"—one each for "home, school, and friends"—to make the point that there are many different ways to be "articulate." And she's articulate, all right, in three different dialects.

↪ *WATCH THE VIDEO of Jamila Lyiscott's TED talk by visiting* <u>everyonesanauthor</u>
<u>.tumblr.com</u>. *Why do you think Lyiscott chose a spoken-word essay as her medium? How does watching and listening to her performance (versus reading words on a page) change the way you understand her message? Why do you think Lyiscott chose to mix dialects? How would it change her message if she chose just one dialect instead of mixing several?*

Drawing Attention

Here is Buthainah, a Saudi Arabian student writing a literacy narrative for an education class at an American college:

ومن يتهيّب صعود الجبال   ~~~   يعش ابد الدّهر بين الحفر

"I don't want to" was my response to my parents' request of enrolling me in a nearby preschool. I did not like school. I feared it. I feared the aspect of departing my comfort zone, my home, to an unknown and unpredictable zone. . . . To encourage me, they recited a poetic line that I did not comprehend as a child but live by it as an adult. They said, "Who fears climbing the mountains~~~ . . . Lives forever between the holes." As I grew up, knowledge became my key to freedom; freedom of thought, freedom of doing, and freedom of beliefs.

—BUTHAINAH, "Who Fears Climbing the Mountains
Lives Forever between the Holes"

In this instance, opening with the Arabic proverb (which also serves as the title of Buthainah's essay) draws readers' attention and announces the importance of Arabic in the author's journey to become the writer she is while also letting non-Arabic speakers feel a bit of what it's like to encounter a foreign language without an immediate translation. At the same time, she makes a point of translating the proverb for her readers as the essay progresses—"They said 'Who fears climbing the mountains ~~~ Lives forever between the holes.'" Buthainah's essay illustrates how switching to a different language or way of speaking can grab attention and show—instead of tell—your audience something that's important to you.

Quoting People Directly and Respectfully

If you are writing about a person or group of people you have interviewed or who have been interviewed by others, you will want to let those people speak for themselves. From 1927 to 1931, Zora Neale Hurston, the famed African American folklorist, cultural anthropologist, and novelist, interviewed Cudjo Lewis, one of the last known slaves to have made the journey across the Atlantic. Lewis's story, told from Hurston's perspective, appears in *Barracoon: The*

Story of the Last "Black Cargo," a book published after Hurston's death. Hurston takes care to let the subject of her interview speak his mind, and in his own words. She begins by documenting her initial interaction with Lewis, telling us, "I hailed him by his African name" (Oluale Kossula) which she had learned from others while conducting prior research. In the next paragraph, Lewis speaks:

> Oh Lor', I kno it *you* call my name. Nobody don't callee me my name from cross de water but you. You always callee me Kossula, jus' lak I in de Affica soil! —ZORA NEALE HURSTON, *Barracoon: The Story of the Last "Black Cargo"*

Hurston alternates between edited academic English and a representation of the actual speech of the person whose words she quotes. These quotations report what she heard, which helps build her ETHOS as a careful listener and researcher. Finally, the use of quotations appeals to her audience's emotions; we can *hear* Lewis's surprise and delight. Readers familiar with the varieties of English Lewis uses might sense kinship with him, while those who are not will be reminded that Hurston is writing about a context different from their experience—but in a way that is always respectful.

When you're quoting others, let them speak for themselves not only in their own words but also in their own language. Whenever possible, ask your subjects to review the quotations you use to ensure they find the representation accurate and respectful.

Evoking a Particular Person, Place, or Community

Using the language of a specific community or group is a good way to evoke the character and sounds of the place. In the following passage, journalist David Thompson is interviewing Lee A. Tonouchi, author of *Living Pidgin: Contemplations on Pidgin Culture.* Responding to a question about his work, Tonouchi uses Hawai'ian Pidgin to evoke family relationships in his particular Hawaiian community:

> [This book is] about finding humor in tragedy. It's about da relationship between one son and his uncommunicative faddah in da wake of da maddah's early passing. An den, it's also about da son's relationship with his grandmas as he discovers what it means for be Okinawan in Hawaii.
> —DAVID THOMPSON, "Lee Tonouchi: Pidgin Poet," *Honolulu Magazine*

Notice that Tonouchi mixes more academic English and Hawai'ian Pidgin within sentences and not just between them, bringing the two into even closer contact and familiarity. When using the language of a community or group you don't belong to yourself, take care to do so with respect. When possible, ask someone who does speak the language to provide feedback on what you've drafted to ensure it's accurate and respectful.

As we've tried to demonstrate, using your own idiolect and shifting between styles are powerful tools for communicating what you have to say. Consider the following questions as you think about mixing languages, dialects, and registers in your own writing:

- *Who's your target* AUDIENCE*?* Are there places where you can shift styles to connect with them? to get and keep their attention? to illustrate a point? What expectations does your audience have about language? Are you meeting or challenging those expectations?

- *What's the larger* CONTEXT*?* Are readers likely to find your language choices appropriate? Is anything at risk, like your credibility or clarity? What's your PURPOSE for taking such risks?

- *Are readers likely to understand your words?* Do you need to provide translations? If you're using a specific style, like MLA or APA, are there conventions—like italicizing unfamiliar words—you need to follow?

- *Have you treated languages, dialects, and registers that are not your own with respect?* When quoting, have you let subjects speak for themselves? Have you solicited feedback from someone who speaks the language, dialect, or register to be sure your text is accurate and respectful?

REFLECT. Think about one or two ways of speaking you encounter that are different from your own—in places you work, movies you watch, or groups you are familiar with but don't belong to. Then find out as much as you can about that way of speaking and gather examples of it in use. What can you determine about how widely the dialect is used, who uses it, when it's used, what characteristics define it, and how it's perceived by different audiences? Write a brief reflection summarizing what you've found.

THIRTY-TWO

How to Craft Good Sentences

HEN A STUDENT asked author Annie Dillard, "Do you think I could become a writer?" Dillard replied with a question of her own: "Do you like sentences?" French novelist Gustave Flaubert certainly did, once saying that he "itched with sentences." Itching with sentences probably isn't something you've experienced—and liking or not liking sentences might not be something you've ever thought about—but we're willing to bet that you know something about how important sentences are. Anyone who has ever tried to write the perfect tweet or, better yet, the perfect love letter knows about choosing just the right words for each sentence and about the power of the three-word sentence "I love you"—or the even shorter sentence that sometimes follows from such declarations: "I do."

In his book *How to Write a Sentence*, English professor Stanley Fish declares himself to be a "connoisseur of sentences" and offers some particularly noteworthy examples. Here's one, written by a fourth grader in response to an assignment to write something about a mysterious large box that had been delivered to a school:

▶ I was already on the second floor when I heard about the box.

This sentence reminded us of a favorite sentence of our own, this one the beginning of a story written by a third grader:

▶ Today, the monster goes where no monster has gone before: Cincinnati.

Here the student manages to allude to the famous line from *Star Trek*—"to boldly go where no man has gone before"—while suggesting that Cincinnati is the most exotic place on earth and even using a colon effectively. It's quite a sentence.

Finally, here's a sentence that opens a chapter from a PhD dissertation on literacy among young people today:

▶ Hazel Hernandez struck me as an honest thief.

Such sentences are memorable: They startle us a bit and demand attention. They make us to want to read more. Who's Hazel Hernandez? What's an honest thief, and what makes her one?

As these examples suggest, you don't have to be a famous author to write a great sentence. In fact, crafting effective and memorable sentences is a skill everyone can master with careful attention and practice. Sometimes a brilliant sentence comes to you like a bolt of lightning, and all you have to do is type it out. More often, though, the perfect sentence is a result of tweaking and tinkering during your revision stages. Either way, crafting good sentences is worth the effort it may take. You may not come up with a zinger like the famous sentence John Updike wrote about Ted Williams's fabled home run in his last at bat at Fenway Park—"It was in the books while it was still in the sky"—but you can come close.

Just as certain effects in film—music, close-ups—enhance the story, a well-crafted sentence can bring power to a piece of writing. So think about the kind of effect you want to create in what you're writing—and then look for the type of sentence that will fit the bill. Though much of the power of the examples above comes from being short and simple, remember that some rhetorical situations call for longer, complex sentences—and that the kind of sentence you write also depends on its context, such as whether it's opening an essay, summing up what's already been said, or something else. This chapter looks at some common English sentence patterns and provides some good examples for producing them in your own work.

FOUR COMMON SENTENCE PATTERNS

We make sentences with words—and we arrange those words into patterns. If a sentence is defined as a group of words that expresses a complete thought, then we can identify four basic sentence structures: a **SIMPLE SENTENCE** (expressing one idea); a **COMPOUND SENTENCE** (expressing more than one idea, with the ideas being of equal importance); a **COMPLEX SENTENCE** (expressing more than one idea, with one of the ideas more important than the others); and a **COMPOUND-COMPLEX SENTENCE** (with more than one idea of equal importance and at least one idea of less importance).

Simple Sentences: One Main Idea

Let's take a look at some simple sentences:

▶ Resist!

▶ Consumers revolted.

▶ Angry consumers revolted against new debit-card fees.

▶ A wave of protest from angry consumers forced banks to rescind the new fees.

▶ The growth of the internet and its capacity to mobilize people instantly all over the world have done everything from forcing companies to rescind debit-card fees in the United States to bringing down oppressive governments in the Middle East.

As these examples illustrate, simple sentences can be as short as a single word—or they can be much longer. Each is a simple sentence, however, because it contains a single main idea or thought; in grammatical terms, each contains one and only one **MAIN CLAUSE**. As the name suggests, a simple sentence is often the simplest, most direct way of saying what you want to say—but not always. And often you want a sentence to include more than one idea. In that case, you need to use a compound sentence, a complex sentence, or a compound-complex sentence.

Compound Sentences: Joining Ideas That Are Equally Important

Sometimes you'll want to write a sentence that joins two or more ideas that are equally important, like this one attributed to former president Bill Clinton:

▶ You can put wings on a pig, but you don't make it an eagle.

In grammatical terms, this is a compound sentence with two main clauses, each of which expresses one of two independent and equally important ideas. In this case, Clinton joined the ideas with a comma and the coordinating conjunction *but*. But he had several other options for joining these ideas. For example, he could have joined them with only a semicolon:

▶ You can put wings on a pig; you don't make it an eagle.

Or he could have joined them with a semicolon, a conjunctive adverb like *however,* and a comma:

▶ You can put wings on a pig; however, you don't make it an eagle.

All of these compound sentences are perfectly acceptable—but which seems most effective? In this case, we think Clinton's choice is: it is clear and very direct, and if you read it aloud you'll hear that the words on each side of *but* have the same number of syllables, creating a pleasing, balanced rhythm—and one that balances the two equally important ideas. It also makes the logical relationship between the two ideas explicit: *but* indicates a contrast. The version with only a semicolon, by contrast, indicates that the ideas are somehow related but doesn't show how.

Using *and*, *but*, and other coordinating conjunctions. In writing a compound sentence, remember that different **COORDINATING CONJUNCTIONS** carry meanings that signal different logical relationships between the main ideas in the sentence. There are only seven coordinating conjunctions.

COORDINATING CONJUNCTIONS

and	for	or	yet
but	nor	so	

▶ China's one-child policy has slowed population growth, *but* it has helped create a serious gender imbalance in the country's population.

▶ Most of us bike to the office, *so* many of us stop at the gym to shower before work.

▶ The first two batters struck out, *yet* the Cubs went on to win the game on back-to-back homers.

See how the following sentences express different meanings depending on which coordinating conjunction is used:

▶ You could apply to graduate school, *or* you could start looking for a job.

▶ You could apply to graduate school, *and* you could start looking for a job.

Using a semicolon. Joining clauses with a semicolon only is a way of signaling that they are closely related without saying explicitly how. Often the second clause will expand on an idea expressed in the first clause.

▶ My first year of college was a little bumpy; it took me a few months to get comfortable at a large university far from home.

▶ The Wassaic Project is an arts organization in Dutchess County, New York; artists go there to engage in "art, music, and everything else."

Adding a **TRANSITION WORD** can make the logical relationship between the ideas more explicit:

▶ My first year of college was a little bumpy; *indeed,* it took me a few months to get comfortable at a large university far from home.

Note that the transition in this sentence, *indeed,* cannot join the two main clauses on its own—it requires a semicolon before it. If you use a transition between two clauses with only a comma before it, you've made a mistake called a **COMMA SPLICE**.

SOME TRANSITION WORDS

also	indeed	otherwise
certainly	likewise	similarly
furthermore	nevertheless	therefore
however	next	thus

REFLECT. Read through something you've written recently and identify compound sentences joined with and. *When you find one, ask yourself whether* and *is the best word to use: does it express the logical relationship between the two parts of the sentence that you intend? Would* but, or, so, for, nor, *or* yet *work better?*

Complex Sentences:
When One Idea Is More Important than Another

Many of the sentences you write will contain two or more ideas, with one that you want to emphasize more than the other(s). You can do so by putting the idea you wish to emphasize in the **MAIN CLAUSE**, and then putting those that are less important in **SUBORDINATE CLAUSES**.

▶ Mendocino County is a place in California *where you can dive for abalone.*

▶ *Because the species has become scarce,* abalone diving is strictly regulated.

▶ Fish and Wildlife Department agents *who patrol the coast* use sophisticated methods to catch poachers.

As these examples show, the ideas in the subordinate clauses (italicized here) can't stand alone as sentences: when we read "where you can dive for abalone" or "who patrol the coast," we know that something's missing. Subordinate clauses begin with words such as *if* or *because,* **SUBORDINATING WORDS** that signal the logical relationship between the subordinate clause and the rest of the sentence.

SOME SUBORDINATING WORDS

after	even though	until
although	if	when
as	since	where
because	that	while
before	though	who

Notice that a subordinate clause can come at the beginning of a sentence, in the middle, or at the end. When it comes at the beginning, it is usually followed by a comma, as in the second example. If the opening clause in that sentence were moved to the end, a comma would not be necessary: "Abalone diving is strictly regulated because the species has become scarce."

Grammatically, each of the three examples above is a complex sentence, with one main idea and one other idea of less importance. In writing you will often have to decide whether to combine ideas in a compound sentence, which gives the ideas equal importance, or in a complex sentence, which makes one idea more important than the other(s). Looking once more at our sentence about the pig and the eagle, Bill Clinton could have made it a complex sentence:

▶ Even though you can put wings on a pig, you don't make it an eagle.

Again, though, we think Clinton made a good choice in giving the two ideas equal weight because doing so balances the sentence perfectly—and tells us that both parts are equally important. In fact, neither part of this sentence is very interesting in itself: it's the balancing and the contrast that make it interesting and memorable.

Compound-Complex Sentences: Multiple Ideas—Some More Important, Some Less

When you are expressing three or more ideas in a single sentence, you'll sometimes want to use a compound-complex sentence, which gives some of the ideas more prominence and others less. Grammatically, such sentences have at least two **MAIN CLAUSES** and one **SUBORDINATE CLAUSE**.

▶ ———————MAIN CLAUSE——————— ┌SUBORDINATE CLAUSE
We have experienced unparalleled natural disasters that have devastated

————————————— MAIN CLAUSE —————————
entire countries, yet identifying global warming as the cause of these

disasters is difficult.

▶ ——————SUBORDINATE CLAUSE—————— ┌MAIN CLAUSE
Even after distinguished scientists issued a series of reports, critics continued

———————————— SUBORDINATE CLAUSE ————————
to question the findings because they claimed results were falsified;

┌—— MAIN CLAUSE ——┐
nothing would convince them.

As these examples show, English sentence structure is flexible, allowing you to combine groups of words in different ways in order to get your ideas across to your audience most appropriately and effectively. There's seldom only one way to write a sentence to get an idea across: as the author, you must decide which way works best for your **RHETORICAL SITUATION**.

WAYS OF EMPHASIZING
THE MAIN IDEA IN A SENTENCE

Sometimes, you will want to lead off a sentence with the main point; other times, you might want to hold it in reserve until the end. **CUMULATIVE SENTENCES** start with a main clause and then add on to it, "accumulating" details. **PERIODIC SENTENCES** start with a series of phrases or subordinate clauses, saving the main clause for last.

Cumulative Sentences: Starting with the Main Point

In this kind of sentence, the writer starts off with a **MAIN CLAUSE** and then adds details in phrases and **SUBORDINATE CLAUSES**, extending or explaining the thought. Cumulative sentences can be especially useful for describing a place or an event, operating almost like a camera panning across a room or landscape. The sentences below create such an effect:

▶ The San Bernardino Valley lies only an hour east of Los Angeles by the San Bernardino Freeway but is in certain ways an alien place: not the coastal California of the subtropical twilights and the soft westerlies off the Pacific but a harsher California, haunted by the Mojave just beyond the mountains, devastated by the hot dry Santa Ana wind that comes down through the passes at 100 miles an hour and whines through the eucalyptus windbreaks and works on the nerves.
　　　　　　　　　　　　—JOAN DIDION, "Some Dreamers of the Golden Dream"

▶ Public transportation in Cebu City was provided by jeepneys: refurbished military jeeps with metal roofs for shade, decorated with horns and mirrors and fenders and flaps; painted with names, dedications, quotations, religious icons, logos—and much, much more.

▶ She hit the brakes, swearing fiercely, as the deer leapt over the hood and crashed into the dark woods beyond.

▶ The celebrated Russian pianist gave his hands a shake, a quick shake, fingers pointed down at his sides, before taking his seat and lifting them imperiously above the keys.

These cumulative sentences add details in a way that makes each sentence more emphatic. Keep this principle in mind as you write—and also when you revise. See if there are times when you might revise a sentence or sentences to add emphasis in the same way. Take a look at the following sentences, for instance:

▶ China has initiated free-market reforms that transformed its economy from a struggling one to an industrial powerhouse. It has become the world's fastest-growing major economy. Growth rates have been averaging 10 percent over the last decade.

These three sentences are clearly related, with each one adding detail about the growth of China's economy. Now look what happens when the writer eliminates a little bit of repetition, adds a memorable metaphor, and combines them as a cumulative—and more emphatic—sentence:

▶ China's free-market reforms have led to 10 percent average growth over the last decade, transforming it from a paper tiger into an industrial dragon that is now the world's fastest-growing major economy.

Periodic Sentences: Delaying the Main Point until the End

In contrast to sentences that open with the main idea, periodic sentences delay the main idea until the very end. Periodic sentences are sometimes fairly long, and withholding the main point until the end is a way of adding emphasis. It can also create suspense or build up to a surprise or inspirational ending.

▶ In spite of everything, in spite of the dark and twisting path he saw stretching ahead for himself, in spite of the final meeting with Voldemort he knew must come, whether in a month, in a year, or in ten, he felt his heart lift at the thought that there was still one last golden day of peace left to enjoy with Ron and Hermione.   —J. K. ROWLING, Harry Potter and the Half-Blood Prince

▶ Unprovided with original learning, uninformed in the habits of thinking, unskilled in the arts of composition, I resolved to write a book.
—EDWARD GIBBON, Memoirs of My Life

▶ In the week before finals, when my studying and memorizing reached a fever pitch, came a sudden, comforting thought: I have never failed.

Here are three periodic sentences in a row about Whitney Houston, each of which withholds the main point until the end:

> ▶ When her smiling brown face, complete with a close-cropped Afro, appeared on the cover of *Seventeen* in 1981, she was one of the first African-Americans to grace the cover, and the industry took notice. When she belted out a chilling and soulful version of the "Star-Spangled Banner" at the 1991 Super Bowl, the world sat back in awe of her poise and calm. And in an era when African-American actresses are often given film roles portraying them as destitute, unloving, unlovable, or just "the help," Houston played the love interest of Kevin Costner, a white Hollywood superstar.
>
>   —ALLISON SAMUELS, "A Hard Climb for the Girl Next Door"

These three periodic sentences create a drumlike effect that builds in intensity as they move through the stages in Houston's career; in all, they suggest that Houston was, even more than Kevin Costner, a "superstar."

Samuels takes a chance when she uses three sentences in a row that withhold the main point until the end: readers may get tired of waiting for that point. And readers may also find the use of too many such sentences to be, well, too much. But as the example above shows, when used carefully a sentence that puts off the main idea just long enough can keep readers' interest, making them want to reach the ending, with its payoff.

You may find in your own work that periodic sentences can make your writing more emphatic. Take a look at the following sentence from an essay on the use of animals in circuses:

> ▶ The big cat took him down with one swat, just as the trainer, dressed in khakis and boots, his whip raised and his other arm extended in welcome to the cheering crowd, stepped into the ring.

This sentence paints a vivid picture, but it gives away all the action in the first six words. By withholding that action until the end, the writer builds anticipation and adds emphasis:

> ▶ Just as the trainer stepped into the ring, dressed in khakis and boots, his whip raised and his other arm extended in welcome to the cheering crowd, the big cat took him down with one swat.

OPENING SENTENCES

The opening sentences in your writing carry big responsibilities, setting the tone and often the scene—and drawing your readers in by arousing their interest and curiosity. Authors often spend quite a lot of time on opening sentences for this very reason: whether it's a business report or a college essay or a blog posting, the way the piece begins has a lot to do with whether your audience will stay with you and whether you'll get the kind of response you want from them. Here are three famous opening sentences:

> ▶ I am an invisible man.   —RALPH ELLISON, *Invisible Man*

> ▶ The sky above the port was the color of television, tuned to a dead channel.
>   —WILLIAM GIBSON, *Neuromancer*

> ▶ They shoot the white girl first.   —TONI MORRISON, *Paradise*

Each of these sentences is startling, making us read on in order to find out more. Each is brief, leaving us waiting anxiously for what's to come. In addition, each makes a powerful statement and creates some kind of image in readers' minds: an "invisible" person, a sky the color of a "dead" TV channel, someone being shot. These sentences all come from novels, but they use strategies that work in many kinds of writing.

It usually takes more than a single sentence to open an essay. Consider, for example, how Michael Pollan begins a lengthy essay on animal liberation:

> ▶ The first time I opened Peter Singer's *Animal Liberation*, I was dining alone at the Palm, trying to enjoy a rib-eye steak cooked medium-rare. If this sounds like a good recipe for cognitive dissonance (if not indigestion), that was sort of the idea. Preposterous as it might seem to supporters of animal rights, what I was doing was tantamount to reading *Uncle Tom's Cabin* on a plantation in the Deep South in 1852.
>   —MICHAEL POLLAN, "An Animal's Place"

The first sentence presents an incongruous image that holds our attention (he's eating a steak while reading about animal liberation). Then the rest of the paragraph makes this incongruity even more pronounced, even comparing the situation to someone reading the antislavery novel *Uncle Tom's Cabin* while on a slave-owning plantation. It's an opening that makes us read on.

Here is the opening of a blog posting that begins with a provocative question:

▶ Have you ever thought about whether to have a child? If so, what factors entered into your decision? Was it whether having children would be good for you, your partner and others close to the possible child, such as children you may already have, or perhaps your parents? For most people contemplating reproduction, those are the dominant questions. Some may also think about the desirability of adding to the strain that the nearly seven billion people already here are putting on our planet's environment. But very few ask whether coming into existence is a good thing for the child itself.
　　—PETER SINGER, "Should This Be the Last Generation?"

Singer's question is designed to get the reader's attention, and he follows it up with two additional questions that ask readers to probe more deeply into their reasons for considering whether or not to reproduce. In the fifth sentence, he suggests that the answers people give to these questions may not be adequate ones, and in the last sentence he lays down a challenge: perhaps coming into existence is not always good for "the child itself."

Here's another example of an opening that uses several sentences, this one from a student essay about graphic memoirs:

▶ In 1974, before the Fall of Saigon, my 14-year-old father, alone, boarded a boat out of Vietnam in search of America. This is a fact. But this one fact can spawn multiple understandings: I could ask a group of students to take a week and write me a story from just this one fact, and I have no doubt that they would bring back a full range of interpretations.
　　—BRANDON LY, "Leaving Home, Coming Home"

This opening passage begins with a vivid image of a very young man fleeing Vietnam alone, followed by a very short sentence that makes a statement and then a longer one that challenges that statement. This student writer is moving readers toward what will become his thesis: that memoirs can never tell "the whole truth, and nothing but the truth."

Finally, take a look at the opening of the speech Toni Morrison gave when she won the Nobel Prize for Literature:

▶ Members of the Swedish Academy, Ladies and Gentlemen:
Narrative has never been mere entertainment for me. It is, I believe, one of the principal ways in which we absorb knowledge. I hope you will

> understand, then, why I begin these remarks with the opening phrase of
> what must be the oldest sentence in the world, and the earliest one we
> remember from childhood: "Once upon a time . . ."
>
> —TONI MORRISON, Nobel Prize acceptance speech

Morrison begins with a deceptively simple statement that narrative is for
her not just entertainment. In the next sentences, she complicates that
statement and broadens her claim that narrative is the way we understand
the world, concluding with what she calls "the oldest sentence in the world."

You can use strategies similar to the ones shown here in opening your
college essays. Here are just some of the ways you might begin:

- With a strong, dramatic—or deceptively simple—statement
- With a vivid image
- With a provocative question
- With an anecdote
- With a startling claim

Opening sentences online. If the internet lets us send messages to people
all over the world, it also challenges us to get and keep their attention. And
with limited space and time (small screens, readers in a hurry, scanning for
what they need), writers need to make sure the opening sentences of any
online text are as attention getting and informative as possible.

In email, for instance, first sentences often show up in auto-preview
lines, so it's a good idea to write them carefully. Here's the first line of an
email sent recently to everyone at W. W. Norton:

▶ A Ping-Pong table has been set up on the 4th floor in loving memory of
Diane O'Connor.

This email was sent by O'Connor's colleagues, honoring her efforts to persuade Norton to have an annual company Ping-Pong tournament. It might
have said less ("Ping-Pong on 4," "remembering Diane"), as email usually
does—but there was more that they wanted to say.

And then there's *Twitter*. As if it weren't enough of a challenge to say
what you want to say in 280 characters, you'd better begin with a sentence
that will catch readers' attention. Here are two tweets that got ours:

▶ Steve Jobs was born out of wedlock, put up for adoption at birth, dropped out of college, then changed the world. What's your excuse?   —@jwmoss

▶ It's so weird because Rush Limbaugh has been such an awesome human being until now.   —@buck4itt

You'll want to think carefully about how you open any text that you post online—and to craft opening sentences that will make sense in a *Google* search list. Here are two that we like:

▶ Smith Women Redefine "Pearls and Cashmere."

This is the headline for an article in *Inside Higher Ed,* an online magazine read by educators, but it's also the line that comes up in a *Google* search. The article is about a controversy at Smith College—and we think you'll agree that the headline surely got the attention of those scanning the magazine's list of articles or searching *Google*.

▶ *The Art of Fielding* is a 2011 novel by former *n+1* editor <u>Chad Harbach</u>. It centers on the fortunes of <u>shortstop</u> Henry Skrimshander and his career playing <u>college baseball</u> with the Westish College Harpooners, a <u>Division III (NCAA)</u> team.

This is the start of the *Wikipedia* entry for a novel, which comes up in a *Google* search. As you can see, it identifies the book, says who wrote it, and gives a one-sentence description of the story. Safe to say, the authors of this entry were careful to provide this information in the very first sentences.

CLOSING SENTENCES

Sentences that conclude a piece of writing are where you have a chance to make a lasting impact: to reiterate your point, tell readers why it matters, echo something you say in your opening, make a provocative statement, issue a call for action.

Here's Joe Posnanski, wrapping up an essay on his blog arguing that college athletes should not be paid:

▶ College football is not popular because of the stars. College football is popular because of that first word. Take away the college part, add in money, and you are left with professional minor league football. . . . See how many people watch that.   —JOE POSNANSKI, "The College Connection"

These four sentences summarize his argument—and the last one's the zinger, one that leaves readers thinking.

Now take a look at the conclusion to a scholarly book on current neurological studies of human attention, the brain science of attention:

▶ Right now, our classrooms and workplaces are structured for success in the last century, not this one. We can change that. By maximizing opportunities for collaboration, by rethinking everything from our approach to work to how we measure progress, we can begin to see the things we've been missing and catch hold of what's passing us by.

   If you change the context, if you change the questions you ask, if you change the structure, the test, and the task, then you stop gazing one way and begin to look in a different way and in a different direction. You know what happens next:

   Now you see it.   —CATHY DAVIDSON, *Now You See It: How the Brain Science of Attention Will Transform the Way We Live, Work, and Learn*

Cathy Davidson uses two short paragraphs to sum up her argument and then concludes with a final paragraph that consists of just one very short four-word sentence. With this last sentence, she uses a tried-and-true strategy of coming full circle to echo the main idea of her book and, in fact, to reiterate its title. Readers who have worked their way through the book will take pleasure in that last sentence: *Now* they do see her point.

For another example, note how in the ending to a speech about language and about being able to use "all the Englishes" she grew up with, author Amy Tan closes with a one-sentence paragraph that quotes her mother:

▶ Apart from what any critic had to say about my writing, I knew I had succeeded where it counted when my mother finished reading my book and gave me her verdict: "So easy to read."   —AMY TAN, "Mother Tongue"

Tan's ending sums up one of her main goals as an author: to write so that readers who speak different kinds of English will find her work accessible, especially her mother.

Finally, take a look at how Toni Morrison chose to close her Nobel Prize acceptance speech:

▶ It is, therefore, mindful of the gifts of my predecessors, the blessing of my
sisters, in joyful anticipation of writers to come that I accept the honor
the Swedish Academy has done me, and ask you to share what is for me a
moment of grace. —TONI MORRISON, Nobel Prize acceptance speech

In this one-sentence conclusion, Morrison speaks to the past, present, and
future when she says she is grateful for those writers who came before her,
for those who are writing now (her sisters), and for those yet to come. She
ends the sentence by asking her audience to share this "moment of grace"
with her and, implicitly, with all other writers so honored.

You may not be accepting a Nobel Prize soon, but in your college writing you can use all the strategies presented here to compose strong closings:

- By reiterating your point
- By discussing the implications of your argument
- By asking a question
- By referring back to your beginning
- By recommending or proposing some kind of action

*REFLECT. Identify two memorable openings and closings from a favorite
novel, comic book, film, or social media post. What makes them so good? Do they
follow one of the strategies presented here?*

VARYING YOUR SENTENCES

Read a paragraph or two of your writing out loud and listen for its rhythm. Is
it quick and abrupt? slow and leisurely? singsong? stately? rolling? Whatever
it is, does the rhythm you hear match what you had in mind when you were
writing? And does it put the emphasis where you want it? One way to establish the emphasis you intend and a rhythm that will keep readers reading is
by varying the length of your sentences and the way those sentences flow
from one to the other.

A string of sentences that are too much alike is almost certain to be
boring. While you can create effective rhythms in many ways, one of the
simplest and most effective is by breaking up a series of long sentences with

a shorter one that gives your readers a chance to pause and absorb what you've written.

Take a look at the following passage, from an article in the *Atlantic* about the finale of the *Oprah Winfrey Show*. See how the author uses a mix of long and short sentences to describe one of the tributes to Oprah, this one highlighting her support of black men:

> ▶ Oprah's friend Tyler Perry announced that some of the "Morehouse Men," each a beneficiary of the $12 million endowment she has established at their university, had come to honor her for the scholarships she gave them. The lights were lowered, a Broadway star began singing an inspirational song, and a dozen or so black men began to walk slowly to the front of the stage. Then more came, and soon there were a score, then 100, then the huge stage was filled with men, 300 of them. They stood there, solemnly, in a tableau stage-managed in such a way that it might have robbed them of their dignity—the person serenading them (or, rather, serenading Oprah on their behalf) was Kristin Chenoweth, tiniest and whitest of all tiny white women; the song was from *Wicked*, most feminine of all musicals; and each man carried a white candle, an emblem that lent them the aspect of Norman Rockwell Christmas carolers. But they were not robbed of their dignity. They looked, all together, like a miracle. A video shown before the procession revealed that some of these men had been in gangs before going to Morehouse, some had fathers in prison, many had been living in poverty. Now they were doctors, lawyers, bankers, a Rhodes Scholar—and philanthropists, establishing their own Morehouse endowment.
>
> —CAITLIN FLANAGAN, "The Glory of Oprah"

The passage begins with three medium-length sentences—and then one very long one (seventy-two words!) that points up the strong contrast between the 300 black men filling the stage and the "whitest of white" singer performing a song from the "most feminine" of musicals. Then come two little sentences (the first one eight words long and the second one, seven) that give readers a chance to pause and absorb what has been said while also making an important point: that the men "looked, all together, like a miracle." The remainder of the passage moves back toward longer sentences, each of which explains just what this "miracle" is. Try reading this passage aloud and listen for how the variation in sentences creates both emphasis and a pleasing and effective rhythm.

The Morehouse Men surprise Oprah.

In addition to varying the lengths of your sentences, you can also improve your writing by making sure that they don't all use the same structure or begin in the same way. You can be pretty sure, for example, that a passage in which every sentence is a simple sentence that opens with the subject of a main clause will not read smoothly at all but rather will move along awkwardly. Take a look at this passage, for example:

> ▶ The sunset was especially beautiful today. I was on top of Table Mountain in Cape Town. I looked down and saw the sun touch the sea and sink into it. The evening shadows crept up the mountain. I got my backpack and walked over to the rest of my group. We started on the long hike down the mountain and back to the city.

There's nothing wrong with these sentences as such. Each one is grammatically correct. But if you read the passage aloud, you'll hear how it moves abruptly from sentence to sentence, lurching along rather than flowing smoothly. The problem is that the sentences are all the same: each one is a simple sentence that begins with the subject of a main clause (*sunset, I, I, evening shadows, I, we*). In addition, the use of personal pronouns at the beginning of the sentences (three *I*'s in only six sentences!) makes for dull reading. Finally, these are all fairly short sentences, and the sameness of the sentence length adds to the abrupt rhythm of the passage—and doesn't keep readers reading. Now look at how this passage can be revised by working on sentence variation:

▶ From the top of Cape Town's Table Mountain, the sunset was especially beautiful. I looked down just as the fiery orb touched and then sank into the sea; shadows began to creep slowly up the mountain. Picking up my backpack, I joined the rest of my group, and we started the long hike down the mountain.

This revision reduces the number of sentences in the passage from six to three (the first simple, the second compound-complex, the third compound) and varies the length of the sentences. Equally important, the revision eliminates all but one of the subject openings. The first sentence now begins with the prepositional phrase ("From the top"); the second with the subject of a main clause ("I"); and the third with a participial phrase ("Picking up my backpack"). Finally the revision varies the diction a bit, replacing the repeated word "sun" with a vivid image ("fiery orb"). Read the revised passage aloud and you'll hear how varying the sentences creates a stronger rhythm that makes it easier to read.

This brief chapter has only scratched the surface of sentence style. But we hope we've said enough to show how good sentences can be your allies, helping you get your ideas out there and connect with audiences as successfully as possible. Remember: authors are only as good as the sentences they write!

REFLECT. Take a look at a writing assignment you've recently completed. Read it aloud, listening for rhythm and emphasis. If you find a passage that doesn't read well or provide the emphasis you want, analyze its sentences for length (count the words) and structure (how does each sentence begin?). Revise the passage using the strategies presented in this chapter.

THIRTY-THREE

Editing the Errors
That Matter

IN PREPARATION FOR a 2018 Coachella performance, Beyoncé led her team through eleven-hour rehearsal days. LeBron James spends five to seven hours every day training in the gym (in addition to team practices). It takes a lot of hard work to make something look easy. Beyoncé rehearses, LeBron trains; what do authors do? We revise.

Take this book, for example. It was written by experienced authors—skilled teachers and professional writers, all. The page that you're reading right now—how many drafts and revisions did it go through before it reached you? We lose count after three or four. The point is, completing a draft is a great accomplishment, and at the same time, it's only the beginning.

One of the most important parts of your revision process is examining each sentence for structural errors. Don't be afraid of "errors"; we all make them, even the pros. Some of our errors are no big deal, barely noticeable, not worth mentioning. Others, however, are more serious—deal breakers, maybe—and we try hard to avoid them.

One of the great things about writing is that we can edit our work and fix our errors. Our team asked seventy-five writing instructors which errors really matter to them—which ones are most bothersome and do the most damage to a writer's credibility and ideas. Their responses covered a wide gamut, from sentence structure to punctuation. This chapter focuses on those errors that matter, showing how to spot them in a draft, explaining why they're so troublesome, and suggesting strategies for editing them out.

Throughout this chapter, you'll find opportunities for editing practice in adaptive activities called InQuizitive. For more information on how to get started with InQuizitive, see the access card at the front of your book or visit *digital.wwnorton.com/everyone3r.*

EDITING SENTENCES

Fragments, comma splices, fused sentences, and mixed constructions are all types of sentence-structure errors. Such sentences are usually comprehensible in context, so if readers can understand the message, why are they errors? Solid sentence structure matters for two reasons:

- The perception of your competence hangs on it: readers don't trust writers who write sloppy sentences.

- Even if a poorly structured sentence can be understood, your readers have to work a little harder to get there, and they may not want to put forth the effort. Your job is to make it easy for readers, to keep them reading smoothly all the way to the end.

Every sentence is composed of one or more **CLAUSES**, and every clause needs to have a **SUBJECT**, a **VERB**, and appropriate punctuation. Don't underestimate those little dots and squiggles; they often make all the difference in how a sentence is read and understood. Consider these two examples:

▶ Let's eat Grandma.

▶ Let's eat, Grandma.

Are you inviting your grandmother to eat a meal right now, or are you inviting someone else to eat *her*? That one little comma in the right place can save grandma's life (or at least make it clear to your readers that you aren't proposing to make a meal of her). The following advice will help you examine your writing with an eye to four common sentence-structure errors: fragments, comma splices, fused sentences, and mixed constructions.

Fragments

At first glance, a fragment looks like a complete sentence—it begins with a capital letter and concludes with end punctuation—but on closer examination, a key element, usually a **SUBJECT** or a **VERB**, is missing. For example: *Forgot to vote.* Who forgot to vote? We don't know; the subject is missing. *Two bottles of rancid milk.* Wow. That sounds interesting, but what about them? There's no verb, so we don't know. A fragment also occurs when a sentence begins with a **SUBORDINATING WORD** such as *if* or *because*, but the **SUBORDINATE CLAUSE** is not followed by a **MAIN CLAUSE**. *If the ball game is rained out.* Well, what happens if the ball game is rained out? Again, we don't know.

Checking for fragments

Sometimes writers use fragments for stylistic reasons, but it's best to avoid them in academic writing. To check your text for fragments, examine each sentence one by one, making sure there's both a subject and a verb. (It might take you a while to do this at first, but it will go much faster with practice, and it's worth the time.) Check also for subordinating words (see p. 699 for a list of common ones), and if there's a subordinate clause, make sure there's also a main clause.

Editing fragments

Let's look at some fragments and see what we can do about them.

NEEDS A SUBJECT

▶ The Centipedes were terrible last night. *Started late, played three songs, and left.*

Context makes it clear that it was the Centipedes who started late. Still, the italicized part is a fragment because there is no explicit subject. We have two good options here. One is to add a subject to the fragment in order to make the sentence complete; the other is to attach the fragment to a nearby sentence. Both strategies will work, and you can choose whichever sounds better to you.

▶ The Centipedes were terrible last night. ~~Started~~ _{They started} late, played three songs, and left.

▶ The Centipedes were terrible last night/ ~~Started~~ _{because they started} late, played three songs, and left.

In the first example, we've added a subject, *They*, which refers to the Centipedes. In the second, we've attached the fragment to the preceding sentence using a subordinating word, *because*, followed by an explicit subject, *they*.

NEEDS A VERB

▶ Malik heard a knock on the door. *Then a loud thud.*

The example makes sense: we know that Malik heard a loud thud after the knock. But the italicized part is a fragment because between the capital *T* at the beginning and the period at the end, there is no verb. Again, there are two strategies for editing: to add a verb to the fragment in order to make the sentence complete, or to incorporate the fragment into the previous sentence so that its verb can do double duty.

▶ Malik heard a knock on the door. Then ^{came} a loud thud.

▶ Malik heard a knock on the door/, T̶h̶e̶n̶ ^{followed by} a loud thud.

NEEDS MORE INFORMATION

▶ Olga nearly missed her plane. *Because the line at security was so long.* She got flustered and dropped her change purse.

The italicized part of the example above does have a subject and a verb, but it can't stand alone as a sentence because it starts with *because*, a subordinating word that leads readers to expect more information. Did the long security line cause Olga to nearly miss her plane? Or did the long line fluster her? We can't be sure. How you edit this fragment depends on what you're trying to say—and how the ideas relate to one another. For example:

▶ Olga nearly missed her plane/ ^{because} B̶e̶c̶a̶u̶s̶e̶ the line at security was so long.

▶ Because the line at security was so long/, ^{she} S̶h̶e̶ got flustered and dropped her change purse.

The first option explains why Olga nearly missed her plane, and the second explains why she got flustered and dropped her change purse.

Edit
The word *if* leads readers to expect a clause explaining what will happen. Consider the following example:

▶ If you activate the alarm.

This example is a fragment. We need the sentence to show the "what-if": what happens if you activate the alarm? Otherwise, we have an incomplete thought—and readers will be confused.

▶ The whole lab will be destroyed. If you activate the alarm. Spider-Man, you can avert the tragedy.

Will the lab be destroyed if Spider-Man activates the alarm? Or will activating the alarm avert the tragedy? There is no way for readers to know. This example needs to be edited! You try. Edit the example above for both possible interpretations.

↪ For more practice, complete the InQuizitive activity on **sentence fragments**.

Comma Splices

A comma splice looks like a complete sentence in that it starts with a capital letter, concludes with end punctuation, and contains two **MAIN CLAUSES**. The problem is that there is only a comma between the two clauses. Here's an example:

▶ It was the coldest day in fifty years, the marching band performed brilliantly.

Both clauses are perfectly clear, and we expect that they are connected in some way—but we don't know how. Did the band play well because of the cold or in spite of it? Or is there no connection at all? In short, comma splices can leave your readers confused.

Checking for comma splices
Writers sometimes use comma splices to create a certain stylistic effect, but it's best to avoid them in academic writing. To check your work for comma splices, look at each sentence one by one and identify the **VERBS**. Next, look for their **SUBJECTS**. If you find two or more sets of subjects and verbs that form **MAIN CLAUSES**, make sure they are connected appropriately.

Editing comma splices

What are the appropriate ways to connect two independent clauses? Let's look at some of the possibilities.

CHANGE THE COMMA TO A PERIOD

One of your options is to create two separate sentences by inserting a period (.) after the first clause and capitalizing the first letter of the following word.

▶ It was the coldest day in fifty years. ~~the~~ *The* marching band performed brilliantly.

This might be your preferred choice if you want to write tersely, with short sentences, perhaps to open an essay in a dramatic way. Maybe there is a connection between the two sentences; maybe there's not. Readers will want to keep going in order to find out.

CHANGE THE COMMA TO A SEMICOLON

Another simple way to edit a comma splice is to insert a semicolon (;) between the two clauses.

▶ It was the coldest day in fifty years; the marching band performed brilliantly.

The semicolon lets readers know that there is a definite connection between the weather and the band's brilliant performance, but they can't be certain what it is. The sentence is now correct, if not terribly interesting. You can make the connection clearer and even make the sentence more interesting by adding a **TRANSITION** (*nevertheless, still, in any event*; check the Glossary / Index for more examples).

▶ It was the coldest day in fifty years; *nevertheless,* the marching band performed brilliantly.

ADD A COORDINATING CONJUNCTION

You can also insert a **COORDINATING CONJUNCTION** (*and, but, or, nor, so, for,* or *yet*) after the comma between the two clauses.

▶ It was the coldest day in fifty years, *but* the marching band performed brilliantly.

With this option, the two clauses are separated clearly, and the word *but* indicates that the band played brilliantly in spite of the cold weather.

ADD A SUBORDINATING WORD

Another way to show a relationship between the two clauses is with a **SUBORDINATING WORD** (*while, however, thus*; see p. 699 for more examples).

▶ *Although it*
It was the coldest day in fifty years, the marching band performed brilliantly.

Here, the logical relationship between the two clauses is clear and explicit, and the band's performance becomes the important part of the sentence. But what if you wanted to suggest that the cold weather was responsible for the band playing so well? You could use the same clauses, but with a different subordinating word, as in the example below.

▶ *Possibly because it*
It was the coldest day in fifty years, the marching band performed brilliantly.

You may also want to experiment with changing the order of the clauses; in many cases, that will cause the emphasis to change. Sometimes, too, changing the order will help you transition to the next sentence.

▶ *The marching band performed brilliantly, even though it*
It was the coldest day in fifty years, the marching band performed brilliantly.
Fans huddled together under blankets in the stands.

Edit

Consider the following example:

> Transit officials estimate that the new light-rail line will be 20 percent faster than the express bus, the train will cost $1.85 per ride regardless of distance traveled.

Try editing this comma splice in two ways: one that emphasizes the speed of the train and another that emphasizes the cost.

↪ For more practice, complete the InQuizitive activity on **comma splices**.

Fused Sentences

A fused sentence looks like a complete sentence at first glance because it begins with a capital letter, concludes with end punctuation, and contains two **MAIN CLAUSES**. The reason it is problematic is that there is no explicit connection between the two clauses. A fused sentence will make sense to readers most of the time, but most of the time isn't quite often enough, and you don't want your readers to struggle to understand what you're saying. A sentence can contain more than one main clause, no problem, but if it does, there needs to be some signal indicating how the clauses relate to one another. That signal could be a punctuation mark, a word that shows how the clauses are related, or both.

Checking for fused sentences

To check your text for fused sentences, look at each sentence one by one and identify any that have more than one **MAIN CLAUSE**. Then see how the clauses are connected: is there a word or punctuation mark that indicates how they relate? If not, you've got a fused sentence.

Editing fused sentences

Let's look at a typical fused sentence and some ways it can be edited.

▶ The fire alarm went off the senator spilled her latte all over her desk.

Perfectly clear, right? Or did you have to read it twice to make sure? This example is a fused sentence because it contains two main clauses but offers no way of knowing where one stops and the next begins, and no indication of how the clauses relate to one another. Here are some options for editing this fused sentence.

ADD A PERIOD

One option is to make the fused sentence into two separate sentences by inserting a period after the first independent clause and capitalizing the first letter of the following clause.

▶ The fire alarm went off. ~~the~~ **The** senator spilled her latte all over her desk.

Now you have two complete sentences, but they are a little dry and lifeless. Readers may think the two events have nothing to do with one another, or they may think some explanation is missing. In some cases, you may want to choose this solution—if you are merely reporting what happened, for example—but it might not be the best one for this example.

ADD A SEMICOLON

Another option is to insert a semicolon (;) between the two clauses.

▶ The fire alarm went off; the senator spilled her latte all over her desk.

This is another simple way to deal with a fused sentence, although it still doesn't help readers know *how* the two clauses relate. The relationship between the clauses is fairly clear here, but that won't always be the case, so make sure the logical connection between the two clauses is very obvious before you use a semicolon. You can also add a **TRANSITION** (*nevertheless, still, in any event*; see the Glossary/Index for more examples) after the semicolon to make the relationship between the two clauses more explicit.

▶ The fire alarm went off; *as a result,* the senator spilled her latte all over her desk.

ADD A COMMA AND A COORDINATING CONJUNCTION

In order to clarify the relationship between the clauses a little more, you could insert a comma and a **COORDINATING CONJUNCTION** (*and, but, or, nor, so, for,* or *yet*) between the two clauses.

▶ The fire alarm went off, *and* the senator spilled her latte all over her desk.

Here the division between the two clauses is clearly marked, and readers will generally understand that the latte spilled right after (and the spill was possibly caused by) the fire alarm. With this solution, both clauses have equal importance.

ADD A SUBORDINATING WORD

One of the clearest ways to show the relationship between two clauses is by using a **SUBORDINATING WORD** (see p. 699 for more examples).

▶ *When the* ~~The~~ fire alarm went off, the senator spilled her latte all over her desk.

Adding the subordinating word *when* to the first clause makes it clear that the fire alarm caused the senator to spill her latte and also puts emphasis on the spilled coffee. Note that you need to add a comma after the introductory clause. You can also change the order of the two clauses; see how the emphasis changes slightly. Note, too, that in this case, you should not add a comma.

▶ The senator spilled her latte all over her desk *when* the fire alarm went off.

Edit

Using the editing options explained above, edit the following fused sentence in two different ways. Make one of your solutions short and snappy.

In the other solution, show that the banging and the shouting were happening at the same time.

> The moderator banged his gavel the candidates continued to shout at each other.

➤ For more practice, complete the InQuizitive activity on **fused sentences**.

Mixed Constructions

A **MIXED CONSTRUCTION** is a sentence that starts out with one structure and ends up with another one. Such a sentence may be understandable, but more often it leaves readers scratching their heads in confusion. There are many different ways to end up with a mixed construction, and this fact alone makes it difficult to identify one. Here is an example of one common type of mixed construction:

> ▶ Décollage is when you take away pieces of an image to create a new image.

The sentence is clear enough, but look again at the word *when*. That word locates an event in time—*I'll call* when *I get there. The baby woke up* when *the phone rang.* When *the armistice was signed, people everywhere cheered.* In the example above, there is no time associated with décollage; the sentence is simply describing the process. To edit the sentence, replace *when* with a more appropriate word, and adjust the rest of the sentence as needed.

> ▶ Décollage is ~~when you take~~ *the technique of taking* away pieces of an image to create a new image.

Checking for mixed constructions
Let's consider another example:

> ▶ Nutritionists disagree about the riskiness of eating raw eggs and also more healthful compared with cooked ones.

What? It's hard to even know where to start. Let's begin by identifying the **VERB(S)**. There's only one verb here, *disagree*. Next, let's identify the **SUBJECT**. Who disagrees? *Nutritionists*. Now we have a subject and a verb. What do nutritionists disagree about? It's clear enough that they disagree about *the riskiness of eating raw eggs*, but after that, it gets confusing. Consider the next words: *and also*. Also what? Do nutritionists also disagree that raw eggs are more nutritious than cooked eggs? Or is the writer claiming that raw eggs *are* more healthful? It's impossible to tell, which suggests that we have a mixed construction.

Editing mixed constructions
Let's look at a couple of ways we might edit the sentence about raw eggs. Here's one way:

▶ Nutritionists disagree about the riskiness of eating raw eggs and also ~~more healthful~~ *about their healthfulness* compared with cooked ones.

Notice that we added another *about*, which makes it clear that what follows is also something nutritionists disagree about. We also added the suffix *–ness* to *healthful* so that the word would be parallel to *riskiness*. Now the verb *disagree* applies to both *riskiness* and *healthfulness*: nutritionists disagree about the riskiness of eating raw eggs, and they also disagree about the healthfulness of raw eggs compared with cooked ones.

   What if the writer's original intention was to claim that raw eggs are more healthful than cooked ones? Since the two parts of the sentence express two different ideas, an editor might choose to simply make the mixed construction into two separate sentences.

▶ Nutritionists disagree about the riskiness of eating raw eggs. ~~and also~~ *Raw eggs are* more healthful *than* ~~compared with~~ cooked ones.

Just considering sentence structure, now we have two good sentences, but even though they both focus on raw eggs, the two sentences are not clearly connected. And besides, who is saying that eating raw eggs is more healthful? The author or the nutritionists? Adding just a couple of words links the sentences together and helps readers follow the ideas.

▶ Nutritionists disagree about the riskiness of eating raw eggs. *Some claim raw* ~~Raw~~ eggs are more healthful than cooked ones.

Here we've added a new subject, *some* (which refers to nutritionists), and we've also given the second sentence a verb, *claim*. Now the two sentences have a logical sequence and are easier to read. Next, let's look at one other mixed construction:

> ▶ Because air accumulates under the eggshell is why an egg stands up underwater.

This sentence is more or less clear, but its parts don't fit together properly. What can we do about that? Same procedure as before—first, look for the verbs. This time, it's more complicated because there are three: *accumulates, is,* and *stands up.* Next, we look for the subject of each of the verbs. The first one is easy—*air* accumulates; the subject is *air.* The third one is also simple—*an egg* stands up; the subject is *an egg.* But what is the subject of *is?* That's not such an easy question with this sentence because its structure changes in the middle. So let's try a different approach.

What exactly is this sentence trying to say? It's clear that the point of this sentence is to explain why a submerged egg stands up, and we have two clauses: one that tells us that *an egg stands up underwater* and another that tells us that the egg stands up *because air accumulates under the eggshell.* Now we just have to put them together in an appropriate way.

> ▶ Because air accumulates under the eggshell, ~~is why~~ an egg stands up underwater.

Did you notice that this version is almost exactly the same as the original sentence? The main difference is the words *is why*—which turn out not to be necessary. We now have one **MAIN CLAUSE** (*an egg stands up underwater*) and one **SUBORDINATE CLAUSE** (*because air accumulates under the eggshell*), with a comma in between. If it sounds better to you, you can reverse the order of the clauses, and the meaning stays the same. Note that you should not use a comma with this option.

> ▶ An egg stands up underwater because air accumulates under the eggshell.

We can use the same approach for a sentence that starts with a prepositional phrase but changes its structure in the middle: figure out what the sentence is trying to say, identify the phrases and clauses, and edit as needed so that you can put them together in an appropriate way.

> *Parents*
> ▶ ~~For parents~~ of children with a peanut allergy depend on rules that prohibit
>   ^
> nuts in school.

Edit
Try editing the following mixed construction in two ways. First, make one sentence that includes all of the information in the example. Next, present the same information in two separate sentences. Which way do you like better? Why?

> One or two months before mating, male and female eagles together build their nests can be four or five feet in diameter.

▶ For more practice, complete the InQuizitive activity on **mixed constructions**.

EDITING PRONOUNS

Pronouns are some of the smallest words in the language, so you might think they should be among the easiest. Well, no, they're often not. But the good news is that editing your work to make sure all your pronouns are used appropriately is not too complicated. The advise that follows gives you tools for editing three common pronoun issues: pronoun reference, pronoun-antecedent agreement, and pronoun case.

First, let's clarify the terms. **PRONOUNS**, as you probably know, are words that refer to other words or phrases (and occasionally even whole clauses). They're very useful precisely because they're small and they do a lot of work representing larger units. The words that they represent are their **ANTECEDENTS**. Most frequently, the antecedent is something or somebody that has already been mentioned, and English has very specific conventions for signaling to readers exactly what that antecedent is so that they won't be confused. We call that **PRONOUN REFERENCE**. Let's suppose this next example is the first sentence in a news report.

▶ The Procurement Committee meets today to review the submitted bids, and she will announce the winner tomorrow.

Wait. *She? She* who? It's not clear what *she* refers to, and readers are now lost.

Pronoun **AGREEMENT** is another important convention. Pronouns have to agree with their antecedents in number (*I, we*) and in some cases gender (*he, she, it*). *Mr. Klein misplaced her phone again.* If Mr. Klein is in the habit of losing a specific woman's phone, then perhaps the sentence makes sense. If it's his own phone that he misplaced again, then *her* doesn't agree with its antecedent, Mr. Klein, and readers will get confused.

PRONOUN CASE is a concept that you may never have encountered, but it's one that you use every day, probably appropriately and without giving it any thought. For example, you probably say *I bought ice cream* automatically—and are not likely to say *Me bought ice cream* or *Coach wants I to play shortstop.* Those two pronouns—*I* and *me*—refer to the same person, but they're not interchangeable. Still, most of the time we automatically choose the appropriate one for the specific context.

Pronoun Reference

Unclear pronoun reference occurs when readers can't be certain what a **PRONOUN** refers to. Usually this confusion arises when there are several possibilities in the same sentence (or sometimes in the previous sentence). Here's an example: *Andrew and Glen competed fiercely for the office of treasurer, but in the end, he won handily.* If Andrew and Glen are both men, the pronoun *he* could refer to either one of them, so who was it that won? We don't know.

Checking for unclear pronoun reference
To check for unclear pronoun reference, you need to first identify each pronoun and then make sure that it points very clearly to its **ANTECEDENT**. Often, the meanings of the words provide clues about what the pronoun refers to—but not always. Let's look at three sentences that have very similar structures.

▶ My grandparents ordered pancakes because *they* weren't very hungry.

First, we identify the pronouns: *my* and *they. My* clearly refers to the writer, but what about *they?* Although both *pancakes* and *grandparents* are possible antecedents for *they,* we know that the pronoun here has to refer to grandparents because pancakes don't get hungry. Now let's look at another sentence:

▶ My grandparents ordered pancakes because *they* weren't very expensive.

This sentence is almost identical to the first one and has the same pronoun, *they,* but this time, the antecedent has to be *pancakes* because there is no price on grandparents. Sorry to say, though, that antecedents aren't always so obvious. For example:

▶ My grandparents like playing cards with their neighbors because *they* aren't very competitive.

Wait. Who's not very competitive here? The grandparents or the neighbors? Or maybe all of them? We really can't be sure.

Editing unclear pronoun reference
Let's look again at the last example:

▶ My grandparents like playing cards with their neighbors because they aren't very competitive.

To edit this sentence, our best option may be to change the structure, and there are several possibilities:

▶ My grandparents like playing cards with their neighbors, ~~because they~~ *who* aren't very competitive.

This option makes clear that the neighbors are the ones who aren't very competitive.

▶ My grandparents, *who aren't very competitive,* like playing cards with their neighbors, *who are also not too* ~~because they aren't very~~ competitive.

Now we know that everybody mentioned here is noncompetitive. You may not think the sentence sounds as good as the original, but at least the meaning is clear. And of course there are usually other options.

The most important objective is to make clear what word or words each pronoun refers to. You don't want to leave your readers guessing. Here is one more example:

▶ After months of posturing and debate, those planning the expensive new football stadium suspended the project, which students loudly celebrated.

What is the antecedent for *which* in this example? You probably interpret this sentence to say that the students celebrated the suspension of the plans to build the stadium, but in fact, that's not really clearly established in the sentence. Another plausible interpretation is that the students celebrated the building of the stadium. Let's reword the sentence and remove *which* in order to make the meaning perfectly clear.

> ▶ After months of posturing and debate, those planning the expensive
>
>   *and*
>   new football stadium suspended the project, ~~which~~ students loudly
>
>   *the news*
>   celebrated.

Edit
The following sentence uses the words *it* and *which* to refer to . . . well, it's not exactly clear what they refer to.

> A temperature inversion happens when a layer of warmer air is positioned above a layer of cooler air, which is not how it usually occurs.

You have several options here that would make this sentence better, but try this one: rewrite the sentence to eliminate the need for any pronoun at all.

➦ For more practice, complete the InQuizitive activity on **unclear pronoun references**.

Pronoun-Antecedent Agreement

Pronoun-antecedent agreement means that every **PRONOUN** has to agree with its **ANTECEDENT** in gender (*he, she, it*) and number (singular or plural). Some sentences with pronouns that don't agree with their antecedents are relatively easy to understand, and usually readers can figure the meanings out, but they shouldn't have to do that extra work. For your academic writing, you need to make sure that all of your pronouns agree with their antecedents.

Checking for pronoun-antecedent agreement
To check for pronoun-antecedent agreement, you need to first identify the pronouns and their antecedents. Then you need to make sure each pronoun agrees with its antecedent in gender and number. Let's look at a couple of examples:

▶ Trombones might be very loud, but it was drowned out last night by the cheering of the crowd.

This sentence has only one pronoun: *it*. *Trombones* is the only noun that precedes *it*, so *trombones* has to be the antecedent. Do they agree? We don't have to think about gender in this example, but we do have to think about number. And that's a problem, because the numbers don't match: *trombones* is plural, but *it* is singular.

▶ The table is wobbly because one of her legs is shorter than the others.

In some languages, tables, chairs, and other inanimate objects have grammatical gender, but in English, they don't. The legs of a table are never referred to with masculine or feminine gender.

Editing for pronoun-antecedent agreement
In order to fix the trombone sentence, you can change either the antecedent or the pronoun to make them agree in number. In this case, it is clear that the first **CLAUSE** refers to trombones in general, and the second clause refers to a specific trombone at a specific event. Assuming that the more important part is the specific event, and that there was only one trombone, let's change the word *trombones* from plural to singular. We can do that easily in this case without really changing the meaning, although sometimes it might be more difficult to do so.

▶ ~~Trombones~~ *The trombone* might be very loud, but it was drowned out last night by the cheering of the crowd.

Both the pronoun and its antecedent are now singular; that is, they agree in number. Now let's consider several examples where gender is a factor. In the example about the table legs, we simply have to replace the feminine pronoun with the inanimate one.

▶ The table is wobbly because one of ~~her~~ *its* legs is shorter than the others.

Remember that the gender of English pronouns matters only with *he, him, his; she, her, hers; it, its.* No other English pronouns specify gender. Some languages have more gender-specific pronouns, and some languages have fewer, but let's just stick to English right now.

▶ My mom and dad have an arrangement about sausage pizza—
he picks off the sausage, and *she* eats *it*.

This sentence has three pronouns—*he, she*, and *it*—and it's quite evident that *he* refers to *dad*, *she* refers to *mom*, and *it* refers to *sausage*. All the antecedents are clear. But what if we changed the cast of characters in the sentence to two men? It would be confusing to refer to each of them as *he*, so we need a different strategy. One possibility is to use *he* to represent one of the men and to refer to the other man by name. Will that work?

▶ Paul and *his* brother have an arrangement about sausage pizza—Paul picks
off the sausage, and *he* eats it.

Who eats the sausage? Paul or his brother? It's still not clear. In this case, our best option is to eliminate the pronoun and refer to both men explicitly both times.

▶ Paul and *his* brother have an arrangement about sausage pizza—
Paul picks off the sausage, and ~~he~~ *his brother* eats it.

If you'd rather not repeat both phrases, and the arrangement itself is more important than which person eats all the sausage, you can try this option:

▶ Paul and *his* brother have an arrangement about sausage pizza—
~~Paul~~ *one of them* picks off the sausage, and ~~he~~ *the other one* eats it.

Now we've got it; everything is clear. As this last edit shows, making pronouns and antecedents agree sometimes requires reworking the structure of a sentence and occasionally even modifying what it says. Pronouns may be small words, but getting them right is hugely important; don't be afraid to make changes in your writing.

Now let's look at some other contexts where making pronouns agree in gender with their antecedents can be complicated. We'll start with one that's pretty straightforward.

▶ Trey noticed a sunflower growing along the path; *he* grabbed *his* phone and took a picture of *it*.

We know that Trey is a man or a boy—*he, his*—and the flower, of course, is inanimate—*it*. In academic writing, inanimate objects are always referred to as *it*, even though in casual speech, we may use gendered pronouns to refer to things such as cars, boats (almost always *she*), and others. What about animals? If you know the sex of an animal, then by all means, refer to it as *he* or *she*. If you don't know the sex, or if the sex isn't pertinent, just use *it*. Also, it is becoming more common for people to specify (or ask one another about) their pronouns—in person, in email signatures, in social media bios—a practice that is in response to increasing flexibility about gender identity. Some individuals opt to be referred to as *they*, a usage that transforms *they* from its conventional usage as plural to a singular pronoun of unspecified gender. Other people may use other pronouns, such as *ze/hir/hirs*. We recommend that, whenever possible, you use individuals' specified pronouns in your writing about them. And what if you're writing about a person whose sex or gender you don't know? That happens, and that's when it can get complicated. For example:

▶ Anyone who gets three speeding tickets in a year will lose *his* license.

What's wrong with this example? Plenty, unless only men have such a license. If what you are writing applies to both women and men, your pronouns should reflect that reality. One of the easiest solutions is to use plural nouns and pronouns because they do not specify gender:

▶ ~~Anyone~~ who ~~gets~~ three speeding tickets in a year will lose ~~his license~~.
  Drivers ^   *get* ^   *their licenses* ^

You may need to tinker a bit with the structure, but the message can remain the same. Another option is to revise the sentence altogether. Here's one possibility:

▶ Getting three speeding tickets in a year will result in the driver's license being revoked.

Another possible solution is to write *his* or *her*:

▶ Anyone who gets three speeding tickets in a year will lose ~~his~~ license.
                                                            his or her ^

This last solution is fine, although if you have many such instances close together, the writing can start to feel awkward. Another possibility is to employ **SINGULAR THEY**, using *they*, *them*, *their*, or *theirs* with a singular antecedent.

▶ Anyone who gets three speeding tickets in a year will lose ~~his~~ license.
                                                            their ^

Many of us use singular *they* this way in casual speech, and its use is becoming more and more accepted in some newspapers and magazines and other more formal contexts. Singular *they* is a very useful solution, but even though it's becoming ever more common, it's still not always accepted in academic writing. Before you use it in your class work, you might check with your instructor to be sure it will be acceptable in their class.

Edit
Edit the following sentence in two ways. First, make both the pronoun and its antecedent singular; second, make the pronoun and antecedent plural. Both ways are acceptable, but which way sounds better to you?

> Applicants must file the forms before the deadline and make sure that it's filled out correctly.

↪ For more practice, complete the InQuizitive activity on **pronoun antecedent agreement**.

Pronoun Case

Pronoun **CASE** refers to the different forms a **PRONOUN** takes in order to indicate how it functions in a sentence. English pronouns have three cases: subject, object, and possessive. Most of the time, we choose the appropriate pronouns automatically, as in the following sentence:

▶ *I* texted *her*, and *she* texted *me*, but *we* didn't see *our* messages.

This sentence involves two people and six distinct pronouns. *I* and *me* refer to one person (the writer), *she* and *her* refer to the other person, and *we* and *our* refer to both people. Each of the three pronoun pairs has a distinct role in the sentence. *I*, *she*, and *we* are all subjects; *me* and *her* are objects; and *our* is possessive.

Checking for correct pronoun case
You would probably not ever say *Me saw her* because it wouldn't sound right. In casual speech, though, you might hear (or say) *Me and Bob saw her*. While you might hear or say that in informal conversation, it would not be acceptable in academic writing. Here is a simple and reliable technique for

checking your work for case: check for compound subjects like *me and Bob* and cover up everything in the phrase but the pronoun. Read it out loud.

▶ Me ~~and Bob~~ saw her.

Does it sound good to you? Hope not. So how do you change it? Read on.

Editing for pronoun case
To edit for pronoun case, the first step is to identify the pronouns in each sentence. The following example has only one, *us*:

▶ Us first-year students are petitioning for a schedule change.

Remember that the way a pronoun functions in a sentence is the key and that there are three possibilities for case. Is *us* functioning as subject, object, or possessive? In order to answer that question, first we need to identify the verb: *are petitioning*. The subject tells us who (or what) is petitioning—in this sentence, *us first-year students*. If you're not sure if *us* is correct, try it by itself, without *first-year students*.

▶ Us are petitioning for a schedule change.

▶ ~~Us~~ ^We^ are petitioning for a schedule change.

We changed *us* to *we* here because it's the subject of the sentence and thus needs to be in the subject case. For more advice on choosing the correct case, see the table below. Now let's look at two more examples: *Pat dated Cody longer than me. Pat dated Cody longer than I.* The only difference between the two sentences is the case of the pronoun, but that little word gives the sentences totally different meanings because the case lets readers know whether the person—*I* or *me*—is the subject or the object of the verb.

▶ Pat dated Cody longer than me.

Look carefully. There's only one verb, *dated*, and its subject is *Pat*. Now notice the pronoun: *me*. That's object case, right? So, according to the example, Pat dated Cody and also dated *me*. Try the next one.

▶ Pat dated Cody longer than I.

Here the pronoun is in subject case: *I*. Even though it's not followed by a verb, the pronoun tells us that Pat dated Cody and so did I.

Subject	Object	Possessive
I	me	my/mine
we	us	our/ours
you	you	your/yours
he/she/it	him/her/it	his/her/hers/its
they	them	their/theirs
who/whoever	whom/whomever	whose

Edit

Use the technique explained in this section to edit the following sentence for pronoun case.

> Iris was unhappy, but the judges called a tie and gave the award to she and Lu.

➡ For more practice, complete the InQuizitive activity on **pronoun case**.

EDITING VERBS

Verbs. Are any words more important—or hardworking? Besides specifying actions (*hop, skip, jump*) or states of being (*be, seem*), verbs provide most of the information about *when* (happening now? already happened? might happen? usually happens?), and they also have to link very explicitly to their subjects. That's a lot of work!

Because verbs are so important, verb problems are often easily noticed by readers, and once readers notice a verb problem in your work, they may question your competence as a writer. But if your readers can catch these problems, so can you. The following advice will help you edit your work for two of the most troublesome verb problems: subject-verb agreement and shifts in tense.

Subject-Verb Agreement

In English, every **VERB** has to agree with its **SUBJECT** in number and person. That may sound complicated, but it's really only third-person singular subjects—*runner, shoe, he, she, it*—that you have to look out for, and even then, only when the verb is in the simple present tense. Still, the third-person present tense is the most common construction in academic writing, so it matters. Take a look at this example:

▶ First the coach enters, then you enter, and then all of the other players enter.

The verb *enter* occurs three times in that sentence, but notice that when its subject is third-person singular—*coach*—an *-s* follows the base form of the verb, *enter*. In the other two cases, the verb has no such ending. What's so complicated about that? Well, there are two kinds of subjects that cause problems: indefinite pronouns, such as *everyone* and *many*, which may require a singular or plural verb even if their meaning suggests otherwise; and subjects consisting of more than one word, in which the word that has to agree with the verb may be hidden among other words.

Checking for subject-verb agreement

To check for subject-verb agreement, first identify the subjects and their verbs, paying careful attention to **INDEFINITE PRONOUNS** and subjects with more than one word. Then, check to make sure that every subject matches its verb in number and person.

Editing for subject-verb agreement

Let's look at a few common mistakes and see what we can do about them.

INDEFINITE PRONOUNS

Indefinite pronouns are words like *anyone, each, everything,* and *nobody.* When they're used as a subject, they have to agree with the verb. Sometimes that's tricky. For example:

▶ First the coach enters, then you enter, and then each of the other players enter.

We know that the subject of the first clause is *coach* and the subject of the second clause is *you*, but what about the third clause? Is the subject *each*? Or is it *players*? You might be tempted to choose *players* because that's the word closest to the verb *enter*, but that's not correct; the subject is *each*, an indefinite pronoun.

▶ First the coach enters, then you enter, and then each of the other
             enters
   players ~~enter~~.

That *-s* at the end of *enters* is necessary because the **SIMPLE SUBJECT** of the final clause is *each*, which is singular. The phrase *of the other players* is additional information. Now see what happens if we change *each* to *all*:

▶ First the coach enters, then you enter, and then ~~each~~ of the other players ~~enters~~.

(*all* written above *each*; *enter* written above *enters*)

Even though the two phrases—*each of the other players* and *all of the other players*—have essentially the same meaning, the word *each* refers to the members of a group individually so it is always singular and requires the verb to have the *-s* ending. *All* is plural here because it refers to a plural noun, *players*. However, *all* is singular when it refers to a singular noun.

▶ *All* of the strawberries *were picked* today.

▶ *All* of the rhubarb *was picked* yesterday.

In the first sentence, *all* refers to *strawberries* all together, in plural form, while in the second sentence, *all* refers to *rhubarb*, a **NONCOUNT NOUN**, which requires the singular form of the verb. **INDEFINITE PRONOUNS** can be tricky. Most take a singular verb, even if they seem plural or refer to plural nouns. These include *anyone, anything, each, either, everyone, everything, neither, nobody, no one, one, somebody, someone,* and *something*. A few indefinite pronouns are always plural: *both, few, many, others,* and *several*. Some take a singular verb when they refer to a singular or noncount noun, but they take a plural verb when referring to a plural noun. These are *all, any, enough, more, most, none,* and *some*.

SUBJECTS CONSISTING OF MORE THAN ONE WORD

Sometimes a sentence has a subject with more than one word, so you need to determine which of the words is the one that the verb has to agree with and which words simply provide extra information. To do that, pull the subject apart to find which word is the essential one. Let's practice with this sentence:

▶ The guy with the mirrored sunglasses run in this park every morning.

The **COMPLETE SUBJECT** is *the guy with the mirrored sunglasses,* but who is it that does the running? It's the guy, and the fact that he has mirrored sunglasses is simply extra information. You could remove the phrase *with the mirrored sunglasses* and still have a complete sentence—it might not be very informative, but it's not incorrect.

To check for subject-verb agreement when a subject has more than one word, first locate the verb and then the complete subject. Then check each word in the subject until you find the one keyword that determines the form of the verb. Since the **SIMPLE SUBJECT** here—*guy*—is in the third-person singular, and the verb is in the present tense, the verb should also be in the third-person singular:

▶   The guy with the mirrored sunglasses ~~run~~ *runs* in this park every morning.

Let's try one more problem sentence:

▶   The neighbor across the hall from the Fudds always sign for their packages.

First, find the verb: *sign*. The complete subject is *the neighbor across the hall from the Fudds*. What part of that subject indicates who does the signing? *Neighbor*. Everything else is extra. Since it's just one *neighbor*, the subject is singular, and since a third-person singular subject requires a present tense verb to have an *-s* ending, the edited sentence will be:

▶   The neighbor across the hall from the Fudds always ~~sign~~ *signs* for their packages.

Edit

The sentence below has four subjects and four verbs. One (or more) of the subjects is singular, so its verb should have an *-s* ending. Edit and make any necessary changes.

> All of the boxes need to be stacked neatly, and every box need to be labeled; the red box with the taped edges fit on top, and each of the boxes need its own lid.

In casual speech, you may not use the *-s* ending, or it may be hard to hear, so you may not be able to rely on your ear alone to edit this sentence.

➡   For more practice, complete the InQuizitive activity on **subject-verb agreement**.

Shifts in Tense

We live in the present moment; our ideas and our feelings are happening right now. Often, though, our present thoughts—and comments—are responses to things that happened in the past or that haven't happened yet. In conversation, we usually shift our verb tenses smoothly and automatically to account for actions that take place at different times, as in the following example of something you might hear or say:

▶ Flor *is* upset because Justin *informed* her that he *will not be able to come* to her graduation.

In writing, however, we need to take extra care to ensure that our tenses are clear, consistent, and appropriate to what we're describing. In contrast to face-to-face conversation—in which tone of voice, facial expressions, and hand gestures help create meaning—writing has to rely on carefully chosen words. Verb tenses work hard to put complex sequences of events into appropriate context. The previous example has three clauses, each in a different tense: Flor *is* upset (right now); because Justin *informed* her (in the past); that he *will not be able to come* (to an event in the future).

Checking for shifts in tense

In academic writing, you'll often need to discuss what other authors have written, and the different disciplines have different conventions and rules for doing that (see p. 552). In classes that require you to use MLA style, for example, you'll rely heavily on the simple present tense:

MLA   Morton argues that even though Allende's characters are not realistic, they're believable.

Notice how *argues, are not*, and *they're* all use the simple present tense even though Morton's article and Allende's novel were both written in the past. If you mention the date when something was written, however, the verb should be in the past tense. In contrast, disciplines that follow APA style require that references to published sources and research results be stated in the past tense or present perfect tense:

APA   Azele reported that 59% of the control group subjects showed high gamma levels.

Notice here that the two verbs in the sentence—*reported* and *showed*—are both in the past tense because both Azele's research and the report were done in the past. Be careful, though, because your sources may be writing about current or future conditions. If that's the case, be sure to preserve the tense of the original in your work, as the following example does.

APA   Donnerstag and Jueves predicted that another Jovian moon will soon be discovered.

Regardless of what class you're writing for, however, the most important thing about verb tenses is consistency—unless you have a reason to shift tense.

Editing confusing shifts in tense

Much of the editing that you do calls for sentence-by-sentence work, but checking for confusing shifts in tense often requires that you consider several sentences together.

 Starting at the beginning, mark every **MAIN VERB**, along with any **HELPING VERBS**, in every sentence (remembering that there may be more than one clause in each sentence). Don't make any changes yet; just mark the verbs. Next, go back to the beginning and notice what tense you used each time. Examine each tense one by one, and when you notice a shift to a different tense, read carefully what you have written and look for a reason for the shift. If you can explain why the shift makes sense, leave it alone. Then move on to the next verb. Is it in the original tense or the new tense? Can you explain why? Continue all the way through your text, examining every verb tense and making sure that any shifts you find can be explained. Let's practice with two examples:

▶ Bates underestimated the public when she writes disparagingly about voters' intelligence.

First, we mark the verbs—*underestimated*, *writes*—and we notice that the first is in past tense while the second is in present. Is there a clear explanation for the shift? No, not really. If you are using **MLA** style, you'll want to put both verbs in the present: *underestimates* and *writes*. In **APA** style, past tense is more appropriate for both: *underestimated* and *wrote*. In any case, there is no reason to use two different tenses in the sentence. Here is another example, this time a little more complicated:

▶ All of the guests ate the stew, but only two showed symptoms of food poisoning.

It's true that the events (*ate, showed*) in both clauses of the example occurred in the past, but can we be certain that the symptoms were a result of eating the stew? Could the guests have had the symptoms already? The sentence isn't really clear.

▶ All of the guests ~~ate~~ ^had eaten^ the stew, but only two showed symptoms of food poisoning.

By changing the verb tense in the first clause to the past perfect (the tense used to indicate that an action was completed before another action in the past began), we show clearly that the stew was eaten before the food poisoning occurred. (We may never know what caused the illness, but at least we know the sequence of events.)

Edit

Edit the following sentence to eliminate any confusing shifts in tense. Assume that the writing has to follow **APA** format for verb tenses.

> Levi (2013) notes that the trade deficit decreases from 2005 to 2015, but he warns that the improvement may be reversed because the new treaty will go into effect in 2020.

 For more practice, complete the InQuizitive activity on **verb tense**.

EDITING QUOTATIONS

In academic writing, you are required not only to express your own ideas, but also to incorporate the ideas of other authors. In a way, you are engaging in a conversation with your sources, whether you draw from Aristotle, Toni Morrison, or a classmate. Your success as a writer has a lot to do with how well you weave your sources' ideas in with your own without your readers ever having to wonder who said what. Editing your work for citation and documentation issues therefore involves two main tasks:

- incorporating any words of others that you quote into your text so that everything flows smoothly

- making sure the punctuation, capitalization, and other such elements are correct

The conventions for citing and documenting sources in academic writing are very precise—every period, every comma, every quotation mark has its job to do, and they must be in exactly the right place.

Incorporating Quotations

Whenever we quote something someone else has said, we need to structure the sentences that contain the quoted material so that they read as smoothly as any other sentence. As writers, we need to master our use of language in much the same way that musicians have to master their instruments, and in both cases, it's not easy. Just as musicians playing together in an orchestra (or a garage band) have to coordinate with one another in tempo, key, and melody, you have to make sure that your words and those of others that you quote fit together smoothly.

Checking to see that quotations are incorporated smoothly
One good way to begin checking a draft to see how well any quotations have been incorporated is to read it aloud, or better yet, get someone else to read it aloud to you. If the reader (you or someone else) stumbles over a passage and has to go back and read the sentence again, you can be fairly certain that some changes are necessary. We can practice with some sentences that quote the following passage from a 2013 *Atlantic* article about fast food:

> Introduced in 1991, the McLean Deluxe was perhaps the boldest single effort the food industry has ever undertaken to shift the masses to healthier eating.
>
> —DAVID FREEDMAN, "How Junk Food Can End Obesity"

Assume that you might not want or need to quote the entire passage, so you incorporate just one part of Freedman's sentence into one of your sentences, as follows:

► Freedman refers to a failed McDonald's menu item "the McLean Deluxe was perhaps the food industry's boldest single effort to shift the masses to healthier eating."

If you read the sentence aloud, you should be able to notice that it is awkwardly structured and even hard to understand. Also, do you notice that the quoted section doesn't exactly match the author's words? Some of the words from the original are missing and some others have been added. Changing an author's words in a quoted section is only allowed if the original meaning is not altered in any way. Also, you need to indicate to your readers that you've modified the author's words. Let's see how we can go about fixing these things.

Editing sentences that include quotations
There are two ways of smoothly incorporating quoted material. One strategy is to adjust your own words to accommodate the quoted material; another is to lightly modify the quoted material to fit your sentence. Here's one way we might edit our sentence by adjusting our own words:

> ▶ ~~Freedman refers~~ *Referring* to a failed McDonald's menu item, *Freedman notes that* "the McLean Deluxe was perhaps the food industry's boldest single effort to shift the masses to healthier eating."

Let's look at what we did. First, we changed the first two words. The meaning didn't change; only the structure did. Then, we added a **SIGNAL PHRASE** (*Freedman notes that*) to introduce the quoted words.

So far so good. But what about the places where we changed the author's words? If you modify an author's words, you need to signal to your readers what changes you've made, and there are precise conventions for doing that.

Enclose anything you add or change within the quotation itself in square brackets ([ ]), and insert ellipses (. . .) to show where any content from the original has been omitted.

> ▶ Referring to a failed McDonald's menu item, Freedman notes that "the McLean Deluxe was perhaps the [food industry's] boldest single effort . . . to shift the masses to healthier eating."

With minimal changes, the sentence now has all the necessary parts and reads smoothly. Note the two things we've done to modify the quotation. We've enclosed the words we added—*food industry's*—in square brackets, and we've inserted ellipses in place of the six words that were omitted from Freedman's sentence. It's worth repeating here that it is only permissible to add or delete words if the meaning of the quotation isn't substantially altered.

Edit

Here is another sentence based on the Freedman passage:

> Freedman talks about an earlier effort the McLean Deluxe by McDonald's
> was perhaps the boldest try to shift the masses to healthier eating.

First, you'll have to make a few changes to help the sentence read smoothly. There are several ways to do that, but try to make as few changes as possible. Once the sentence reads smoothly, compare it with the original passage to see where you might need square brackets (for added material) or ellipses (to show where words have been removed). By the way, you don't have to put *McLean Deluxe* in quotation marks because it was not a term coined by Freedman.

➦ For more practice, complete the InQuizitive activity on **incorporating quotations**.

Punctuating Quotations

Citation conventions exist to help us clearly distinguish our words from the words of our sources, and one way we do that is by punctuating quotations carefully. When you quote someone's exact words, you need to attend to four elements: quotation marks, capitalization, commas, and end punctuation. These elements let your readers know which words are yours and which are the words of someone else.

Checking to see how any quoted material is punctuated

Here is another sentence taken from the *Atlantic* article about fast food; let's use it in a variety of ways in order to show how to capitalize and punctuate sentences that quote from this passage.

> A slew of start-ups are trying to find ways of producing fresh, local, unprocessed meals quickly and at lower cost.
> —DAVID FREEDMAN, "How Junk Food Can End Obesity"

You might write a sentence such as this one:

▶ It may one day be possible to get fast food that is healthy and affordable since a slew of start-ups are trying to find ways, according to David Freedman.

Structurally, the sentence is fine, but it includes a direct quotation from Freedman without letting readers know which words are his and which are yours. Even if you used Freedman's exact words accidentally, it would still be **PLAGIARISM**, which may carry a stiff penalty. The sentence needs to be edited.

Editing quotations to indicate who said what
There are numerous ways to edit the above sentence to make clear who said what. Here is one option:

> ▶ It may one day be possible to get fast food that is healthy and
> affordable. ~~since~~ slew of start-ups are trying to find ways/. ~~according~~
> *According to David Freedman,* "A ,"
> ~~to Freedman.~~

What changed? First, we added quotation marks to enclose Freedman's exact words. Second, we broke the sentence into two and started the second one with the signal phrase *According to Freedman*, followed by a comma. Third, we capitalized the first letter of the quotation. Since *A* was capitalized in the original quotation, no brackets are necessary. Finally, notice the period. The sentence ends with the quoted material, so the period goes inside the quotation marks. Now let's look at how you might go about editing another sentence.

> ▶ Freedman asserts that many new businesses are working to develop fresh, local, unprocessed meals quickly and at lower cost.

Check your four elements. First, insert any necessary quotation marks; make sure they enclose Freedman's exact words. Second, is any additional capitalization necessary? If so, capitalize the appropriate word(s). Third, if there's a **SIGNAL PHRASE** before the quoted material, does it need to be followed by a comma? Finally, make sure any end punctuation is in the right place. Try editing the sentence yourself before you look at the following revision.

> ▶ Freedman asserts that many new businesses are working to develop
> "fresh, local, unprocessed meals quickly and at lower cost."

The quoted portion is not a complete sentence, and we placed it in the middle of ours, so no capitalization was necessary. We didn't insert a comma because his words flow smoothly within the larger sentence. Since the sentence ends with the quoted material, we put the period inside the quotation marks.

Depending on the documentation style that you are using, you may need to provide parenthetical information at the end of any sentences that include quoted material. Some styles require that you name the author(s) if you haven't named them earlier in the sentence, along with the page number(s) where their words appeared. Here's how you would do so in MLA and APA style requirements.

MLA Freedman asserts that many new businesses are working to develop "fresh, local, unprocessed meals quickly and at lower cost" (82).

APA Freedman asserted that many new businesses are working to develop "fresh, local, unprocessed meals quickly and at lower cost" (2013, p. 82).

One more important point: notice that with parenthetical documentation, the final period of the sentence is no longer inside the quotation marks; it is after the parentheses.

Edit

The following sentences cite the passage from Freedman's essay; they need to be formatted properly in order to read smoothly and also to show more clearly which words are the writer's and which are Freedman's. Remember the four elements: quotation marks, capitalization, commas, and end punctuation.

> Healthy and affordable fast food may not be a reality yet, but we may not have too long to wait. As Freedman explains a slew of start-ups are trying to find ways to bring such meals to market.

It is possible to edit the sentence using only the four elements and not adding, subtracting, or changing any words. Try it.

➤ For more practice, complete the InQuizitive activity on **punctuating quotations.**

EDITING COMMAS

Ideas are made out of words, right? So why should we care about commas? Well, here's why—they help those words make more sense. Nobody wants to have to read the same sentence two or three times in order to get it. Well-placed commas can make your sentence clear and easy to read—and can keep the words (and ideas) correctly grouped together. Read this next sentence out loud:

> ▶ The boxer exhausted and pounded on wearily left the ring.

Did you start off expecting to read about the boxer's opponent who was getting "exhausted and pounded on"? Did you have to go back and start over? Bet you did. Well-placed commas would have immediately pointed us all in the right direction—like this:

> ▶ The boxer, exhausted and pounded on, wearily left the ring.

There are a lot of ways to err with commas. You might omit one that's necessary or place one where it doesn't belong. Even professional writers sometimes have trouble deciding where (and where not) to put a comma, and it's not always a big deal. The advice that follows won't make you a comma superstar, but it will show you how to edit your work for two of the comma problems that matter most to instructors and other readers: the commas that set off introductory information and the commas that distinguish between essential and nonessential information.

Introductory Information

English sentences generally begin with a **SUBJECT**. Without ever really thinking about it, those of us who read and write in English have an expectation that the first thing we read in a sentence will be its subject. Often, however (like right now), we begin a sentence in a different way. In academic writing especially, we might vary the structure of our sentences just to make our writing interesting. One way we vary our sentences is by starting some of them with introductory words, phrases, or even clauses. And usually we use a comma to set off those introductory words. That comma signals to readers that they haven't gotten to the subject yet; what they are seeing is additional information that is important enough to go first. For example:

▶ In Georgia, Lee's book jumped quickly to the top of the best-seller list.

Without the comma, readers might think the author's name was Georgia Lee, and they would get very lost in the sentence. Introductory words don't always cause so much confusion; in fact, some authors omit the comma if the introductory element is very short (one, two, or three words). Still, adding the comma after the introductory information is never wrong and demonstrates the care you take with your work.

Checking for commas after introductory information

▶ Initially the council proposed five miles of new bike paths; they later revised the proposal.

To check for introductory information, you should first identify the **VERB** —in this case, *proposed*. Now what's the subject? (In other words, who or what *proposed*?) The subject here is *the council*. Everything that goes before the subject is introductory information, so the comma goes between that information and the subject.

▶ Initially, the council proposed five miles of new bike paths; they later revised the proposal.

In the example above, the introductory element is only one word, and the comma could have been omitted, but its presence adds a little extra emphasis to the word *initially*, and in fact, that emphasis is probably why the author chose to put that word at the beginning, before the subject. The comma definitely helps. And sometimes, introductory elements can cause confusion:

▶ Tired and discouraged by the unsuccessful search for the fugitive Sgt. Drexler the detective and her squad returned to headquarters.

In this example, the introductory information is much longer, and without an appropriate comma, readers have no way of knowing if Sgt. Drexler is the name of the fugitive, the name of the detective, or someone else entirely. Let's imagine that Drexler is the fugitive. With one well-placed comma, the sentence is now perfectly clear.

▶ Tired and discouraged by the unsuccessful search for the fugitive Sgt. Drexler, the detective and her squad returned to headquarters.

Editing for commas after introductory information

Let's take a look at a few examples to see how we can figure out where to put commas with introductory elements. The following sentence needs a comma; where should it go?

▶ For the first three scoreless innings Clark struggled to stay awake.

How do you know where to put the comma? Let's follow the steps described in this chapter. First, identify the verb: *struggled*. Next, identify the subject—in other words, who or what struggled? The subject here is *Clark*, and everything that precedes it is introductory information.

▶ For the first three scoreless innings, Clark struggled to stay awake.
                                    ^

Here is one more example. Follow the same procedure to determine where to put the comma.

▶ In the chaotic final episode of season 2 the shocking plot twists left viewers breathless.

In this example, the comma should go after *2*; the verb in the sentence is *left*, and the **COMPLETE SUBJECT** is *the shocking plot twists*. Everything that goes before the subject is introductory information, so the comma falls between that information and the subject:

▶ In the chaotic final episode of season 2, the shocking plot twists left viewers breathless.
                                          ^

Edit

Try editing the following sentence by inserting a comma after the introductory information. Remember the technique: first, find the verb; second, find the subject. The comma goes before the subject because everything that precedes it is introductory information.

Behind the parade marshal and the color guard the sponsors' convertible carrying the Founders' Day Queen will proceed along Cunningham Street.

 For more practice, complete the InQuizitive activities on **commas**.

Essential and Nonessential Information

What do we mean by **ESSENTIAL** and **NONESSENTIAL** information? The simplest way to explain the difference is with examples.

▶ My sister Jamilah graduates on Saturday.

If the writer has more than one sister, the name *Jamilah* tells us which one; that's important to know because we don't want to congratulate the wrong sister. Therefore, her name is essential information. When the information is essential, it should not be set off with commas. But if the writer has only one sister, writing her name there is simply extra information; it's not essential. When the information is nonessential, we set it off with commas:

▶ My sister, Jamilah, graduates on Saturday.

Checking for essential and nonessential information
To check your work for these kinds of commas, read over what you've written and identify the **NOUNS**. When a noun—*stadium*, *achievement*, *amino acids*, whatever—is followed immediately by additional information about it, ask yourself if the information is essential: does it tell you which stadium, which achievement, which amino acids? If so, it shouldn't be set off with commas. If, however, the information is nonessential, and the sentence would still be fine without that information, it should be set off with a pair of commas. Let's examine two examples:

▶ The neighbors, who complained about parking, called a meeting to discuss the problem.

▶ The neighbors who complained about parking called a meeting to discuss the problem.

In these examples, the noun *neighbors* is followed by additional information. Which sentence talks about a situation where all of the neighbors complained? Which one describes a situation where only some of them did? Remember that the commas set off information that is extra and not essential. In the first sentence, the commas indicate that the information *who complained about parking* is extra, nonessential; it doesn't tell us which neighbors, so we can safely conclude that all of the neighbors complained. In the second sentence, the absence of commas lets us know that the information is essential; the clause *who complained about parking* tells us which neighbors called the meeting—only the ones who complained.

Editing commas with essential and nonessential information
Here is an example to practice with:

▶ Vitamins, such as B and C, are water-soluble and easily absorbed by the body; excess amounts are eliminated in the urine.

In order to edit the example, you will need to know if the phrase *such as B and C* is essential or if it's only additional information. In order to save you from looking it up, here it is: not all vitamins are water-soluble; some are fat-soluble and are stored in the body rather than quickly eliminated. Now, is the phrase *such as B and C* essential information? And if it is, should this sentence have commas? Here is the edited version:

▶ Vitamins⁄ such as B and C⁄ are water-soluble and easily absorbed by the body; excess amounts are eliminated in the urine.

Edit
The two sentences below are nearly identical; the difference is that one has essential information about its subject, while the other one's subject has extra information. Put commas in the appropriate places.

> Missy Elliott who will perform in the opening act will do her sound check at 5:30.

> The backup singers who will perform in the opening act will do their sound check at 5:30.

➡ For more practice, complete the InQuizitive activity on **commas**.

EDITING WORDS THAT ARE OFTEN CONFUSED

English has more than a million words, and any one of them could be used appropriately—or inappropriately—in a variety of ways, so no book could possibly help you edit all of the "wrong words" that might turn up in your writing. A few basic strategies, however, can help you with many of those problems. Here you'll find tips for identifying a few of those in your own work—and then editing as need be. Although there are countless ways to get a word wrong, many such problems can be traced back to two causes: words that sound like other words (homophones) and apostrophes (which don't have any sound at all). Here's an example:

▶ Joe should of told them to buy there TV there because its cheaper and its screen is bigger.

Read that sentence out loud and it sounds exactly as the writer intended it; the meaning is perfectly clear. But your writing can't just "sound" right—it has to look right, too. In other words, the written words have to be correct. There are three wrong words in that sentence: *of*, *there*, and *its*. Let's look at each one.

Of/Have

The useful little word *of*, which is a preposition, sounds a lot like another very useful and common word, the verb *have*, especially in rapid or casual speech. The two are often confused when *have* is used as a **HELPING VERB** with the **MODALS** *can, could, may, might, must, should, will,* or *would*—especially in contractions, such as *could've* or *should've*. How do you know if the appropriate word is *of* or *have*? Try reframing your sentence as a question. That should tell you right away which one is the right choice.

▶ Should Joe of told them?

▶ Should Joe have told them?

You can probably tell right away that *have* is the better choice. When you're editing, develop the habit of noticing whenever you use a modal, and make sure the words that follow it are appropriate. *Have* can be written out in its full form or combined with the preceding word to form a contraction—*should've, would've*. Try it without the modal. *Have you told them?* That's good. *Of you told them?* Not so good. That's because *have* is a helping verb, and *of* is not.

There/Their/They're

There is a common and useful word that sounds exactly like another common word, *their*, and those two sound the same as a third common word, *they're*, the contracted form of *they are*. So not only do we have three homophones, but each of the three words is used very frequently in both speech and writing. That leads to a large number of wrong word problems. For example:

▶ For security screening, passengers must put all cell phones in the trays, and now *there* required to put *there* shoes *there*, too.

You'll notice three instances of *there* in the example, and two of them are "wrong words." The sentence should have one each of *they're*, *their*, and *there*, so let's take a closer look at each use of *there*.

THEY'RE

Let's start with the first one. That part of the sentence is trying to say that the passengers—*they*—are required to do something, so the appropriate word would be the contraction of *they are*: *they're*. The word *they're* has only that one meaning, so using it is very simple. Just see if you can substitute "they are" for the word in question and still have the meaning you intended. If not, you'll need to make a change.

THEIR

Now let's look at the second instance of *there*: *there shoes*. That part of the sentence is talking about the shoes that belong to the passengers, so the appropriate word would be a possessive: *their*. The word *their* has only that one uncomplicated meaning—it always indicates possession, as in the following examples:

▶ *Their* feet were swollen and *their* toes were numb, but the hikers were determined to reach Vogelsang before dark.

▶ The birds are squawking because the wind blew *their* nest down.

▶ Both of the radios still work, but *their* clocks are wrong.

When you're trying to decide if *their* is the right word, try asking if the word you are using is intended to show possession. In the examples above, *their* is correct because it indicates possession: Whose feet and toes? *Their* (the hikers') feet and toes. Whose nest? *Their* (the birds') nest. Whose clocks? *Their* (the radios') clocks.

THERE

That leaves us with the final instance of *there* in our example sentence. That *there* is correct. Most of the time, as in our example, *there* simply indicates a place, telling *where* something is: Where's my phone? It's *there*, on the table. Sometimes, though, *there* is used to introduce information that's provided later in the sentence. For example:

▶ Whenever *there* was a big snowstorm, the neighbors all helped clear the street.

▶ *There* are three candidates in the race, but only one has the right experience.

That meaning of *there* simply indicates the existence of something—*a big snowstorm, three candidates.* Here's an example that uses both meanings:

▶ *There* is a coatrack behind the door; you can hang your jacket *there*.

To check whether *there* is the appropriate word, ask whether the word indicates either the existence of something or a place. If the word indicates either of those two things, *there* is the correct choice.

When editing your own work, check each instance of *there, their,* and *they're* to make sure that you've written the one you really mean. That may sound tedious, but here's a handy shortcut: use the Find function in your word processing program to search for each instance of *there, their,* and *they're.* That way, you won't miss any.

Now let's revise our original example sentence. Try it yourself before you look at the edited version below.

▶ For security screening, passengers must put all cell phones in the trays,
and now ~~there~~ *they're* required to put ~~there~~ *their* shoes there, too.

It's / Its

It's and *its* make for many "wrong word" problems. Although they're pronounced exactly the same, they really are two distinct words with distinct uses: *its* is the possessive form of *it*, and *it's* is a contraction of *it is*. That difference makes it easy to know which one is appropriate for your sentence. Let's look at one problematic sentence:

▶ When my phone fell, *its* screen shattered, but luckily, *its* still working.

There are two instances of *its* in the sentence, but one of them should be *it's*. How can you tell which is which? Check to see which one can be replaced by *it is*. The second one—*it is* still working. The one without the apostrophe, *its,* is the possessive form of *it*: the screen that belongs to *it* (the phone). So here's how you'd edit this sentence:

> ▶ When my phone fell, its screen shattered, but luckily, ~~its~~ still working.
> it's

Wait. Haven't you been told to use an apostrophe to indicate possessives, as in *the priest's robe, the frog's sticky tongue*? So how can it be that the version *without* the apostrophe is the possessive one? *It* is a **PRONOUN**, along with *he, I, she,* and *you,* for example. What are the possessive forms of those pronouns? *His. My. Her. Your.* Do you notice that those possessives don't have an apostrophe? Neither does *its.*

If you know or suspect that you have problems confusing *it's* and *its* in your work, you can check for them using the Find function of your word processor. Search your text for each of the two words, and make sure that the possessive *its* has no apostrophe and that the contracted form of *it is* always appears as *it's.*

Edit
Return now to the first problem sentence at the top of page 751, and try editing it using all of the techniques discussed above:

> Joe should of told them to buy there TV there because its cheaper and its screen is bigger.

↪ For more practice, complete the InQuizitive activity on **words often confused**.

PART VIII

Design and Delivery

ASKED TO NAME the three most important parts of rhetoric, the famous Greek statesman and orator Demosthenes is said to have replied: "Delivery, delivery, delivery." Not too many years ago, that assessment might have seemed overdone: Delivery, more important than content? Delivery, more important than the inventiveness of the message? Delivery, more important than style? But those were the years when print texts still claimed pride of place, when what was most important was "put in writing," and when most messages came to us in black print on white pages. In these instances, the message was carried by words alone, and those words were "delivered" in print texts. Period.

But today, Demosthenes is right on target. With messages of every imaginable sort packaged in ever more alluring garb vying for our attention, just how those messages are delivered matters—a lot. So just what do we mean by "delivery"? For the purposes of this book, we have two senses of the word in mind.

The first refers to how the message is communicated: in what *mode* and through what *medium*. Mode refers to what makes up the message and communicates its meaning: words, sounds, gestures, still and moving images, or some combination of those. Medium is the form in which the audience receives it: these days, that's print, oral, or digital. So a political candidate delivering a campaign speech (the medium) might use words, gestures, and a series of images (the modes) to make a vivid and personal appeal to her audience.

But there's another important sense of the word "delivery," one that comes down to us through the history of human communication. This sense of the word refers to the *performance* of a text and captures the speaker's tone, pacing, and quality of voice as well as a full range of facial and bodily gestures and movements. In Demosthenes's time, such delivery was of paramount importance in connecting to an audience and gaining its assent, approval, or understanding. And given the ubiquity of television, film, and video (not to mention *YouTube* and *Instagram*), these elements of communication are taking on greater significance.

Savvy authors understand that messages today don't just lie there on the page and wait for readers to discover them. Rather, it's up to you as author to capture and hold the attention of your audience. For authors of texts in all media, that means paying careful attention to *design*. A text's design— whether it be the use of color and fonts in a print text, the choice of music and moving images in a video, or the slides and handouts in an oral presentation—often determines your audience's first and lasting impressions. An effective design can draw the notice of your audience, keep their attention on your message, and help you achieve your purpose.

This section of *Everyone's an Author* aims to get *your* attention and to focus it on what delivery can mean for you as an author. The chapters that follow will ask you to consider the choices you'll need to make as an author who is designing texts, and how those choices affect the delivery and reception of your messages. In addition, we will examine the role of delivery in successful oral presentations, multimodal compositions, and portfolios. And last but not least, we'll urge you to deliver some of your ideas to audiences by way of publication, proving once again that, today, everyone's an author.

THIRTY-FOUR

Designing
What You Write

ESIGN. IT'S A WORD YOU HEAR ALL THE TIME, one you use without thinking about it. "Meghan Markle walked down the aisle in a wedding dress designed by Clare Waight Keller for Givenchy." "Have you seen the design for Stephen Colbert's new book?" "Frank Gehry's design of the Disney Concert Hall astonished critics with its waves of gleaming stainless steel." "My essay was designed to get the attention of the college admissions committee."

Fashion, technology, architecture, toys: everything is designed, and that includes everything you write. A slide presentation, a *YouTube* video, an essay—you design it, whether you are conscious of doing so or not. You select a medium and tools: a lined notebook and a pencil, a text message and a smartphone, white paper and black printer ink. You choose fonts and colors: big red capital letters for a poster, 12-point black Times New Roman for an essay, your neatest cursive for a thank-you note. You think about including visuals: a bar graph on a slide, a cartoon in a blog, a photo in an essay. You consider whether to use multiple columns, bullet points, numbered lists—and where to leave some white space. You decide what you want readers to notice first and how to make it catch their eye.

This chapter discusses several key design elements: typography, color, visuals, and layout. Whatever fonts or images you choose, though, remember that they are not mere decoration. However you design a text, you need to be guided by your purpose, your audience, and the rest of your rhetorical situation.

THINKING RHETORICALLY ABOUT DESIGN

Researchers point out that being able to design your writing gives you more control over your message than writers had in the past, when they had fewer options and tools at their disposal. That's because your design choices can play a big role in the way your audience receives your message and whether your text achieves its purpose. Look, for example, at the different ways that Coca-Cola was advertised in 1913 and in 2014.

In 1913, Coke was relatively new, and its ads relied on words to introduce it to an audience that was not yet familiar with the drink, telling them it had "character" and was "delicious," "refreshing," and "thirst-quenching." The ad shown here was designed so that these words would pop and be easy to read.

To reach today's audiences, however, advertisers use multiple media—in the case of this 2014 ad aired just before the World Cup in Brazil, print as well as video. Coca-Cola knew the world would be watching the World Cup, and this ad launched a special celebration of the event: mini bottles featuring designs inspired by the flags of World Cup host nations past, present, and future. The message: Coca-Cola is global, reaching potential customers all over the world.

A print ad for Coca-Cola in Georgia Tech's 1913 yearbook and a video ad presented during the telecast of the 2014 FIFA World Cup.

One thing the two ads have in common, though, is the logo. Whether it's in black ink on white paper or red and white pixels on a screen, the Coca-Cola logo was *designed* to be instantly recognizable.

In designing what you write, think about how you can best reach your audience and achieve your purpose. Given the deluge of words, images, and other data, readers today are less likely than they once were to read anything start to finish. Instead, they may scan for just the information they need. So as an author, you need to design your documents to be user-friendly: easy to access, to navigate, to read—and to remember.

Considering Your Rhetorical Situation

- *Who is your* AUDIENCE, and are there any design elements they expect or need? Large type? Illustrations? Are there any design elements that might not appeal to them—or cause them to question your authority?

- *What is your* PURPOSE, and what design elements can help you achieve that purpose? If you're trying to explain how to do something, would it help to set off the steps in a numbered list? Is there anything that would work against your goals—using a playful typeface in a business letter, for example?

- *What's your* GENRE, and does it have any design requirements?

- *What's your* STANCE *as an author,* and how do you want to come across to your audience? Do you want to seem businesslike? serious? ironic? practical and matter-of-fact? How can your use of fonts, color, images, and other design elements reflect that stance?

- *Consider the larger* CONTEXT. Does your assignment specify any design requirements? What design elements are possible with the technology you have available?

- *What* MEDIA *will you use*—print? digital? spoken?—and what kinds of DESIGN elements are appropriate (or possible)? A print essay, for example, could include photographs but not video.

CHOOSING FONTS

Authors today have hundreds of fonts to choose from, and the choices you make affect the message your readers receive—so it's important to think carefully about what's most appropriate for the particular rhetorical situation.

Serif fonts (fonts with small decorative lines, called serifs, added to the ends of most letters) such as Times New Roman or Bodoni have a traditional look, whereas sans serif fonts (those without serifs) such as Arial or Futura give a more modern look. Your instructors may require you to use a specific font, but if you get to choose, you'll want to think about what look you want for your text—and what will be most readable. Some readers find serif fonts easier to read in longer pieces of writing. Sans serif, on the other hand, tends to be easier to read in slide presentations. Save novelty or decorative fonts such as **Impact** or *Allegro* for your nonacademic writing—and even there, use them sparingly, since they can be difficult (or annoying!) to read.

Most fonts include **bold**, *italics*, and underlining options, which you can use to highlight parts of a text. In academic writing, bold is generally used for headings, whereas italics or underlining is used for titles of books, films, and other long works. If you're following MLA, APA, or another academic style, make sure that your use of fonts conforms to the style's requirements.

Readability matters. For most academic and workplace writing, you'll want to use 10-to-12-point type, and at least 18-point type for most presentation slides. Academic writing is usually double-spaced; letters and résumés are single-spaced.

ADDING HEADINGS

Brief texts may need no headings at all, but for longer texts, headings can help readers follow the text and find specific information. Some kinds of writing have set headings that authors are required to use— **IMRAD** reports, for instance, require introduction, methods, research, and discussion headings. When you include headings, you need to decide on wording, fonts, and placement.

Wording. Make headings succinct and parallel. You could make them all nouns ("Energy Drinks," "Snack Foods"), all gerund phrases ("Analyzing the Contents of Energy Drinks," "Resisting Snack Foods"), or all questions ("What's in Energy Drinks?" and "Why Are Snack Foods So Hard to Resist?").

Fonts. If you've chosen to divide your text further using subheadings under larger headings, distinguish different level headings from one another typographically by using bold, italic, underlining, and capitalization. For example:

FIRST-LEVEL HEADING
Second-Level Heading
Third-Level Heading

When you get to choose, you may want to make headings larger than the main text or to put them in a different font or color (as we do throughout this book). But if you're following **MLA** or **APA** styles, be aware that they require headings to be in the same font as the main text.

Placement. You can center headings or set them flush left above the text, or place them to the left of the text; but whatever you do, treat each level of heading consistently throughout the text. If you're following MLA or APA styles, be aware that first-level headings must be centered.

USING COLOR

Sometimes you'll be required to write in black type on a white background, but many times you'll have reason to use colors. In some media, color will be expected or necessary—on websites or presentation slides, for instance. Other times it may be inappropriate—in a thank-you note following a job interview at a law firm or in an application essay to business school. As with any design element, color should be used to help you get a message across and appeal to an audience, never just to decorate your text.

Be aware that certain colors can evoke specific emotional reactions: blue, like the sky and sea, suggests spaciousness and tranquillity; red invokes fire and suggests intense energy and emotions; yellow, the color of our sun, generates warmth and optimism. Also remember that certain colors carry different associations across cultures—to Westerners, white suggests innocence and youth, but in China white is traditionally associated with death (which is why Chinese brides wear red).

Especially if you use more than one color in a text, you'll want to consider how certain colors work together. Look at the color wheel on the next page to see how the colors are related. *Primary colors* (red, blue, and yellow) create

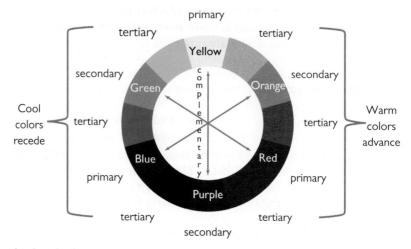

A color wheel.

an effect of simplicity and directness. The more *secondary* and *tertiary colors* you use, the more sophisticated the design. *Complementary colors*, located opposite each other on the color wheel, look brighter when placed next to each other but can sometimes clash and look jarring. (Black and white are also considered complementary colors.) Cool and dark colors appear to recede, whereas warm and bright colors seem to advance. So using both cool and warm colors can create a feeling of movement and energy.

Remember that any color scheme includes the type, the background, and any images or graphics that you use. If colorful photos are an important part of your website, they'll stand out most strongly on a white background and with black type—both of which you may want to use for that reason alone. If you're writing a report that includes multicolored pie charts and want to have color headings, you wouldn't want to use primary colors in the headings and pastels in the charts. In short, if you use colors, make sure they work well with all the other design elements in the text.

Using color to guide readers. Like bold or italic type, color can help guide readers through a text. In fact, that's the way color is used in this book. The headings are all red to make them easy to spot, and keywords are color-coded a pale orange to signal that they're defined in the glossary/index. In addition, we've color-coded parts of the book—roadmaps are on yellow pages, readings are light blue, research chapters are green, style chapters are lavender, design and delivery chapters are aqua—to help readers find them easily.

Color is an important navigational element on websites as well, sometimes used to indicate links and to highlight headings. For such uses of color, it's important to choose colors that are easy to see.

Considering legibility. Using color can make your writing easier—or harder—to read. Use type and background colors that are compatible. Dark type on a light background works best for lengthy pieces of writing, while less text-heavy projects can use a light text on a dark background for visual effect. In either case, be sure that the contrast is dramatic enough to be legible. Keep in mind that some people can't see or distinguish certain colors (notably, red and green).

USING VISUALS

Authors today write with more than just words. Photos, charts, tables, and videos are just some of the visual elements you can use to present information and to make your writing easier or more interesting to read. Would a photo slideshow help listeners see a scene you're describing in an oral presentation? Would readers of a report be able to compare data better in a table or chart than in a paragraph? Would a map or diagram help readers see how and where an event you're describing unfolded? These are questions you should be asking yourself as you write.

Be sure that any visuals you use are relevant to what you have to say—that you use them to support your point, not just to decorate your text. And remember that even the most spectacular images do not speak for themselves: you need to refer to them in your text and to explain to readers what they are and how they support what you're saying.

Kinds of Visuals

You may be assigned to include certain kinds of visuals in your writing—but if not, a good way to think about what sorts of visuals to use (or not) is by considering your rhetorical situation. What visuals would be useful or necessary for your topic and purpose? What visuals would help you reach

A photo of street art in a Texas parking lot demonstrates the layering effect of graffiti in a way that would be difficult to do with words alone.

your audience? What kinds of visuals are possible in your medium—or expected in your genre?

Photographs can help an audience envision something that's difficult to describe or to explain in words. A good photo can provide powerful visual evidence for an argument and can sometimes move readers in a way that words alone might not. Think of how ads for various charities use photos of hungry children to appeal to readers to donate.

Photos can be useful for many writing purposes, letting readers see something you're **DESCRIBING** or **ANALYZING**, for instance, or even something you're **REPORTING** on. (See how Melissa Rubin needed to include a photo of the ad that she analyzes on p. 276, and how Katherine Spriggs included photos of two different kinds of farms in her argumentative essay on p. 177.) You can take your own photos or use ones that you find in other sources. Remember, however, to provide full documentation for any photos that you don't take yourself and to ask permission before photographing people and using their image in your writing.

Videos are useful for demonstrating physical processes or actions and for showing sequences. Your medium will dictate whether you can include videos in a text. The print version of a newspaper article about aerialist skiers, for instance, includes a still photo of a skier in mid-jump, whereas the same article on the newspaper's website and on a TV news report features videos showing the skier in action. Your topic and genre will affect whether or not you have reason to include video if you can. If you were writing a **PROCESS ANALYSIS** to teach a skier how to perform a certain aerial maneuver, a video would be far more useful than the still photo you might include if you were writing a **PROFILE** of a professional skier.

Graphs, charts, and tables. Numerical and statistical data can be easier both to describe and to understand when they are presented visually. See the fantasy sports graphics on this page, for example—and imagine trying to present that data in a paragraph. You'll often have occasion to present data in graphs or charts, in bar graphs, pie charts, and the like, especially in **REPORTS** and **ANALYSES**. In many cases, you'll be able to find tables and graphs in your research and then incorporate them into your own writing. You can also use templates found in *Excel*, *Word*, *PowerPoint*, and other programs to create charts and tables yourself. Whether you find or create them, be sure to indicate in your text where the information comes from and how they support your argument.

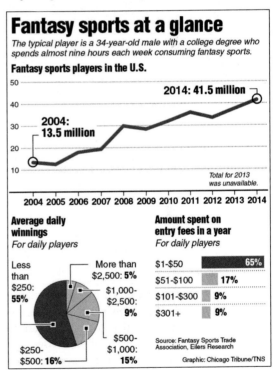

Line graphs are useful for illustrating trends and changes over time—how unemployment fluctuates over a period of years, for instance. By using more than one line, you can compare changes in different variables, such as unemployment for those with a college education and those with only a high school education. When comparing more

A line graph shows the rising number of fantasy sports players over a period of 10 years; a pie chart and a bar graph break down average winnings and entry fees.

than one variable, the lines should be in two different colors so that readers can easily see the comparison.

Bar graphs are useful for comparing quantitative data, such as for different age groups or different years. In the example about fantasy sports, the bars make it easy to see how much most players spend to participate in fantasy sports leagues. It would be easy enough to convey this same information in words alone—but more work to read and harder to remember.

Pie charts give an overview of the relative sizes of parts to a whole, such as what share of a family budget is devoted to food, housing, entertainment, and so on. Pie charts are useful for showing which parts of a whole are more or less significant, but they are less precise (and harder to read) than bar graphs. It's best to limit a pie chart to six or seven slices, since when the slices become too small, it's difficult to see how they compare in size.

Tables are an efficient way of presenting a lot of information concisely by organizing it into horizontal rows and vertical columns. Table 1 below presents data about home internet access in the United States, information that is made easy to scan and compare in a table.

Table I
US Home Internet Access by Age Group, 2009

Age of Householder	No In-Home Internet (%)	In-Home Internet (%)
Under 25 years	33.0	67.0
25-34 years	25.8	74.2
35-44 years	22.2	77.8
45-55 years	24.2	75.8
55 years and older	41.8	58.2

Source: United States Dept. of Commerce, Census Bureau; "Internet Use in the United States: October 2009," Current Population Survey; US Dept. of Commerce, Oct. 2009; Web; 11 June 2012; table 1.

Maps provide geographic context, helping to orient your audience to places mentioned in your text. A report on the 2011 earthquake in New Zealand, for example, includes the maps on the facing page showing where the earthquake was centered and where the most damage was done. Include a map when location is important to your point.

CHRISTCHURCH BUILDINGS DAMAGE

Buildings damaged   Buildings collapsed

The Christchurch Press

Backpacker hostel

Pyne Gould Guinness building

Forsyth Barr building

Canterbury Provincial Chambers

Piko Wholefoods

Hotel Grand Chancellor 26-storey hotel teetered to near collapse

200m

Kilmore St   Madras   Barbadoes St

Central Christchurch

Christchurch Cathedral

Armagh St
Gloucester St
Worcester St
Hereford St
Cashel St

Manchester St

Colombo St

N

Avon River

Christchurch Hospital

Saint Asaph St   Montreal St

Christ's College

Arts Centre

Bus crushed by falling building

Canterbury Television building which housed language school where 10 Japanese students remain unaccounted for

⊕ Christchurch International Airport

Worst-affected areas

● Building damage

CHRISTCHURCH

Detailed map

Pacific Ocean

NEW ZEALAND

Wellington

Opawa

Sumner

2 km

Epicentre Tuesday's 6.3 magnitude quake struck at lunchtime

Christchurch

Lyttelton

Sources: Reuters, NZ Herald   *Graphic: Fabian Chan/RNGS*   ⊘ REUTERS

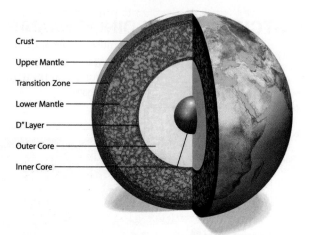

Crust
Upper Mantle
Transition Zone
Lower Mantle
D" Layer
Outer Core
Inner Core

A diagram of the earth's internal structure shows the various layers.

Diagrams are useful for illustrating details that cannot be shown in a photograph. A carefully drawn diagram can deliver a lot of information in a small amount of space.

Infographics bring together several different types of visuals—charts, tables, photos, and so on—to give detailed information and data. They can help simplify a complex subject—or make a potentially dull topic visually interesting. Because infographics can be so densely packed with information, make sure that they are large enough for your audience to be able to read and arranged in a way that they can follow.

Creating Visuals

You can find visuals online, scan them from print sources, or create them yourself using basic software or a camera. If you come across an illustration you think would be useful, make or save a copy. Scan or photocopy visuals from print sources, and save a link or take a screen grab from digital sources. Label everything clearly. Be aware that visuals and any data you use to create them need to be **DOCUMENTED** in a **CAPTION** or source note—so keep track of where you found everything as you go.

- *Photographs and videos.* If you plan to print an image, save each file in as high a resolution as possible. If a photo is only available in a very small size or low resolution, try to find a more legible option. Be careful about cropping, adjusting color, and altering images or videos in other ways that could change the meaning; straying too far from the original is considered unethical.

This infographic on the cherry blossom season in Washington, DC, includes photos, diagrams, maps, and a bar chart.

- *Graphs, charts, and tables.* Be consistent in your use of fonts and colors, especially if you include more than one graph, chart, or table. Be sure that the horizontal (x) and vertical (y) axes are labeled clearly. If you use more than one color, add labels for what each color represents. When you have many rows or columns, alternating colors can make categories easier to distinguish.

- *Maps.* Provide a title and a key explaining any symbols, colors, or other details. If the original is missing these elements, add them. If you create the map yourself, be sure to highlight notable locations or information.

- *Diagrams.* Use a single font for all labels, and be sure to make the diagram large enough to include all of the necessary detail. Make sure these details are clearly and neatly represented, whether they're drawn or created on a computer.

Introducing and Labeling Visuals

Introduce visuals as you would any other source materials, explaining what they show and how they support your point. Don't leave your audience wondering how a photo or chart pertains to your project—spell it out, and be sure to do so *before* the visual appears ("As shown in fig. 3, population growth has been especially rapid in the Southwest"). Number visuals in most academic writing sequentially (Figure 1, Figure 2), counting tables separately (Table 1, Table 2). If you're following MLA, APA, or another academic style, be sure to follow its guidelines for how to label tables and figures.

MLA STYLE. For tables, provide a number ("Table 1") and a descriptive title ("Population Growth by Region, 1990–2010") on separate lines above the table; below the table, add a caption explaining what the table shows and including any source information. For graphs, charts, photos, and diagrams, provide a figure number ("Fig. 1"), caption, and source information below the figure. If you give only brief source information in a parenthetical citation, include the source in your list of works cited.

APA STYLE. For tables, charts, diagrams, graphs, and photos, provide a number ("Table 1" or "Figure 1") and a descriptive title on separate lines above the table or figure; below the table or figure, include a note explaining any elements whose meanings are not apparent in the table or figure and providing source information if the table or figure is adapted or reprinted from another source.

PUTTING IT ALL TOGETHER

Once you've chosen fonts, colors, and visuals, you need to think about how they all come together as a text. Look, for instance, at the homepage of TED, a nonprofit group dedicated to disseminating "ideas worth spreading." It's easy to read with a sans serif font and minimal text. The logo draws your eye because it's large, red, capitalized, and positioned in the upper left corner of the screen. The soft gray "ideas worth spreading" complements the red and leads your eye to the bold black text below—"Riveting talks by remarkable people, free to the world"—which defines the group's purpose and audience. Each of the images is a link to a specific TED talk. Note how white space separates the parts and makes the page easy to read. No surprise that this site won a Webby Award, the online equivalent of an Oscar.

You may not have occasion to design anything as large or complex as the TED site, but the same design principles will apply for all the writing you do. Whether you're designing a report, a photo essay, or a slide presentation, chances are you'll be working with some combination of words, images, graphs, and other graphic elements that you'll need to put on paper or screen in order to reach a certain audience to achieve a certain purpose.

Look beyond the details and think about what you want your design to accomplish. Do you want it to help your audience grasp a message as fast as possible? convey your identity as a creative author? conform to the requirements of a certain academic style? be appealing yet simple enough to implement by an approaching deadline? Thinking about what you want your design to do can help you determine how to put it all together in a way that achieves your end goal.

Keep it simple. Sometimes you'll need to follow a prescribed organization and layout, but if you get to decide how to design your document, here's a piece of advice: don't make your design any more complex than it has to be. Readers want to be able to find the information they need without having to spend time deciphering a complex hierarchy of headings or an intricate navigational system.

Think about how to format your written text. Should it all be in paragraphs, or is there anything that should be set off as a list? If so, should it be a bulleted list to make it stand out, or a numbered list to put items in a sequence? If your text includes numerical data, should any of it be presented in a graph, chart, or table to make it easier for readers to understand? Is there any information that's especially important that you'd like to highlight in some way?

Position visuals carefully. Keep in mind how they will look on a page or screen. Placing them at the top or bottom of a print page will make it easier to lay out pages. If your text will be online, you have more freedom to put visuals wherever you wish. Reproduce visuals at a large enough size so that readers will be able to see all the pertinent detail, but be aware that digital images become fuzzier when they are enlarged. Reduce large image files by saving them in compressed formats such as JPEGs or GIFs; you don't want readers to have problems loading the image. And once everything is in place, look over your text carefully to be sure that nothing is too small or blurry to read.

Use white space to separate the parts of your text. Add some extra space above headings and around lists, images, graphs, charts, and tables. This will keep your text from looking cluttered and make everything easier to find and read.

Organize the text. Whether your text is a simple five-page report or a full website, readers will need to know how it's organized and how to find the information they're looking for. In a brief essay, you might simply indicate that in a sentence in your introduction, but in lengthier pieces, you may need headings, both to structure your text and to make it easy for readers to navigate.

If you're creating a website, you'll need to figure out how you're dividing materials into pages and to make that clear on the site's homepage. Most homepages have a horizontal navigation bar across the top indicating and linking to the main parts and often another navigation menu going down the left side of the screen, with links to specific materials on the site. These menus should appear in the same position on every page of the site—and every page should include a link to take readers back to the homepage. Take a look at the examples from *National Geographic* on the following page and you'll see the consistent elements that help readers navigate the site: navigation bars at the top, links to popular information in bulleted lists, ads in the bottom right corner, consistent colors and fonts on all the pages.

GETTING RESPONSE TO YOUR DESIGN

Whether you're composing a report, an illustrated essay, or a blog post, try to get response to the design. Enlist the help of friends or classmates, asking them what they think of the "look" of your text, how easy it is to read, and so on. Following are some specific things they (and you) should consider:

- Is the design appropriate to the text's **PURPOSE**, **AUDIENCE**, **GENRE**, and **MEDIUM**? Consider the fonts and any use of color: do they suit your rhetorical situation?

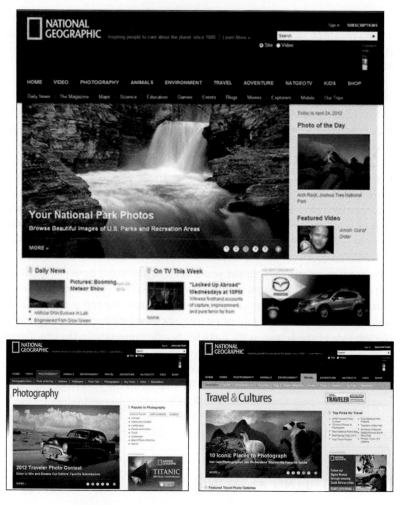

Examples from the *National Geographic* website.

- Does the design make the main parts of your text easy to see? If not, would it help to add headings?

- Is there any information that should be set off as a list?

- Does the text include any data that would be easier to follow in a chart, table, or graph?

- If you've included images, what purpose do they serve? How do they support the point of your text? If some are only decorative, should you delete them?

- Does the overall "look" of your text suit the message that you want to convey?

Remember: your design is often the first impression readers get, and it can make all the difference in getting your message across. There may be a lot at stake in the simple choice of a font or color or image, so make these choices carefully—and make your design work for you.

REFLECT. Find a design that you think is attractive (or not)—a book cover, a magazine spread, a brochure, a poster, a blog, a website, whatever. **ANALYZE** *its use of fonts, colors, and visuals. What works, and what doesn't? How would you revise the design if you could?*

THIRTY-FIVE

Writing in Multiple Modes

Ever since the days of illustrated books and maps, texts have
included visual elements for the purpose of imparting
information. The contemporary difference is the ease with
which we can combine words, images, sound, color, animation,
and video . . . so that they are part of our everyday lives.

—NCTE ON MULTIMODAL LITERACIES

 HE **NATIONAL COUNCIL OF TEACHERS OF ENGLISH** made
this statement more than a decade ago, and in the years
that have passed, multimodal literacies have indeed become part of the "everyday lives" of students everywhere.
Take a look at the cartoon on the next page, for example.
The little boy in this cartoon illustrates the NCTE statement perfectly: he lies in bed, listening to his dad read him a story. But the boy
does more than just listen: he compliments his dad on his reading ("darn
good job") and offers to record him reading and then "podcast" him on his
website. Multimodal, indeed.

Defining Multimodal Writing

So just what are these multimodal texts? Put most simply, they are texts
that draw on more than words, bringing in still or moving images, sound,
and so on. Researcher Cynthia Selfe identifies five modes writers can use
to convey their messages: linguistic (that's words, written or spoken);
visual (colors, fonts, images, and so on); audio (tone of voice, music, and

"You know, Dad, you do a darn good job.
You should let me record you sometime, and
I'll podcast you on my website. Just a thought."

other sounds); gestural (body language and facial expression); and spatial
(the way elements are arranged on a page or screen).

For hundreds of years, writers have relied primarily on two of these
modes, the linguistic and the visual. In this sense, all writing uses multiple modes, so multimodality is nothing new. And just like traditional
print texts, more complex multimodal ones call for careful attention to
the same conventions of good writing, research, and argument expected
of all college writing.

But today writers have easy access to all five modalities and can produce texts that convey meaning not only through words but also through
sounds, moving and still images, animations, and more—delivered
through print, spoken, and digital media. For you as a writer, that opens
up an infinite number of options. This chapter offers some tips for deciding among those options and for making best use of the various technologies available for writing in multiple modes.

*REFLECT. Make a list of writing assignments you've done this term and
of any writing projects you have worked on out of class. How many of them rely on
printed words on a page? How many use multiple modes—and what are they? On the
basis of this exercise, write (or draw, or record) a reflection about yourself as a writer of
multimodal texts. Then consider the next piece of writing you're preparing to do. How
might you use sounds, images, and other modes to get your message across?*

Considering Your Rhetorical Situation

Writing in multiple modes calls for the same close attention to rhetorical principles that all writing does. Whatever your topic, the following questions can help you think about your purpose, audience, and the rest of your rhetorical situation:

Consider your PURPOSE. Why are you creating this project? What are your purposes or goals? No doubt one purpose is to fulfill an assignment—and do a good job of it. But you may have other purposes as well: to raise awareness about a problem on campus; to convince someone to support a project you have in mind; to provide information. Consider the message you want to communicate. What do you want to see happen as a result of what you write?

Think about your AUDIENCE. Whom are you aiming to reach, and how can you best reach them? If you're writing to all members of your campus community, you'll probably want to post your message online, but if you're writing to neighbors about a lost dog, posters might work better. If your intended audience is limited to people you know (such as on a website accessible only to students at your school), you may make some assumptions about them and how they're likely to respond. But remember that most projects you put online may well be accessible to the public—that is, to people you don't and can't know. In this case, it's important not to make assumptions about what they know and to be respectful of the diverse audience that may read what you write.

Think about your STANCE. What is your attitude toward your topic, and how do you want to present yourself as an author—as well-informed? outraged? perplexed? How can you convey that stance? Certain fonts look serious while others look silly; same thing with colors. If you're including music, that too affects the tone. If you're giving an oral presentation, your facial expression and gestures can signal something about your stance.

Choose your GENRE. The kind of writing you're doing can sometimes determine the form that your multimodal project will take. If you're **REPORTING** information, a wiki might be an appropriate choice. But if you're delivering a **PROPOSAL** asking for funding for an event, a print text may be most appropriate. And if afterward you want to create a **NARRATIVE** documenting the event, a video essay might capture the experience most vividly.

Consider the larger **CONTEXT**. How much time do you have, and is your topic narrow enough that you can do a good job in that amount of time? Do you have access to whatever technology you will need? If you'll need to learn new software, remember to build in time for that. Does your campus offer any services (perhaps at a writing center) where you can get help?

Consider **MEDIA**. What media will best serve your audience, purpose, and topic? If you're writing about Bollywood films, you might create a blog, which would enable you to embed video clips and to reach a community of fans. If you want to inform fellow students about ways to save water, you might create an infographic to post in restrooms around campus.

KINDS OF MULTIMODAL PROJECTS

A wide range of multimodal projects have made their way into classrooms at colleges and universities across the country. The most prevalent and popular of these projects are illustrated essays, blogs, wikis, audio essays, video essays, and posters. Following are some tips for composing each of these kinds of writing.

Illustrated Essays

Probably the simplest and most likely multimodal assignment you will encounter is an essay in which you're asked to embed illustrations—photos, drawings, maps, graphs, charts, and so on. Illustrated essays offer you a chance for creativity and for getting your point across in multiple ways; in fact, such writing is a staple in all newspapers and most magazines today. So there's no reason why your college assignments should be words only, not when you have so many other elements to work with.

See how one student used images in an essay about how Japanese video games are no longer being "localized," that is, remade so as to better appeal to foreign audiences.

Even companies like Nintendo, which had previously relied on the denationalized nature of their characters for international success, have begun capitalizing on uniquely Japanese concepts. For example, the Tanooki Suit is an item introduced with *New Super Mario Bros. 3* that allows Mario to

Figure 1. The box art for *Super Mario Bros. 3* prominently featured Raccoon Mario . . .

Figure 2. . . . while art for later releases focused on Tanooki Mario, who, although present in *Super Mario Bros. 3*, was not nearly as prominent as in *3D Land* or *3D World*.

transform into a tanuki, or Japanese raccoon dog. In the original release of *Super Mario Bros. 3*, Tanooki Mario was de-emphasized in favor of Raccoon Mario, which was prominently featured on the cover art, since Americans were more likely able to identify a raccoon rather than a tanuki (see Figure 1). However, with the release of *Super Mario 3D Land*, which some consider to be a spiritual successor to *Super Mario Bros. 3* (Sterling), Nintendo fully embraced the Tanooki power-up and made it the primary focus both in their advertising and in-game, with many enemies gaining Tanooki tails. This newly realized proliferation of Tanooki extended into its sequel, *Super Mario 3D World* (see Figure 2) and related games, such as *Mario Kart 7*. By embracing their cultural heritage rather than disguising it, Nintendo helps introduce Western gamers to elements of Japanese culture they may otherwise not be aware of, no longer fearful of culture shock.

—RUIZHE (THOMAS) ZHAO, "Word for Word: Culture's Impact on the Localization of Japanese Video Games"

Notice how Zhao has carefully incorporated the two images into his argument, labeling them with figure numbers, referring to them in the text, and providing captions for each one. Though it's not shown here, he also included documentation information in a works cited list. Far from being mere decoration, these images provide essential support for his argument.

Some Tips for Writing Illustrated Essays

- Make sure all illustrations help communicate your message. You never want to use illustrations as mere decoration.
- Refer to each illustration in the text and position each one carefully so that it appears near the text where it's discussed.
- Give each illustration a figure number and a caption that tells readers what it is.
- Provide documentation for any illustrations that you don't create yourself, either in a caption or in a works cited list.

Blogs

Blogs—an abbreviation of "weblogs"—are regularly updated sites on which writers post reflections, ideas, information, and arguments. They often include images, embedded audio or video clips, and links to other sites. Some blogs focus on a single topic (Deb Perelman's *Smitten Kitchen* blog focuses on home cooking; Nate Silver's *FiveThirtyEight* analyzes politics, economics, and sports), but those run by newspapers, advocacy organizations, or other institutions cover a wide range of topics (the *Huffington Post* hosts dozens of blogs by politicians, academics, celebrities, and many ordinary folks who have something to say). Almost all blogs allow readers to comment and thus function as sites where people share and discuss information and ideas. Blogs are a part of the everyday landscape of the web: as of May 2019, the blogging platform *Tumblr* hosted well over 467 million blogs—including *everyonesanauthor.tumblr.com*, the companion site to this book.

Blogs are frequently assigned in college classes. You may have been assigned to post responses to one, or maybe you have a blog yourself. Check out the following excerpt from a blog posting in the *Huffington Post* by Julia Landauer, who was a college student as well as a NASCAR driver when she wrote this post:

The Lady Up Front

"Boogity boogity boogity, let's just go racing!" screams Darrell Waltrip from the booth. That's when you know the green flag has flown and the Daytona 500 is under way.

Julia Landauer,
NASCAR driver.

Normally Waltrip says, "Boogity boogity boogity, let's go racing, boys!" But from here on out his trademark phrase will have to be slightly altered to include the sole lady racer, Danica Patrick.

I was thrilled when Danica qualified on pole [won the number one starting position by having the fastest qualifying time] for the 55th running of the Daytona 500. Yes, I wanted to be the first woman to do that, but women in racing is bigger than me. In the effort to draw in more female racers, crewmembers and race/safety officials to the sport, Danica's history-making pole was a huge contribution. Hopefully this contribution will help catapult more women into the sport.

People will critique it, saying that a pole on a super speedway (oval tracks that are over 2 miles long, such as Daytona or Indy) is irrelevant to the rest of the season, so Danica's accomplishment is not a big deal. How wrong! The fact is that success is success and if people consider super speedway poles and wins to be "easy accomplishments," then they should be taken out of the schedule. Or people shouldn't make a big deal about other racers finding success on them. But clearly there is a prestige that goes along with setting pole and winning at Daytona, which can't be taken away from Danica.

The big picture is that Danica showed that women can run up front at the highest levels of racing. There were concerns as to whether she'd

Danica Patrick's race car.

be able to stay up front, and she did; she was in the top five for the majority of the race and even became the first woman to lead laps at the Daytona 500.

Despite finishing 8th, which is still quite respectable, Danica did a great job and set the stage for the future of women in racing. Lyn St. James, retired racer and first female to win the Indianapolis 500 Rookie of the Year award, stated in an interview with CNN, "[Danica] did everything right for the whole race . . . she learned a lot and earned respect from so many people that it was a terrific start of the season and a positive example for women everywhere."

To piggyback off of Lyn's comment, my favorite result from Danica winning the pole comes in something Ella Gordon, Jeff Gordon's daughter, finally realized. As the *Atlantic* pointed out, Danica's pole brought widespread publicity to the fact that women can be racecar drivers too, something that 4-year-old Ella hadn't previously understood to be a possibility. Now think of what all the other little girls who grow up around racing are thinking! We can do it too.

—JULIA LANDAUER, "The Lady Up Front"

Note that the photo of Landauer is one she includes on the blog, in racing gear—a personal touch that helps to build her readership, especially among the women she wants to see join this sport. Her title, "The Lady Up Front," gives a clue about the topic and is meant to intrigue any readers who assume that racing is a man's sport. In providing detailed information about a Daytona 500 race, she quotes from CNN and includes a link to an article in the *Atlantic*. Landauer's writing is informal and friendly, and her point is clear: girls "can do it too."

While you may create a blog of your own, you'll probably also find yourself responding to other people's posts or being assigned to do so for a class. See one response to a post on the *Web of Language* blog run by linguistics professor Dennis Baron. The response is to a posting he wrote in 2010, "Should Everybody Write?"

shon.bacon@ttu.edu Mar 9, 2010 12:08 am
Nice post. This makes me think about a question I've had for a while now with participatory culture and everyone being a producer—producer and user. With the internet and social media, the idea of "audience" has blurred quite a bit considering, as this post notes, that anyone can create content. The idea of a participatory culture, of everyone

having a voice, sounds great in theory, but I'm not sure how beneficial it is to have all voices create a cacophony instead of a well-blended harmony. I guess this is my longwinded way of answering your question. My short version: "Yes, but . . ."

Note that the author of this response raises a question of his own that relates to Baron's post, about the blurring of the line between author and audience. He builds on what Baron has written and then concludes by answering Baron's original question about whether everyone should write: "Yes, but . . . "

Some Tips for Posting to a Blog

- Blog posts are usually fairly brief and to the point because bloggers assume that their readers are reading for specific information. With this in mind, make sure your posts have a point—and that you make that point clear.
- Blogs tend to be written in fairly informal, conversational language.
- Many readers scan blogs for information, so use lists, headings, italics, and other design elements to make your text easy to scan.
- When appropriate, include images or embed audio or video clips to help make your message clear.
- Include links to guide your readers to additional information.
- Invite feedback: ask questions so that readers will naturally want to comment and respond.
- Give your post a compelling title, one that will make readers want to read on. Try to use keywords that will help your post turn up on a search site.

Wikis

Wikis are collaborative websites that invite readers to add and edit content, allowing them to make changes to an existing page, link to other pertinent pages, or even create new pages. Wikis serve as running records of information that is shared within online communities of various kinds: doctors, gamers, students and staff of a college—or, in the case of *Wikipedia*, the entire internet.

You're no doubt familiar with *Wikipedia*, the "free encyclopedia that anyone can edit." Since it started in 2001, it has grown from a site that many were suspicious of (Can you trust the information is correct?) into the first place many people go when looking for information. *Wikipedia* now contains over 5.8 million entries in its English version alone, the majority of which, it turns out, are reliable. And it has set a precedent for just how effective collaboration can be in creating and sharing knowledge. Here is part of *Wikipedia*'s entry on "wiki," showing how this particular web format works.

A **wiki** is a website on which users collaboratively modify content and structure directly from the web browser. In a typical wiki, text is written using a simplified markup language and often edited with the help of a rich-text editor.[1]   —WIKIPEDIA.ORG, "Wiki"

This entry gives readers options to click for more information. Highlighted terms indicate links to pages about key concepts, and clicking on the numbers takes you to a list of references. The entry also includes—in true multimodal fashion—a video interview with Ward Cunningham, inventor of the wiki.

Some instructors use wikis to collect and add to class notes, creating a collaborative record of what is taught and said in class during the term. Maybe you've been assigned to contribute to an entry on *Wikipedia* or to a wiki for a class.

Whether you build a wiki or add to an existing one, you should think carefully about what community it serves. Wikis are never private sites—they're meant to be collaborative and shared! So in contributing to a wiki, you potentially become part of a huge collaborative project.

Some Tips for Contributing to a Wiki

- Be sure any information you present is authoritative and credible. Information should come from reliable sources, and you should check multiple sources before presenting it as fact.

- Remain fair and be respectful, both in your choice of topic and in what you say about it. Some wikis have rules for what content is allowed, and remember that while you may write whatever you wish, other editors can choose to delete it.

- Anticipate a broad audience. Don't assume others have background knowledge of your subject. Explain terms or events that may be unfamiliar, or link to pages on those topics.

- Offer information that will be useful to others. Write about something others will want to learn about!

- Add links, references, and citations that lead to reliable sources for more information.

- If you are adding links to a wiki entry, be sure that you have correctly coded the links so that they work, and make sure that the pages linked to actually exist.

- Remember that wikis are usually sites for shared revision. You will need to think carefully and respectfully before editing or changing other authors' contributions.

Audio Essays

The University of Wisconsin's Design Lab defines audio essays as ones that "explore topics using spoken text, audio interviews, archival recordings, music, environmental sounds, and/or sound effects" and notes that they "can make unfamiliar materials more accessible to new audiences and/or reveal new perspectives on familiar subjects."

↪ Russel Honoré's essay on p. 162 was written for *This I Believe*. Read it, and then listen to the audio version at everyonesanauthor .tumblr.com. What does he do differently for those listening to his text?

National Public Radio has helped popularize audio essays with its *This I Believe* and *This American Life* series. One of NPR's most popular pieces is humorist David Sedaris's readings from his "Santaland Diaries," which chronicle his experiences working as a department store elf one holiday season. Listen to the audio at everyonesanauthor.tumblr.com, paying attention to how the piece is structured in 45-to-50-second segments and how that structure affects the way you follow the story. Here's one segment of Sedaris's tale:

> Twenty-two thousand people came to see Santa today, and not all of them were well-behaved. Today I witnessed fistfights and vomiting and magnificent tantrums. The back hallway was jammed with people. There was a line for Santa and a line for the women's bathroom. And one woman, after asking me a thousand questions already, asked, "Which is

the line for the women's bathroom?" And I shouted that I thought it was the line with all the women in it. She said, "I'm going to have you fired."

I had two people say that to me today: "I'm going to have you fired." Go ahead. Be my guest. I'm wearing a green velvet costume; it doesn't get any worse than this. Who do these people think they are? "I'm going to have you fired."

And I want to lean over and say, "I'm going to have you killed."

—DAVID SEDARIS, "The Santaland Diaries"

Notice how the music at the beginning and the end of this segment helps bring together the narrative. And listen to Sedaris's voice: how it changes as he imitates the voice of the woman who threatens to have him fired—and then lowers and becomes more menacing at the end, concluding the segment with an unexpected shift in the narrative that keeps listeners engaged (and makes us laugh). That's good radio.

Some Tips for Composing an Audio Essay

- Decide on the software you will use. (*Audacity* and *GarageBand* are widely used.)

- Write out a script, using everyday language, short sentences, strong verbs, and active voice.

- If you are using sources, introduce them at the beginning of the sentence and paraphrase rather than quote.

- Use concrete examples and vivid imagery to help listeners see or imagine what you're describing. Sound effects can help establish setting.

- Organize your audio essay in chronological order, allowing for flashbacks and flashforwards if they are necessary to your story.

- Practice reading your script. Vary your tone of voice to keep listeners engaged. You might change your tone to imitate someone else speaking. (Or better yet, edit in sound clips of others speaking for themselves.)

- Follow *This American Life* host Ira Glass's "45-second rule": listeners expect some kind of break or change of pace every 45 to 50 seconds. Try to pace your essay accordingly.

- Use music to establish a mood, to mark transitions, and to keep your listeners engaged.

Video Essays

Video essays are popular, and not just on *YouTube*. Some students submit video essays as part of their college applications, and some employers are asking for videos as part of job applications. While anyone with a smartphone can create a video essay, it's not always easy.

Just like traditional essays composed with written words alone, video essays need to make some kind of point, to offer good reasons and evidence in support of that point, to acknowledge other points of view, and so on. Unlike print essays, however, video essays can use a combination of images, sounds, and words to make their point.

And you can present these images, sounds, and words in many different ways. Take images: you can use still images, moving images, and stop-motion images. Sounds can include people speaking on camera, voiceover, music, and background sounds. Words can be spoken, or they can be put on-screen as titles, subtitles, credits—even in thought bubbles. All these elements add up to infinite possibilities for authoring.

Multimedia journalist Adam Westbrook combines still photos, moving images, music, maps, charts, and more with spoken commentary in *Cause / Effect: The Unexpected Origins of Terrible Things*, a video essay arguing that World War I was caused not by the assassination of Archduke Franz Ferdinand but by Germany's desire for sea power. The video format allows Westbrook to present audio and visual evidence that makes a persuasive (and engaging) case for his argument—and to use both spoken and written language, from voiceover narration to labels identifying those pictured in historic photos.

Go to everyonesan author.tumblr.com to watch *Cause / Effect: The Unexpected Origins of Terrible Things*.

A map and photograph from the video essay *Cause / Effect*.

Westbrook's example shows how complicated video essays can be to do, with words, images, and sounds all at work in multiple ways. A good way to plan out how all these elements will fit together is by creating a **STORY-BOARD**, a series of sketches that shows the sequence of scenes and actions in a film. Take a look at the storyboard on the next page showing five camera shots that follow a man as he walks down a hallway into his office, sits down, and is approached by someone holding a gun. The written words provide directions for the camera operator, noting places where there should be wide-angle shots, close-ups, and so on. A storyboard like this will serve as a blueprint as you shoot and edit a video essay.

Some Tips for Composing a Video Essay

- Decide which program you will use: *iMovie*, *Final Cut Pro*, and *Windows Live Movie Maker* are popular choices.

- Try to show much of the evidence for your argument visually, with images rather than just words.

- Think about the tone you want to project and how color, lighting, pacing, and music might evoke that tone.

- Draft a script for any text that will be spoken on camera or read as a voiceover—and practice reading it aloud.

- Create a storyboard to map out how the parts of your video essay will fit together. Use your storyboard to plan the shots you need before you begin shooting, and always shoot more than you think you'll need. It's easy to delete footage, much harder to get a single shot you missed.

- Consider a variety of camera angles. Wide-angle shots are useful for setting a scene; medium shots, for framing someone speaking to the camera; close-ups, for showing important details.

- Experiment also with moving the camera—following the subject, zooming in or out, panning left or right—but do so sparingly. You don't want to make your viewers dizzy!

- Use title cards to display written text if needed. You'll probably want to open with your title, and you might add text to identify the setting, time, and the name and title of someone speaking; to add captions or subtitles; or to mark transitions.

- Provide a written list of credits on the screen at the end, citing any sources you use and thanking those who helped.

Go to everyonesanauthor.tumblr.com to browse examples of multimodal projects created by students.

A storyboard lays out the sequence of camera shots and transitions.

Posters

You're likely to have opportunities—and assignments—to create posters for classroom presentations, campus organizations, or academic conferences. And posters aren't what they were years ago when all that was needed was poster board and some markers; posters today have become sophisticated and multimodal ways of communicating information. Take a look at the poster on the following page that three students created in order to present the results of a research study. The topic is clearly stated in a heading at the top. The text is organized in three columns: one devoted to the motivation for the project, the second to the methods used, and the third to results and future directions. Data is presented in bar graphs, and other images illustrate and underscore key points in the report.

A poster created by a student research group to present its study.

Some Tips for Creating a Poster

- People often read posters at a glance, so present the information you want your audience to take away clearly and simply.

- Check to see if there are any guidelines for the size of the poster and whether it should be on a tabletop, an easel—or somewhere else.

- Think hard about how you can get your audience's attention: by asking a provocative question in a large bold font at the top of the poster? with color? an eye-catching image? something else?

- Keep the design simple: too many images, too much text, or distracting fonts make for a cluttered look that can be hard to follow.

- Be sure that any text is large enough to read—and that it is organized in a way that makes it easy to scan and understand quickly.

- Choose colors that will be easy to see. Primary colors are easier to see than pastels, as is dark text on a light background.

MANAGING A MULTIMODAL PROJECT

Managing a multimodal project is a bit like juggling: at any one time, you have multiple balls in the air, each one needing attention, and altogether it takes a lot of skill to keep them all airborne. While we can't provide guidelines for every step of every multimodal project you may encounter, we can offer some general advice about how to approach them.

Whether you're composing an illustrated essay, a blog, a video, or any other multimodal text, you will want to plan carefully for how your project will achieve your purpose with a particular audience and in a particular context. To do so, you'll need to carefully manage your time, your files, your project content, your sources, and more.

Managing your time. Make sure you know exactly how much time you have before your project is due and then be realistic about how to manage that time. Set up a calendar and block out specific times when you know you can work on the project; consider whether you'll have any class time to devote to it. If you're assigned to work with other students, set regular meeting times and draw up a schedule and task list together so that you each know your responsibilities. Breaking a project down into parts and setting deadlines for each part can help keep you on track. And don't forget to build in time to get response to a draft of your project—from your instructor if possible as well as from classmates and friends.

Managing project files. Writers traditionally used 3 × 5 index cards to keep track of information and sources, which were almost always print. But for many multimodal projects, it's likely you'll be using digital sources: GIF or JPEG image files, M4V or MOV video files, and so on. Create a folder on your computer where you can save in one place all the files you may want to use. Organize files according to type (images, charts, video clips, audio clips, and so on) and according to the organization of your project (clips for scene 1 of a video essay, graphs for the results section of a research poster). Be sure to label each file in a way that makes sense to you and to make note of where you found it, the date you downloaded it, and any other relevant source information—so that you can cite your sources properly and go back to them if need be. Your school might provide project management software access, but if not you'll want to look at free online options. A site like top5projectmanagement.com that offers descriptions and reviews can help you sort through the multiple possibilities.

Organizing your content. Some writers begin with nothing more than a pack of sticky notes, putting main points and sub-points and supporting reasons and evidence on individual stickies and arranging them on a larger surface. You might begin with an outline of the main points you want to make and the support for each one. This kind of careful organizing is crucial because it creates a "big picture" of your message and all its parts.

If you're creating a *video essay*, you might create a storyboard to put everything in sequence; another possibility would be a two-column script to line up the video and audio portions. *Audio essays* need some kind of script as well, one that accounts for both words and any music or other sounds. For an *illustrated print essay*, you'll need to decide where to put the images. For *wiki entries*, *blog posts*, and other kinds of online texts that readers navigate by links, you might map out your organization on a large sheet of paper, putting the main page at the center top and then drawing lines out to the various pages you will link to.

Crediting your sources. Be sure to credit your sources. You can do so at the bottom of a poster, as the last slide in an oral presentation, as footnotes in a wiki or links on a blog, or as credits at the end of a video or audio essay.

REFLECT. "This is the time for exploration, for experimentation. This is the time when we can create and risk, when we can write graffiti on the walls and color outside the lines. . . . If we are going to fly and find new intellectual spaces . . . we must expand our notion of academic discourse." That's a challenge that Stanford professor Adam Banks issued in 2015 to an audience of college writing instructors. How would you answer his challenge? Find a piece of academic writing you've done and imagine how you could re-create it using multiple modes.

THIRTY-SIX

Making Presentations

HAT GOES INTO a sure-fire great presentation? Author and consultant Nancy Duarte wanted to find out. So she set out to study some great presentations, hundreds of them, beginning with Martin Luther King Jr.'s "I Have a Dream" speech and Steve Jobs's iPhone launch, two speeches that seemed so different to her that she couldn't imagine she would find anything in common. But she did.

She found that these two speeches—and hundreds of other terrific presentations—shared one common structure. Each speech begins by describing "what is"—and then goes on to suggest what it could (or should) be. That's in the introduction. Then in the middle of the speech, the presenter moves back and forth between discussing that status quo and what it could or should be. And in most cases, the conclusion vividly evokes what could be and calls for action.

Duarte's research shows that this basic structure (from what is to what could be) is very widely used, and especially so by activists, politicians, and businesspeople proposing change of some kind. In fact, it's a structure that may work well for many of the presentations you make in your college classes. And there are two common variations on this structure that you may be familiar with. One begins with what *was*, in the past, and then moves on to explain how it changed. The other opens by noting what others have said about a topic and then moves on to what you want to say about it, focusing on the benefits of your position. Starting with what is, what was, or what's been said and then suggesting

Martin Luther King Jr.

Steve Jobs.

something "better" uses a classic storytelling technique: setting up a conflict that needs to be resolved. And presenting your main point as a story works well in a spoken presentation because stories are easier to follow and remember than other kinds of evidence and are often more persuasive.

In 2014, Michelle Obama used such a story in a high school graduation speech in Topeka, Kansas, where the famous 1954 Supreme Court case *Brown v. Board of Education* originated, in which separate schools for black and white students were ruled unconstitutional. In that speech, she told the story of how that case came into being, what Topeka was like then, and how it had changed since. She brought her main point home at the speech's conclusion by telling the graduates about the grandniece of Lucinda Todd, the very first parent to sign on to the *Brown* lawsuit: that young woman was Obama's "right-hand woman" in the White House. It's this storyline, reaching from the original court case to the present moment, that summed up her point: change is possible, and the students in that audience could help bring it about.

Sounds simple, doesn't it? State your main point, find a story to help get that point across, and inspire the audience to accept what you say. But coming up with these elements in ways that will capture and hold an audience's attention—well, that's not simple. Still, there are some structures and techniques that will help you create presentations that audiences will listen to and remember and that might even call them to action. This chapter provides guidelines to help you do so.

ACROSS DISCIPLINES

You'll likely be required to give oral presentations, using slides or posters, in courses across different fields. This is because of the growing awareness that in the world of work, nearly everyone ends up sharing specialized knowledge with colleagues, (potential) clients, or the public through presentation. Different disciplines and professions have preferred practices. In fields like engineering and the lab sciences, presentations are often team affairs. In these and, in fact, many other fields, the preferred method of presentation is the "assertion-evidence" style: a speaker makes a claim and immediately presents the evidence to support that claim, often in visual form or with the aid of a visual. The website *Assertion-Evidence Approach*, created by Michael Alley at Penn State University, offers tutorials, sample slides, and videos of presentations by students. By watching the videos, you can get ideas about how to develop an effective presentation style that works for you. Seeking at models of effective presentations in your field is a good way to learn what's expected of you.

First, let's take a look at the script one of our students prepared for a presentation on Japanese manga. As you'll see, she used a "what was and how it changed" structure as a foundation for her presentation.

The Rise of Female Heroes in Shoujo Manga

HALLE EDWARDS

HERE'S A QUESTION FOR YOU: [SLIDE] Where are all the strong women heroes in popular comics? In our class we've seen some talented female authors of graphic narratives, but in terms of popular comic book characters (not to mention writers and fans), the girls have been outnumbered.

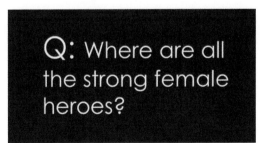

[SLIDE] So guess what? When I started looking, I found the strong female heroes in comics! The place—Japan. The time period—the 1990s. The genre—Shoujo manga. Literally "girls' comics" in Japanese, Shoujo manga is a

HALLE EDWARDS composed this presentation for a second-year writing course that focused on graphic narratives. For this assignment, she first wrote an academic essay and then "translated" it into a ten-minute oral presentation with seventeen slides. As you'll see, we've included only a few of these slides.

popular form of comics in Japan typically written by women for women. Prior to the 1990s, Shoujo typically featured weak heroines and plots that revolved around romance. Then, in the 1990s, Shoujo started showing strong female heroes whose first priority wasn't romance. But what did that change look like and, more importantly, why did it happen?

Today I'll explore the answers. First I'll show you an example of this phenomenon, from Naoko Takeuchi's smash hit manga *Sailor Moon*. Then I'll explain what was happening in Japan in the 1990s and why this allowed Shoujo manga to change so drastically.

[SLIDE] Part one. *Sailor Moon* tells the story of Usagi, a clumsy and not particularly smart schoolgirl with a heart of gold. She discovers that she has a secret identity—Sailor Moon—and is destined to fight the forces of evil. [SLIDE] While *Sailor Moon* does have a love story, much of the manga is devoted to expanding on Sailor Moon's relationship with her eventual comrades—Sailors Mars, Mercury, Jupiter, and Venus. [SLIDE] The relationship of these five heroes is usually prioritized over the romance.

Wait a minute. Five female heroes? The romance is just a side plot? Girls described as soldiers who physically fight bad guys? For anyone familiar with traditional Shoujo manga, it's obvious that *Sailor Moon* pushed boundaries.

[SLIDE] This boundary-pushing can be seen in the introduction of the second female hero, Ami, or Sailor Mercury. Introduced as an aloof genius, Ami quickly reveals Takeuchi's friendly, playful side. [SLIDE] From the outset, Sailor Mercury cannot be pinned down to a stereotype—she's neither a cold nerd nor a bubbly teenager. She's very flawed and very real. Takeuchi's female heroes are layered, interesting, and compelling.

Throughout the story, we see Ami develop a close friendship with Usagi, [SLIDE] ultimately ending in a battle where Ami discovers her identity as Sailor Mercury. Meanwhile, Usagi's budding romance is barely a side plot. Throughout *Sailor Moon*'s five-year run, its female heroines were always the heart of the story—not the romance. The funny thing? Despite this drastic departure from typical Shoujo norms, *Sailor Moon* was a smash hit.

[SLIDE] So why was *Sailor Moon* so warmly received, given that it defied so many norms in Shoujo manga? To understand, you need to know a bit about Japan in the early 1990s. [SLIDE] In 1989, the Asset Price Bubble broke—essentially a huge economic bubble that vastly inflated real estate prices. [SLIDE] This sent Japan's economy spiraling into a recession that lasted throughout the entire 1990s, a decade now known as Japan's "lost decade."

[SLIDE] The recession changed many aspects of life in Japan. Before the recession, men could expect to get hired at a company out of college and work there for their whole lives. Meanwhile, women held mainly part-time jobs—think secretaries and office ladies—with few opportunities for advancement. However, once the recession hit, layoffs became rampant. Companies tanked. Men could no longer rely on having lifetime careers, and many in Japan questioned the long hours that were customary in Japan's workplaces.

> ## What made the 1990s in Japan the "Era of Women"?
>
> - Economic recession lowered job security for men
>
> - More women worked outside the home
>
> - More women voted
>
> - Several female candidates were elected in 1989

[SLIDE] Meanwhile, in the 1989 elections, several female candidates were elected. Also, voter turnout among women was higher than ever. Because of this, the media predicted that the 1990s would be the "era of women." Women were suddenly seen as capable: they could hold real jobs outside the home, run for office, and help save Japan's stumbling economy. These new women were featured in popular soap operas known as "morning dramas" on the government-funded NHK channel.

[SLIDE] Given this media-propelled image of the new, strong woman, several of the major Shoujo magazines began to take note. Thus, when Toshio Irie, the newly minted editor of *Nakayoshi* magazine, learned of *Sailor Moon*, a story with five strong female heroes, he jumped at the opportunity. Not only did he publish Takeuchi's manga; he embraced a mixed-media strategy, including *Sailor Moon*–themed toys with the magazine (to encourage fans to buy their own copies and limit sharing) and selling additional *Sailor Moon* merchandise. [SLIDE] Also, when Toei Animation snapped up the rights to create an animated *Sailor Moon* series, Irie worked with the company to closely match the release of the new *Sailor Moon* chapters and episodes.

Such a media blitz was unheard of for a work of Shoujo manga, and it paid off. By the end of 1995, *Sailor Moon* had made over 300 billion yen in profits and was expanding rapidly worldwide. Circulation figures for the magazine reached an all-time high of 2 million per month. The thirteen volumes that had been released by then had sold over a million copies each and been exported to twenty-three countries.

[SLIDE] The recession, and the media's message that the 1990s would be the "era of women," caused forces in the media to realize that the image of strong women could be popular—and more importantly, profitable. As a result, other manga editors were willing to publish works that featured strong female heroes—knowing that they would make money. This is one way that Shoujo sparked important change.

But why, you might be wondering, does it matter? This was just one time period in one country where comics featured strong women. Was it a phenomenon that spread to other countries? Did more girls start reading comic books and graphic narratives? And did life really change for women in Japan?

The simple answer is no. The "era of women" did not lead to significant change in the lives of women in Japan. They were still mostly relegated to part-time jobs and to most domestic responsibilities. And after the magical girl heroine trends of the 1990s, Shoujo in the 2000s became more focused on "slice of life" stories. This is not to say it went backwards—it just stopped moving forward so daringly.

However, the 1990s in Japan proved that there is a place, and an audience, for strong heroines in graphic narratives. Although there was little or no precedent for introducing strong women characters, a few key people took risks on some new stories, and they paid off. I think this is a lesson we can apply to the graphic novel market today. Just because there are still more male readers and characters in US comics does not mean that the market for strong female characters does not exist. In fact, the success of authors Lynda Barry and Alison Bechdel as well as of the hit TV series Marvel's *Agent* (Peggy) *Carter* suggests that the time may be ripe for many more strong women in graphic narratives. So let's heed the story of Sailor Moon and her crew and read and encourage others to buy works that feature strong women. Then when we're asked "where are all the strong women heroes in popular comics?" we can answer, "They're everywhere!"

[SLIDE] Thank you for listening. I'll be glad to take questions.

Halle Edwards opens her presentation with a statement about "what is"—that is, the status quo, which finds few strong female heroes in popular comic books. She then tells about a similar situation in Japan, and how it changed, exploring some of the issues in Japanese society that allowed women heroes to emerge and using the story of *Sailor Moon*'s success as the major example. Throughout, she poses questions to involve her audience, beginning by asking "Where are all the strong women heroes in popular comics?" Take a moment to count the number of questions in this presentation and where they occur and you'll see that they act as "signpost language," helping the audience follow the presentation and focusing their attention on its most important points. Notice as well that Edwards uses good presentational style: short sentences, simple syntax, clear transitions and other signpost language, active verbs, and vivid description—all things that make the presentation easy to listen to and to follow.

REFLECT. Halle Edwards's presentation grew out of a research paper she had written on the same topic. Look back at an academic essay you have written and then, using this chapter as a guide, make notes on what you would need to do to transform it into a memorable oral presentation.

MAKING A PRESENTATION / A Roadmap

Begin by considering your rhetorical situation

Anticipate who will be in your **AUDIENCE**. What do they already know about your topic, and what other information might they need? What kinds of evidence are most likely to appeal to them? You can keep your audience engaged by establishing eye contact and addressing them directly from time to time. If you're addressing your audience via video, make "eye contact" by looking into the camera.

Be clear about your **PURPOSE**. Make sure you understand any assignment you've been given for this presentation. Is your goal to provide information? to persuade? to propose some kind of action?

Think about your **STANCE**. How are you presenting yourself: as an expert? an interested novice? a researcher? an advocate? Be sure that the stance you are taking is appropriate for your topic and audience. Halle Edwards presents herself as a peer and classmate who has researched her topic and can thus speak with authority about it.

Consider the **CONTEXT**. Where will the presentation take place? What equipment will you need? Whatever it is, be sure to test it in advance—and keep in mind that technology glitches happen, so be sure to have a backup plan. How much time will you have? Who will introduce you?

Think about your **GENRE**. If you've been assigned a specific genre, say to report on a topic or to present a proposal, consult those chapters in this textbook for guidance. If not, see Chapter 11 for help choosing a genre.

Will you be using any **MEDIA** elements that need to be **DESIGNED**? Would showing images or information on a slide or flip chart help your audience follow your presentation? Will they expect some kind of visual aids? Will you be referring to a text or something else that you could put on a handout? Remember that slides and flip charts need to be simple enough and large enough for your audience to read as you speak.

Prepare your presentation

Focus on one main point, and then orchestrate everything else to support it. Halle Edwards begins with a question that signals her main point: where are all the strong women heroes in popular comics? In the rest of the presentation, she provides answers to this question in a story about the appearance of women heroes in Japanese manga, using *Sailor Moon* as her main example.

Gather EVIDENCE to support your point. Once you've decided on your main message, look for examples, statistics, stories, and other evidence that illustrates your point. Halle Edwards uses facts and statistics to support her main point—that, despite some changes, there are still not enough strong female heroes in comic books. Even the huge success of *Sailor Moon* failed to turn the tide in any permanent way.

Develop a clear structure. You can try using the structure Nancy Duarte recommends, focusing on what is (or was) and moving to what it could or should be (or how it changed). If that doesn't suit your topic, you might start by noting what else has been said about your topic as a way of introducing what you want to say about it. Any of these structures will set up a tension that your presentation then resolves—a storytelling technique that will make your argument easier for your audience to follow.

Use TRANSITIONS and other techniques to help listeners follow your presentation. It's always helpful to provide an overview of your talk, saying something like "I have four points to make," and then use those points as signposts in the presentation. One other useful technique is repetition. Halle Edwards repeatedly poses questions that mark turning points in her talk. Another good technique is to explain what you're saying as you go, using expressions such as "in other words." Provide printouts of your scripted presentation to hand out as access copies so your talk is accessible to everyone.

Use vivid language, images, and metaphors to hammer home your point clearly and memorably. The vivid language ("neither a cold nerd nor a bubbly teenager," "smash hit") and metaphors ("boundary-pushing") that Halle Edwards uses help her audience visualize and follow her argument.

But keep it simple. Remember that your audience doesn't usually have a script to read, so you need to speak in a way that will be easy to understand.

Notice that Halle Edwards uses fairly simple diction throughout—and that her sentences are short and follow a straightforward subject-verb-object structure. Even her paragraphs are short, some only a sentence or two—which helped her keep to her script without having to refer to it often as she spoke.

Develop a dynamic **INTRODUCTION**, one that will engage your audience's interest and establish some kind of **COMMON GROUND** with them. You'll also want to establish your **CREDIBILITY**, to show that you've done your homework and can speak knowledgeably about your topic. Halle Edwards was addressing her classmates, so she could assume common ground, but she engaged their interest by asking a provocative question: "Where are all the strong women heroes in popular comics?" The way you open will depend on your topic and rhetorical situation, but whether you start by telling a story, making a startling claim, or summarizing what someone has said about your topic, your goal is to interest your audience in what is to come.

CONCLUDE in a way that leaves your audience thinking. Whether you conclude by reiterating your main point, saying why your argument matters, or some other way, this is a moment when you can make sure your presentation has some kind of impact. Halle Edwards faced a challenge: her research had turned up strong female heroes in Japanese manga, but in the end they did not change the status quo. So she concluded by pointing out that her research showed that there's "a place, and an audience, for strong heroines in graphic narratives." She then turned to her audience and challenged them to seek out such characters and to read the works they appear in.

Think about whether and where you need any visuals. Images can bring your presentation to life, illustrate important points, and engage your audience. Any slides should support or explain a point you are making and need to be clear and easy to see so that your audience can process the information in a couple of seconds. It's therefore often better to convey one idea per slide than to provide a list of bullet points on a single slide. If you need to communicate complex information, putting it in a chart or graph can make it easier for you to explain—and for your audience to understand. More detailed information or material you want your audience to read is best presented on handouts. Try to distribute the handouts at the point when your audience needs them: if you give them out before then, some in the audience may be focusing on the handouts rather than on what you say.

If you'll be using slides or other media, you'll need to design them carefully.

- All slides need to be clearly visible to everyone in your audience, so use at least 24-point fonts. Simple bold fonts are easiest to read; avoid italic fonts, which can be difficult to read.

- Don't depend too much on templates for slides: the choices they build in—colors, fonts, layout, and so on—may not be appropriate for your topic or purpose.

- The most effective slides are simple enough for the audience to process the information they contain in a couple of seconds. As a general rule, it's better to convey one idea per slide than to provide a list of bullet points.

- At the same time, avoid walls of text. In other words, don't fill slides with long sentences.

- It's generally best to begin with a slide that includes the title of your presentation, your name (and those of your team members, if this is a group presentation), and any other relevant information such as the course or your institution if you're presenting to an outside group. If you are using a design such as a university logo, use it on only the opening slide.

- Make sure that any audio or video clips embedded in your presentation relate directly to the point you are making and that they are clear and easy to see and hear.

- Additionally, make sure any embedded audio or video clips will work properly on the technology you'll actually be using to give your presentation.

- Be sure that any visual you use contributes to your argument. Don't use visuals, especially clip art, that does not add value to your presentation.

- When you take visuals from other sources, acknowledge those sources, either on the slide in a small font or in the references at the end.

- Decorative backgrounds can be distracting, so avoid them unless they add something very specific to your presentation. In general, avoid special effects.

- When possible, present ideas in diagrams or charts that will be easy for the audience to understand.

- Be consistent. Using one font or color for headings and making them parallel in structure will help your audience follow what you are saying. Remember that some audience members may be color-blind, a fact that should influence your choice of color palette.

- Provide descriptions of your visuals in printed access copies so that those in the audience who can't see the slides can still follow your argument.

- Finally, be sure to get responses to your slides just as you would to drafts of your script. Note that Halle Edwards made her slides simple and clearly focused, intended to raise a question or illustrate or underscore a point. She used *PowerPoint* because she was making a linear argument; for less linear structures, you might use *Prezi*, which allows you to zoom in and out, looking at images in detail and from different perspectives.

Give your presentation

Practice, practice, practice. There is no substitute for practice. None. So schedule time to rehearse and make sure you can articulate your main message loud and clear at a moment's notice. Ask friends to serve as an audience for a full rehearsal, and be sure to time your presentation so that you don't go beyond the limit. When you're done, ask your friends to tell you your main point. If they can do so, then you've made an impression! Ask them as well how you came across—as friendly? authoritative? something else? If it's not what you're aiming for, talk through how you *want* to come across and how to get there.

Listen to how you use your voice. Record yourself speaking and then listen to what you sound like. Is your voice clear and loud enough to hear? Do you speak very quickly, or too slowly? Do you vary your tone of voice or tend toward a monotone? What can you do to improve this aspect of your delivery? If you're presenting alone, begin by introducing yourself and announcing the topic of your talk to get some idea of how your voice is projecting in the space where you're presenting. For a team presentation, all members should introduce themselves in order to hear their own voice and adjust their volume appropriately. After the introductions, the first speaker can announce the topic of the presentation for team presentations.

Establish eye contact with the audience by quickly scanning the audience at eye level. If you're uncomfortable making direct eye contact, focus a little higher than their heads at the back of the room. Do not look down at the floor; do not look up at the ceiling. Don't turn your back to the audience to read slides.

Stand up straight! And look at your audience. Try to avoid shifting from foot to foot or jingling change in your pockets. You want the focus to be on you and your message.

Move around. Especially if you are going to speak for more than five minutes, you won't want to stand cemented in place. Depending on the configuration of the room where you're presenting, be careful to avoid blocking the audience's view of the slides. In these cases, stand to the right or the left of the slides, out of the line of sight of the audience members.

THIRTY-SEVEN

Assembling a Portfolio

 OR HIS FIRST-YEAR WRITING CLASS, Julio Martinez was required to create a portfolio of his work to demonstrate how his writing had improved over the term. He included the drafts and final revision of a rhetorical analysis, along with two peer reviews he received; an annotated bibliography; and the drafts and final revision of a research report. Finally, he wrote a cover letter to his instructor in which he described, evaluated, and reflected on his writing—and set out several goals to work on after the term was over. He submitted his portfolio in print.

Not so for Susanna Moller, an art major who created a website during her sophomore year to host her portfolio of artwork. She included only finished works, organized by subject and style, and updated the site with new pieces throughout college. When she had her first solo show, she posted the review from the college newspaper. As graduation approached, she put her résumé on the site—and added the URL to résumés she sent to potential employers so they could see her work.

Deborah Burke began her portfolio blog with a first-year essay she was very proud of. The next year, she wrote a radio essay on the same topic; this became another item in her portfolio. Continuing her research, she wrote a play and added the script to her blog, along with a *YouTube* video of a scene from the play. Finally, she added her résumé and a statement reflecting on her work in college. This portfolio helped her to get an internship—and later a job.

Today, portfolios exist on paper and online. You may be required to keep a portfolio of your work for a writing course as a way of thinking about what you've learned, demonstrating and delivering to your instructor what you've written, and reflecting on your strengths and weaknesses as a writer. Or you may assemble a portfolio to showcase your best work to prospective employers. Whatever your purpose, assembling a portfolio offers an excellent opportunity to reflect on your writing and to chart goals for yourself as a writer. This chapter provides guidelines to help you compile a writing portfolio.

What to Include in a Writing Portfolio

A portfolio submitted to your instructor at the end of a course should represent your best work and demonstrate your growth as a writer, so you'll probably include some of the following materials:

- A number of your best essays and other projects
- Writing representing several genres and media
- Freewriting and other notes
- Various drafts, from first to final
- Response from readers
- A statement reflecting on your work

Your instructor may specify what you need to include, but often you'll get to choose. In that case, what you include will depend on what you're trying to show. If you're trying to show your best work, you might include three pieces that you like best; if, on the other hand, you're trying to show a range of what you've written, you would probably choose writing in various GENRES and MEDIA. If you're trying to show how you've improved, you'll want to include work in several drafts. Just remember that your portfolio is an opportunity for you to evaluate and deliver your own writing: choose work that demonstrates what you want to show.

If you are preparing a portfolio not for class but to highlight your accomplishments for future employers, you will probably make different choices. These choices would be informed by the skills required for the positions you are applying for, and by what you wish to demonstrate to potential employers. If you want to show your abilities as a journalist, you might include in your portfolio a narrative that you wrote for a writing course or a video that you shot and edited. If you are applying for a position in a research lab, you might include a report of a research study and the written proposal that led to that project. Depending on what technology or social media skills employers ask for, you might also include work you've done in multiple modes, such as websites or blogs. You'll certainly want to include a carefully constructed résumé and a cover page introducing yourself and providing an overview of your skills.

Collecting Your Work

Start collecting pieces for your portfolio early in the term. Organization is critical, so create a specific computer folder for the portfolio and give it a name (like "My Portfolio") that you can easily find; inside the folder, create a sub-folder for each piece of writing you include. Identify all drafts with a title and date, as shown in the following example.

```
▼ 📁 My Portfolio
   ▼ 📁 Analysis
      📄 Analysis_draft_final_28Sept
      📄 Analysis_draft1_14Sept
      📄 Analysis_draft2_21Sept
      📄 Analysis_notes_10Sept
   ▼ 📁 Position
      📄 Position_draft_1_9Oct
      📄 Position_draft_2_16Oct
      📄 Position_draft_final_23Oct
      📄 Position_notes_5Oct
```

If you're required to include a statement reflecting on your writing, take notes on your process and your work *throughout the term*. Also keep copies of any peer responses you receive in your file.

You may also find that you want to add new pieces to your portfolio even after you've submitted it for an assignment, in which case it's all the more important to keep your files neat and organized from the beginning. Adding work is easy, especially to an online portfolio, but anyone visiting your site should see an organized, polished collection of work instead of a site that looks to be under construction.

Reflecting on Your Writing

An essential component of your portfolio is a statement that introduces and reflects on the work that's included in the portfolio. Such a statement should explain what's included and why you included the pieces you did, describe your writing process, assess what you've learned, reflect on your development as a writer, and perhaps establish goals for yourself.

Writing such a statement gives you the opportunity to take a good look at your writing and to evaluate it on your own terms. Maybe the essay on which you received your lowest grade was one where you experienced a breakthrough in your writing process. You may well want to discuss this breakthrough in your statement. Did you discover that freewriting worked better than outlining as a way to generate ideas? These are the kinds of insights you can include in your statement to demonstrate to your instructor that you have thought carefully about your writing and your writing process. Following are some prompts to help you think critically about both:

- **REVIEW** *each piece of writing in your portfolio.* What are the strengths and the weaknesses? Which is your best piece? Explain why it is the best and what it demonstrates about what you've learned. Which would you say is the weakest—and how would you change it if you could?

- **ANALYZE** *your writing process.* Study any drafts, responses, and other materials you're including. How did any responses you received help you revise? Which of them helped the most? Were any not helpful?

- **DESCRIBE** *the strategies you use to write.* Which ones have been most helpful, and which have been less helpful? Which ones do you enjoy?

- **REFLECT** *on your work as an author.* What does the writing in your portfolio show about you? What do you do well—and less well? What kinds of writing do you like the most? Is there any kind of writing that you struggle with or dislike—and if so, why?

- **DEFINE** *goals.* What has your portfolio helped you understand about yourself as a writer? What strengths or weaknesses do you now see? Based on this analysis, what do you now want to work on?

This statement is usually written either as a letter or as an essay. You may or may not have an explicit **THESIS**, but you need to make clear what your portfolio demonstrates about you as a writer. Remember that the statement itself demonstrates your writing ability: write it thoughtfully and carefully.

A Sample Portfolio Statement

December 7, 2019

Dear Reader,

Writing used to be one of those things I never gave much time to. I'd get it done but without thinking much about how to do it better. It wasn't until coming to Ball State and taking a class with Professor Clark-Upchurch that writing started to be more than just a nuisance. For the first time, I was forced to look at the inner workings of formal writing, to analyze and examine each part, and to learn what each one is supposed to contribute and why it's important. Slowly over the course of this semester, I have moved beyond the simple five-paragraph essay I learned in high school. All in all, I have become a stronger writer.

Writing the first paper, the literacy narrative, came easily to me . . . or so I thought. When my paper came back to me with Professor Clark-Upchurch's comments about my thesis and organization, some irrelevant incidents I included, the lack of illustrations to support my points, and my "repetitive and simplistic sentence structures," I knew I needed to work harder. On the second paper, an analysis of a magazine ad, my thesis was clearer and my paragraphs "flowed, one into the next" with good examples from the ad as support, but I still needed to work on using a variety of sentences to "make the reader want to read on."

It was on my last paper, the research-based essay, that I finally pulled everything together: an engaging introduction, a clear thesis, logical organization, solid development with lots of supporting examples, and (finally!) varied sentences.

Although my writing style has improved and my understanding of all that goes into a paper is at an all-time high, I still struggle with writing a proposal. I'm not sure why, but for some reason writing an essay about writing a future essay leaves me confused. I'd rather just write the essay in the first place instead of wasting time and effort proposing what I'm going to write about. As a result, I never really made a decent effort at the third writing project—the proposal for the research paper. Thus I have decided to exclude that paper from my portfolio as I am sure it is my weakest.

In addition to these three papers, I include drafts with peer responses and Professor Clark-Upchurch's suggestions in order to provide a clear picture of how much I learned this term. One of the most helpful parts of the class was the peer responding sessions, when we analyzed each other's essays. Doing this helped me think about what I do in my own writing and showed me that other people can learn from what I write—it's not just for the teacher or to get a grade.

The essays you are about to read are just a start, a sturdy base for me to continue developing my writing into something more. Whether willingly or unwillingly, I learned that good writing takes work, but that it also starts to work better when I think about how the parts of my writing fit together. Now whenever I need to write a formal paper, I have some tools I have learned and can use to write for a purpose instead of simply writing to fill the page and finish the assignment.

Sincerely,
Kameron Wiles

Organizing a Portfolio

The way you organize and deliver your portfolio is important; it's part of how you present yourself as a writer. There's no one way to organize a portfolio, but it needs to be carefully arranged so that it's easy to read. Be sure you know if your instructor expects a certain format or system.

Print portfolios can go in a folder (for a small portfolio) or a binder (for a longer one). Begin with a title page that includes your name, the course title and number, the instructor's name, the date, and the portfolio's title. Follow the title page with a table of contents. Next comes your statement, and finally the writing. Unless your instructor asks for papers in a different order, organize the writing by assignments, putting all the materials from each assignment together, with the final draft on top. If you're using a binder, add tabbed dividers, one for each assignment. Number the pages consecutively. Label everything.

E-portfolios can be as basic as *Word* documents uploaded to *Blackboard* or some other online course management system. Or you might post texts to an e-portfolio platform like *Google Docs* or use a blogging site like *WordPress*, *Scribd*, or *Tumblr*. You can create a personal website using a building platform like *Wix*, *Google Sites*, *Squarespace*, or *Weebly*.

And just like a print portfolio, your e-portfolio should be organized by year, course, assignment, or the kind of content on each page. See on the following page how Rae'Johne Smith, an economics major at Spelman College, organizes her e-portfolio. Her homepage features a prominent banner with her name, her photo, and an introductory statement saying who she is and what her portfolio will show—all organized by a menu of links across the top.

As an economics major preparing for a career in finance, Smith presents her writing using the metaphor of a J-curve, one that will make good sense to potential employers. And for those unfamiliar with economics concepts, she clearly explains that a J-curve represents investments and returns over time—and that she's using it here to reflect her growth as a writer

Smith collects her writing—work in which she has obviously invested a lot of time and energy—on the second page, titled "investments," and organizes it into yearly "capital calls," an economics term for money that is put into an investment fund. Then comes a link to "distributions," which is econspeak for the rewards that have come her way from improving her writing. Next comes an "annual report" that sums up her growth as a student and writer, followed by a page with her contact information.

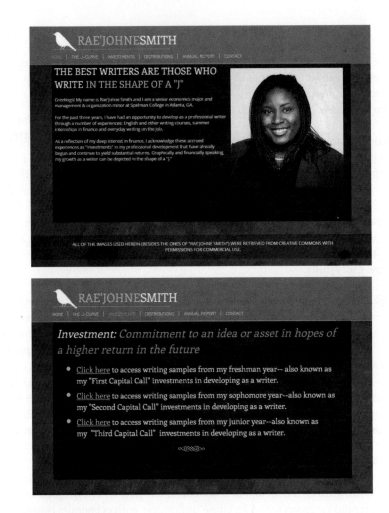

Some Tips for Compiling an E-portfolio

- Figure out exactly what you're going to put in your portfolio and how you're going to organize it before uploading anything.

- Be sure you know what system your instructor expects you to use, and contact your school's tech desk if you need help.

- If you need to upload files, know what type of file you should use: *Word* documents, PDFs, or something else?

- Double-check that the file you are uploading is the final version.

- If you are working on an e-portfolio website, set up a homepage with your basic information and include links to your statement and to each piece of writing, each on its own page.

- To be sure all of the links work and everything looks the way you expect, check your site in different browsers and on different devices (laptops, tablets, and phones); you don't want to find out after you've submitted your portfolio that links don't work or some parts aren't visible.

- If you're using a school website or platform to host your work and want to preserve your e-portfolio or continue to add to it, ask your instructor or the tech desk if it will remain online after the term ends. If it will be deleted, you will need to move it to a more permanent platform.

Portfolios are becoming increasingly necessary, both in school and on the job. Your portfolio is more than an archive of your writing—it's a way of looking systematically at your work. Keeping a portfolio of your writing projects enables you to reflect on your development as a writer—on what you've learned and what you need to work on.

REFLECT. Suppose you're putting together a writing portfolio as part of an application for a summer job or a job after graduation. Go through your files to determine which writing samples you would want to include for the kind of job you are applying for. Consider writing in various modes, genres, and media. Read over each piece carefully and then write a brief comment on each one, pointing out its strengths and what it shows about you as a writer.

THIRTY-EIGHT

Publishing Your Writing

NCE UPON A TIME you had to get a newspaper, magazine, or book editor to read and accept your writing in order to be published. Go back further, and even talent wasn't enough to get your work into print—you usually had to be a man as well. Even further back in time, writers who wanted to share their ideas with others often had to hire a scribe to handwrite their work since writing was a skill not many people mastered. Clearly, getting published wasn't easy. But today things have changed. You're only a few clicks away from delivering your writing to audiences far and wide online.

The internet not only allows writers to publish their work but also has changed how we define "publishing": it no longer only means seeing your work distributed in print by an authoritative source. Today publishing your work means making it available to an audience, whether in print or online.

Want to become a published author? As a writer today, you have many ways to share your work with an audience. This chapter lists a sampling of print and online venues where you can do so. We invite you to join the fun and publish what you write. It's easier than you may think!

Essay competitions. Most colleges and universities have newspapers and journals that publish selected student writing—and many have literary magazines that focus on creative writing and art. It's common to gather submissions by holding annual writing competitions—featuring the winners' work online, in a printed collection, or at an event. For example, DePaul University holds an annual writer's showcase where chosen writers who submit their work are invited to present. Search your school's website to see if there's an opportunity to submit writing for publication on your campus.

In fact, W. W. Norton, the publisher of this book, sponsors an annual prize for an outstanding essay written by an undergraduate student. You can read all the previous winning essays—and submit your own work—by visiting everyonesanauthor.tumblr.com.

Undergraduate writing publications. You aren't restricted to publishing opportunities on your own campus; the following publications accept submissions from undergraduate writers around the country:

- *Young Scholars in Writing: Undergraduate Research in Writing and Rhetoric*, supported by Montana State University, publishes "research and theoretical articles from undergraduates on writing, writers, rhetoric, discourse, language, and related topics." Despite the journal's title, undergraduate students of all ages are invited to submit.

- *Queen City Writers*, an online journal at the University of Cincinnati, publishes undergraduate research and "thought-provoking pieces that explore questions and problems related to writing, rhetoric, reading, literacy broadly conceived, popular culture and media, community discourses, and multimodal and digital composing."

- The following schools offer detailed lists of additional publishing opportunities for student writers: Southern Utah University's list of creative writing opportunities; University of Nebraska–Lincoln's list of undergraduate research journals organized by topic; and University of Notre Dame's list of undergraduate research journals divided by discipline.

Publish yourself! Kindle Direct Publishing and other self-publishing platforms make it possible to self-publish works and then sell them directly to readers. Blogs and social networking sites are quick and easy ways to share your ideas with a wide audience for free, as are websites built to collect and publish user reviews such as *Yelp, Google, Amazon,* and *Trip Advisor.* And don't discount the commenting space most newspapers, magazines, and video- and image-sharing sites like *YouTube* offer. Some sites like the *New York Times* even curate comments, highlighting those worth considering and responding to. Finally, don't forget fan fiction sites like *FanFiction.net* for spaces to discuss your favorite works, receive writing tips, and contribute your own fiction based on works you admire. Fan fiction sites offer a good way to practice as well as find an audience and supportive community of writers with like interests.

If everyone's an author, that includes you! So get busy. Now's the time to publish something you've written. We hope this book will help you do so.

Credits

TEXT

Chapter 7: Yuliya Vayner: Sample Annotated Text. Copyright © 2019 by W. W. Norton & Company.

Chapter 12: Jennifer Delahunty: "To All the Girls I've Rejected." Originally published in *The New York Times*, March 23, 2006. Reprinted by permission of the author. **Russel Honoré:** "Work Is a Blessing" from *This I Believe: On Fatherhood*, eds. Dan Gediman, John Gregory, Mary Jo Gediman. Copyright © 2011 by This I Believe, Inc. All rights reserved. Reproduced with permission of John Wiley & Sons, Inc. **Jaron Lanier:** Excerpts from "Welcome to the Cage That Goes Everywhere with You" and "Bummer Anti-Magic" from the book *Ten Arguments for Deleting Your Social Media Accounts Right Now*. © 2018 by Jaron Lanier. Used by permission of Henry Holt and Company, Random House Ltd. and William Morris Endeavor Entertainment, LLC. **Katherine Spriggs:** "On Buying Local." Copyright © 2008 by Katherine Spriggs.

Chapter 13: Connor Coyne: "Bathtime." Originally published in *Belt Magazine*. Reprinted by permission. **Raya Elfadel Kheirbek:** Copyrighted and published by Project HOPE/Health Affairs as "At the VA, Healing the Doctor-Patient Relationship" by Raya Elfadel Kheirbek. *Health Affairs*, October 2017, 36(10):1848–1851. The published article is archived and available online at www.healthaffairs.org/. Reprinted with permission. **Larry Lehna:** "The Look." Copyright © 2014 by Larry Lehna. **Melanie Luken:** "Literacy: A Lineage." Copyright © 2009 by Melanie Luken. **Minh Vu:** "Dirty Nails." Copyright © 2018 by Minh Vu.

Chapter 14: David Brooks: "Third-Party Option." From *The New York Times*, July 30, 2018. © 2018 The New York Times. All rights reserved. Used under license. www.nytimes.com. **Jerome Conlon:** "Analyzing Nike's Controversial Just Do It Campaign," by Jerome Conlon. Branding Strategy Insider, September 5, 2018. Reprinted by permission of The Blake Project. **Eamonn Forde:** " 'Happy' by Pharrell Williams: Why This Song Has Grabbed the Nation." *The Big Issue*, February 11,

2014. Reprinted by permission of The Big Issue. **Alberta Negri:** "Underneath the Leather Jackets and Chrome Pipes: Research into a Community of Local Bikers," by Alberta Negri. Originally published by *Queen City Writers*, November 9, 2017. Reprinted by permission of the author. **Darlene E. Jenkins, Ph.D.:** Excerpts from "Tightening the Turns in Speed Skating: Lessons in Centripetal Force and Balance," www.ScienceBuddies. org. Reprinted with permission. **Will Moller:** Excerpts from "A Painful Posting," It'sAbouttheMoney.net, Feb. 4, 2011. Reprinted by permission of the author. **Johna Paolino:** "Google Home vs. Alexa," by Johna Paolino. Originally published on *Medium*, January 4, 2017. Reprinted by permission of the author. **Melissa Rubin:** "Advertisements R Us." Copyright © 2011 by Melissa Rubin. **Somini Sengupta:** "Why Is Everyone Focused on Zuckerberg's Hoodie?" From *The New York Times*, May 11, 2012. © 2012 The New York Times. All rights reserved. Used under license. www.nytimes. com. **Eric Williams:** "Five Things All Tennis Players Can Learn from Serena Williams." Originally published on Examiner.com, April 30, 2013. Reprinted by permission of the author.

Chapter 15: Barry Estabrook: "Selling the Farm." Originally published on Gourmet.com, August 13, 2009. Reprinted by permission of the author. **Ryan Joy:** "The Right to Preach on a College Campus." *Portland Spectrum*, June 2015. Copyright © 2015 by Ryan Joy. Reprinted by permission of the author. **Bill Laitner:** "Heart and Sole: Detroiter Walks 21 Miles in Work Commute." From *Detroit Free Press*, February 2, 2015. © 2015 Gannett-Community Publishing. All rights reserved. Used under license. www.freep.com.

Chapter 16: Tim Alamenciak: "*The Monopolists* by Mary Pilon: Review." *Toronto Star*, March 20, 2015. Reprinted by permission of the author. **Marc Bernardin:** "*Black Panther* Gets So Much Right, and One Crucial Thing Wrong," by Marc Bernardin, Nerdist.com, February 6, 2018. Reprinted by permission of Nerdist. **Crystal Aymelek:** Introduction from "The Effects of Mindfulness Meditation and Exercise on Memory." Copyright © 2014 Crystal Aymelek. **Lou Kesten:** "Nintendo Switch Is impressive, but Needs More Games," Associated Press, 1 March 2017. Reprinted by permission. Copyrighted 2017. Associated Press. 2105578:0919PF **Areyon Jolivette:** " 'Spider-Man: Into the Spider-Verse' Is as Extraordinary as It Allows Its Audience to Be," by Areyon Jolivette. Originally published in *The Daily Californian*, December 19,

About the Authors

 ANDREA LUNSFORD is Professor Emerita of English at Stanford University and is on the faculty at the Bread Loaf School of English. Her scholarly interests include rhetorical theory, women and the history of rhetoric, collaboration, style, and technologies of writing. She's received the Braddock and Shaughnessy awards for her research on audience and classical rhetoric, and the CCCC Exemplar Award. She is currently at work on *The Norton Anthology of Rhetoric and Writing.*

 MICHAL BRODY is a linguist. She was a founding faculty member of the Universidad de Oriente in Yucatán, Mexico. Her scholarly work centers on language pedagogy and politics in the United States and Mexico, and she recently led a writing workshop for personnel of the secretaría de las Mujeres in Mérida, Yucatán. She's a co-author of *What's Language Got to Do with It?* and *The Little Seagull Handbook,* and the editor of the *Everyone's an Author Tumblr* and *They Say / I Blog.*

 LISA EDE is Professor Emerita of English at Oregon State University, where she directed the Center for Writing and Learning and taught courses in composition, rhetoric, and literacy studies. She's received the Braddock and Shaughnessy awards for her research on audience and classical rhetoric. Her recent books include *Situating Composition: Composition Studies and the Politics of Location* and (with Andrea Lunsford) *Writing Together: Collaboration in Theory and Practice.*

BEVERLY MOSS is Associate Professor of English at The Ohio State University, where she teaches in the Rhetoric, Composition, and Literacy program, and is director of the Bread Loaf Teacher Network for the Middlebury Bread Loaf School of English. Her research and teaching interests focus on community literacy, composition theory and pedagogy, and writing center theories and practices. Her books include *Literacy across Communities* and *A Community Text Arises: A Literate Text and a Literacy Tradition in African-American Churches*.

CAROLE CLARK PAPPER has spent four decades teaching writing and rhetoric. Prior to retiring from Hofstra University, where she directed the University Writing Center, she served for many years as the Director of the Ball State University Writing Program (winner of the CCCC Certificate of Excellence 2006–2007). Her continuing scholarly interests include visual literacy, composition theory and pedagogy, and writing center theories and practices.

KEITH WALTERS is Professor Emeritus of Applied Linguistics at Portland State University, where he taught courses in sociolinguistics, discourse analysis, and professional communication. Much of his research has focused on issues of language and identity in Tunisia, where he served as a Peace Corps volunteer, and the Arab world more broadly. He's a co-author of two other textbooks, *Everything's an Argument with Readings* and *What's Language Got to Do with It?* Prior to teaching at PSU, he taught in the Linguistics Department at the University of Texas at Austin and in the English Department at The Ohio State University. Most recently, he was a Fulbright scholar in the English Department at Bethlehem University in the West Bank.

About the Alphabet

THE ALPHABET song may be one of the first things you learned to sing: *a - b - c - d - e - f - g / h - i - j - k - l - m - n - o - p / q and r and s and t / u - v - w - x - y - z / Now I know my abc's / Next time won't you sing with me?* And maybe you had a set of alphabet blocks, 26 little letters you could use to make words of your own. Combined, those letters yield everything from the word *Google* to the complete works of Shakespeare. So alphabets are versatile, and perhaps that's part of their fascination. In our grandmothers' day, young women often made alphabet samplers, using fancy stitches to create the letters. Earlier, in medieval times, scribes labored to create highly ornate letters to adorn manuscripts whose words were "illuminated" by the intricate letters, often done in silver and gold.

We had these illuminated letters in mind when we asked Carin Berger to create a modern-day illuminated alphabet for this book. You'll see the results in every chapter, each of which begins with one of the letters Berger created. To us, they represent our old alphabet blocks, our grandmothers' samplers, and the illuminated letters that still dazzle us after many hundreds of years. But look again and you'll see that these letters are also striking images. And instead of being decorated with precious silver and gold leaf, our letters are decorated with bits of everyday text—maps, comics, stationery, receipts, school papers, checks, and so on. In our alphabet, old and new, low tech and high tech, word and image come together to create evocative, timely letters for our book.

And just as modern-day type fonts have names, so too does our alphabet. We call it Author.

Submitting Papers for Publication by
W. W. Norton & Company

We are interested in receiving writing from college students to consider including in our textbooks as examples of student writing. Please send this form with the work that you would like us to consider to Marilyn Moller, Student Writing, W. W. Norton & Company, 500 Fifth Avenue, New York, NY 10110. For questions, or to submit electronically, email us at composition@wwnorton.com.

Text Submission Form

Student's name _____

School _____

Address _____

Department _____

Course _____

Writing assignment the text responds to _____

_____

_____

_____

_____

_____

Instructor's name _____

Please write a few sentences about what your primary purposes were for writing this text. Also, if you wish, tell us what you learned about writing from the experience of writing it.

_____

_____

_____

_____

_____

_____

_____

_____

_____

_____

Contact Information

Please provide the information below so that we can contact you if your work is selected for publication.

Name _____

Permanent address _____

Email _____

Phone _____

Author / Title Index

A

"About Men" (Ehrlich), 464
"Abraham Lincoln" (Du Bois), 417
"ADAPTS, the First Evacuation Sling for Wheelchair Users" (Wearly), 375–76
Adegboyega, Ade, 55–56, 59
"Advertisements R Us" (Rubin), 276–81
"After the Cameras Leave" (Hrabowski), 161
Agnes Scott College Commencement Address 2017 (Winfrey), 18, 19
"Ain't I a Woman?" (Truth), 471
Akukwe, Chinua
    "H.I.V. and AIDS in Africa: Ten Lessons from the Field," 470
Alamenciak, Tim, *345*
    "Monopoly: The Scandal Behind the World's Favorite Board Game," 345–47
Alley, Michael, 796
"Analyzing Nike's Controversial Just Do It Campaign" (Conlon), 238–39
"An Animal's Place" (Pollan), 704
Anthony, Mariah, 338
"Aretha Franklin Obituary" (Williams), 187
"Are We Alone in the Universe?" (Krauthammer), 547–50
Aristotle, 2, 6, 101, 425
    Rhetoric, 552
Arkle, Peter, 338
The Art of Slow Reading (Newkirk), 71
"At the VA, Healing the Doctor-Patient Relationship" (Kheirbek), 202–7

Note: Page numbers in *italics* indicate figures.

Austen, Jane
    Pride and Prejudice and Zombies, 535
Aymelek, Crystal, *350*
    "The Effects of Mindfulness Meditation and Exercise on Memory," 350–55

B

Balko, Radley
    "What You Eat Is Your Business," 438, 439
Bamboo
    "Mama Africa," 686, 687, 689
Baron, Dennis
    "Should Everybody Write?," 783–84
Barracoon: The Story of the Last "Black Cargo" (Hurston), 691–92
Barry, Dave
    "Beauty and the Beast," 457
    "Guys vs. Men," 460
"Bathtime" (Coyne), 219–23
"Beauty and the Beast" (Barry), 457
Becker, Amy
    "Employment Discrimination, Local School Boards, and LGBT Civil Rights: Reviewing 25 Years of Public Opinion Data," 559–60
Bennett, Lerone Jr.
    "Blacks in Chicago," 473
Berliner, David
    "High-stakes Testing and Student Achievement," 536
Bernardin, Marc, *362*
    "*Black Panther* Gets So Much Right and One Crucial Thing Wrong," 362–66

"Beyond the Ivory Tower: The Scientific Consensus on Climate Change" (Oreskes), 158–59

Birkenstein, Cathy
   "They Say / I Say," 17

"*Black Panther* Gets So Much Right and One Crucial Thing Wrong" (Bernardin), 362–66

"Blacks in Chicago" (Bennett), 473

Blanda, Sean
   "The 'Other Side' Is Not Dumb," 10

The Blind Side (Lewis), 197–99

"Blocky Empires" (Woolsey), 340

Blount, Julia
   "Dear White *Facebook* Friends: I Need You to Respect What Black America Is Feeling Right Now," 8–9

Booth, Wayne, 5, 6
   The Rhetoric of Rhetoric, 15–16

Borowitz, Andy, 103

Bower, Bruce
   "Female Chimps Play with 'Dolls,'" 429

Branding Strategy Insider (blog), 238

Brandt, Deborah
   "Writing at Work," 62–63

"Broken English" (Lyiscott), 689–90

Brooks, David, *414*
   "Nonconformity Is Skin Deep," 414–15
   "Third-Party Option," 234–36, 249–51

Burke, Deborah, 809

Burke, Kenneth, 1, 143, 538
   The Philosophy of Literary Form, 7

Buthainah
   "Who Fears Climbing the Mountains Lives Forever between the Holes," 691

C

"Call It Blindness" (Kleege), 196–98

"Call to Action to Prevent Gun Violence" (Interdisciplinary Group on Preventing School and Community Violence), 376–77, 383–85

The Canterbury Tales (Chaucer), 110, *111*, 685

Capitalism vs. the Climate (Klein), 469

Carlin, John
   Playing the Enemy: Nelson Mandela and the Game That Made a Nation, 424–25

Cause/Effect: The Unexpected Origins of Terrible Things (Westbrook), *538*, *788*, 788–89

"Celebration" (Madonna), 534

Chast, Roz
   "New Movie Genres," *138*

Chaucer, Geoffrey
   The Canterbury Tales, 110, *111*, 685

Chomsky, Noam
   Language and Politics, 460

Cicero, 9, 448, 673

Cisneros, Sandra
   Woman Hollering Creek and Other Stories, 686–87

City of Appleton On-Street Bike Plan (Wisconsin Department of Transportation), 378–80, *381*

"The Clan of One-Breasted Women" (Williams), 462–63

Climate Change 2014: Synthesis Report (United Nations), 454

Clinton, Bill, 696–97, 700

Colberg, Chloe
   "What Can You Do to Make a Difference?," 470, *471*

"The College Connection" (Posnanski), 707–8

"College Drinking Hazardous to Campus Communities: Task Force Calls for Research-Based Prevention Programs" (National Institutes of Health), 469

"Color Blind or Color Brave?" (Hobson), 154–56

A Community Text Arises (Moss), 240–42, 247

Conlon, Jerome
   "Analyzing Nike's Controversial Just Do It Campaign," 238–39

Con Respeto: Bridging the Distances between Culturally Diverse Families and Schools (Valdés), 687–89

Conversations with People Who Hate Me (Marron), *22*, 22–23

Cooper, Lane, 552

Cossery, Albert, 342

Coyne, Connor, *219*
"Bathtime," 219–23

Crain, Caleb
"There She Blew: The History of American Whaling," 341

"Crap Detection 101" (Rheingold), 102

Creswell, Robyn
"Undelivered," 342

Cullors, Patrisse, 678

D

Da Corte, Alex
Rubber Pencil Devil, *331*

"Damage Control" (Sainani), 430

"Dancing Past the Boundaries" (Hinojosa), 417–18

Dargis, Manohla
"Herzog Finds His Inner Man," 338–39

Davidson, Cathy
Now You See It: How the Brain Science of Attention Will Transform the Way We Live, Work, and Learn, 129, 708

Davis, Daryl, *25*
"How to Argue," 24–25

"Dear White *Facebook* Friends: I Need You to Respect What Black America Is Feeling Right Now" (Blount), 8–9

Delahunty, Jennifer
"To All the Girls I've Rejected," 156–57, 159, 160

"Delete Your Social Media Accounts Right Now" (Lanier), 172–76

Didion, Joan
"Some Dreamers of the Golden Dream," 701

Dillard, Annie, 694
A Writing Life, 451–52

"Dirty Nails" (Vu), 193–94

Dive Bar Girl (DBG; CherryTheDiveBarGirl), 675–76

Donne, John, 112

"Don't Blame the Eater" (Zinczenko), 427

"Do the Right Thing" (Simoneaux), 666

Dreher, Rod
"Same Food Planet, Different Food Worlds," 674–76

Duarte, Nancy, 794–95

Du Bois, W. E. B.
"Abraham Lincoln," 417

E

"Early Word Production: A Study of One Child's Word Productions" (Sheppard), 295, 647–61

"Eboo Patel" (Interfaith Youth Core), 422

"The Economic Impact of Investing Public Funds in Sports Franchises" (Pasini), 387–90

The Economics of Attention (Lanham), 67

Edwards, Halle, *797*
"The Rise of Female Heroes in Shoujo Manga," 797–802

"The Effects of Mindfulness Meditation and Exercise on Memory" (Aymelek), 350–55

Ehrlich, Gretel
"About Men," 464

Ellison, Ralph
Invisible Man, 704

"Employment Discrimination, Local School Boards, and LGBT Civil Rights: Reviewing 25 Years of Public Opinion Data" (Becker), 559–60

Epictetus, 8

e-Portfolio (Smith), 815, *816*

"Establishing Identities" (Fox), 294–95

Estabrook, Barry, *318*
"Selling the Farm," 318–23

F

Falcon, Ted
Getting to the Heart of Interfaith: The Eye-Opening, Hope-Filled Friendship of a Pastor, a Rabbi and a Sheikh, 233

"Farewell Letter to America" (McCain), 673–74

Farid, Hany, 105–6

"Female Chimps Play with 'Dolls'" (Bower), 429

Fish, Stanley
    How to Write a Sentence, 694

"Five Things All Tennis Players Can Learn from
    Serena Williams" (Williams), 231–32

FiveThirtyEight, 781

Flanagan, Caitlin
    "The Glory of Oprah," 710
    "The Madness of Cesar Chavez," 431–32

Fleming, David
    "Sports' Perfect 0.4 Seconds," 194–96

Florida, Richard
    "Where the Brains Are," 459

"Florida State University to Phase Out Academic
    Operations" (*The Onion*), 467

Forde, Eamonn, *252*
    "Why Pharrell's 'Happy' Has Grabbed the
    Nation," 252–55

Fountain, Henry
    "Up in the Air, and Down, with a Twist," 285,
    293–97

Fox, Kelley
    "Establishing Identities," 294–95

*Framework for Success in Postsecondary
    Writing*, 36

Freedman, David H.
    "How Junk Food Can End Obesity," 375, 379,
    741–45

Friedman, Thomas
    "The Inflection Is Near?," 148, 149, 156

G

Ganz, Steven
    *Valley Speak: Deciphering the Jargon of Silicon
    Valley*, 689

Garza, Alicia, 677–78

Gay, Roxane
    speech to *Publishers Weekly*'s Winter Institute,
    200–201

"Gender" (*Wikipedia*), 298–300

*Getting to the Heart of Interfaith: The Eye-
    Opening, Hope-Filled Friendship of a Pastor,
    a Rabbi and a Sheikh* (Rahman, Mackenzie,
    and Falcon), 233

Gibbon, Edward
    Memoirs of My Life, 702

Gibson, William
    Neuromancer, 704

"Girls Suffer Sports Concussions at a Higher
    Rate than Boys. Why Is That Overlooked?"
    (Snyder), 438

Glass, Gene
    "High-stakes Testing and Student
    Achievement," 536

Glass, Ira, 787

"The Glory of Oprah" (Flanagan), 710

Goldwasser, Amy, 338

"The Good Immigrant Student" (Nguyen),
    468

"Google Home vs Alexa" (Paolino), 272–75

Gopnik, Adam
    "How the Internet Gets Inside Us," 455–56

Gorlick, Adam
    "Media Multitaskers Pay Mental Price," 431

Gourevitch, Philip
    "Mr. Brown," 301–3

Graff, Gerald
    They Say / I Say, 17

Grahame-Smith, Seth
    Pride and Prejudice and Zombies, 535

Grant, Adam, *396*
    "Speaking While Female," 396–99

Gray, Sarah
    "Why LeBron James' Move to Los Angeles
    Could Boost the City's Economy," 149

Griffin, Cindy, 446

"Guys *vs.* Men" (Barry), 460

H

Hagerty, Marilyn, *675*
  "Long-awaited Olive Garden Receives Warm
    Welcome," 674–75
Hamlet (Shakespeare), 142
Hampton University, 186
"Handel in Good Hands" (Taylor), 336
"'The Handmaid's Tale': A Dystopian Tale of
    Female Subjugation That Hits Close to
    Home" (McFarland), 329–30
"A Hard Climb for the Girl Next Door" (Samuels),
    703
Harry Potter and the Half-Blood Prince (Rowling),
    702
Hasset, Kevin A.
  "Why We Shouldn't Raise the Minimum
    Wage," 168
"Heart and Sole: Detroiter Walks 21 Miles to
    Work" (Laitner), 304–10
Here Comes Everybody (Shirky), 123
"Herzog Finds His Inner Man" (Dargis), 338–39
Hicks, Randall, 153, 154
"The Higher Price of Buying Local" (Vayner),
    93–97
Highfield, Ashley
  "Why the Digital Revolution Is Only Just
    Beginning," 458–59
"High-stakes Testing and Student Achievement"
    (Nichols, Glass, and Berliner), 536
Hinojosa, Maria
  "Dancing Past the Boundaries," 417–18
"H.I.V. and AIDS in Africa: Ten Lessons from the
    Field" (Wangila and Akukwe), 470
Hobson, Mellody, *155*
  "Color Blind or Color Brave?," 154–56
Hofstra University, 186
"Holding Up the Hollywood Stagecoach: The
    European Take on the Western" (Przyby-
    lowski), 601–17

Honoré, Russel, *162*
  "Work Is a Blessing," 162–63
hooks, bell
  "Work Makes Life Sweet," 199–201
Hopkins, Megan
  "Training the Next Teachers for America,"
    380, 382
"How Junk Food Can End Obesity" (Freedman),
    375, 379, 741–45
"How the Internet Gets Inside Us" (Gopnik),
    455–56
"How to Argue" (Davis), 24–25
How to Write a Sentence (Fish), 694
Hrabowski, Freeman A., III
  "After the Cameras Leave," 161
Hurston, Zora Neale
  Barracoon: The Story of the Last "Black Cargo,"
    691–92

I

Ibrahim, Sonallah, 342
Ice Cube, 6
"I Have a Dream" (King), 471–72, 794–95
"Immigrants (We Get the Job Done)" (Miranda),
    149–52, *151*, 156, 160
"Incentive for Developers Would Spur Affordable
    Housing" (Saltzman), 377–78
"Indie Gem *Please Knock on My Door* Expertly
    Captures Mental Illness" (Ummadi), 367–70
"The Inflection Is Near?" (Friedman), 148, 149, 156
*In Search of Solutions: A New Direction in Psy-
    chotherapy* (O'Hanlon and Weiner-Davis),
    625–26
Interdisciplinary Group on Preventing School and
    Community Violence
  "Call to Action to Prevent Gun Violence,"
    376–77, 383–85
Interfaith Youth Core
  "Eboo Patel," 422

Interview with David Sumner (Williams), 463–64
Invisible Man (Ellison), 704
iPhone launch speech (Jobs), 794–95
Ivins, Molly
    Nightline interview, 466

J

Jackson, Shirley Ann
    "Leaders in Science and Engineering: The
        Women of MIT," 152–53
Jenkins, Darlene
    "Tightening the Turns in Speed Skating:
        Lessons in Centripetal Force and Balance,"
        246
Jenkins, Henry, 125
Jenks, Christopher, 39
Jobs, Steve, *464, 795*
    iPhone launch speech, 794–95
    Stanford University commencement address,
        464–65
Johnson, Steven, 112
Jolivette, Areyon
    "*Spider-Man: Into the Spider-Verse* Is as
        Extraordinary as It Allows Its Audience to
        Be," 342
Jordan, Barbara, *544*
    1976 keynote address to the Democratic
        National Convention, 544
Joy, Ryan, *324*
    "The Right to Preach on a College Campus,"
        324–27

K

Karr, Mary, 338
Kesten, Lou
    "Review: Nintendo Switch Is Impressive, but
        Needs More Games," 334
Key, Francis Scott
    "Star-Spangled Banner," 534

Kheirbek, Raya Elfadel, *202*
    "At the VA, Healing the Doctor-Patient
        Relationship," 202–7
King, Martin Luther Jr., *409, 795*
    "I Have a Dream," 471–72, 794–95
    "Letter from Birmingham Jail," 408–10
K'Lee, review of Texas A&M for *U.S. News & World
        Report*, 337
Kleege, Georgina
    "Call It Blindness," 196–98
Klein, Naomi
    Capitalism vs. the Climate, 469
Kopp, Rochelle
    *Valley Speak: Deciphering the Jargon of Silicon
        Valley*, 689
Krauthammer, Charles
    "Are We Alone in the Universe?," 547–50

L

"The Lady Up Front" (Landauer), 781–83
Laitner, Bill
    "Heart and Sole: Detroiter Walks 21 Miles to
        Work," 304–10
Landauer, Julia, *782*
    "The Lady Up Front," 781–83
    "War, Cartoons, and Society: Changes in
        Political Cartoons between World War II
        and the Iraq War," 539–40
Language and Politics (Chomsky), 460
Lanham, Richard, 665
    The Economics of Attention, 67
Lanier, Jaron, *172*
    "Delete Your Social Media Accounts Right
        Now," 172–76
"Leaders in Science and Engineering: The Women
        of MIT" (Jackson), 152–53
"Leaving Home, Coming Home" (Ly), 705
Lee, Jerry Won, 39
"Lee Tonouchi: Pidgin Poet" (Thompson),
        692–93

Lehna, Larry, *224*
   "The Look," 224–28
Leone, Steven
   "The Likelihood of Homeowners to Implement
      CIGS Thin-Film Solar Cells," 512–13
"Letter from Birmingham Jail" (King), 408–10
Letter to Robert Hooke (Newton), 13
Lewis, Michael
   The Blind Side, 197–99
"The Likelihood of Homeowners to Implement
    CIGS Thin-Film Solar Cells" (Leone),
    512–13
"Literacy: A Lineage" (Luken), 209–13
Liveable City, *289, 296*
   "Reclaiming Affordability in Today's Austin,"
    288–89, 292–93, 296, 297
Lives on the Boundary (Rose), 192–93, 199
Living Pidgin: Contemplations on Pidgin Culture
   (Tonouchi), 692
"Long-awaited Olive Garden Receives Warm Wel-
   come" (Hagerty), 674–75
"The Look" (Lehna), 224–28
Luken, Melanie, *209*
   "Literacy: A Lineage," 209–13
Ly, Brandon
   "Leaving Home, Coming Home," 705
Lyiscott, Jamila, *690*
   "Broken English," 689–90

M

MacFarland, Jack, 192–93
Mackenzie, Don
   *Getting to the Heart of Interfaith: The Eye-
    Opening, Hope-Filled Friendship of a Pastor,
    a Rabbi and a Sheikh*, 233
MacNamara, Ellen, 35, 36, 38
"The Madness of Cesar Chavez" (Flanagan),
   431–32
Madonna
   "Celebration," 534

Maeda, John
   "On Meaningful Observation," 545
"Making Friends Who Disagree with You (Is the
   Healthiest Thing in the World)" (Vert),
   20–21
"Mama Africa" (Bamboo), 686, 687, 689
Margarita Philosophica (Reisch), *664*
Marron, Dylan, 21–23, 26
Martin, George R.R.
   A Song of Fire and Ice, 236–37
Martinez, Julio, 809
McCain, John
   "Farewell Letter to America," 673–74
McComb, Karen, 246, 250
McFarland, Melanie
   "'The Handmaid's Tale': A Dystopian Tale
    of Female Subjugation That Hits Close to
    Home," 329–30
McKee, Ann, 521
Mead, Margaret, 17
"Media Multitaskers Pay Mental Price" (Gorlick),
   431
Memoirs of My Life (Gibbon), 702
Mernit, Judith Lewis
   "Seismology: Is San Francisco Next?," 436–37
Miller, Susan
   Textual Carnivals, 524
Minard, Charles Joseph, 455
Mincey, Sofi
   "On Climate Change and Hurricanes," 167
Miranda, Lin-Manuel
   "Immigrants (We Get the Job Done)," 149–52,
    151, 156, 160
"Mr. Brown" (Gourevitch), 301–3
Moller, Susanna, 809
Moller, Will
   "A Painful Posting," 247–49, 251
   "Moment of Joy," 415–17, *416*
"Monopoly: The Scandal Behind the World's
   Favorite Board Game" (Alamenciak),
   345–47

Morrison, Toni, 68, 78
  Nobel Prize acceptance speech, 705–6, 708–9
  Paradise, 704
Moss, Beverly
  A Community Text Arises, 240–42, 247
"Mother Tongue" (Tan), 708
Moynihan, Daniel Patrick, *284*

N

Nabokov, Vladimir, 667
Nass, Clifford, 431
National Institutes of Health
  "College Drinking Hazardous to Campus
    Communities: Task Force Calls for Research-
    Based Prevention Programs," 469
Negri, Alberta
  "Underneath the Leather Jackets and Chrome
    Pipes: Research into a Community of Local
    Bikers," 242–44
Net Smart (Rheingold), 126
Neuromancer (Gibson), 704
Newkirk, Tom
  The Art of Slow Reading, 71
"New Movie Genres" (Chast), *138*
Newton, Isaac
  letter to Robert Hooke, 13
Nguyen, Bich Minh
  "The Good Immigrant Student," 468
Nichols, Sharon
  "High-stakes Testing and Student
    Achievement," 536
Nightline interview (Ivins), 466
1976 keynote address to the Democratic National
    Convention (Jordan), 544
Nobel Prize acceptance speech (Morrison), 705–6,
    708–9
"Nonconformity Is Skin Deep" (Brooks), 414–15
Novak, Michael
  "The Spirit of Capitalism," 460–61
*Now You See It: How the Brain Science of Attention
    Will Transform the Way We Live, Work, and
    Learn* (Davidson), 129, 708

O

Obama, Michelle, 795
O'Connor, Flannery, 669
O'Hanlon, Bill
  In Search of Solutions: A New Direction in
    Psychotherapy, 625–26
"On Buying Local" (Spriggs), 88, 150, 177–85,
    672–73
"On Climate Change and Hurricanes" (Mincey),
    167
The Onion
  "Florida State University to Phase Out
    Academic Operations," 467
"On Meaningful Observation" (Maeda), 545
Oreskes, Naomi
  "Beyond the Ivory Tower: The Scientific
    Consensus on Climate Change,"
    158–59
"The 'Other Side' Is Not Dumb" (Blanda), 10

P

"A Painful Posting" (Moller), 247–49, 251
Paolino, Johna, *272*
  "Google Home vs Alexa," 272–75
Paradise (Morrison), 704
"Paradise, Paved," *258*
Pasini, David, *387*
  "The Economic Impact of Investing Public
    Funds in Sports Franchises," 387–90
Patel, Eboo
  "To Narrow Toxic Divides, Students Build
    Bridges between Faiths," 423–24
Pellman, Elliott, 521
Perelman, Deb, 781
Persepolis I (Satrapi), 472, *472*
The Philosophy of Literary Form (Burke), 7
*Playing the Enemy: Nelson Mandela and the Game
    That Made a Nation* (Carlin), 424–25
Pollack, Neal
  "Why Your Kids Are Addicted to *Cars*,"
    438

Pollan, Michael
"An Animal's Place," 704
Portfolio Statement (Wiles), 813–14
Posnanski, Joe
"The College Connection," 707–8
Powers of Two (Shenk), 124
Pride and Prejudice and Zombies (Austen and
Grahame-Smith), 535
Przybylowski, Walter
"Holding Up the Hollywood Stagecoach:
The European Take on the Western,"
601–17

Q

Queen
"We Will Rock You," 534

R

Rahman, Jamal
Getting to the Heart of Interfaith: The Eye-
Opening, Hope-Filled Friendship of a Pastor,
a Rabbi and a Sheikh, 233
"Reclaiming Affordability in Today's Austin"
(Liveable City), 288–89, 292–93, 296, 297
Reisch, Gregor, 664
Margarita Philosophica, 664
"Remembering My Childhood on the Continent of
Africa" (Sedaris), 457–58
"Renewable and Sustainable Energy in Rural
India" (Vaish), 531–32
"Review: Nintendo Switch Is Impressive, but
Needs More Games" (Kesten), 334
Review of Walk the Line (Smith), 334, 336
Rheingold, Howard, 67–68, 520, 665
"Crap Detection 101," 102
Net Smart, 126
Rhetoric (Aristotle), 552
The Rhetoric of Rhetoric (Booth), 15–16
Rhys, Jean, 66
"The Right to Preach on a College Campus" (Joy),
324–27

"The Rise of Female Heroes in Shoujo Manga"
(Edwards), 797–802
"Robin Williams Remembered by Critics, Close
Friends" (Svetkey), 536–37
Rogers, Carl, 445
Rolle, Jamaal, 187, 188
Rose, Mike
Lives on the Boundary, 192–93, 199
Rosenblatt, Louise, 70–71
Rowling, J. K.
Harry Potter and the Half-Blood Prince,
702
Rubber Pencil Devil (Da Corte), 331
Rubin, Melissa, 276, 764
"Advertisements R Us," 276–81

S

Sainani, Kristin
"Damage Control," 430
Saltzman, Dan
"Incentive for Developers Would Spur
Affordable Housing," 377–78
"Same Food Planet, Different Food Worlds"
(Dreher), 674–76
Samuels, Allison
"A Hard Climb for the Girl Next Door," 703
Sandberg, Sheryl, 396
"Speaking while Female," 396–99
Sanders, Elizabeth, 60
"The Santaland Diaries" (Sedaris), 786–87
Satrapi, Marjane
Persepolis I, 472, 472
Schmolli, DJ
"Super Bowl Anthem," 534
Scott, A.O., 488, 490
Sedaris, David
"Remembering My Childhood on the
Continent of Africa," 457–58
"The Santaland Diaries," 786–87
"Seismology: Is San Francisco Next?" (Mernit),
436–37
"Selling the Farm" (Estabrook), 318–23

Sengupta, Somini, *259*
   "Why Is Everyone Focused on Zuckerberg's
      Hoodie?," 259–61
Seuss, Dr., 66
Shakespeare, William
   Hamlet, 142
Shapiro, Shawna, *400*
   "Snowflakes and Free Speech on Campuses,"
      400–404
Shea, Don, 338
Shenk, Joshua Wolf
   Powers of Two, 124
Sheppard, Katryn
   "Early Word Production: A Study of One Child's
      Word Productions," 295, 647–61
Shirky, Clay
   Here Comes Everybody, 123
"Should Everybody Write?" (Baron), 783–84
"Should This Be the Last Generation?" (Singer), 705
Silver, Nate, *232*, 781
Simmons, Laurie, 476
Simoneaux, Brent
   "Do the Right Thing," 666
Singer, Peter
   "Should This Be the Last Generation?," 705
Smith, Rae'Johne
   e-portfolio, 815, *816*
Smith, Zadie
   Review of *Walk the Line*, 334, 336
Smitherman, Geneva, *670*
   *Talkin and Testifyin: The Language of Black
      America*, 670–71
Smitten Kitchen, 781
*Smoking and Health: Report of the Advisory
      Committee of the Surgeon General of the
      Public Health Service* (U.S. Surgeon General),
      157–58, 160
"Snowflakes and Free Speech on Campuses"
   (Shapiro), 400–404
Snyder, Marjorie A.
   "Girls Suffer Sports Concussions at a Higher Rate
      than Boys. Why Is That Overlooked?," 438

"Some Dreamers of the Golden Dream" (Didion),
      701
Song, Shuqiao, 54–55
A Song of Fire and Ice (Martin), 236–37
"Speaking while Female" (Sandberg and Grant),
      396–99
Speech to *Publishers Weekly*'s Winter Institute
      (Gay), 200–201
"*Spider-Man: Into the Spider-Verse* Is as
      Extraordinary as It Allows Its Audience to
      Be" (Jolivette), 342
"The Spirit of Capitalism" (Novak), 460–61
"Sports' Perfect 0.4 Seconds" (Fleming), 194–96
Spriggs, Katherine, *177*, 764
   "On Buying Local," 88, 150, 177–85, 672–73
Stanford commencement address (Jobs), 464–65
"Star-Spangled Banner" (Key), 534
Stowe, Harriett Beecher
   Uncle Tom's Cabin, 704
Strain, Michael
   "Why We Shouldn't Raise the Minimum
      Wage," 168
Sumner, David, 463–64
"Super Bowl Anthem" (Schmolli), 534
Svetkey, Benjamin
   "Robin Williams Remembered by Critics, Close
      Friends," 536–37
Swift, Jonathan, 98

T

*Talkin and Testifyin: The Language of Black
      America* (Smitherman), 670–71
Tan, Amy
   "Mother Tongue," 708
Taylor, Katie
   "Handel in Good Hands," 336
Textual Carnivals (Miller), 524
"There She Blew: The History of American Whal-
      ing" (Crain), 341
"*They Say / I Say*" (Graff and Birkenstein), 17
"Third-Party Option" (Brooks), 234–36, 249–51

Thompson, David
"Lee Tonouchi: Pidgin Poet," 692–93
"Tightening the Turns in Speed Skating: Lessons in Centripetal Force and Balance" (Jenkins), 246
"To All the Girls I've Rejected" (Delahunty), 156–57, 159, 160
Tometi, Opal, 678
"To Narrow Toxic Divides, Students Build Bridges between Faiths" (Patel), 423–24
Tonouchi, Lee A.
Living Pidgin: Contemplations on Pidgin Culture, 692
Tosh, Peter, 686
Toulmin, Stephen, 442
"Training the Next Teachers for America" (Hopkins), 380, 382
Truth, Sojourner, 66
"Ain't I a Woman?," 471
Tucker, Ken
"Why Is Game of Thrones So Popular?," 236
Twain, Mark, 545
2005 commencement speech (Wallace), 546–47
2013 Speech at the United Nations (Yousafzai), 452–53

U

Ummadi, Manisha, 367
"Indie Gem Please Knock on My Door Expertly Captures Mental Illness," 367–70
Uncle Tom's Cabin (Stowe), 704
"Undelivered" (Creswell), 342
"Underneath the Leather Jackets and Chrome Pipes: Research into a Community of Local Bikers" (Negri), 242–44
United Nations
Climate Change 2014: Synthesis Report, 454
Updike, John, 695
"Up in the Air, and Down, with a Twist" (Fountain), 285, 293–97

U.S. Surgeon General
Smoking and Health: Report of the Advisory Committee of the Surgeon General of the Public Health Service, 157–58, 160

V

Vaish, Saurabh, 531
"Renewable and Sustainable Energy in Rural India," 531–32
Valdés, Guadalupe
Con Respeto: Bridging the Distances between Culturally Diverse Families and Schools, 687–89
Valley Speak: Deciphering the Jargon of Silicon Valley (Kopp and Ganz), 689
Vayner, Yuliya, 84–85, 93
"The Higher Price of Buying Local" (Vayner), 93–97
Vert, Shauna
"Making Friends Who Disagree with You (Is the Healthiest Thing in the World)," 20–21
Vu, Minh
"Dirty Nails," 193–94

W

Wallace, David Foster
2005 commencement speech, 546–47
Wangila, Rhoi
"H.I.V. and AIDS in Africa: Ten Lessons from the Field," 470
"War, Cartoons, and Society: Changes in Political Cartoons between World War II and the Iraq War" (Landauer), 539–40
Wearly, Robin, 373
"ADAPTS, the First Evacuation Sling for Wheelchair Users," 375–76
Weiner-Davis, Michele
In Search of Solutions: A New Direction in Psychotherapy, 625–26
Westbrook, Adam
Cause/Effect: The Unexpected Origins of Terrible Things, 538, 788, 788–89

"We Will Rock You" (Queen), 534

"What Can You Do to Make a Difference?" (Colberg), 470, *471*

"What You Eat Is Your Business" (Balko), 438, *439*

"When You Are Old" (Yeats), 544

"Where the Brains Are" (Florida), 459

"Who Fears Climbing the Mountains Lives Forever between the Holes" (Buthainah), 691

"Why Is Everyone Focused on Zuckerberg's Hoodie?" (Sengupta), 259–61

"Why Is *Game of Thrones* So Popular?" (Tucker), 236

"Why LeBron James' Move to Los Angeles Could Boost the City's Economy" (Gray), 149

"Why Pharrell's 'Happy' Has Grabbed the Nation" (Forde), 252–55

"Why the Digital Revolution Is Only Just Beginning" (Highfield), 458–59

"Why We Shouldn't Raise the Minimum Wage" (Hasset and Strain), 168

"Why Your Kids Are Addicted to *Cars*" (Pollack), 438

"Wiki" (*Wikipedia*), 785

Wikipedia
   "Gender," 298–300
   "Wiki," 785

Wiles, Kameron
   portfolio statement, 813–14

Williams, Eric
   "Five Things All Tennis Players Can Learn from Serena Williams," 231–32

Williams, Richard
   "Aretha Franklin Obituary," 187

Williams, Scott, 57

Williams, Terry Tempest
   "The Clan of One-Breasted Women," 462–63
   Interview with David Sumner, 463–64

Wineburg, Sam, 102–3

Winfrey, Oprah
   Agnes Scott College Commencement Address 2017, 18, 19

Wisconsin Department of Transportation
   City of Appleton On-Street Bike Plan, 378–80, *381*

Woman Hollering Creek and Other Stories (Cisneros), 686–87

Woolsey, Cameron
   "Blocky Empires," 340

"Word for Word: Culture's Impact on the Localization of Japanese Video Games" (Zhao), 779–80

"Work Is a Blessing" (Honoré), 162–63

"Work Makes Life Sweet" (hooks), 199–201

"Writing at Work" (Brandt), 62–63

A Writing Life (Dillard), 451–52

Wuerker, Matt, *99*

Y

Yeats, William Butler
   "When You Are Old," 544

Yousafzai, Malala, *452*
   2013 Speech at the United Nations, 452–53

Z

Zhao, Ruizhe (Thomas)
   "Word for Word: Culture's Impact on the Localization of Japanese Video Games," 779–80

Zinczenko, David
   "Don't Blame the Eater," 427

Glossary / Index

A

abbreviations, 42–43

ABSTRACT, 645 A GENRE of writing that summarizes a book, an article, or a paper, usually in 100–200 words. An *informative abstract* summarizes a complete report; a briefer *descriptive abstract* works more as a teaser; a standalone *proposal abstract* (also called a PROJECT PROPOSAL) requests permission to conduct research, write on a topic, or present a report at a scholarly conference. Features: a SUMMARY of basic information • objective description • brevity

Academic Search Complete (EBSCO), 502

academic success, habits for, 36–38

academic writing, 35–49

   characteristic features, 42–49

   defined, 38–39

   genres

      analyses, 230

      arguments, 144

      narratives, 189

      proposals, 372

      reports, 284–85

      reviews, 330

   habits for academic success, 36–38

Note: This glossary / index defines key terms and concepts and directs you to pages in the book where you can find specific information on these and other topics. Please note the words set in SMALL CAPITAL LETTERS are themselves defined in the glossary / index. Page numbers in *italics* indicate figures.

presentations, 795–96

reading, 77–78

style, 679–80

in US academic contexts, 39–42

   asking questions, 40

   focusing from the start, 40

   responding, 39

   saying what you think, 40

   stating a point explicitly, 42

acknowledging sources, 13, 48–49, 556–57

ACTIVE VOICE, 679–80 When a verb is in the active voice, the subject performs the action: *He sent a gift.*

ADAPTS transfer sling, *373*, 375–76

Adbusters, 449–50, *450*

ad hominem fallacy, 433

Adobe Acrobat Reader, 83

advertisements

   Adbusters, 449–50, *450*

   argument and, 468, *468*

   Kobe Bryant video for Nike, 106, *106*

   Camel cigarettes, *435*, 435–36

   Coca-Cola, 276–81, *277*, *758*, 758–59

   Nike's Just Do It campaign, 238–39, *240*

   The Shelter Pet Project, *468*

   Shinola, 74, *75*

   2011 Super Bowl Chrysler ad, 12, *12*

   in works cited (MLA style), 593

African American English, 670–71

afterwords, in works cited (MLA style), 588

AGREEMENT, 708–32, 734–37 The correspondence between a SUBJECT and VERB in person and number (*the <u>dog chases</u> the children down the*

street) or between a PRONOUN and its ANTECED-
ENT in gender and number (*the cat nursed her
babies; the children flee because they are afraid*).
    pronoun-antecedent, 728–32
    subject-verb, 734–37

AIDS, in Africa, 470, *470*
AllSides, 21, 103
The Amazing Race (television show), 486
Amazon, 272–74, 820
American Association of University Professors, 153
American Journal of Human Genetics, 491, *492*
American Psychological Association (APA), 562,
    618. *See also* APA STYLE

ANALOGY, 451–53 A STRATEGY for COMPARISON
by explaining something unfamiliar in terms of
something that is more familiar. *See also* faulty
analogy

ANALYSIS, 229–81 A GENRE that breaks something
down into its component parts so that those parts
can be thought about methodically in order to
understand the whole. Features: a question that
prompts a closer look • DESCRIPTION of the subject
being analyzed • EVIDENCE drawn from close
examination of the subject • insight gained from
the analysis • clear, precise language. *See also*
CAUSAL ANALYSIS; DATA ANALYSIS; INFORMATIONAL
ANALYSIS; INSTRUCTIONAL ANALYSIS; PROCESS
ANALYSIS; RHETORICAL ANALYSIS; VISUAL ANALYSIS
    across academic disciplines, 77–78, 230
    across cultures and communities, 233
    across genres, 233–34
    across media, 230–32
    analyzing arguments, 411–50
    annotated example, 252–55
    characteristic features, 234–51
    kinds of analysis
        causal, 246–47, 266–67
        data, 247–49, 267–68
        discourse, 242–44, 265–66

        process, 244–46, 266
        rhetorical, 238–42, 265
        visual, 256–61, 268
    readings
        "Advertisements R Us," 276–81
        "Google Home vs Alexa," 272–75
        "Should Everybody Write?," 783–84
        "Why Is Everyone Focused on Zuckerberg's
            Hoodie?," 259–61
        "Why Pharrell's 'Happy' Has Grabbed the
            Nation," 252–55
    roadmap to writing analytically, 262–71

ANECDOTE, 46 Brief NARRATIVE used to illustrate
a point.

ANNOTATE, 80–85 The process of taking notes,
underlining key information, and marking aspects
of a text that strike you as important while reading.

ANNOTATED BIBLIOGRAPHY, 529–33 A writing GENRE that gives an overview of published
research and scholarship on a topic. Each entry
includes complete publication information
for a source and a SUMMARY or an ABSTRACT. A
descriptive annotation summarizes the content
of a source without commenting on its value; an
evaluative annotation gives an opinion about the
source along with a description of it. Features:
complete bibliographic information • a brief
SUMMARY or DESCRIPTION of the work • evaluative
comments (for an evaluative bibliography) • some
indication of how the source will inform your
RESEARCH • consistency
    annotated example, 531–33
    characteristic features, 529–30
    descriptive, 531–32
    evaluative, 533

annotating, 80–85, 83
    defined, 79
    for engagement, 70
    reflection exercise, 85

sample text, 84–85
    in slow reading, 71
    steps in, 80–83
    and summarizing, 86
annotation, by readers, 70, 80–85

ANTECEDENT, 728–32 The NOUN or PRONOUN to
which a pronoun refers: *Maya* lost *her* wallet.
anthologies
    in MLA style in-text documentation, 568
    in works cited (MLA style), 584–85

APA STYLE, 562, 618–61 A system of DOCUMENTA-
TION used in the social sciences. APA stands for
the American Psychological Association.
    directory, 618–20
    formatting a research essay, 644–46
    in-text documentation, 620–24
    list of references, 625–44
        articles and other short works, 629–33
        audio, visual, and other sources, 639–44
        authors and other contributors, 626–29
        books, parts of book, and reports, 633–39
        sources not covered by APA, 644
    notes, 625
    parenthetical documentation, 553
    quotations, 543, 544, 645, 745
    sample research essay, 646–61
    signal phrases, 621
    verb tenses, 552–53, 738–40
    visuals, 770–71

appeals
    emotional, 421–22
    ethical, 422–25
    logical, 425, 427–32
    to readers' values, 160–61

APPENDIX A section at the end of a written work
for supplementary material that would be distracting in the main part of the text.
application letters, 55–56
appropriateness, 668–71

ARGUING A POSITION, 143–85 A GENRE that
uses REASONS and EVIDENCE to support a CLAIM.
Features: an explicit POSITION • a response to
what others have said • appropriate background
information • a clear indication of why the topic
matters • good REASONS and EVIDENCE • attention
to more than one POINT OF VIEW • an authoritative TONE • an appeal to readers' values.
    across academic disciplines, 144
    across cultures and communities, 146
    across genres, 147
    across media, 144–46
    annotated example, 162–63
    characteristic features, 147–61
    readings
        "Delete Your Social Media Accounts Right
            Now," 172–76
        "On Buying Local," 177–85
        "Work Is a Blessing," 162–63
    roadmap to arguing a position, 164–71

ARGUMENT, 405–73 Any text that makes a CLAIM
supported by REASONS and EVIDENCE.
    analyzing and constructing, 411–50
    claims, 415–19
    classical, 440–42
    classification and, 337–39
    common ground and, 424–25
    invitational, 446–48
    means of persuasion, 421–34
        emotional appeals, 421–22
        ethical appeals, 422–25
        logical appeals, 425, 427–32
    multiple points of view, 434–37
    purposes, 407
    Rogerian, 445–46
    stance and, 412–15
    stasis theory, 419–20
    strategies for supporting an argument, 451–73
    structuring, 438–48
    Toulmin, 442–44

Aristotle, 2, 6, 101, 425

art, in works cited (MLA style), 593–94

ARTICLE The word *a*, *an*, or *the*, used to indicate that a NOUN is indefinite (*a writer*, *an author*) or definite (*the author*).

articles
    in lists of references (APA style), 629–31
    as sources, 495
    in works cited (MLA style), 577–80
Assertion-Evidence Approach, 796
assignments, understanding, 115
@Raicestexas, 678
attitude, 33. *See also* STANCE

ATTRIBUTION BIAS, 100 The tendency to think that our motivations for believing what we believe are objectively good while thinking that those who we disagree with have objectively wrong motivations.

Audacity, 787

AUDIENCE, 31–32 Those to whom a text is directed—the people who read, listen to, or view the text. Audience is a key part of any RHETORICAL SITUATION.
    analysis and, 187–89
    collaboration and, 125–26
    connecting to, 671–73, 686–87
    considering, 31–32

audio essays, 786–87
audio recordings, documenting, 553–54

AUTHORITY, 521–25 A person or text that is cited as support for a writer's ARGUMENT. A structural engineer may be quoted as an authority on bridge construction, for example. Authority also refers to a quality conveyed by writers who are knowledgeable about their subjects.

author searches, 505–6
autobiographies, 187

B

background research, 482
bandwagon appeals, 433
Banks, Caitlin, 507
bar charts, *765*
bar graphs, 766
the Beatles, *124*
Bedwell, Linda, 507
begging the question, 433
Bert (*Sesame Street* character), 415, *416*, 417
Beyoncé, 713
bibliographies. *See also* REFERENCES
    annotated, 529–33
    as sources, 494
    working, 518–19
Bing, 497
Bing Translator, 4
Blackboard, 815
#BlackLivesMatter, 677–78
Black Panthers, 670

BLOCK QUOTATION, 599 In a written work, long QUOTATIONS are indented and set without quotation marks: in MLA STYLE, set off text more than four typed lines, indented five spaces (or one-half inch) from the left margin; in APA STYLE, set off quotes of forty or more words, indented five spaces (or one-half inch) from the left margin. *See also* QUOTATION

BLOG, 815 An abbreviation of *weblog*. A regularly updated website on which writers post their work, often including images, embedded audio or video clips, and links to other sites.
    embedding links, 13
    in lists of references (APA style), 640–41
    tips for writing, 781–84
    in works cited (MLA style), 591

boldface, 760
book review, in lists of references (APA style), 632

books, documenting
    in lists of references (APA style), 633–39
    as sources, 494
    in working bibliography, 519
    in works cited (MLA style), 584–89
Boolean operators, 504
brackets, to indicate changes in quotations, 545

BRAINSTORMING, 116 A process for GENERATING IDEAS AND TEXT by writing down everything that comes to mind about a topic, then looking for patterns or connections among the ideas.

brands, *439*
broadcast interviews, in works cited (MLA style), 595
Brown, James, 301–3, *303*
Brueghel, Pieter, the Elder, *3*
Bryant, Kobe, 106, *106*
Bush, Kelly, *129*

C

CAB Abstracts, 502
Camarillo, David, 430
capitalism, 460–61

CAPTION, 554 A brief explanation accompanying a photograph, diagram, chart, screen shot, or other visual that appears in a written document.
cartoons, in works cited (MLA style), 594

CASE, 726, 732–34 The different forms some PRONOUNS can take to indicate how they function in a sentence—for example, as the SUBJECT or OBJECT. *I* and *me* refer to the same person, but they are not interchangeable in a sentence: *Joanne offered me one of the puppies, but I am allergic to dogs.*

Cash, Johnny, 334, *335*, 336

CAUSAL ANALYSIS, 246–47, 266–67, 453–55 A kind of ANALYSIS that explains why something occurs or once occurred. Also a STRATEGY for supporting an argument about a topic where questions of causality are relevant. *See also* faulty causality

cause and effect. *See* CAUSAL ANALYSIS
Cave of Forgotten Dreams (film), 338–39, *339*
cave paintings, *2*
CDs, in works cited (MLA style), 597
Charlie Hebdo, 407–8
charts, 765, 766, *769*, 770
    as evidence, 432
Chavez, Cesar, *431*, 431–32

CHRONOLOGICAL ORDER, 119, 193 A way of organizing text that proceeds from the beginning of an event to the end. Reverse chronological order proceeds in the other direction, from the end to the beginning.

Cicero, 9, 448, 673

CITATION, 555–62 In a text, the act of giving information from a source. A citation and its corresponding parenthetical DOCUMENTATION, footnote, or endnote provide minimal information about the source; complete information appears in a WORKS CITED or REFERENCES list at the end of the text.

CLAIM, 45–46, 415–19 A statement that asserts a belief or POSITION. In an ARGUMENT, a claim needs to be stated in a THESIS, or clearly implied, and requires support by REASONS and EVIDENCE.
    in academic writing, 42, 45–46
    in argument and, 415–19
    qualifying, 45, 419

clarity, 46–47, 250–51

CLASSICAL ARGUMENT, 440–42 A system of ARGUMENT developed in Greece and Rome during the classical period. It features an introduction that states the CLAIM; a body that includes background information, good REASONS and EVIDENCE, and attention to COUNTERARGUMENTS; and a CONCLUSION.

classical literature, in lists of references
(APA style), 637

CLASSIFICATION, 455–56 A STRATEGY that groups
numerous individual items by their similarities
(for example, classifying cereal, bread, butter,
chicken, cheese, cream, eggs, and oil as carbohy-
drates, proteins, and fats). Classification can serve
as the organizing principle for a paragraph or
whole text.

CLAUSE, 696 A group of words that consists of at
least a SUBJECT and a predicate; a clause may be
either MAIN or SUBORDINATE.
  main clause, 699, 700, 715, 717, 719, 720, 724
  subordinate clause, 699–700, 715, 724

Cleveland Cavaliers, 149
CLICKBAIT, 697

CLUSTERING, 116, 117 A process for GENERATING
IDEAS AND TEXT, in which a writer visually connects thoughts by jotting them down and drawing lines between related items.

CNET, 229–30
Coca-Cola, 276–81, *277*, *758*, 758–59

CODE-MESHING, 684 A way of weaving together
languages and DIALECTS.

CODE-SWITCHING, 684 The practice of
shifting from one language or DIALECT to another.
collaboration, 27, 123–31
  audience and, 125–26
  authors and, 125–26
  students and, 127
  tips for, 130–31
  at work, 128–29, *129*

COLLECTIVE NOUN A NOUN—such as *committee,
crowd, family, herd,* or *team*—that refers to a group.

College of Southern Nevada, 499, 500, *500*, *501*
color, 761–63, *762*

commas, 714, 746–50
  after introductory information, 746–48
  comma splices, 717–19
  fused sentences, 721
  quotations and, 546
  to set off nonessential elements, 749–50

COMMA SPLICE, 698, 717–19 Two or more MAIN
CLAUSES joined with only a comma: *I came, I saw,
I conquered.*

comments, 820
  in lists of references (APA style), 632
  in works cited (MLA style), 583
common errors, 122, 713–54
  commas after introductory information, 746–48
  comma splices, 717–19
  commas with essential and nonessential
    information, 749–50
  fused sentences, 719–22
  incorporating quotations, 741–43
  mixed constructions, 722–25
  pronoun case, 732–34
  pronoun reference, 726–28
  punctuating quotations, 743–45
  quotations, 740–45
  sentence fragments, 715–17
  shifts in tense, 738–40
  subject-verb agreement, 734–37
  verbs, 734–40
  words often confused, 750–54

COMMON GROUND, 24–26, 424–25 Shared values.
Writers build common ground with AUDIENCES
by acknowledging others' points of view, seeking
areas of compromise, and using language that
includes, rather than excludes, those they aim to
reach.

common knowledge, 556
communication, 1–2, 6, *135*. *See also* RHETORIC
  global culture and, 128–29
  professional, 50, *51*, 52 (*see also* teamwork)

COMPARISON AND CONTRAST, 457–59 A STRATEGY that highlights the points of similarity and difference between items. Using the block method of comparison and contrast, a writer discusses all the points about one item and then all the same points about the next item; using the point-by-point method, a writer discusses one point for both items before going on to discuss the next point for both items, and so on. Sometimes comparison and/or contrast can serve as the organizing principle for a paragraph or whole text.

COMPLETE SUBJECT, 736–37, 748 The SIMPLE SUBJECT plus any MODIFIERS. The complete subject can be one word (*I enjoy carrots*), two words (*The girls* went to the grocery store), or many words: *The old farmer with the multi-colored carrots* has a booth at the market.

COMPLEX SENTENCE, 699–700 A single MAIN CLAUSE plus one or more DEPENDENT CLAUSES: *When the United States holds a presidential election once every four years, citizens should vote.*

COMPOUND-COMPLEX SENTENCE, 700 Two or more MAIN CLAUSES plus one or more DEPENDENT CLAUSES: *When the United States holds a presidential election once every four years, citizens should vote, but voter turnout is often disappointing.*

COMPOUND SENTENCE, 696–98 Two or more MAIN CLAUSES joined by a comma and a COORDINATING CONJUNCTION or by a semicolon: *The United States holds a presidential election once every four years, but voter turnout is often disappointing.*

CONCLUSION The way a text ends, a chance to leave an AUDIENCE thinking about what's been said. Five ways of concluding a college essay: reiterating your point, discussing the implications of your ARGUMENT, asking a question, referring back to your OPENING, or proposing some kind of action.

closing sentences, 707–9
drafting, 120
conference proceedings
    in lists of references (APA style),
        639, 642
    in works cited (MLA style), 588–89

CONFIRMATION BIAS, 100–101, 104 The tendency to favor and seek out information that confirms what we already believe and to reject and ignore information that contradicts those beliefs.
conjunctions, coordinating, 697–98, 718, 721

Consumer Reports, 332, 343

CONTEXT, 33 Part of any RHETORICAL SITUATION, conditions affecting the text such as what else has been said about a topic; social, economic, and other factors; and any constants such as due date and length.
online, 161

contrast. *See* COMPARISON AND CONTRAST

COORDINATING CONJUNCTION, 697–98, 718, 721 One of these words—*and, but, or, nor, so, for,* or *yet*—used to join two elements in a way that gives equal weight to each one (*bacon* and *eggs; pay up* or *get out*).

correctness, 668–71
Council of Science Editors (CSE), 562

COUNTERARGUMENT, 437, 440 In ARGUMENT, an alternative POSITION or objection to the writer's position. The writer of an argument should not only acknowledge counterarguments but also, if at all possible, accept, accommodate, or refute each counterargument.

COUNT NOUN A word that names something that can be counted (*one book, two books*). *See also* NONCOUNT NOUN

court case
    in MLA style in-text documentation, 569
    in works cited (MLA style), 594

CREDIBILITY, 422–32 The sense of trustworthiness
that a writer conveys through the text.
    in arguments, 160
    in reports, 294–95
    in research, 562

credit, giving, 13, 555–62
Crick, Francis, 15–16

CRITERIA, 336–37 In a REVIEW, the standards
against which something is judged.

crowdfunding, 372, 373
CSE (Council of Science Editors), 562
cultures and communities, 692–93
    analyses, 233
    arguments, 146
    narratives, 190–91
    proposals, 372–74
    reports, 285
    reviews, 332

CUMULATIVE SENTENCE, 701–2 A sentence that
begins with a main idea expressed in a MAIN
CLAUSE and then adds details in PHRASES and
DEPENDENT CLAUSES that follow the MAIN CLAUSE.
See also PERIODIC SENTENCE

current sources, 491–93
Curry, Steph, 194–95, 195

D

Daily Californian, 342
Daily Wallpapers blog, 461
Dame Rhetorica, 663, 664

DATA ANALYSIS, 247–49, 267–68 A kind of ANALY-
SIS that looks for patterns in numbers or other
data, sometimes in order to answer a stated or
implied question.

databases
    documentation of, 578, 580, 582
    finding sources with, 501–3
    general, 502
    subject-specific, 502–3
data set, in lists of references (APA style), 644
Day After Tomorrow (film), 104, 105
definite article. See ARTICLE

DEFINITION, 460–61 A STRATEGY that says what
something is. Formal definitions identify the
category that something belongs to and tell
what distinguishes it from other things in that
category: A worm is an invertebrate (a category)
with a long, rounded body and no appendages
(distinguishing features). Extended definitions
go into more detail: a paragraph or even an essay
explaining why a character in a story is tragic.
Stipulative definitions give a writer's own use of a
term, one not found in a dictionary. Definition can
serve as the organizing principle for a paragraph
or whole text.

delivery, 755–56. See also DESIGN
    portfolios, 809–17
    presentations, 794–808
    publishing, 818–20
Demosthenes, 755, 756
DePaul University, 819
Descartes, René, 13

DESCRIPTION, 462–64 A STRATEGY that tells how
something looks, sounds, smells, feels, or tastes.
Effective description creates a clear DOMINANT
IMPRESSION built from specific details. Description can be objective, subjective, or both. Description can serve as the organizing principle for a
paragraph or whole text.
    analyses and, 236–37
    narratives and, 194–96
    visuals and, 462–64, 463

descriptive annotations, 531–32

DESIGN, 755–820 The way a text is arranged and presented visually. Elements of design include fonts, colors, illustrations, LAYOUT, and white space. *See also* MEDIUM
    color, 761–63
    fonts, 760
    getting a response to, 773–75
    headings, 760–61
    layout, 771–73
    thinking rhetorically about, 758–59
    visuals, 763–71

details, narratives and, 194–96
Detroit News, 332
diagrams, 768, *768*, *769*, 770

DIALECT, 683–93 Varieties of language that are spoken by people in a particular region, social class, or ethnic group.

DICTION, 665 Word choice.

dictionaries
    in lists of references (APA style), 636
    in MLA style in-text documentation, 569
    in works cited (MLA style), 580
Digital Archive of Literacy Narratives, 189
digital texts, 34, 72–74
directness, 46–47
Directory of Open Access Journals, 501–2
discipline librarians, 499
discourse analysis, 242–44, 265–66
dissertations
    in lists of references (APA style), 638–39
    in works cited (MLA style), 589
DNA, 15–16, *16*

DOCUMENTATION, 552–62 Publication information about the sources cited in a text. The documentation usually appears in an abbreviated form in parentheses at the point of citation or in an endnote or a footnote. Complete documentation usually appears as a list of WORKS CITED or REFERENCES at the end of the text. Documentation styles vary by discipline. *See also* MLA STYLE and APA STYLE.
    using appropriate citation style, 48–49

DOI, 519
    MLA style, 574
    APA style, 626, 630, 660

DOMINANT IMPRESSION, 462 The overall effect created through specific details when a writer describes something.

DRAFTING, 120 The process of putting words on paper or screen. Writers often write several drafts, REVISING each until they achieve their goal or reach a deadline. At that point, they submit a finished final draft.

drawing, 1–2, *2*, 117
Duarte, Nancy, 794
DuckDuckGo, 498
DVDs
    in lists of references (APA style), 641
    in works cited (MLA style), 597

E

Ebola outbreak, *421*, 421–22

EDITED ACADEMIC ENGLISH, 42–43, 669–71, 685 The conventions of spelling, grammar, and punctuation expected in academic discourse, which tends to be more formal than conversational English. Academic English varies from country to country and changes over time. *Edited* refers to the care writers take in reviewing their formal written work.

edited collections, in lists of references
    (APA style), 636

EDITING, 122 The process of fine-tuning a text—examining each word, phrase, sentence, and paragraph—to be sure that the text is correct and precise and says exactly what the writer intends. *See also* DRAFTING; PROOFREADING; REVISION

editions
    in lists of references (APA style), 636
    in works cited (MLA style), 587
editorials
    in lists of references (APA style), 632
    in works cited (MLA style), 580
Educational Resource Information Center
    (*ERIC*), 503
either-or fallacy, 433
electronic books, in lists of references (APA style), 633
electronic sources. *See* online sources
Elizabeth II, Queen, 667, *668*
ellipsis marks, 545
email, 62
    opening sentences of, 706
    in works cited (MLA style), 592
Emig, Janet, 112
emoji, 43

EMOTIONAL APPEALS, 421–22 Ways that authors appeal to an AUDIENCE's emotions, values, and beliefs by arousing specific feelings—for example, compassion, pity, sympathy, anger, fear. *See also* ETHICAL APPEALS; LOGICAL APPEALS

empathy, 21–23
encyclopedias
    in lists of references (APA style), 636
    in MLA style in-text documentation, 580
    as sources, 493–94
engagement, reading rhetorically for, 69–70
English
    breaking the rules, 670–71
    edited academic, 42–43, 669–71, 685
Environmental Protection Agency (EPA), 100
e-portfolios, 815–17
e-publishing, 819–20

ERIC (Educational Resource Information
    Center), 503
Ernie (*Sesame Street* character), 415, *416*, 417
errors. *See* common errors
essay competitions, 818–19
essays
    audio, 786–87
    illustrated, 779–81
    summary/response, 90–97
    video, 788–90

ESSENTIAL ELEMENT, 749–50 A word, PHRASE, or CLAUSE with information that is necessary for understanding the meaning of a sentence: *French is the only language* that I can speak.

ETHICAL APPEALS, 422–25 Ways that authors establish CREDIBILITY and AUTHORITY to persuade an AUDIENCE to trust their ARGUMENTS—by showing that they know what they're talking about (for example, by citing trustworthy SOURCES), demonstrating that they're fair (by representing opposing views accurately and even-handedly), and establishing COMMON GROUND. *See also* EMOTIONAL APPEALS; LOGICAL APPEALS

ethos, of reviewing, 343–44. *See also* ETHICAL
    APPEAL
evaluation. *See also* REVIEW
    criteria for, 336–37
    of sources, 520–28, *522*
    support for, 337–39
evaluative annotations, 533

EVIDENCE, 425, 427–32, 451–73 In ARGUMENT, the data you present to support your REASONS. Such data may include statistics, calculations, EXAMPLES, ANECDOTES, QUOTATIONS, case studies, or anything else that will convince your readers that your reasons are compelling. Evidence should be sufficient (enough to show that the reasons have merit) and relevant (appropriate to the argument you're making).

in academic writing, 45
across academic disciplines, 77
in analyses, 237–49
in arguments, 156–58
in defensive reading, 103–4
in proposals, 378–79
in summary/response essay, 91–92

EXAMPLE, 464–65 A strategy that illustrates a point by giving specific instances.
visual, *465*

Excel, 765
exclamation points, 546–47
experiments, as evidence, 430–31

F

Facebook
and #BlackLivesMatter, 678
in lists of references (APA style), 643
and research, 498
tone, 676
in works cited (MLA style), 592–93
FactCheck.org, 102–4, 413, 499, 524, 526

FACTS, 420, 427 Information that can be backed up and verified by reliable evidence. For example: *Robert F. Kennedy was killed in 1968.*
defining, 98–100
distinguishing misinformation from, 98–107

fair use, 557–58

FAKE NEWS, 100, 495 A kind of misinformation made to look like authentic news. *See also* MISINFORMATION

FALLACY, 432–34 Faulty reasoning that can mislead an AUDIENCE. Fallacies include ad hominem, bandwagon appeal, begging the question, either-or argument, faulty analogy, faulty causality (also called "post hoc, ergo propter hoc"), hasty generalization, slippery slope, and straw man.

false dilemma. *See* either-or fallacy
FanFiction.net, 820
fan fiction websites, 820
fast reading, 70–71
faulty analogy, 434
faulty causality, 433

FIELD RESEARCH, 506–14 The collection of first-hand data through observation, interviews, and questionnaires or surveys.
interviews, 508–10
observations, 507–8
surveys and questionnaires, 510–14

figures, documenting, 553
films
in lists of references (APA style), 641
in works cited (MLA style), 594–95
Final Cut Pro, 789
first person. *See* POINT OF VIEW

FLASHBACK, 193 In NARRATIVE, an interruption of the main story in order to show an incident that occurred at an earlier time.

FLASH-FORWARD, 193 In NARRATIVE, an interruption of the main story in order to show an incident that will occur in the future.

flash mobs, 125–26, *126*
Flickr, 498
focus, 40
fonts, 760, 761
APA style, 644
MLA style, 598
Food Science and Technology Abstracts, 502
Ford, Harold, 155–56
forewords, in works cited (MLA style), 588

FORMAL WRITING, 673–74 Writing intended to be evaluated by someone such as an instructor or read by an AUDIENCE expecting academic or businesslike argument and presentation. Formal writing should be carefully EDITED, REVISED, and PROOFREAD.

formatting. *See also* DESIGN
    APA style, 644–46
    MLA style, 598–600
Fortnite (video game), 125

FRAGMENT, 715–17 A group of words that is capitalized and punctuated as a sentence but is not one, either because it lacks a SUBJECT, a VERB, or both, or because it begins with a word that makes it a SUBORDINATE CLAUSE.

Franklin, Aretha, 23, *23*, 187–89, *188*

FREEWRITING, 117 A process for GENERATING IDEAS AND TEXT by writing continuously for several minutes without pausing to read what has been written.

FUSED SENTENCE, 719–22 Two or more MAIN CLAUSES with no punctuation between them: *I came I saw I conquered.*

Fyre Festival, 465, *465*

G

Game of Thrones, 236–37, *237*
GameSpot, 137, 340
GarageBand, 787
gender, 729–32
general databases, 502

GENERATING IDEAS AND TEXT, 116–18 Activities that help writers develop a topic, EXAMPLES, REASONS, EVIDENCE, and other parts of a text by BRAINSTORMING, CLUSTERING, FREEWRITING, LOOPING, OUTLINING, and QUESTIONING.

GENRE, 133–404 A way of classifying things. The genres this book is concerned with are kinds of writing that writers can use to accomplish a certain goal and to reach a particular AUDIENCE. As such, they have well-established features that help guide writers, but they are flexible and change over time, and can be adapted by writers to address their own RHETORICAL SITUATIONS. Genres covered in this book include ANALYSES, ANNOTATED BIBLIOGRAPHIES, ARGUMENTS, NARRATIVES, PROPOSALS, REPORTS, and REVIEWS. Subgenres covered include LITERATURE REVIEWS, LITERACY NARRATIVES, PROFILES, PROJECT PROPOSALS, and VISUAL ANALYSES.
    academic writing and, 47–48
    analyses, 229–81
    arguments, 143–85
    choosing, 137–42
    narratives, 186–228
    proposals, 371–404
    reports, 282–327
    reviews, 328–70

GERUND A VERB form ending in *-ing* that functions as a NOUN: *Swimming improves muscle tone and circulation.*

global culture, 128–29
González, Emma, 106
Google, 707
    checking evidence, 104
    finding sources, 487, 497, 503
    Google Home, 272–74
    user reviews, 820
Google Arts and Culture, 497
Google Books, 494
Google Docs, 131, 815
Google Forms, 511
Google Images, 105
Google Maps, 498
Google News, 480, 495, 498
Google Scholar, 495, 497, 524
Google Sites, 815
Google Translate, 4
government documents
    in lists of references (APA style), 638
    as sources, 496
graphic narratives, 472, *472*
    in works cited (MLA style), 587

graphs, 765–66, 770
Gray, Freddie, 8
The Guardian, 107
Guggenheim Museum Bilbao, *554*

H

The Handmaid's Tale, 328–30, *329*

HASHTAG A metadata tag created by placing a number sign (#) in front of a word or unspaced phrase (for example, #BlackLivesMatter), used in social media to mark posts by KEYWORD or theme and make them searchable by these tags. Also used to add commentary on a web text outside of the text itself.
    and tone, 676

hasty generalization, 434
have/of, 751
headings, 760–61
    APA style, 645

HELPING VERB, 739 A VERB that works with a MAIN VERB to express a tense and mood. Helping verbs include *do*, *have*, *be*, and MODALS: *Elvis has left the building. Pigs can fly.*

Herzog, Werner, 338–39
his or her, 731
historical documents, as sources, 496–97
Hitler, Adolf, 6
Hooke, Robert, 13
Howard, Rebecca Moore, 558
Huffington Post, 781
humor, argument and, 466–67
Hurricane Katrina, 419–20
Hypothesis, 83

I

ideas
    emphasizing main idea, 701–3
    expressing clearly, 46–47

formulating, 40
generating, 116–18
organizing, 119–20
presenting in response to others, 46
synthesizing, 534–40
IEEE Xplore, 502
illustrated essays, 779–81
illustrations
    APA style, 646
    MLA style, 599–600
images. *See* visuals
imagination, 13–15
IMDb (Internet Movie Database), 343
iMovie, 789

IMRAD, 44, 284–85, 760 Acronym representing sections of scientific reports conveying information: introduction (asks a question), methods (tells about experiments), results (states findings), and discussion (tries to make sense of findings in light of what was already known).

indeed, 698
indefinite articles. *See* ARTICLE

INDEFINITE PRONOUN, 735–36 A PRONOUN—such as *all*, *anyone*, *anything*, *everyone*, *everything*, *few*, *many*, *nobody*, *nothing*, *one*, *some*, and *something*—that refers to a nonspecific person or thing.

indents
    APA style, 644–45
    MLA style, 598
infographics, 470, *471*, 768, *769*
information
    controversial, 557
    managing information overload, 515–19
    reporting, 282–83
    trustworthiness of, 294–95
    well-known, 556

INFORMATIONAL ANALYSIS, 266 A kind of PROCESS ANALYSIS that tells how something works.

information technology, 62–63, 127, *129. See also* social media

infotention, 67

inquiry letters, 54–55

Inside Higher Ed, 707

Instagram, 134, 139
    and argument, 406
    collaboration on, 127
    in lists of references (APA style), 643
    and narrative, 186
    profile for, 301
    and research, 497, 498
    responding on, 88
    in works cited (MLA style), 592–93

Institutional Review Board, 506

INSTRUCTIONAL ANALYSIS, 266 A kind of PROCESS ANALYSIS that tells how to do something.

internet. *See also* online sources; social media; WIKI
    fair use, 557–58
    opening sentences online, 706–7
    publishing on, 818–20
    style, 677–79

Internet Movie Database (*IMDb*), 343

interviews
    as evidence, 429–30
    in field research, 508–10
    in a job search, 61
    in works cited (MLA style), 595

in-text documentation
    APA style, 620–24
    MLA style, 565–71

introductions. *See also* OPENING
    drafting, 120
    in works cited (MLA style), 588

intuition, 13–15

INVITATIONAL ARGUMENT, 446–48 A system of ARGUMENT based on the work of Sonja Foss and Cindy Griffin that aims for understanding and shared goals by listening carefully to all concerned.

Invitational arguments introduce the issue, present all perspectives on it fairly, identify any commonalities among the perspectives, and conclude by seeking a resolution that is agreeable to all.

IRREGULAR VERB A VERB that does not form its past tense and past participle by adding *-ed* or *-d* to the base form (for example, *eat, ate, eaten*).

it, 728, 730–31

italics, 760

It Gets Better Project, 191

it's/its, 753–54

J

James, LeBron, 148–49, 713

Jamison, Judith, 417–18, *418*

Japanese video games, 779–80, *780*

Jensen, Arthur, 670

job interviews, 61

job letters, 53–57

Jobs, Steve, 794, *795*

journals. *See also* articles; periodicals
    in lists of references (APA style), 629, *631*
    in works cited (MLA style), 577, 580

JSTOR, 502

JURN, 495, 497

K

Kaepernick, Colin, 238–39, *240*

KAIROS, 122, 666 An ancient Greek term meaning "the opportune moment." Authors look for just the right moment to make a particular ARGUMENT, appeal to a particular AUDIENCE, and so on.

Kennedy, Robert F., 100

key terms, definitions of, 292–94

KEYWORD, 58 A term that a researcher inputs when searching RÉSUMÉS, databases, and the internet for information.

keyword searches, 503–4

Kickstarter, 124, 372, 373, *373*, 375

Kindle Direct Publishing, 819–20

King, Martin Luther, Jr., 794, *795*

Kokenis, Toni, 430

Kossola, Oluale (Cudjo Lewis), 691–92

L

LAB REPORT, 284 A GENRE of writing that covers the process of conducting an experiment in a controlled setting. Features: an explicit title • ABSTRACT • PURPOSE • methods • results and discussion • REFERENCES • APPENDIX • appropriate format

language, 2. *See also* English; RHETORIC; STYLE

language mixing
    connecting with audiences, 686–87
    drawing attention, 691
    edited academic English and other dialects, 685
    evoking person, place, or community, 692–93
    illustrating a point, 689–90
    providing translation, 687–89
    quoting directly with respect, 691–92

LAYOUT, 757–75 The way text is arranged on a page or screen—for example, in paragraphs, in lists, on charts, with headings, and so on.

LCSH (Library of Congress Subject Headings), 505

Leeper, Stacy, *483*

legal sources, 496
    in MLA style in-text documentation, 569

Lennon, John, *124*

Leone, Steven, 512–13

letters
    application, 55–56
    inquiry, 54–55
    job, 53–57
    in lists of references (APA style), 624

    thank-you, 57
    in works cited (MLA style), 583, 588, 591

Lewis, Cudjo (Oluale Kossola), 691–92

libraries
    finding sources, 499–501
    library catalogs, 500–501, *501*
    library websites, 499–500, *500*

Library of Congress subject headings (LCSH), 505

Lin, Jian, 436–37

Lincoln, Abraham, 417

line graphs, *765*, 765–66

LinkedIn, 301

listening, 8–10, 130

LITERACY NARRATIVE, 208–13 A GENRE of writing that tells about a writer's experience learning to read or write. Features: a well-told story • a firsthand account • an indication of the narrative's significance.
    annotated example, 209–13
    characteristic features, 208
    reading
        "Literacy: A Lineage," 209–13

literary works, in MLA style in-text documentation, 568

LITERATURE REVIEW, 348–55 A GENRE of writing that surveys and synthesizes the prior research on a topic. In the sciences, a literature review is a required part the introduction to an IMRAD report; in all disciplines, scholars write article-length literature reviews devoted to specific topics. Features: a survey of relevant research on a carefully focused topic • an objective summary of the literature • an evaluation of the literature • an organization appropriate to your assignment and PURPOSE • appropriate DOCUMENTATION.
    annotated example, 350–55
    characteristic features, 348–49

Liveable City, 288–89, 292–93, 296, 297

Living Room Conversations project, 21

LOGICAL APPEALS, 425, 427–32 Ways an author uses REASONS and EVIDENCE to persuade an AUDIENCE to accept a CLAIM: facts, images, observations, statistics, testimony, etc. *See also* EMOTIONAL APPEALS; ETHICAL APPEALS

logos. *See* logical appeals

LOOPING, 117 A process for GENERATING IDEAS AND TEXT in which a writer writes about a subject quickly for several minutes and summarizes the most important or interesting idea in a sentence, which becomes the beginning of another round of writing and summarizing, and so on, until an angle for a paper is found.

Los Angeles Times, 449

M

Magazine Index, 495
magazines
　　in lists of references (APA style), 630
　　in works cited (MLA style), 577–78,
　　　581

MAIN CLAUSE, 696, 700, 715, 717, 719, 720, 724 A CLAUSE, containing a SUBJECT and a VERB, that can stand alone as a sentence: *She sang. The world-famous soprano sang several arias.*

main idea, emphasizing, 701–3

MAIN VERB, 739 The verb form that presents the action or state. It can stand alone or be combined with one or more HELPING VERBS. *My dog might have <u>buried</u> your keys. Leslie Jones <u>is</u> a comedian. Alexa was <u>wearing</u> a gown by Milly. The agent didn't <u>appear</u> old enough to drive.*

Mandela, Nelson, 424–25, *426*
maps, 766, *767, 769, 770*
　　in lists of references (APA style), 642-43
　　in works cited (MLA style), 595

margins
　　APA style, 644–45
　　MLA style, 598
Marjory Stoneman Douglas High School shooting, 383
Martin, Trayvon, 261, 678
mash-ups, 534, *535*
Massachusetts Institute of Technology (MIT), 98–99
matter, nature of, 453–54
McCartney, Paul, *124*
Medical Subject Headings (MeSH), 505
Medium, 123, 125

MEDIUM, 755–56 A means for communicating—for example, in print, with speech, or online. *See also* DESIGN

　　analyses, 230–32
　　arguments, 144–46
　　design and delivery, 756
　　narratives, 189–90
　　proposals, 372
　　reading across media, 72–76
　　reports, 285
　　reviews, 331–32
　　style across media, 677–79

MEMOIR, 468 A GENRE that focuses on something significant from the writer's past. Key features include good story, vivid details, and clear significance.

Mendeley, 516
Metacritic.com, 330
Miller, Carolyn, 137
Miller, Susan, 524
Minecraft: Playstation 4 Edition, 340
minus signs, in keyword searches, 504

MISINFORMATION, 98–107, 491 False or inaccurate information that may or may not be intended to deceive (lies, on the other hand, are always told deliberately).

MIT (Massachusetts Institute of Technology), 98–99

MIXED CONSTRUCTION, 722–25 A sentence that starts out with one structure and ends up with another one: *Although bears can be deadly is not a good reason to avoid camping altogether.*

MLA International Bibliography, 503

MLA STYLE, 562, 563–617 A system of DOCUMENTATION used in the humanities. MLA stands for the Modern Language Association.
    directory, 563–65
    formatting a research essay, 598–600
    illustrations, 599–600
    in-text documentation, 565–71
    notes, 571
    parenthetical documentation, 553
    quotations, 543, 544, 745
    sample research essay, 600–617
    verb tenses and, 552, 739
    visuals, 770
    works cited, 572–98
        articles and other short works, 577–84
        audio, visual, and other sources, 593–98
        authors and other contributors, 574–76
        books and parts of books, 584–89
        core elements, 572–74
        personal communication and social media, 591–93
        websites, 589–91

MODAL, 751 A HELPING VERB—such as *can, could, may, might, must, ought to, should, will,* or *would*—that does not change form for person or number and indicates probability or necessity.

MODE, 776–77 A way of conveying a message. Writing often uses multiple modes: linguistic, audio, visual, spatial, and/or gestural. *See also*

STRATEGIES FOR SUPPORTING AN ARGUMENT, which are also referred to as modes.
    multimodal writing, 776–93

Modern Language Association (MLA), 562, 563.
    See also MLA STYLE
motivation, examining, 10–11, 32

MULTIMODAL WRITING, 776–93 Writing that uses more than one MODE of expression, including some combination of words, images, audio, video, links, and so on. Sometimes called "multimedia writing."
    audio essays, 786–87
    blogs, 781–84
    defined, 776–77
    illustrated essays, 779–81
    posters, 790–91
    video essays, 788–90
    wikis, 784–86

multivolume works
    in lists of references (APA style), 637
    in MLA style in-text documentation, 570
    in works cited (MLA style), 585
musical scores, in works cited (MLA style), 596
music recordings, in lists of references (APA style), 641
Mutt Love Rescue, 145

N

NAACP (National Association for the Advancement of Colored People), 670
Napoleon I, *454,* 455

NARRATION, 468–69 A STRATEGY for presenting information as a story, for telling "what happened." It is a pattern often associated with fiction, but it shows up in all kinds of writing. When used in a REVIEW, a REPORT, or another academic GENRE, narration is used to support a point—not merely to tell an interesting story for its own sake.

Narration can serve as the organizing principle for a paragraph or whole text.

NARRATIVE, 186–228 A GENRE that tells a story for the PURPOSE of making a point. Features: a clearly defined event • a clearly described setting • vivid, descriptive details • a consistent POINT OF VIEW • a clear point. *See also* LITERACY NARRATIVE

    across academic disciplines, 189
    across cultures and communities, 190–91
    across genres, 191–92
    across media, 189–90
    advertisements and, 468
    annotated example, 202–7
    characteristic features, 192–201
    graphic narratives, 472, *472*
    literacy narratives, 208–13
    readings
        "At the VA, Healing the Doctor-Patient Relationship," 202–7
        "Bathtime," 219–23
        "Literacy: A Lineage," 209–13
        "The Look," 224–28
    roadmap to writing a narrative, 214–18

National Aeronautics and Space Administration (NASA), 520, *522, 527*
National Association for the Advancement of Colored People (NAACP), 670
National Council of Teachers of English, 776
National Geographic, 491, *492,* 773, *774*
National Library of Medicine, 505
National Newspaper Index, 495
National Public Radio, 480, 786
National Weather Service, 456, *456*
Netflix, 137
NewsNow, 498
newspapers
    in lists of references (APA style), 630
    in works cited (MLA style), 578
New York Times, 343, 495, 820
New York Times Book Review, 338

Nexis Uni, 502
9/11, 5
Nintendo, 334, *334,* 779–80, *780*
Nixon, Richard, *284*

NONCOUNT NOUN, 736 A word that names something that cannot be counted or made plural with certain modifiers or units: *information, rice.*

NONESSENTIAL ELEMENT, 749–50 A word, phrase, or CLAUSE that gives additional information but that is not necessary for understanding the basic meaning of a sentence: *I learned French, <u>which is a Romance language,</u> online.* Nonessential elements should be set off by commas.

nor, 697
Norton Writer's Prize, 819
notes
    APA style, 625
    MLA style, 571
note taking, 121–22, 516–18, 561

NOUN A word that refers to a person, place, animal, thing, or idea (*director, Stephen King, forest, Amazon River, tree frog, notebook, democracy*).
    noncount, 736

novels, in MLA style in-text documentation, 568
NPR Research News, 480

O

Oakland Promise, 289–92, *290, 291,* 295–96, 313
Obama, Barack, 187
obituaries, 187
object case, 732–34
observations
    as evidence, 428–29
    in field research, 507–8
O'Connor, Diane, 706
of/have, 751
older sources, 491–93

One Billion Rising, 126, *126*

The Onion, 103

online contexts, 161

online sources

    avoiding plagiarism, 561

    evaluating, 520–28, *522*

    keeping track of, 515–16

    in lists of references (APA style), 626, 629–34, 639–44

    in works cited (MLA style), 589–91

on-screen reading, 72–76

OPENING, 704–7 The way a text begins, which plays an important role in drawing an AUDIENCE in. Some ways of opening a college essay: with a dramatic statement, a vivid image, a provocative question, an ANECDOTE, or a startling CLAIM.

    online, 706–7

    sentences, 704–7

or, 697–98

oral presentations, in works cited (MLA style), 596

organization, 43–47

    chronological, 193

    general to specific, 45–46

    IMRAD, 44

    spatial, 315

    of summary/response essays, 92

organizing

    analyses, 269–70

    arguments, 169

    drafts, 120

    narratives, 216–17

    oral presentations, 794–95

    proposals, 394

    reports, 295–97, 314–15

    reviews, 359

OUTLINING, 118 A process for GENERATING IDEAS AND TEXT or for examining a text. An informal outline simply lists ideas and then numbers them in the order that they will appear; a working outline distinguishes support from main ideas by indenting the former; a formal outline is arranged as a series of headings and indented subheadings, each on a separate line, with letters and numerals indicating relative levels of importance.

Ovechkin, Alexander, *14*

P

page numbers

    APA style, 644

    MLA style, 598

    works without, 570–71

papers from conference proceedings

    in lists of references (APA style), 639

    in works cited (MLA style), 588–89

PARAPHRASE, 541–43, 547–49, 551–54 To reword a text in about the same number of words but without using the word order or sentence structure of the original. Paraphrasing is generally called for when a writer wants to include the details of a passage but does not need to quote it word for word. As with QUOTING and SUMMARIZING, paraphrasing requires DOCUMENTATION. *See also* PATCHWRITING

    deciding whether to quote, paraphrase, or summarize, 542–43

    signal phrases and, 551–52

parentheses, in keyword searches, 504

"parlor" metaphor (Burke), 7

PASSIVE VOICE, 679–80 When a VERB is in the passive voice, the subject is acted upon: *A gift was given to Oliver.*

PATCHWRITING, 558–60 PARAPHRASES that lean too heavily on the words or sentence structure of the source, adding or deleting some words, replacing words with synonyms, altering the syntax slightly—in other words, not restating the passage in fresh language and structure.

Patel, Eboo, 422–24, *423*

pathos. *See* EMOTIONAL APPEALS

Patrick, Danica, 781–83, *782*

peer review. *See* response

periodicals, documenting, 494–95

    in lists of references (APA style), 629–30

    in working bibliographies, 519

    in works cited (MLA style), 577–84

PERIODIC SENTENCE, 702–3 A sentence that delays the main idea, expressed in a MAIN CLAUSE, until after details given in phrases and SUBORDINATE CLAUSES. *See also* CUMULATIVE SENTENCE

periods, 546, 718, 720

personal experience

    as evidence, 431–32

    as support for an argument, 464–65

personal interviews, in works cited (MLA style), 595

perspectives. *See also* POINT OF VIEW

    in arguments, 158–59

    considering multiple perspectives, 9–10, 45, 434–37

persuasion, 5. *See also* RHETORIC

Pettitte, Andy, 247–49, *249*, 251

Phoenix, Joaquin, 334, *335*

photographs, 105–6, 764, *764*, 769

pie charts, *765*, 766

Pienaar, Francois, *426*

PLAGIARISM, 555–62 Using another person's words, syntax, or ideas without giving appropriate credit and DOCUMENTATION. Plagiarism is a serious breach of ethics.

    avoiding, 558–61, 744

    fair use and the internet, 557–58

    patchwriting, 558–60

Playing for Change, 126

plus signs, in keyword searches, 504

podcasts

    in lists of references (APA style), 640–41

    in works cited (MLA style), 596

poems, in MLA style in-text documentation, 568

POINT OF VIEW A position from which something is considered. The common points of view are first person, which uses *I* or *we*, and third person, which uses *he*, *she*, or *they*. *See also* perspectives

    in narratives, 196–99, 216

popular sources, 490–91, *492*

PORTFOLIO, 809–17 A collection of writing selected by a writer to show their work, sometimes including a statement assessing the work and explaining what it demonstrates.

    e-portfolios, 815–17, *816*

    organizing, 815–17

    portfolio statements, 813–14

    reflecting on your writing, 812–14

    sample portfolio statement, 813–14

    what to include, 810–11

POSITION, 167–69 A statement that asserts a belief or CLAIM. In an ARGUMENT, a position needs to be stated in a THESIS or clearly implied and requires support with REASONS and other kinds of EVIDENCE.

possessive case, 732–34

posters

    for presentation, 790–91, *791*

    in lists of references (APA style), 639

posts to online forums

    in lists of references (APA style), 640

    in works cited (MLA style), 592

PowerPoint, 145, 765, 807

    in lists of references (APA style), 642

prefaces, in works cited (MLA style), 588

presentations, 794–808

    across disciplines, 795–96

    common structure, 794–95

    roadmap to making a presentation, 803–8

    sample presentation, 797–802

    in works cited (MLA style), 596

Prezi, 677, 807

primary documents, as sources, 496–97

PRIMARY SOURCE, 488, 490 A source such as a literary work, historical document, work of art, or performance that a researcher examines firsthand. Primary sources also include experiments and FIELD RESEARCH. In writing about the Revolutionary War, a researcher would probably consider the Declaration of Independence a primary source and a textbook's description of the writing of the document a SECONDARY SOURCE.

PROBLEM AND SOLUTION, 469–70 A STRATEGY for supporting an ARGUMENT by framing it as a way of solving a problem, or of introducing a change of some kind. If a writer can first convince readers that there's a problem (and that it matters), they'll be more likely to read on to hear about how it can be solved. In fact, this is a classic storytelling technique, setting up a conflict that needs to be resolved. It's a technique that can help capture and hold an AUDIENCE'S attention.

proceedings of conferences
    in lists of references (APA style), 639
    in works cited (MLA style), 588–89

PROCESS ANALYSIS, 244–46, 266 A kind of ANALYSIS that closely examines the steps of a process. *See also* INFORMATIONAL ANALYSIS; INSTRUCTIONAL ANALYSIS

professional communication, 50, *51. See also* teamwork
    collaboration in, 128–29
    job interviews, 61
    job letters, 53–57
    rhetorical situations at work, 52
professionalism, 53

PROFILE, 301–10 A REPORT about people, places, events, institutions, or other things. Features: a firsthand account · detailed information about the subject · an interesting angle

annotated example, 304–10
characteristic features, 301–3
readings
    "Heart and Sole: Detroiter Walks 21 Miles to Work," 304–10
    "Selling the Farm," 318–23

Project Gutenberg, 494
Project Information Literacy, 447

PROJECT PROPOSAL, 386–90 A writing GENRE that describes the PURPOSE of a research project, the steps of the project, and its goal. Features: a discussion of the topic · an indication of a specific focus · the REASON for interest in the topic · a research plan · a schedule
    annotated example, 387–90
    characteristic features, 386

PRONOUN, 725–34 A word that takes the place of a NOUN or functions the way a noun does.
    clear pronoun reference, 726–28
    gender and, 729–32
    indefinite pronouns, 735–36
    pronoun-antecedent agreement, 728–32
    pronoun case, 732–34

PRONOUN REFERENCE, 726–28 The way in which a PRONOUN indicates its ANTECEDENT. Pronoun reference must be clear and unambiguous in order to avoid confusing readers.

PROOFREADING, 122 Process that includes checking for correct spelling and punctuation as well as for page order, missing copy, and consistent use of typefaces and fonts. *See also* EDITING; REVISION

PROPOSAL, 371–404 A GENRE that argues for a solution to a problem or suggests some action. Features: a precise description of the problem · a clear and compelling solution to the problem · EVIDENCE that your solution will address the problem · acknowledgment of other possible solutions • a statement of what your proposal will accomplish. *See also* PROJECT PROPOSAL

across academic disciplines, 372
across cultures and communities, 372–74
across genres, 374
across media, 372
annotated example, 383–85
characteristic features, 374–82
project proposal, 386–90
readings
"Call to Action to Prevent Gun Violence," 383–85
"The Economic Impact of Investing Public Funds in Sports Franchises," 387–90
"Snowflakes and Free Speech on Campuses," 400–404
"Speaking While Female," 396–99
roadmap to writing a proposal, 391–95

ProQuest One, 502
protesters, 5–6, *6*
PsycINFO, 502
Publication Manual of the American Psychological Association. See APA STYLE
Public Citizen, *413*, 413–14
published interviews, in works cited (MLA style), 595
publishing, 818–20
on fan fiction websites, 820
on the internet, 819–20
reviews, 820
self-publishing, 819–20
punctuation, 42
commas, 714, 746–50
ellipsis marks, 545
exclamation points, 546–47
periods, 546, 718, 720
question marks, 546–47
quotation marks, 543–44, 545–47
of quotations, 543–47
semicolons, 546, 698, 718, 720–21

PURPOSE, 28–29 A writer's goal: to explore; to express oneself; to entertain; to demonstrate learning; to report; to persuade; and so on. Purpose is one element of the RHETORICAL SITUATION.

Putin, Vladimir, 105, *105*

Q

QUALIFYING WORD, 45, 419 A word such as *frequently*, *often*, *generally*, *sometimes*, or *rarely* that indicates the strength of a CLAIM.

QUALITATIVE DATA, 267, 336–37 Data that describe something in unquantifiable terms—for example, with DESCRIPTION, ANECDOTES, and other nonnumerical information, including that found through FIELD RESEARCH.

Qualtrics, 511

QUANTITATIVE DATA, 267, 336–37 Data that can be presented in concrete, measurable ways, such as statistics and measurements.

Queen City Writers, 819

QUESTIONING, 117–18 A process of GENERATING IDEAS AND TEXT about a topic—asking, for example, What? Who? When? Where? How? and Why?
articulating questions, 482–84
in defensive reading, 103–4
generating ideas, 117–18
in interviews, 509
in surveys and questionnaires, 512–13

question marks, 546–47
questionnaires
as evidence, 428, *428*
in field research, 510–14

QUOTATION, 541–47, 551–54, 691–92 Someone's words used exactly as they were spoken or written. Quotation is most effective when wording is worth repeating or makes a point so well that no rewording will do it justice or when you want to cite someone's exact words or to quote someone

whose opinions disagree with others. Quotations need to be acknowledged with DOCUMENTATION. *See also* in-text documentation
  acknowledging sources, 557
  APA style, 620–21, 645, 745
  block quotations, 544
  deciding whether to quote, paraphrase, or summarize, 542–43
  incorporating quotations, 741–43
  indicating changes, 545
  indicating who said what, 744
  MLA style, 599, 745
  punctuating quotations, 543–47, 743–45
  short quotations, 543–44
  signal phrases, 551–52, 742, 744–45

quotation marks
  in keyword searches, 503–4
  for short quotations, 543–44

R

radio programs, in works cited (MLA style), 597
random samples, 510
Ratcliffe, Krista, 8
readability, 760, 763
The Readers' Guide to Periodical Literature, 495
reading
  across academic disciplines, 77–78
  across genres, 76
  across media, 72–76
  annotating, 80–85
  considering your rhetorical situation, 69
  distinguishing facts from misinformation, 98–107
  efferent, 71
  fast vs. slow, 70–71
  and infotention, 67–68
  on- vs. off-screen texts, 72–76
  reading process, 65–107
  reading rhetorically, 67–78

  reflection exercises, 78
  responding to readings, 88–97
  summarizing, 86–88, 90–97
  of unfamiliar/difficult text, 72
  writing as reciprocal of, 65–66

READING DEFENSIVELY, 101–4, 491 The kind of reading that doesn't take things at face value, that questions underlying assumptions, that scrutinizes claims carefully, and that does not rush to judgment.

REASON Support for a CLAIM or POSITION. A reason, in turn, requires its own support.
  in arguing a position, 156–58
  faulty reasoning, 432–34

recorded source material, incorporating, 553–54
reference librarians, 499
references (in job searches), 60

REFERENCES, 625–44 The list of sources at the end of a text prepared in APA STYLE. *See also* bibliographies
  annotated example, 660–61

REFERENCE WORKS, 493–94 SOURCES such as encyclopedias, handbooks, atlases, directories of biographical information, and almanacs that provide overviews of a topic.
  as sources, 493–94
  in works cited (MLA style), 580

reflecting on your writing, 812–14

REGISTER, 683–84 Varieties of language associated not with particular people or users but with a particular activity or occupation—like soccer or chemical engineering.

REITERATION, 471–73 A STRATEGY for SUPPORTING AN ARGUMENT that uses the repetition of a KEYWORD, phrase, image, or theme throughout a text to drive home a point.

RELATIVE PRONOUN A PRONOUN, such as *that*, *which*, *who*, *whoever*, *whom*, and *whomever*, that introduces a SUBORDINATE CLAUSE: *The professor who gave the lecture is my adviser.*

religious works, in lists of references (APA style), 638

REPORT, 282–327 A writing GENRE that presents information to inform readers on a subject. Features: a topic carefully focused for a specific AUDIENCE • definitions of key terms • trustworthy information • appropriate organization and DESIGN • a confident TONE that informs rather than argues. *See also* IMRAD; PROFILE
    across academic disciplines, 284–85
    across cultures and communities, 285
    across genres, 287
    across media, 285
    annotated example, 298–300
    characteristic features, 288–97
    IMRAD, 284–85
    profiles, 301–10
    readings
        "Gender," 298–300
        "Heart and Sole: Detroiter Walks 21 Miles to Work," 304–10
        "The Right to Preach on a College Campus," 324–27
        "Selling the Farm," 318–23
    roadmap to writing a report, 311–17

representative samples, 510
republished work, in works cited (MLA style), 588

RESEARCH, 475–662 The process of gathering information from reliable SOURCES to help in making decisions, supporting ARGUMENTS, solving problems, becoming more informed, and so on. *See also* FIELD RESEARCH
    annotating a bibliography, 529–33
    avoiding plagiarism, 555–62
    documenting sources
        APA style, 618–61
        MLA style, 563–617
    evaluating sources, 520–28
    field research, 506–14
    finding sources, 486–514
    giving credit, 555–62
    keeping track, 515–19
    quoting, paraphrasing, and summarizing, 541–54
    scheduling, 485
    starting, 477–85
    synthesizing ideas, 534–40

RESEARCH QUESTION, 482–84 A question that guides research. A good research question should be simple, focused, and require more than just a "yes" or "no" answer.

research sites, 497–503

RESPECT, 15 The act of giving someone or something your careful attention, listening with an open mind, being polite and considerate, and according someone else the same right to speak that you wish for yourself.
    demonstrating, 23–24
    engaging respectfully with others, 18–27

response, getting and giving, 88–90, 121
    analyses, 270–71
    arguments, 169–71
    to a design, 773–75
    inviting a response, 26–27
    narratives, 217–18
    proposals, 394–95
    reports, 315–17
    reviews, 360–61
    writing process, 121
restrictive element. *See* ESSENTIAL ELEMENT

RÉSUMÉ, 58–59 A GENRE that summarizes someone's academic and employment history, generally written to submit to potential employers. DESIGN and word choice depend on whether a résumé is submitted as a print document or in an electronic or scannable form. Features: an organization that suits goals and experience • succinctness • a design that highlights key information (for print) or that uses only one typeface (for scannable)

    design, 58

    example, 59

    formats, 58

    objectives, 58

REVIEW, 328–70 A writing GENRE that makes a judgment about something—a film, book, product, restaurant, whatever —based on certain CRITERIA. Features: relevant information about the subject • criteria for the evaluation • a well-supported evaluation • attention to the AUDIENCE's needs and expectations • an authoritative TONE • awareness of the ethics of reviewing. *See also* LITERATURE REVIEW

    across academic disciplines, 330

    across cultures and communities, 332

    across genres, 332

    across media, 331–32

    annotated example, 345–47

    characteristic features, 333–44

    literature reviews, 348–55

    publishing reviews, 820

    readings

        "*Black Panther* Gets So Much Right, and One Crucial Thing Wrong," 362–66

        "The Effects of Mindfulness Meditation and Exercise on Memory," 350–55

        "Indie Gem *Please Knock on My Door* Expertly Captures Mental Illness," 367–70

        "Monopoly: The Scandal Behind the World's Favorite Board Game," 345–47

    roadmap to writing a review, 356–61

    in works cited (MLA style), 583

REVISION, 121–22 The process of making substantive changes, including additions and cuts, to a draft so that it contains all the necessary information in an appropriate organization. During revision, a writer generally moves from whole-text issues to details with the goals of sharpening the focus and strengthening the ARGUMENT.

    analyses, 270–71

    arguments, 169–71

    narratives, 217–18

    proposals, 394–95

    reports, 315–17

    reviews, 360–61

    writing process, 122

RHETORIC, 1–63 One of the three original disciplines in the ancient world (along with grammar and logic), rhetoric has been defined in many ways through the centuries. In this book, we define it as the art, practice, and theory of ethical communication.

    need for, 1–63

    reading rhetorically, 67–78

    rhetorical situations, 28–34

    thinking rhetorically, 5–17

    in the workplace, 50–63

RHETORICAL ANALYSIS, 238–42, 265 A kind of ANALYSIS that takes a close look at how a text communicates a message to an AUDIENCE.

RHETORICAL SITUATION, 28–34, 115–16 The circumstances that affect writing or other communication, including PURPOSE, AUDIENCE, GENRE, STANCE, CONTEXT, MEDIA, and DESIGN.

    considering your rhetorical situation

        analyses, 262–64

        arguments, 164–66

        design, 759

        multimodal writing, 778–79

        narratives, 214–15

        presentations, 803

        proposals, 391–92

        reports, 311–13

        research, 479–80

        reviews, 356–57

        at work, 52

rhetorical situation *(cont.)*
 elements of
  audience, 31–32
  context, 33
  genre, 30–31
  medium/design, 34
  purpose, 32–33
  stance, 33

ROGERIAN ARGUMENTS, 445–46 A system of ARGU-MENT based on the work of Carl Rogers that stresses fairness and compromise and persuasion by non-confrontational strategies such as showing respect and establishing COMMON GROUND. The introduction presents the issue fairly, the body discusses various POSITIONS on the issue including the author's own, and the CONCLUSION presents a resolution.

Rolling Stone, 316

S

sacred texts
 in MLA style in-text documentation, 569
 in works cited (MLA style), 587
samples, in field research
 random, 510
 representative, 510
Sandy Hook Elementary School shooting, 411–12, *412*
sans serif fonts, 760
schedules, 485
scholarly sources, 490–91, *492*
Science Buddies, 244–45
Scribd, 815
searches, 503–6. *See also* KEYWORD
 author, title, and subject searches, 505–6
 keyword searches, 503–4
 search engines, 707
 wildcard, 504
search sites, 497–98

SECONDARY SOURCE, 488, 490 An ANALYSIS or interpretation of a PRIMARY SOURCE. In writing about the Revolutionary War, a researcher would probably consider the Declaration of Independence a primary source and a textbook's description of how the document was written a secondary source.

Selfe, Cynthia, 776–77
self-publishing, 819–20
self-representation, 15
semicolons, 546, 698, 718, 720–21
sentences, 714–25
 closing, 707–9
 comma splices, 717–19
 cumulative, 701–2
 emphasizing main idea, 701–3
 fused, 719–22
 mixed constructions, 722–25
 opening, 704–7
 periodic, 702–3
 sentence fragments, 715–17
 varying, 709–12
serif fonts, 760
setting, 193–94
setting up a strawman, 434
Sheperd, Scott, *25*
shifts in tense, 738–40
Shinola, 74, *75*
Shockley, William, 670

SIGNAL PHRASE, 551–52, 742, 744–45 A phrase used to attribute quoted, paraphrased, or summarized material to a source, as in "she said" or "he claimed."

signal verbs, 551–52, 621

SIGNPOST LANGUAGE Words and phrases meant to help listeners follow an oral presentation. Some functions of signpost language include introducing or concluding a presentation ("My topic today is . . ."), providing an overview ("I will make three major points"), or marking TRANSITIONS ("My third and final point is . . .").

SIMPLE SENTENCE, 696 A single MAIN CLAUSE, which contains at least a SUBJECT and a VERB.

The main clause must stand alone: *Citizens vote. The United States holds a presidential election once every four years.* For sentences with more than a single main clause, *see* COMPOUND SENTENCE; COMPOUND-COMPLEX SENTENCE; COMPLEX SENTENCE.

SIMPLE SUBJECT, 736, 737 The word that determines the form of the VERB: *The young farmer from Ten Barn Farm has the best tomatoes at the market.* The simple subject is *farmer*, a singular NOUN; for that reason, the verb *has* is singular.

since, 699

SINGULAR *THEY*, 731–32 The use of *they*, *them*, and *their* to refer to a person whose gender is unknown or not relevant to the context. Traditionally, *they* has referred only to plural items, but the use of singular *they* is now becoming more accepted.

sketching, 117
Skype, 61, *62*
slippery slope fallacy, 433–34
slow reading, 70–71
Snopes, 102, 103, 106, 499, 524, 526
social media, 5–6, 112, 127, 186
    Black Lives Matter, 677–78
    for finding sources, 498–99
    in lists of references (APA style), 643
    style, 677–79
    in works cited (MLA style), 592–93
SocINDEX, 503
software, computer programs, or apps, in lists of
        references (APA style), 642
solutions
    acknowledging other possible, 379–80
    clear and compelling, 376–78
sound recordings, in works cited
        (MLA style), 597
sources, 486–528
    acknowledging, 556–57
    citing, 555–62
    crediting, 555–62
    documenting (*See* APA STYLE; MLA STYLE)
    evaluating, 520–28, *522*
    finding, 486–514, *489*
    incorporating, 551–54
        deciding whether to quote, paraphrase, or
                summarize, 542–43
        paraphrasing, 547–49, 551–54
        quoting, 543–47, 551–54
        summarizing, 549–54
    interviews, 508–10
    keeping track, 515–19
    observations, 507–8
    older vs. current, 491–93
    paraphrasing, 547–49
    primary vs. secondary, 488, 490
    quoting, 543–47
    reading critically, 526–28
    research sites, 497–503
    scholarly vs. popular, 490–91, *492*
    searches, 503–6
        author, title, and subject searches, 505–6
        keyword searches, 503–4
    social media, 487
    summarizing, 549–54
    surveys, 510–14
    synthesizing, 534–40
    trustworthy, 102–3
    types of, 493–97
        audio, 553–54
        books, 494
        electronic, 515–16
        government and legal documents, 496
        periodicals, 494–95
        primary and historical documents,
                496–97
        reference works, 493–94
        visual, 553–54
Southern Utah University, 819
spacing
    APA style, 644–45
    MLA style, 598

SPATIAL ORGANIZATION, 315 A way of ordering a text that mirrors the physical arrangement of the subject, for instance from top to bottom, left to right, outside to inside.

specificity, 42
speech, recording of, in lists of references
        (APA style), 642
spelling, 42
Spider-Man: Into the Spider-Verse (film), 342, *343*
spoken texts, 34, 76
SPORTDiscus, 502
sports coverage, 189
Sports Illustrated, 13–15, *14*
Spotify, 137
Squarespace, 815
St. Onge, Ryan, 285, *286*, 293–94

STANCE, 10–11, 33 An author's attitude toward the subject—for example, reasonable, neutral, angry, curious. Stance is conveyed through TONE and word choice.
        analytical writing, 294–95, 302

Stanford University, 101
Star Trek, 668–69, *669*

STASIS THEORY, 419–20 A simple system for identifying the crux of an ARGUMENT—what's at stake in it—by asking four questions: (1) What are the facts? (2) How can the issue be defined? (3) How much does it matter, and why? (4) What actions should be taken as a result?

statistics, as evidence, 427
Stein, Ross, 436–37

STORYBOARD, 789, 790 A series of sketches used in planning a film or video essay to map out the sequence of camera shots, movement, and action.

STRATEGIES FOR SUPPORTING AN ARGUMENT, 451–73 Patterns for organizing and providing EVIDENCE to support a POSITION: ANALOGY, CAUSE AND EFFECT, CLASSIFICATION, COMPARISON AND CONTRAST, DEFINITION, DESCRIPTION, EXAMPLE, NARRATION, PROBLEM AND SOLUTION, and REITERATION.
        analogy, 451–53
        cause and effect, 453–55
        classification, 455–56
        comparison and contrast, 457–59
        definition, 460–61
        description, 462–64
        examples, 464–65
        humor, 466–67
        narration, 468–69
        problem and solution, 469–70
        reiteration, 471–73

straw man fallacy, 434
Street Roots, 377
students, 127

STYLE, 663–754 The particular way something is written or communicated that includes all the elements—such as sentence structure, TONE, and word choice—that make the communication distinctive.
        academic writing and, 35–49, 679–80
        appropriateness and correctness, 668–71
        argument and, 448–50
        connecting with audiences, 671–73
        defined, 667–82
        design, 598–617
        formality, 673–74
        good sentences, 694–712
        personal, 680–82
        sentence style, 694–712
        stance, 674–76
        tone, 676–77

style guides. *See* APA STYLE; MLA STYLE

SUBJECT, 734–37 A word or word group, usually including at least one NOUN or PRONOUN plus its modifiers, that tells who or what a sentence or CLAUSE is about. In the sentence *A frustrated* *group of commuters waited for the late bus,* the subject is *A frustrated group of commuters.*

  sentence fragment, 715–16
  subjects consisting of more than one word, 736–37
  subject-verb agreement, 734–37

subject case, 732–34
subject librarians, 499
subject searches, 505–6
subject-specific databases, 502–3

SUBJECT-VERB AGREEMENT, 734–37 The agreement in number (singular or plural) and person (first, second, or third) of a SUBJECT and its VERB: *Danny rides his bike to school; his brothers ride the bus.*

SUBJUNCTIVE MOOD The MOOD of a VERB used to express wishes or requests or to indicate unlikely conditions: *Most people wish that global warming were not so evident.*

SUBORDINATE CLAUSE, 699–700, 715, 724 A CLAUSE that begins with a SUBORDINATING WORD and therefore cannot stand alone as a sentence: *She feels good when she exercises. My roommate, who was a physics major, tutors students in science.*

SUBORDINATING WORD, 699, 719, 721–722 A word or phrase, such as *because, in order that,* and *while* that introduces a SUBORDINATE CLAUSE: *The ice sculpture melted because the room for the wedding reception was too warm.*

summarizing, 542–43, 549–54
  as a reading strategy, 86–88

SUMMARY, 541–43, 549–54 The use of one's own words and sentence structure to condense someone else's text into a version that gives the main ideas of the original. As with paraphrasing and quoting, summarizing requires DOCUMENTATION.

  deciding whether to quote, paraphrase, or summarize, 542–43
  signal phrases and, 551–52

summary/response essays, 90–97
  annotated example, 93–97
  characteristic features, 91–92
  reading
    "The Higher Price of Buying Local," 93–97
Super Mario Bros. 3, 779–80, *780*
Superstorm Sandy, *104,* 105
Surf Market, *672,* 672–73
SurveyMonkey, 511
surveys
  as evidence, 428
  in field research, 510–14

SYNTAX, 665 Sentence structure.

SYNTHESIZING IDEAS, 534–40 Bringing together ideas and information from multiple sources, exploring patterns in order to discover new insights and perspectives.

  sources in, 535–37
  your own ideas, 537–40

T

tables, 765, 766, *766,* 770
  APA style, 646
  documenting, 553
Taylor, Lawrence, 197–98, *198*
Teach for America (TFA), 380, 382
teamwork, 128–29, *129*
technical or research reports, in lists of references (APA style), 638
technology, 3–4
TED.com, 479, *771,* 771–72
telecommuting, 128–29
television programs
  in lists of references (APA style), 641
  in works cited (MLA style), 597–98

TENSE A characteristic of VERBS that indicates the time when action occurs or expresses a state of being. The three main tenses are the present

(*I play*), the past (*I played*), and the future (*I will play*). Each tense has perfect (*I have played*), progressive (*I am playing*), and perfect progressive (*I have been playing*) forms. *See also* VERB
    with APA style, 738–40
    with MLA style, 739
    past perfect, 740
    past tense, 738–40
    present perfect, 738–39
    present tense, 738
    shifts in, 738–40

tentative thesis, 118–19
testimony, as evidence, 430
Texas A&M University, 336–37
text message, in works cited (MLA style), 592
texts
    difficult, 72
    digital, 34, 72–74
    print, 72–76
    sacred, 569, 587
    spoken, 34, 76
    unfamiliar, 72
    visual, 74, *75*
TFA (Teach for America), 380, 382
thank-you letters, 57
Theismann, Joe, 197–98, *198*
therefore, 698
there/their/they're, 751–53

THESIS, 45, 168, 417 A statement that identifies the topic and main point of a piece of writing, giving readers an idea of what the text will cover.
    plotting out a working thesis, 484–85
    tentative, 118–19, 168

they, 726–27
    singular, 731–32
they're/there/their, 751–53
thinking rhetorically, 5–17
    about design, 758–59
    being imaginative, 13–15
    considering alternative points of view, 9–10
    giving credit, 13
    listening, 8–10
This American Life, 786, 787
This I Believe, 786
Time (magazine), 316
Tin Eye, 105
title pages
    APA style, 644
    MLA style, 598
title searches, 505–6
Todd, Lucinda, 795

TONE, 33 A writer's or speaker's attitude toward the audience and subject. Tone reflects the writer's STANCE: critical, playful, reasonable, ironic, and so on.
    appropriate, 676–77
    authoritative, 160, 341–42
    confident and informative, 297

top5projectmanagement.com, 792
topics, 118–19
    choosing, 115
    narrowing, in research, 480–81
    research for, 478–79
    selection of, 115
    for specific genres
        analyses, 262
        arguments, 164, 166–67
        narratives, 216
        profiles, 301
        project proposals, 386
        proposals, 391
        reports, 288–92, 311, 313–14
        reviews, 356

TOPIC SENTENCE, 43 A sentence, often at the beginning of a paragraph, that states the paragraph's main point. The details in the rest of the paragraph should support the topic sentence.

Tosh, Peter, 686

TOULMIN ARGUMENT, 442–44 A system of ARGUMENT developed by Stephen Toulmin that features a qualified CLAIM; REASONS and EVIDENCE in support of the claim; underlying assumptions that aren't explicitly stated but that also support the claim; further evidence or backing for those underlying assumptions; and a CONCLUSION.

Tower of Babel, 3

TRANSITION, 698 A word or PHRASE that helps to connect sentences and paragraphs and to guide readers through a text. Transitions can show COMPARISONS (*also, similarly, likewise, in the same way*); CONTRASTS (*but, instead, although, however, nonetheless*); EXAMPLES (*for instance, in fact, such as*); place or position (*above, beyond, near, elsewhere*); sequence (*finally, next, again, also*); SUMMARY or conclusion (*on the whole, as we have seen, in brief*); time (*at first, meanwhile, so far, later*); and more.
    in academic writing, 44

translations, 4, *4*, 687–89
    in lists of references (APA style), 637
    in works cited (MLA style), 576
Trip Advisor, 820
Trump, Donald, 105, *105*
truncation, in searches, 504
Tumblr, 678, 781, 815
tutoring sessions, 127–28
tweets, in works cited (MLA style), 592–93
Twitter, 677–78
    and #BlackLivesMatter, 678
    collaboration, 123
    in lists of references (APA style), 643
    misinformation, 98–99
    and research, 497, 498
    reviews, 336
    and sentences, 706–7
    in works cited (MLA style), 592–93
typography, 760

U

undergraduate writing publications, 819
underlining, 760
University of Nebraska–Lincoln, 819
University of Notre Dame, 819
University of Wisconsin, Design Lab, 786
U.S. News & World Report, 336–37

V

values, appealing to readers', 160–61

VANTAGE POINT The physical position from which a writer describes something. *See* perspectives; POINT OF VIEW

VERB, 734–40 A word that expresses an action (*dance, talk*) or a state of being (*be, seem*). A verb is an ESSENTIAL ELEMENT of a sentence or CLAUSE. Verbs have four forms: base form (*smile*), past tense (*smiled*), past participle (*smiled*), and present participle (*smiling*). *See also* HELPING VERB; IRREGULAR VERB; TENSE
    APA style, 738–40
    common errors, 734–40
    MLA style, 739
    sentence fragment, 716
    signal verbs, 551–52
    subject-verb agreement, 734–38

verb tenses, 552–53, 738–40
    with APA style, 738–40
    with MLA style, 739
    past perfect, 740
    past tense, 738–40
    present perfect, 738–39
    present tense, 738
    shifts in, 738–40
Veronica Mars (television series), 124
verse plays, in MLA style in-text documentation, 568

video conferencing, 61, *62*, *129*
video essays, 788–90
video games, 125
    in works cited (MLA style), 598
videos
    distinguishing facts from misinformation in, 106–7
    in lists of references (APA style), 640
    and narratives, 189
    quoting, 553–54
    and reports, 285
    in works cited (MLA style), 596
violence, 5

VISUAL ANALYSIS, 256–61 A **GENRE** of writing that examines an image, video, or some other visual text and how it communicates a message to an **AUDIENCE**. Features: a description of the visual • some contextual information • attention to any words • close **ANALYSIS** of the message • insight into what the visual "says" • precise language.
    annotated example, 259–61
    characteristic features of, 256–58
    readings
        "Advertisements R Us," 276–81
        "Why Is Everyone Focused on Zuckerberg's Hoodie?," 259–61

visuals, 763–71
    creating, 768–70
    definition and, 461
    description and, 462–64
    diagrams, 768, 770
    as evidence, 432
    graphs, charts, and tables, 765–66, 770
    incorporating, 553–54
    infographics, 768, *769*
    introducing, 770–71
    labeling, 770–71
    maps, 766, *767*, 770
    photographs, 764, 769
    tables, *766*
    videos, 765, 769
    visual arguments, 449–50
    visual examples, *465*
visual texts, 74, *75*

W

Walk the Line (film), 334, *335*, 336
Watson, James, 15–16
Webb, Jack, 282, *283*
webinar, recording of, in lists of references (APA style), 642
weblog. *See* BLOG
Web of Language, 783–84
webpage, in lists of references (APA style), 633
websites. *See also* online sources
    in works cited (MLA style), 589–91
web sources, in working bibliography, 519
Weebly, 815
which, 727–28

WIKI, 784–86 A website format, often consisting of many linked pages on related topics, that allows readers to add, edit, delete, or otherwise change the site's content.
    in lists of references (APA style), 639
    as sources, 493–94
    in works cited (MLA style), 591

Wikipedia, 707
    collaboration, 123, 125–27
    reporting information, 298–300, 784–85
    in research, 482, 487, 493–94, 497, *522*
Wikitorial, 449
wildcard searches, 504
Williams, Robin, 537–38
Williams, Serena, *231*, 231–32
Williams, Ted, 695
Window Rock writing conference, 687, *688*
Windows Live Movie Maker, 789
Winfrey, Oprah, 710–11, *711*

Winter Olympics (2018), *245*
Wix, 815
Word, 765
WordPress, 815

WORKING BIBLIOGRAPHY, 518–19 A record of all sources consulted during research. Each entry provides all the bibliographic information necessary for correct DOCUMENTATION of each source, including author, title, and publication information. A working bibliography is a useful tool for recording and keeping track of sources.

working thesis, 484–85

WORKS CITED, 572–98, 600, 617 The list of full bibliographic information, for all the sources cited in the text, which appears at the end of a researched text prepared in MLA STYLE. *See also* bibliographies
    annotated example, 617

World without Oil, 125
writing, at work, 50–63
writing analytically, 229–81. *See also* ANALYSIS
writing centers, tutoring sessions, 127–28

writing processes, 109–31
    in Middle Ages, 109–10, *110*
    need for collaboration, 123–31
    roadmap to writing process, 113–22
writing samples for a job search, 60

Y

Yelp, 820
yet, 697
Young Scholars in Writing, 819
YouTube, 137, 150
    collaboration, 127
    fabricated videos, 107
    portfolios for, 809
    publishing on, 820
    and research, 487, 498
    and style, 679

Z

ze/hir/hirs, 731
Zotero, 516
Zuckerberg, Mark, 259–61

MLA DOCUMENTATION DIRECTORY

MLA In-Text Documentation

1. Author named in a signal phrase *566*
2. Author named in parentheses *566*
3. Two or more works by the same author *566*
4. Authors with the same last name *567*
5. Two or more authors *567*
6. Organization or government as author *567*
7. Author unknown *567*
8. Literary works *568*
9. Work in an anthology *568*
10. Encyclopedia or dictionary *569*
11. Legal and historical documents *569*
12. Sacred text *569*
13. Multivolume work *570*
14. Two or more works cited together *570*
15. Source quoted in another source *570*
16. Work without page numbers *570*
17. An entire work or one-page article *571*

MLA List of Works Cited

Core Elements *572*

Authors and Other Contributors *574*

1. One author *575*
2. Two authors *575*
3. Three or more authors *575*
4. Two or more works by the same author *575*
5. Author and editor or translator *576*
6. No author or editor *576*
7. Organization or government as author *576*

Articles and Other Short Works *577*

Documentation Maps *579, 581, 582*

8. Article in a journal *577*
9. Article in a magazine *577*
10. Article in a newspaper *578*
11. Article accessed through a database *578*
12. Entry in a reference work *580*
13. Editorial *580*
14. Letter to the editor *583*
15. Review *583*
16. Comment on an online article *583*

Books and Parts of Books *584*

Documentation Map *586*

17. Basic entries for a book *584*

18. Anthology *584*
19. Work in an anthology *585*
20. Multivolume work *585*
21. Book in a series *587*
22. Graphic narrative *587*
23. Sacred text *587*
24. Edition other than the first *587*
25. Republished work *588*
26. Foreword, introduction, preface, or afterword *588*
27. Published letter *588*
28. Paper at a conference *588*
29. Dissertation *589*

Websites *589*

Documentation Map *590*

30. Entire website *589*
31. Work on a website *591*
32. Blog entry *591*
33. Wiki *591*

Personal Communication and Social Media *591*

34. Personal letter *591*
35. Email *592*
36. Text message *592*
37. Post to an online forum *592*
38. Post to *Twitter*, *Facebook*, or other social media *592*

Audio, Visual, and Other Sources *593*

39. Advertisement *593*
40. Art *593*
41. Cartoon *594*
42. Supreme Court case *594*
43. Film *594*
44. Interview *595*
45. Map *595*
46. Musical score *596*
47. Online video *596*
48. Oral presentation *596*
49. Podcast *596*
50. Radio program *597*
51. Sound recording *597*
52. TV show *597*
53. Video game *598*